The European Mosaic

Contemporary Politics, Economics and Culture

third edition

David Gowland,
Richard Dunphy and Charlotte Lythe

School of Contemporary European Studies, University of Dundee

FT Prentice Hall
FINANCIAL TIMES

An imprint of Pearson Education

Harlow, England • London • New York • Boston • San Francisco • Toronto • Sydney • Singapore • Hong Kong
Tokyo • Seoul • Taipei • New Delhi • Cape Town • Madrid • Mexico City • Amsterdam • Munich • Paris • Milan

Pearson Education Limited
Edinburgh Gate
Harlow
Essex CM20 2JE
England

and Associated Companies throughout the world

Visit us on the World Wide Web at:
www.pearsoned.co.uk

First published 1995
Second edition published 2000
Third edition published 2006

ISBN-10 582-47370-5
ISBN-13 978-0-582-47370-6

British Library Cataloguing-in-Publication Data
A catalogue record for this book is available from the British Library

Library of Congress Cataloging-in-Publication Data
The European mosaic : contemporary politics, economics, and culture / [edited by] David
  Gowland, Richard Dunphy, Charlotte Lythe.-- 3rd ed.
      p. cm.
  Includes bibliographical references and index.
  ISBN 0-582-47370-5 (pbk.)
   1. Europe--Civilization--1945- 2. Europe--Economic conditions--1945- 3.
  Europe--Politics and government--1945- I. Gowland, D. A. II. Dunphy, Richard. III.
  Lythe, Charlotte.

  D1055.E84 2006
  940.55--dc22

                                                                    2005053916

10 9 8 7 6 5 4 3 2 1
08 07 06

Typeset in 10pt Sabon by 30
Printed and bound in Great Britain by Ashford Colour Press, Hants

The publisher's policy is to use paper manufactured from sustainable forests.

Contents

Contents

Preface

This is the third edition of a book originally published in 1995 with a second edition in 2000. Each five-year interval has involved considerable updating, but in this edition we have also been able to expand the text to introduce a substantial amount of new material. Parts 1 and 5 are almost entirely new, as is most of Part 4; in Part 2 we have major new sections on Russia and on Turkey and Cyprus, and in Part 3 we consider a broader spectrum of policies than in previous editions.

However, we have retained two features of the previous editions. The first is our pan-European approach. In the changes for this edition, this is signalled most clearly in Part 1, where we move from a discussion of the enlargement of the European Union to ask what Europe is, what it is to be European and how Europe interacts with the rest of the world. Our wide concept of Europe is also demonstrated by our new sections in Part 2.

The second feature we have retained is the strongly interdisciplinary focus of the book. As with previous editions, the text is the work of a team. All bar two of the team are current or recently retired members of staff of the University of Dundee, and most of us are involved with the work of the School of Contemporary European Studies. All the members of the team agreed to give the editors a free hand to modify their drafts, so the editors bear full responsibility for the final text. However, it could not have been produced without the expertise of the team.

The team members, and the main areas in which they prepared first drafts, are:

- Brian Baxter, Department of Politics, University of Dundee: EU environmental policy; EU fisheries policy; co-author on European democracy.

- Angela Bourne, Department of Politics, University of Dundee: recent history of the EU; EU institutions; co-author on political Europe.

- Richard Dunphy, Department of Politics, University of Dundee: France, Germany, Italy, UK; Greece, Portugal, Spain; co-author on political Europe, on European democracy and on living with diversity (also co-editor).

- Neil Elder, Department of Politics, University of Hull: co-author on Denmark, Finland, Iceland, Norway, Sweden.

- Adrian Flint, Department of Politics, University of Dundee: EU and the Third World.

- David Gowland, Department of History, University of Dundee: enlargement; history of EU; chronology (also co-editor).

- Susan Isherwood, Department of Politics, University of Dundee: EU and USA; NATO; Cyprus and Turkey; EU security and defence policy.

- Charlotte Lythe, Department of Economic Studies, University of Dundee: European economy and East–West economic comparisons; EU commercial, monetary and economic integration; the euro zone (also co-editor).
- David Mallion, Department of Politics, University of Dundee: social Europe; EU industrial and social policy; social structure and change.
- Lee Miles, Department of Politics, University of Liverpool: co-author on Denmark, Finland, Iceland, Norway, Sweden.
- Basil O'Neill, Department of Philosophy, University of Dundee: cultural Europe; visions of Europe; religious and cultural fault lines; co-author on living with diversity.
- Cameron Ross, Department of Politics, University of Dundee: enlargement (Czech Republic, Hungary, Poland, Slovakia, Slovenia); EU and Russia; East/West political comparisons; Russia; Central and Eastern European countries.
- Fiona Smith, Department of Geography, University of Dundee: concepts of Europe; human rights and migration.
- Alex Wright, Department of Politics, University of Dundee: regions and stateless nations.

We would like to dedicate this book to all who have worked with us in the School of Contemporary European Studies – to the academic and the clerical staff, but above all to the students, with whom we have learned so much.

In memory of David Mallion (1938–2005).

David Gowland, Richard Dunphy and Charlotte Lythe
2006

Acknowledgements

We are grateful to the following for permission to reproduce copyright material:

Table 1.1 and Table 1.4, from *Portrait of the EU* at http://www.epp.eurostat.cec.eu.int/cache/ITY_PUBLIC/KS-60-04-523/EN/KS-60-4-523-EN.PDF, Office for Official Publications of the European Communities (Eurostat 2004); Map 1.1a and 1.1b, from *Key Facts and Figures about the European Union*, http://europa.eu.int/comm/publications/booklets/eu_glance/44/en-1.pdf, Office for Official Publications of European Communities (European Commission 2004); Table 1.2, from *The Newcomers in the Future of Europe: Europeanisation and Domestic Change*, edited by F. Cameron, Routledge (Grabbe, H. 2003); Figure 1.2, from *Historical Geography in Europe in the 1990s: A Geographic Analysis*, 6th edn, edited by George W. Hoffman, copyright © John Wiley & Sons Inc. (East, W. Gordon 1989), reprinted with permission of John Wiley & Sons, Inc; Figure 1.3, from The Mansell Collection, copyright Getty Images; Table 1.5 and Table 1.6, from Richard Rose, Centre for the Study of Public Policy, New Europe Barometer, 2001; Figure 1.6 and Figure 1.7, from http://www.hm-treasury.gov.uk/media/5AA/B3/euroc1.9.gif, Crown copyright material is reproduced with the permission of the Controller of HMSO and the Queen's Printer for Scotland; Figure 1.12, from the website of *The Guardian*, copyright © Steve Bell 2000/All Rights Reserved; Figure 2.2, published in *The Spectator*, 24 February 1990 (Brookes, Peter 1990); Figure 2.3 and Figure 2.4, from Debardeleben, Joan, *Russian Politics in Transition*, 2nd edn, copyright © 1997 by Houghton Mifflin Company, reprinted with permission; Table 2.6 and Table 2.8, from WORLD BANK ONLINE by THE WORLD BANK, copyright 2005 by WORLD BANK, reproduced with permission of WORLD BANK in the format Other Book via Copyright Clearance Center; Table 2.12, from International Monetary Fund Report no. 04/315, Russian Federation: Statistical Appendix, International Monetary Fund (IMF 2004); Table 2.17, from 'Eastern Europe after Communism' in *Developments in East European Politics*, edited by S. White, J. Bat and P. G. Lewis, MacMillan (White, S. 1993), reproduced with permission of Palgrave MacMillan; Table 2.18, from *Revolution in East-Central Europe* by David S. Mason, copyright © 1992 by Westview Press, reprinted by permission of Westview Press, a member of Persus Books, L.L.C; Table 2.19, from *Managing Transition Economies in Developments in Central and East European Politics – 3*, edited by S. White, J. Bat and P. G. Lewis, MacMillan (Blycza, G. 2003), reproduced with permission of Palgrave MacMillan; Table 2.23, from *Political Parties in Post-Communist Eastern Europe*, Routledge (Lewis, P.G. 2000); Table 2.24, adapted from Table 1, p. 18 of *Nations in Transit: Democratisation in East Central Europe and Eurasia, Freedom House*, Rowman & Littlefield Publishers Inc.

(2004); Table 2.25, from *Poland in Developments in East European Politics*, edited by S. White, J. Bat and P. G. Lewis, MacMillan (Millard, F. 2003), reproduced with permission of Palgrave MacMillan; Table 3.2, from Eurobarometer, May 2004, EB61-CC-EB 2004, p. 1, at http://www.europa.eu.int/comm/public_opinion/archives/cceb/2004/cceb_2004.1_highlights.pdf, Office for Official Publications of the European Communities (EU 2004); Figure 3.2, from http://www.europa.eu.int/comm/mediatheque/photo/select/eurosmile/p-008509-00-01.jpg, accessed 18 February 2005, Audiovisual Library of the European Commission; Figure 3.3 and Figure 4.5, from *The ABC of Community Law*, European Commission (Borehardt, Klaus-Diezer 2000); Table 3.6, from *The Co-Decision (Article 251) Procedure Post-Amsterdam in The EU and Politics of the EU*, MacMillan (Nugent, N. 1999), reproduced with permission of Palgrave MacMillan; Table 3.7, from *Regional Socio-Economic Studies on Employment and the Level of Dependency on Fishing*, at http://www.europa.eu.int/comm/fisheries/doc_et_publ/liste_publi/studies/regional/finalreport.pdf, Office for Official Publications of European Communities (Commission of the European Communities, Directorate-General for Fisheries 2000); Table 3.8, from *Jobs, Jobs, Jobs: Creating More Employment in Europe* (Chart 13, annex 2), at http://www.europa.eu.int/comm/employment_social/employment_strategy/pdf/etf_en.pdf, Office for Official Publications of European Communities (Kok, W. 2003); Opinion 4.1, from *Social Change and Innovation in the Labour Market*, Oxford University Press (Hakim, C. 1998), by permission of Oxford University Press; Figure 4.1, from *Britain in Europe: An Introduction to Sociology*, edited by T. Spybey, Routledge (1997); Figure 4.2, from *Revolutions in Our Time: Capitalism*, Victor Gollancz, a division of the Orion Publishing Group (Vaizey, J. 1971); Table 4.3 and Table 4.4, from *Post European Election 2004 Survey* (Flash Eurobarometer: 162), at http://www.europarl.eu.int/press/Eurobarometer/pdf/en/PostEuropeElections2004ReportEN.pdf, Office for Official Publications of European Communities (EU 2004); Figure 4.3 by John Berridge; Figure 4.4, from *A Social and Economic History of Twentieth-Century Europe*, Harvard University Press (Ambrosius, G. and Hubbard, W.H. 1989); Table 4.5, from *Elections Around the World*, at http://www.electionworld.com, accessed on 4 January 2005; Table 4.6, from *European Union Politics*, edited by M. Cini, Oxford University Press (2003), by permission of Oxford University Press; Figure 4.6, from *The Guardian*, 14 February 1994, copyright David Simonds 1994; Figure 4.7 and Figure 5.1, by Katy Jones; Fig. 5.2, from http://www.europa.eu.int/comm/mediatheque/photo/select/eurosmile/p-008509-00-06.jpg, accessed 18 February 2005, Audiovisual Library of the European Commission; Figure 5.3, from *L'Express*, 14 March 2005, Plantu; Table 5.4, from Eurostat's Database 'New cronos', at http://www.europa.eu.int/comm.//eurostat/newcronos, Office for Official Publications of European Communities (EU); Table 5.5, from Eurostat's website, Office for Official Publications of European Communities (EU); Table 5.6, from http://www.europa.eu.int/.constitution/ratification_en.htm, Office for Official Publications of European Communities (EU).

Plate 1.1 and Plate 2.2, copyright AM/EMPICS; Plate 1.2, from http://www.europa.eu.int/comm/mediatheque/p-011422/00-0, Audiovisual Library of the European Commission; Plate 1.3, from http://www.europa.eu.int/comm/mediatheque/oracle/WebTek/APPL.IdToFullScr?pTp+1&p, accessed 18 February

2005, Audiovisual Library of the European Commission, Plate 1.4, from NATO website, NATO; Plate 2.3, from AP/ Wide World Photos; Plate 2.5, from http://www.europa.eu.int/comm/mediatheque/photo/commprodi/prodi/p-009137-00-1.jpg, Audiovisual Library of the European Commission; Plate 2.6, from The Finnish Parliament (2002), Parliament of Finland; Plate 3.2, from http://www.europa.eu.int/comm/mediatheque/photo/select/founding fathers/p-002763-00-1.jpg, accessed 17 February 2005, Audiovisual Library of the European Commission; Plate 3.3, from http://www. europa.eu.int/comm/mediatheque/photo/select/neweucon/h-488.jpg, accessed 19 April 2005, Audiovisual Library of the European Commission; Plate 3.4, from http://www.europa.eu.int/comm/mediatheque/photo/select/formerpresid/p-002614-01-25.jpg, accessed 2 May 2005, Audiovisual Library of the European Commission; Plate 3.5, from http://www.europa.eu.int/comm/mediatheque/photo/select/neweucon/97-d05-34.jpg, accessed 19 April 2005, Audio-visual Library of the European Commission; Plate 3.6, from http://www.europa.eu.int/comm/mediatheque/photo/select//treaty/92-d10-55.jpg, accessed 17 February 2005, Audiovisual Library of the European Commission; Plate 3.7, from http://www.europa.eu.int/comm/mediatheque/photo/select/symbol99/p-007623-01-01.jpg, accessed 19 February 2005, Audiovisual Library of the European Commission; Plate 3.8, from http://www.europa.eu.int/comm/mediatheque/photo/select/founding fathers/b-435-o7b.jap, accessed 17 February 2005, Audiovisual Library of the European Commission; Plate 3.10, Dutch police officer holds EU flag, reproduced by permission of Reuters/Danilo Krstanov, 1 January 2003; Plate 4.1, copyright: Jewish Museum, Berlin, Photo: Jens Ziehe, Berlin; Plate 5.1, Old Mostar Bridge by Sheldon Breiner/Reconstructed Mostar bridge by Alexandra Henriques.

Office for Official Publications of the European Community for extracts from various EU publications; HMSO for an extract from a country profile of Moldavia published by the Foreign and Commonwealth Office; and Sage Publications Limited for an extract from 'Sweden "hitchhiking" and the Euro referendum', by I Miles published in *Co-operation and Conflict*, vol. 39, no. 2, © NISA: Nordic International Studies Association 2004.

In some instances we have been unable to trace the owners of copyright material, and we would appreciate any information that would enable us to do so.

Editor's acknowledgements

We would like to express our thanks to Morten Fuglevand of Pearson Education for his unfailing advice and assistance, to Katie Jones for providing drawings that vividly illustrate several major themes, to Alison Gowland and Rob Porter of Jesus College, Oxford University, for translating some French text, and to John Berridge of Dundee University for permission to use and to modify his unique diagrams on the institutions of the European Union, which also appeared in the second edition of this book.

List of abbreviations

ACP	African, Caribbean and Pacific
AFD	Alliance of Free Democrats (Hungary)
AKP	Justice and Development Party (Turkey)
AN	National Alliance (Italy)
ANAP	Motherland Party (Turkey)
APL	Albanian Party of Labour
ASP	Albanian Socialist Party
AWS	Solidarity Electoral Action (Poland)
BBP	Grand Unity Party
BSP	Bulgarian Socialist Party
CAP	Common Agricultural Policy
CEAS	Common European Asylum System
CCP	Common Commercial Policy
CD	consolidated democracy
CDE	Conference on Disarmament in Europe
CDR	Romanian Democratic Convention
CDU	United Democratic Coalition (Portugal)
CDU	Christian Democratic Union (FRG/Germany)
	Christian Democratic Union (Hungary)
CEAS	Common European Asylum System
CEE	Central and Eastern Europe
CEFTA	Central European Free Trade Agreement
CFE	Conventional Forces in Europe
CFP	Common Fisheries Policy
CFSP	Common Foreign and Security Policy
CHP	Republican People's Party (Turkey)
CIS	Commonwealth of Independent States
CJTF	Combined Joint Task Force
CMEA/Comecon	Council of Mutual Economic Assistance
COMESA	Common Market for Eastern and Southern Africa
CoR	Committee of the Regions
COREPER	Committee of Permanent Representatives
CPNT	Pro-hunting Party in France
CPRF	Communist Party of the Russian Federation
CPSU	Communist Party of the Soviet Union
CSCE	Conference on Security and Cooperation in Europe
CSR	Common Strategy on Russia
CSU	Christian Social Union (FRG)

CSV/PCS	Christian Social People's Party (Luxembourg)
CzSSD	Czech Social Democratic Party
DA	Justice and Truth (Romania)
DC	Christian Democracy (Italy)
	Democratic Convention (Romania)
Dehap	Democratic People's Party (Turkey)
DF	Danish People's Party
DL	Liberal Democracy (France)
DNSF	(Democratic) National Salvation Front (Romania)
DP	Democratic Party (Albania)
DS	Democratic Party (Serbia and Montenegro)
DSP	Democratic Left Party (Turkey)
DU	Democratic Union (Poland)
DUP	Democratic Unionist Party (Northern Ireland)
EAC	East African Community
EAEC	European Atomic Energy Community
EAPC	European–Atlantic Partnership Council
EAR	Greek Left Party
EC	European Community
ECB	European Central Bank
ECHR	European Convention on Human Rights
ECJ	European Court of Justice
ECOFIN	European Council of Finance Ministers
ECOWAS	Economic Community of West African States
ECSC	European Coal and Steel Community
ECU	European Currency Unit
EBA	'Everything But Arms'
EDC	European Defence Community
EDF	European Development Fund
EEA	European Economic Area
EEC	European Economic Community
EEP	Single Economic Space
EFTA	European Free Trade Association
EMS	European Monetary System
EMU	Economic and Monetary Union
EPAs	Economic Partnership Agreements
EOKA	National Organisation of Cypriot Fighters
EPC	European Political Cooperation
ERM	Exchange Rate Mechanism
ERRF	European Rapid Reaction Force
ESCB	European System of Central Banks
ETA	Basque Homeland and Freedom
EU	European Union
FCMA	Treaty of Friendship, Cooperation and Mutual Assistance
FDP	Free Democratic Party (FRG)
FIDESZ	Alliance of Young Democrats (Hungary)
FINEFTA	Finland and the EFTA special arrangement

FN	National Front (France)
	National Front (Belgium)
FP	Virtue Party (Turkey)
FPÖ	Freedom Party of Austria
FRG	Federal Republic of Germany
FRY	Federal Republic of Yugoslavia
FSB	Russian Security Forces
FYROM	Former Yugoslav Republic of Macedonia
GATT	General Agreement on Tariffs and Trade
GDP	gross domestic product
GDR	German Democratic Republic
GNI	gross national income
GP	Youth Party (Turkey)
HDF	Hungarian Democratic Forum
HDZ	Croatian Democratic Alliance
HR	High Representative
HSBC	Hong Kong and Shanghai Banking Corporation
HSWP	Hungarian Socialist Workers' Party
HZDS	Movement for a Democratic Slovakia
IBRD	International Bank for Reconstruction and Development
IMF	International Monetary Fund
IMP	Integrated Mediterranean Programme
INF	Intermediate Nuclear Forces
IMRO	Internal Macedonian Revolutionary Organisation
IRA	Irish Republication Army
IU	United Left (Spain)
JHA	Justice and Home Affairs
KKE	Greek Communist Party
KLA	Kosova Liberation Army
KOR	Workers' Defence Committee (Poland)
KPD/DKP	Communist Party of Germany (FRG)
LCY	League of Communists of Yugoslavia
LDCs	less developed countries
LDDP	Lithuanian Democratic Labour Party
LDPR	Liberal Democratic Party of Russia
LN	Northern League (Italy)
LO	Workers' Struggle (France)
LCR	Revolutionary Communist League (France)
LPR	League of Polish Families
MDF	Hungarian Democratic Forum
MDS	Movement for a Democratic Slovakia
MEP	Member of the European Parliament
MFA	Armed Forces Movement (Portugal)
MFN	most favoured nation
MHP	Nationalist Action Party (Turkey)
MNR	Republican National Movement (France)
MRF	Movement for Rights and Freedoms (Bulgaria)

MSI	Italian Social Movement
MSP	National Salvation Party (Turkey)
MSzP	Hungarian Socialist Party
MTS	medium-term strategy for development of relations with the EU
NACC	North Atlantic Cooperation Council
NATO	North Atlantic Treaty Organisation
ND	New Democracy (Greece)
NGO	non-governmental organisation
NSF	National Salvation Front (Romania)
OCTs	overseas countries and territories
ODS	Civic Democratic Party (Czech Republic)
OECD	Organisation for Economic Cooperation and Development
OEEC	Organisation for European Economic Cooperation
OPEC	Organisation for Petroleum Exporting Countries
OSCE	Organisation for Security and Cooperation in Europe
PASOK	Pan-Hellenic Socialist Movement (Greece)
PCA	Partnership and Cooperation Agreement
PCE	Communist Party of Spain
PCF	French Communist Party
PCI	Italian Communist Party
PCP	Portuguese Communist Party
PD	Democratic Party (Romania)
PDS	Democratic Party of the Left (Italy)
	Party of Democratic Socialism (Germany)
PDSR	Democratic Social Pole of Romania
PHARE	Poland and Hungary Assistance for Economic Restructuring Programme
PiS	Law and Justice (Poland)
PMR	Greater Romania Party
PNL	National Liberal Party (Romania)
PO	Civic Platform (Poland)
PP	Popular Party (Spain)
PPI	Italian Popular Party
PR	proportional representation
PRC	Party of Communist Refoundation (Italy)
PRG	Left Radical Party (France)
PS	Socialist Party (formerly SFIO, France)
PSD	Social Democratic Party (Portugal)
	Social Democratic Party (Romania)
PSI	Italian Socialist Party
PSL	Polish Peasant Party
PSOE	Spanish Socialists Workers' Party
PSP	Portuguese Socialist Party
PUNR	Party of Romanian National Unity
PUR	Humanist Party of Romania
PUWP	Polish United Workers' Party
QMV	qualified majority voting

RP	Welfare Party (Turkey)
RPR	Rally for the Republic (France)
SACU	Southern African Customs Union
SADC	Southern African Development Community
SAP	Social Democrats (Sweden)
SARK	Serbian Autonomous Region of Krajina
SCA	Special Committee for Agriculture
SCD	semi-consolidated democracy
SDLP	Social Democratic and Labour Party (Northern Ireland)
SDL	Party of the Democratic Left (Slovakia)
SEA	Single European Act
SED	Socialist Unity Party (GDR)
SFIO	Section Francaise de l'Internationale Ouvrière
SIS	Slovak Information Service
SLD	Union of the Democratic Left (Poland)
SMD	single-member district
SO	Self-Defence (Poland)
SP	Felicity Party (Turkey)
SPD	Social Democratic Party (FRG, Germany)
SPS	Union of Right Forces (Russia)
TACs	total allowable catches
TRNC	Turkish Republic of North Cyprus
UCD	Democratic Centre Union (Spain)
UDF	Union for French Democracy
	Union of Democratic Forces (Bulgaria)
UDMR	Democratic Alliance of Hungarians in Romania
UMP	Union for the Presidential Majority (France)
UP	Labour Union (Poland)
USSR	Union of Soviet Socialist Republics
UUP	Ulster Unionist Party (Northern Ireland)
UW	Freedom Union (Poland)
VAT	value-added tax
VB	Flemish Block (Belgium)
WEU	Western European Union
WTO	Warsaw Treaty Organisation
	World Trade Organization
YTP	New Turkey Party

List of figures and plates

list of text boxes

Part 1

Europe and the wider world

Plate 1.1 Chelsea Football Club players celebrating winning the English Premiership title on 30 April 2005. The team is owned by a Russian oil tycoon and managed by a Portuguese, and the native countries of the playing squad for this match were Cameroon, The Czech Republic (2), England (3), France (2), Germany, Iceland, Italy, Ivory Coast, Portugal (2), Russia, and Serbia and Montenegro. In what senses is this an *English* football club? In what senses is it *European*? Is it *global*?

Source: © EMPICS; picture by Mike Egerton

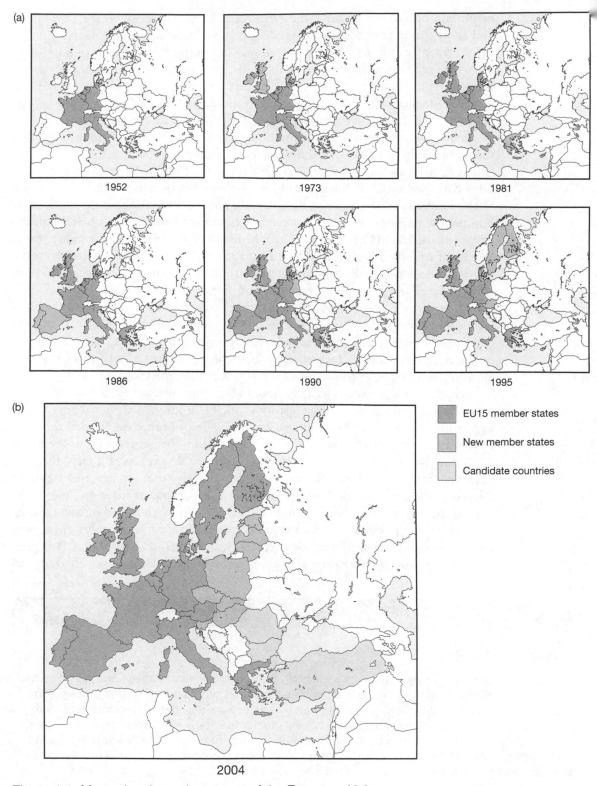

Figure 1.1 Maps showing enlargement of the European Union

Source: Europa (2005).

membership. In the meantime, these countries have free access to the EU market and an opportunity to negotiate 'Stabilisation and Association agreements' with the EU, as Croatia and the FYR of Macedonia have already done, before eventually applying for EU membership. In the more distant future, EU membership is a possibility for the Ukraine but remains unlikely for Belarus and almost out of the question for Russia by virtue of its size and standing as a world power. Other possible candidates for EU membership include the four EFTA countries. Norway has, by referendum, rejected membership on two occasions, while Switzerland applied for membership in 1992 but did not pursue the matter.

The EU's future expansion plans, especially the decision to open EU membership talks with Turkey, raise the question as to whether it is ever possible to draw the final boundaries of the EU, and that, in turn, poses questions about the meaning of Europe, the purpose of European integration and the nature of EU interests in the wider world. The EU has never defined the limits of its possible territorial coverage and has formally advocated an inclusive rather than exclusive approach to the question of enlargement. It invites any European state to join the organisation, without specifying what is to be understood as European (see Key fact 1.2). In territorial terms, the shape of the EU is ultimately determined by the governments of the member states. The open-endedness of the enterprise means that it is unclear whether any state can apply for membership provided that it meets the declared criteria (see Key fact 1.3) and whether, for example, the admission of Turkey makes it all the more difficult to refuse membership to Russia or the Ukraine.

Such questions are not new. They have to a greater or lesser extent accompanied each phase of enlargement in the history of the EU from the first failed attempts at expansion in the 1960s, when President de Gaulle of France questioned the UK's European credentials and vetoed the UK's application for membership of the EC in 1963 and again in 1967. At the same time, de Gaulle expressed a view that has accompanied each proposed enlargement, namely that enlargement would adversely affect the economic arrangements, the geographical focus and the workings of the organisation (see Opinion 1.1). De Gaulle's brutal use of the national veto and of the power to label an applicant state European or non-European was an early demonstration of a continuing contrast between the rhetoric of European unity and inclusiveness and the politics of division and exclusion, which are based

Key fact 1.2

How to join the EU

Any European State may apply to become a Member of the Union. It shall address its application to the Council, which shall act unanimously after consulting the Commission and after receiving the assent of the European Parliament, which shall act by an absolute majority of its component members. The conditions of admission and the adjustments to the Treaties on which the Union is founded which such admission entails shall be the subject of an agreement between the Member States and the applicant State. This agreement shall be submitted for ratification by all contracting States in accordance with their respective constitutional requirements.

(Source: Article O of the Treaty on EU.)

Opinion 1.1

The first failed attempt at enlargement

Extracts from a press conference (14 January 1963) at which President de Gaulle of France questioned the UK's European credentials and justified his decision to veto the first UK application to join the EC:

England in effect is insular, she is maritime, she is linked through her exchanges, her markets, her supply lines to the most diverse and often the most distant countries; she pursues essentially industrial and commercial activities, and only slightly agricultural ones. She has in all her doings very marked and very original habits and traditions. In short, the nature, the structure, the very situation (conjuncture) that are England's differ profoundly from those of the continentals . . . .

It must be agreed that first the entry of Britain, and then these States [Denmark, Ireland, Norway], will completely change the whole of the actions, the agreements, the compensations, the rules which have already been established between the Six, because all these States, like Britain, have very important peculiarities. Then it will be another Common Market [European Community] whose constructions ought to be envisaged; but one which would be taken to 11 and then 13 and then perhaps 18 would no longer resemble, without any doubt, the one which the Six built.

(Source: WEU Assembly 1963 (1964): 20–2.)

Was de Gaulle right?

on the drawing of arbitrary lines between insiders and outsiders (Heffernan 1998). Studies of the background to the recent enlargement of the EU (Kok 2003; Nugent 2004; Cameron 2004) have raised several questions about this development, most notably about whether it will strengthen or weaken the EU, about the impact of expansion on the new and old member states, and about the particular implications of enlargement for EU policies and policymaking. Each phase of the EU's expansion has challenged the EU's capacity to absorb new members while maintaining the momentum of European integration. One view is that the processes of enlargement and deepening are complementary. Another view, evident in de Gaulle's handling of the first UK application for EC membership, is that enlargement leads to a wider but weaker EU. Over the years, the main thrust of this argument has more or less been to the effect that an expanding EU is more susceptible to disintegrative forces and can be held together only on the basis of a multi-speed approach to policy integration whereby a hard core of member states acts as the spearhead of integration, leaving other states to catch up later. It can be argued that a multi-speed Europe already exists in several main policy areas, such as the single currency, Schengen and defence (all of which will be discussed later). A multi-speed Europe is not necessarily a problem from an integrationist perspective (Cameron 2004). Furthermore, there is strong evidence to suggest that the relationship between enlargement and integration has varied over time and in different cases. In the 1970s, the implications of the first enlargement generally overshadowed the process of integration. In the 1980s, however, the EU expanded at the same time as it embarked upon the single market programme, and in the 1990s the decision to form the euro zone preceded the enlargement of 1995. However, the most recent enlargement of the EU has occasioned further expressions of the view that 'more [Europe] means less [integration]'. According to this view, therefore, the larger the EU becomes the more likely it will come to resemble a cumbersome international organisation supervising little more than a free trade area.

A further aspect of the wider but weaker view of enlargement concerns institutional integration and the effectiveness of the EU's institutions and decision-making system. Whether enlargement has an invigorating or paralysing effect in this and in other respects is a matter of speculation. To date, the rate of expansion of the EU has formed a marked contrast to the laggardly efforts of the governments of the member states to undertake fundamental reforms of the EU organisation. Some of the EU institutions have long pressed the case for reorganisation in the belief that the combination of a largely uninformed system and an increased membership could jeopardise the process of integration (see Opinion 1.2). The impact of institutional changes in recent years is considered in Part 3. At the very least, there is a major question mark against whether the new constitution of the EU (if ratified) will deliver a system capable of managing a membership of 25 plus states in the near future. There is in this respect much adherence to the view that while the EU strongly encouraged the new member states to prepare for membership, its own preparations for enlargement were very limited and did little more than meet the minimum requirements for an effective EU to function (Cameron 2004).

Opinion 1.2

The process of enlargement

Prior to the enlargement of the European Community to include Greece (1981) and Portugal and Spain (1986), an EC Commission paper commented on the implications of enlargement:

> The institutions and organs of the present Community cannot ensure that the process of integration will continue in an enlarged Community; on the contrary there is reason to [fear] that the Community decision-making procedures will deteriorate. If this happened, it would be difficult or even impossible to create a Community based on the rule of law . . . The institutions and organs of the enlarged Community must accordingly be decisively strengthened.
>
> (source: European Commission paper 78)

Do you agree? Is this a rationale for the Constitutional Treaty?

The process of enlargement also involves questions about the membership. While EU governments have never defined what a European state [is], they have nevertheless specified what is required [of a] state in order to meet the conditions of membership (see Key Facts ...) [condi]tions were first explicitly defined in 1993 in the face of the desire [of the] former communist states of Eastern Europe in joining the E[U] equally applicable in the earlier cases of Greece, Spain and Portugal. They will also apply to any future applicant states and are likely to loom particularly large, whether in view of human rights record or democratic procedures, in judging the merits of the case for agreeing EU membership for Turkey, some of the states in the western Balkans, or still further afield, Ukraine.

Key fact 1.3

The Copenhagen and Madrid criteria for EU membership

A meeting of EU leaders in Copenhagen (June 1993) set out for the first time the conditions for EU membership. The Copenhagen criteria, as they became known, set the following standards for countries wishing to join the EU:

- Stability of institutions guaranteeing democracy, the rule of law, human rights and respect for, and protection of, minorities.
- The existence of a functioning market economy as well as the capacity to cope with competitive pressure and market forces within the Union.
- The ability to take on the obligations of membership, including adherence to the aims of political, economic and monetary union.

At a subsequent meeting in Madrid, a fourth criterion was added:

- Candidate countries had to prove that they had put in place the administrative and juridical structures necessary to implement the EU's 'acquis communautaire' (see Key concept 1.1).

Key concept 1.1

The 'acquis communautaire'

This French phrase, the nearest English translation of which is 'common (or communal) inheritance', refers to the existing EU legislative texts. Put together, these are a massive document of 80,000 pages divided into 31 thematic chapters. (See Cameron 2004: 119.)

Another aspect of the recent enlargement of the EU concerns the application of the special conditions that apply to any new member state with respect to full membership of the euro zone. The new member states are expected to adopt the euro when ready to do so and not immediately upon accession. Each state will join according to its own timetable, and no state has an opt-out from the euro as was obtained by the UK and Denmark. To qualify for euro-zone status, however, each state is required to meet a number of detailed conditions involving several stages (see Key fact 1.4). Whether such conditions as low inflation and limited budget deficits will facilitate the growth and investment required by the former communist states of Eastern Europe remains to be seen as do the longer-term effects of enlargement on EU budgetary and other policies.

Key fact 1.4

New member states of the EU and the euro

New member states of the EU are expected to adopt the euro when ready to do so, not immediately upon accession. For a new member state, there are detailed conditions involving several stages:

1. the pre-accession stage, during which the country must demonstrate irreversible progress towards a functioning market economy and competitiveness as well as sustainable macro-economic stability;

2. in intermediary phase following accession, in which the new member participates fully in the single market and demonstrates progress towards achieving the conditions necessary to adopt the euro;

3. a minimum of two years successful participation in the exchange rate mechanism;

4. fulfilment of the criteria that apply to current members for the adoption of the single currency, including a budget deficit of less than 3 percent of GDP, a debt ratio of less than 60 percent of GDP, low inflation and interest rates close to the EU average; the essential condition is a sufficient degree of sustainable real convergence.

(Source: Kok 2003a: 42.)

Key concept 1.2

GDP

Gross domestic product (GDP) measures the total economic activity of a country in any time period, usually a year. It is the country's national income.

GDP figures are often used to measure a country's growth or to compare one country with another. When the calculation is of growth, care has to be taken to correct the figures for inflation. Note that growth rates can vary sharply from one period to another, and can, as for Malta in Table 1.1, be negative when output is declining.

When different countries are being compared, their GDP figures have to be expressed in the same currency. Often this is done just by using exchange rates, but this can be misleading – for example, where exchange rates are artificially controlled. There is a further issue. If you want to compare living standards or calculate how competitive an economy is, it is more useful to make comparisons after correcting for differences in price levels. Unless otherwise indicated, the GDP data used in this book are measured in euros adjusted for price levels – purchasing power standard (PPS) euros.

The enlargement process also raises questions about why states wish to join the EU in the first place and why the existing member states are willing to contemplate enlargement. A particular mix of factors at the national and international levels accounts for an individual state's decision to seek membership. Yet all applicant states have to a greater or lesser extent had to address similar questions about how best to interact with their neighbours, especially because they need to advance their own economic and security interests. What remains to be seen in the longer term is how successful the new member states in Eastern Europe are in their attempts to reverse some of the restricted terms of entry that they were offered, particularly on the EU's budgetary, regional, agricultural and free movement of labour policies. Meanwhile, member states have had to address questions not only about the positive advantages of membership for themselves but also about the likely consequences of the failure to press ahead with enlargement for themselves and for the applicant states. Some of the common problems and issues have changed over time, most notably the greater prominence given in recent years to combating organised crime and illegal immigration. Yet this type of cost/benefit analysis is at the heart of any enlargement exercise. Each of Opinions 1.3 and 1.4 provides an example of one official representation of this type of assessment, the validity of which is considered below. An important feature of enlargement for the EU concerns the economic impact of this process, especially in view of the laggardly growth rates of major economies like France and Germany in recent years and the declared aims of the Lisbon agenda to make the EU the most competitive and dynamic knowledge-based economy in the world by 2010. According to EU Commission estimates, EU membership will add up to 1 percent extra growth annually for the new member states during the first ten years of membership (based on the experience of Greece, Ireland, Portugal and Spain as new member states), while the amount of extra growth in the other EU states will be lower but still significant.

Opinion 1.3

European Commission assessment of the benefits of enlarging the EU from 15 to 25 member states

- The extension of the zone of peace, stability and prosperity in Europe will enhance the security of all peoples.
- The addition of more than 100 million people, in rapidly growing economies, to the EU's market of 370 million will boost economic growth and create jobs in both old and new member states. [Note that the enlargement from 15 to 25 in fact brought in about 75 million, not 100 million, people.]
- There will be a better quality of life for citizens throughout Europe as the new members adopt EU policies for protection of the environment and the fight against crime, drugs and illegal immigration.
- The arrival of new members will enrich the EU through increased cultural diversity, interchange of ideas and better understanding of other peoples.
- Enlargement will strengthen the Union's role in world affairs – in foreign and security policy, trade policy and the other fields of global governance.

(Source: http://www.europa.eu.int/comm/enlargement/arguments/index.htm.)

What might the main counter-arguments be?

Opinion 1.4

European Commission assessment of the costs of non-enlargement of the EU (from 15 to 25 member states) for the Union and for the applicant countries

- Delay in enlarging the single market, and lower economic growth in the applicant countries, would deprive member states of the economic benefits.
- For the applicant countries, failure to join the Union would weaken the incentive for economic reform, discourage foreign investment and reduce economic growth.
- It could thus create political instability in Europe, and even undermine the process of democratisation, with potential repercussions for the Union.
- Without enlargement, the Union would be less able to combat the problems of organised crime, illegal immigration and terrorism.
- Disillusion with the Union in the applicant countries would feed Euroscepticism in the member states.

(Source: http://www.europa.eu.int/comm/enlargement/arguments/index.htm.)

What might the main counter-arguments be?

Key fact 1.5

The Lisbon agenda

At a meeting in Lisbon in March 2000, the European Council was concerned about evidence that the EU was becoming uncompetitive in world terms. The USA was maintaining its productivity lead over the EU, and its economy was growing faster than those of EU countries. At the same time, the rapidly growing Asian economies were posing an increasing threat to EU production. The Council agreed that the EU needs a modern, efficient economy. It set a goal that the EU would become, within ten years, 'the most competitive and dynamic knowledge-based economy in the world, capable of sustainable growth with more and better jobs and greater social cohesion'. The 'Lisbon strategy' set out specific targets for matters such as research, education and training, and on-line and Internet activities, and established a programme of annual review of progress.

Finally, the recent enlargement poses questions about the EU's standing in the wider world and what is often noted as the contrast between its economic clout and its lightweight political and diplomatic standing in foreign and security policy. An immediate implication of enlargement is that the extension of the EU borders to new neighbours (Belarus, Croatia, Romania, Serbia and Ukraine) and the lengthening of the EU border with Russia (enclosing part of Russia in the case of Kaliningrad) focuses attention on the nature and extent of cross-border co-operation and on such matters as border management, immigration procedures, environmental policy and measures to combat international crime.

In 2002, the EU European Council agreed that the EU should not only avoid drawing new dividing lines but should also act to promote stability and prosperity on both sides of its new borders. As part of its 'European Neighbourhood Policy', the EU plans to extend to its neighbours to the east (Moldova, Russia, Ukraine and eventually Belarus) and to the south (the Mediterranean countries) many of the benefits of the EU's internal market together with trade concessions and financial assistance in return for commitments by these countries to a programme promoting democratic reform, a market economy and human rights. EU–Russia relations will be a matter of particular concern to the former communist Central and Eastern European states within the EU in view of the long history of troubled relationships between Russia and those states. In the case of the Mediterranean countries, the EU is committed to setting up a free trade area by 2010 to include the Arab countries around the southern and eastern Mediterranean together with Israel and the Palestinian Territories.

In the wider international system beyond Europe, it remains to be seen whether the enlarged EU can exercise a greater degree of power and influence. The deep divisions exposed before, during and after the US-led invasion of Iraq in April 2003 indicated all too clearly that the enlarged EU was far from speaking with one voice on major issues. Whether the Iraq war was a special case rather than indicative of a trend in EU external relations and especially EU–US relations is among the questions discussed in detail below.

Enlargement of the EU in Central and Eastern Europe

We will now examine in more detail the five Central and Eastern European states of the Czech Republic, Hungary, Poland, Slovakia and Slovenia, which joined the EU in May 2004. These five accession states vary widely in the size of their territories and in their populations, and in economic development (see Table 1.1). Three gained their independence only after the collapse of communism in 1989: the Czech Republic and Slovakia (formerly Czechoslovakia), and Slovenia (formerly part of Yugoslavia). Poland has by far the largest population (38.2 million) of the five, while Slovenia, one of the most prosperous, has a population of only two million.

The five Central and Eastern European states are much poorer than the 15 countries (EU15) that made up the EU before May 2004 – see the GDP column in Table 1.1. They all have GDP per head below the EU average, and only the Czech Republic and Slovenia are near three-quarters of the EU average. Unemployment varies considerably, with Poland and Slovakia (together with Estonia, Latvia and Lithuania, to be discussed later) having unemployment rates notably higher than other EU countries. Inflation rates also vary, but inflation is high in Hungary and Slovakia (and Latvia). Approximately one in five members of Poland's workforce is engaged in agriculture, but this is not greatly above the proportion in Greece.

The path to EU membership has been complex and protracted for all five Central and Eastern European states. It was only in 1998, nine years after the collapse of communism, that the EU finally entered into detailed accession negotiations with the Czech Republic, Hungary, Poland, and Slovenia, and it was not until

Table 1.1 Demographic and economic data

Country	Population ('000) 2004	Unemployment rate % Sept. 2004	Inflation rate % Sept. 2004	GDP per capita in PPS* EU=100 2003	GDP yearly growth, %, second quarter of 2004	Labour force working in argiculture (%)
The EU15						
Austria	8,114	4.5	1.9	122	1.8	12.9
Belgium	10,396	7.7	1.8	116	2.4	2.2
Denmark	5,398	5.3	0.9	123	2.6	3.3
Finland	5,220	8.4	0.2	110	2.7	5.1
France	61,685	9.6	2.2	113	2.8	4.1
Germany	82,532	9.9	1.9	108	1.5	2.4
Greece	11,041	9.3	2.9	80	3.9	16.0
Ireland	4,028	4.4	2.4	133	4.1	6.5
Italy	57,888	8.5	2.1	108	1.2	4.4
Luxembourg	452	4.3	3.1	212	n.a.	1.3
Netherlands	16,258	4.7	1.1	120	1.4	3.3
Portugal	10,475	6.5	2.1	75	1.5	12.6
Spain	42,345	10.6	3.2	95	2.6	5.7
Sweden	8,986	6.8	1.2	115	3.5	2.3
UK	59,652	4.6	1.1	118	3.6	0.9
The 10 countries that joined the EU in May 2004						
Cyprus	730	5.1	1.8	83	4.3	n.a.
Czech Republic	10,212	8.4	2.8	73	4.1	4.5
Estonia	1,351	8.9	3.8	46	5.9	6.1
Hungary	10,117	5.9	6.7	61	4.1	5.8
Latvia	2,319	9.7	7.7	42	7.7	13.4
Lithuania	3,446	10.4	3.0	46	7.4	17.8
Malta	400	8.4	3.2	74	−1.5	n.a.
Poland	38,191	18.7	4.7	46	6.1	18.4
Slovakia	5,380	18.0	6.4	51	5.4	4.4
Slovenia	1,996	5.9	3.4	77	4.6	10.9

* Purchasing power standad
(Source: Eurostat 2004.)
Note that the data for Cyprus refer to the 'government-controlled area' only – i.e. they exclude the part of the island under Turkish control – see later.

2000 that negotiations began with Bulgaria, Romania and Slovakia. By May 2004, Bulgaria and Romania had still not met all the conditions for EU membership but were considered to be on track for accession in 2007.

We have already seen that, in order to be admitted to the EU, each of the candidate states had to satisfy the Copenhagen and Madrid conditions. Many of the candidate countries rightly complained that the conditions set out in Copenhagen and Madrid were much more demanding than those for previous enlargements. As Rupnik (2004: 79) observes, the candidate states were asked 'to apply standards that none of the current EU members could live up to'. Thus, according to a report by the European Commission, none of the EU15 states actually enforced or applied more than 80 percent of the *acquis*. Moreover, the accession conditions have been interpreted progressively more widely. New areas added since 1993 include those of justice and home affairs, and the Schengen area of passport-free travel; a common foreign and security policy, with a defence identity; and a common currency (Grabbe 2003: 255–6).

The European Commission's Comprehensive Monitoring Report, issued in October 2003, provides an in-depth assessment of each of the candidate countries and their readiness for accession. The report detailed those areas where work was still required before accession. Thus, for example, it called upon Slovenia, the Czech Republic and Poland to take 'immediate action with regard to training requirements and mutual recognition of qualifications for professionals'. Slovakia was urged to speed up its provision of 'fiscal aid to the steel industry, legislation pertaining to food safety and health, and procedures dealing with payments to farmers'. The Czech Republic was called upon to make changes 'in food safety, health matters and road transport', while Hungary was told that it must speed up 'the distribution of rural development aid and payments to farmers'. Poland was required to 'implement legislation governing the certification of veterinarians, the movement of animals, the disposal of animal waste, food safety and health issues, procedures for making payments to farmers, and inspection and control of the fishing fleet' (report findings summarised in Cameron 2004: 120).

Support for EU accession

In referenda held across the region in 2003, support for EU membership was very strong, ranging from 77 percent in the Czech Republic and Poland to 86 percent in Hungary, 90 percent in Slovenia and 92 percent in Slovakia (see Table 1.2). These results were far higher than any of the numerous opinion polls had predicted in the run-up to the referenda. However, turnout was rather low, particularly in Hungary, where less than half of the electorate participated. Poland's referendum was also rather tense, as a 50 percent turnout was required for the results to be valid (Grabbe 2004: 70).

Table 1.2 Referenda in accession countries

Country	Whether binding	Date in 2003	Result %	Turnout %
Slovenia	Not Binding	23 March	90 Yes	60
Hungary	Binding	12 April	84 Yes	46
Slovakia	Binding	16–17 May	92 Yes	52
Poland	Binding	7–8 June	77 Yes	59
Czech Republic	Binding	13–14 June	77 Yes	55

(Source: Grabbe 2004: 70.)

As Grabbe observes, strong euro-scepticism has generally been 'confined to fringe parties' in most of the new member states (*ibid.*). The most senior politician to speak out against the EU was the Czech president, Vaclav Klaus, who repeatedly warned his countrymen that after accession the Czech Republic would cease to exist as an independent country (Shafir 2004a: 11). Thus, while former president Vaclav Havel celebrated accession day (on 1 May 2004) with the speakers of both houses of the Czech parliament, Klaus declared that he saw no need to take part in such festivities (*ibid.*). However, Klaus also argued that the Czech Republic had no real choice over the matter of EU accession, and that it had to join the EU if it did not want to be left politically and economically isolated.

Fuelled by rumours of economic hardship and high unemployment and fears that land and property would be sold off to foreigners, support for EU membership fell precipitously in the run-up to accession. In Poland, support for Self-Defence, the virulently anti-EU party (which won 10 percent of the vote in the 2001 parliamentary elections) and for the ultra-nationalist League of Polish Families (which gained 7.8 percent of the vote) increased sharply as the date of accession drew nearer (Cameron 2004: 125). Polish farmers were among the most strident euro-sceptics, fearing that they would not be able to compete with their Western counterparts in the EU. Over two million farms in Poland are small and poorly equipped to deal with competition from Western Europe (Maksymiuk 2004: 6).

In a poll conducted in March 2004, less than half of Poles (42 percent) believed that enlargement would benefit their country, while 33 percent were against. In Hungary, 34 percent of those polled were optimistic, and 27 percent regarded the expansion with scepticism. In the Czech Republic, the number of euro-optimists (35 percent) was roughly equal to the number of euro-sceptics (33 percent) (Buechsenschuetz 2004: 1). Three main factors appear to have contributed most strongly to the drop in popularity of EU membership:

1. the immediate costs of enlargement for the Czech taxpayer;
2. panic among the EU's 15 'old' members over a possible invasion of cheap labour from the 'new' members;
3. persistent squabbles over the postwar settlements with neighbouring Germany and Austria, but also with segments of the Hungarian political elite (Shafir 2004a: 12).

Moreover, support for the EU is liable to drop even further as the economic costs of membership become clearer in the post-accession period. The sceptics are right to be worried. The five Central and Eastern European states, plus Estonia, Latvia and Lithuania, 'will receive a total of some 27 billion euros in commitments from all EU programmes, plus a special cash-flow facility and temporary budgetary compensation in the first three years of membership'. But they will also have to pay 'approximately 14 billion euros to the EU, resulting in a net budgetary gain of 13 billion euros' (Cameron 2004: 123). The cash-flow facility for Poland will be approximately one billion euros 'for 2004, plus 650 million euros in 2005 and 550 million in 2006'. In addition, all the new members will get 'temporary compensation to ensure that no new member becomes a net contributor' (Grabbe 2004: 68). However, countries with rising budget deficits, such as the Czech Republic, Hungary and Poland, will sooner or later have to cut back on their expenditure for health, education, social security, and other welfare policies. Polish farmers will initially be handicapped by the EU's system of direct farm subsidies. They will receive just 25, 30 and 35 percent of full EU subsidies in 2004, 2005 and 2006, respectively. The richest of the candidate countries, the Czech Republic and Slovenia, stand to gain the least from the economic package.

Promotion of democratic reform in Central and Eastern Europe

One positive aspect of EU enlargement in Central and Eastern Europe has been the impact of the accession process on democratisation and economic reforms. The quest for EU membership has undoubtedly speeded up the development of democracy and the rule of law in the region. As Romano Prodi observed: 'There can be no doubt that the enlargement of the EU has been a powerful stimulus for political and economic reforms that have buttressed democratic institutions and respect for human rights in the accession countries. It has also supported the creation of competitive, socially oriented market economies' (Prodi 2004: 2).

Each of the candidate countries has sought to adopt EU laws and regulations, to open markets to EU goods and services, and to settle internal and external disputes peacefully, and they have also had to bring their legislation into line with the EU *acquis* (Zielonka 2004: 23). Thus, for example, under pressure from the EU, the Czech Republic, Hungary and Slovakia have introduced measures to improve the situation of the Roma (see Key fact 1.6). The EU has also 'denounced politically motivated corruption, and criticised the manipulative and illiberal way in which the public media were run in Hungary and Slovakia' (Pehe 2004: 38). Twice the EU accession process has contributed to the defeat of authoritarian governments led by Prime Minister Vladimir Meciar in Slovakia (Rupnik 2004: 78). Slovakia had originally been left out of the 'fast-track' candidates for EU membership because of 'Meciar's hectic policies of nationalism and cronyism, his harassment of political opponents' and human rights violations perpetuated against the Roma, who comprise 9 percent of the population (Shafir 2004b: 13–14). Thanks to pressure from the EU, the Meciar government was defeated in 1998, and the new government of

---

Key fact 1.6

The Roma

The Roma, also known by many other names, such as Gypsies, Romanies and Tzigani, are a people originally from northwest India who migrated to Europe, reaching Western Europe by the fourteenth century. (The name 'Gypsy' came from a mistaken belief that they originated in Egypt.) They are now mostly settled, although it is thought that about 5 percent of the European Roma are still nomadic. Throughout their history in Europe they have been subjected to persecution – for example, it is estimated that at least 250,000, perhaps up to 500,000, Roma were exterminated in the Nazi Holocaust. They still face discrimination, especially in some Central and Eastern European countries – notably Bulgaria, Romania and Serbia.

(Source: For more information, see http://www.romani.org/.)

Prime Minister Mikulas Dzurinda, which was returned to power in 2002, was able to speed ahead with the implementation of radical economic and political reforms, eventually overtaking Bulgaria and Romania in the race to satisfy the Copenhagen conditions for EU membership.

In addition, judicial reforms have been implemented in all five Central and Eastern European states under the scrutiny of the EU, and many 'judges and prosecutors with compromised records from communist times' have been removed from office. In addition, the civil service was depoliticised with the introduction of 'merit-based criteria for advancement', and 'nepotism, misfeasance, and inefficiency' have been rooted out of state bureaucracies. Thus, for example, the Czech Republic hurriedly pushed its civil service law through parliament on the eve of an important European Council meeting in Copenhagen in 2002 that invited it to join the EU. Poland, the Czech Republic and Slovakia have also created regions and regional governments under pressure from the EU (Pehe 2004: 40). However, there is still much work to be done, and corruption and government control over the media are still major concerns in all five Central and Eastern European states.

Economic reforms

It is fair to say that in the case of economic reforms, 'all the candidate countries had to overcome rampant corruption, dubious privatisation deals, and questionable banking practices under which money was loaned solely on the basis of political connections' (Pehe 2004: 40). Under pressure from the EU, the Czech Republic and Slovakia also conducted major reforms of their banking systems. Market economies are now firmly in place in all five Central and Eastern European states, and we have seen an end to the 'mafioso capitalism', which was common in the early transition period at the beginning of the 1990s (Pehe 2004: 40).

However, while enlargement may have boosted democratic fortunes in Central and Eastern Europe, it is far from clear that it will enhance democracy within the EU itself. There are fears among the older members that this latest round of enlargement will provide an avenue through which Central and Eastern European 'paternalism, populism, and corruption' will infiltrate the EU. Furthermore, enlargement could:

- harm democracy by moving governance even farther from citizens' reach;
- erode democratic practices that existed between and within the old members;
- make politics more remote from citizens;
- add to the considerable levels of democratic deficit already present in the EU (Zielonka 2004: 30, 33).

From the Baltic to the Mediterranean

The wide territorial coverage of the May 2004 enlargement of the EU is particularly evident in its inclusion of three Baltic states (Estonia, Latvia and Lithuania) and two Mediterranean states (Cyprus and Malta). All of these states and especially the Baltic states are among the poorest and smallest states in the enlarged EU (see Table 1.1). They also share other common features, including a recent history as part of large empires and a keen regard for independence in the light of this experience. The Baltic states were annexed by the Soviet Union during the Second World War and finally achieved independence in 1990–91, while Cyprus and Malta were UK possessions until 1960 and 1964, respectively.

Referenda in the Baltic states resulted in substantial majorities for EU membership – Estonia (66.9 percent), Lithuania (91 percent) and Latvia (67 percent). In Malta, however, there was a much smaller majority (53 percent). Deep divisions of opinion on membership dated back to 1990, when Malta first applied to join the EU, but this application was suspended under the Labour government of 1996–98. In a bitterly contested referendum campaign, the conservative Nationalist Party supported membership, while the Labour Party called for a 'No' vote and advocated a loose, ill-defined 'partnership' between Malta and the EU that would allow the island to keep its options open and remain a 'Mediterranean Switzerland'.

Cyprus did not hold a referendum. The island constitutes the most problematical feature of the recent enlargement because of its division since 1983 between Turkish Cypriots (whose Turkish Republic of Northern Cyprus is not recognised by any state except Turkey) and Greek Cypriots in the southern part of the island (whose Republic of Cyprus is internationally recognised as the official state). The troubled history of relations between Greece and Turkey following a Greek-engineered coup against the island's democratically elected government and Turkey's invasion of the island in response (1974) has implications for Turkey's current efforts to join the EU. Prior to the entry of Cyprus into the EU in May 2004, a United Nations plan (Kofi Annan Plan) to reunite the island via a bi-communal federation of two largely autonomous states was approved by the Turkish Cypriots but rejected by the Greek Cypriots (April 2004). Consequently, although Cyprus joined the EU in May 2004, that part of the island under Turkish occupation does not enjoy *de facto* membership. Turkey's support for the Annan plan strengthened its case for opening negotiations for EU membership and contributed to the EU's decision to do so (December 2004). Before full membership of the EU becomes possible, however, Turkey will have to undertake a major policy change towards the question of Cyprus. In short, it could not join the EU with its army still occupying the northern part of the island in contravention of international law.

Further reading

The most useful recent book is Cameron, F. (ed.) (2004) *The Future of Europe: Integration and Enlargement*, Taylor & Francis, London. This book contains essays by a range of scholars.

Use relevant websites to keep up to date – particularly, the relevant part of the EU Commission's site http://www.europa.eu.int/comm/enlargement.

Section 1.2

What is Europe?

Tracing the changing understandings of the idea of Europe requires consideration of shifting relations within Europe and between Europe and the world beyond. Such changes from ancient times to the present day are illustrated below in relation to key shifts in the geographical imagination of Europe.

Origins of the idea of Europe

Origins of the name for the continent today called Europe and located in the western end of the Eurasian land mass are obscure, as is the idea of Europe being a separate continent at all. In ancient Greek mythology, 'Europa' was the daughter of a Phoenician king abducted by Zeus in revenge for the abduction of Io (Unwin 1998: 2). How and why the name became attached to the continent is not clear. One suggestion is that the name comes instead from Phoenician words for 'evening land', or from the Greek meaning 'dark looking one' (Unwin 1998). Such puzzles find mention in classical Greek geographies. Herodotus (fifth century BC) mentions a division of the known world into three continents – 'Asia', 'Europe' and 'Libya' (in northern Africa) – but concedes that he has little idea how the names came about. Nor did Herodotus know why Europe was seen as a continent rather than part of a larger land mass, nor why particular rivers were seen to divide these continents. Furthermore, he admitted having little idea how the western and northern fringes of Europe looked. Typically, his world view reflected an existence centred on the Mediterranean Sea, with its importance for trade, communication and what the Greeks regarded as civilisation. There was little notion of Europe as a continent having significance in and of itself.

However, Greek civilisation and the later Roman Empire together provided powerful cultural legacies that shape later concepts of Europe:

- First, Romans and Greeks saw the qualities, rights and duties of their urban-based societies as marks of 'civilisation', and distinguished themselves from those they regarded as less 'civilised', the 'barbarians'. For the Greeks, this distinction between civilised and less civilised realms came over time to be associated, often through early examples of political propaganda, with geographical distinctions between the 'European' lands to the west of the Bosphorous where they lived and the lands to the east, in areas known by the Greeks as Asia (Delanty 1995). It would be going too far to suggest that any clear 'European' identity developed at this time, but cultural distinctions and their association with particular parts of the Eurasian land mass can be found.

- Second, the rise of the Roman Empire incorporated large swathes of land and people across Europe under a unified 'cultural complex' (Unwin 1998: 2). Influential elements included use of a shared language (Latin), administrative and legal system and cultural attitudes. The Roman Empire also introduced a shared religious world view following the adoption of Christianity as the official religion of the Roman Empire by Emperor Constantine in AD 391.

Medieval Europe and the rise of Christendom

Emerging out of the so-called Dark Ages following the fall of Rome in AD 476, medieval world views show a shift away from the central position of the Mediterranean to an emphasis on continental distinctions between Europe, Asia and Africa. Heffernan (1998) argues that this began in the seventh and eighth centuries AD and is represented in the T-and-O maps and *mappae mundi* (world maps) produced by medieval scholars (see Figure 1.2). Reflecting the religious orientation of the world view in this period, these are typically oriented with east, the direction of Jerusalem, at the top rather than north. The world was depicted as divided into three segments representing Asia, Africa and Europe, with a clear continental divide in which, in particular, the Christian realm, or 'Christendom', became ever more strongly associated with the continent of Europe.

However, the term 'Europe', was only rarely used in the medieval period and had little geopolitical significance compared with the idea of 'Christendom'. Within Europe, at least among educated elites, 'Christendom' was cemented by elements of a shared 'super-culture' based around the *lingua franca* of Latin, shared adherence to Christianity and shared cultural and symbolic practices originating in these and underpinned by the structures of the Church. The idea of Christendom was also associated with territorial struggles between Christian forces and those of diverse Muslim powers. Muslim powers had conquered Iberia in the eighth century AD, controlled Jerusalem, triggering the Crusades, and at a later period conquered Constantinople, and with it the seat of eastern Byzantine Christianity in 1453 (Heffernan 1998). Common opposition to an external force created a Christian realm ever more closely associated with European territories and a westward movement of the realm of Europe over this period (Delanty 1995).

However, it would be wrong to suggest that Christendom formed a united, harmonious territory. Duchies, kingdoms, church lands, lands controlled in different places by a single dynasty, and diverse and changing alliances, all overlapped and intersected to produce a fragmented, hierarchically organised system of political territories that bore little resemblance to the modern state system. The dominant understanding and use of space in political terms was pre-modern, organised around a multi-level, religious-centred world view and feudal social structures.

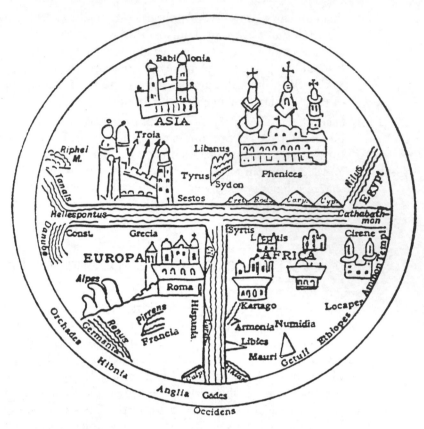

Figure 1.2 T and O map

Source: East (1989: 48)

Europe and the wider world – secular Europe emerges

The Renaissance and early modern period in Europe mark a shift from pre-modern territoriality towards new concepts of the place of Europe in the world and the meaning of being European that were in turn related to the beginning of the modern state system.

• The idea of 'Europe' as a secularly defined continent emerged to displace the older notion of 'Christendom', although Christianity remained important in the development of the continent thereafter. In part influenced by the breakdown of the unity of the Christian Church following the Reformation, this secularisation is also associated with fundamental changes to the political economy as exploration, colonialism and expanded trade routes laid the basis for capitalist economic growth in Europe. Exploration and improved cartographic techniques led to the production of new world maps that were very different from those of the medieval period. The new maps positioned Europe at the centre of a much-expanded world and typically placed north, rather than east, at the top. Such maps represented views centred not on Rome and Jerusalem but on the needs and interests of the new mercantile and trading centres of Northern Europe and the Atlantic such as Amsterdam, Hamburg, Lisbon and London.

- Through exploration, trade and colonial rule, Europeans developed new views of themselves compared with other populations in the world, particularly those they conquered. This new geographical imagination saw Europe as politically dominant over other parts of the globe and was accompanied by a developing sense of Europe having a common set of cultural characteristics distinct from those of non-Europeans. Etienne Balibar (1991) argues that it was really only in contact with non-Europeans that the idea of a shared sense of being 'European' came to be meaningful, representing a way of distinguishing the colonisers from the colonised. Blake's illustration from 1796 (which appeared in *Engravings for J. G. Stedman, Narrative, of a five years' expedition, against the Revolted Negroes of Surinam, in Guiana, on the Wild coast of South America; from the year 1772, to 1777*) represents this in the embodied relationships between Africa, America and Europe. Europe appears as the central figure, distinctive and idealised, needing its links to Africa and America but fundamentally different from the darker-skinned Africa and America.

A Europe of nation-states – coexistence or conflict?

However, the new geographic imagination of Europe was fractured for centuries by wars and conflicts between the different political forces that emerged in the new structures of the modern state system in Europe. It has been argued, for example, that the idea of 'Europe' as a secular geopolitical concept emerged from the early modern attempt to create an international system in which conflict and warfare between emerging nation-states would be, if not eradicated, then at least controlled (Heffernan 1998: 92). Competition within and beyond Europe (through increasingly global trading empires and territorial conquests), the emergence of the capitalist economy and the Reformation and Counter-Reformation (shattering the previous unifying force of the Church) increased rivalries between European states and empires. Such struggles are typified by the conflicts of the Thirty Years War (1618–48). At the end of that war, the Treaty of Westphalia established key principles of territorial sovereignty and international law that came to underpin the developing modern state system in Europe. Central to this was Machiavelli's idea of the balance of power. He argued that since rival states had apparently in-built tendencies towards conflict, the power of a state should be held in balance by a system of other roughly equally powerful states. Action by any one state would be counteracted by an alliance of other states to restore balance.

While the balance of power represented the dominant underpinning of the state structure, over the following centuries a number of commentators sought alternative overarching politico-territorial solutions to promote peaceful coexistence. These solutions were forerunners of contemporary ideas about shared security and prosperity in Europe (see Opinion 1.5). None of these grand designs was implemented, since, as Frederick the Great of Prussia remarked, 'the thing is very practicable: all it lacks to be successful is the consent of all Europe and a few other small details' (cited in Heffernan 1998: 31). Instead, the first unification of much of Europe in the modern period came with the conquest of the Napoleonic armies (1792–1814) following the French Revolution. The Napoleonic Wars marked a failure of the balance of power and its displacement by the expansionist drives of one state.

Opinion 1.5

Grand plans for Europe

The Duc de Sully (early seventeenth century) suggested that Europe be divided equally among a certain number of powers and in such a manner that none of them might have cause to either envy or fear from the possessions or power of others. He proposed 15 states, a common European army and delegates to a general council to resolve conflicts.

William Penn (1693) said that there was an urgent need for a European diet or parliament to remove the possibility of war; he also proposed a common European army.

The Abbé de Saint-Pierre (1712) added the suggestion of legally binding codes through which warfare would be conducted.

Claude-Henri de Saint-Simon (1814) proposed the reorganisation of European society around shared economic and transport interests.

(Source: For further details, see Heffernan 1998.)

How do these ideas relate to the current debates about the way forward for the EU?

The Congress of Vienna (1815) at the end of the Napoleonic wars marked an attempt by the major powers in Europe to reassert the balance of power, seeking to hold French power in control. However, perhaps equally significant in the long run were the political implications of the French Revolution, which had demonstrated, in its ideals at least, that the old regimes of Europe could be replaced by new forms of government based on modern ideals of citizenship and liberty. Such ideas of liberation and the political expression of national cultures in the shape of a modern state underpinned nationalist movements in the early nineteenth century, which focused either on seceding from the old territorial empires (the Habsburg or the Ottoman Empire), or on building nation-states out of splintered national groupings (Italy and Germany). Early nationalist movements saw little tension between ideals of nationalist uprising and a desire for harmonious coexistence with other states. Young Europe (1834), involving nationalist movements in Italy, Germany, Poland and elsewhere, called for the creation of a United States of Europe to match the United States of America, which was seen as an example of possible forms of cooperation.

Despite this pan-Europeanism, as the nineteenth century progressed there was increasingly intense rivalry between the major powers over European, colonial and economic interests. This rivalry was fuelled by increasingly aggressive forms of nationalism and by self-interest and pushed aside any ideas of European unity. Alongside its role as the core of major global empires and cultural movements, Europe was increasingly associated with rivalries and open conflicts, which eventually escalated into the enormous destruction of the two world wars of the twentieth century.

Figure 1.3 Old conflicts in Europe

Source: *Independent on Sunday* (18 February 1990) © The Mansell Collection, Getty Images.

European integration – a new beginning?

Out of the ruins of the Second World War and the emerging continental divisions of East and West in the Cold War came attempts to create new territorialities for Europe to form some kind of basis for peaceful coexistence and economic recovery. From the start, moves to postwar integration involved tensions between differing concepts of Europe, for example around whether integration should be European in orientation or have a transatlantic focus. The EC's early focus on economic cooperation as a basis for mutual security in the western part of a divided Europe gradually drew in more countries to be part of an 'ever closer union' (as expressed in the Treaty of Rome in 1957), and the end of the Cold War eventually allowed expansion of membership to countries across the old East–West divide. Yet, as discussions elsewhere in this book show, contemporary concepts of Europe remain highly contested despite the institutional unity of the EU. For example, should Europe be a 'multi-speed' Europe with some countries heading more quickly towards integration than others, as in the case of the euro zone? How can Europe create openness and integration while protecting its borders without becoming a 'fortress Europe'? How can the differences in foreign and security policy, captured by US Defense Secretary Donald Rumsfeld's comparison of 'New Europe' and 'Old Europe', be reconciled?

Development of the EU might be interpreted as a move to a 'postmodern territoriality' in Europe, shifting from the modern centrality of the nation-state to new post-national political structures (Ruggie 1993) and reducing the significance of the nation-state (Anderson 1995). This in turn raises questions about the balance between states and the EU that are central to current debates about the sovereignty of member states, or the discussions around the European constitution. However, seeing the EU as a new super-state arguably overstates the mark somewhat, since much of the political structure of the EU depends on intergovernmental cooperation.

Open Europe or new boundaries?

Thinking of the EU as one big country is only one particular representation of the changing spaces and places of Europe, and other trends in European territoriality can be identified. It has been argued, for example, that 'while we can point to a map and identify Europe, or we can complain about it or celebrate it as an institution, in many ways Europe is brought into being, brought alive, by a series of practices of mobility' (McNeil 2004: 121). Through tourism and migration across open borders within the EU, either for work or a better quality of life, new patterns of 'transnational' belonging may be producing a new concept of Europe as an interconnected set of networks, or a 'space-of-flows' (Ruggie 1993). Likewise, such networks connect well beyond the boundaries of the EU through the impacts of global migration patterns into and out of Europe. This notion of Europe as a 'space-of-flows' is also prevalent in discussions of the integration of European economic spaces with globalised networks of trade, business and capital (Hudson 2004).

However, such fluid and open processes are countered by tendencies to seek to fix boundaries, to limit flows and interconnection, to reassert the political borders of the nation-state or to bound the edges of Europe more tightly. Ethno-nationalist and regional movements, the political salience of anti-immigration parties, debates about threats to national sovereignty from European integration, moves to control migration into Europe, and economic debates about protectionism and free trade all suggest that the supposed move to open boundaries and a post-national form of political territoriality in Europe is far from a completed project. Europe today involves a complex set of competing and contested processes about the nature and identity of the political spaces and territories of the continent. Current debates centre on questions of how open or closed, fluid or fixed the spaces of Europe should be, how they should be governed and what makes them 'European'.

Figure 1.4 The states of Europe 1994

Is there a cultural Europe?

Culture as determining identity

Everyone has a sense of what he or she is as a person. But although we are all different, the identity we form is not made up by each individual. It is built up from the culture. So to some extent we share our identities with those whose culture is similar to our own. Culture determines or influences a social (shared) identity.

The faith in a European cultural identity and its political roots

In the long European peace lasting from 1815 to 1914, many Europeans came to think that Europe, which dominated the whole world apart from what had been its own colonial area of North America, was the centre of a secure civilisation of a high culture of modernity, advancing in peace and progress. The disasters of the two world wars of the twentieth century smashed this comfortable belief. Both wars arose from the mutual jealousies and fears of European nation-states, and they were accompanied by dreadful massacres, racism and totalitarian brutality. Thinkers realised with horror that the political and perhaps cultural divisions within Europe were deep enough to have produced the most destructive wars and some of the most barbarous regimes in history. And on one common interpretation of this, these wars were caused above all by the nationalism of the states of Europe, the extreme loyalty of many Europeans to their separate national states, which then developed into hostility to other nations. For example, many Germans in the 1920s and 1930s may have felt their own identity as a person as specifically German, because the symbols and cultural spectacles and trivia of everyday life reinforced this feeling and portrayed the lifestyles and ideas of non-German people as alien. So their primary sense of identity would be a sense of national identity. Consequently, they would think of themselves as part of the German nation and be ready to resent or fear any political events that they thought might be signs of a threat to Germany. In this way, a kind of culture was thought to lie at the root of the destructive wars of European nations with each other, a culture determining national identities for the separate nations of Europe. So towards the end of the Second World War, some thinkers hoped for a new culture in Europe that would determine a new, European identity so that, for example, Germans would no longer feel their identity as exclusively German, and French people would no longer think of their identity as exclusively French. This new culture would not replace the national cultures but would situate them within an overarching European identity. People would have a sense of themselves as European over and above their German-ness or French-ness, so the European identity would stand over all the separate national identities of Europe.

Key concept 1.4

National identity

Since 1815 many states, and since 1918 most states, have been nations and have tried to strengthen their national character This means that their citizens have shared a culture that reinforces the sense of identity as a sense of being a member of that nation.

Key concept 1.5

Overarching identity

An identity of an area containing separate identities, felt as such by its inhabitants but not at the expense of the separate contained identities.

The political institutions of the EC (or more recently, the EU) would help to foster this sense of an overarching identity; indeed, that was one of their main purposes. The political and economic structure of the EU was to be the institutional embodiment of the overarching identity. The aim was to substitute for age-old rivalries the merging of their essential interests; to create, by establishing an economic community, the basis of a broader and deeper community among people long divided by bloody conflicts; and to lay the foundations for institutions that will give direction to a destiny henceforward shared. In turn, the overarching European culture would generate further popular support for the institutions of the EU.

However, this new culture was not to be a sheer invention – if it were, it might only be resented. The overarching European identity was to build on a European culture that, people thought, already existed but that was not sufficiently recognised or thought of as determining a kind of identity. The European flag, the European currency, the European anthem, and European sporting and cultural events and competitions would make it more visible, more proud of itself, more a part of people's everyday consciousness; but it was already there as part of a European cultural heritage. Thus the claim that there is an essential European culture, not merely one invented by officials of the EU, is vital for the whole project of United Europe as originally conceived. But is the claim justified? Is there really an essential European culture? And if there is, does it determine some kind of identity? Indeed, is it true that in general there are separate cultures for peoples occupying separate areas of land (such as Europe), and that each one of these determines a separate social/political identity?

An essential European culture?

What is the distinctively European cultural heritage? In the past, people have thought that it is the inheritance of ideas, of law, and of moral order, from ancient Greece and Rome ('classical' culture). But although this inheritance is indeed part of European history (as it is also of Islamic history in the Middle East), a background of classical ideas and habits of thought is now common to the whole world; it cannot be the mark of what is specifically European. Or one might identify Christianity as the cultural heart of Europe. But other parts of the world at present have populations more widely committed to Christianity than Europe, there are major non-Christian elements in Europe's populations, and there are secular and predominantly Islamic countries wholly or partly in Europe – Albania, Bosnia and Turkey, although this cultural concept of Christian Europe is a reason why some people want to keep Turkey out of the EU. However, others vehemently reject this concept of Europe as essentially Christian, thinking it potentially racist and exclusivist. The most plausible idea of an essential European culture builds on the idea of the Enlightenment, which was originally (in the eighteenth century) a European cultural development, and – it is claimed – is still Europe's central cultural force in the world.

Key concept 1.6

The Enlightenment

A movement of thought and political action that began in Europe in the eighteenth century. It respects individual judgement rather than submission to authority, judgement based on reason focused on human happiness, equal rights for all, and eventually democracy.

Moreover, it identifies Europe as it essentially is now with something in its history that is progressive, rather than with darker aspects of its history like colonialism, fascism or racism. The very identity of Europe (for this way of interpreting it) is something progressive and good; and it is quite in keeping with this that the music chosen as the EU's anthem is Beethoven's 'Ode to Joy', with text by Schiller, which appeals to all men of the whole world, who are (it proclaims) all brothers. The Enlightenment holds that each individual should make up his or her own mind about anything important, such as moral and religious issues and how a shared society should be ruled. So each individual (and his or her opinions) should be respected, and respected equally. Political and moral ideas are not to be accepted or imposed by authority (for instance, not by religious leaders or dictators or aristocrats) but reached by each individual making up his or her own mind, on the basis of reason applied to all the evidence. But each individual must respect all other individuals; all must have equal rights.

By the mid-twentieth century, modern political programmes for a democratic society had grown out of this Enlightenment philosophy, reflecting both its liberal and socialist variants, and the EU demands acceptance of certain elements of this for all its members: human rights, freedom of speech, the rule of law, gender equality, the secular state, and democratic rule. We can see a twenty-first-century expression of the EU's expectations and its claims of their ancestry in Opinion 1.6.

Opinion 1.6

The preamble of the Constitutional Treaty

DRAWING INSPIRATION from the cultural, religious and humanist inheritance of Europe, from which have developed the universal values of the inviolable and inalienable rights of the human person, freedom, democracy, equality and the rule of law,

BELIEVING that Europe, reunited after bitter experiences, intends to continue along the path of civilisation, progress and prosperity, for the good of all its inhabitants, including the weakest and most deprived; that it wishes to remain a continent open to culture, learning and social progress; and that it wishes to deepen the democratic and transparent nature of its public life, and to strive for peace, justice and solidarity throughout the world,

CONVINCED that, while remaining proud of their own national identities and history, the peoples of Europe are determined to transcend their former divisions and, united ever more closely, to forge a common destiny,

CONVINCED that, thus 'United in diversity', Europe offers them the best chance of pursuing, with due regard for the rights of each individual and in awareness of their responsibilities towards future generations and the Earth, the great venture which makes of it a special area of human hope ...

(Source: *Official Journal of the European Union*, 16 December 2004, C310/3.)

How would you define being European?

The problem of 'the West': North America and Europe

But does the Enlightenment heritage and its modern continuance as democratic society belong to Europe especially, or to the world? Since it proclaims universal values (such as the rights of man) and favours internationalism, it can hardly be regarded as a culture that non-Europeans cannot share equally. The Enlightenment wants to share enlightenment with all men and women. So should we say instead that in Europe there is a continuing tradition of Enlightenment, continuous from the eighteenth century and the European thinkers and activists who founded the Enlightenment (and setting aside the almost equally long European tradition of opposing the Enlightenment)? Perhaps that is right; but it conceals a major problem. Even in the eighteenth century, a major contribution to the Enlightenment was made by Europe's colonies across the Atlantic, which became independent as the USA. Indeed, the very first revolution built on the principles of the Enlightenment was the American Revolution (1776–83), whose Declaration of Independence proclaimed Equality and the Rights of Man. Since then, the development of the

Enlightenment (democracy, rights for women, freedom of the press, etc.) has progressed as much in North America as in Europe, and the USA has become more powerful and wealthy than Europe. Increasingly, people came to speak of 'the West' as the centre of the Enlightenment and democracy, meaning roughly Western Europe, the USA and Canada. So the cultural basis for what we might think of as Europe's identity is not specifically Europe's at all; rather, it is the tradition of 'the West'. Hence, if there really is an essential European identity that is distinct from the USA, it must seek to distinguish itself, as the bearer of the tradition of the Enlightenment, from a powerful rival claimant. How can this be done?

Typically, it is done by emphasising the (predominantly) European sources of the Enlightenment. Locke and John Stuart Mill were English; Hume and Adam Smith were Scottish; Voltaire and Rousseau were French; Beccaria was Italian; Pestalozzi was Swiss; Kant and Schiller and Beethoven were German. The European political struggles for liberalism and democracy – the French Revolution, the Italian Risorgimento, the Parliamentary Reform movement in the UK, German and Austrian liberalism, etc. – constituted the largest part of the movement of the world's social and political structures towards democracy. The socialist wing of the labour movement, with its tradition of collective struggle against economic exploitation and a politics based on class consciousness, constituted another part. But this way of thinking based on history has its own disadvantages. Tradition is important, but most people do not think of themselves primarily in terms of the history they learn at school or university. Every genuine cultural identity must be as much forward-looking as it is conscious of its history, an understanding of who we are now rather than merely an understanding of who our ancestors were. The more European identity is defined in terms of history alone, the more it risks losing touch with who we are now and where we are going.

Opinion 1.7

Europe's uncertain place

Europe has no natural eastern boundary, and as you go east the sense of being culturally (and perhaps politically) part of Europe diminishes. So there is a tendency to think of Europe as a cultural entity firmly located in Western and Central Europe and fading away eastwards. The fact that the EU does not (in 2005) include important parts of Eastern Europe (notably Russia and the Ukraine) and Turkey reinforces this tendency. So there is a vagueness in talking about 'Europe'. People often mean 'that part of Europe included in the EU', or 'Europe except for Belarus, the Caucasus states, Russia, Turkey and Ukraine'. So the word 'Europe' sometimes designates a region on the map stretching East to the Urals and the Caucasus, and sometimes it designates an area where a certain culture is supposed to prevail. Sometimes, also, it designates the EU (although usually without intending to exclude Norway and Switzerland). But if it is defined by a culture (as is most often the case in political discussions), what exactly is this culture, and is it clear which countries have it? 'The Enlightenment' is one answer; but people have also wanted to say 'Christianity', or 'a mature political culture'.

How would you define Europe?

Furthermore, large parts of Europe do not seem to be clearly part of 'the West'; they are more on the periphery. People – even some of the inhabitants of these regions themselves – often feel this way about Russia, the Caucasian countries, Eastern Europe, the Balkans and Turkey. If the identity of Europe is specified in terms of the Enlightenment, then some countries in it (indeed, some people in it) will be more European than others, and some not very European, in this sense, at all. But is this what an identity for a population occupying a space of land ought to be? It becomes more like an *ideal standard* that some segments of it attain better than others, thereby downgrading as marginal those who do not seem to be established members of the Enlightenment tradition.

European identity and European culture in a globalised world

If culture is to be the basis for a sense of identity for a population in a region of the world, it has to be concentrated within that region. If the people within it all speak the same language, this will help to focus many aspects of a culture within that region, and national identities were often given greater cultural impact by a wide sharing of the same language in their boundaries. But there have always been linguistic minorities in every nation, and many nations share their language with other nations. So sharing the same language is not essential to a sense of identity. But in the globalised world that has increasingly come to prevail since about 1960, the elements of culture are constantly exchanged across state boundaries and become part of the cultural world of very different peoples in many parts of the world. (CNN and Harrison Ford are watched all over the world; 'The Archers' is popular in Afghanistan; and the same pop music is found everywhere.)

Key concept 1.7

Globalisation of culture

Culture in every part of the world is now strongly influenced by culture in other parts because of rapid and widespread communication throughout the globe. Consequences are (1) tendency towards one world culture (often predominantly that of the USA); and (2) a counter-tendency towards local partially differentiated cultures within global culture.

So people often think that there is a pressure towards a single homogeneous culture all over the world. Often, they identify this world culture as American, and often they think it should be resisted to preserve the native (European) culture from this cultural threat from abroad. Many European cultural leaders (especially French leaders) think this and try to protect European culture from US films and TV programmes, etc. by subsidising European (or French, etc.) films and TV production to counter the competitive advantage that US producers gain from their large home market. This programme is not very successful, not at any rate with the mass market, which produces the largest profits and has the widest influence. But in a globalised world, we should expect this. Modern technologies of communication make it impossible to resist the pressure of global culture. Cultural products and ideas just spread too fast, on too wide a range. Only a partial and limited preservation of separate national traditions (or a separate European tradition) will be possible. If separate identities for spatially separate regions of the world – whether nations or unions like the EU – depend on separated cultures, then the time for them has gone; the globalised world has dissolved the separateness on which they depended.

But we should look more closely at what the cultural effects of globalised culture actually are. In fact, globalisation does not tend towards a single homogeneous culture, although it does tend towards much cultural borrowing and much awareness of rich and powerful cultures (like that of America). People receive and understand the ideas and signs that they encounter in a way that is often strongly tilted in the direction their local culture favours. Moreover, there is a strong counter-tendency in the globalised world to a kind of localism – promoting a local culture or region as a tourist destination or as a labour market by emphasising its distinctiveness, its attractive difference from the usual. What is determined as local in this way may be a region within a country ('Stratford country', Lombardy, Catalonia), or even a city, or it may be a nation and a national area. But such local cultural distinctiveness in the globalised world is only partial, like a local colour on ideas and music that circulate generally in the world.

Thus the very idea of a separate culture prevailing on a segment of land, and generating a sense of identity, may be out of date; or at any rate any supposedly separate culture will be much more mixed and will involve much more exchanging and borrowing with other cultures than used to be the case. It is not that there is no such thing as a British or French culture, or in a looser way a European culture, but that in the globalised world it will not be so separate and distinctive, and to some extent it will be just a particular flavour to or perspective on universally shared cultural elements.

European cultural leadership

For many centuries, Europe dominated the world in many ways, notably through trade dominance, colonisation, and political and military control. However, Europe's domination of the Americas ended in 1783 with the American Declaration of Independence and in 1823 with the Monroe Doctrine, asserting the USA's determination to prevent European interference in Central and South America. Partly (but not only) because of its trade, colonial, political and military role, Europe also dominated the world culturally; political and cultural elites in Africa, Asia and South America largely took their ideas, in the twentieth century, from Europe's Enlightenment and other European cultural ideas and arts. Many Europeans took for granted their cultural leadership in the world, and often also their superiority and their right to dominance over it; hence arose a long and unhappy history of colonialism and racism by Europeans. Regrettably, these assumptions are still powerful among some Europeans.

Opinion 1.8

Europe's cultural dominance: fundamental truth or dangerous illusion?

From the sixteenth century to the mid-twentieth century, Europe (later Europe and North America) dominated the world politically and militarily. Colonialism (conquest and control of and sometimes European immigration into non-European countries) was only one aspect of this. Europeans generally believed that Europe also had the 'highest' culture or civilisation, and that imparting this to the natives of other countries was unequivocally a benefit to them. Many non-Europeans also believed this and studied European cultural knowledge so as to acquire this higher culture.

Is this the case now, and if so is it decisive for European identity, e.g. in making Europe *the* centre of Enlightenment culture? Or is it a complacent and backward-looking illusion, when the globalised world has moved on?

Opinion 1.9

The last Utopian project?

The belief that the US or the European Union, in their various forms, have achieved a mode of government which, however desirable, is destined to conquer the world, and is not subject to historic transformation and impermanence, is the last of the utopian projects so characteristic of the last century. What the 21st needs is both social hope and historical realism.

(Source: Eric Hobsbawm, quoted in *The Guardian*, 9 March 2005.)

Do you agree with Professor Hobsbawm?

So European thinkers got used to European cultural dominance, except that North American culture – though equally part of 'the West' – was and is seen as the great cultural rival to Europe, especially in the fields of television programmes, films and music. But this assumption that only the big boys (Europe and North America) count culturally is rapidly becoming out of date. Peruvian and Nigerian novelists and Lebanese poets have won Nobel prizes; Japanese musicians are highly regarded; Chinese, Indian and Iranian films are hugely successful; Australian sportsmen are among the best; and Indian economists have made major contributions to their discipline. So it is no longer the case that merely being a repository of 'high culture' especially marks out Europe in the world.

Nevertheless, European thinkers and artists remain very important, and the intellectual elite of Europe does very often still think of Europe as the location of the high point of world culture (and sometimes fails to appreciate the value of other cultures because of this). But popular culture in Europe is not centred on poetry and classical music, and the project of defining European culture and European identity from the elite culture of a minority risks leaving most people in Europe feeling that this culture has nothing to do with them. Moreover, about 10 percent of the population of Europe is now of non-European origin. For many of these people, their culture is a mix of that of their old home and what they have assimilated of their new European homes. Something remains of the old assumption that Europe is the centre of sophisticated Enlightenment culture, but it is weakening slowly. It is doubtful whether European identity should be based only on this.

Is there a European culture?

It is therefore difficult to pin down a distinctively European cultural identity, but it is not clear that this issue is so crucial as to whether the European project is viable. Perhaps it is the global structures of interconnectedness of trade, finance, and personal travel and communication that will (we hope) prevent any new war between major European nations, rather than any cultural unity as something distinctive of Europe. But there is culture in Europe, many different elements of culture shared and partly shared among its people. And to some extent people will be aware of these cultural elements as especially European. The EU tries to encourage this cultural image of Europe, but this is quite difficult because any particular person or event that the EU might think of celebrating will be associated with one among the nations of Europe. So the EU cannot make use of any hero figures to appear on banknotes lest people from other nations might feel slighted by Monnet being French or Adenauer being German or Britannia being British, if their images were depicted. Instead, the euro banknotes bear images of bridges and buildings. Furthermore, unlike the nations of Europe, Europe as an overarching identity cannot invoke the historical memories and images that nations can celebrate and that tug at the heart-strings, creating powerful emotional attachments – memories of sacrifices and heroism in past wars, national songs, images of loved landscapes, etc. So it does not seem likely that a European cultural identity can be a powerful focus of popular loyalty as national identities have been and to some extent still are, at least in the medium term. But it can be another, looser kind of identity, a partial sharing of understanding in a globalised world. And it is arguable that it is the larger, looser groupings gathering together social, economic and strategic connections in a network rather than a unitary structure that best suit the needs of our time in this interconnected world. Such groupings might include the EU, for example, together with the still looser partnership connections that it probably has to construct with the regions and states that surround it, like Morocco, Russia and Ukraine.

European culture at the beginning of the twenty-first century

Bearing in mind this looseness of any possible cultural identity for Europe, is there anything we can say about what it is like? Clearly, it has to understand itself in terms of the positive aspects of its Enlightenment inheritance (rather than the dreadful traditions of fascism and totalitarianism, for example), an inheritance that leads to commitment to the requirements of a modern democratic society. But it is interesting to focus more particularly (on a very general overview) on how it is different from the comparable tradition of the other great power centre of the West, the USA. Both Europe and the USA incorporate major cultural differences within their populations. But for the US individualist culture, these differences do not need to be accommodated; within the framework of market capitalism each individual competes with every other, and how that works out is how the market decides. For the social model of capitalism that prevails in European thinking, however, it is hoped or expected that the differences between people will form stresses indeed, but stresses within networks of relationships, still pointing towards a kind of community, a community that still contains unresolved differences but where all component cultures and peoples must be somehow brought into a community of mutual responsibility and care.

Key concept 1.8

Forms of capitalism

- *Market model capitalism*: society in which people's income is determined by the labour market and by their personal capital (accumulated or inherited), while the distribution of goods is determined by supply and demand in a market.
- *Social model capitalism*: a capitalist economy in which the state attempts to ameliorate the impact of the market economy on the weakest and more vulnerable parts of the population by employing redistributive policies.

In practice, all societies are somewhere in between these models, but the models still play a major role in focusing how society may be thought of and how policy directions can be determined.

Thus the literature, film-making, philosophy, and art of Europe show a greater tendency than those of America to emphasise unresolved differences of perspective and points of view, rather than follow heroic narratives of individual struggles and achievements. And the political understanding on which the EU is built is one of partial and negotiated connection built up through discussion in the interrelations of the European partner states and partner peoples, rather than decisive action by a unitary government. Obviously, this understanding fits well with the constitutional structure and origins of the EU, but it also has strong roots in the cultures of Europe and was given new strength by Europeans' determination to avoid the horrors of the Second World War and totalitarianism in the future.

The conception of Europe as essentially Christian in culture tends towards treating atheists, agnostics and secularists, Jews and Muslims as peripheral to the true European culture (although many Christian leaders do not intend to see it that way). Thus this way of thinking of Europe takes some differences as being within the core culture of Europe, other differences as marking off members of the core from outsiders, who are (perhaps) accepted as citizens but who are not part of the essentially European society as defined culturally. This attitude has the potential for encouraging ethnic and religious jealousies, in particular against the many Muslims now settled in Europe. Thus the debate on the admission of Turkey to the EU, in which some prominent Europeans want to exclude Turkey just because its population is predominantly Muslim, raises the most fundamental issues about whether the essential European culture is Enlightenment culture leading to secular modernity, or whether we should qualify this as also essentially Christian, thus limiting the range of differences to be regarded as fully within the community.

Opinion 1.10

Is Europe Christian?

In the debates leading up to the Constitutional Treaty, there was much discussion about whether one of the preambles of the treaty should refer to Europe's Christian heritage and whether some religious criterion should be added to the Copenhagen and Madrid criteria for new members applying to join the EU. See opinion 1.6 and key fact 1.3 to check that there is no explicit reference to Christianity in either case.

Should there be?

Is Turkey European?

The recent history of Turkey has been dominated by the search for stability and the struggle for a recognised identity. Here, we will introduce these quests. Later, in Part 2, we will look in much more depth at Turkey's pursuit of political and democratic stability and at Turkish identity through a brief analysis of Turkey's relationship with the EU and its ongoing pursuit of EU membership.

Turkey: a brief overview

Turkey is a country caught between two continents. It straddles the boundary between Europe and Asia yet does not see itself as a true member of either. The contradictions brought about by this lack of clear identity are reflected in Turkish society. While the Turkish population is overwhelmingly Islamic, the role of Islam in Turkish society and politics has been, and continues to be, hotly debated. Islam-based political parties, along with prominent individuals, have been banned several times from political office with the justification that they are anti-secular so threaten the continuance of Turkey's secular political society. Turkey is a democracy, with elections to the Grand National Assembly held every five years, yet the military continues to have an important role in domestic politics, with the last of a series of coups taking place in 1980.

However, there have also been benefits to Turkey of these contrasts and its geostrategic location. Turkey has been able to exploit these to its own advantage. Turkey borders the Middle East and has often projected itself as part of the Islamic world, as well as being part of 'the West'. Turkey was also able to take advantage of its strategic location bordering both the Middle East and the USSR during the early years of the Cold War when it became a member of the North Atlantic Treaty Organisation (NATO) in 1952. Since then, Turkey has continued to align itself with the USA and Western Europe on issues of international security. In more recent times, it has been an important ally of the USA and some European countries in the 'War on Terror', which followed the events of '9/11' (see Key fact 1.7). Turkey itself is no stranger to terrorist attacks; for many years, it was exposed to attacks from the separatist Kurdish organisation, the PKK. More recently, in November 2003, Istanbul was the scene of attacks by Islamic extremists on synagogues, the British Consulate and the headquarters of the British bank, HSBC. These attacks have served only to confirm Turkey's orientation towards 'the West'.

Key fact 1.7

'9/11' and the 'War on Terror'

On 11 September 2001, terrorists hijacked four passenger aircraft in the USA. Two of the planes smashed into the World Trade Center (WTC) in New York; the twin skyscraper towers of the WTC were dominant on the New York skyline, and space in the WTC was let to various financial and commercial institutions. A third plane demolished part of the Pentagon, the US military headquarters. The fourth plane, reportedly on course to collide with the White House, crashed in open country. In total, over 3,000 people were killed, and the WTC towers were destroyed. Images of the planes flying into the WTC towers and their subsequent collapse were broadcast live to an incredulous worldwide TV audience. The attack was the responsibility of al-Qaeda, a hitherto obscure Islamist terrorist group.

Public and political opinion in the USA was shocked by the events, usually known as '9/11' (following the US convention of dating with the number of the month first and then the number of the day). The last large-scale loss of civilian lives and property in the USA had been during the American Civil War, in the 1860s, and the USA had never experienced significant civilian losses from *foreign* enemy action; even during the Second World War, the USA had been almost immune from attack because the US mainland was out of reach of bomber aircraft. (By contrast, in Europe in the Second World War many towns and cities suffered serious bombing raids, with many civilian casualties and much destruction of property, and throughout the twentieth century persistent cross-border terrorist activity – especially by the Basque separatist group ETA and the Irish Republican Army (IRA) – provided a continued background of some loss of civilian life and damage to property.) The WTC attack in particular brought about a profound change in US attitudes by showing that the USA was no longer invulnerable to international terrorists.

The reaction of US President George W. Bush and the US Congress was to declare a 'War on Terror'. The first stage in the 'war' was to invade Afghanistan, because Afghanistan had provided a refuge for Osama Bin Laden, who appeared to be the leader of al-Qaeda. There was general world sympathy with the desire of the USA to punish those responsible for 9/11, and the invasion of Afghanistan commanded widespread support, through NATO and the United Nations, and some European countries were partners to the USA in attacking Afghanistan. The second phase of the 'war' was the invasion of Iraq in April 2003 – as we shall see below, this was much more controversial and had major implications for NATO, for US–EU relations and for the EU itself.

The legacy of Atatürk

The Republic of Turkey came into being in 1923 under the leadership of Kemal Atatürk. Atatürk had been declared the head of government of what remained of the Ottoman Empire in April 1920. He was fiercely nationalist in his policies, which led to him negotiating the return of much of the Ottoman territories in the Treaty of Lausanne in 1923. Even now, Kemalism continues to have a large impact on Turkish society and politics nearly 70 years after his death. Three areas of his legacy are particularly important for today's Turkey:

1. Secularism. As seen later in this book, Turkish political society remains secular, with the role of religion marginalised, although this has been challenged in the recent past.

2. The influence of the military in Turkish domestic politics. When he took power, Atatürk was an officer in the military and remained at the centre of a single-party government until his death. As explored later in this book, the military continues to remain influential in Turkish politics.

3. Atatürk envisaged Turkey as a modern society that, in many areas, although not all, looked towards the West.

Later in this book, we will look at the more modern history of Turkey and discuss how far Atatürk's inheritance is reflected in modern Turkish attitudes to how far the country regards itself as being European.

Turkish democracy

In terms of security, therefore, it is fair to say that Turkey identifies itself with 'the West' i.e. Europe and the USA. On the surface, Turkey is also a liberal democracy, with an elected parliament, the Grand National Assembly.

Whether or not Turkey fully adheres to European democratic and pluralist values and norms is nevertheless open to serious question. It is not at all just a matter of the country's Islamic background and traditions. There are aspects of Turkish political culture and political history – with nothing at all to do with Islam – that give cause for concern. Part of the legacy of Atatürk is an intense and chauvinistic nationalism that seeks to impose a cultural homogeneity by force where none really exists. This chauvinistic nationalism refuses to accept, let alone respect, the plurality of nations within the Turkish state. Thus, modern Turkey has so far refused to face up to the historical responsibility of the Turkish state for the genocide committed against the Armenian population of the Ottoman Empire (and the young post-Ottoman Turkish Republic). Between 1915 and 1918, and again between 1920 and 1923, a brutal campaign of genocide unleashed against Armenians resulted in the deaths of an estimated one and a half million people – three-quarters of the total Armenian population of the Ottoman Empire. Turkey continues to deny that this crime took place, let alone seek to make reparations. More recently, the legacy of national chauvinism has resulted in repression of the country's large Kurdish minority.

The conflict between the Turkish state and its millions of Kurdish citizens started in 1924, when Atatürk's aggressive secularism destroyed the foundations of Turk–Kurd union, which had been rooted in the Islamic faith. Subsequently, the Kurdish language and culture were brutally suppressed, Kurdish political organisations were driven underground, and several Kurdish groups reacted by resorting to armed force, or terrorism. Atatürk's legacy meant that war against the Kurds was seen as an assertion of Turkish superiority, and the campaigns of repression took on increasingly racist and imperialist overtones. It was not until 1991 that the legal ban on the Kurdish language was lifted. Turkey's support for the US-led war in Iraq in 2003 was motivated in no small measure by its desire to prevent the emergence of a strong Kurdish national entity in post-Saddam Iraq.

There is no doubt that Turkey has made major democratic advances in recent years. It abolished the death penalty in 2004 and signed various protocols on minority rights. A military state of emergency in the Kurdish lands has been lifted, and the government has promised to eliminate torture and protect press freedom. A new penal code, promised in 2005, will improve the rights of women (for example, by making rape within marriage illegal) and outlaw so-called 'honour' killings. Many of these advances have been bolstered – perhaps, influenced – by moves towards EU membership. Yet the signs are contradictory.

For example, in September 2004, the Turkish government seriously considered legislation to criminalise marital infidelity, to appease religious fundamentalists, only drawing back at the last minute. The proposed new criminal code will continue to allow judges to order 'virginity tests' on young women, even if they refuse consent, if their prospective future husbands demand this. The laws still discriminate against homosexuals. Women remain deprived of many rights – 19 percent of Turkish women are illiterate. A peaceful demonstration of Turkish women on International Women's Day, 8 March 2005, was baton-charged by police with great brutality, suggesting to commentators that the police were signalling their unease at proposed curbs on their hitherto absolute power. Trade unions remain very weak and deprived of many fundamental rights. And the electoral law, which requires parties to gain 10 percent of the national vote before they get representation, while not unusual in European terms by requiring a threshold, has the result of excluding Kurds and Armenians from the Turkish parliament. In conclusion, much has been achieved, but much remains to be done.

Is Russia European?

To this very day, the question of whether Russia is a part of Europe or is predominantly an Asiatic power is a highly contentious issue that is continually debated in the Russian press and among academic circles. To answer this question, we need to examine not only the geographical location and geopolitics of the Russian Federation but also questions of Russia's identity, which are rooted in its history, culture and politics.

Opinion 1.11

Russia and the West

Consider the following two views:

1. Russia's relationship with the West, and especially the related question of whether Russia is part of Europe, has had the most profound impact on how the Russians have viewed themselves and the outside world, how they have interpreted their own history and how they have defined possible paths for their country's development over the past three hundred years.

(Source: Tolz 2001: 69.)

2. The inconsistency and complexity of the Russian soul may be due to the fact that in Russia two streams of world history – East and West – jostle and influence one another. The Russian people is not purely European and it is not purely Asiatic. Russia is a complete section of the world – a colossal East–West. It unites two worlds, and within the Russian soul two principles are always engaged in strife – the Eastern and the Western.

(Source: Berdyeav, quoted in Danks 2001: 68.)

Can you think of examples, from Russian literature or Russian history, to illustrate these views?

Geography and geopolitics

With a population of 145 million, the Russian Federation is one of the most populous and ethnically diverse states in the world. Within its vast territory, which encompasses one-eighth of the world's land surface, reside 128 officially recognised nations and ethnic groups. Geographically, this vast country straddles both Europe and Asia and borders no less than six geopolitical regions of the world: Europe, the Middle East, the Mediterranean, Central Asia, China and the rest of the Far East. While most of Russia's land mass is in Asia, and Russia's border with China is more than 4,000 kilometres long, the vast majority of Russian citizens live in the European part of Russia, situated to the west of the Urals.

The post-communist Russian Federation

The new Russian Federation, which emerged out of the ashes of the USSR in January 1992, comprised just 76 percent of the area and 60 percent of the population of the USSR (see Figures 2.4 and 2.5). With the loss of the Slavic countries of Ukraine and Belarus, as well as the three Baltic states of Estonia, Latvia and Lithuania, Russia's borders were 'pushed' 1,000 kilometres to the east and were thus moved back 'to the European frontiers it had in the middle of the seventeenth century' (Smith 1999: 70). 'Russia's relations with the core states of western Europe were now conducted from behind a "double belt" of independent Central and East European states, and states of the former Soviet Union' (Berryman 2000:

Table 1.3 The former USSR

Republic/Country	Now (April 2005) in	Continent
Armenia	CIS	Europe
Azerbaijan	CIS	Europe and Asia
Belarus	CIS	Europe
Estonia	EU	Europe
Georgia	CIS	Europe
Kazakhstan	CIS	Asia
Kyrgyzstan	CIS	Asia
Latvia	EU	Europe
Lithuania	EU	Europe
Moldova	CIS	Europe
Russia	CIS	Europe and Asia
Tadjikstan	CIS	Asia
Turkmenistan	CIS	Asia
Ukraine	CIS	Europe
Uzbekistan	CIS	Asia

CIS = Commonwealth of Independent States, a Russia-led grouping for trade and other purposes of some of the former USSR republics (for more details, see http://www.cisstat.com/eng).

336). These momentous developments forced Russia once again to question its identity and to ask whether it was still a part of Europe, or if 'the loss of empire had turned it into an Asian or an Eurasian power' (Light 2001: 422).

Russia's contested identity

Throughout its history, Russia has always had an ambivalent relationship with Europe. Until the nineteenth century, it had been isolated from the events that influenced the development of the rest of Europe. 'As a result, Russia was shaped by profoundly different political, economic, religious, and cultural forces than those that moulded Western Europe' (Smith 1988: 8).

> For Russia, Europe was always both charming and frightening, appealing and repulsive, radiating light and incarnating darkness. Russia was anxious to absorb Europe's vitality – and to ward off its contaminating effects; to become a fully fledged member of the European family of nations and to remain removed from it.
>
> (Source: Baranovsky 2001: 430.)

Today, we can follow Smith (1999: 50) in identifying three schools of thought over Russia's identity and relationship with Europe:

1. those who regard Russia as part of Europe and the West (the Westernisers);
2. those who see Russia as distinctively different from both Europe and Asia (the neo-Slavophiles);
3. those who envisage Russia as a bridge between the two (the Eurasianists).

As Tolz notes, 'The famous Slavophile–Westerniser debate of the nineteenth century was precisely about Russia's difference or similarity with Europe' (Tolz 2002: 281). The *Westernisers* held that Russia's destiny was to follow the Western model of development:

> While the Westernisers promoted industrialisation, secularisation, and the rise of a middle class, the Slavophiles stressed the simple idealistic virtues of the Russian peasant, the peasant commune (*mir*), Orthodoxy, and rural life.
>
> (Source: Smith 1988: 10.)

In the early years of post-communist Russia (1992–96), the Westernisers were the dominant force in the Yeltsin government, and the Russian Foreign Minister Andrei Kozyrev pursued an overtly pro-Western agenda. Russia's aim at this time was to rejoin the European 'family of civilised nations' and to integrate its economy and polity with the advanced countries of 'the West'. In 1994, Russia signed a Partnership and Cooperation Agreement with the EU, and in 1996 it became a member of the Council of Europe. For a time, it looked as if Russia would seek full EU membership. However, in the mid-1990s the influence of the Westernisers in Russian foreign policy began to wane and a new more nationalist foreign policy emerged. After President Putin came to power in March 2000, it was made clear that Russia had no intention of seeking EU membership.

In contrast to the Westernisers, proponents of the second school of thought, the *neo-Slavophiles*, are highly suspicious of the West. For this school, Russia is a world apart from Europe and is culturally and geopolitically distinct. Russia, the neo-Slavophiles argue, must follow its own unique path of development rather than slavishly follow the capitalist West (Smith 1999: 51).

Members of the third school of thought (the *Eurasianists*), which has had a major influence on members of the current political elite, view Russia as 'a great Eurasian power whose role is to organise and stabilise Eurasia's heartland, and to operate as a buffer or bridge between Europe and Asia' (*ibid.*: 51–2). According to this school, Russia will not subordinate itself to Europe and the West; rather, it will fight to maintain its dominant control over the territories of the post-Soviet space, and particularly in the Commonwealth of Independent States (CIS). But unlike the neo-Slavophile school, Russia will not reject Europe according to the eurasianists. Thus, Putin has been at pains to emphasise Russia's European credentials. For example, at the EU–Russia summit in May 2000, he stressed that Russia 'was, is and will be a European country by its location, its culture, and its attitude towards economic integration' (Tolz 2001: 284).

With the enlargement of the EU in May 2004 and the entry of the three Baltic states (Estonia, Latvia and Lithuania), the Czech Republic, Hungary, Poland, Slovakia and Slovenia into the EU, the EU now shares a border with Russia. But as we have demonstrated, the question of whether Russia is 'a part of Europe or apart from Europe' is not simply a geographical one, and Russia's identity is still highly contested (Baranovsky 2001: 417).

Is there a European economy?

To answer this question, we need to consider what defines similarity and difference in economies. Later in Part 1, we will look at the specific differences between Eastern and Central Europe on the one hand and Western Europe on the other, so our focus here is on a more general picture.

Economies can be very different in size – for example, the economy of Scotland is about a tenth of the size of the economy of England – but still similar in structure, as the Scottish and English economies are. They can be similar in size but have different timing of their cycles of prosperity and depression – like the EU and the USA. They can even have quite different levels of income per head and yet be closely inter-twined – Luxembourg's income per head is double that of Belgium or the Netherlands, but Belgium, the Netherlands and Luxembourg have had a very close economic relationship since 1948. The important respect in which economies are or might be similar is how they behave, particularly in response to unexpected events.

Various criteria can be used to determine the likely degree of similarity of behaviour. The most important rest on analysis of:

- industrial structure
- trade interdependence
- policy stances.

We will look at these in turn.

Industrial structure

If two economies are very different in structure, for example one being very agricultural and the other very dependent on services, a sudden downturn in global prosperity is likely to affect them differently. If one is a service economy, the downturn will damage it more than the agricultural economy (because if people's income falls they will cut back more on luxury expenditure than on food consumption). However, a service economy is more likely to experience long-term economic growth than an agricultural one (because as people become richer the proportion of their income they spend on services rises, and the proportion spent on food falls). With the exception of Albania, about half of whose output comes from agriculture, in the European economies not more than about 15 percent of output comes from agriculture (all data are from Department of Economic and Social Affairs 2004) – so the economies of Europe are all (except for Albania) firmly industrialised, with varying dependence on manufacturing as against services.

Within this general similarity, however, there are significant variations. One scenario often posed is how economies would react to a future 'oil price shock' – e.g. what would happen if oil prices doubled? On this criterion, it is clear that European economies would be differently affected, because some are and others are not significant oil producers – for example, Norway and Russia would benefit because their oil exports would be worth more, and France and Poland would lose because their oil imports would cost more.

So on this first criterion the evidence is mixed. There are indeed general similarities of economic structure between the European countries, but once we look at details the evidence is more mixed. How far this really matters depends on our findings on the two remaining criteria.

Trade interdependence

The more economies trade with each other, rather than with other countries, the more likely they are to experience rises and falls in prosperity together. Exports by any country increase its economic activity (because the goods being made are sold to the citizens of other countries, thus increasing sales for home producers). Imports reduce its economic activity (because its citizens are buying goods produced in other countries rather than made by domestic producers). Suppose, for example, that France and Germany trade intensively with each other and very little with the USA. If France experiences some chance rise in income, its citizens will be better off and spend more on services and goods, including imports. The effect will be felt much more strongly by German than by US producers, so the rise in income in France will tend to raise German income but have little effect on US income. If the USA were to experience a similar chance rise in income, there would be relatively little effect on either France or Germany. In practice, despite the rise in manufacturing in the Far East, both within the EU and beyond it, intra-European trade is much more important than trade between European and non-European economies, so the European economies broadly satisfy this criterion for similarity.

This is most strikingly true for the EU countries. One of the fundamental rationales for the creation of the EC, particularly the EEC, was the promotion of trade between members. Successive enlargements make the data slightly complicated to interpret. As more countries join the EU, the proportion of the trade of existing EU members that is intra-EU (within the EU) rather than extra-EU (outside the EU) almost automatically rises. For example, on the day when Denmark, Ireland and the UK joined the original six members, trade between Germany and Denmark became intra-EU rather than extra-EU, so the proportion of Germany's trade that was intra-EU rose overnight without any change in actual trade flows. This has to be borne in mind when looking at the evidence, but it is still quite clear that EU countries trade much more with each other than with other countries. Table 1.4 presents some relevant evidence. Only Cyprus (defined to exclude the Turkish-controlled part of the island), Greece, Lithuania and the UK conducted less than 60 percent of their trade with other EU countries, and even for these four countries intra-EU trade was more than half their total trade. It is striking how far the countries that joined the EU in 2005 had already established strong trade links with EU countries by 2003.

Policy stances

This criterion tries to assess how similarly political decision makers will react to a particular shock causing, say, a rise in unemployment. As we shall see, the structures of the EU, and especially the commitments of members of the euro zone,

Table 1.4 Intra-EU trade

Country	Intra-EU trade as a percentage of total trade, 2003
Austria	77.2
Belgium	75.3
Cyprus	59.3
Czech Republic	78.7
Denmark	71.5
Estonia	72.0
Finland	63.7
France	67.4
Germany	64.7
Greece	55.4
Hungary	71.7
Ireland	62.2
Italy	60.0
Latvia	76.7
Lithuania	58.6
Luxembourg	82.3
Malta	60.1
Netherlands	68.0
Poland	74.3
Portugal	79.9
Slovakia	79.2
Slovenia	71.4
Spain	71.5
Sweden	63.7
UK	56.9
EU average	66.5

(Source: Eurostat 2004.)

impose quite considerable similarity of response, and since the euro zone accounts for a lot of European economic activity, that of itself, coupled with our first two criteria, tends to lead to similarity of behaviour within Europe. Most of the European countries that are not in the euro zone tend to behave to some extent as if they were. For some, as we have seen, this was a condition of their recent accession to the EU. Others wish to become members of the EU and hence are trying to meet the conditions of entry (which constrain their economic responses to shocks). For the remainder of the Western European countries, it is convenient for traders to ensure that their currencies do not fluctuate too wildly against the euro, and hence they adopt policies that are not too far from those of the euro zone. Only in a very few Central and Eastern European economies is there no great political imperative to follow to some extent the euro-zone countries' policies.

So, on all three criteria we have seen that in principle there are fairly strong similarities between European economies. The best evidence in practice is probably the degree of similarity in timing of the trade cycle. Here, the evidence seems to be that most of continental Europe experiences booms and slumps at about the same time, but the UK and Irish economies are on a different cycle, much more closely related to that in the USA. Concern about the lack of synchronisation of the business cycle was part of the UK's reluctance to join the euro zone. In 1997, the UK Treasury set out 'five economic tests' of whether entry to the euro zone would be in the interests of the UK; much the most important of these economically was the degree of convergence, principally trade cycle convergence, between the UK and euro-zone economies. The Treasury publishes periodic reports on these tests, and Figures 1.5 and 1.6 are drawn from the 2003 report. Figure 1.6 compares the UK, EU15 (i.e. averages for the 15 countries in the EU prior to the 2004 enlargement), German and US trade cycles over the period 1975–99. It shows clearly that the timing of cyclical peaks and troughs in the UK is similar to that in the USA and rather different from that of the EU15. It also shows that the timing of the German cycle is similar to but not quite identical to the EU15 – the differences arise principally because of the effects of German unification (1990). Figure 1.6 sets out more recent evidence (1988–2003 and forecasts to 2006) comparing the UK with the euro zone and appearing to show the UK economy experiencing swings much more in line with those in the euro zone since about 1999. So Figure 1.6 suggests that in practice the European economies are behaving more similarly to each other.

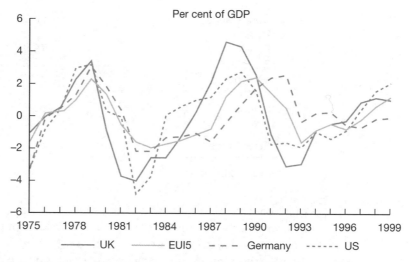

Figure 1.5 UK, EU, German and US trade cycles 1975–99

Source: HM Treasury (2003). Crown copyright material is reproduced with the permission of the Controller of HMSO and the Queen's Printer for Scotland.

Key fact 1.8

The Treasury's 'five economic tests' for whether entry to the euro zone would be in the interests of the UK.

The 'economic tests' set out by the Treasury in 1997 were:

1. Are business cycles and economic structures compatible so that the UK and other euro-zone members could live comfortably with euro interest rates on a permanent basis?

2. If problems emerge, is there sufficient flexibility to deal with them?

3. Would joining EMU create better conditions for firms making long-term decisions to invest in the UK?

4. What impact would entry into EMU have on the competitive position of the UK's financial services industry, particularly the City of London's wholesale financial markets?

5. In summary, would joining EMU promote higher growth, stability and a lasting increase in employment in the UK?

The Treasury's periodic reports on these tests can be found at **http://www.hm-treasury.gov.uk**

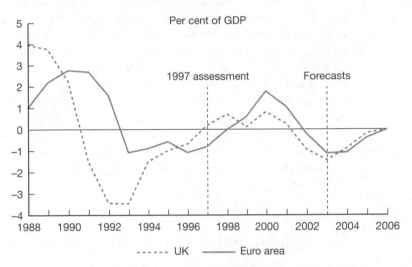

Figure 1.6 UK and euro zone trade cycles, 1988–2006

Source: HM Treasury (2003). Crown copyright material is reproduced with the permission of the Controller of HMSO and the Queen's Printer for Scotland.

Is there a social Europe?

Every society is shaped by its own unique history. As sociology, the systematic study of society, has developed it has tended to identify society and nation, referring rather loosely to American society, Russian society, Spanish society, etc. However, each of these has regional variations in culture and social structure, some parts being rural, others industrial, some inhabited by particular ethnic or religious groups. A complex nation-state like the United Kingdom could be said to enclose separate societies of Scottish, Welsh, and Northern Irish as well as the majority English, and some would want to designate separate social systems for the Channel Islands, the Isle of Man and the Scottish islands.

Is it sensible, then, to talk about a European society? Allowing for all the differences in regional and national patterns of social life and culture, can we find some lowest common denominator, some 'ingredient X', which separates all European societies from all non-European ones? This question has become more relevant as the EU has enlarged towards the east, and enthusiasts for this economic and political union assume that out of it will grow a greater sense of European citizenship, a feeling that all Europeans now belong to a pan-European society. In this section, this question will be explored mainly by contrasting the USA, which will be portrayed as a fairly coherent single society, with what some are now calling the 'United States of Europe'.

Where is European society?

Before embarking on such a comparison, it is necessary to deal first with a fundamental objection that comparing the USA with the EU is like comparing one's leg with one's body. Surely, some will argue, the USA is an extension of European society, as are Australia, Canada, New Zealand and many parts of South America. It is true that Europe spread its people throughout the globe, especially in the nineteenth century, when millions left to seek political asylum or became economic migrants from famine or to seek their fortunes abroad. These European migrants helped to build new nations, but once these nations had matured they created new societies that are distinct from the European homeland. This occurred because exposure to new geographical, economic and political environments alters the way people think and relate to each other. For example, the pioneering spirit of American settlers has left its mark on their attitudes towards individualism and opportunity, the role of government, and the right to bear arms, to mention only a few US idiosyncrasies.

The historical origins of national differences in Europe

Seeking to generalise about the Europeans who remained in Europe would require a full comparative history of nations over centuries or even millennia. The peculiarities of each nation or region would have to take into account the waves of conquest by the Romans, the eastern hordes that destroyed the Roman Empire, the dynastic struggles between empires, which subjected some to rule by Russia, Sweden, the Ottoman Empire, the Habsburg Empire, Napoleon, and, more recently, Hitler or Stalin. Such historical influences would help to explain why some parts of Europe are Roman Catholic, others Protestant or Greek Orthodox, etc. A useful exercise for any student new to the study of Europe would be to turn back the pages in a good historical atlas to see what remarkable changes have occurred over the centuries, leaving their mark on the present map of Europe. As there is not space enough here to attempt such a historical portrait, students should also refer to such authorities as Hobsbawm (1994) and his earlier works on the nineteenth century.

Europe as modern society

The one generalisation that can safely be made is that, in so far as such a thing as European society exists it is modern. Indeed, the process of modernisation, a combination of industrialisation, urbanisation and democratisation, began in Europe and then spread to the rest of the world, partly by means of the emigration of Europeans referred to above. However, the development of modern society (discussed at greater length in Part 4) took time to spread through Europe, beginning in northwest Europe, particularly the UK and Belgium, more than two centuries ago and spreading gradually east and south, reaching its more remote areas only in the second half of the twentieth century. Apart from lagging behind Western Europe in the development of modernity the eastern countries reached their present stage of development after an interlude of communist rule lasting, in the case of Russia, from 1917 and for most of Eastern and Central Europe from soon after the Second World War. It is only since the fall of the communist regimes after 1989 that these countries have begun to join the capitalist societies that had developed in most of the rest of Europe by the start of the twentieth century. However, parts of southern Europe, Portugal, Spain, southern Italy and Greece were slower to develop modern economies.

So we have a Europe of countries at different stages on the path of modernisation, some long-established urban industrial democracies, others in a slow transition towards democracy from rural backwardness and authoritarian rule. Despite the differences in their political histories, most of the nations of Europe have experienced some common trends in recent years, such as:

- a declining birthrate;
- an ageing population;
- a slow decline in religious observance and marriage;
- widespread exposure to the new mass media.

Does all of this amount to the arrival of a European society? The answer is 'no', for several reasons.

Linguistic barriers to a common European society

Unlike the USA, Europe does not share a common language. Agreed, many people share a second language, English (or American), French, German, Russian, etc., which can be useful in doing business with other EU citizens, but in private life people relax back into their native tongue. One important economic consequence is that Europeans are reluctant to move permanently to other parts of the continent to work unless forced to do so by economic calamity back home. Europe does have a small cosmopolitan elite that jets about the continent and beyond in their global worlds of business and international politics, but most people travel abroad only occasionally, to watch a football match or to go on holiday, usually spending all their time in the company of their compatriots. It is possible that more frequent trips into neighbouring countries will eventually breed a new Europhile identity, but there is little sign of this happening yet.

The mass media as a unifying influence?

It is sometimes claimed that the mass media have brought Europeans together, supplying much more information about each other's countries. However, most people watch their own national or regional television and listen to local or national radio stations, except when seduced by US cultural channels. When abroad on holiday, few Europeans can bear to tune into local radio stations in a foreign language; even if they can understand the words, the music is discordant and the sense of humour puzzling. These differences in national tastes are rooted in national cultures that developed as part of the nation-building process, mainly in the nineteenth century. By 1900, each nation had adopted its favourite poets, playwrights, novelists and classical composers (often incorporating national folk tunes into their music) and had developed its own style of popular entertainment as well as celebrating its own tastes in food and drink and its own peculiar ideas on fashionable clothing. These influences still persist, despite the infusion of largely US culture through the mass media. The differences between Italian, Swedish and German films cannot be obliterated by subtitles. French and British intellectuals still see the world differently. Europe remains a collection of national societies. One only has to watch the Eurovision song contest to drive the point home.

The unity of US society

In the USA there is a relatively common culture. Despite the disparate immigrant groups that went into the so-called 'melting pot' of US cities, they eventually all became Americanised (although some would say that the internal African-American migrants from the former southern slave states are still excluded). Cohen (1990) has graphically described this process in the city of Chicago in the 1920s and 1930s. Immigrant groups initially settled in separate parts of the city, specialising in different trades and building around them a ghetto culture reflecting their country of origin. Each group had its own shops selling familiar food and clothing, they developed local newspapers and radio stations broadcasting their own language and music, and they supported their own native brand of local theatres, bars and restaurants. However, in the 1930s these immigrant communities were weakened by commercial and technological forces. Nationwide chains of shops and mail-order firms undercut the local grocers and clothiers. New powerful radio transmitters, able to broadcast coast to coast, beamed out all-American programmes about baseball and American football. Hollywood and national advertising campaigns disseminated a new American dream of material progress and unlimited individual opportunities. The process of Americanisation was also helped by everyone attending the local high school to learn to speak American and to salute the Stars and Stripes every morning. Fighting side by side in the Second World War almost certainly intensified the feeling of national unity.

By contrast, most Europeans learn their own native language and, having fought wars against each other within living memory, still honour their own national flag; who really cares about that blue flag with all the stars on? Whereas a Californian out of work would seriously consider moving to the east coast in search of employment, there are much greater obstacles to mobility within Europe, where differences of language, religion and culture inhibit movement. We shall look later at examples of the behaviour of the expatriates in Europe and note their typical failure to integrate well into the communities in which they are living. Where there is already an established community, e.g. of Britons living in southern Spain, migration seems less inhibiting – the process migration economists dub 'the beaten path effect' – but movement to other countries for work is difficult for most people unless they are going to join others from their own country or some clearly established professional community.

Is there a political Europe?

Throughout the modern period, the nation-state has been the largest, most inclusive, of the political groupings with which people have identified. But, as we have seen, in Europe since the time of the ancient Greeks people have also had some sense of being 'European' as a significant kind of identity. The European leaders who set out to build up a European Community (as opposed to merely a pattern of arrangements for limited economic cooperation) sought to build on this sense of 'European-ness' by making the EC a political unit, with which people could identify politically. Partly they did so to bind together the quarrelsome European nations and so reduce the risk of a recurrence of the European wars that had been so disastrous in 1914–18 and 1939–45. But the project also arose from a deeper sense that the age of the nation-state of moderate size was over. It was felt that the political and economic troubles of Europe of the 1930s had resulted from the attempt to organise life in separate units (when in fact their activities intersected so much that they could not construct coherent policies as separate units) and so fell blindly into destructive policies of injuring each other's interests. The technical, economic and military conditions of the twentieth century made organised cooperation essential.

In this way, the idea of Europe as an overarching political unit, encouraging a plurality of identities in its peoples, came to seem the best solution to Europe's problems. So from the start the EC was conceived as an overarching entity, a unit of cooperation, and not as a replacement for the European nations. It was envisaged that people would feel more vividly the plural character of their identities; that they would feel themselves to be both French and European (as well as, say, Breton, and a citizen of Dinard, and so on). Such a programme can work only if people feel happy to accept the overarching unit, 'Europe', and if they feel involved in it as participants.

From the outset, there were problems with this vision:

1. Until the start of the twenty-first century, the EU was limited to a relatively small group of relatively developed countries in Western Europe. The tendency to conflate 'Europe' with the 'EU', and by extension to ignore or consign to the margins of European political realities all those countries that were not EU members, was not only historically and culturally inaccurate, it was potentially imperialistic. Even today, with EU membership expanded to include 25 countries by 2004, the EU is not synonymous with Europe. The former excludes many European countries, not only in the east of the continent and Western European mini-states but also some well-established Western European democracies such as Iceland, Norway and Switzerland.

2. It is difficult to speak of a 'political Europe' when there is so little agreement on what the core political values and traditions of such a Europe should be. Even after the end of the Cold War, Europe is still bitterly divided politically in many

ways – between, for example, secular and religious, left and right, progressive and reactionary. In many ways, the debates of the eighteenth-century European Enlightenment are still being played out. Moreover, even if agreement could be forthcoming on what constitutes Europe's core political values, it is hard to see what would make such values specifically European.

3. The degree of popular acceptance of an overarching European political identity, embodied in the EU, has always been problematic.

By the turn of the century it was clear that there had been a tendency for the EU to be built from above, and that the decision-making processes of the EU were seen as technocratic and elitist and were often heedless of the needs and feelings of the different nations and of large sections of the peoples of the EU. Indeed, as the constitutional structure of the EU changes from unanimity to majority decisions, the prospect of substantial clashes of policy between some member states or parts of the EU's population and the EU as a whole increases; and the larger the EU becomes, and the more extensive the range of competence of its policies, the more such clashes are likely to happen. Thus the sense of an overarching European identity is damaged or overthrown by a fairly widespread feeling that it is associated with structures that are not sufficiently accountable to the peoples of the EU. The scene is thus set for an accumulation of grievances that nationalistic forces, and those nostalgic for the past, may seek to exploit.

So what policy might now be adopted for Europe? On the one hand, federalists argue that incremental progress in the direction of economic integration has reached the point where a relaunch of the EU along democratic federalist lines is necessary in order to safeguard and protect European democracy. They envisage a federal EU, in which a European government elected by and accountable to the European Parliament would share power with regional and national governments and parliaments. Such a union would have the power to operate a positive policy to ameliorate the ills of European society, to combat regional and sectoral imbalances and to tackle the problems of mass unemployment and migration. On the other hand, anti-federalists argue that we should construct an EU-wide free market based on free movement of labour, capital, goods and services. Following the Gaullist slogan of '*Europe des patries*', they seek to retain control over political and social matters at the level of the nation-state.

Recent EU treaties – Maastricht, Amsterdam and Nice – leave the institutional framework of the EU intergovernmental, rather than supranational, in character. The European Parliament, for example, is still a long way from becoming transformed into a legislature; people refer to the 'democratic deficit': the fact that control of European institutions is a long way from the democratic control of the people because the European Parliament has so little power. Marquand (1995) argues that the European project found itself confronted by four paradoxes at the end of the twentieth century:

1. There is a paradox of identity. Born in the shadow of the Cold War, the identity of the EU was implicitly accepted, originally, as essentially Western European, developed and mainly Roman Catholic. Expansion towards the Protestant north and the non-Western and underdeveloped east obviously forces reconsideration of a European identity. Clearly, what it is to be European as a citizen of the EU

has now become more complex and problematic culturally, socially and historically. This point is sharply illustrated by unease in some quarters about Turkey's future membership of the EU.

2. There is a paradox of territory: the more the EU expands and grows, both economically and geographically, the greater the potential imbalance between its prosperous core and its dependent periphery, with all the potential for political tension that this brings. To overcome this paradox would require mechanisms of redistribution, which in turn requires some significant transfer of power from national governments to EU institutions.

3. There is the paradox of supranationalism. So long as the political control of the EU remains substantially devolved to its member states, it can operate effective policies only if the more powerful of its member states (i.e. especially France and Germany) exert firm and dynamic pressure to get such policies accepted. These states have not ceased to be sovereign or grown weaker. Indeed, they have, through European integration, become stronger and more effective.

> This, however, is where the paradox comes into the story. The nation states of Carolingian little Europe, of the Europe of the six which is still and will, for the foreseeable future, remain the heartland of the Union, have become stronger because they have created a chain of interdependencies which has made it impossible, or at the very least extremely expensive, for them to act unilaterally in certain key areas – notably in the key area of macro-economic management and latterly even in the key area of industrial policy'. Although these states 'remain overwhelmingly the most important focus for political loyalty and political activity ... the very processes through which they have regained the legitimacy and efficacy which they lost during the Second World War have made it increasingly difficult for them to act in the ways in which the social-democratic state of the post-war period used to act.
>
> (Source: Marquand 1995.)

At the same time, several such strong states, acting together, can slow down or paralyse EU development, perhaps contributing to widespread popular unease or disenchantment with the whole European project. Although they remain the focus for citizens' political loyalties, these interdependencies limit the capacity of nation-states to put in place policies that could effectively resolve the other paradoxes.

4. Finally, Marquand refers to the paradox of functionalism. The very success of the European project to date has brought us to the point where it is no longer clear that the hidden hand of economic integration can of itself deliver an answer to the question, 'What is Europe?' But it is not clear how the political basis for a more extensive function for European institutions could be constructed. The drafting of an EU constitution in the period 2003–04 was an attempt to address these issues. However, it is unclear whether the constitution (if adopted into law by all member states) will help to foster the strong sense of EU citizenship – of identification with the EU as a political entity – that is currently lacking, or whether it will be used by member states to delineate and defend their rights and powers, thus bolstering primary political identification with the nation-state.

Clearly, we cannot really speak of a political Europe – of European culture, democracy, or civil society – unless we accept that there is more to Europe than just a marketplace, and more to being a European than just being a consumer – albeit a consumer of a greatly increased range of goods and services. As Jacques Delors, the former president of the European Commission, warned: 'You can't fall in love with a single market!'

The construction of the EU has, until recently, been guided largely by technocratic logic. Political elites in the EU have begun to show recognition of the fact that new ways will have to be found of listening to the peoples of Europe – particularly the tens of millions of unemployed, low-paid and marginalised who feel most threatened and betrayed by socio-economic change – and engaging them seriously with the project of the construction of Europe. This is likely to be the greatest political challenge in the years ahead. As European history shows, the price of failure could be high.

Further reading

This section has introduced you to some challenging concepts. Select one or two of the following books and chapters to add more depth to your understanding:

Haseler, S. (2004) *Superstate: the New Europe and its Challenge to America*, I.B. Tauris, London and New York.

Marquand (1995), which is a chapter in D. Milliband (ed.) *Europe and the Left*, Polity Press, Cambridge.

Shore, C. (2000) *Building Europe: the Cultural Politics of European Integration*, Routledge, London and New York.

Stern, S. and Seligman, E. (eds) (2003) *Desperately Seeking Europe*, Archetype Publications, London.

Section 1.3

How different are Western and Eastern Europe?

The collapse of communism in Central and Eastern Europe in 1989 and the eastern enlargement of the EU in May 2004 have now made much of the earlier thinking about the differences between 'East' and 'West' redundant. As we discuss below, all of the countries in Central and Eastern Europe are now committed to upholding the principles of democracy and the rule of law, and market economies are now in place all across the former communist bloc. Moreover, just as there are important differences in the political cultures and institutions in countries such as Denmark, Italy and Greece, there are also wide variations in the political systems and political cultures of Central and Eastern Europe. Some Western European states, such as Greece (which is actually geographically further east than most Central European states), Portugal and Spain, have also only relatively recently (in the 1970s) completed their own transitions from authoritarianism.

In the early 1990s, there was deep pessimism among many Western academics and politicians about the future of democracy in Central and Eastern Europe. Three factors, it was feared, would prevent the totalitarian communist regimes from developing consolidated democracies:

1. the need to reform the economy at the same time as democratising the polity;

2. the difficult task of creating democratic institutions and norms in states with authoritarian political cultures and weak civil societies; and

3. the problem of carrying out democratic transitions in multi-ethnic states.

In contrast to previous transitions from authoritarianism in the capitalist states of Greece, Portugal and Spain, which necessitated a single reform of the polity, the transition from communism in Central and Eastern Europe required a double reform of the economy and the polity. It was feared that citizens there would turn to new populist parties and authoritarian leaders to protect them from the inevitable hardships that would accompany the rapid move to a market economy. Soaring unemployment, rising levels of poverty and the collapse of the welfare state, it was argued, would lead many of the newly dispossessed subjects to reject both capitalism and democracy.

A second factor that distinguished the transitions in the communist states of Central and Eastern Europe from previous transitions in southern Europe was the weakness of civil society and the authoritarian nature of the political cultures. In many of the totalitarian states of Central and Eastern Europe (Albania, Bulgaria, Czechoslovakia, the GDR and Romania), there was a fusion of party and state, and the Communist Party in these states dominated all aspects of a citizen's life. All of the organisations of civil society, such as political parties, trade unions and the press, were under the tight control of the Communist Party. Thus, when communism collapsed, there was no civil society to fall back upon to help to rebuild democratic institutions. In other states, such as Hungary, Poland and Slovenia, there was some liberalisation of the economy and the polity in the latter part of the communist era; not surprisingly, these states have been among the front-runners in developing consolidated democracies. In addition, four decades of authoritarian rule left a legacy of citizen distrust of political institutions and in particular political parties. Thus, it was argued that the development of multi-party pluralist democracies in Central and Eastern Europe would be much more difficult than was the case in southern Europe and would take decades to complete.

The third unique feature of the transitions in Central and Eastern Europe is the importance of the ethnic factor. Countries such as Czechoslovakia and Yugoslavia had been artificially stitched together in the aftermath of the First World War, and during the communist period they had been held together more by coercion than by consent. Once communism had collapsed, they simply fell apart. Yugoslavia disintegrated into a number of ethnic states amid the horrors of civil wars and 'ethnic cleansing'. Czechoslovakia split into separate Czech and Slovak states in the more amicable 'velvet divorce' of January 1993.

There were also fears that ethnic violence would erupt in other states where there were sizeable ethnic minorities, such as in Hungary, Romania and Slovakia. Some commentators feared that ultra-nationalist leaders would come to the fore and that authoritarianism of the left would now be replaced by authoritarianism of the right.

However, 15 years after the 1989 revolutions, the pessimists have been proved wrong. After a difficult and protracted transition process, which continued into the mid-1990s and which undoubtedly brought economic hardship to millions, Central and Eastern European citizens have now thrown their support behind democracy rather than dictatorship. Ultra-nationalist right-wing parties have indeed emerged in countries throughout the bloc, and a number of former communist leaders have used the nationalist card to gain power (e.g. Iliescu in Romania, Meciar in Slovakia). However, outside the Balkans, none of the ultra-nationalist anti-system parties has come close to winning power, although a number have participated in coalition governments. It should also be remembered that ultra-nationalist parties are also to be found in Western Europe. Thus, for example, parties such as the National Front in France and the Northern Leagues in Italy have been able to garner relatively high levels of public support.

Consolidated democracies

Democratic constitutions have been ratified in a majority of the countries of Central and Eastern Europe, and most elections throughout the region have been free and fair. As in Western Europe, there is a great variety of electoral systems across the region, but most countries adopted either a proportional representation or a mixed electoral system in which part of the parliament is elected on the basis of proportional representation and the other part by single-member constituencies (Kopecky 2003: 140). Although turnout at elections has declined somewhat from the heady days of the early 1990s, it is still comparable with, and in many cases higher than, turnout in Western Europe, where there has been a marked decline in the number of citizens voting in national and local elections. Moreover, all of the Central and Eastern European states have now had more than two rounds of elections, and we have witnessed more than one peaceful turnover of government in all of them.

The consolidation and institutionalisation of parties and party systems is now well under way, and legislative bodies throughout the region are more stable and productive and thus better equipped to carry out their key tasks of holding their executives to account. While membership of political parties is low in Central and Eastern Europe, this is also increasingly the case in Western Europe. Parties in Central and Eastern Europe can now be considered 'key agencies of representation, similar to most countries in Western Europe' (Kopecky 2003: 141). The professionalisation of the members of parliament has been promoted by significant increases in their salaries, the introduction of travel and accommodation allowances, and general improvements in their working conditions. It is also interesting to note that the number of women members of parliament in Central and Eastern Europe is at least comparable with that in the West. Thus, in 2002, Western European countries had an average of 17 percent of women MPs, while in Central and Eastern Europe the percentage in Bulgaria (26 percent) and Poland (22 percent) was higher than this, although the proportion was much lower in Albania (6 percent) and Hungary (9 percent).

However, we must distinguish between procedural and substantive notions of democracy.

> Setting up the procedures for a democracy i.e., creating democratic institutions and elections does not guarantee a democracy. In this case all the emphasis is placed upon the procedures established and less attention is paid to the quality or substance of the 'democracy' introduced.

> (Source: Crawford 1996: 84.)

Thus, while free and fair elections are undoubtedly key attributes of democracy, other factors need to be taken into consideration, such as levels of press freedom, respect for the rule of law and constitutional norms, levels of corruption, and the development and protection human rights. When we measure these additional categories, we find important variations across the region, but we also find that the quality of democracy in many Central and Eastern Europe states is now classified as being on a par with the consolidated democracies of Western Europe.

Support for democracy and its alternatives

Political culture in Central and Eastern Europe is not as static or authoritarian as was earlier feared. The opening up of the countries in the region to the outside world, alongside economic modernisation and the development of a much freer and pluralist press, has had a major impact on citizen support for democracy. As Table 1.5 shows, there are major differences across the region in citizens' attitudes towards their old communist regimes, their current systems and hopes for the future. Thus, for example, over two-thirds of citizens in Hungary remain positive about both the old regime and their current system, and 87 percent are positive about the future, while in the Czech Republic, where citizens suffered far greater repression after the Soviet invasion of the country in 1968, only 31 percent have a positive attitude towards the old regime while 76 percent are positive about the current political system, and 83 percent are positive about the future. Indeed, across the bloc as a whole, an average of 68 percent of Central and Eastern European respondents gave a positive assessment of the future.

Table 1.5 Attitudes towards old and new regimes and the future (percent positive)

	Old regime	Current system	Future
Czech Republic	31	76	83
Slovenia	64	75	73
Hungary	68	76	87
Poland	61	66	77
Bulgaria	57	59	58
Romania	55	50	62
Slovakia	61	39	49

(Source: Rose 2004: 1.)

Moreover, Table 1.6 shows more than four-fifths on average reject a return to communist rule, and 94 percent reject the army taking control of the country. A majority of citizens throughout the region also reject dictatorship, with the highest levels of opposition occurring in Slovakia, the Czech Republic and Hungary. In Romania, where the worst traditions of despotism and Stalinism were to be found, over two-thirds of those polled gave a resounding rejection to dictatorship, and over 80 percent were against communism.

Table 1.6 Endorsement of undemocratic alternatives (percent regarding as better)

	Communist	Military	Dictator
Slovakia	30	32	5
Bulgaria	27	32	28
Slovenia	23	6	27
Poland	23	6	33
Czech Republic	18	1	13
Romania	19	14	32
Hungary	17	2	17

(Source: Rose 2004: 2.)

The development of consolidated democracies

Freedom House is a US-based trust funded by various trusts but also by the US State Department. It publishes ratings of the countries of the world in terms of how democratic their institutions are. In its 2004 Freedom in the World ratings, Freedom House classified Bulgaria, the Czech Republic, Croatia, Hungary, Poland, Romania, Slovakia and Slovenia, as 'free'. Moreover, Slovenia was classified as being on a par with France, Germany, Italy and the United Kingdom. Bulgaria, the Czech Republic, Hungary, Poland and Slovakia are also classified as 'free' but come slightly lower down the scale, being situated in the same band as Greece. Albania and the former Yugoslav republics of Bosnia-Herzegovina and Macedonia are classified as 'partly free' (Freedom House 2004).

Freedom House also classifies Poland (1.75), Slovenia (1.75), Hungary (1.96), Slovakia (2.08) and the Czech Republic (2.33) as consolidated democracies. Bulgaria (3.25) and Romania (3.58) are classified as semi-consolidated democracies, and Albania (4.13) as a transitional government. The scores are an average of the ratings for electoral process, civil society, independent media, governance, constitutional, legislative and judicial framework, and corruption, and are based on a scale of 1 to 7, with 1 representing the highest level and 7 the lowest level of democratic development.

Finally, five Central and Eastern European states (the Czech Republic, Hungary, Poland, Slovakia, Slovenia) were admitted to the European Union in May 2004 and were thus deemed to have met the stringent Copenhagen membership criteria. According to the EU, all five of these new member states have now achieved stability of institutions guaranteeing democracy, the rule of law, human rights, and respect for and protection of minorities. Bulgaria and Romania are not far behind and are set to join the EU in 2007. In conclusion, we have witnessed a remarkable convergence in the political systems of the 'West' and the 'East'. Consolidated democracies are now the norm rather than the exception in Central and Eastern Europe.

How different are Western and Eastern Europe economically?

Fifteen years ago, we would have noted a very major difference in the fundamental principles on which the economies of European countries were run. In the West, the economies were market-driven; in the East, they were still centrally planned. Because these differences still leave a legacy in the performance of the economies now and in EU policy, we need to start with a brief discussion of this background.

Markets versus central planning

In a market-driven economy, the set of goods and services produced is the result of market forces – both how much of any good or service consumers want to buy and how much producers are prepared to supply varies according to the price charged, and in a market system prices adjust to balance supply to demand. The outcome is that what is produced, and at what prices, and thus who is employed, and at what rate of pay, is determined by market forces and not by any conscious decision of government or any other agency.

In a centrally planned economy, by contrast, it is government that decides what is produced and influences the prices charged, and similarly government decides who is employed and at what rate of pay. Many European economies have on occasion been run on more or less centrally planned lines. For example, during the Second World War, most European governments operated legislation that restricted the amounts of goods that consumers could buy (they operated a system of rationing); this was in order to devote resources to the war effort, so the state was in effect deciding how much of the available resources was to be devoted to fighting the war and how much to individual consumption.

However, in peacetime the economies of the Western European countries have been run on broadly market principles. In all Western European economies, there has always been a role for the state in determining its own expenditure on the provision of public services, in achieving some redistribution of income to achieve social justice, and in trying to prevent the production, distribution and consumption of goods regarded as socially damaging such as illegal drugs. In many Western European economies, the state has also from time to time chosen to run certain key industries in what was thought to be the national interest – often by a process of nationalisation, sometimes by using persuasion on private companies – but in general the market has been the dominant force in peacetime Western European economies. The fundamental belief underpinning this approach is that markets are efficient and flexible and that the best way to run an economy is generally to let households make whatever decisions they wish.

Why are there markets?

In any society, families play two economic roles. They are consumers of the goods and services that are available, and they make (or help to make) them. Let us start by thinking about a family, which does not trade at all but is dependent simply on what it can produce itself. Any society, which our family symbolises, faces what economists regard as the basic economic problem – it would like to have more goods and services than can be made with the available resources, so choices have to be made about what is to be produced, including how this is to be done and who is to receive the goods and services when they are available.

Consider, for example, the family groupings in Europe in the late Stone Age. They grew crops, such as grain, and they made various tools, including polished stone axes. In order to quarry the stone and then shape it to make the axes, they needed to devote labour and other resources to the task. The axes were used to help to clear the ground for new areas of cultivation; so more axes enabled more food to be grown in the long term. At any one time, however, the resources used to make axes had to be diverted from other activities, such as growing grain and making it into bread. The problems confronting any Stone Age family in any year can be considered in a stylised way as the choice between making axes and making bread, as represented in Figure 1.7.

The curve in Figure 1.7, known as a production possibility curve, represents the range of possibilities open to a family or community at any one time – for example, it could choose to make no axes, in which case it could have ten loaves (point A). It could also make no axes and only seven loaves (point B), but in that case it would not be using all its resources and would not be operating efficiently. A second economically efficient combination is point C, where there are four loaves and three axes.

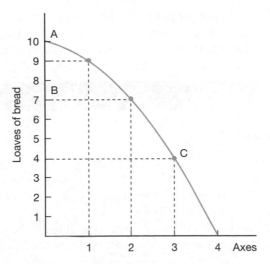

Figure 1.7 The production possibility curve

The production possibility curve can also be used to identify how much of any one commodity the family has to give up to get more of the other. Look at Figure 1.8, which repeats points A, B and C from the first diagram. Starting at A, with ten loaves and no axe, if the family wants one axe it has to give up one loaf of bread (because at point D there is one axe but only nine loaves). A second axe (point E) requires a greater sacrifice of bread, because devoting enough resources to make two axes leaves the family able to make only seven loaves, so in moving from D to E the extra axe requires resources that could have made two loaves. Except in very unusual circumstances, the efficient combinations will all lie along a curve, as in Figures. 1.7 and 1.8. When axe production is very low (e.g. at point D), more axes can be made using labour that is not very useful for baking bread and by quarrying the stone from land that is not very good for growing wheat; but when more axes

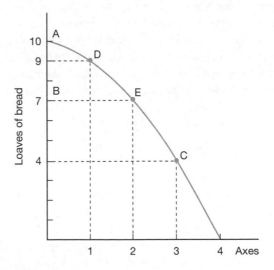

Figure 1.8 Opportunity cost

are made (e.g. at point C), the labour and other resources that need to be diverted into extra axe production are more and more efficient at making bread, so more bread is lost for each axe as axe production rises.

Opinion 1.12

What is efficient?

It should be noted that 'efficient' is here being used in the quite restricted sense that at any time with predetermined resources and technology as much is produced as possible, or any achievable output is made with as few resources as possible. It usually excludes problems such as the depletion of natural resources or pollution, because it limits itself to relatively immediate matters. It also assumes that resources are available in the right mix and of the right quality to be fully used, and that what is produced will be demanded. Neither part of this assumption is necessarily valid, so there may be unemployment.

Should all economic relationships be efficient? If not, how do we decide which should, and which should not, be efficient?

Bearing these qualifications in mind, one can conceive a production possibility curve, drawn in multidimensional space to allow for a whole range of commodities, as representing the set of choices open to the family. If it is operating efficiently as defined here – but see Opinion 1.12 – it can select any combination on the curve, but it cannot go beyond it unless its options are increased. If the family remains isolated from other families, it can obtain goods and services in greater quantity if the technology available to it improves or if it increases the resources available to it – if more of its members can work, or it acquires more of the means of production, like more axes to clear land. The choice between bread and axes can be regarded as illustrating the choice between consuming as many goods as possible now (bread) or forgoing some present consumption to increase resources (axes) to enable more bread to be consumed in the future. Pushing the curve out, by increasing the resources available, or by improving technology so as to enable more to be made with given resources, or both, is the process of growth. However, there is another way in which the family can increase the range of choices confronting it – by trading with others. The process of trading is that of taking part in a market.

How do markets work?

As soon as families move away from self-sufficiency, they will wish to exchange their surpluses of unwanted goods for goods of which they would like more. Those with surpluses wish to supply goods; those who want more demand them. The exchange can happen in two ways.

In theory, the more straightforward method of exchange is barter – the swapping of goods at some agreed rate: for example, one axe for ten loaves of bread.

However, simple bilateral swaps may not be possible. Once barter involves several swaps, it can become very complicated (see Key concept 1.9).

Key concept 1.9

Barter

The practical complications of barter can be illustrated by an example from the early career of Robert Maxwell. In the early 1950s, most international trade had to be conducted by barter because of currency restrictions. In one deal brokered by Maxwell, chemicals were exported from the UK to East Germany in exchange for an assortment of china, glass and textiles, which were sent to Argentina. In return, Argentina sent pork to the UK. Unfortunately for Maxwell, the pork was condemned by the UK authorities as unfit for human consumption, but nothing daunted he arranged for it to be re-exported, some to the Netherlands (where it was canned and sent to East Germany in exchange for cement, which was eventually sold to Canada) and the rest to Austria in exchange for prefabricated houses.

(Source: Bower 1991.)

Can you think of examples of barter in your everyday transactions?

Because of the difficulties of barter, economies have evolved the use of a specialised good – money – to act as a medium of exchange. Whether with a barter system or with a monetised one, the principles are similar: those who demand goods and those who wish to supply them meet to try to arrive at a deal. This process of meeting, whether it takes place physically in a marketplace or without buyer and seller ever coming into direct contact with each other, is called a market. Figures 1.9 and 1.10 illustrate the principles.

Figure 1.9 shows the operation of barter in the Stone Age community. The family that wants to supply axes and receive bread will be willing to supply more axes the more bread it gets for each axe, so the supply curve for axes slopes up

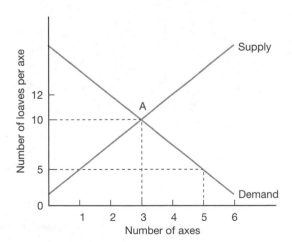

Figure 1.9 Barter

from left to right. The family that wants to obtain axes and to barter its surplus bread for them will demand more axes the fewer the loaves it has to pay for each axe, so the demand curve for axes slopes down from left to right. If, as in the diagram, the two curves intersect, it is possible to find an equilibrium price for axes in terms of bread – here ten loaves, so at the equilibrium point three axes will be exchanged for ten loaves each, thirty loaves in total. At any other price, one or both of the families will not be satisfied; for example, if the price of each axe is five loaves, only one axe will be supplied but five axes will be demanded, so there will be an excess demand of four axes. Similarly, if the price is above equilibrium, for example at twelve loaves per axe, there will be an excess supply of axes. Only at the equilibrium price can the families strike a bargain by agreeing on the number of axes to be exchanged.

Figure 1.10 illustrates exactly the same principle for a modern economy – the price in the UK of mobile phones. The equilibrium price is P_e and quantity Q_e; at prices below equilibrium, such as P_1, there will be excess demand (Q_2–Q_1) and at prices above equilibrium there will be excess supply (Q_4–Q_3).

We can use the same economic reasoning to talk about each market in a modern economy, where the markets are not just for goods like mobile phones but also for services like haircuts. The same principle also applies in markets where households are the suppliers – of their own labour and other resources to make the goods and provide the services. So the market system can be envisaged as one where a whole set of transactions is taking place simultaneously. What each household chooses to buy depends on its tastes and its income. Its income comes indirectly from what other households choose to buy, because its income comes from selling its labour and other resources to producers. So the process is circular and driven fundamentally by what households want to consume – a 'consumer sovereignty' system.

There is another important feature of the market system. Where there are many firms trying to sell some particular good, those who can offer it most cheaply will be successful, and those whose prices are too high will find that they cannot sell the good. Firms can offer goods cheaply if they produce them efficiently. Where the good is produced in a range of qualities, then the successful firms will be those that produce efficiently at each quality standard.

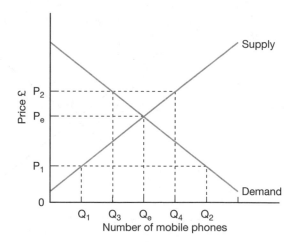

Figure 1.10 Markets in a modern economy

As we shall see, there may be distortions, but in principle the market system responds quickly and efficiently to changes in consumer tastes or to the appearance of new goods and services.

Central planning

By contrast with Western Europe, in the USSR from 1917 (apart from a brief flirtation with markets in the 1920s) and in the countries of Eastern and Central Europe that fell under USSR hegemony in 1945, the system of fundamental beliefs that operated was different in two major respects:

1. The view was that the most important aim of an economy was to achieve an appropriate distribution of income, so the state was the dominant force in determining what was produced and who was to receive the products.

2. Economic policy started from a concept of public ownership of most of the means of production (except people's labour).

To operate this system, price signals are almost irrelevant, and an elaborate structure of central planning had to be introduced. (Note that Yugoslavia adopted its own solution, market socialism, which combined elements of market and of planned economies.)

The most famous planning agency was Gosplan, which was responsible for the highest level of planning in the USSR and was responsible for the USSR's series of five-year plans. In order for the central plan to work, the planners had to calculate how much of each good and service was needed and then give each producer instructions of how much to make, what materials to use and how much labour they could have. For an economy with fairly straightforward objectives, like trying to win a war or trying to expand basic industries quickly, such planning can work quite well, but it becomes very difficult to operate in a sophisticated modern economy. When there is a huge range of consumer goods and services on offer, it is very difficult to work out how much of each item is needed and particularly hard for planners to cope with the whims of fashion. It was also increasingly difficult for the planners to work out how many resources producers really needed to make their products – producers had a strong incentive to make life as easy for themselves as possible by being given undemanding targets, and as a result production became increasingly inefficient. The problems were compounded because the maximum prices of many products were controlled, as a matter of social policy, the idea being that basic requirements, such as food and housing, would be available to people on low incomes. However, the result was shortages of goods, with long queues as people tried to buy the goods when they became available and the development of (illegal) black markets, as rich families that did not want to queue bought goods from poorer families that were prepared to spend the time to queue. The increasing dissatisfaction felt by citizens of the USSR and other Central and Eastern European countries was an important cause of the gradual abandonment of the old-style planning system and its substitution by a market system from the very late 1980s.

A further problem of shortages is that, when durable goods are available, buyers hoard them. This is true both for producers, hoarding supplies of raw materials, and for households. The average Soviet family in 1990, fearing even worse shortages or sharp price rises, was storing about 6 kg of soap and washing powder and vast holdings of toilet rolls and sugar. The confusion in the retail market effectively turned Soviet flats into small warehouses. However, hoarding serves only to make the shortages worse for those not holding stocks.

Economic reform in Central and Eastern Europe

As we have seen, the old planning system left a legacy of old-fashioned products, produced inefficiently, in the Central and Eastern European countries. As a result, in many of them the adjustment to a market system was very painful – not only did producers have to learn to respond to market signals, they also had to revamp their product range and to abandon inefficient methods of production if they were to meet the challenge of imports from Western Europe and the rest of the world.

Across Eastern and Central Europe, various attempts had been made, intermittently from the mid-1960s but in a more sustained way from the early 1980s, to make the planning system less unwieldy and more responsive to consumer tastes and to reduce the inefficiency that was becoming endemic in production. The mechanisms of incentives for producers were modified many times to try to make them operate more efficiently. Markets were increasingly being given at least semi-official recognition, particularly for small-scale producers and farmers. However, the economic reforms were mainly tinkering with detail rather than addressing the fundamental problems, and by the late 1980s they were overtaken by political events.

There was a further problem. The USSR and the other Central and Eastern European economies were members of the Council for Mutual Economic Assistance (CMEA, also known as Comecon), which they had formed to counter the economic groupings in Western Europe. Because the USSR was in both political and economic terms the dominant member of the CMEA, the non-USSR members became more dependent on trade with the USSR than the USSR did on trade with them. The CMEA links were strong, however: in 1988, about half of the USSR's trade was with other European CMEA members, and nearly 70 percent of the other CMEA members' trade was with the USSR. Therefore, the general collapse of the Soviet-style economies had profound effects on all of them, because they all simultaneously saw their major export markets shrinking. They could not develop new markets quickly, because many of their products were too old-fashioned to be attractive, at any price, to Western markets. At the same time, the new liberalisation of trade enabled consumers who could afford to do so to buy imports from the West.

Their difficulties were compounded by rapid inflation. To understand why, we will need to consider the role of prices in a planned economy. If the planning is strictly enforced, prices are set to enable poor households to buy basic goods. If this entails shortages, as we have seen, richer households may bypass the price ceilings by operating in the illegal black market. The decision of a government to operate official price ceilings but to acquiesce in the existence of a black market can serve both to make most of the goods available at low prices to those who are prepared to queue and to make small quantities (sometimes of superior quality) available at a much higher price to those who are prepared to pay for it. However, richer households are likely still to have difficulty in spending all their income, particularly in an economy where there is no private ownership of assets such as housing.

Why was economic reform associated with rapid inflation? When planning was abandoned and the market mechanism introduced in its place, demand adjusted much more quickly than domestic supply. Richer households had substantial savings to spend. The black markets meant that at least the more affluent households in cities had some experience of the price mechanism, but producers (especially those in what was the USSR, who had known nothing but central planning for up to 70 years) were used to being told what to make (and, sometimes, how to make it) and found it difficult to learn how to adapt output to demand. That meant that for commodities whose price had been set artificially low, output remained very low so the free market price was very high. Once output adjusted, prices would fall, but the initial price rises were very steep. Key fact 1.9 illustrates the problem. Faced with steep price rises, workers demanded substantial pay rises, thus fuelling the whole process of inflation. Families with two or more members in employment fared reasonably well, with pay rises about matching those in prices, but those with no or limited earning capacity suffered badly, so total demand fell for many products.

Key fact 1.9

The inflationary effects of price liberalisation in Russia

Let us look at some evidence of prices in the USSR/Russia. To start with, many of the price ceilings on basic foodstuffs were probably not all that far below market prices. But, as we have seen, in the USSR's planning system it was very difficult to determine what market-clearing prices would have been. The state-controlled prices were more or less constant over the years, while market-clearing prices probably rose slowly. As a result, when price ceilings were abandoned with the collapse of planning and the introduction of markets, prices shot up enormously. The table below illustrates the situation. The January 1990 prices are the old controlled prices. On 2 January 1991, the prices of all these commodities were freed; since there had been thriving black markets, the black market prices were used by traders as their first guess of what they should charge.

Prices in St Petersburg (all prices in roubles)

Price on:	2/1/90	2/1/91	2/1/92
Bread, 1 kg	0.13	0.65	2.92
Cheese, 1 kg	3	9	144
Beef, 1 kg	2	7	60
Tomatoes, 1 kg	0.5	9	120
Milk, l litre	0.36	0.65	7

We can see from the table some of the details that made for horrifying rates of inflation in Russia in the early 1990s.

Falling demand makes it less attractive for producers to expand output and thus prolongs the problem. Furthermore, the government, knowing that prices should fall when output grows, will be reluctant to see incomes rise very far because of the inflationary consequences. This will result in particular in a squeeze on public sector pay, adding to the depression in the economy. All this is compounded by a further problem. To meet the excess of demand over supply, more goods are imported; for example, in Russia in early 1993 much of the supply of vodka and spirits, and nearly all paper handkerchiefs, were imported, as were vast quantities of consumer durables. The growth in imports, together with inflation, led to rapid devaluation of currencies such as the rouble.

In the immediate aftermath of the collapse of Soviet-style socialism, few Central and Eastern European economies escaped a combination of sharp declines in real output and inflation of at least 100 percent (i.e. prices doubling in a year). For many countries, unemployment, which in theory and to some extent in practice was unknown under the planning system, became a serious problem. The reality for individuals was that the abolition or drastic modification of social security arrangements meant that many people went hungry, and some starved to death. We shall look at the evidence in much more detail in Part 2.

In all the Eastern and Central European countries, the ending of communism was marked by extensive privatisation of hitherto state-owned means of production and by the creation of financial markets to deal, for example, in the shares of the newly privatised companies. But these financial markets were thin – in many cases, there were still few quoted companies and few people interested in buying and selling shares – so the markets were very vulnerable to destabilising forces, and it was easy for some individuals to become very wealthy. The newly reconstituted banking system lacked experience; in particular, the central banks were ill-equipped to perform their main functions:

- to act as banker to the state;
- to oversee and control the money supply;
- to act as effective regulators to prevent doubtful practice by privatised financial institutions.

In consequence, the Russian rouble crashed in value yet again because of (well-founded) fears about the capacity of Russia to honour its debts.

The West sought to ensure that Russia adhered to the market system by linking assistance to promises that there would be no turning back from reform. Countries that believed that there was a realistic prospect for them of early membership of the EU similarly faced strong pressure not to deviate from the path of capitalism. As we have already seen, the European Council meeting in Copenhagen and later in Madrid laid down four criteria for new EU membership; these were to be applied generally but were written specifically to meet concerns about the countries of Eastern and Central Europe; one of these criteria requires that the applicant has a functioning market economy and can cope with competitive pressure and market forces within the EU. For many of the Eastern and Central European economies, the worst of the pain of reform is almost certainly now over. However, there remains a strong temptation for the people of Russia and some other ex-USSR countries to conclude that the miseries of their experiment with capitalism are never-ending and that they would be better off resurrecting some sort of communist system, even if it does mean cutting themselves off from the West and sinking into further long-term decline (see Part 2 for further discussion). Although many other elements are involved, this debate is part of the background to the recent hotly disputed presidential election in Ukraine.

In general, however, and if they keep their nerve, the Eastern and Central European economies have the potential for rapid and sustained growth once the world economy, and particularly that of Western Europe, starts to recover. They start with the flexibility that springs from a major refocusing of their economic activity. Their pay levels are, by Western European standards, still low, and their workforce is generally well educated. Their main current problem is that they are still hampered by poor capital equipment. Investment from outside into the Eastern and Central European economies will lead to high returns for the investors and will modernise the host economies.

Summary: the East–West comparisons

Differences remain, but they are diminishing. In terms of income per head, the poorest major Western European countries are Greece and Portugal (with an annual income per head in 2000 of around $10,600) (all data are from Department of Economic and Social Affairs 2004). In the same year, the richest of the Eastern European countries was Slovenia, with income per head of $9,120, but no other Central or Eastern European economy had income per head as high as $5,000. However, inward investment and the general potential for economic growth have meant that the Central and Eastern European economies are growing faster than those in the West, so the gap between them in income per head is declining quite rapidly. For those Central and Eastern European countries that have joined the EU, we have seen in Table 1.1 evidence of the rapid growth rates that most of them have been achieving recently. Table 1.1 has also shown us that, when price levels are taken into account, their income per head is rather closer to Western European standards than the raw data earlier in this paragraph imply.

Further reading

If you are new to economics, you may find a good introductory economics textbook helpful in telling you more about the market system. Older editions of such books may also explain more fully how central planning operated.

If you have studied some economics, add depth to this discussion by thinking about the mix of markets and state intervention that is typical of modern European economies; some commentators argue that there is too much state intervention, and there should be less – Europe should be more like the USA – whereas others believe that there is great value in the European traditions of a more socially aware economic system. Where do you think the balance lies?

For the politics part of this section, the following references are the most useful:

Crawford, K. (1996) *East Central European Politics Today,* Manchester University Press, Manchester.

Rose, R. (2004) 'Advancing into Europe? The contrasting goals of post-communist Countries', in *Nations in Transit, Democratisation in East Central Europe and Eurasia,* Freedom House, Washington, DC.

White, S., Batt, J. and Lewis, P.G. (eds) (2003) *Developments in Central and East European Politics 3,* Palgrave Macmillan, Basingstoke – contains useful studies, particularly those by Grabbe and Kopecky.

The European Union's external relationships

Background

This chapter focuses on the EU's relations with other countries. It concentrates on EU relations with the USA, with Russia and with 79 African, Caribbean and Pacific (ACP) countries that were previously colonies of EU member states. This treatment is necessarily selective in view of the numerous and wide variety of EU ties with countries throughout the world. Nevertheless, our examination of EU relations with the USA, Russia and the ACP countries captures much of the breadth and variable depth of the EU's relations with the wider world and covers many of the issues and problems involved in these relations.

Any study of the EU's external relations, whether with countries as in this section or with international bodies as in the next section, raises questions about the competence and identity of the EU. What exactly the EU can and cannot do in the international sphere ranges from exclusive power in some policy areas like trade relations to little or no competence in other policy areas like defence (see next section). There has been much debate about how best to describe the EU as an international actor, especially since its emergence as a participant in international trade negotiations in the 1960s and its adoption of a more political role via the European Council and European Political Cooperation in the 1970s. According to some accounts, the EU is primarily a 'civilian power' with a particular focus on civil, political, economic, social and cultural rights. Its strengths and emphases are said to lie mainly in the area of 'low politics' or the 'soft power' of economic, commercial and welfare matters, often summed up in the image of the EU as an economic superpower but a political dwarf in the international system. However, other accounts view the EU as a 'superpower in the making' that is gradually engaging in the area of 'high politics' or 'hard power' relating to core state activities like military, defence and security matters. More recent characterisations refer to the EU as an international 'presence' or as an international 'identity'. Any generalisation about the EU's role in external relations is also complicated by the different perspectives of interested parties. State-centred national policymakers and media, for example, may obscure the achievements of the EU on the international stage (Carlsnaes *et al.* 2004), while EU institutions and personnel may exaggerate the importance of the EU's international standing and achievements. We need to bear this in mind when considering each set of relations below.

The EU–USA relationship demonstrates both the strengths and limitations of the EU's role on the international stage. It is also an indicator of the nature and extent of changing perspectives, interests and attitudes on both sides. The EU and the USA are roughly equal as the largest players in global trade. They are each other's main trading and investment partners, accounting for approximately 20 percent of each other's bilateral trade and for over 50 percent of each other's total foreign investment. As a single trading entity, the EU is able to match US bargaining power in this field. However, other aspects of the transatlantic relationship are far more problematical. Major events in recent years, most especially '9/11' and European divisions over the US-led invasion of Iraq, have prompted much debate about:

- whether the proliferating political, cultural, economic and diplomatic disputes since 2000 mark a fundamental departure from the close ties of the past 60 years;

- whether we are witnessing a period of 'transatlantic drift' (Lundestad 2003) that is comparable to past squally episodes in this relationship and that may not amount to a sea-change in the relationship;

- whether the basic interests of Europe and the USA in the international system will continue to coincide or complement each other;

- whether US and European approaches to international problems will increasingly differ and result in a more adversarial relationship.

EU–USA relations have evolved against the background of US support for European integration since 1947. However, EU–Russia relations were subjected to Cold War antagonism in the form of Soviet opposition to the EC, at least until the emergence of Mikhail Gorbachev as Soviet leader in 1985 and his vision of a 'common European home'. In the post-Cold War period, Russia has abandoned its hostility to the EU, which is Russia's main trading partner and a major source of foreign direct investment in Russia and which also has a particularly strong interest in securing Russian energy supplies. In both Russian and EU circles, however, security worries and lingering suspicions remain. Russia is particularly concerned about the implications of an enlarged EU for Russian influence on neighbouring states. Meanwhile, there is continuing anxiety in EU circles about the future development of Russian polity and foreign policy, which is all the greater with the recent admission to the EU of eight of the Central and Eastern European ex-communist states and also in view of the EU's emphasis on human rights and Western democratic values.

Relations between the EU and the ACP countries provide yet another contrasting set of conditions. Some of the key issues in this context concern the role and importance of the EU as a global trading power in shaping trade relations with the ACP countries. Over the past 40 years, the EU–ACP countries relationship has invariably been an unbalanced one, but while the EU has retained the upper hand in trade and aid negotiations, the bargaining power of the ACP countries has fluctuated for reasons discussed below. The nature of this relationship has been viewed in a number of ways against the background of changing circumstances and from the very different perspectives of the EU and the ACP states. Early relations between the EU and the ACP countries during the late 1950s and 1960s frequently attracted criticism on the grounds of being a neo-imperialist relationship dressed up as benevolent paternalism. France was particularly intent on forging association agreements between the EU and former French colonies, thereby ensuring, according to critics at the time, that one impoverished French African ex-colony spoke French unto its equally impoverished neighbour. Political independence for these colonies, changing economic conditions and the inclusion of other former (British) colonial possessions in the 1970s gave rise to a relationship known as the Lomé system. The advantages and disadvantages of this system were much debated in the final quarter of the twentieth century. Supporters of the Lomé system viewed it as a model of cooperation between the EU and the ACP in that it gave the ACP countries the best possible terms of access to the EU market and also much development aid. However, critics of this arrangement regarded it as either a means whereby the EU countries reaped far greater political and economic advantages than the ACP states or as a form of 'managed' trade relations that failed to relieve the dire poverty of the ACP countries and that needed to give way to a neo-liberal or free-market approach.

The EU's relationship with the USA

The most important aspects of the relationship between Western Europe and the USA are political, especially in terms of security, and economic, through trade. The relationship between the USA and Europe is multifaceted, complex and essential for both the USA and EU. Not only did the USA support and encourage European integration in the early days of the ECSC and EEC, but this support has remained more or less constant over the last 60 years. In addition, US economic and military support for Western Europe was a crucial aspect of the Western European postwar recovery. However, despite this general support for Western Europe and European integration, the early years of the twenty-first century have been marked by speculation about the state of relations between the USA and the EU. Questions have surfaced about whether the relationship will survive its current tensions. This section will look at the development of transatlantic relations since the end of the Cold War. It will argue that this has been a relationship in transition rather than a relationship in terminal decline.

Since the end of the Cold War, the relationship between the USA and Western Europe has undergone a number of significant changes. One of the major modifications has been caused by the end of the Cold War. After 1945, the Cold War shaped much of the transatlantic bond, but following the collapse of communism in Central and Eastern Europe, it was clear that the relationship needed to be renegotiated in some way in order for it to adapt successfully to the post-Cold War world. The second major change in the transatlantic relationship has been the expansion of the activities of the EU. For much of the past 60 years, the USA conducted its diplomacy and policy towards Europe through individual countries. However, since the Maastricht Treaty the activities of the EU have expanded, and consequently Washington has dealt less with individual member states and more with the EU as a single body. Thus, there were several attempts by the USA and countries in Western Europe to provide a written framework for the relationship in the 1990s; these led up to the New Transatlantic Agenda (NTA) between the USA and the EU as a whole, signed in 1995. Although the NTA was greeted by both parties with enthusiasm, it has not proved to be as effective as was hoped in providing a model for the contemporary transatlantic relationship.

Other examples of the USA dealing with the EU as a whole are:

- the World Trade Organization (WTO), where the EU negotiates as one body on behalf of its member states; and

- the Kyoto Protocol concerning the reduction of greenhouse gas emissions, where the EU again negotiated as one.

This has meant that the USA has had to adapt its approach in some aspects of its relationship with the EU. Nevertheless, it is still a crucial aspect of US diplomacy that it conducts relations with individual Western European countries as appropriate. So what is the current state of transatlantic relations?

EU–US relations since September 2001

There has been much debate, particularly since the election of George W. Bush as president of the USA in 2000, about the future of relations between the EU and the USA. Many writers have focused on whether there is a case for the relationship to be considered to be in crisis (Daalder 2001; Gordon 2001; Steinberg 2003; Moisi 2001; Blinken 2001). It is easy to see how these debates have developed, because there appear to have been an increasing number of areas where there has been transatlantic divergence:

- the Kyoto Protocol on cutting greenhouse gas emissions;

- the use of the death penalty for some federal and state crimes in the USA (EU member states will not extradite people to the USA if they would be subject to the death penalty);

- the divergence in views over GM food.

Some writers claim that there is a difference in the 'world views' of the USA and Western Europe on these and other issues (Blinken 2001; Daalder 2001). Current writing on transatlantic relations in the Bush era may lead one to think that the relationship is in decline, but that would be a vast oversimplification of the situation. In many areas, the relationship between the USA and Europe remains strong and constant, for example in economic and trade issues (Baldwin *et al.* 2003).

The debates about the future of the relationship between the USA and Europe have only increased since '9/11'. Immediately after this event, it seemed that Europe and the USA would become closer and united in combating the threat of terrorism. Many supportive statements were made by European leaders, and there was great sympathy from Europe directed towards the USA. Evidence of the uniting influence of '9/11' was seen within NATO, which invoked, for the first time, Article 5, the mutual defence aspect of the North Atlantic Treaty. By this action, '9/11' was regarded by members of NATO as an attack not just on the USA but on all NATO members. Yet, just a short time later, once again questions were being asked about the transatlantic relationship. Since '9/11', the debates about the current, and future, state of the relationship have continued and, in some ways, have become more intense.

Plate 1.2 Condoleezza Rice, US Secretary of State, and Benita Ferrero-Waldner, European Commissioner for External Relations, at an international conference on Iraq in 2005

Source: Audiovisual Library of the European Commission (2005).

Many writers look to '9/11' as a turning point in relations between the USA and Europe. But has the case been overstated? Daalder focused on '9/11' as reflecting what he calls 'the end of Atlanticism'. This, he claims, means that Europe is no longer the primary focus of US foreign and security policy, as it had been during, and immediately after, the Cold War (Daalder 2003). The fight against international terrorism has, following '9/11', become centre stage in the US view of the world. In the same way that during the Cold War global events were seen by the USA as part of the ongoing ideological conflict against communism, today, global events are often seen as part of the Bush administration's 'War on Terror'. The refocusing of US foreign policy has clear ramifications for the US–EU relationship. The EU has to adjust to the new realities of 'the end of Atlanticism'; it has to accept that it is now not as important to Washington as it once was and that it may find it harder to influence Washington politically. Similarly, the USA has to adjust to the EU's development of its own Common Foreign and Security Policy (see Part 3).

It is difficult to deny that '9/11' has impacted on the transatlantic relationship in the short term. However, the long-term effects are a matter for speculation. But are the issues that have come to the fore in the relationship since '9/11' new, or are they issues that were already present in the transatlantic relationship before September 2001 and have simply been given new emphasis? There is evidence to suggest that it is the latter. Concerns about divergence and lack of direction in the transatlantic relationship had begun to surface before the US presidential elections in November 2000, for example differences in policy towards so-called 'rogue states', and it is naive to place all the problems seen in the transatlantic relationship at the door of George W. Bush. So what issues did '9/11' expose as being

Figure 1.11 President Bush reacts to Russian, French and German criticisms of the Iraq war

problematic in the transatlantic relationship? Writers such as Cox have attempted to identify a number of areas, including:

- the different views of the world and global organisation;
- the moves away from multilateralism by the USA since the 1990s; and
- the increasing military capabilities gap between the USA and Europe (Cox 2003).

If differences within the transatlantic relationship had been exposed by '9/11', the lead-up to the conflict in Iraq magnified them. The relationship between some European states and the USA reached its lowest level for some time, with very bitter and divisive language used on both sides of the argument. For most of this section, it has been viable to talk about 'Europe' or the EU as being united in its relationship with the USA, but when the 2003 conflict in Iraq is analysed, it is impossible to talk about the relationship between a united Europe and the USA. Europe was hopelessly divided on the issues, with some states, including Italy, Poland, Spain and the UK, expressing their support for the USA and others, including France and Germany, leading the opposition to the US-led invasion. The dispute over Iraq has been bitter and ongoing and prompted Donald Rumsfeld (US Defense Secretary) to refer to 'Old Europe' (those states who opposed the US action) and 'New Europe' (the supporters of the US-led coalition). The division within Europe during the run-up to the conflict in Iraq was confirmed in January 2003 in an open letter supporting the US approach signed by the leaders of 'New Europe' states (the letter was signed by the leaders of the Czech Republic, Denmark, Hungary, Italy, Poland, Portugal, Spain and the UK) (FCO 2003) – eight of the 25 current EU member states. It was also clear that the USA was subtly shifting its alliances within Europe. Poland, with its consistent support for recent US policy and membership of NATO, had become a more important player in the transatlantic relationship, and the influence of France, in particular, with the Bush administration had declined.

The relationship between Europe and the USA is, as said previously, complex and multifaceted, and disagreements over international security have not affected the trade and economic relationship. Trade between the USA and EU is vital to both markets: in 2003, exports from the EU to the USA were worth €151 billion and from the USA to EU, €220.2 billion (*European Union in the US* 2004). The relationship between the USA and Europe is a close one, and it has endured many periods of disagreement, but it has continued to change and adapt to events and circumstances and will endure.

The EU and the Third World

The EU is the world's fourth-largest international aid donor, with a development budget of €8.31 billion. Since the late 1950s, development aid has played an important role in shaping the EU's relationship with developing countries and continues to do so. Historically, there have been close links between Europe and the South, in many instances spanning centuries. A number of European countries, the UK and France in particular, held colonial possessions until the second part of the twentieth century, and cultural and economic ties with the ex-colonies have endured. The decolonisation process that began with the granting of independence to India and Pakistan in 1947 gained pace in the 1950s and 1960s, resulting in the creation of a large number of newly independent states, many of which chose to retain close links – including trade – with their former 'mother' countries. When the EEC was formed, Belgium and France argued that some agreement would need to be reached between member states in order to accommodate these former colonial ties. These ties were with what are commonly called Third World countries (see Key concept 1.10 for clarification).

Key concept 1.10

Third World, developing countries and the South

There is frequently confusion as to what the terms 'Third World', 'developing countries' and the 'South' encompass. This confusion is often exacerbated by the fact that these descriptions are routinely employed interchangeably, both in the media and in the academic sphere.

Credit for coining the term 'Third World' is usually attributed to the French economist, Alfred Sauvy, who introduced the phrase in a magazine article in *L'Observateur* in 1952. The term rapidly entered political parlance during the period following decolonisation and remains in common use. However, it has increasingly come to be viewed as pejorative, evoking as it does images of poverty, disease,

▶

corruption, war and famine. Furthermore, with the disappearance of the 'Second World' (the former Eastern bloc communist countries), many analysts have come to argue that the term 'Third World' is now obsolete.

Popular alternatives to 'Third World', such as 'developing countries' and 'the South', are now generally used in its stead. However, there are a number of problems with these umbrella terms. Many poorer countries in Africa cannot accurately be described as 'developing'. In fact, many are stagnating or experiencing negative economic growth. This discrepancy has prompted the creation of a further category, that of 'least developed countries' (or, as some have described it, the Fourth World). Likewise, 'the South' is a geographic misnomer given that a number of poor countries are situated to the north of the equator.

There is thus no single accepted term that adequately brackets countries not previously classed as First World or Second World. While none of the three descriptions highlighted is 'incorrect', people should be aware that each has its shortcomings and that these should be taken into account when these terms are employed.

Historical background

The Treaty of Rome, which established the EEC in 1957, incorporated articles relating to 'Overseas Countries and Territories' (OCTs) and made provision for the funding of these areas. Consequently, in 1958 the first European Development Fund (EDF) was established, a significant proportion of which was distributed in the form of grants to France's overseas possessions. When the majority of these OCTs were afforded independence, economic ties with the EC were maintained by virtue of the Yaoundé Conventions (Yaoundé I, 1963–69; Yaoundé II, 1969–75) which established the basis for future cooperation with developing countries. The stated aim of these conventions was to enable all newly independent former colonies to achieve significant levels of economic development and thus economic independence.

When the UK was finally admitted to the EC in 1973, it was clear that a new, more encompassing agreement would need to be negotiated in order to accommodate Commonwealth interests. The Commonwealth was deemed too large and too disparate in nature to be dealt with as a single bloc. Consequently, the EC decided to divide the Commonwealth into two groups, the associables and the non-associables. The associables group incorporated the undeveloped African, Caribbean and Pacific (ACP) Commonwealth members, and these countries were invited to negotiate potentially lucrative association agreements with the EC. The non-associables, such as India, were judged too developed to warrant inclusion in any such agreements and were restricted to negotiating standard bilateral trade agreements with the EC.

To the surprise of many in Europe, the ACP countries decided to negotiate as a bloc rather than in regional groupings when trade talks began in July 1973. This show of unity led to the formalisation of the ACP group when 46 developing countries signed the Georgetown Agreement in June 1975. The fact that these countries chose to negotiate an association agreement as a single group significantly bolstered their leverage during talks. Consequently, the resulting convention, Lomé I, offered ACP countries a number of favourable concessions, including non-reciprocal privileged access to EC markets, as well as compensation mechanisms designed to help to offset commodity price instability. In part, the ACP countries were able to extract such concessions from the EC as a result of anxieties fostered by the 1973 oil crisis and the ensuing spectre of raw material shortages. Cold War geopolitical considerations also played a role. The first Lomé Convention was duly signed in 1975 between the nine member states of the EC and the 46 ACP states and subsequently renegotiated at five-yearly intervals, in 1980 (Lomé II), 1985 (Lomé III), 1990 (Lomé IV) and finally 1995 (Lomé IV-bis). During this period, ACP membership expanded considerably, and the bloc currently comprises 79 states (Key fact 1.10).

Key fact 1.10

African, Caribbean and Pacific (ACP) countries

Angola – Antigua and Barbuda – Bahamas – Barbados – Belize – Benin – Botswana – Burkina Faso – Burundi – Cameroon – Cape Verde – Central African Republic – Chad – Comoros – Congo – Cook Islands – Côte d'Ivoire – Cuba – Democratic Republic of Congo – Djibouti – Dominica – Dominican Republic – Equatorial Guinea – Eritrea – Ethiopia – Fiji – Gabon – Gambia – Ghana – Grenada – Guinea – Guinea–Bissau – Guyana – Haiti – Jamaica – Kenya – Kiribati – Lesotho – Liberia – Madagascar – Malawi – Mali – Marshall Islands – Mauritania – Mauritius – Micronesia – Mozambique – Namibia – Nauru – Niger – Nigeria – Niue – Palau – Papua New Guinea – Rwanda – St Kitts and Nevis – St Lucia – St Vincent and the Grenadines – Samoa – São Tomé and Principe – Senegal – Seychelles – Sierra Leone – Solomon Islands – Somalia – South Africa – Sudan – Suriname – Swaziland – Tanzania – Timor Leste – Togo – Tonga – Trinidad and Tobago – Tuvalu – Uganda – Vanuatu – Zambia – Zimbabwe.

Of all the ensuing accords, Lomé I was the closest to an agreement between partners. There was little or no conditionality, and ACP members were free to formulate their own economic policies without undue outside interference. However, each successive renegotiation of Lomé diminished the power of the ACP within the relationship. The debt crisis of the 1980s, the collapse of world commodity prices and the end of the Cold War all eroded the bargaining power of the ACP countries. As a result, the EU was able to incorporate conditionality into later versions of the treaty, thereby limiting the ability of the ACP states to formulate home-grown policies. It can thus be argued that over time the relationship between the EU and the ACP countries has become increasingly one-sided. The position secured by the bloc during the negotiations in the build-up to Lomé I was systematically rolled back with each successive renegotiation of the convention. Yet despite increasing disparities in power relations, most ACP countries were dismayed when it became apparent that the convention would not be renewed after the expiry of Lomé IV-bis in 2000.

The post-Lomé era

The Lomé era of cooperation officially came to an end on 23 June 2000 with the signing of a new agreement between the EU and the ACP countries in Cotonou, Benin. The Lomé regime had been under sustained pressure from 1994 onwards, when a General Agreement on Tariffs and Trade (GATT) panel ruled that the non-reciprocity elements contained within the convention, as well as its discriminatory nature, meant that it was incompatible with the multilateral trading system (see the discussion later about the 'banana wars'). Consequently, before it could be implemented, Lomé IV-bis required a waiver from the World Trade Organization (WTO), the then newly created successor to the GATT. Largely as a result of the GATT panel's findings, the EU decided that Lomé would not be renewed after 2000 and stressed that any future EU–ACP agreement would need to fall within WTO parameters.

While WTO rules do not allow for non-reciprocal trade agreements, they do allow for economic partnership agreements (EPAs) – agreements between economic blocs – that facilitate the mutual lowering of tariffs and trade barriers. It is for this reason that the post-Lomé strategy is one built upon regionalism. Article 35 of the Cotonou Agreement emphasises that

> economic and trade co-operation shall be built on regional integration initiatives of ACP States, bearing in mind that regional integration is a key instrument for the integration of ACP countries into the world economy.

The proponents of increased regional cooperation in the EU maintain that economic integration initiatives will provide the ACP countries with markets of scale and improve their competitiveness, as well as attracting additional investment from abroad.

However, as the Cotonou Convention makes special allowances for least (or less) developed countries (LDCs), its dictates do not apply equally to all ACP states. The LDC category, created by the United Nations in 1971, currently comprises 49 of the poorest countries in the world, 40 of which are already ACP members (see Key fact 1.11). The Cotonou Agreement encompasses the EU's 'Everything but Arms' (EBA) initiative, which affords all LDC exports, barring weapons manufactures, tariff-free entry into the EU without the need for reciprocity. This initiative is intended to be fully operative by 2009. EBA is possible because such concessions to LDCs are sanctioned by the WTO and do not require a waiver. However, the net result has been that the Cotonou Agreement has created a two-tier ACP group, namely LDC and non-LDC countries. The latter are obliged to operate within the narrow constraints set by the WTO, while the former are not. The unity of the ACP bloc has thus been severely undermined.

Key fact 1.11

ACP least developed countries

Angola – Benin – Burkina Faso – Burundi – Cape Verde – Central African Republic – Chad – Comoros – Democratic Republic of Congo – Djibouti – Equatorial Guinea – Ethiopia – Eritrea – Gambia – Guinea-Bissau – Guinea – Haiti – Kiribati – Lesotho – Liberia – Madagascar – Malawi – Mali – Mauritania – Mozambique – Niger – Rwanda – Samoa – São Tomé and Principe – Senegal – Sierra Leone – Solomon Islands – Somalia – Sudan – Tanzania – Togo – Tuvalu – Uganda – Vanuatu – Zambia.

For non-LDCs, the Cotonou strategy represents a major departure from the Lomé regime and, at the time of the negotiations, many ACP states felt that the timetable for terminating non-reciprocal trade links was too inflexible. As a result, the ACP countries campaigned vigorously for an extension to the WTO waiver relating to the Lomé system of preferences. An extension was eventually secured, facilitating the gradual implementation of the Cotonou Agreement over a period of eight years, ending in 2008. This extension has allowed ACP countries a certain degree of breathing space, and, it is argued, will enable them to prepare their economies for the loss of tariff revenues and duties brought about by their acceptance of the new agreement. Moreover, ACP members can now, in theory, negotiate regional partnerships in an unhurried, systematic manner, without fearing a loss of income in the interim.

Future outlook

It is imperative that the ACP countries be prepared for post-2008 realities if they are not to suffer financial losses. During the WTO waiver negotiation process, Latin American countries such as Bolivia, Guatemala, Honduras and Paraguay all argued strongly against the extension of the Lomé system of preferences. Furthermore, even EU members such as Spain indicated that an eight-year extension of preferential access was too generous; a future agreement extending the waiver beyond 2008 thus seems very unlikely. Unfortunately, preparation in anticipation of the new regime is behind schedule as ACP members struggle to conduct evaluation studies and, moreover, to muster the necessary political will to implement the timetable framework. An additional complication for the ACP countries is that they need to participate in parallel multilateral discussions as part of the ongoing Doha Round if they are to gain any further concessions from the WTO. These negotiations are problematic with regard to the implementation of the new convention because, if the new EU–ACP agreement is to be WTO-compliant, regional initiatives should arguably be suspended until the new WTO rules are formalised. The Doha Round, originally planned for completion by 1 January 2005, is behind schedule – mainly because very little progress has been made on trade in services – and it is currently hoped that the round will be completed some time in 2006. The negotiations could yet have important ramifications for any EU–ACP EPAs, given that the aspects of the Doha Agreement that relate to regional trading blocs still require clarification.

There are additional difficulties associated with the regional strategy put forward by the EU. While there are many regional groupings involving ACP members, very few are in any real position to negotiate EPAs. Regional groups involving ACP countries have historically been weak. Africa, for example, has an extensive record of multilateral economic agreements, probably fielding more examples than any other continent, with more than 200 regional agreements having been established in the last 30 years. Examples of regional groups currently active in Africa include the West African Economic and Monetary Union (WAEMU), the Economic Community of West African States (ECOWAS), the East African Community (EAC), the Common Market for Eastern and Southern Africa (COMESA), the

Southern African Customs Union (SACU) and the Southern African Development Community (SADC). Of these, only the SACU can be said to be a truly successful venture. Given that the ACP countries' scope for deriving benefits from the Cotonou Agreement depends largely upon functioning regional groupings, such weaknesses represent cause for concern.

The reason regional strategies have performed poorly in the past, especially in Africa, has been a lack of political will. African governments have traditionally derived a significant proportion of their income from duties and tariffs and have been shown to be loath to give up this source of revenue. Furthermore, experience has shown that by dropping trade barriers poor countries leave their often fragile domestic industries exposed to competition from more efficient foreign firms and to 'dumping' from abroad. This is particularly true for agricultural goods from the EU, subsidised by the Common Agricultural Policy (CAP). The Cotonou regime has thus not proved to be a popular successor to the Lomé Convention.

Conclusion

The Cotonou Agreement, which heralded the end of 25 years of Lomé cooperation, will have a number of important implications for relations between developing countries and the EU. All future EU–ACP cooperation must now conform to WTO precepts, and if developing countries are to benefit from the new regime, then they must embrace the EU's vision of regional EPAs. It is therefore crucial that the ACP regional groupings be in place and functioning as soon as possible in order to meet the 2008 deadline when the Lomé system of preferences expires. It is possible to keep abreast of the state of the EPA negotiations by making reference to the *Trade Negotiation Insights*, the *EPAwatch* and the WTO websites listed in the bibliography.

Opinion 1.13

The effects of the Cotonou Agreement on ACP countries

- *Regionalism*: creates markets of scale for ACP countries; boosts trade. Historically, there are few successful examples of regional groupings among ACP states.
- *Reciprocity*: EU–ACP trade relations now conform to WTO rules. ACP economies may be vulnerable to penetration by foreign firms.
- *Tariffs*: by liberalising their economies, ACP countries will become integrated into the global economy. ACP countries will no longer be able to rely on revenues derived from duties on EU goods.
- *Least developed countries*: extremely poor countries now have easier access to EU markets. This action by the EU has split the ACP group in two.

Should the ACP countries have accepted this agreement? What choices did they have?

The EU's rocky relations with the Russian Federation

Up until the end of the Cold War, the EEC was viewed by Soviet officials as the 'economic wing of the Atlantic alliance', an organisation of the enemy camp that could not be trusted, and it was not until 1989 that formal relations were codified in a limited trade and cooperation agreement (Gower 2004: 14). However, the disintegration of the Soviet Union in December 1991 paved the way for more meaningful negotiations to take place between the EU and the new Russian Federation, which had emerged as an independent sovereign state in January 1992. After an exhaustive round of meetings, a historic Partnership and Cooperation Agreement (PCA) was eventually signed between the EU and Russia in 1994.

Russia saw the PCA primarily as a means by which it could gain access to European and global markets to compensate for the collapse of its traditional markets in Central and Eastern Europe (Timmins 2003: 81). Indeed, most of the 112 articles, ten annexes, two protocols and the joint declaration of 178 pages were devoted to trade relations (Linch 2003: 55). However, the EU viewed the PCA in much broader terms. It sought to use the agreement to promote European democratic values and institutions eastwards across the former Iron Curtain. Thus, the PCA called upon Russia to commit itself 'to political and economic freedoms, the promotion of international peace and security, and respect for democratic principles and human rights' (Timmins 2003: 82).

In order to facilitate the goals of the PCA, a number of top-level institutional forums were created, including 'biannual presidential summits, annual meetings of a Cooperation Council (at ministerial level), biannual meetings of a Cooperation Committee (at the level of senior officials), regular meetings of nine functionally designated Sub-Committees, and the launch of a Parliamentary Cooperation Committee to meet annually' (Linch 2003: 55). In 2004, the Cooperation Council was upgraded to Permanent Partnership Council. However, Russia's military excursion into Chechnya in 1994, and the subsequent international outcry over human rights violations by Russian troops, delayed ratification of the PCA until December 1997.

Two years later in June 1999, the EU published a major document, the Common Strategy on Russia (CSR), which outlined its key foreign policy goals. The CSR has four main aims:

1. the consolidation of democracy, the rule of law and public institutions in Russia;

2. the integration of Russia into a common European economic and social space;

3. cooperation to strengthen stability and security in Europe and beyond;

4. cooperation in responding to common challenges on the European continent, such as on nuclear safety, organised crime and environmental problems (Linch 2003: 56).

In addition, the CSR stressed that any relationship with Russia would have to be based on shared democratic values, and Russia was called upon to bring its political and legal systems into line with the EU.

However, just as the Chechen conflict had obstructed the ratification of the PCA, the 'CSR was hindered' by the start of the second Chechen war in autumn 1999

(Timmins 2003: 86). At the European Council meeting in Helsinki in October 1999, the bombing of the Chechen capital, Grozny, was condemned by the EU, which declared:

> Russia is a major partner for the EU. The Union has constantly expressed its willingness to accompany Russia in its transition towards a modern democratic state. But Russia must live up to its obligations if the strategic partnership is to be developed. The EU does not want Russia to isolate herself from Europe

(Source: Timmins 2003: 86.)

The declaration was followed up in January 2000 by proposals for a series of trade sanctions against Russia.

Russia's medium-term strategy

In October 1999, Russia gave its response to the CSR with the publication of its *Medium-Term Strategy for Development of Relations with the EU* (MTS). This document was the first official pronouncement by the authorities that the Russian Federation had no intention of seeking membership of the EU. The MTS stressed that Russia, as 'a world power situated on two continents should retain its freedom to determine and implement its domestic and foreign policies, its status and advantages of a Euro-Asia state and the largest member of the Commonwealth of Independent States, independence of its position and activities at international organisations' (Timmins 2004: 240). As Linch notes, while the CSR focused on shared values and Russia's need to instigate major economic and political reforms, the MTS stressed the primacy of Russian national interests and sovereignty (2003: 58). Moscow was not going to be bullied into reforming its economic and political systems according to the dictates of the EU. Instead, the MTS sought

> the development of a collaborative pan-European security defence identity to counterbalance 'NATO-centrism in Europe'; the creation of 'a Russia–EU free trade zone', including an energy dialogue; and EU support for Russia's entry into the World Trade Organization.

(Source: Timmins 2004: 365.)

The foreign policy concept

Since the election of Vladimir Putin as Russian president in March 2000, there has been a much more consistent pro-Western foreign policy line and a more positive stance towards the EU than was the case under President Yeltsin. This new approach to the EU was graphically illustrated in Russia's Foreign Policy Concept, adopted in June 2000, which now underlined that 'the Russian Federation views the EU as one of its main political and economic partners and will strive to develop with it an intensive, stable and long-term co-operation devoid of expediency fluctuations' (Timmins 2004: 365).

The EU's eastward expansion and Russia–EU relations

The 1 May 2004 expansion of the EU to include ten new members, eight of which are either former Soviet republics or former Soviet satellite states, opened a new era in Russia's relations with the rest of Europe. Enlargement has brought the EU much closer to Russia, and its common borders with the EU have now increased to 2,200 km. There are new borders between the Pskov region in Russia and Estonia, which is a new EU member state. Moreover, a new EU 'blue curtain' (of Poland and Lithuania) now separates the Russian enclave of Kaliningrad from the rest of Russia.

> The question of transit access for Russian citizens wishing to travel by land between the detached Russian region of Kaliningrad and the Russian 'mainland' dominated the Russia–EU agenda during 2001–2002. The Russian government demanded that access should be visa-free, while the EU Commission demanded that Russian citizens would have to abide by the Schengen regime and obtain visas before they could cross EU territory.
>
> (Source: Holtom 2005: 1.)

However, agreement over transit rights was settled amicably in 2003, and this dispute did not turn into a major stumbling block in EU–Russian relations, as many had feared before EU enlargement.

Plate 1.3 President Putin of Russia at an EU–Russia summit, 2003

Source: Audiovisual Library of the European Commission (2005).

As EU Commission President Romano Prodi noted, the new borders provide new opportunities for cooperation between the EU and Russia 'in areas such as border management, migration controls, and the fight against organised crime' (Prodi 2004: 2). Enlargement will also have a significant impact on EU–Russia trade. 'Direct proximity to the world's largest Single Market with a single set of rules presents Russian companies with new opportunities for trade and investment' (*ibid.*: 2). Before the enlargement, trade with the EU accounted for 46 percent of Russia's foreign trade turnover. Since enlargement, the figure has risen to 54 percent. By comparison, Russia's share of the EU's total trade volume, excluding energy, is just 4 percent. However, Russia provides 42 percent of the EU's natural gas requirements and 18 percent of its oil imports. Energy supplies, which currently make up 55 percent of Russia's exports to the EU, are completely free of tariffs and quotas. Moreover, conditions for Russian exports to the EU are more favourable now than before enlargement. The average level of tariffs is expected to be reduced from 9 to 4 percent (*ibid.*: 6).

In a joint statement on EU enlargement and EU–Russia relations in April 2004, Russia and the EU reaffirmed their commitment to ensure that EU enlargement will bring the EU and Russia closer together in a Europe without dividing lines, *inter alia* by creating a common space of freedom, security and justice. The joint statement also noted that agreement had been reached on extending the PCA to include the ten new EU member states (see *Joint Statement* 2004). However, enlargement has thrown up a set of thorny issues over the EU's relations with its new neighbours to the east and south. Thus, for example, the former Soviet republics of Belarus, Moldova and Ukraine are now classified by the EU as belonging to what it calls 'wider Europe'. These new EU neighbours are now considered to be within the expanded EU's legitimate sphere of interests. However, it can be argued that Moscow has more or less openly stated its intention of restoring its dominance of the territory of the former Soviet Union (the Commonwealth of Independent States), with the exception of the Baltic states (Yasman 2004).

We have already witnessed tensions over the settlement of the Transdniester conflict in Moldova (see Key fact 1.12). In November 2003, Russia's proposed solution to border disputes was rejected outright by the EU (Yasman 2004). Nor were relations between the two sides improved when in September 2003 Russia signed a Single Economic Space agreement with Belarus, Kazakhstan and Ukraine. This agreement followed a separate agreement that Russia had signed with the EU on 'four common spaces' at the St Petersburg summit in May 2003. The four common spaces cover:

1. economic issues and the environment;

2. issues of freedom, security and justice;

3. external security, including crisis management and non-proliferation; and

4. research and education, including cultural aspects.

There are now questions over which of these two agreements is to be given priority by Russia.

In the most recent EU–Russia summit, in the Hague in November 2004, the thorny issue of the promotion of democratic values once again came to the fore as the EU tried to link together the implementation of the four common spaces, while

Key fact 1.12

The frozen conflict in Transdniester

In the wake of the nationalist unrest that spread across the USSR in the late 1980s and early 1990s, the Soviet Republic of Moldova emerged as an independent state in January 1992. Fearing that Moldova would be reunited with Romania (as was the case before the Second World War) non-Moldovan citizens, primarily Russians and Ukrainians, formed the breakaway republic of Transdniester in 1992. The population of Transdniester is 40 percent Moldovan, 28 percent Ukrainian and 23 percent Russian.

After a period of civil war, a peace treaty was signed in April 1992. The Transdniester Republic maintains close relations with the Russian Federation, and indeed Russian troops have been based in the country since 1992, creating tensions between the EU and Russia.

In 1997, Moldova and Transdniester signed a Memorandum on Normalisation of Relations, with Russia, Ukraine and the OSCE acting as mediators. But there was little headway. In 2003, the Moldovan government invited the Transdniester authorities to participate in the setting up of a new federal state with Transdniester as a fully fledged federal subject. But again deadlock ensued.

In November 2003, the Russian government produced a new document setting out parameters for a settlement that was rejected by the OSCE. Formal negotiations resumed in April 2004 but then broke down again in July. In November, a meeting of the two parties (Moldova and Transdniester) and three mediators (Russia, Ukraine and OSCE) took place in Varna, Bulgaria, but again there was no agreement. The Transdniester Republic steadfastly refuses to give up its sovereignty, and Russia insists that it has the right to maintain troops in the breakaway republic.

(Source: Foreign and Commonwealth Office: Country Profiles, Moldova **http://www.fco.gov.**)

Russia, true to form, sought to prioritise separate agreements on the economic and security spaces while playing down the importance of political and legal reforms. Relations at this summit were also soured over the conflicting interpretations of the legitimacy of Ukraine's presidential elections. In the post-summit press conference, Russian officials declared that the election of Viktor Yanukovich as president was legitimate, while EU officials declared that the elections were far from free and fair. The EU later steadfastly refused to recognise the validity of the election results and gave its full support to the campaign of the opposition candidate, Viktor Yuschenko, in his quest to nullify the results of the elections. Both sides accused the other of undue interference in the domestic affairs of a sovereign state.

As Dmitri Trenin stresses:

Russia's rapprochement with Europe is only in the second instance a foreign policy exercise. Its success or failure will primarily depend on the pace and depth of Russia's economic, political and societal transformation. Russia's entry into Europe cannot be negotiated with Brussels. It has to be first 'made in Russia itself'.

(Source: Gower 2004: 249.)

In conclusion, however, it is highly unlikely that Russia will take heed of EU demands to democratise its polity or improve its human rights record in Chechnya. The Russian Federation, under the leadership of President Putin, 'is not prepared to sacrifice part of its sovereignty, adopt European legislation, or make human rights a priority' (Yasman 2004: 1). Russia has also clearly staked out its position as the dominant power in the Commonwealth of Independent States; this is liable to bring it into collision with the EU's Wider Europe policy. Thus the road ahead for EU–Russia relations looks as rocky as ever.

Further reading

For this section, there are very few books that are sufficiently up to date. Use the full list of references to find the sources of the useful articles that are cited in the text.

Section 1.5

Europe and international bodies

Background

This section examines the nature and extent of Europe's, and more particularly the EU's, relationships with several major international bodies. Some of the least visible yet highly important aspects of the EU's activities feature under this heading. For example, international trade issues involving the EU's Common Commercial Policy (CCP) rarely figure prominently in the media except in the business sections or in the event of a threatened 'trade war'. However, the EU is an established and very powerful participant in the management of the global trade system. Why this is the case and whether it is likely to remain so are among the questions addressed below.

First, we look at the relationship between the EU and NATO and the subject of Europe's defence and security. The possibility of a common defence and security policy has figured to a greater or lesser extent throughout the history of the EU since the collapse of the European Defence Community project (1954). However, the legal basis for such a policy was established only with the adoption of the Maastricht Treaty (1993), when the EU was charged with defining and implementing a common foreign and security policy, including the progressive framing of a common defence policy that might lead to a common defence. Whether or not this will amount to anything substantial in the longer term is a matter of debate. Achievements to date in terms of operational capabilities as opposed to declaratory rhetoric are discussed below. The formal or institutional relationship between the EU and NATO commenced in January 2001. It is very limited and is largely defined by what NATO permits and what the EU member states are willing to undertake in terms of collective defence via the EU; it is the EU member states (not all of which belong to NATO) rather than the EU that contribute to NATO. In some respects, as in the case of southern Serbia or the FYR of Macedonia, practical cooperation between the EU and NATO has occurred in the absence of agreement on formal modalities for EU–NATO cooperation.

NATO is the longest-surviving military alliance of its type in modern history, yet its seemingly uncertain future has been much discussed (more so in European than in US circles) in each decade since its formation (1949). Thus it was asked whether NATO could survive:

Key fact 1.13

Membership of NATO

1949 founding members – Belgium, Canada, Denmark, France, Iceland, Italy, Luxembourg, Netherlands, Norway, Portugal, UK, USA.
1952 Greece, Turkey.
1955 FRG.
1982 Spain.
1999 Czech Republic, Hungary, Poland.
2004 Bulgaria, Estonia, Latvia, Lithuania, Romania, Slovakia, Slovenia.

- the Suez crisis (1950s);
- the policies of French President de Gaulle (1960s);
- *détente* in East–West relations (1970s);
- the deployment of US missiles in Western Europe (1980s);
- the end of the Cold War (1990s);
- US unilateralism (2000s).

Any current doubts about NATO's future, therefore, are scarcely novel. However, it remains to be seen whether NATO can forge a new, major, long-term role comparable to its original Cold War role or whether it will increasingly resemble a monument to the Cold War age that survives by inertia, by lack of use (as in the case of the Iraq war) or by continued divisions over its use in 'out of area' operations.

What is also unclear is the nature of the relationship between NATO and the EU if the latter advanced from its current limited role in defence and security matters, which is primarily focused on peacekeeping and conflict prevention and is based on using the military capabilities of the member states, to the formation of an independent EU military force. This prospect arguably remains as distant as ever and for several reasons. On the European side, there remains a marked preference for national military forces within NATO rather than for some kind of EU military force, for relatively cheap defence via the US commitment to Europe, and for the USA as the arbiter in European affairs. Furthermore, in the treaty establishing an EU constitution (still unratified at the time of writing), the member states declared that a common defence must be compatible with NATO's security and defence policy. On the US side, the possibility of an independent EU military force or bloc has long been viewed with suspicion as likely to undermine alliance unity and, more seriously, pose a threat to US leadership of NATO. In countering such a possibility, the USA has frequently exploited divisions between European governments and applied a divide and rule strategy in its management of European allies. Prior to the invasion of Iraq in 2003, for example, US Defense Secretary Donald Rumsfeld advised the world that there was a distinction between 'Old' and 'New' Europe; the European commissioner responsible for the EU's external relations was so unimpressed by the Pentagon's management of relations with European allies that he reportedly commented in the aftermath of the invasion of Iraq: 'The Pentagon is to diplomacy what the chainsaw is to chiropody'.

The EU as a single entity within the international system is at its strongest in it relations with a constellation of international economic organisations, notably the Organisation for Economic Co-operation and Development (OECD), the International Monetary Fund (IMF), the World Trade Organization (WTO) and the International Bank for Reconstruction and Development (IBRD). The EU functions as a single actor in the WTO, where it is represented by the European Commission in the various rounds of multilateral trade negotiations, the current round being known as the 'Doha Development Agenda'. It is also through the WTO framework that many trade disputes are settled, as for example, between the EU and the USA over steel imports into the USA, the export of US agricultural goods (especially genetically modified food) to the EU, and the subsidising of the exports of US multinational companies by the US government.

The OECD and the IMF are organisations that regularly monitor and assess economic policy developments in their member states. The forerunner of the OECD, the Organisation for European Economic Co-operation, was considered so limited in its potential that the founder member states of the EU bypassed it and embarked on a more intensive form of economic integration. Some of the EU's formal relations with the OECD and the IMF are conducted through the European Central Bank (ECB), although it is individual countries, rather than the EU as an entity, that are members of both the OECD and the IMF. The ECB and the national central banks of the countries that are in the euro zone together constitute what is known as the Eurosystem, the central banking system of the euro area whose main objective according to its mission statement 'is to maintain price stability: safeguarding the value of the euro' (Scheller 2004). (The European System of Central Banks comprises the Eurosystem together with the national central banks of the EU member states that are not in the euro zone.) The ECB currently has observer status in the IMF, this arrangement being devised (1998) because IMF membership is restricted to countries; the ECB's role here is likely to become increasingly important, because monetary policy for the euro zone is one of the 'exclusive' competences where only the EU may act.

NATO

From the perspective of Europe, NATO is the dominant international organisation in the field of security. It was formed in 1949 with the signing of the North Atlantic Treaty and was a direct response to the worsening Cold War. NATO is a mutual defence and security organisation; Article 5 of the North Atlantic Treaty states that an armed attack against one or more of the signatories in Europe or North America shall be considered an attack against them all (North Atlantic Treaty 1949). The mutual defence aspect of the North Atlantic Treaty clearly reflected the concerns of Western Europe, the United States and Canada when they faced the perceived threat from the USSR and its satellite states.

NATO was founded specifically to protect and defend Western Europe, and the majority of its members are European (along with Canada and the USA). NATO was also important because it confirmed the US commitment to Western Europe, and the USA continues to play the lead role in NATO today.

Plate 1.4 The NATO headquarters building in Brussels

Source: NATO website (2005).

With the recent increase in emphasis on defence and security policy within the EU and the setting of the 'Headline Goal' (see Part 3) or the development of a European Rapid Reaction Force (ERRF), there has been much speculation that the relationship between NATO and the EU has become increasingly competitive. This, it is claimed, may weaken the relationship (Lindley-French 2003). The relationship between the EU and NATO has been largely cooperative and complementary. This is reflected in several agreements, the most important of which is the March 2003 Berlin-Plus Agreement, which, among its measures, allows the EU to utilise NATO's operational planning facilities, along with NATO capabilities and common assets (De Witte 2003).

Since the Cold War ended in the early 1990s, NATO has faced many questions about its future. There is no doubt that NATO was a Cold War organisation, and this led to one of the crucial questions that NATO members had to address following the collapse of communism in Central and Eastern Europe: 'Was there a future for NATO and, if so, what would be its future role?' The fact that NATO still exists answers part of this question, as European and North American governments clearly feel that there is a place for NATO in the contemporary world. However, whether NATO has found a clear role for itself in the last 15 years remains open to question.

One clear success for NATO has been its enlargement programme, which has widened its relationship with European states. NATO preceded the EU in welcoming ex-communist states from Central and Eastern Europe as members, with the first enlargement taking place in 1999 (the Czech Republic, Hungary and Poland), with a further enlargement taking place in May 2004 (Bulgaria, Estonia, Latvia, Lithuania, Romania, Slovakia and Slovenia). This is one area where the political, rather than the military, aspect of NATO came to the fore. The transformation of the ex-communist states was a complex process and included democratisation of all aspects of society. NATO has played a significant part in this transformation by encouraging and facilitating democratic civilian control of the armed forces in the former communist states (Edmunds 2003).

Despite NATO's enlargement and its role in Central and Eastern Europe, debates continue about what NATO's future role should be. Following NATO's intervention in Bosnia and, more significantly, in Kosovo, many thought that NATO would develop a role in guaranteeing Europe's wider security and in peacekeeping and conflict management. However, this role has been eclipsed following the events of '9/11', resulting in renewed speculation about the future of NATO. We have already seen that following '9/11' NATO invoked Article 5 of the North Atlantic Treaty for the first time. This was intended to show political and military support by NATO members for the USA. Through the invoking of Article 5, the military assets of NATO were placed at the disposal of the USA to defend itself against any future attack. However, this offer was declined by the USA, which, instead, asked for help in eight areas and preferred to form a loose coalition, which included UK forces, to undertake the campaign in Afghanistan. Some viewed this as a rejection by the USA of the formal alliance structure of NATO (Gordon 2001).

NATO is now playing an important role in Afghanistan through its leadership of ISAF (International Stabilisation and Assistance Force) and has also begun to adapt its forces to be more flexible and quicker in response to the threat posed by terrorism. Some authors have asked whether '9/11' will have a negative impact on NATO as a military force (Rees 2003; Dockrill 2003; Cox 2003). They point to the inflexibility of NATO decision-making structures, which means that decision making is slow and that a resolution can be blocked by a minority of members. In order to fight the 'War on Terror', military forces need to be flexible, able to respond quickly and have a global outreach. The reluctance of some European members of NATO to see the organisation as a global rather than regional player that would increasingly act 'out of area' (that is outside the borders of NATO members) may also be a problem in the future. It is also unclear what relevance the USA thinks NATO now has, since the USA chose not to use the full assets of NATO following '9/11' but focused instead on loose, informal 'coalitions of the willing' both in Afghanistan and in Iraq. These doubts both in Europe and in the USA have the potential to transform European security. If the USA decided to reduce its commitment to NATO, the organisation would have to adapt to this. One impact of this may be that Europe may rapidly have to develop its own capacity for the security and defence of the continent. This raises further questions about European security and defence policy, which will be discussed later in the book.

The IMF, WTO and OECD

Towards the end of the Second World War, representatives of the allied powers agreed to create a set of international economic institutions to try to ensure that world trade operated smoothly after the war. The most important of these institutions are:

- the International Monetary Fund (IMF) – to bring about stability of exchange rates;
- the International Bank for Reconstruction and Development (IBRD) – to help postwar reconstruction in Europe and Asia and world development;
- the General Agreement on Tariffs and Trade (GATT), now broadened and run by the World Trade Organization (WTO) – to promote freedom of trade by the elimination of barriers such as tariffs (taxes on imports) and quotas (quantitative restrictions on imports).

Together with most countries in the world, all the EU countries are members of the IMF, the IBRD and the WTO.

The IMF

The exchange rate stability operated by the IMF depended crucially on the US dollar. Money – for domestic or for international trade – serves its purpose by being acceptable to the parties to the trade. Many commodities – such as iron bars or cowrie shells or even cigarettes – have been acceptable as money in some circumstances. However, from early times bars or coins made from precious metal, silver and especially gold, were generally recognised as the most generally acceptable form of money. Paper money, or 'fiat' money, evolved simply as a method of establishing ownership of gold or silver. For domestic purposes, while banknotes declare a promise to pay money to the bearer, nobody expects to go to their bank and get gold for their notes, because countries have reliable banking systems. For international trade, however, there is no similar banking system, and the basic role of the IMF was to fill that gap. It took many centuries for domestic banking systems to cease to be dependent on gold, and it could not be expected that the IMF could establish a system independent of gold. So the system set up was that all currencies were pegged to the US dollar, with a small permitted adjustment margin, and the value of the US dollar was fixed in gold. The IMF could itself create credit, valued in dollars, to help to finance trade. The system therefore depended on the willingness, and ability, of the USA to exchange dollars for gold. The stresses on the US economy created by involvement in the Vietnam War (in the 1960s) meant that the USA no longer held the gold reserves needed to meet its IMF obligations, so in 1971 it changed the value of the dollar in gold. This severely damaged the (roughly) fixed exchange rate system that the IMF operated. The fixed exchange rate system finally collapsed in 1973 because it could not withstand the stresses brought about by the first major oil price rise. As far as the EU countries are concerned, they were in any case exploring their own fixed exchange rate system – now the euro – which we will discuss in Part 3.

The IMF still exists, but it now has more of a monitoring function on exchange rates and the general financing of world trade. However, it still acts as an important source of lending to countries experiencing economic difficulties. These are loans, at commercial rates of interest, and frequently come with quite stringent conditions. Its role as lender was important in the 1990s to some of the countries of Central and Eastern Europe in their transition to a market system – Key fact 1.14 looks at the most striking example, the IMF loan to Russia in 1996, which is the largest loan the IMF has ever made.

Key fact 1.14

The IMF and Russia

In March 1996, the IMF made a loan of $10 billion to Russia to support that country's medium-term economic programme. The most acute problem that the Russian economy was experiencing was inflation – at the time of the loan, the Russian government predicted inflation in 1996 would be a little over 50 percent per annum, down from 896 percent in 1993, 302 percent in 1994 and 190 percent in 1995. However, the IMF was also concerned that Russia address other issues – especially, the extent of public sector debt, which had been running at between 10 and 15 percent of GDP in 1993–95 and was expected to be about 40 percent in 1996. This focus of the IMF on Russian government borrowing was very much in line with its policy prescriptions for most countries – its general approach has been to regard government borrowing as the fundamental cause of the problems for which help is sought, so it insists on rises in taxation and cuts in public spending as a condition of its assistance. The loan was for three years. Russia was subsequently given further loans by the IMF, and it paid off the last IMF loan in February 2005.

(Source: For further details, see the IMF website: http://www.imf.org/external/.)

The IBRD

The IBRD is also known as the World Bank – a slightly confusing term since the IMF carries out many of the conventional banking operations for the world. The IBRD did indeed help the postwar reconstruction of Europe – for example, its first loan was to France in 1947 – but its focus now is on the much more complex problems of developing Third World countries, particularly in Africa. Bilateral help, in the form of Marshall Aid, was much more significant in the rebuilding of Europe after the war. The Marshall Plan aid came from the USA and Canada and was administered through the Organisation for European Economic Co-operation

Key fact 1.15

OECD membership

1960 20 original members – Austria, Belgium, Canada, Denmark, France, Germany, Greece, Iceland, Ireland, Italy, Luxembourg, Netherlands, Norway, Portugal, Spain, Sweden, Switzerland, Turkey, UK, USA
1964 Japan
1969 Finland
1971 Australia
1973 New Zealand
1994 Mexico
1995 Czech Republic
1996 Hungary, Korea, Poland
2000 Slovakia

(Source: For more information, see the OECD website: http://www.oecd.org/.)

(OEEC). The OEEC in due course developed into the Organisation for Economic Co-operation and Development (OECD), which is now primarily a forum where member countries (most of the prosperous market economies of the world) exchange ideas and information; it is also a valuable source of economic statistics.

The countries of Europe work with the IBRD and other countries and international agencies in the provision of development aid to the poorest countries of the world. The countries that are most important aid donors are those in Western Europe, Japan and the USA. In practice, donor countries tend to concentrate their efforts geographically, with the Western European countries giving assistance particularly to Africa (rather than Asia or Central and South America, which receive most of the aid given by Japan and the USA). We have already looked at the links between the EU (and its member states) and the ACP group. The total aid to some ACP states that comes from the EU, either through member countries directly or indirectly through the European Commission, is significant. The poorest region of the world is sub-Saharan Africa, which contains many ACP countries. On average, in 2001 and 2002, the EU accounted for 51 percent of total overseas development aid to this region; in the same years, IBRD aid was 15 percent of the total and US aid 12 percent (all data are drawn from *EU Donor Atlas: Mapping Official Development Assistance* at http://www.europa.eu.int/development/).

However, overseas development assistance from the EU is also directed towards other countries, including those in Central and Eastern Europe. For example, in 2001–02, the biggest aid donation from EU countries was to Serbia and Montenegro, which received an average over those two years of $1,172 million from the EU ($307 million through the EU Commission, the rest from member states). The EU Commission and EU member states accounted for 64 percent of the aid received by Central and Eastern European countries in 2001 and 2002.

Key fact 1.16

EU aid to other countries

The top ten recipients of aid from the EU Commission in 2001 and 2002 were (in order of magnitude) Serbia and Montenegro, Turkey, Tunisia, Morocco, South Africa, Bosnia-Herzegovina, the Palestine administrative areas, Mauritania, Ethiopia and Mozambique; and the top ten recipients of total EU aid (Commission and member states together) were (in order of magnitude) Serbia and Montenegro, Mozambique, Tanzania, Ivory Coast, Afghanistan, Morocco, Egypt, South Africa, Nicaragua and India.

(Source: *EU Donor Atlas: Mapping Official Development Assistance* at http://www.europa.eu.int/development/.)

The WTO

The WTO is now the most active and, as we have already seen, controversial of the set of international agencies. It embraces trade not just in goods (the original GATT) but also in services and intellectual property. WTO members bind themselves not to raise barriers against each other except in special circumstances. The special circumstances in which they can raise barriers include retaliation to barriers raised by another country. They meet periodically for worldwide negotiations about cutting barriers. These are conducted in 'rounds', usually named after the city or country in which they are held or some major person who promoted them, so the current round is named after Doha, in Qatar. The WTO runs dispute settlement procedures in which individual disputes are referred to dispute settlement bodies, which use panels and 'appellate bodies' to do the technical work and produce reports. A recent bitter dispute between the EU and the USA was over the unlikely topic of bananas (see Opinion 1.14).

Opinion 1.14

The 'banana wars'

The background to the 'banana wars' lies in the Lomé Convention, whereby EU countries maintain special relationships with some former colonies. This arrangement gives preferential access to EU markets for some developing countries – the African, Caribbean and Pacific (ACP) group. ACP exporters are offered duty-free access to EU markets and can impose tariffs on imports to them from EU members.

A special arrangement was made for bananas. Some of the Caribbean countries are very heavily dependent on banana exports – for St Lucia, St Vincent and Dominica, bananas represent over half of export earnings. The main alternative source of bananas in the world is Central and South America, where large US multinational companies have financed big plantations with a cost advantage over the Caribbean – the 'dollar' bananas. For many years, Germany has imported 'dollar' bananas, and Germany accounts for a third of the EU banana imports. The UK, France and Italy have historically imported their bananas from the Caribbean. Under the Lomé Convention, special access to the EU markets was kept for Caribbean bananas; Caribbean bananas were imported into the EU duty-free. Initially, these bananas were imported at a special guaranteed price, higher than the 'dollar' banana price. (The guaranteed price also applies to the EU's own banana production, which takes place mainly in the French associated territories.) At the same time, bananas were being imported into Germany at the 'dollar' banana price. This dual pricing of banana imports became untenable when the 'Single Market' was completed by the end of 1992. So the whole arrangement had to be revised. The EU Commission proposed that ACP bananas would continue to have tariff-free access to EU markets, and a moderate tariff would be imposed on non-EU and non-ACP bananas for up to 2 million tonnes of imports per annum, and a very high tariff on any additional imports over 2 million tonnes. In 1992, the EU consumed about 4.12 million tonnes of bananas, of which EU production accounted for about 0.7 million, Caribbean imports about 0.64 million, other – principally 'dollar' – bananas 2.77 million. If total banana sales were unchanged, the effect therefore would be to stimulate EU and Caribbean production to increase by about 0.77 million tonnes because the very high tariff rate would make the 'dollar' bananas uncompetitive.

The USA and four major multinational banana producers (with interests in the 'dollar' banana plantations) asked the WTO to rule that this action by the EU violated the EU's obligations under the GATT. The WTO ruled in 1998 that the EU proposals did indeed violate the GATT. In consequence, the EU modified the arrangements in July 1998 by changing the details in various ways but still keeping the principle of an effectively guaranteed share of the market

▶

for EU and ACP bananas, arguing that these arrangements protect the legitimate interests of producers in the ACP countries against the industrial might of the 'dollar' banana distributors. In response, Ecuador, Guatemala, Honduras, Mexico and the USA claimed that the new EU arrangements were still illegal, and the WTO agreed. The USA threatened to impose barriers to selected EU imports (e.g. bath products made by the Body Shop and Gucci handbags), claiming legitimacy to do so because the EU was in violation of its own obligations under the GATT – i.e. a trade war. The matter was ultimately solved by a climb-down by the EU; as we have seen, this entailed the abandonment of the Lomé Convention and its substitution by an agreement which drops the preferential access to EU markets for the ACP countries.

The long dispute produced an atmosphere of some mutual suspicion between the USA and the EU and thus indirectly led to more recent disputes between them, such as on steel and potentially on the safety of foodstuffs.

What do you think should have been concluded in the banana case?

The WTO has proved controversial in recent years because critics have viewed it as 'captured' by big business interests. In the 'banana wars' case, for example, it appeared that the WTO was ruling in favour of big US-based multinationals against Caribbean banana farmers. It is also claimed that WTO rulings are insensitive to environmental considerations. The basic rationale of the WTO, expressed in many of its documents, is that competition supported by free trade is best for the world as a whole and for each individual country; however, critics argue that this approach is too broad and does not pay sufficient attention to the imperfections of the market system. The strength of opposition to the WTO manifested itself in growing protests at some of its meetings. The prospect of riots, with about 30,000 protesters, caused the abandonment of the 'millennium round' meeting scheduled to be held in Seattle in 1999. The WTO meeting in 2003 in Cancun, Mexico, collapsed after the representatives from developing countries refused to open their agricultural markets to competition, fearful for the future for their farmers – even though it had seemed likely that the meeting would bring about an end to EU and US farm subsidies. More recently, however, the WTO has twice ruled against the policy of the USA in giving subsidies to its cotton farmers. Once the USA accepts this ruling, world cotton prices will probably rise a little, thus making it easier for Third World cotton producers to make a living.

Further reading

For this section, the most useful sources are websites. However, remember that each site represents the views of the organisation sponsoring it, so you should read several sources to make sure you have obtained an objective view.

EU Commission website: (http://www.europa.eu.int/comm).

IBRD website: (http://www.worldbank.org).

IMF website: (http://www.imf.org).

NATO website: (http://www.nato.int).

OECD website: (http://www.oecd.org).

UK Foreign and Commonwealth Office website: (http://www.fco.gov.uk).

WTO website: (http://www.wto.org).

Part 2

Country studies

Plate 2.1 A mosaic map of the world, near the monument to the discoveries, in Lisbon. The design of the mosaic is a large compass rose, with the map in the centre and Europe in the centre of the map. Do Europeans still think Europe is the centre of the world?

Source: FOTOSEARCH® (2005).

Section 2.1

Introduction

Part 2 of the book focuses on introducing students to processes of political, economic and social change in a range of European countries. Our case studies include countries from all parts of the continent. We start by examining the four largest countries of Western Europe – France, Germany, Italy and the United Kingdom. Because of their population size, level of economic development, cultural dominance, and, not least, because of the legacy of history, these four countries might be spoken of as constituting a European 'core'. Acting together – something that they do not always manage to do – they certainly have the capacity to exercise a decisive influence on the rest of the continent. Two of these countries (France and the UK) are longstanding democracies, and two (Germany and Italy) faced the challenge of democratic reconstruction and consolidation after the defeat of Nazism and fascism in 1945 (as did France after the short period of Nazi occupation and territorial division).

We then focus on a group of countries that includes some of the oldest European democracies – the Nordic countries. The Nordic region is formed by the four Scandinavian countries (Denmark, Iceland, Norway and Sweden) plus Finland. (For cultural, linguistic and historical reasons, Finland is not a Scandinavian country, although it is often inaccurately referred to as such). These countries have enjoyed highly developed welfare states and stable consensus politics for many years, both of which are now under strain. They have also, for various reasons, been considered 'reluctant Europeans'.

We then move our attention to Southern Europe, studying three countries – Greece, Portugal and Spain – that have experienced the heavy hand of right-wing dictatorships in the late twentieth century, undergoing transitions to democracy within a year of each other (1974–75). These countries also entered the EC in the early to mid-1980s. Less affluent and less well developed than the Northern and Western European countries, they formed, for many years, a sort of peripheral sub-region within the EC/EU. They have had to struggle with issues of democratic consolidation and economic underdevelopment in the period from the mid-1970s to the mid-1990s, especially.

Many of these same issues have faced the ex-communist countries of Central and Eastern Europe and Russia since 1989, as our next set of case studies reveals. Indeed, a substantial body of research has emerged that explores the lessons to be learned from comparing democratic transitions and democratic consolidation in Eastern, Central and Southern Europe (and other regions of the globe, such as

Latin America, parts of Africa, and Southeast Asia). There is one major difference between the Southern and Eastern European experience. Unlike Southern Europe in the mid-1970s (and Germany and Italy in 1945), the countries of Central and Eastern Europe and Russia have had to undergo two processes of dramatic transformation simultaneously: a political and cultural transition from dictatorship to liberal democracy, and an economic transition from centrally planned economies to free-market capitalism. For many citizens, the impact has often been as painful as it has been liberating, if not more so. As our study also shows, there are substantial differences between the countries of Central and Eastern Europe – and between them all and Russia. These differences relate to levels of economic development,

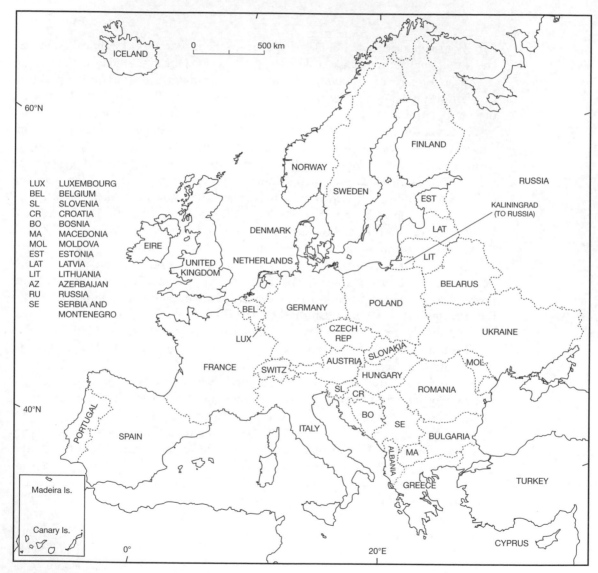

Figure 2.1 Political map of Europe

Source: Unwin (1998: 5).

differing historical experience (or lack of it) of democratic institutions and a democratic political culture, and the strength of civil society. Even the very size of a state can be important – Russia's sheer vastness makes both its stable democratic governance and its future absorption by a body such as the EU (even if both the EU and Russia itself desired such an objective) highly problematic.

Finally, we turn our attention to a populous and largely Islamic country (Turkey) which sits uneasily at the point of intersection between Europe and Asia and whose application for EU membership has raised heated debates about the meaning of European identity. We also look at a country (Cyprus) that is both a new member of the EU and a small state that has been torn apart tragically in recent decades by the poisonous history of conflict between Greece and Turkey. The ability of that beautiful but long-suffering island to achieve a conflict settlement that allows its Greek Cypriot and Turkish Cypriot communities to live in peace, security and harmony may well prove to be an early test case for the effectiveness of the expanded EU as a force for democratic stability and pluralism.

Our range of country studies does not claim to be exhaustive. However, it is substantial and we hope sufficiently inclusive of all parts of the continent to give a flavour of both the achievements of European democracy and the sorts of challenges and problems facing Europe in the years ahead. Many of these challenges and problems are related to the much-debated phenomenon of globalisation, on which there is now a vast literature (see Key concept 2.1).

Globalisation casts a long shadow over all political debates in Europe today. Our studies of various European countries will show that many of the challenges they face are similar and are affected by factors that are no longer easily influenced by action at the level of national government. Within the EU, the debate has sometimes been between those who argue that the EU must embrace globalisation with enthusiasm and become more like the USA, with greater labour market flexibility (often code for making it easier to hire and fire workers and alter their working conditions), if it is to compete globally, and those who argue that a stronger and more effective EU is needed to stand up to global corporations and defend European standards of welfare provision and workers' rights against further erosion.

Key concept 2.1

Globalisation

Studies range from those that see globalisation as the defining characteristic of our age to those that deny there is anything really new about the phenomenon at all. They also run from those that hail globalisation as liberating to those that see it as undermining democracy, eroding workers' and citizens' rights and enslaving millions. In a nutshell, we might describe globalisation as an attempt to conceptualise and understand the processes by which economic, cultural and political power has come to be concentrated in the hands of multinational corporations and media conglomerates that operate and compete with each other on a global basis, measure their success in terms of their share of a global market and increasingly evade the constraints of any nation-state. It has led to the perception that nation-states (and hence democratically elected governments) are increasingly powerless and unable to stand up to corporate power. However, many challenge this perception.

Above all, it could be argued, globalisation has affected the language of politics, the space for real political disagreement and choice, and the attitude that many Europeans have towards political parties and their leaders. We are witnessing a crisis of some importance as many people 'turn off' politics, not bothering to vote and dismissing all parties as being basically the same and failing to deliver their manifesto promises. There is no doubt that this is a Europe-wide phenomenon. It is reflected in the huge change that has taken place in just a generation in what many people perceive by the political terms 'left' and 'right'.

A generation ago, it was reasonably clear what 'left' and 'right' meant. On the left of the political spectrum were two main 'families' of political parties – communists and socialists (or social democrats).

In Central and Eastern Europe, communist parties exercised state power. They proclaimed the dominance of the working class and the superiority of the values of equality, solidarity and the elimination of economic exploitation. The reality, following the deformation of Marxist ideals by the Stalinist dictatorship in the USSR and its subsequent imposition on the countries of Central and Eastern Europe, was very different. Repressive one-party dictatorships led by a privileged party apparatus paid only lip service to the ideals of communism.

In Western Europe, communist parties that were loyal to Moscow were largely insignificant in electoral terms, although they sometimes enjoyed pockets of support. Exceptions included the communist parties of Greece and Portugal, which, although hard-line, enjoyed enormous prestige because of their role in opposing the right-wing dictatorships in their countries. Elsewhere, as in France, Finland, Iceland, Italy and Spain, large and popular communist parties existed but had mostly taken their distance from the Soviet model by the late 1970s and embraced parliamentary democracy and pluralism. They preached a combination of defence of workers' rights and a strong public sector, economic equality and support for the cooperative sector, and support for democracy. In reality, these democratised communist parties were distinguished in degree only from the second 'family' of the left, whose ranks they would for the most part join in the 1990s – the socialists or social democrats.

In Western Europe a generation ago, socialist, social democratic or labour parties (the terms are virtually interchangeable) dominated the left of the political spectrum in all countries except Italy. They were often linked to strong trade union movements and enjoyed support from workers in manufacturing industry, as well as white-collar workers, intellectuals and (sometimes) small farmers. They stood for wealth redistribution, a strong welfare state, defence of trade union rights, social equality and a strong sense of collectivist identity.

On the right of the political spectrum in Western Europe were three main 'families' of political parties: Christian Democrats, liberals (sometimes called radicals) and conservative nationalists. The Christian Democrats were a dominant centre-right force in a number of countries, such as Austria, Belgium, the FRG and Italy, and were important actors in several other countries. For the most part, they had their origins in Catholic social activism in the early twentieth century, often encouraged by the Vatican. (An important exception was in Germany, where the CDU always drew support from both Catholic and Protestant communities, although its Bavarian sister organisation, the CSU, was more recognisably Catholic.) They preached a blend of Catholic idealism, conservative social policies (on abortion and divorce, for example), and support for welfare capitalism. They courted support from both employers' organisations and Catholic trade unions. They were strongly middle-class parties but often with substantial working-class support.

The liberal (or radical) parties tended to be smaller, as often as not junior partners in right-of-centre coalitions, as in the FRG and some Nordic countries. They tended to be strongly bourgeois parties that supported free-market or neo-liberal economic policies. They appealed to a rugged individualism and were sceptical of collectivist identities or traditions. In Europe, such parties also tended to be secular, and many had their origins in nineteenth-century struggles against the absolute power of the Catholic Church. As often as not, the liberal parties appealed to the anti-clerical sentiments of the individualist-minded educated bourgeois voter.

Conservative or nationalist parties enjoyed widespread appeal in countries where nationalism (and perhaps the legacy of imperial glory) was popular. An obvious example is the UK. Although such parties differed significantly in their economic policies, they enjoyed considerable cross-class support and espoused a blend of respect for tradition, aggressive patriotism and paternalistic capitalism.

A generation ago, an overwhelming majority of European voters would have identified with one of the above traditional families of the left or the right and known more or less what the parties stood for. Party identification was, in most cases, handed down from generation to generation. Not all voters thought of themselves as being on the left or on the right – there have always been 'floating' voters and supporters of parties that transcended the left/right divide (for example, regionalist parties) – but most certainly did.

A great deal has changed. First, the collapse of the communist regimes in Central and Eastern Europe, the decline in support for communist parties in Western Europe, and the transformation of many of these parties into social democratic parties has been part of a wider process of deradicalisation, especially on the left. Nowadays, ex-communist parties in countries such as Poland and Hungary actively support the US-led war in Iraq and implement policies of privatisation. Social democratic parties everywhere in Europe have agreed to policies of welfare cuts and privatisation. Few parties call nowadays for a strong public sector. In an era of globalisation, large sections of the traditional left, it seems, have accepted that there is no real economic alternative to capitalist free-market economics. However, social inequalities and marginalisation continue to exist. Capitalist globalisation has its many critics, as seen in the large numbers of people prepared to take part in anti-globalisation marches and demonstrations, but political parties of the left seem uncertain as to what to offer by way of a clear alternative. In consequence, many traditional left-wing voters have become disillusioned and cynical. Others, who feel strongly about an issue such as the war in Iraq, may feel that there is no way of expressing this feeling in voting terms that will make a difference.

Other important social changes in recent decades that have affected parties of the left include:

• growing affluence, which has transformed many working-class families into a new middle class;

• declining numbers of workers who belong to trade unions;

- weakening class consciousness;
- increased reliance on immigrant workers in low-paid jobs who may not be socialised into the traditions of the labour movement and may not even have the right to vote.

As left-wing parties have taken their distance from their working-class roots, they have tended to shed their traditional ideological trappings and appeal to the 'centre ground' in politics. Overall, they have maintained their relative share of the European electorate (albeit on the basis of an ever-decreasing turnout) but have changed beyond recognition. Moreover, the centre ground in European politics has shifted significantly towards the right. A generation ago, a UK politician such as Roy Hattersley (deputy leader of the Labour Party from 1983 to 1992) was on the moderate, right wing of his party; nowadays, he is considerably to the left of Tony Blair and Gordon Brown. Hattersley's views have not changed in any significant way; rather, his party has changed utterly.

Globalisation has also affected parties of the right in a number of ways. First, it might be expected that the apparent triumph of capitalist economics would hugely benefit right-of-centre parties, perhaps even seal their electoral triumph everywhere. Yet this has not been the case. Overall, their share of the vote has not increased significantly, even if they have fared rather better in the battle of ideas.

Centre-right parties have been badly divided on several important matters pertaining to globalisation. We will look in turn at four questions:

1. What should their view be about free markets?
2. Should they compete for the centre ground?
3. Should they support welfare capitalism?
4. How should they respond to the increasing secularisation of society?

Should they embrace global free markets or resort to protectionism in order to safeguard domestic capitalism? And does an embrace of global free markets necessarily imply an embrace of supranational political institutions? In Europe this has resulted in bitter splits and divisions within the right over the issue of EU integration. Moreover, should they welcome increased labour migration, as a logical outcome of globalisation, or support populist campaigns against immigration?

Second, should they respond to the centre-left's courtship of the centre ground in politics by competing for that centre ground – or by moving further to the right? This raises the important question of alliance strategies on the right. Recent decades have seen the emergence of extremist, often racist and xenophobic and sometimes even neo-fascist, parties on the right. Such parties offer scapegoats for society's problems and simple solutions to complex issues. They benefit from voter disillusionment with the mainstream parties. Centre-right parties face a difficult choice between forming alliances with these extremist parties (and perhaps legitimising their extremism), or joining forces with the centre-left to oppose them (and perhaps losing any distinctive identity).

Third, the collectivist traditions and paternalistic welfare capitalism of several of the centre-right families of parties – Christian Democrats and some 'one-nation' conservative parties – have been as badly hit by the rise of globalisation as have been the collectivist traditions and values of the left. In France, Germany,

Plate 2.2 Racism in Europe
Source: © EMPICS; picture by Joerg Sarbach.

Italy and other countries, Catholic trade unionists, traditionally loyal to Christian Democratic parties, have taken to the streets in protest against welfare cuts alongside their left-wing colleagues.

Fourth, some wider social and cultural trends in Europe have particularly hit the centre-right. One example is the widespread secularisation of European society. While this is not a problem for traditionally secular liberals, it is for many Christian Democrats and conservative nationalists. Organised religion, especially Christianity, has lost a lot of ground in many European countries in recent decades. Fewer and fewer Europeans go to church. Fewer and fewer are prepared to be told by the clergy what to think, how to behave, or who to vote for. Parties of the right that have in the past relied on clerical support, or invocation of religious values, now face a dilemma.

Such parties have sought to maintain their support by broadening their horizons. They have been anxious not to be seen to be too closely tied to traditional religion for fear of alienating growing numbers of liberal and secular voters. Taking a hard line against gay rights, abortion or contraception may well repel many voters who might otherwise find the economic policies of these parties quite attractive. On the other hand, breaking free of the churches altogether, even if the churches are a declining force, may cause disruption and division. The dilemma for such parties is increased by the fact that as organised religion has declined in size and influence in Europe, it has often become more shrill and fundamentalist in outlook. The election of the conservative German cardinal Joseph Ratzinger as Pope Benedict XVI in April 2005 (in succession to the already conservative Pope John Paul II), is an example. Pope Benedict XVI has staunchly refused to compromise with an increasingly liberal and secular Europe and has even gone on record (before his election as pope) as opposing Turkey's membership of the EU on the grounds that 'Europe' is Christian, and Turkey is not. If such an uncompromising line emanates from the Vatican in the years ahead, it is likely to cause difficulties for Christian Democratic parties that have been associated with the Vatican in the past but that must tread a very different line in the future if they wish to maintain their vote share. An example is the current debate in the Netherlands, where some Christian Democrat leaders have openly appealed to Muslim voters and have debated whether the party should change its image from that of Christian Democrats to 'Faith Democrats' in recognition that there are probably as many practising Muslims as practising Christians in the Netherlands nowadays. Admittedly, the Dutch Christian Democrats have always drawn heavily on Protestant as well as Catholic support, but the basic point remains valid.

As parties of both left and right struggle to define what exactly they stand for nowadays, a certain fragmentation at both ends of the political spectrum has taken place. On the left, the old two-party competition between communists and socialists has given way to what the French call '*la gauche plurielle*' (the pluralist left). The rise of the Greens has been important. In many countries, new left-wing formations, progressive regionalist parties and left-leaning social movements have also emerged. On the right, conservative regionalist parties (such as Italy's Northern

Leagues), anti-EU parties (such as the UK Independence Party) and racist and xenophobic parties have all complicated the picture. Although the left has perhaps suffered the greater loss of radicalism as a result of globalisation's impact, this has sometimes made the formation of coalition alliances easier. Electoral systems do vary enormously and are important in determining the real range of choices facing the electorate. In a first-past-the-post system, such as the UK's, effective choice may well be limited for many voters to two big parties that converge on many issues.

In conclusion, as our country studies will show, the past few decades have seen unprecedented shifts in political and cultural identities in Europe. Many of these shifts have been affected by the phenomenon of globalisation. The implications for political parties and for voters' faith in the value of democratic politics and the efficacy of political involvement have been considerable. Centre-left and centre-right all too often seem to be offering the same, largely technocratic, message, narrowing or even removing any element of real choice. This has encouraged a fragmentation of party systems and a growth in right-wing extremism. This, in turn, has complicated the business of alliance strategy and coalition government formation. As party identification has declined, Europeans have often found themselves questioning the extent to which either their national governments or the EU are willing and/or able to meet the challenges posed by globalisation.

Section 2.2

The core democracies of Western Europe: France, Italy, Germany, the UK

Introduction

Since 1945, the four major democracies of Western Europe have confronted similar problems and challenges:

- democratic consolidation and economic reconstruction;
- the building of political and social consensus;
- urbanisation, modernisation and changes to the social structure;
- the impact of recession and economic crisis since the 1970s, and in particular the growing burden on the welfare state;
- the increasing internationalisation of both politics and economics; and
- the challenges of European integration.

These developments have been associated with major transformations in cultural and social life – for example:

- the decline in the social and political influence of the main churches through widespread secularisation;
- the move from large-scale and labour-intensive manufacturing industry to light industry, computerisation and the service sector, with a concomitant decline in traditional working-class subcultures and change in the relationship between social class membership and political behaviour;
- the political impact of feminism, with challenges to patriarchal privilege;
- the changing ethnic and racial composition of societies; and
- the momentous challenge posed by the growth in the power of the mass media and the impact of new forms of marketing and communications upon politics.

More recently, the collapse of communist rule in Eastern and Central Europe, and the reopening of old and seemingly intractable ethnic conflicts, as well as the eastern countries' need for economic aid, have added to the debate about the future of European democracy. Traditional parties and ideologies have been forced, with varying degrees of enthusiasm and success, to respond to new political agendas, centred on topics such as ecological concerns, race and ethnicity, regionalism, and gender politics; and to organise around new socio-political cleavages, many of which are as yet only semi-formed. Whereas some parties have sought to transform their ideologies and structures totally, others have been content to adapt to change more slowly. New political forces have sought to enter the mainstream – the Greens, for example, but also, most dramatically in the 1990s, a resurgent extreme right in several countries. The major European democracies face mounting evidence of voter volatility and unrest.

This section presents a synopsis and analysis of the main contours of political developments in each of the four major Western European democracies since 1945. It examines each country in turn before turning to a comparative analysis of the challenges confronting the major democracies at the start of the new millennium.

France

The experience of war, occupation, and liberation left deep scars upon the French body politic: in 1945, the country was divided between those who had resisted the Nazis and those who had collaborated, either actively or passively. This political dichotomy was compounded by divisions within the victorious resistance movement between a nationalist right wing, loyal to General Charles de Gaulle, and a communist-led left wing. The French Communist Party (PCF) emerged in elections held in October 1945 as the biggest single party, with 26 percent of the popular vote. However, the political life of the Fourth Republic – inaugurated in October 1946 – was to be dominated by a series of shaky coalition governments, often led by the moderate and pro-Western Socialist Party (SFIO); and both the Gaullist and communist movements were to experience marginalisation following de Gaulle's withdrawal from active politics in 1946 (in disagreement with the new constitution) and the PCF's removal from the postwar government in 1947. Importantly,

Government 2.1

Government in France

France is a republic, with a president directly elected for five years (until recently, seven years).

The parliament has two chambers. The National Assembly has 577 members, elected for a five-year term in single-seat constituencies. The Senate has 331 members, 319 elected for a nine-year term from local electoral colleges, one third coming up for election each three years; the remaining twelve members represent citizens living abroad.

(Source: http://www.electionworld.org.)

the wartime experience had discredited those substantial sections of the French right that had collaborated with the Nazi occupation and that adhered to an almost pre-revolutionary creed that conflated racial purity with true Frenchness and national glory with respect for hierarchy. Although such sentiments would resurface in the 1950s in the far right Poujadiste movement, and even in some parts of the Gaullist movement, and again more recently in Jean-Marie Le Pen's Front National, for the most part the post-1945 French right would embrace a conservative variant of the democratic republicanism of 1789.

A key priority of the governments of the Fourth Republic was economic reconstruction. From 1945 to 1947, the National Resistance Council nationalised many key industries and banking and insurance concerns. Although the pace and direction of nationalisations changed after 1947, state intervention and direction remained a cornerstone of the French drive to rebuild and modernise the economy. A modernisation plan was launched by Jean Monnet in 1945 based on the premise that the only way to catch up with countries such as the UK and USA was through development of large corporations that could introduce technological innovations and benefit from economies of scale. From 1946, governments sought to raise investment and production in the private sector by assistance and encouragement of mergers. A series of five-year plans from 1947 prioritised industrial growth, to be achieved initially through the development of French industry behind the barriers of protection. Politicians such as Pierre Mendès-France and Guy Mollet sought to speed up modernisation throughout the 1950s. Industry grew rapidly; living standards rose, and from 1952 increased urbanisation began to change the social structure dramatically. On the negative side, rural depopulation saw many small farmers forced off the land, small businesses suffered from the policy of industrial and commercial concentration, and the new city dwellers frequently suffered from urban congestion. Moreover, the planning process was entrusted to civil servants and technocrats, who were often accused of top-down, authoritarian management. The *dirigiste* foundations of French-style corporatism were laid in this period, pre-empting later Gaullist tendencies to bypass traditional interests and elites by dealing with sympathetic professional associations.

The Fourth Republic was politically unstable. A strong parliament, inclusive of all shades of opinion through proportional representation, had been envisaged in the constitution of the republic. However, parties in parliament remained deeply polarised. Weak governments, unable to straddle the great political cleavages, further reproduced chronic instability. France had no fewer than 25 governments and 15 prime ministers between 1945 and 1958. Even more worrying, from the point of view of the political establishment, was that by 1951 nearly half the electorate was voting for parties – communist or extreme right – that rejected the postwar political system; indeed, the 1950s saw a rise in support for the right-wing Poujadiste movement, which appealed to those lower middle classes adversely affected by economic restructuring.

It is possible that the Fourth Republic might have endured longer but for the crisis that erupted in Algeria in 1954. The outbreak of a violent and bloody colonial war there had a profound effect upon French society, polarising the country between supporters and opponents of French imperial rule. By 1957–58, it was clear that elements of the French military were out of control and willing to resort to open rebellion and threats of assassination against cabinet ministers; France's moral standing in the world was collapsing as reports of torture of Algerians reached the outside; and right-wing terrorist groups at home were targeting opponents of the colonial war. Fears rose that the civilian authorities were in danger of losing power to the army in a coup.

When a coup came, in May 1958, it did not inaugurate a military-style dictatorship. Rather, Charles de Gaulle, helped by his wartime prestige and by the fact that he had stood above the chaos of the Fourth Republic, took power, promising a new constitution for a Fifth Republic. That constitution, promulgated in September, introduced a strongly centralised presidential democracy with a directly elected head of state (de Gaulle became president in December). The powers of parliament *vis-à-vis* the executive were reduced. De Gaulle consolidated his position by removing the military threat to democracy, and he ended the war in Algeria by granting that country its independence (1962).

The Gaullist decade saw substantial elements of continuity in economic policy. State direction of private sector operations through technocratic planning continued to act as a motive force of development. With the foundation of the EEC in 1957, the French economy was opened up, step by step, to greater competition; however, caution and compromises with those business interests that felt threatened by international competition were necessitated by political as well as economic criteria. In 1963, a new regional planning agency was created – DATAR – with the intention of further bypassing local elites and developing the more backward areas of the country. Its operations also tended to undermine political parties and reinforce the irrelevance of parliament as a forum where regional problems could be aired and resolved. Throughout the 1960s, the regime sought to strengthen industry by encouraging mergers and shutdowns, which led to mounting unemployment and a lengthening of the working week – the longest in Western Europe by 1968.

Economic modernisation was not accompanied by a modernisation of social structures. Indeed, Gaullism exuded paternalism and populist appeal to traditional morality, patterns of social behaviour and respect for authority. The combination of rapid economic growth with social stagnation created several sources of powerful discontent. Workers, especially the newly urbanised, were angered by rising unemployment, low wage increases and cuts in public spending on health and housing after 1963. Students railed against a university sector in which numbers had expanded rapidly without a corresponding increase in spending on education. The effects of land clearances alienated small farmers. These grievances came to a head in May 1968, when France was rocked by virtual revolution. Tens of thousands of students and workers occupied universities and factories, and for a period it seemed as if the Fifth Republic would fall. Eventually, de Gaulle called a general election, which was won by the right-wing parties, capitalising upon the fear of revolution and chaos. However, the regime had been badly shaken, and in April 1969 de Gaulle resigned the presidency, being succeeded after elections by Georges Pompidou.

May 1968 represented a revolt against the stifling paternalism of postwar French society. In the early 1970s, French governments moved to introduce a number of changes, including greater trade union rights, educational reforms and progressive social legislation, including the legalisation of abortion and freer access to birth control. However, under the presidencies of both Georges Pompidou (1969–74) and Valéry Giscard d'Estaing (1974–81), France remained a highly centralised state.

During the 1970s, a number of important developments changed the nature of political competition. On the right of the political spectrum, the remains of the

Gaullist movement had to compete with a non-Gaullist right wing that saw itself as more modern, liberal and pro-European and less nationalist. Such forces were organised by Giscard d'Estaing into the Union for French Democracy (UDF), a

---

Biography 2.1

Georges Pompidou (1911–74)

President of France, 1969–1974, Pompidou served as an aide to General de Gaulle during and after the Second World War, and this helped to launch his political career. In 1962, he was appointed premier by President de Gaulle but was dismissed from this office following the demonstrations and strikes in France in 1968. Pompidou was widely regarded as a steadying influence in this crisis, and on de Gaulle's resignation from the presidency in 1969 he was elected president with the strong support of the Gaullist party. He immediately sought to address France's economic problems at this time by devaluing the franc and introducing price controls. He also brought a renewed impetus to EC affairs and was largely responsible for calling the important Hague summit of the six EC states in December 1969, which resulted in a strong commitment to the completion, enlargement and deepening of the EC.

Pompidou was far more disposed than de Gaulle had been to consider enlargement and UK membership. However, he was as determined as de Gaulle had been to ensure that the EC served French material interests. For example, he was primarily responsible for the introduction of permanent arrangements for the funding of EC activities such as the Common Agricultural Policy immediately before the EC's enlargement and thus before UK membership was likely to complicate the issue of a permanent financing mechanism or the EC's 'own resources'.

Plate 2.3 This McDonald's restaurant on the most famous boulevard in Paris, the Champs-Élysées, has aroused the ire of some French nationalists opposed to American influence in French life

Source: AP/Wide World Photos. ©AP/EMPICS.

centre-right coalition that supported his presidential bid in 1974. Gaullist forces, reorganised by Jacques Chirac into the Rally for the Republic (RPR) in 1976, would have both to compete against, and to cooperate with, this new centre-right in order to hold on to power.

Biography 2.2

Jacques Chirac (1932–)

French politician and conservative (Gaullist) president of the Fifth Republic (1995–). The son of a Parisian banker, Chirac trained as a technocrat. After a youthful flirtation with socialism, he embraced Gaullism and was National Assembly deputy for the rural department of La Corrèze from 1967 until 1995. He was a protégé of President Georges Pompidou (1969–74), under whom he served as minister of the interior. In 1974, Chirac supported Giscard d'Estaing for the French presidency and was rewarded with the office of prime minister. The two men fell out in 1976, whereupon Chirac founded the neo-Gaullist Rassemblement pour la République (RPR) party and challenged Giscard d'Estaing for leadership of the French right. Chirac served as Mayor of Paris between 1977 and 1995, building up a huge patronage machine. Allegations of corruption from those days have haunted his presidency, and there is a possibility that he may yet face criminal charges upon leaving office. Chirac was parliamentary leader of the right-wing opposition to President Mitterrand's government in the National Assembly from 1981 to 1986. Following the right's victory in National Assembly elections in 1986, he served as prime minister in 1986–88 and unsuccessfully challenged Mitterrand in the 1988 presidential elections. He was finally elected president in 1995 and returned to office in 2002. He was forced to 'cohabit' with a socialist prime minister, Lionel Jospin, from 1997 (following the left's victory in National Assembly elections) until 2002. Chirac is a controversial character. Skilful, amiable and charismatic, he has a well-earned reputation for ruthless pragmatism and ideological inconsistency. His many policy changes include moving from mild euro-scepticism to ardent support for European integration. He has also faced constant allegations of corruption and an extravagant lifestyle. In the second round of the 2002 presidential elections, when he faced far right leader Le Pen in a run-off, centre-left supporters reluctantly supported him only after declaring 'better the thief than the fascist'.

In 1972 the Communist and Socialist Parties signed a Common Programme of the Left, which facilitated greater cooperation, from which the Socialist Party (PS) of François Mitterrand would emerge as the main victor. Despite a flirtation with the more open-minded and liberal positions of 'Eurocommunism' during the 1970s, the French communists, under Georges Marchais, had reasserted their hard-line and sectarian reflexes by the end of the decade and were unable to compete with Mitterrand's PS. It was the PS, preaching social modernisation, regional reform, workers' self-management and redistribution of wealth, that benefited most from the post-1968 change in atmosphere.

Positive election returns for the left in 1978 were followed by Mitterrand's election in May 1981 as the first socialist president of the Fifth Republic. The PS then achieved a majority in parliament, and a government that included four communist ministers took office.

Biography 2.3

François Mitterrand (1916–96)

French politician and socialist president of the Fifth Republic (1981–95). Mitterrand fought in the French army in the Second World War but later served as a minor official in the Vichy regime. Elected to the National Assembly in 1946 for a small centrist party, he served as minister of the interior (1954–55) and minister for justice (1956–57). He stood unsuccessfully against de Gaulle as the main left-wing candidate in 1965. In 1970, Mitterrand helped to found the modern French Socialist Party (PS) and became its first secretary in 1971, again standing unsuccessfully in the presidential elections of 1974. He was elected president in 1981 and again in 1988, his 14 years in office making him the longest-serving president of the Fifth Republic. His early years in power saw radical measures implemented, including a strengthening of welfare provision, nationalisations and regional reforms. From 1984, his administration moved towards the centre ground, abandoning socialist radicalism and embracing European integration. Several periods of 'cohabitation' between Mitterrand as president and centre-right governments further eroded the differences between centre-left and centre-right. A pragmatist, Mitterrand once famously declared that 'French socialism is not my Bible.' He left office in 1995 as an enigmatic figure, partly discredited by evidence of corruption. He died in 1996 after a long battle against cancer. His legacy has been a difficult one for his Socialist Party.

The early Mitterrand government had many radical innovations to its credit, including:

- a strengthening of workers' rights and a raising of the wages of many workers;
- attempted reflation of the economy through increased public spending;
- increases in social welfare provision;
- the introduction of legislation to increase women's rights in the economic and social spheres;
- long-overdue regional reforms, which, though criticised in their implementation, provided for democratically elected regional authorities for the first time and represented a step away from the old tradition of centralising all power in Paris.

By early 1983, the reform programme was in trouble. The international climate worked against radical economic policies, which depended upon increased borrowing and higher taxes, and in 1983–84 Mitterrand rejected Keynesian economics in favour of austerity. Realisation that the government could not deliver socialism while ignoring external pressures also led to a greater enthusiasm for European cooperation and integration. In July 1984, the communists resigned from government, Mitterrand replaced his prime minister, Pierre Mauroy, with the young technocrat Laurent Fabius, and the administration moved towards the centre. Elections in 1986 returned a right-wing parliamentary majority and ushered in a period of cohabitation between a right-wing government (with the Gaullist, Chirac, as prime minister) and a socialist president. Although the new government carried out some privatisations, the ground had already been prepared by the Fabius administration, and the U-turn was less dramatic than might have been expected.

Mitterrand's re-election in 1988 brought the PS back to office, but this time there was little of the earlier idealism; the communists – reduced to less than 10 percent of the vote – remained firmly in opposition; and Mitterrand included several centre-right figures from the UDF in his new, pragmatic administration. His appointment of a succession of moderate prime ministers – Michel Rocard, Edith Cresson, Pierre Bérégovoy – seemed to confirm to some commentators that French politics was undergoing a process of de-ideologisation, with centre-left and centre-right agreeing on the fundamentals of policy. To others, the impression was created of a Socialist Party unsure of how to react to the country's economic problems or (after 1990) the challenge of a united Germany.

A wild card in French politics was a resurgent extreme right in the form of the racist Front National (FN), led by Jean-Marie Le Pen. Benefiting from the persistence of mass unemployment and the decline of the PCF as an effective vehicle for the protest vote, the FN, preaching hostility towards immigrants and calling for social authoritarianism, was to achieve 10–15 percent of the vote in elections from the mid-1980s. Its rise succeeded to some extent in setting the political agenda in the early 1990s, tempting politicians such as Chirac and Cresson to pander to anti-immigrant sentiments. The FN also sought to exploit growing fears of a loss of national sovereignty, which it claimed was inherent in the Maastricht Treaty on European Union; the treaty was only very narrowly approved by the French in a referendum in September 1992 following a campaign against ratification by the FN, the PCF and some Gaullists.

Although a mass anti-racism movement was formed in response to the FN, a clear turn to the right in French politics was apparent in the early 1990s, and this was confirmed by the election of a right-wing government in March 1993 under the Gaullist Edouard Balladur. Another period of cohabitation began. The socialists had fallen to around 19 percent of the popular vote in the 1993 elections, their worst performance in over 20 years, and had suffered a rout in terms of parliamentary seats. Nevertheless, the volatility of the political situation meant that by the end of 1993, the new government had already been forced to stage two humiliating retreats in the face of popular opposition to its education reforms and its plans to reduce the wages of young workers. Local elections in early 1994, which saw a modest left-wing revival, confirmed the impression of volatility.

In May 1995, the Mitterrand era finally came to an end when the Gaullist Jacques Chirac was elected president. By now, Mitterrand was terminally ill with cancer, and his last years in office had seen growing unease with the moral and political behaviour of members of his entourage and a widespread feeling that his regime had run out of ideas. This reflected badly on his Socialist Party, as did the party's failure to stem the tide of rising unemployment during the 1988–93 period. Nevertheless, the PS presidential candidate – the widely respected Lionel Jospin – did much better than expected in 1995; he actually topped the poll in the first round of the presidential elections and polled 45.8 percent in the second, running Chirac a close second. The outcome allowed Jospin to establish his control over the notoriously fissile PS party machine and to prepare the ground for a post-Mitterrand PS revival.

He did not have to wait long. By late 1995, the tide had already turned against the right, and Chirac and his Gaullist prime minister, Alain Juppé, were embroiled in the worst period of social unrest that France had seen for nearly 30 years. A programme of drastic public spending cuts, which included lowering pensions, cutting social services, reducing the rail network and privatising telecommunications, provoked trade union and student anger. Opinion polls saw Juppé's popularity ratings slump to an all-time low. Chirac's argument that the cuts – and increased taxes – were needed to qualify for European monetary union cut little ice in a country where euro-scepticism was growing and where pride in France's welfare state transcended the usual left/right divide. By April 1996, the PCF (under its new leader, Robert Hue) had explicitly ditched its hard-line stance and was seeking a new government alliance with Jospin's socialists and other centre-left forces.

In early summer 1997, President Chirac made a disastrous tactical blunder by calling a general election. A left-wing alliance of PS, PCF, Greens, Radicals and the tiny Citizens' Movement scored an impressive victory over the right-wing coalition of Gaullists and centrists. The left won 319 seats in the National Assembly to the right's 257, and Chirac had to appoint Jospin as prime minister at the head of a government that included two communist ministers and Dominique Voynet, the young female Green leader, as environment minister. A third of Jospin's cabinet were women – a very significant advance for women at the top of French politics.

The first two years of the Jospin government saw many tensions within the left:

- over European monetary union, to which the PCF and the Citizens' Movement were opposed;
- over increases in pensions and welfare contributions;
- over the speed with which the government was moving to reduce France's dependence on nuclear energy (a key Green Party demand);
- over whether proposals to tackle unemployment went far enough.

Plate 2.4 The German troops visiting Paris to mark Franco-German rapprochement would recall to older French people the sight of German troops parading down the Champs Élysées after conquering France in 1940

Source: *The Independent* (31 January 1998; Dyclos-Merilon-Turpin/FSP).

However, the willingness of the government partners to make compromises and to hold together was impressive and was helped perhaps by the gradual transformation of the PCF into a more moderate force. Party leader Robert Hue pledged his strategic commitment to the government in October 1997, determined not to repeat the PCF–PS internecine feuding of the 1978–83 period; coincidentally, the death of his hard-line predecessor Georges Marchais in November 1997 seemed to symbolise the passing of the communist old guard. Not even PCF dismay over France's support for NATO's bombing of Yugoslavia in 1999 could undermine the PCF's commitment to the government.

Jospin's government was also helped by a near miraculous recovery of the French economy in late 1997: a boost in French exports and tourism receipts and a pick-up in domestic demand helped the government to cut the budget deficit and so meet the Maastricht criteria for entry to the single currency without the sort of drastic social spending cuts that might have destabilised the left. A relatively painless 1998 budget meant that, despite continuing protests over France's 3.2 million unemployment figure, Jospin's popularity and the unity of his government both remained high. It was also possible for Jospin to keep his promise to his Green and communist allies to introduce a phased move to a 35-hour working week, which it was hoped would help to create new jobs.

The election of a Labour government in the UK in May 1997 and of a centre-left coalition government in Germany in September 1998 boosted French hopes of a centre-left agenda across the EU, which prioritised the fight against mass unemployment and social inequality. However, the UK Labour Government, which had gone much further than its French or German comrades in accepting neo-Thatcherite strictures on curbing public spending, was most reluctant to embrace French proposals here.

The last years of the Jospin government (1999–2002) were marked by mounting popular disappointment and discontent with its performance. Jospin himself was a popular prime minister; his personal honesty and integrity were regarded as above reproach. However, his government's embrace of a programme of privatisations and public spending cuts (partially in order to prepare France for participation in the euro zone) offended many of the left's natural supporters. In particular, on the eve of the 2002 presidential elections, two big problems remained for the left. First, there was the central question of mass unemployment, which the centre-left parties across the EU had failed to combat successfully. Second, the PS's smaller coalition allies – especially the PCF and the Greens – faced something of a crisis of political identity. The PCF, especially, had swallowed policy after policy – from joining the euro zone to privatisations of large parts of the economy – with which it had passionately disagreed in the recent past, all in order to remain in government. Jospin, who emerged as the left's obvious leading candidate in the presidential elections, had two big advantages: his personal popularity (though lacking in charisma, he remained highly respected), and signs of continuing division on the right of French politics. These divisions had seen several new parties appear and disappear in the 1990s: the Gaullists split over whether or not to change the party's name and profile; the centrist UDF split over alliances with the FN. The FN itself suffered a split when Le Pen's deputy, Bruno Mégret, led a sizeable section of the party in revolt against the old leader. As Chirac strongly endorsed European monetary union and attacked racism, his party tried to avoid collapse by abstaining on the question of the euro, and Chirac found himself estranged from Charles de Gaulle – the former president's grandson – who ran as an FN candidate in the 1999 European Parliament elections.

In the event, neither Jospin's popularity nor divisions on the right were enough to save the centre-left from a voters' backlash against its failure to cut unemployment or to appeal to its natural supporters. In the first round of the 2002 presidential elections in April (see Table 2.1), Jospin made the tactical mistake of moving towards the centre ground too quickly, failing to mobilise disenchanted left-wing voters. Candidates on both the extreme left and extreme right polled heavily. Although the PCF suffered a huge setback, two Trotskyist candidates on the far left polled 10 percent of the total vote. Most dramatically, and unexpectedly, the extreme right candidate Jean-Marie Le Pen narrowly forced Jospin into third place, costing him his place in the vital second round of voting a fortnight later, when only the two top-placed candidates go forward.

Table 2.1 Results of the first round of voting, French presidential election, 21 April 2002

Candidate	Party	% of votes cast
J. Chirac	Gaullist (RPR)	19.9
J.-M. Le Pen	far right (FN)	16.9
L. Jospin	Socialist (PS)	16.2
F. Bayrou	centre-right (UDF)	6.8
A. Laguiller	far left (LO)	5.7
J.-P. Chevènement	centre-left (PR)	5.3
N. Mamère	Greens (les Verts)	5.2
O. Besancenot	far left (LCR)	4.2
J. Saint-Josse	pro-hunting (CPNT)	4.2
A. Madelin	centre-right liberal (DL)	3.9
R. Hue	communist (PCF)	3.4
B. Mégret	far right (MNR)	2.3
C. Taubira	left radical (PRG)	2.3
Others		3.7

(Source: http://www.electionworld.org.)

For the first time ever, the expected second-round contest between a centre-right and a centre-left candidate now turned into a battle between a centre-right and an extreme right candidate. The shock waves felt, in France and abroad, by Le Pen's stunning success in making it into the second round of voting were considerable and the implications profound. By a tantalisingly small margin, Jospin – the left's great hope – had failed to qualify for the second round. If he had done so, he might very well have beaten outgoing president Jacques Chirac, whose popularity had been badly damaged by a succession of political and financial scandals dating back to his time as mayor of Paris. In the event, Chirac now went forward as the undisputed champion of democracy against a resurgent extreme right. Hundreds of thousands of concerned French citizens took to the streets to protest against what they saw as a fascist threat to democracy. In the second round of voting, even dismayed left-wing electors were forced to back Chirac, although many saw it as a painful choice between 'the thief' and 'the fascist'. Chirac had the most comfortable victory of any French president on the second round of voting (See Table 2.2). It is also worth noting that turn-out increased from 71.6 percent in the first round to 79.7 percent in the second, reflecting a widespread belief that this was a vitally important election for the future of French democracy.

Table 2.2 Results of the second round of voting, French presidential election, 5 May 2002

Candidate	party	% of votes cast
J. Chirac	Gaullist (RPR)	82.2
J.-M. Le Pen	far right (FN)	17.8

(Source: http://www.electionworld.org.)

Back in power, Chirac reorganised his Gaullist party and other centre-right elements into a new political formation – the Union for the Presidential Majority (UMP), and appointed a prime minister, Jean-Pierre Raffarin, from one of the non-Gaullist elements (the centrist Liberal Democracy Party) that threw in its lot with him. However, the period 2002–05 saw the Chirac presidency plagued by a host of problems. In particular, mass unemployment and public opposition to plans to reduce France's generous welfare entitlements led to a downturn in the president's popularity and the near-collapse of that of his prime minister. In March 2004, the left secured a sweeping triumph in regional elections, winning control over all but one of the country's regional parliaments; and European Parliament elections in June 2004 saw further setbacks for Chirac's allies. President Chirac's opposition to the US-led war in Iraq from April 2003 was certainly a popular policy stance at home, but it was not sufficient to allay fears about the country's economic and social problems. Moreover, French public opinion remained divided over the course of European integration, and especially the question of Turkey's EU membership; the president's support for Turkey's membership application was unpopular with many French voters. From 2004 onwards, Chirac faced stiff political competition on two main fronts: from a rejuvenated Socialist Party in which, after Lionel Jospin's retirement from front-line politics in May 2002, power passed to a younger generation with the election of François Hollande as secretary; and from a powerful internal rival within the UMP – the young, energetic and popular Nicholas Sarkozy.

In December 2004, Hollande reinforced his authority over the Socialist Party when he triumphed decisively in a referendum among party members that was held to determine the party's stand on the proposed new EU constitution, regarding which he had campaigned vigorously for a 'yes' vote. Hollande's success in securing the backing of 59 percent of the party faithful strengthened his prospects of fending off a challenge from former PS leader and prime minister Laurent Fabius for the 2007 presidential nomination. (A constitutional reform has reduced the presidential term of office from seven to five years, meaning that the next election will take place in 2007, not 2009.)

Sarkozy, meanwhile, has established himself as by far the most popular figure on the centre-right. Appointed interior minister by Chirac after June 2002, Sarkozy earned a reputation as hard-working, efficient and charismatic. His hard-line law and order policies outraged civil liberties campaigners but seemed to be popular with voters. His unconcealed ambition to replace Chirac as president led the latter to move him, first to the finance ministry and then to the chairmanship of the UMP. In January 2005, Sarkozy used that position to challenge Chirac to a popularity contest by arguing that UMP members should decide by a popular vote on who should be the presidential candidate in 2007; and to advocate new policies on Europe, the economy and security that almost amounted to an alternative governmental programme. The bitter rivalry between the two men again became apparent in the aftermath of the French referendum on the EU constitution on 29 May 2005. After a bitterly fought referendum campaign, in which popular anger over high unemployment and worries about an erosion of social welfare provision was focused on the governing elite that Chirac personified, French voters rejected the EU constitution by 55 percent to 45 percent (the campaign and the result are discussed in greater detail in Part 5). The result was widely interpreted as a personal rejection of Chirac, whose popularity fell to a new all-time low. In the aftermath, Chirac dismissed his prime minister, Raffarin, but he chose not to appoint Sarkozy, whom sections of the right-wing media had clamoured for; instead, he opted for the centrist politician Dominique de Villepin, a Chirac loyalist.

President Chirac's political standing was undoubtedly damaged by the outcome of the May 2005 referendum, but the opposition Socialist Party was also exposed as badly divided. The Socialist leadership, under François Hollande, had campaigned for a 'yes' vote. But other prominent figures, including Laurent Fabius, led the 'no' campaign. A majority of Socialist voters – around 56 percent according to exit polls – voted 'no'. This fact robbed Hollande of the advantage that his victory in the internal party poll in December 2004 had given him. It was the opponents of the EU constitution, not its supporters, who seemed to be more in tune with the Socialist electorate.

Politics and society in France at the beginning of the twenty-first century were diversified and fragmented with the potential for unforeseen challenges to the major parties being launched by new forces seeking to mobilise around the big issues of unemployment, Europe and immigration. Although the logic of presidential elections has once again reinforced competition between right-wing and left-wing alliances, bitter divisions remain within those alliances, and French society is scarcely less fragmented politically than in the days of the Fourth Republic. In particular, the extremes of both left and right have shown that they continue to be capable of mounting formidable electoral challenges.

Italy

From Mussolini's downfall in July 1943 – after which he fled behind German lines, presiding in name over a Nazi puppet regime – until final liberation from fascism on 25 April 1945, Italy was involved in civil conflict, although the increasing domination of the Germans over the remnants of Italian fascism allowed the conflict to be articulated by the anti-fascist side as a war of national liberation. Both the communist and Christian Democrat wings of the Italian resistance movement were to emphasise the patriotic nature of the anti-fascist struggle. Democratic patriotism was seen as a useful way of constructing a new Italian national identity that was not merely post-fascist but decidedly anti-fascist, thus denying the hard right patriotic legitimacy in post-1945 Italy.

Government 2.2

Government in Italy

Italy is a republic, with a president elected for seven years by an electoral college. The parliament has two chambers. The Chamber of Deputies has 630 members, elected for a five-year term, 475 in single-seat constituencies and 155 by proportional representation. The Senate of the Republic has 326 members, 315 of whom are elected for a five-year term, 232 in single-seat constituencies, 83 by proportional representation; the remaining eleven are senators for life.

(Source: http://www.electionworld.org.)

While such political myths played a positive role in binding some of the wounds of the previous 20 years, the reality was a lot more complex. An extreme right wing, nostalgic for Mussolini's rule, remained an enduring force in Italian politics; reorganised in December 1946 as the Italian Social Movement (MSI) in order to circumvent the constitutional ban on the old Fascist Party, it would wait for nearly 50 years until the collapse of the Christian Democrat system of power in the early 1990s gave it an opportunity to expand its social base, entering the Italian government in May 1994 with five cabinet ministers. It was then reborn as the 'post-fascist' National Alliance (AN).

The Italian people voted in June 1946 to abolish the monarchy and a new constitution established Italy as a democratic republic. The Christian Democrats (DC), under Alcide de Gasperi, who became prime minister in December 1945, engineered (with Washington's approval) the expulsion of the Italian Communist Party (PCI) from the postwar government in 1947, and in 1948 the long period of Christian Democrat dominance began in earnest when the party won general elections with nearly 50 percent of the vote. The DC would remain in power, at the head of a series of mostly coalition governments, until its collapse amid massive corruption scandals in 1993–94.

Italian economic policy after 1945 sought regeneration through integration with the world capitalist economy. Italy pursued an 'open doors' policy, which emphasised competition in external markets. Northern Italian industry was encouraged to take advantage of low wages paid to southern migrant labour and to act as the motive force of a growth drive led by exports. This policy necessitated internal migration from south to north, heavy external emigration of 'surplus' workers, weakened trade unions and relative neglect of agriculture, especially the notoriously inefficient southern agricultural sector.

After 1953, the DC felt that political circumstances necessitated greater state intervention in the economy. Elections in 1953 saw the DC slide to 40 percent, and the PCI increase its vote to nearly 23 percent, eclipsing the Socialists on the left. Having failed in an attempt to manipulate the electoral law in its favour, the DC moved to entrench itself in power against the danger of an eventual left-wing victory at the polls by exploiting the full potential for patronage of giant state corporations created during fascism – such as the Institute for Industrial Reconstruction (IRI) – or instituted by the DC – such as the State Hydrocarbons Corporation (ENI). Public works programmes contributed to the economic boom in the 1950s and 1960s. The DC under Amintore Fanfani brought the state and semi-state sectors under party control, patronage becoming a mainstay of the party's system of power. Public sector jobs were increasingly awarded on the basis of political loyalty rather than merit.

From 1957 to the mid-1960s, high growth rates transformed Italy into a modern industrial economy, but serious social and economic problems were exacerbated during the 1960s:

- in the cities, appalling conditions and low wage rates prevailed for many of the hundreds of thousands of newly urbanised poor;
- the longstanding imbalance between the rich north and the underdeveloped south became, if anything, even more critical as Italy emerged as a major economic power;
- unemployment in the 1950s reached four times the European average;
- social problems were neglected – provision of public housing was negligible, and no national health service existed until the late 1970s.

From the mid-1960s, wages picked up and trade unions became more vocal. The DC responded to a rise in PCI support by seeking to isolate the Communists through incorporation of the Socialist Party (PSI) in coalition governments from 1963. This move was facilitated by the election of a more liberal-minded pope, John XXIII, in 1958; his predecessor, Pius XII, had vigorously opposed any *rapprochement* between the DC and the PSI. The new coalition merely encouraged expectations of social reforms, which the PSI was unable to deliver while the DC controlled the purse strings. In the longer term, the PSI was drawn into the web of patronage and corruption that came to characterise the Italian ruling elite, a process that was facilitated by Bettino Craxi's election as PSI leader in 1976.

Biography 2.4

Bettino Craxi (1934–2000)

Italian socialist politician and prime minister (1983–87). Craxi became leader of the Italian Socialist Party (PSI) in 1976, following years of factional infighting. He sought to move the party decisively towards the right, away from an alliance with the powerful Italian Communist Party (he was a fierce anti-communist) and towards a strategic alliance with the Christian Democrats (DC). During the 1980s, he formed a close relationship with DC leaders Andreotti

▶

and Forlani (the trio were known collectively as CAF). This gave the PSI a key role in government but also meant that it ultimately became as corrupt as the DC, competing for the spoils of office. In 1983, Craxi became Italy's prime minister. He pursued relatively right-wing economic policies but also occasionally stood up to the USA in foreign policy. In the early 1990s, anti-corruption judges investigating corruption and Mafia influence in Italian politics turned their attention on Craxi. His unusual defence was that all parties needed to extort illegal bribes – that he was guilty, but that so was everyone else. This did not persuade public opinion, or the judges. His party, which had never polled more than 14 percent, collapsed overnight. Some of its remnants joined Silvio Berlusconi's new Forza Italia party. Craxi, who was renowned for his arrogance, sought to blame his juniors for corruption within the PSI. He then fled into exile in Tunisia (1994) to avoid imprisonment; he died there in 2000. Berlusconi's government has sought to rehabilitate Craxi since his death, prompting the Italian joke that the Post Office had to abandon plans to issue a stamp with Craxi's profile on it because too many people would have spat on the wrong side.

By 1969, the economic miracle was in trouble. Attempts to buy social peace and political stability by expanding the numbers in higher education and the state bureaucracy, and by paying hidden subsidies to dependent social groups (in the form of 'invalidity' payments to semi-employed small farmers, for example) could not prevent a social explosion in 1969. The so-called 'Hot Autumn' of that year saw massive industrial unrest, with more hours lost in strikes than in any other country in the developed world.

The early 1970s saw some social reforms that strengthened workers' rights, establishing a new institutionalised role for the trade unions. The perceived shift in the balance of power towards the labour movement, together with continuing good election results for the PCI, provoked an extreme right-wing backlash: neo-fascist terrorists bombed civilian targets from 1969, hoping to provoke political chaos and calls for an authoritarian government, and both far right and far left terrorism plagued Italian politics during the 1970s and 1980s.

The 1970s saw social change. Despite opposition from both the DC and the Vatican, a majority of Italian voters approved the legalisation of divorce (1974) and abortion (1981) in referenda. Together with evidence of falling attendances at church services, these developments highlighted the widespread secularisation of Italian society. The election of a conservative pope, John Paul II, in 1978 failed to reverse the trends. During the 1970s, a large and vocal feminist movement campaigned successfully for changes in family law and the laws on rape, which had effectively condemned women to second-class citizenship. However, it was to prove more difficult to change societal attitudes, especially in the conservative south.

In the wake of the social and economic change that characterised the early 1970s, electoral support for the Italian left wing grew impressively. The PCI scored more than 34 percent in elections in 1976, within 4 percent of the DC. The PCI, pioneers of independent-minded reform communism long before Gorbachev, called for a 'historic compromise' with the DC. A powerful array of forces – the economic and financial establishment, the Church, the DC and its allies, the security services, the US embassy, the Mafia, and the shadowy far-right masonic lodge known as P2 (to which nearly 1,000 of the most influential figures in Italian public life belonged)

– opposed the election of any left-wing government. According to PCI leader Enrico Berlinguer, a successful democratic reform of the Italian state, to tackle corruption and the Mafia (see Key fact 2.1) and to strengthen democratic institutions, could not be undertaken by the Communists alone in the face of such opposition. It required the two big parties to work together. If the DC would commit itself to political reform, the PCI would agree to postpone socialism. A period of 'national solidarity' opened during which the DC, under Giulio Andreotti, continued to exclude the Communists from government but obtained their support in parliament in return for consultation. Such a formula caused considerable tension within both parties: the right wing of the DC resented and opposed any 'legitimation' of the Communists; and the left wing of the PCI feared that their party would simply be used by the establishment to undermine the gains of the labour movement and then be cast aside. The murder in 1978 of leading DC reformer Aldo Moro, an advocate of dialogue with the PCI, was followed by a turn to the right. Moro was kidnapped and murdered by the left-wing terrorist group, the Red Brigades. Subsequent revelations suggested that elements of the state security services and some of his own DC colleagues were implicated in the events leading to his death.

Key fact 2.1

The Mafia

The origins of the Mafia – a vast network of organised crime, political intrigue and covert power – are obscure, as is the very meaning of the word. Some date its genesis to the thirteenth century, but it was in the late nineteenth century that Mafia power engulfed the island of Sicily. Today, the Sicilian Mafia (known locally as *Cosa Nostra* – 'our affair'), is still regarded as the Mafia proper, although the term is also widely applied to organised crime networks in two other areas of southern Italy – the *Camorra* in Naples and the *'ndrangheta* in Calabria.

These criminal networks are protected by self-serving myths that portray them as 'men of honour' protecting the poor (the Calabrian word *'ndrangheta*, of Greek origin, means an honourable or virtuous society), and by a ruthlessly enforced code of silence, known as *omertà*. Far from being honourable, however, the reality is that the Mafia clans have become vicious and murderous parasites that perpetuate the underdevelopment of southern Italy, the exploitation of its people, and the fragile and corruption-prone state of Italian democracy.

Following Italian unification in the period 1860–71, the Mafia emerged as the hired thugs of Sicilian landowners or men of status (known as 'dons') who were determined to hold on to their power in a united Italy. They entered the Italian political system in the years 1876–1914, delivering votes to ambitious politicians in return for protection and power. Under fascism (1923–43), Mussolini claimed to have smashed the Mafia. In reality, they were at best dormant. In some instances, they simply entered the Fascist Party.

Liberation from fascism after 1943 simply increased the Mafia's powers, as the US army in particular used local Mafia networks to secure US influence. Italian emigrants to the USA had given birth to an Italian-American Mafia, which benefited from Prohibition in the 1920s to extend its control over organised crime in Chicago, New York and elsewhere. After 1943, links between this American Mafia and the home-grown Mafia back in Italy increased.

In Italy, the Mafia became associated with political parties on the right, especially the ruling Christian Democrats (DC). It carried out massacres of trade unionists and communist supporters, as in the Portella della Ginestra massacre in May 1947, when trade unionists assembling for a picnic were machine-gunned, leaving eleven dead, including four children. The Mafia's power grew considerably in the 1950s and 1960s. It expanded from control over the building and construction industry and protection rackets into drugs and prostitution.

Wars between rival Mafia clans in the 1960s to the 1980s left hundreds dead. At the same time, Mafia infiltration of the political system led to an endemic degeneration of Italian politics. The Mafia assassinated politicians who stood up to it, and sometimes even politicians it had corrupted (in order to set an example to others in its pay). In the early 1990s, Mafia corruption contributed to the collapse of the Italian political elite as revelations of Mafia association led to the implosion of several hitherto powerful parties, including the Christian Democrats (DC). The Mafia, meanwhile, assassinated several very brave judges and prosecutors who had tried to clean up Italian politics, including Judge Giovanni Falcone (May 1992) and Judge Paolo Borsellino (July 1992).

In the late 1990s, there was substantial evidence that the Mafia had shifted its political patronage and control to Silvio Berlusconi's right-wing Forza Italia party, which won every parliamentary seat in Sicily in 2001, allegedly with Mafia backing. Berlusconi, indicted for corruption, accused the judiciary of a 'communist plot' against him.

The Mafia remains a very powerful economic and political force in Italy. Its control over the black (illegal) and grey (semi-legal, or unregulated) economies in Italy make millions dependent on its patronage or protection. It has exploited immigrants, both in terms of its involvement in the trafficking of people and in terms of using immigrants to sell its drugs and goods on the streets of Italy, thus deflecting anger at its criminal activities on to the unfortunate immigrants. Its power undermines local and national government, in many instances. It retains the ability to impede and subvert democratic progress.

Biography 2.5

Giulio Andreotti (1919–)

Italian Christian Democrat politician and seven times prime minister (between 1972 and 1992). Andreotti is one of Italy's most powerful and most controversial – and some would say, most corrupt – politicians of the postwar era. He served as a deputy minister in various postwar governments, rising through the ranks of the Christian Democratic Party (DC). He has sat in parliament without interruption since 1946, first as a member of the Chamber of Deputies (1946–91) and then as a senator for life. He was foreign minister from 1983 to 1989. During the 1980s, he was one of a trio of powerful politicians (known collectively as CAF – Craxi, Andreotti, Forlani) that dominated Italian politics. Andreotti's faction of the DC was notoriously close to the Mafia. Sicilian Christian Democrat politician Salvatore Lima was believed to have been Andreotti's key go-between with the Mafia (Lima was subsequently murdered by the Mafia, allegedly as a warning to Andreotti not to disappoint the godfathers of crime). Andreotti was the last DC prime minister of Italy from 1989 to 1992, and his last government was undermined by massive corruption and evidence of Mafia collusion. This ultimately destroyed the DC. In November 2002, Andreotti was convicted of ordering the 1979 murder of a journalist who had published allegations about Andreotti's ties to the Mafia and sentenced to 24 years in prison. In October 2003, an appeal court overturned the conviction and he walked free.

The 1980s opened with the PCI back in opposition and isolated. The party's loss of any sense of strategic direction was bitterly exposed after the sudden death of its leader, Berlinguer, in 1984; thereafter, open factionalism gradually robbed the party of its once proud unity. The party's defeat in a referendum on wage cuts in 1985, and its inability to halt job losses or privatisations, was followed by an electoral setback in 1987, when the PCI share of the vote fell back to 26.6 percent.

In 1983, the DC agreed to the appointment of Socialist leader Bettino Craxi as prime minister, although Christian Democrats continued to dominate the cabinet. Craxi had led the PSI steadily to the right, acquiring a reputation for fierce anti-communism and ruthless pragmatism. He sought to project the PSI as a decisive force for change, attractive to the young professionals and middle classes and contemptuous of socialist ideology and political moralism – which he associated with the PCI. Under his leadership, the Socialists played a double role in government. They claimed to be a more modern alternative to both the Communists and the Christian Democrats, yet they cooperated closely with the latter in keeping the former isolated. They demanded economic rationalisation yet became ever more embroiled in the system of corruption and patronage, with which they came to be as closely associated as the Christian Democrats. Craxi's party succeeded in winning wealthy backers, such as the media mogul Silvio Berlusconi. (This explains the apparent paradox whereby many ex-Socialists who had supported Craxi joined Berlusconi's fiercely right-wing Forza Italia party, which he launched in the 1990s.) Nevertheless, for all its new influence and powers of patronage, the PSI was unable to exceed around 15 percent of the popular vote.

By the early 1990s, the Italian political system was showing signs of considerable strain. No real change of government had been achieved since 1947. The Mafia remained a powerful threat, not only to democracy and the rule of law but also to the very survival of the Italian state. The system of political patronage, based upon high levels of public spending, was difficult to sustain in times of economic recession, and Italy entered the 1990s with the highest level of public debt in Western Europe. The decision of PCI leader Achille Occhetto to rename and relaunch the party as the post-communist Democratic Party of the Left (PDS) in February 1991 was intended as an initiative to break the log jam and create a new centre-left majority. In the event, the party split with radicals leaving to form the Communist Refoundation Party, and a divided left suffered further losses in elections in 1992.

Meanwhile, a revolt against government corruption got under way in the north. The populist Northern Leagues, centred in wealthy Milan and led by the outspoken Umberto Bossi, exploited the well-documented connections between government parties and the Mafia to accuse Rome of draining the north of resources and pumping them into the south, where the Christian Democrats had their power base. The Leagues veered between calls for a new federal Italy and threats of outright northern secession. Appealing to the self-interest of the northern middle classes but also capturing working-class support with a heady mixture of regionalist fervour and hostility towards 'immigrants' from the south, the Leagues won nearly 9 percent of the total national vote in 1992. Thereafter, they suffered electoral setbacks, falling to around 4 percent in 2001.

In 1991–94, investigations into political corruption by a number of outstandingly brave Italian magistrates – their resolve strengthened, if anything, by Mafia assassination of several of their colleagues – revealed massive networks of bribery and theft of public funds and ensnared hundreds of leading politicians. Virtually the entire ruling political elite was exposed as corrupt. Left-wing hopes of a thorough democratic revolution, perhaps involving a move to the left, were dashed by a growing exasperation with all politicians and with politics in general – expressed in a longing for a 'saviour' from without who would smash the old system. A popular referendum on electoral reform in June 1993 produced a massive majority in favour of a move away from proportional representation – seen as leading to weak and corrupt cabinets. Serious discussion of the implications of various reforms tended to get brushed aside by a tidal wave of negative feeling towards the entire political class.

Local elections in November 1993 produced victory for a left-wing alliance, led by the PDS. However, a huge increase in the neo-fascist vote was also recorded; the neo-fascist MSI was visibly replacing the crumbling Christian Democrats as the main right-wing force in the south of the country. The DC was now disintegrating, with a rump renaming and relaunching itself early in 1994 as the Italian Popular Party (PPI) and several other factions giving birth to smaller right-wing parties.

In February 1994, Silvio Berlusconi launched a new political movement, Forza Italia, with the intention of blocking an anticipated left-wing victory in general elections scheduled for March. The movement was aggressively right-wing, preaching free-market economics, business success and anti-communism and promising instant cures for the country's economic and political crises. It benefited from the backing of Berlusconi's vast media and business empire. Although Berlusconi was associated with the old regime – a member of the P2 masonic lodge and a friend to many of the disgraced political elite – he managed to project an image of success and dynamism. In alliance with the Northern Leagues and the neo-fascists, his movement harnessed a popular mood of weariness with political squabbling, desire for strong government and longing for economic prosperity to inflict a heavy defeat on the left-wing alliance in March; Berlusconi subsequently became prime minister.

Biography 2.6

Silvio Berlusconi (1936–)

Italian conservative politician and prime minister (April–December 1994 and 2001–). Berlusconi is one of Italy's wealthiest businessmen, a multi-millionaire media mogul whose vast business empire includes television and radio stations, advertising and publishing outlets, a daily newspaper (*Il Giornale*), cinema and home video distribution firms, insurance and banking, and AC Milan football club. He built his fortune from the 1960s to the 1980s and was associated in the 1980s with the ruling (and corrupt) Italian parties, especially the Christian Democrats (DC) and Bettino Craxi's PSI. He was revealed to have been a member of the secret, quasi-masonic P2 organisation, which included in its membership lists powerful politicians, generals, Catholic churchmen and business figures, and was suspected of plotting a coup in the event of a left-wing victory at the polls. Following the collapse of the ruling parties in the early

1990s, Berlusconi entered politics himself, founding his own party, Forza Italia, just months before the 1994 elections, which he won. He posed as the saviour of the Italian economy and protector against a communist takeover. His government was an alliance between his Forza Italia, the neo-fascist National Alliance and the racist Northern Leagues. By the end of 1994, it had collapsed, following controversy over Berlusconi's conflicts of interests. He returned to power in 2001 at the head of the same coalition. His policies have included tax cuts, reduction in welfare spending, a tough line on immigrants' rights and support for the war in Iraq. Berlusconi has survived several attempts by magistrates to indict him for corruption, has been suspected of Mafia collusion (his party won every parliamentary seat in Sicily in 2001, allegedly with *Cosa Nostra* support), and has reformed the law to allow himself to retain control over the mass media. As prime minister, he has established effective control over the state-owned RAI broadcasting corporation, resulting in a dangerous and unprecedented concentration of power in one person's hand. By 2005, his government was bitterly divided and suffered badly in regional polls.

His cabinet was the first in any European country since 1945 to include fascist ministers, causing concern in many European capitals. Moreover, it represented an unprecedented concentration of political, economic and media power in the hands of one man. Ultimately, the contradictions of this position were to lead to Berlusconi's fall from office after less than a year – when the Northern Leagues withdrew their support. An interim government of non-party technocrats, led by Lamberto Dini, was appointed by President Scalfaro to lead Italy from the end of 1994. Berlusconi was subsequently implicated in a series of corruption and bribery scandals, all the time alleging that he was the victim of smears by 'communist' judges and public prosecutors – and refusing to relinquish the leadership of his increasingly volatile Forza Italia movement.

In April 1996, a centre-left coalition of parties led by the PDS – the so-called 'Olive Tree' – won elections. Italy's first government including former communists in senior ministerial positions was formed, although the PDS offered the prime minister's job to a moderate and highly respected former Christian Democrat, Romano Prodi. Over the next two years, the Prodi government chalked up considerable success in preparing Italy for entry to the euro zone, beginning the slow reform of the Italian bureaucracy and, to a lesser extent, tackling the reform of the country's bloated pensions system. However, it relied for its parliamentary majority on the small Party of Communist Refoundation (PRC). The price that the PRC exacted was a commitment to move towards a 35-hour working week (French-style) and a watering down of cuts in social spending that the PRC feared would hit the poor and the vulnerable. Never that enthusiastic about the euro, the PRC saw its role as ensuring that the price of preparing Italy for the euro did not fall on the shoulders of the working class.

In 1997, PDS leader Massimo D'Alema persuaded his party to move towards the centre, attacking trade union leaders and proclaiming his ambition to lead a 'Blairite' moderate centrist party. In early 1998, the PDS changed its name to the 'Left Democrats' (DS), replaced the hammer-and-sickle symbol with a red rose and even encouraged speculation that its ultimate ambition was to unite all moderates in a US-style Democratic Party. The new DS absorbed some small ex-Socialist and

Plate 2.5 Romano Prodi, President of the European Commission, addressing a meeting
Source: Audiovisual Library of the European Commission (2005).

ex-Christian Democrat factions, although the price paid for this was renewed fac-tionalism and internal disunity, which ultimately thwarted its ambition to become an expanded political force.

In October 1998, D'Alema achieved a major step forward towards his ambition for his party when he replaced Prodi as prime minister. He headed a coalition gov-ernment that, although based on the previous Olive Tree forces, was broader in its appeal, including both former conservatives led by ex-president Francesco Cossiga and a group of Marxists who had broken away from the PRC over that party's opposition to the centre-left government. The period 1999–2001 saw the centre-left racked by internal divisions and rivalries. D'Alema seemed to lack both the charisma and the authority needed to contain these division, and although his gov-ernment had considerable achievements to its credit – such as successfully preparing Italy for adoption of the euro – it lost power in May 2001 to a rightist coalition led once again by Silvio Berlusconi (see Table 2.3).

The second Berlusconi government, still in office at the time of writing, has undoubtedly been the most right wing in Italy since 1945. The leader of the ex-fas-cist National Alliance, Gianfranco Fini, became deputy prime minister and (in 2004) foreign minister. The government's main achievements have included tough policies on law and order and immigration, but in many other respects Berlusconi's brash populism has not always been rewarded with political success. Throughout his second term in office, he has repeatedly been involved in clashes with the judici-ary, with several leading members of his party arrested for corruption and Mafia

Table 2.3 Results of the Italian general election, 13 May 2001 (elections to the lower house of parliament, the Camera dei deputati)

'House of Liberties' (right-wing coalition led by Berlusconi) –		49.5%	368 seats
main components include:	Forza Italia (centre-right)	29.4%	
	National Alliance (far right)	12.0%	
	Lega Nord (regionalists)	3.9%	
	Biancofiore (Christ. Dems.)	3.2%	
	New PSI (ex-Craxi)	1.0%	
'Olive Tree' (centre-left coalition led by D'Alema) –		35.1%	247 seats
main components include:	DS (ex-communists/social democrats)	16.6%	
	La Margherita (progressive Catholics)	14.6%	
	Il Girasole (greens)	2.2%	
	PCd'I (communists)	1.7%	
Party of Communist Refoundation (PRC)		5.0%	11 seats

(Source: http://www.electionworld.org.)

association. The prime minister's attempts to change the law so as to guarantee himself immunity from prosecution when he leaves office brought him into conflict with the president of Italy, Carlo Azeglio Ciampi, whose duty it is to uphold the constitution. In November 2004, more than half of Italy's 8,000 magistrates and judges signed a petition protesting against attacks on the independence of the judiciary by the Berlusconi government and went on strike, closing the courts for a day.

Berlusconi's strong support for the US-led war in Iraq in 2003 earned him the friendship of President Bush and Tony Blair but was far from popular at home. His relations with other EU leaders deteriorated after several undiplomatic outbursts and an unfortunate showdown with the European Parliament after its rejection of his nomination of the ultra-conservative Catholic Roberto Buttiglione as Italy's EU commissioner in 2004. (After the European Parliament threatened to bring down the entire Commission, Buttiglione's nomination was eventually withdrawn.) Moreover, the economic miracle that he had promised had not materialised by 2005. On the contrary, many Italians felt that inflation had risen steeply since the introduction of the euro and that their job security had decreased. For the first time since 1945, Italian voters reported feeling that their children faced a bleaker future than they had. In December 2004, the Catholic charity Caritas reported that seven million Italians were living in poverty and warned of mounting social unrest ahead.

The failure of some government policies and the controversial nature of others meant that the prime minister's position was by no means as unassailable by 2004 as it had seemed just a few years earlier, despite an unprecedented concentration of power in his hands. In June 2004, the centre-left scored major gains in regional and European Parliament elections. With the return of Romano Prodi to Rome (after completion of his stint as EU Commission president), the centre-left finally had a leader once again with the charisma seriously to threaten Berlusconi. Moreover, the government was plagued by internal divisions between supporters and opponents of deeper European integration. It had only the reluctant and unreliable support of the Northern Leagues, which, though a diminished force and with its leader Umberto Bossi seriously ill, still had the capacity to split the right-wing vote in some areas of northern Italy. Above all, the government's economic strategy lacked cohesion. Fini and the National Alliance placed the priority on cutting the budget deficit. Berlusconi remained convinced, in early 2005, that only sweeping tax cuts could deliver the election victory in 2006 of which he dreamed. At the time of writing, whether Berlusconi's second government would enter the history books as the first postwar Italian government to complete its full term of office, let alone secure a subsequent electoral victory, was still very much an open question. Politics in Italy, as in France, remain fragmented and unpredictable.

The Federal Republic of Germany

After the defeat of the Nazi regime in 1945, Germany found itself under the military and political sway of the four liberating allied powers: France, the UK the USA and the USSR. Although the preservation of German unity remained on the agenda in the immediate postwar period, Western reluctance to accept Soviet demands that any united Germany should be neutral and demilitarised, together with the dynamics of the Cold War that soon developed, effectively sealed the division of the country.

The new Federal Republic of Germany (FRG) adopted a Basic Law in May 1949. This provided for a parliamentary democracy, with a cabinet government, accountable to parliament. The country was divided into states, or *Länder*, governed by their own parliaments and enjoying considerable powers. At the federal level, a two-chamber parliament consisted of a lower house (Bundestag), directly elected every four years by the people, and a much smaller upper house (Bundesrat), comprising representatives of the various state governments. A federal president is elected every five years by the Bundestag, augmented by an equal number of *Länder* representatives. The head of government, the chancellor, enjoys considerable authority. A dual electoral system provides for half the seats in the Bundestag to be filled on the basis of a constituency-based vote and half on the basis of a party list system. However, parties polling less than 5 percent of the total national vote are excluded from winning party list seats. This measure, it was claimed, would ensure stability and governability; it also penalises smaller parties and narrows the range of views that are represented in parliament.

Also in 1949, the German Democratic Republic (GDR, or East Germany) was established from the area of Germany occupied by the USSR. East Berlin became its capital city, while to all intents and purposes West Berlin became part of the FRG. The capital thus became the cause of much tension and conflict. Political life in the GDR was dominated by the communist Socialist Unity Party (SED), which was formed following the forced merger (on Soviet instructions) of branches of the old German Communist and Social Democratic Parties in the East. East German members of the Social Democratic Party (SPD) who resisted absorption into the communist SED had to operate underground, as the SPD was declared illegal following the 'merger'.

Although the GDR became in effect a one-party state, it was not formally so. The SED held all real power, dominated all mass organisations and had an in-built permanent guaranteed majority in the unicameral People's Parliament. But other 'puppet' or 'satellite' parties were allowed to exist and recruit members up to a maximum quota (always less than 10 percent of the two million members that the SED would eventually claim). These were the Christian Democrats (CDU), the Liberals (LDPD), the Democratic Farmers' Party (DBD) and the National Democrats (NDPD). Although these parties sometimes had names that resembled those in the FRG, they were isolated from the FRG parties until the 1980s and operated as extensions of the communists. The idea was that they would represent social groups – such as intellectuals or workers – other than the 'dominant' working class. They were not allowed to contest multi-party elections. Instead, they formed a 'National Front' alongside the communist SED and were each allocated 52 seats in the GDR parliament, regardless of popularity. Heavily infiltrated by the secret police, the Stasi, they operated loyally as extensions of the communists. In the 40 years of its existence, the GDR parliament passed all but one bill with 100 percent of the votes.

In June 1953, mass demonstrations against increased work quotas rocked the GDR and threatened political stability when calls were made for free elections. The Soviet army suppressed the demonstrations with the loss of 50 lives. Thereafter, the GDR became one of Moscow's most loyal allies and the SED one of the most Stalinist of ruling communist parties. The SED and the GDR were led by Walter Ulbricht (1946–71) and Erich Honecker (1971–89). On the surface, the regime was certainly repressive, and public life was rigorously controlled and monitored. However, the GDR also for a time enjoyed the highest living standards in the Soviet bloc and managed to foster a degree of legitimacy among its citizens. It did this partly by tapping into the longstanding Prussian tradition of discipline and social conformity and partly by celebrating in ritualistic fashion the German traditions of socialism that had enjoyed genuine widespread popularity (especially in 'red' Berlin) before Hitler's rise to power. The GDR made much of its claim to be an anti-fascist and 'de-Nazified' German state, accusing the FRG of rehabilitating and recycling old Nazis.

One of the first tasks to be faced by the FRG was de-Nazification – the removal from positions of authority and bringing to justice of those guilty of crimes under the Nazi dictatorship. However de-Nazification soon fell victim to the logic of the Cold War. Although 13 million people had been screened by 1949, less than 2,000 were considered major offenders. As the USSR came to be regarded as the new enemy, and the FRG as being on the front line of the new East–West potential conflict, fierce anti-communism, rather than thorough-going catharsis *vis-à-vis* the Nazi past, came to characterise the political life of the FRG. The Communist Party of Germany (KPD) was banned in 1956 – although it soon resurfaced under a new name, the DKP.

Until 1969, the political life of the FRG was dominated by the Christian Democratic Union (CDU) and its conservative ally in Bavaria, the Christian Social Union (CSU). The CDU/CSU was a centre-right force, firmly committed to the Western alliance under US leadership and strongly anti-communist. Although it embraced capitalist economic rationale and was committed to private sector-led economic growth, it also sought a measure of social partnership between employers and trade unions, and it articulated the concept of a social market economy. This was in essence a kind of paternalistic capitalism, in which the state assumed some responsibility for regulating prices in the housing and farm sectors, for social insurance, and for offering protection to the lower income groups.

Key fact 2.2

Hyperinflation and German attitudes to inflation

The strongly anti-inflationary policy pursued by Konrad Adenauer, incorporated in workings of the Bundesbank and now, at least to some extent, in the ECB, has its ancestry in bitter experience of hyperinflation in the 1920s in several European countries – notably Austria, Germany, Hungary, Poland and Russia. The experience was most acute in Germany in the second half of 1923.

There is no agreed numerical cut-off to distinguish hyperinflation from simply very high inflation, but hyperinflation is usually identified by how people behave in the economy. When hyperinflation occurs, prices rise so fast that money loses its worth very quickly. Those who can do so shift their savings from the country's money to some other asset – perhaps foreign currency, or gold, or diamonds – because their savings if held in local currency will rapidly be worth nothing. Employees demand to get paid daily, or even twice a day, so that they can spend their pay before it loses too much of its value. Some people, especially those on fixed incomes, lose out very badly. Most of those in work have some protection, because their pay will rise more or less in step with prices, but when prices are rising really fast it is hard for employees and employers alike to work out how fast pay should rise and for shopkeepers to keep abreast of the prices they should charge.

The roots of the German hyperinflation in the 1920s lie in the Treaty of Versailles at the end of the First World War. Germany was required to make heavy reparation payments, and when it refused to do so France and Belgium occupied the industrial area of the Ruhr. This deprived the German government of tariff revenue and in consequence it was short of funds; it sought to solve the problem by printing more money, which rapidly lost its value. There are various ways of measuring inflation – by using price indices or by looking at exchange rates, but they all show prices in Germany relatively stable from February 1920 to May 1921, rising by between 400 and 600 percent from May 1921 to July 1922, by between 13,000 and 22,000 percent from July 1922 to June 1923 and between 381,000,000,000 percent and 854,000,000,000 percent from July 1923 to 20 November 1923 (these data were calculated by the German statistical agency). The order of magnitude of these figures is hard to grasp but can be illustrated by one example. In 1920, the highest-value postage stamp was for 4 marks. In 1923, the highest-value postage stamp was for 50,000,000,000 marks. In November 1923, a new currency, the *renten-pfennige*, supposedly backed by gold, was introduced and the hyperinflation brought to an end.

Adenauer was well aware that the hyperinflationary period had been disastrous for Germany and was one of the causes for the social dissatisfaction that fed into the Third Reich, and he was therefore determined that the FRG would be a model of anti-inflationary rectitude.

CDU leader Konrad Adenauer was chancellor from September 1949 until October 1963. The period witnessed the consolidation of CDU supremacy as the party led the FRG through a sustained economic boom. The model of economic management adopted allocated huge powers to an independent central bank, the Bundesbank, which was charged with keeping inflation under control at all costs. A strongly centralised trade union movement, the DGB, was enlisted by the state to assist in guaranteeing labour discipline in return for a recognised place at the negotiating table; collective bargaining over wages was regulated by law.

The period of economic success and capitalist stabilisation and the growing consolidation of CDU power forced a historic rethink within the ranks of the main opposition party, the Social Democratic Party (SPD). Moving towards the centre, the SPD dropped its support for widespread nationalisation of the economy, accepted the capitalist market economy and abandoned its militant secularism, accepting religious instruction in schools. This process came to a head at the SPD congress in Bad Godesberg in 1959, when the party turned its back on Marxism and embraced reform. The following year saw the SPD effectively accept the main outlines of Adenauer's foreign policy.

In 1960–66, the CDU governed in coalition with the centrist Free Democrats (FDP). As elsewhere in Western Europe, the decade saw considerable social and cultural change, which presented a challenge to the CDU. In 1963, Adenauer was succeeded as chancellor by Ludwig Erhard. Policy divisions within the government, the growing confidence of the SPD (which elected Willy Brandt as its leader in 1963) and the easing of the Cold War in the 1960s all contributed to a CDU loss of confidence in 1966, which was followed by a period of 'grand coalition' between the CDU–CSU and the SPD. In 1969, the popularity of Brandt's policy of improved relations with the East (*Ostpolitik*) saw the SPD clinch victory. An SPD–FDP coalition followed with Brandt as chancellor. The SPD remained in power until 1982, Brandt being succeeded as chancellor by Helmut Schmidt in 1974.

Biography 2.7

Willy Brandt (1913–92)

German Social Democrat politician and chancellor of the Federal Republic of Germany (1969–74). Brandt was an anti-Nazi activist in the socialist youth movement who had to leave his native land in 1933 following Hitler's assumption of absolute power. He sought exile in Norway, becoming a Norwegian citizen. He was later active in the anti-Nazi resistance movement in both Norway and Germany, returning to Berlin in 1945 and resuming his German citizenship in 1947. He was elected to the Bundestag for the SPD in 1949, served as mayor of West Berlin (1959–66) and as chairman of the SPD (1964). He was appointed minister for foreign affairs and vice chancellor in 1966 and became the first Social Democrat chancellor in 1969. A passionate advocate of peaceful coexistence between East and West (the cornerstone of his '*Ostpolitik*', or attempts at reconciliation with the GDR and the Soviet bloc), he championed disarmament and global social justice. He resigned as chancellor in 1974 following revelations that a GDR spy had penetrated his inner circle. He remained active in politics, becoming honorary chairman of the SPD in 1987. His Brandt Commission on the World Economy published its report on justice and development issues in 1980.

The 1970s saw substantially improved relations with the USSR and Eastern Europe, including the GDR. In 1970, Chancellor Brandt negotiated an agreement with the USSR involving the *de facto* acceptance of all state boundaries in Europe, and he also signed a Basic Treaty with the GDR, recognising the reality of its existence. In the eyes of the GDR leadership, this helped to establish the legitimacy of their state's right to exist and meant that they could henceforth hope to negotiate directly with 'the other Germany' instead of always having Moscow negotiate on their behalf. In 1972, the GDR entered the United Nations, further seen as a 'coming of age' for the self-proclaimed 'socialist state of the German nation'.

While consensus among the main parties, political stability and mounting acceptance of the FRG internationally, combined with substantial economic recovery, represented a success story, there was another side to West German life. Revolt against the stifling conformism and orthodoxy of politics and society was commonplace in the late 1960s and early 1970s among young people, especially students. In its most extreme manifestation, this led to urban terrorism by far-left groups such as the Baader–Meinhof gang. The heavy-handed response of the authorities included much-criticised police measures and the introduction of notorious laws banning left-wing radicals from holding public sector jobs. Such measures caused concern among intellectuals and civil liberties groups about the extent to which authoritarian impulses still characterised the official response to political dissent.

In the 1970s the FRG, in common with its partners throughout Western Europe, suffered the effects of the oil crisis and recession. A nuclear energy programme was one response to this situation. Opposition to nuclear energy, to growing involvement in NATO and to the environmental pollution caused by industrial growth produced a vocal Green movement in the early 1980s. The Greens soon established a reputation as being among the most politically effective and formidable of European environmental movements, heralding a new brand of politics that soon found echoes in other European countries. Mobilisation against NATO plans to modernise nuclear weapons on FRG soil gave the Greens a popular cause, and in 1983 they entered the national parliament.

In 1982, the FDP moved to the right, responding to a combination of circumstances: the ascendancy of 'new right' ideas elsewhere, the renewed Cold War following the Soviet invasion of Afghanistan and martial law in Poland, and clashes with the SPD over the funding of welfare programmes. As a result, the FDP brought down the SPD-led government and returned the CDU, under Helmut Kohl, to power. The new government reduced social welfare spending and increased incentives to the private sector. Throughout the 1980s, the Kohl administration's primary objective was to maintain the country's economic standing in the face of international recession and mounting unemployment at home. The FRG had established itself as a highly successful exporter, dominating the markets of its neighbours. Not surprisingly, the Kohl governments would display support for the completion of a unified European market, and by the end of the 1980s European political union had become a key and strategic policy goal.

During the 1980s, political and economic problems in the GDR came to a head; political stagnation combined with a growing economic crisis. The GDR leadership had tried to 'buy' social peace by borrowing heavily from the West. Political dissidents had been allowed to travel to the FRG and reunite with family members there in exchange for payments from the FRG government. Even works of art from GDR museums had been sold by the Stasi secret police on the black market to Western dealers in order to raise hard currency such as deutschmarks (DM) and dollars.

None of this worked. As the Soviet bloc slid towards disaster, the ageing GDR leadership was unable to embrace the new thinking advocated by Mikhail Gorbachev (Soviet leader from 1985).

By 1989, Gorbachev made it clear that the USSR would not intervene to maintain an unreformed GDR regime. From the summer of 1989, a mass civil organisation, Neues Forum (New Forum), organised huge peaceful demonstrations calling for political reform and peaceful change. Even some senior SED figures (including outgoing Stasi police chief Markus Wolf) joined the demonstrations, which at first did not call for the GDR to be dismantled but merely reformed. Some, perhaps many, still hoped for a democratic form of socialism, rather than a takeover by the FRG, at this stage. For example, in October 1989 New Forum published plans for a new democratic GDR constitution, with a new GDR flag (replacing the communist symbol with a pacifist 'swords into ploughshares' symbol).

The GDR leadership appeared paralysed. It was unwilling to risk repression without Moscow's backing, but it was unable to pursue bold reform. Events in Hungary (see Key fact 2.3) overtook the leadership. In late 1989, the SED's puppet or satellite parties broke with the GDR regime and embraced the opposition. They were subsequently merged with the FRG parties and received lavish funding from the FRG Christian Democrats and Liberal Democrats, even though they had been as compromised by association with the old regime as many members of the SED. The SED dumped the Honecker leadership, renamed itself the Party of Democratic Socialism (PDS) and tried to reform the GDR. But it was all too little, too late. The pulling power of the DM proved stronger than the idealistic hopes for a reformed socialism. The FRG flag and calls for German unification soon dominated mass demonstrations.

Figure 2.2 West Germany swallows East Germany. Brookes makes use of a classic form of caricature in the manner of James Gillray's cartoons of the Napoleonic Wars. West Germany personified as Chancellor Kohl swallows East Germany

Source: Peter Brookes, *The Spectator* (24 February 1990).

Biography 2.8

Helmut Kohl (1930–)

German Christian Democrat politician and chancellor of the Federal Republic of Germany (1982–98). Kohl joined the Christian Democratic Union (CDU) in 1947. From 1959 to 1976, he served in the regional parliament of Rhineland-Palatinate, becoming regional president in 1969. He became CDU chairman in 1973 and was CDU candidate for chancellor in 1976, when he lost to the Social Democrat Helmut Schmidt. He led the centre-right opposition in the Bundestag until 1982, when he was elected chancellor. His administrations pursued public spending cuts and a pro-NATO foreign policy, although he was also a passionate champion of European integration and emerged as one of the driving forces behind closer and deeper European integration during the 1980s and 1990s. His proudest moment came in 1990 when he presided over German unification. He was elected chancellor of a united Germany later that year. However, the spiralling economic costs of German unification badly affected his popularity and, although he was re-elected in 1994, it was with a much-reduced majority. High unemployment and unpopular economic and social reforms, which he deemed necessary to prepare for the single European currency, continued to erode his popularity, and in 1998 he lost power to a coalition of Social Democrats (SPD) and Greens.

In November 1989, Chancellor Kohl seized the initiative and published a ten-point plan for German unification. The USA supported him. The UK and France were sceptical, as were many left-of-centre West Germans, mindful of the historical legacy of a strong German state in the twentieth century (the writer and intellectual Günther Grass famously remarked that he loved Germany so much, he was glad there were two of them). In July 1990, Kohl met Gorbachev, and Soviet objections to German unity were overcome. The USSR had little option but to accept a united Germany within NATO and the withdrawal of all Soviet troops from the GDR territory. In July, the DM was extended to the GDR, and on 31 August Kohl and Hans Modrow, the last SED–PDS prime minister of the GDR, signed a unification treaty. On 3 October 1990, the two German states were united. Essentially, the GDR ceased to exist and was absorbed into the FRG.

The collapse of the GDR presented the FRG with unanticipated challenges and opportunities at the beginning of the 1990s. Kohl's promises of instant economic improvements to the people of the East, the prestige he enjoyed as the man who presided over unification, and the hesitancy and uncertainty of the SPD in the face of unification, all contributed to a CDU victory in all-German elections held in December 1990. In the early 1990s, the SPD moved somewhat to the left, voicing well-founded (but at the time unpopular) concerns about the pace and direction of German unification and fielding the socialist SPD party chairman, Oskar Lafontaine, as candidate for the post of federal chancellor in 1994. In the event Kohl, still buoyed by his image as the architect of both German and European unification, led the CDU and its allies to another victory, although their parliamentary majority was slashed. Despite that success, it was becoming clear that united Germany faced a number of difficulties that were to blight the last years of Kohl's reign.

Government 2.3

Government in Germany

Germany is a republic, with a president elected for five years by an electoral college based on the federal and *Länder* parliaments. The parliament has two chambers. The Bundestag has 603 members, elected for a four-year term, 299 in single-seat constituencies and the remainder by proportional representation. The Bundesrat has 69 members, representing the governments of the *Länder*.

(Source: http://www.electionworld.org.)

Unification had plainly not involved a fusion between two equal partners; rather, it has resembled a takeover of the GDR by the FRG – symbolised by the simple extension of the FRG's Basic Law to cover the GDR rather than the promulgation of a new constitution for the united Germany. The impression of West German arrogance and insensitivity led to resentment among those strata in East Germany that suffered most economically. A backlash in eastern Germany against perceived neglect by Bonn has seen a steady level of support for the Party of Democratic Socialism (PDS). In early 1994, the PDS scored impressive local government gains: in general elections in September 1998 (which ended Kohl's period in power), it not only retained a level of support in eastern Germany of above 20 percent but surprised the political establishment in Bonn by exceeding the 5 percent barrier on a national level and winning more than 35 seats in the Bundestag; it followed this within weeks by re-entering the government of an eastern German *Land* in coalition with the SPD, establishing a considerable measure of legitimacy for the PDS. The heavy-handed approach of Kohl and the CDU to the former Communists during the 1990s, involving threats to proscribe the PDS and repeated insults to their electorate, had clearly backfired on the CDU. Partly also because of the failure of the promised economic miracle in the east, the CDU lost heavily there in 1998.

Moreover, unification imposed heavy economic costs on the German economy at a time of recession. Many West Germans were unwilling to pay higher taxes or suffer reductions in living standards in order to subsidise the recovery in eastern Germany. Reports of resentment towards East Germans, stereotyped as lazy or parasitical, underlined the enormous scale of the effort required to build a truly unified nation.

Unification also saw an alarming rise in neo-Nazi violence and racist propaganda, with an escalation of murderous attacks upon immigrants, Jews, homosexuals and other vulnerable groups calling into question the willingness or ability of the authorities to respond decisively to right-wing violence. A substantial growth in electoral support for the far right in parts of eastern Germany in the 2000s underlined the potential for such groups to exploit economic hardship in order to undermine democracy.

Finally the costs of unity have cast a shadow over German enthusiasm for European union. The period 1993–98 saw a significant drop in public support for the euro – Chancellor Kohl's most cherished project. Although Germany remains

Key fact 2.3

The fall of the Berlin Wall

The Berlin Wall, known in the German Democratic Republic (GDR) as the Anti-Fascist Protection Barrier, was built in 1961. It was a time when the 'brain drain' of skilled people, especially doctors and scientists, from East to West was seriously weakening the GDR economy (between 1949 and 1961, the GDR lost three million people to the West). The GDR leadership claimed that the wall was needed to 'protect' the GDR from subversion by unreconstructed fascists in the FRG. In reality, its purpose was to prevent the continuing population loss of skilled workers.

Between 1961 and 1989, the Berlin Wall snaked around West Berlin like an ugly scar, isolating it from East Berlin, which was the capital city of the GDR (Bonn was then the FRG capital). Special, heavily guarded corridor roads linked West Berlin (in reality, an enclave surrounded by GDR territory) with the FRG. The Berlin Wall was in reality two walls – one manned by GDR border guards, the other by allied forces stationed on FRG territory – with a heavily mined thin strip of 'no man's land' in between. The Berlin Wall came to symbolise divisions between East and West, the very division of Europe by the Cold War, and the lack of freedom of movement and other basic human rights within the Soviet bloc.

During the 28 years of its existence, several hundred people were killed while trying to cross the Wall from East to West. (After the wall's fall, the guilt or innocence of the GDR border guards involved in shooting would-be escapees – they maintained that they had merely carried out their duty according to the laws of the GDR – would be a burning issue in a unified Germany).

In September 1989, the reformist communist government in Hungary opened its borders with Austria and allowed thousands of GDR citizens (who enjoyed freedom of travel to Hungary, a fellow member of the Soviet bloc) to traverse its territory *en route* for the FRG. The GDR government rapidly lost control of its borders. Huge demonstrations in Berlin, Dresden, Leipzig and other GDR cities demanded reform and human rights. Even GDR leaders such as Markus Wolf, head of the secret police, the Stasi, concluded that reform was inevitable. On 9 November 1989, the wall started to crumble. GDR border guards were told to stand aside as thousands of people began to tear down the hated symbol of Europe's postwar divisions.

fully committed to European economic, monetary and political union, the growing sense of uncertainty engulfing Europe and the growing economic burden at home mean that it will calculate carefully whether it can afford to foot the bill for European union. Germany, for example, made a net contribution of around DM25 billion (£10 billion) to the EU budget in 1994 – a figure that will increase further following the admission of ten new EU member states in May 2004.

All of these problems and concerns, plus a general sense of weariness with the ageing Kohl after so long in office, contributed to a spectacular turnabout in fortunes for Germany's left-wing parties in federal elections held in September 1998. The SPD had prepared the way for its resurrection by endorsing as its candidate for chancellor the media-friendly and moderate regional party leader Gerhard Schröder. He fought a clever campaign, promising modest reforms and coining the slogan 'the New Centre' to signify his moderate credentials. He also permitted speculation of a possible post-election deal with the CDU to form a so-called 'Grand Coalition' to grow, distancing himself from the scaremongering on the right wing about the effects of a 'Red–Green' government between the SPD and the Greens (or possibly even the East German PDS). In the event, the scale of the

Biography 2.9

Gerhard Schröder (1944–)

German Social Democrat politician and chancellor of the Federal Republic of Germany (1998–). Born in North Rhine-Westphalia, Schröder joined the SPD in 1963. He was a radical young socialist in his youth. He was elected president of the Young Socialists (SPD youth section) in 1978 and entered the Bundestag in 1980. Elected to the party executive in 1986 and to its praesidium in 1989, he became regional president of Lower Saxony in 1990 at the head of an SPD–Green coalition. In the mid-1990s, Schröder, who had long since abandoned his youthful radicalism, challenged the left wing of his party, led by Oskar Lafontaine, and from 1997 he elaborated his rhetoric on the need for a 'new centre' in German politics. Essentially, he was involved in attempts to move his party towards the centre ground, along the lines of Tony Blair's 'New Labour' or Bill Clinton's 'New Democrats'. In 1998, he was elected chancellor, leading a coalition with the Greens at federal level. His first government had a mixed record, introducing progressive reforms in the environmental and citizenship rights fields but proving unable to halt the steady rise in unemployment. In 2002, he narrowly retained power, thanks to a combination of two factors: the popularity of his opposition to the US-led war in Iraq and the excellent performance of his coalition partners, the Greens.

CDU's defeat saw the SPD and Greens win a comfortable overall majority in the Bundestag, with the PDS also doing well.

The new government took office in October 1998 on a centre-left platform, but one with many radical elements. It should not be forgotten that this was the first time ever that the SPD had gone into government with a coalition partner that was not to its right in terms of ideology. Oskar Lafontaine, the left-wing chairman of the SPD, became finance minister and immediately began calling for interventionist policies to tackle mass unemployment and social injustice. Joschka Fischer, Green Party leader and an enthusiastic European federalist, became minister for foreign affairs. The government's platform pledged that every economic policy would be judged on whether it reduced unemployment. Tax reform aimed at reducing the burden on low- and middle-income families and at making the rich pay more as many tax write-offs were removed. Germany's citizenship laws were to be changed to allow millions of immigrants to acquire new rights, and the country was to receive its first ever anti-discrimination law. All nuclear power stations would be shut down, gradually but irreversibly, and green taxes on petrol, electricity and gas were pledged. A new partnership with unions and employers to fight unemployment was promised. In summary, it was clear that Germany had taken a clear move to the left.

Needless to say, the new government also faced huge problems. In the face of massive unemployment, a budgetary situation inherited from Kohl that Schröder described as 'a mess', and continuing social malaise, the centre-left was rather less united on firm policies than on rhetoric. There were four major areas of difficulty:

1. There were tensions within the SDP over economic policy. The clear preference of the finance minister, Lafontaine, for Keynesian-style interventionist policies designed to boost jobs and tackle social injustice presaged a struggle with not

only the Bundesbank but also the powerful European Central Bank. Lafontaine, speaking for many of the centre-left in Europe, called for the statutes of both to be redrafted so that they had an obligation to tackle unemployment and marginalisation – and not merely, as at present, seek low inflation regardless of the social costs. The bankers dug their heels in at the start of 1999, refusing to budge and accusing the politicians of 'interference'. The fact that such strictures seemed to have the backing of the more 'moderate' or Blairite wing of the SPD itself (including Schröder) meant that divisions within the new German government over basic policy and ideological issues were almost inevitable from the outset. In spring 1999, Lafontaine paid the price for this radicalism; publicly chastised by the chancellor for his outspokenness, he resigned from all government and party posts. His resignation dismayed the SPD left and seemed a major victory for the bankers.

2. Tensions were present from the beginning within the Green Party. Joschka Fischer had always represented the more pragmatic wing of the Greens – the so-called 'realos', who had faced continuing internal opposition from the Greens' fundamentalist wing, or 'fundis'. Fischer's embrace of compromise and moderation alienated many Greens; for example, many were unwilling to accept a long-term (rather than immediate) timetable for the elimination of nuclear power and were resolutely opposed to Germany's membership of NATO and to the deployment of German troops in peacekeeping operations abroad (both policies that Fischer, in his capacity as foreign minister, would be personally responsible for overseeing). Fischer's support for NATO's bombing of Yugoslavia in spring 1999 led to much protest and soul-searching within the Greens. Nevertheless, most Green MPs seemed to believe that the price for bringing the government down over this issue would be electoral annihilation.

3. Tensions were perceptible from the beginning over European policy. On the eve of Germany's EU presidency in January 1999, Fischer, a European federalist, outlined an ambitious plan for a democratic and federal, socially just and environmentally friendly European Union with a single constitution, government, army and foreign policy. Undoubtedly, many in the German government shared this vision. Nonetheless, Schröder sought on occasions to rein in his more idealistic colleagues and tone down talk of a single European state. Partly for tactical reasons, and partly because of his own innate pragmatism, he preferred to stress national advantage over strategic vision. While assuring Germany's allies that he had no intention of allowing the country to become semi-detached from the European project or to turn inwards on itself, it seemed likely that a more pragmatic and self-confident approach to European policy would characterise Schröder's government, with politicians such as Fischer providing elements of ideological impetus and moral conscience.

4. The continuing resilience of the eastern German PDS provided both a parliamentary focus for opposition to the Schröder government, should it stray too far towards the centre, and a point of pressure on the government should it fail to deliver greater prosperity in eastern Germany.

The Schröder government faced elections in September 2002 with its popularity badly damaged by the factors discussed above and with discontent within both government parties – the SPD and the Greens – mounting. That the chancellor and his centre-left coalition managed to snatch victory from the jaws of defeat (see Table 2.4) was partly (perhaps even largely) due to the very strong popularity of one clear decision he had taken – his opposition to the war in Iraq and refusal to commit Germany to the UK–US cause. More than any other issue, this managed to appease his critics within both the SPD and Greens and to rally public support.

As can be seen from Table 2.4, Chancellor Schröder was saved from defeat by two factors above all: the excellent performance of his Green coalition partners; and the fact that the former East German communists, the PDS, narrowly failed to pass the 5 percent threshold required to win seats on the proportional party list system – a failure that might be explained by many left-wingers wishing to show support for the government's stance on the Iraq war.

Table 2.4 Results of the German general election, 22 September 2002 (lower house of parliament, the Bundestag)

Party	% of votes cast	Seats won
SPD (social democrats)	38.5	251
CDU–CSU (Christian democrats)	38.5	248
Greens	8.6	55
FDP (liberals)	7.4	47
PDS	4.3	2

(Source: http://www.electionworld.org.)

The first half of Chancellor Schröder's second term in office saw his government take a battering at the polls. The SPD suffered disastrously in regional polls, and in June 2004 both the SPD and the Greens lost seats in the European Parliament elections; the opposition CDU–CSU was not alone in making gains; the PDS won seven seats in the European Parliament with around 7 percent of the total vote. A modest revival in SPD fortunes in late 2004 was threatened by the release, in January 2005, of the worst unemployment figures since Hitler came to power in the early 1930s. The federal labour office announced that unemployment had topped five million (12.1 percent of the labour force). In January 1998, an unemployment figure of 4.8 million had helped to seal the fate of Helmut Kohl's CDU–CSU government in polls later that year. The SPD had come to power with Schröder promising to reduce unemployment to 3.5 million. By 2005, it was clear that he had failed spectacularly to achieve this goal; economic growth projections were gloomy; and the government's austerity measures – cutting welfare entitlements and making it easier for workers to be laid off – had alienated many SPD supporters to such an extent that figures on the party's left were speculating about the possible launch of a new party. As well as internal divisions within the government parties, the resilience of the PDS, and the possibility that the CDU–CSU under its first ever female leader, Angela Merkel, might prove an attractive alternative to the SPD, there was another cloud on the horizon: a neo-Nazi revival. German democrats of all political persuasions reacted with horror to regional gains by neo-Nazis in late 2004 and early 2005, which saw the neo-Nazi vote reach 9.2 percent in regional elections in

Saxony, in eastern Germany. With unemployment standing at more than 20 percent in eastern Germany, the prospect of neo-Nazis feeding off despair and discontent had, by 2005, become very real.

The United Kingdom

Alone among the major Western European democracies, the United Kingdom entered the postwar era without having to embark on the search for new political institutions. The UK had experienced neither fascist dictatorship nor enemy occupation (apart from the Channel Islands). Nor, for that matter, had it experienced a far-reaching democratic political revolution in modern times; a hallmark of the UK political system has been its gradualist evolution, embracing democratic reforms without ever fully shedding its aristocratic and elitist origins. The UK, for example, does not have a written constitution; the upper house of its two-chamber parliament is an unelected House of Lords; and although its constitutional monarchy is politically powerless and largely symbolic, the prime minister, or head of the executive, can exercise considerable powers of patronage and decision making in the name of the crown prerogative (i.e. outside parliamentary accountability). The political system has been praised for stability and durability but criticised for secrecy, elitism and centralisation of power.

Government 2.4

Government in the UK

The UK is a monarchy. The parliament has two chambers. The House of Commons has 659 members, elected for a five-year term in single-seat constituencies. The House of Lords is undergoing constitutional reform, from a largely hereditary chamber with a minority of life peers. Its 2005 composition was 700 members: 600 life peers and 92 hereditary peers elected by the hereditary peers, with the remainder being bishops and law lords.

In 1945, the UK had entered an era of long-term decline as a world power, although the extent of this was only to become apparent later. Although Conservative prime minister Winston Churchill presided over victory in the Second World War, the radicalising and levelling effect of the war upon UK society, and the enormous hopes raised for social progress in the postwar era, delivered election victory in 1945 to the Labour Party led by Clement Attlee. Committed in theory to wholesale nationalisation of the economy, Labour in practice followed a much more moderate course, embracing the mixed economy but dedicating itself to social amelioration through welfare provision and wealth redistribution. The Labour government carried out a number of major social reforms, including most famously the foundation of a National Health Service to provide free and comprehensive health coverage for all. In many respects, Labour was building on earlier reports produced by the national coalition government of the war years (and enjoying Conservative and Liberal support), which had recommended the formation of a welfare state to provide healthcare and education, and insurance coverage 'from the cradle to the grave'. The Attlee government also strove to deliver full employment.

Inevitably, the cost of such measures forced a devaluation of the currency in 1949 and a reduction in the UK's overseas and defence commitments. The period from 1945 to the 1960s saw the UK withdraw from, and preside over the dismantling of, its empire. Decolonisation, and close and growing dependence on the USA, tended to dominate UK foreign policy. The UK mostly stood aside from efforts at European integration in the 1950s.

Internal divisions within the Labour Party over cuts in social welfare spending and foreign policy led to the return of the Conservative Party to power in 1951. Four subsequent Conservative prime ministers – Churchill (until April 1955), Anthony Eden (April 1955–January 1957), Harold Macmillan (January 1957–October 1963) and Alec Douglas-Home (October 1963–October 1964) – presided over administrations that followed consensus politics: accepting the welfare state, pursuing stability and partnership between government, employers and the trade unions, and seeking to build upon economic growth. Realisation that industrial growth necessitated entry to European markets led in 1961 to an application to join the EEC, which was vetoed by France until 1969.

Following the collapse of the Conservative government in 1964, amid economic woes and moral scandal, Labour returned to power. The new prime minister, Harold Wilson, captured the imagination of the country with a call for a scientific–technological revolution. The 1960s saw far-reaching social change. The rise of a youth culture and the challenge of the feminist movement confronted old, traditional values. The so-called sexual revolution saw greater access to birth control, while a consumer boom partially transformed the nature of domestic labour for many women by bringing labour-saving machinery within their budgets. Educational reforms included the foundation of the Open University, extending the possibility of participation in tertiary education.

Despite a generally favourable economic situation, Labour lost the election in 1970, and a Conservative Government led by Edward Heath took office. The 1970s were to prove a disastrous decade for the UK economically. Recession and the impact of the oil crisis forced power cuts and the introduction of a three-day working week in late 1973; wages and prices were temporarily frozen. Conflict with the trade unions over Heath's 1971 Industrial Relations Act culminated in a miners' strike that eventually brought his government down in 1974.

Back in power between 1974 and 1979, Labour faced mounting economic problems. Balance of payments problems, high inflation, faltering productivity, rising unemployment and the widespread perception that trade unions enjoyed too much power bedevilled efforts at recovery. Labour was forced increasingly to borrow heavily from the IMF and to plead with the unions for social peace. The Labour government's economic policies were increasingly influenced by the IMF, and it introduced monetarist policies that bitterly divided the Labour Party. The Conservatives then fought an aggressive campaign that returned Margaret Thatcher to power as the country's first woman prime minister.

Until her removal from office in November 1990, Thatcher, a free-market right-winger, presided over a series of governments that set out to change the face of the UK, abandoning consensus politics. In her economic policy:

- she sought to reduce public ownership, embarking on a sustained programme of privatisation of nationalised industries;
- she cut income tax and raised indirect taxes;
- she removed controls on prices and wages, leaving the free market to determine their levels;
- adopting a monetarist policy, she attacked public spending;
- efforts to control the money supply were prioritised;
- the trade unions were targeted by measures that sought, for example, to reduce their right to secondary picketing and to regulate their internal affairs.

Biography 2.10

Margaret Thatcher (Baroness Thatcher) (1925–)

British politician and Conservative prime minister (1979–90). She studied chemistry at Oxford and became a research chemist. She ran unsuccessfully for parliament in 1950 and from 1951 (after marriage to a millionaire, Denis Thatcher), she devoted herself full time to politics. Elected as Conservative MP for Finchley in 1959, she served as a minister for pensions under Macmillan. She became secretary of state for education and science in 1970 and joint shadow chancellor in 1974–75. She was elected Conservative Party leader in 1975 and prime minister in 1979. A staunch right-winger, she advocated privatisation of state-owned industry and utilities, reduction in trade union powers and rights, and pursuit (more in theory than in practice) of a monetarist economic policy (policies sometimes collectively known as 'Thatcherism'). In the early years of her government, manufacturing industry suffered severe decline, and unemployment rose to three million. She was not expected to secure re-election in 1983, but victory in the Falklands War (1982) and a disorganised opposition Labour Party helped her to secure an electoral triumph. She was a staunch anti-communist (dubbed 'the Iron Lady' by the Soviets) and a friend of US president Ronald Reagan. Although she signed the Single European Act in 1986, she was an instinctive 'euro-sceptic' and English nationalist (her unpopularity in Scotland and Wales left her party facing electoral rout in both those parts of the UK). Divisions over EU policy and the unpopular poll tax led to her removal in an internal Conservative Party putsch in November 1990. She left parliament in 1992 and became a baroness in 1994. Her legacy is a divisive one. She moved the UK decisively towards the right and became an enduring heroine of supporters of free-market policies. She also became a figure of loathing for those who saw her years in power as synonymous with greed, selfishness and lack of compassion for the poor.

Politically, Thatcher earned a reputation as a UK nationalist and a centraliser of power. Hostile to demands from Scotland and Wales for regional devolution, she considerably reduced the powers of local government. Engaging in fiercely nationalistic rhetoric, she attacked the threat to UK sovereignty allegedly posed by the EC. Returned to power in 1983 following victory over Argentina in the Falklands

War, she cultivated strong personalistic leadership. Calls for a return to 'traditional family values' and attacks on the rights of homosexuals and other groups brought forth accusations of moral authoritarianism. However, the rhetoric and the reality were not always matched. By the end of the 1980s, the economy was again in recession. Manufacturing output had decreased considerably, and evidence suggested that both regional and social class imbalances had grown. Inflation had indeed been reduced. The trade unions had been greatly weakened (perhaps her most lasting achievement). But nothing like the promised economic miracle to restore lost national greatness had materialised. Unemployment, which had stood at one million in 1979, had by 1990 reached between three and four million.

Thatcher fell from power when her own party became convinced that the vastly unpopular poll tax, which she had introduced to finance local government, would cost it the next election. Her successor, John Major, retained power with a much-reduced majority in 1992. His government continued with Thatcherite policies in most spheres but was plagued by indecisive leadership, splits over policy (especially on European unity), various moral and political scandals, and a general air of incompetence and loss of direction. In particular, the UK's exit from the EC's Exchange Rate Mechanism in September 1992 was an embarrassment for Major's government. The Conservatives' support fell to 27 percent in local government elections in May 1994, and they suffered serious losses in European Parliament elections the following month, when their 28 percent of the vote was their worst national election result for more than a century. The next three years saw the Major government practically paralysed by growing internal party splits over Europe, mounting corruption and sleaze allegations against Conservative MPs and government ministers, and apparent mishandling of important policy issues such as food safety and the fate of UK agriculture. In the general election of May 1997, the Conservatives faced a resurgent and revitalised Labour Party and were undermined in some constituencies by defections to the fiercely euro-sceptic Referendum Party, founded by millionaire businessman Sir James Goldsmith. As Labour swept to power with its biggest ever parliamentary majority, the Conservatives lost nearly half of their House of Commons seats, failing to win a single seat in either Scotland or Wales. In the aftermath of the defeat, and a divisive leadership battle, John Major was succeeded as party leader by the young and decidedly uncharismatic William Hague. Hague further alienated moderate Conservatives, such as former cabinet ministers Kenneth Clark and Michael Heseltine, by shifting the party to the right, pledging opposition to the European single currency. This was precisely the sort of euro-sceptical policy that pro-European Conservatives felt had lost them the 1997 election by ceding the centre ground in politics to Labour. The years 1997–2001 saw Conservative divisions over Europe compounded by Hague's controversial and, in the event, unwise decision to conduct a campaign against UK membership of the euro zone in such a seemingly obsessive and nationalistic way as to make the Conservatives seem both a single-issue party and one that had failed to learn the lessons of its 1997 defeat. A second spectacular election defeat in 2001 was followed by a further move to the right with the election of Iain Duncan Smith as Hague's successor. Described, a little uncharitably, by some sections of the UK media as 'William Hague without the charisma', Duncan Smith led his party through two years of mounting crisis and electoral failure, being forced to resign the leadership in October 2003 when 90 of his 165 MPs voted against his

Biography 2.11

Sir John Major (1943–)

British politician and Conservative prime minister of the UK (1990–97). Elected to parliament in 1979, Major became a minister for social security (1986–87), chief secretary to the Treasury (1987–89), foreign secretary (1989), and chancellor of the exchequer (1989–90). Following Margaret Thatcher's downfall as prime minister and Conservative Party leader in November 1990, Major emerged as her successor, with her backing. As prime minister, Major distanced himself from some of Thatcher's most unpopular policies, abolishing the hated poll tax and taking a more conciliatory line on Europe. He secured a surprise election victory in 1992. Thereafter, his government rapidly became engulfed in economic crisis, bitter disunity over Europe and constant scandals involving evidence of wrongdoing on the part of ministers. Major's reputation never recovered from the economic crisis of 'Black Wednesday' (September 1992), when sterling was forced out of the European Exchange Rate Mechanism and the government's economic policy lay in ruins; or from his own off-the-cuff description of some of his cabinet colleagues as 'bastards'. In 1997, he led the Conservatives to their worst election defeat in more than a century.

leadership. His successor, Michael Howard, a hard-line home secretary in the administration of Margaret Thatcher, was widely regarded as a stop-gap leader whose chances of defeating the Labour Party in elections expected in 2005 were, barring a political miracle, not highly rated.

The Conservatives had not managed to confront the legacy of their own past – the reasons for their overwhelming rejection in 1997 and 2001 – or to broaden their support base beyond their loyal core of voters. Unsteady attempts to project a more socially liberal image were prone to be undermined by maverick MPs. The party was unable to take advantage of the growing mood of public disillusionment with Labour, and with Tony Blair in particular, during Blair's second administration. Some commentators were even moved, by early 2005, to speculate as to whether the Liberal Democrats could eclipse the Conservatives as the second political party in the UK in the medium to long term.

The 1980s was a traumatic decade for Labour. In the early 1980s, under the influence of its left wing, the party embraced policies such as opposition to membership of the EC and support for unilateral nuclear disarmament that proved unpopular with the electorate. Internal divisions culminated in a split in 1981, when several Labour right-wingers formed the breakaway Social Democratic Party (SDP). This short-lived phenomenon eventually merged with the Liberals to form the Liberal Democrats in the late 1980s. However, the split certainly damaged Labour. Under first Neil Kinnock (1983–92) and then John Smith (1992–94), Labour sought to modernise and moderate its image and programme, supporting European integration, accepting that an immediate reversal of all Conservative economic changes was not feasible and seeking to appeal to the middle classes. Defeat in 1992 was a bitter blow to the hopes of Labour's modernisers, but by the mid-1990s under its new leader Tony Blair it appeared a more credible party of government than it had done for many years.

Biography 2.12

Tony Blair (1953–)

British politician and Labour prime minister of the UK (1997–). Born into a Conservative-voting middle-class family, he studied law at Oxford and became a barrister. He was elected Labour MP for Sedgefield in 1983. Blair rose rapidly through the Labour Party ranks, his career being promoted by then Labour leader Neil Kinnock. He served as a member of the shadow Treasury team in 1984 and became shadow secretary of state for energy in 1988. In 1989, he moved to the employment brief. In 1992, the new Labour leader, John Smith, promoted Blair to shadow home secretary. In this role, he made his famous pledge to be 'tough on crime, and tough on the causes of crime'. Following Smith's sudden death in 1994, Blair was elected Labour leader. He moved the Labour Party further towards the centre-right, ditching the commitment to public ownership and coining the phrase 'New Labour' to emphasise the break with the party's past. In 1997, he led Labour to its biggest ever election victory, and he repeated this triumph in 2001. His government's achievements included successful management of the economy, with low unemployment and low interest rates; constitutional reform with devolved parliamentary assemblies in Scotland, Wales, Northern Ireland and Greater London; greater investment in health and education; and the peace process in Northern Ireland. However, his second term in office (2001–05) was marred by mounting disappointment and disillusionment. Constitutional reform and the peace process in Northern Ireland both stalled. Better results in public services were not immediately apparent to all. Many traditional Labour voters were alarmed by quasi-Thatcherite private finance initiatives, which were seen as eroding public sector values. Above all, an unpopular war in Iraq in 2003, when Blair defied both public opinion and a substantial section of his party to rally to the support of President George W. Bush, cast a long shadow over Blair. The inability of the opposition Conservatives to escape their past unpopularity and divisions remained his greatest asset. In May 2005, Blair won a widely expected victory in a general election that he had called almost a year early. He will thus be remembered as the first Labour leader ever to secure three consecutive terms in office for his party. However, as also expected, his majority was severely cut, falling by almost 100 seats to just 66.

By the time a new Labour government took office in May 1997, the UK faced several formidable challenges. While some of the country's severest economic problems – such as endemic mass unemployment – could be said to reflect international realities, in several other respects the UK was falling behind its partners and competitors: for example, in education and training, investment in public transport and infrastructure, and provision of social services. The Conservatives, kept in power due to their dominance in the heavily populated south of England and never polling more than 43 percent of the vote since 1979, had bequeathed a highly centralised political system from which many people felt alienated, especially in the north of England and in Scotland and Wales. The new Labour government was determined to honour its election pledges to devolve power to regional assemblies in Scotland and Wales, as well as to strengthen local government in England, before a build-up of frustration might threaten the unity of the UK. Labour also faced demands for modernisation of the UK political system, including the difficult issue of electoral reform. Meanwhile, in Northern Ireland, murderous sectarian violence, which had first erupted in 1969, had abated somewhat in the period 1994–97 as dialogue between the UK and Irish governments, Northern Irish politicians, and some of the terrorist organisations involved in the conflict had got under way.

When Labour came to power, this so-called 'peace process' was looking increasingly fragile. The prime minister, Tony Blair, made the search for an agreed settlement of the province's conflict a top priority of his government. Indeed, the urgency and energy with which Blair, following on initial steps taken by Major, addressed the crisis in Northern Ireland won him respect. In April 1998, a peace agreement was finally signed between the Irish and UK governments and most of the main Northern Ireland political parties. This agreement provided for a directly elected Northern Ireland assembly, a power-sharing executive led by a first minister and including all democratic parties that agreed to implement the agreement in full, a strong north–south dimension, and a Council of the Isles involving the UK and Irish parliaments and the assemblies of Scotland, Wales and Northern Ireland. Opposed bitterly by hard-line republicans and unionists, the agreement was ratified by clear majorities both north and south of the Irish border in May 1998. The moderate attitude of the Ulster Unionist leader, David Trimble, had been crucial in securing the support of most Ulster Protestants for the agreement, and Blair and his new Northern Ireland secretary of state, Mo Mowlam, had played key roles in securing Trimble's support. Pro-agreement forces won a majority of seats in the new Northern Ireland assembly in elections held in June 1998. However, the peace process faced horrendous obstacles. A brutal bomb attack by renegade IRA members in Omagh, County Tyrone, in August 1998 left 29 people dead and over 300 injured; although the bombing failed in its immediate purpose – to derail the peace process and provoke renewed sectarian conflict – it underlined the need for decommissioning of terrorist arms before admitting their political wings to the new Northern Ireland government. On this point, the peace process repeatedly stalled from late 1998 right through until 2003; and the early release of terrorist prisoners, under the agreement, further increased suspicion and unease in the province. The Labour government had nevertheless achieved a huge deal in moving the process forward in its first 18 months, and Blair's personal commitment to making the peace agreement stick remained high.

On several occasions, most recently in 2003, the UK government felt obliged to suspend the institutions of the devolved government, or executive, in Northern Ireland due to the impasse between Sinn Féin and the Unionist parties. New elections to the Northern Ireland Assembly in late 2003 saw the political eclipse of the relatively moderate Ulster Unionist Party (UUP) and (mainly Catholic) Social and Democratic Labour Party (SDLP) by the more hard-line Democratic Unionist Party (DUP) and Sinn Féin. Under the terms of the 1998 'Good Friday' Agreement, this meant that an executive led by the DUP leader, the Rev. Ian Paisley, as first minister and a Sinn Féin nominee as his deputy first minister would have to take office if devolved government was to be restored. The refusal of these two parties – long mortal enemies – to reach agreement on power sharing, despite coming tantalisingly close to a deal in a series of talks sponsored by the UK and Irish governments throughout 2004, meant that in early 2005, Northern Ireland continued to be ruled directly from Westminster, in the form of a secretary of state. With the IRA and loyalist terrorist groups now on (more or less permanent) ceasefire, the province was more peaceful and stable than in several decades. But with the IRA refusing to decommission its weapons, and with suspected IRA involvement in a number of bank robberies and 'punishment attacks', suspicions on both sides of the divided community remained high and political progress blocked.

Biography 2.13

Rev. Dr Ian Paisley (1926–)

Northern Irish politician and hard-line Protestant Unionist leader. Ordained a minister in 1946, Paisley became moderator (leader) of the Free Presbyterian Church in Ireland in 1951. Imprisoned twice in the 1960s for militant anti-Catholic activity, he was elected to the devolved Northern Ireland Parliament at Stormont in 1970. He founded the Protestant Unionist Party (known as the Democratic Unionist Party from 1974), in opposition to the Ulster Unionist Party, which he considered too moderate. Paisley has been a member of the UK Parliament since 1970 and was a member of the European Parliament from 1979 to 2004. A prominent and outspoken opponent of Irish nationalism and of the Catholic Church, he has opposed every attempt at a solution to Northern Ireland's problems that has involved concessions to the province's minority community. In late 2003, the DUP achieved its objective of overtaking the more moderate UUP as the main voice of the Unionist community. Under the terms of the 'Good Friday' agreement, which has guided the Northern Ireland peace process, Paisley (or his nominee) would therefore become first minister in any devolved power-sharing government that might be restored to Northern Ireland, were agreement to be reached with nationalists and republicans. However, the peace process has continued to stall ever since.

In many other policy areas, the first Blair government was to prove an administration of contradictions. A cornerstone of 'New Labour' thinking was that the party had finally won office by appealing to the centre ground – a centre ground that had allegedly accepted the privatisations, anti-union policies and reductions in personal taxation of the Thatcherite years but wanted a more caring version of capitalism. Yet it was far from clear how policies that mounted a real challenge to poverty, inequality and social exclusion could be pursued if the government was unwilling to raise the revenue to pay for them; and Labour's acceptance of the spending constraints of its Conservative predecessor was to lead to much disillusionment on the part of its traditional supporters. It was also part of the New Labour mantra that the party had lost four successive elections partly because of indiscipline on its own part, the hostility of the tabloid media and its loss of touch with the public mood. Yet Blair's attempts to ensure that such perceived shortcomings were not repeated were also to expose contradictions at the heart of government. By the end of its first term in office, the Blair government faced accusations of:

- top-heavy centralisation of power and decision making within the Labour Party;
- too cosy a relationship with the (traditionally) right-wing press, especially those papers owned by media mogul Rupert Murdoch;

- too close a relationship with big business, as Labour apparently tried to supplant the Conservatives as the favoured party of the rich and powerful;
- a tendency towards government by 'spin doctors'.

These contradictions and problems would all be exacerbated during the second term in office from 2001 to 2005. This can be illustrated by a brief look at some policy areas.

Labour had come to power promising to be a radical and reforming government that would modernise and democratise the UK's rather outdated constitution. Commentators were soon able to point to hesitations and contradictions. The party sought to reform the House of Lords – the UK's unelected second chamber – but while legislating for the abolition of hereditary peers' voting rights in the face of Conservative opposition, it drew back from proposing a democratically elected senate. Blair's strong personal support for the monarchy meant that any republican views of Labour politicians were fully reined in. Deeply divided on electoral reform, Labour did legislate for forms of proportional representation for the Scottish Parliament and Welsh Assembly and for European Parliament elections; but its insistence on a closed party list system for the latter provoked criticism of centralised control over the party's candidates and a desire to stamp out dissent. In government, the party moved with less speed to introduce freedom of information legislation and other measures to promote 'active citizenship' than had been promised when in opposition. Its plans for elected regional assemblies in England were (apart from the successful launch of a London Assembly) largely abandoned indefinitely following defeat in a referendum on the issue in northeast England in 2004.

Perhaps the government's most undeniable constitutional reform achievement was the establishment of a Scottish Parliament with tax-raising powers and a Welsh Assembly with narrower legislative powers. Both proposals were approved by voters in Scotland and Wales in referenda held in September 1997 – by an overwhelming majority of Scots and by a slender majority of voters in Wales, which had always been more closely integrated with England. Both bodies came into being in 1999 following direct elections in May. Labour also introduced a directly elected mayor for London and promised a 'rolling programme' of directly elected mayors for other large English cities where local opinion seemed favourable. However, once again the party drew back from more far-reaching proposals. The Welsh Assembly was relatively toothless. The party fought shy of suggestions – from the Liberal Democrats and others – that democratic decentralisation logically necessitated introduction of an English parliament and a fully federal system of government. And, in the face of growing Scottish nationalism, Blair sought to impose centralised control on the Scottish Labour Party and to seek ways of drawing back from the full implications of devolution.

On economic and social policy the government also faced some contradictions and hesitancies. Its attempts to reform the welfare state smacked of a mixture of truly radical measures – such as proposals designed to make it easier for single parents to enter the labour force, and to encourage young workers to find jobs – and penny-pinching proposals that even the Conservatives had not sought to introduce, such as making it harder for many people to claim social welfare benefits. It could boast of increased spending on health and education and a reduction in hospital waiting lists; but it also stood accused of authoritarian social impulses and 'nannying'. For example, Blair's personal advocacy of Christian moral values and talk of 'family values' left many libertarians and feminists outraged and worried. In September 1998, Blair published a pamphlet advocating his so-called 'third way' in politics – essentially a rejection of many of the key tenets of traditional social democracy or democratic socialism and an embrace of a Clinton-style blend of free-market economics and 'caring' social policies. Rejected by many European social-ists as a surrender to Thatcherism, this 'third way' was significant as an indication of the Labour government's economic thinking. Blair praised Thatcher's privatisa-tion programme and anti-union legislation as 'necessary acts of modernisation' and pledged to move beyond the so-called Old Left's alleged support for 'state control, high taxation and producer interests'. In essence, this represented wholesale accept-ance of key tenets of Thatcherite free-market ideology, and the Labour government gave every sign of regarding its remaining links with the trade union movement as an embarrassment.

On Europe, too, the heavy hand of previous Conservative administrations could be felt. Labour's general tenor since coming to power was clearly more pro-European than the Conservative Party's. And Blair had pledged to place the UK in the driving seat of European affairs. Although his election was widely welcomed in Europe, his government was soon adopting a cautious note. Wary of offending the euro-sceptical Murdoch press, it refused to commit the UK unequivocally to mem-bership of the single currency while indicating that in principle it favoured joining. What this meant in practice was that the UK would not join in the first wave but might join afterwards; however, a feeling that the single currency was being intro-duced by stealth in order to avoid a national debate on the issue that might damage the Labour Party was hard to avoid. Blair's government also adopted a strident defence of what it perceived as the UK's national interests: refusing to agree to common tax policies, for example; suggesting that aspects of the Social Chapter to the Maastricht Treaty might be watered down in practice; and disappointing its centre-left allies in France and Germany by refusing to agree to higher public spending by the EU to tackle unemployment. During the second Labour term, Blair seemed to lose control of the single currency issue. Partly due to a fear of losing a promised referendum and damaging Labour's chances of a historic third term, and partly perhaps because of the cooler stand of his ambitious chancellor of the Exchequer and potential Labour leadership rival Gordon Brown, the question of the euro seemed to slide into abeyance. No national debate to convince the UK public of its merits was launched. Any referendum campaign to win public support for ratification of the proposed new EU Constitutional Treaty was postponed until after a hoped-for third Labour election victory.

Labour had comfortably returned to power with a second huge majority in June 2001, although this owed more to the peculiarities of the UK electoral system than to widespread enthusiasm for the incumbent government. Disenchantment with Blair's rule was already growing and would continue to grow dramatically during the second term. Yet Labour's greatest asset was perhaps the absence of a convinc-ing alternative government. For most voters, the Conservatives were a long way from being accepted as such.

During the second Blair administration, many of the contradictions and prob-lems mentioned above were intensified. Above all, the government was increasingly prone to petty scandals and to a sense of 'spin doctors' spiralling out

Table 2.5 Results of the UK general election, 5 May 2005 (lower house of parliament, the House of Commons)

Parties	% of votes cast	Seats won
Labour Party	35.2	356
Conservative Party	33.3	198
Liberal Democratic Party	22.1	62
Scottish National Party	1.5	6
Plaid Cymru (Welsh nationalists)	0.7	3
UK Independence Party	2.3	0
Northern Irish parties	3.0	18
Others	2.9	3

(Source: http://www.electionworld.org.)

of control. But one issue above all would dominate the second term – and perhaps come to define the Blair prime ministership. This was Blair's enthusiastic support for the alliance with the USA, especially after '9/11'. This enthusiasm would lead Blair and his cabinet to commit UK forces to a US-led war in Iraq (without UN backing) in April 2003. The war in Iraq proved immensely unpopular with many UK voters – perhaps a majority. It produced some of the largest protest marches ever seen in the UK. Involvement in a bloody, costly and (in many party members' eyes) illegal and immoral war also badly split the Labour Party, leading to the resignation of two senior cabinet members and a loss of thousands of party members. It damaged relations between the UK and its European allies, such as France and Germany, which opposed the US-led war. But above all, perhaps, it ended the long love affair that many middle-class UK voters had had with the personal charisma of Tony Blair. Widely believed to have led the country to war on the basis of intelligence information about alleged 'weapons of mass destruction' that he knew to be false, Blair suffered a huge drop in his personal popularity. Increasingly, he was distrusted and disbelieved by voters on a range of issues. His insistence on the righteousness of the war to remove the then Iraqi government struck many voters as self-delusional and out of touch with popular opinion. The war overshadowed many real achievements of the Labour government during its second term; for example, massive investment in the national health system was finally beginning to show concrete results. But Labour voters remained alienated. The party suffered setbacks in local and European Parliament elections in June 2004. By early 2005, it was clear that UK troops might have to remain in Iraq on a much longer-term basis than originally foreseen, and that the war would continue to cast a shadow over Blair and Labour as they geared up for an imminent general election. Their biggest asset remained the continuing failure of Michael Howard's Conservatives – who had also supported the Iraq war – to make much of an impact on public opinion. The first-past-the-post electoral system also cushions a government from voter anger over a policy such as the war by reducing voters' effective options (in terms of a governing party) to a stark choice between the 'big two'. However, British politics was increasingly volatile, with ever growing numbers of voters expected to abstain, or to a lesser extent opt for one of the smaller parties.

The election, held on 5 May, confirmed these expectations. Labour was returned to power for a third term but its share of the popular vote fell to a mere 35.2 percent – the lowest share ever attained by a victorious party. Labour's parliamentary majority was reduced from 165 to 66 seats. The opposition Conservatives failed to make any signficant electroral progress, remaining stuck on 32.3 percent. However, they did capture an additional 33 seats. The Liberal Democrats benefited from an anti-war vote, increasing their electoral share and winnng ten extra seats. Small parties also did better but failed to translate this improved performance into parliamentary seats (see Table 2.5).

Towards the end of his second term in office, it had become clear that Tony Blair's espousal of 'third way' economics and strong support for US foreign policies had effectively transformed Labour into one of the most right-leaning of Europe's social democratic parties. On matters such as tightening border controls, deploying tough controls on immigration, and curbing civil liberties on the basis of the need to fight terrorism, Blair and his government went much farther than most other centre-left parties in office were prepared to go – and were accused by minor parties of engaging in a 'bidding war' with the Conservatives to talk tough on such issues. In 1997, many Labour voters had believed that Blair and his team had, in stealing some of Thatcher's policies and rhetoric, engaged in a tactical manoeuvre to outwit the Conservative Party. By 2005, it seemed increasingly likely that the espousal of these policies was strategic, rather than tactical, and conviction-led. It was perhaps a sign of just how far the fundamental shift to the right in UK politics that had occurred with Thatcherism still affected UK politics after eight years of a Labour government that commentators could write of Blair's role in completing the Thatcherite revolution, rather than reversing it.

Into the new millennium: the challenges facing the major multi-party democracies in comparative perspective

Western Europe's four biggest democracies, in common with their smaller neighbours, face a number of considerable challenges in the years ahead. The European economy has undergone a period of prolonged recession, which may be intensified in the short to medium term by uncertainty about the pace and outcome of European monetary and economic union, and the demands of lower-income countries in Eastern and Central Europe. A key factor undermining economic security for many has been mass unemployment, which had reached an estimated 23 million in the EU by late 2004. Europe in the postwar period has known economic restructuring and upheaval before – the 1950s and 1960s were decades of rapid economic change, when millions of people were uprooted. Then, however, the problem was one of the imbalances caused by societal modernisation and economic growth; the mood was generally one of optimism for the future, and politicians could point to the promise of future rewards. Now, no easy solution to mass unemployment seems at hand; indeed, for many people no solution at all seems possible. Not since the 1930s has economic insecurity and uncertainty so greatly coincided with political pessimism.

Economic crisis is accompanied in many countries by a growing sense of political crisis. The main parties of both left and right face the consequences of the perceived failure of their ideologies to explain or make sense of reality. The growing complexity of policymaking and the globalisation of economic processes contribute to a sense of parties being unable to deliver their election promises. Although centre-right parties that are prepared to 'go with the flow' of the international markets are perhaps less immediately challenged by such developments than left-wing parties, which see their dreams of radical social change through controlled economic management implode, in the longer term all democratic parties must struggle to convince the electorate that democracy can still deliver in sufficient measure for people to feel that they have a stake in its defence and preservation. Cynicism and nihilism are directed at politics in general, and there is mounting evidence of voter alienation, volatility and protest voting.

The secularisation of society, the rise of a market-based consumer culture and the erosion of longstanding political identities and subcultures have all to some extent contributed to a sense of a loss of community. It is perhaps those social groups adversely affected by economic decline that are most vulnerable to moral panic.

This combination of circumstances creates a potentially lethal cocktail of resentment, despair and sullen alienation on the part of millions of Europeans, which extremist groups that do not share the values of liberal democracy seek to exploit. The spectre of communism may no longer haunt Europe, but the spectres of racism, neo-fascism and intolerance would appear to be back. Neo-fascist parties have scored considerable electoral success in France and Italy and are also growing in Germany and, to a lesser extent, the UK. Everywhere, there has been a marked increase in extremist violence against minorities, The search for scapegoats is on.

Opinion 2.1

Causes of the crisis of parliamentary democracy in the UK

In his diaries (p. 24), Robin Cook commented:

There is no glib solution to this trend [of falling participation rates in UK elections]. It is in part a product of other deep-seated developments in modern society. The growth of an individualistic culture makes it more challenging to sell the relevance of participation in a mass ballot, which is the mother of all collective decision-making. In an era in which the extended family has largely vanished, union solidarity has decreased and community groups often struggle to find activists, it would be naive to expect participation in official elections to be bucking the decline in social capital. And the inevitable tendency of decision-making in the modern world to recede to European and even global forums makes political power appear even more remote to individual electors and even further beyond the practical influence of their votes.

(Source: Cook 2004.)

Do you agree? Do measures like extending the use of postal (or on-line) ballots help?

At the end of the twentieth century, centre-left governments held office for the first time ever in all four of Western Europe's major democracies simultaneously. The common problems they faced were matched by a common set of values and of priorities – tackling unemployment, overcoming social exclusion, reinvesting in health and education, reforming the welfare state without dismantling or undermining it, and building an EU that was not just a free market but also a community in which the left's traditional values – solidarity, social justice and full employment – could find expression. But on many of these questions, the centre-left forces were critically divided in terms of their strategic vision and ideological outlook between those who were inspired by Blair's pragmatic 'third way', with its embrace of free-market capitalism, and those who looked to the radical, feminist, Keynesian and ecological strands of centre-left thinking that were articulated by many within the German and French left-wing parties. These divisions largely paralysed the centre-left at a pan-European level and rendered powerless their potential challenge to the monetarist ideology of the European Central Bank as the single currency was introduced. The centre-right had returned to power in France and Italy by 2002; in the UK, Labour still held power in 2005, but on the basis of foreign and domestic policies that appealed to many Thatcherites and dismayed many traditional Labour voters; and in Germany, the SPD–Green coalition clung on despite suffering harsh defeats in many regional elections and a sharply reduced majority at the national level. A failure to deliver real change had clearly disillusioned many left-wing voters in all four major democracies and contributed to a strengthening of the extreme right. Most seriously, if the democratic political parties do not appear to be capable of offering voters a real and effective choice, then voters are likely to switch off politics altogether in increasing numbers, or act with growing volatility.

About the state of democracy in general, it does not pay to be too pessimistic. The political culture of the major European democracies has proved to be very resilient since 1945. Europeans have fought and died for the values of pluralism, democracy, solidarity, and individual and collective liberties, and those values will not be surrendered easily. But the challenges facing the major democracies are obviously great. Western Europe's four major democracies have considerable achievements to their credit in the postwar era, not least the attainment of greater security for the mass of their citizens, the preservation of basic civil liberties, and the acceptance of norms of at least minimum social justice and social responsibility. The struggle to defend and build upon those achievements may well be the overriding priority in the coming years.

Further reading

We list the most useful recent books comparing the countries considered in this section, together with a sample of good recent books on the individual countries.

Bell, D.S. (2000) *Parties and Democracy in France: Parties under Presidentialism*, Ashgate, Aldershot.

Coxall, B. and Robins, L. (2003) *Contemporary UK Politics*, 4th edn, Palgrave Macmillan, Basingstoke.

Dunleavy, P. *et al.* (2003) *Developments in UK Politics – 7*, Palgrave Macmillan, Basingstoke.

Gildea, R. (2002) *France Since 1945*, 2nd edn, Oxford University Press, Oxford.

Ginsborg, P. (2001) *Italy and its Discontents,* Allen Lane/Penguin Press, London.

Ginsborg, P. (2004) *Silvio Berlusconi: Television, Power and Patrimony*, Verso, London.

Guyomarch, A. *et al.* (2001) *Developments in French Politics – 2*, Palgrave Macmillan, Basingstoke.

Jones, B, *et al.* (2004) *Politics UK*, 5th edn, Pearson Education, Harlow.

Jones, T. (2003) *The Dark Heart of Italy*, Faber and Faber, London.

Kesselman, M. *et al.* (2002) *European Politics in Transition*, 4th edn, Houghton Mifflin, Boston, MD.

Knapp, A. and Wright, V. (2001) *The Government and Politics of France*, 4th edn, Palgrave Macmillan, Basingstoke.

Mény, Y. and Knapp, A. (1998) *Government and Politics in Western Europe: The UK, France, Italy, Germany*, 3rd edn, Oxford University Press, Oxford.

Sassoon, D. (1997) *Contemporary Italy: Politics, Economy and Society*, Longman, London.

Padgett, S., Paterson, W. and Smith, G. (2003) *Developments in German Politics – 3*, Palgrave Macmillan, Basingstoke.

Tiersky, R. (ed.) (2004) *Europe Today: National Politics European Integration and European Security*, 2nd edn, Rowman & Littlefield, Lanham, MD.

Section 2.3

The Nordic countries: still reluctant Europeans?

Introduction

Since the publication of a book by Toivo Miljan (1977), the phrase 'reluctant Europeans' has been closely associated with the Nordic countries in one form or another (see also Gstöhl 2002). At the time that Miljan's book appeared, one of these states – Denmark, the original 'reluctant European' – had already joined the EC (1973). The main thrust of Miljan's argument was that the remaining states of the region were slowly but inexorably being propelled in the same direction as Denmark by powerful economic forces. The states in question were Finland, Norway and Sweden; the fifth and last state in the region – Iceland – was left out of the reckoning as a special case. In each of these states, there were considerable political and cultural obstacles in the way of following Denmark's example. Obstacles of this kind had not been able to outweigh the force exerted by economic factors. Now, two of the remaining states, Finland and Sweden, have joined the EU after holding public referenda on the issue. Iceland and Norway remain outside. Let us take a closer look, starting with a brief survey of the key characteristics of the Nordic region.

The Nordic region lies on – or in the case of Iceland, off – the northwestern periphery of continental Europe. The combined total population of the five Nordic states is a little under 25 million (see Table 2.6). Three of the five states achieved independence only in the twentieth century: Norway (1905), Finland (1917) and Iceland (1944). It is not surprising, then, that the preferred course of action for all these states in the realm of foreign policy during the twentieth century would have been to stay out of disputes between the great powers. During the First World War they were able to manage it, although Finland suffered a short yet bitter civil war in the wake of the 1917 Bolshevik revolution in neighbouring Russia. However, during the Second World War, the Danish position as the stopper in the bottle of the Baltic, and Norway's strategic importance for Atlantic trade routes, ensured that both countries fell under German occupation. Similarly, allied forces occupied Iceland, while Finland was embroiled in two major wars with the Soviet Union. Only Sweden managed to stay neutral this time. The different states eventually evolved varying security policies in the light of their experiences, yet they worked out these policies with consideration for their regional neighbours' defence worries and established what became known as the 'Nordic balance' as a result.

Table 2.6 The Nordic countries

Country	Population (millions)	Area (sq. km)	Capital city
Denmark	5.4	43,376	Copenhagen
Finland	5.2	338,145	Helsinki
Iceland	0.29	103,300	Reykjavik
Norway	4.6	323,802	Oslo
Sweden	9.0	450,295	Stockholm

Note: figures for 2003

(Source: World Bank Group: http://www.worldbank.org/data/.)

Key concept 2.2

The Nordic balance

This concept seeks to explain why the Nordic region remained an area of low tension in the Cold War period of 1945–91. It was argued that, in security terms at least, the Atlanticist-oriented NATO members of Denmark, Iceland and Norway in the western Nordic region were balanced by the eastern-focused security concerns of Finland. The latter had negotiated a special arrangement in the 1948 Finno-Soviet Treaty of Friendship, Cooperation and Mutual Assistance (FCMA), which ensured that Finland would take Soviet security concerns into account when conducting Finnish foreign and security policy. In the central Nordic region, pivotal non-aligned Sweden operated a voluntary security policy of 'active neutrality' in order to lessen the worries of involvement in the region by either NATO or the Soviet Union and to defuse any frictions in the region. With the end of the Cold War, the concept of the 'Nordic balance' has become less relevant given that NATO's roles are changing, the Swedes have adopted a more flexible definition of 'non-alignment', and the influence on Finnish foreign and security policy has altered with the disintegration of the Soviet Union in 1991.

The gist of this was that Denmark, Iceland and Norway joined NATO, but first Denmark and then Norway rejected military bases on their territory unless tension escalated dangerously. Denmark and Norway also refused to have nuclear weapons on their soil. The intention was to try to minimise Cold War tensions in the region and to avoid shifting the balance to the detriment of Finland and Sweden.

The prevailing political temper of this region is pragmatic. There is a strongly marked preference for the functionalist rather than federalist approach in the field of international cooperation. Nordic politicians (with the possible exception of the Finns) therefore tended to be more than halfway sympathetic to the cautious UK attitude towards the pursuit of ambitious initiatives coming out of the EU.

This cast of mind can be clearly illustrated by reference to the creation of the Nordic Council in 1952. In 1949, Sweden proposed a Nordic Defence Pact that would have brought Denmark and Norway into a non-aligned military alliance. This seemed to the latter two powers to offer considerably less security than NATO membership, which would guarantee supplies of defence equipment under the powerful US shield. So when the project failed, Denmark took the initiative in creating a new regional organisation designed to multiply grass-roots contacts between the regional states based purely on the principle of close regional cooperation for the advantage of all members. Foreign policy and defence policy were excluded from the competence of this Nordic Council.

Government 2.5

Government in Denmark

Denmark is a monarchy. The parliament has one chamber, with 179 members, 175 elected for a four-year term (all by versions of proportional representation); there are two representatives each from the Faroe Islands and Greenland.

(Source: http://www.electionworld.org.)

Because of this, it was possible for Finland, which always had to keep a wary eye on the security worries of the (then) Soviet Union next door, to join the other four states in the organisation in 1955. The calculation was that a steady flow of carefully thought-out yet unspectacular initiatives would create a network of interdependencies knitting the states in the region ever more closely together – 'cobweb integration' (Andrén 1967). But if this meant creating a new politically integrated regional grouping, it was never feasible. The defence and security policies of the member states diverged too sharply to foster political integration. Moreover, national feelings ran too strongly for any political merger to be in question. The appropriate metaphor is probably one of a family of states with each member jealous of its independence but conscious of a fellow feeling with the others. Meanwhile, the Nordic Council brought about a modest improvement in the level of human happiness in the region. For example, it created a passport union among the member states, carried out a reciprocal extension of social security rules and introduced a common regional labour market. These are no small matters for the inhabitants of the five states, and they have been annually buttressed by further examples of mutually advantageous agreed cooperation, especially cross-border collaboration at grass-roots level.

Government 2.6

Government in Finland

Finland is a republic. Its president is elected directly for a six-year term. The parliament has one chamber, with 200 members, elected for a four-year term by proportional representation in multi-seat constituencies.

(Source: http://www.electionworld.org.)

Government 2.7

Government in Iceland

Iceland is a republic. Its president is elected directly for a four-year term. The parliament has one chamber, with 63 members, elected for a four-year term by proportional representation.

(Source: http://www.electionworld.org.)

Linguistically, Finland is exceptional within the Nordic region, and its language is unintelligible to most of the peoples of the other states. Nevertheless, what makes Finland a genuine and non-artificial member of the region is historical circumstance and cultural inheritance. From the fourteenth century until 1809, it was predominantly a province of Sweden. From 1809, when Sweden lost a war with Russia, the country came under the rule of the Russian tsars until it won its independence in the aftermath of the Bolshevik revolution. Throughout the long period of Russian rule, however, the country maintained the legal and administrative institutions that it had inherited from Sweden, so that its political inheritance in the twentieth century can certainly be called Western democratic rather than Eastern autocratic. It has a small but significant Swedish-speaking minority – currently around 6 percent of the population; this has declined from its mid-nineteenth-century position of a dominant political and business elite to become roughly a centrist pivotal force in Finland's political scales.

Government 2.8

Government in Norway

Norway is a monarchy. The parliament has one chamber, with 165 members, elected for a fixed four-year term by proportional representation in multi-seat constituencies.

(Source: http://www.electionworld.org.)

The other four countries of the region are linguistically akin. Icelandic, the closest to Old Norse, is the remotest in more senses than one, and spoken Danish, for example, is not so easy for the average Swede to understand. But the written languages have a close similarity, and written Danish, Norwegian and Swedish present no great difficulties for mutual comprehension.

Three of the states – Denmark, Norway and Sweden – have constitutional monarchies. Finland and Iceland are republics. The monarchies are purely symbolic and dignified parts of their political systems. It is of more political significance that all five have deeply entrenched liberal democratic values. Finland got off to a shaky start in this respect with a bitter civil war between 'Reds' and 'Whites' in the early months of 1918 and a briefly threatening spell of right-wing extremism a decade or so later (the 'Lapua Movement'). Subsequently, however, the country totally accepted the democratic norms of its neighbours to the west. All five states operate some form of proportional representation electoral system at the national and local level. This has resulted in multi-party political systems, with many coalition governments most commonly in Denmark, Finland and Iceland but much less so in Norway and Sweden. This, in turn, has tended to produce political progress, so to speak, in a straight line – free, until recently, of the reversals associated with adversarial politics in a predominantly two-party political system. The main dysfunction has perhaps been that the political elites have sometimes established so cosy a relationship among themselves as to provoke occasional explosions of electoral anger, as in the Danish general election of 1973.

Government 2.9

Government in Sweden

Sweden is a monarchy. The parliament has one chamber, with 349 members, elected for a four-year term by proportional representation in multi-seat constituencies.

(Source: http://www.electionworld.org.)

The multiplication of parties has not led to weak and ineffective government in the Nordic region, because their political and electoral systems are underpinned by a strong, if perhaps declining, social cohesion, with the partial and temporary exception of interwar Finland. The Norwegian national day, for example, is 17 May and commemorates the adoption of the Eidsvoll constitution of 1814. The constitution was approved by a national assembly in the brief interlude before Norway fell under Swedish rule until finally winning independence in 1905. It is still the basis of the country's fundamental laws. Similarly, Denmark's national day, 5 June, marks the adoption of a strikingly liberal constitution on that date in 1849 and also the adoption of the present constitution in 1953. The symbolism is significant and unifying. Ordinary citizens of all five countries fly their national flags in their gardens to a degree unimaginable in a country like the UK.

National sentiment, then, cements. Yet, in addition, the advent of democracy in the Nordic countries in the early twentieth century was antedated by the growth of vigorous grass-roots popular movements that were self-governing and spontaneous. These included:

- temperance societies, which developed a strong input into the self-improvement of working people through education;
- agricultural cooperative movements, which encouraged rural populations to self-help and to participation in democratic processes;
- folk high schools;
- most of all, trade unions, which increasingly mobilised the working class in the pursuit of political influence.

The dominant parties in much of the region in the second half of the twentieth century have been social democratic, most clearly so in Norway and Sweden, increasingly so in Finland, at or near the centre of gravity of the political system in Denmark, and a significant (though far from dominant) player in Iceland (see Table 2.7). Sweden holds the record: here the Social Democrats have been the natural governing party since 1933. Everywhere, the Social Democrats have been concerned to build up and to preserve the welfare states that have become almost synonymous with the region. Nevertheless, as we touch upon the economic dimension, it becomes clear that there also exists an inexorable pull on all these states exerted by the EU. Above all, there is considerable doubt about the merits and indeed sustainability of any kind of 'Nordic model'.

Table 2.7 Nordic governments since the 1980s

Year	Prime minister	Party composition
Denmark		
1982	Schlüter, P.	Conservatives, Liberals, Christian People's Party, Centre Democrats
1988	Schlüter, P.	Conservatives, Social Liberals, Liberals
1990	Schlüter, P.	Conservatives, Social Liberals
1994	Rasmussen P. Nyrup	Social Democrats, Social Liberals, Christian People's Party, Centre Democrats
1998	Rasmussen P. Nyrup	Social Democrats, Social Liberals, Radicals & Unity List
2001	Rasmussen A. Fogh	Liberals, Conservatives
2005	Rasmussen A. Fogh	Liberals, Conservatives
Finland		
1982	Sorsa, K.	Social Democrats, Democratic League, Centre Party, Swedish People's Party
1982	Sorsa, K.	Social Democrats, Centre Party, Swedish People's Party
1983	Sorsa, K.	Social Democrats, Centre Party, Swedish People's Party, Rural Party
1987	Holkeri, H.	Conservatives, Social Democrats, Swedish People's Party, Rural Party
1990	Holkeri, H.	Conservatives, Social Democrats, Swedish People's Party
1991	Aho, E.	Centre Party, Swedish People's Party, Conservatives, Christian League
1995	Lipponen, P.	Social Democrats, Left Alliance, Swedish People's Party, Greens, Conservatives
1999	Lipponen, P.	Social Democrats, Left Alliance, Swedish People's Party, Greens, Conservatives

Year	Prime minister	Party composition
2003	Jaatteenmaki, A.	Centre Party, Social Democrats, Swedish People's Party
2003	Kalliomäki, A	Social Democrats, Centre Party, Swedish People's Party
2003	Vanhanen, M.	Centre Party, Social Democrats, Swedish People's Party

Iceland

1980	Thoroddsen, G.	Splinter from Independence Party, Progressive Party, People's Alliance
1983	Hermannsson, S.	Progressive Party, Independence Party
1987	Pálsson, T.	Independence Party, Progressive Party, Social Democrats
1988	Hermannsson, S.	Progressive Party, People's Alliance, Social Democrats
1989	Hermannsson, S.	Progressive Party, People's Alliance, Social Democrats, Citizens' Party
1991	Oddsson, D.	Independence Party, Social Democrats
1995	Oddsson, D.	Independence Party, Progressive Party
1999	Oddsson, D.	Independence Party, Progressive Party
2003	Oddsson, D.	Independence Party, Progressive Party
2004	Asgrimmsson, H.	Progressive Party, Independence Party

Norway

1981	Brundtland, G.H.	Labour Party
1981	Willoch, K.	Conservatives
1983	Willoch, K.	Conservatives, Centre Party, Christian Democrats
1986	Brundtland, G.H.	Labour Party
1989	Syse, J.P.	Conservatives, Centre Party, Christian Democrats
1990	Brundtland, G.H.	Labour Party
1993	Brundtland, G.H.	Labour Party
1996	Jagland, T.	Labour Party
1997	Bondevik, K.M.	Christian Democrats, Liberals, Centre Party
2001	Bondevik, K.M.	Christian Democrats, Liberals, Centre Party
2005	Stoltenberg, J.	Labour Party, Socialist Left, Centre Party

Sweden

1981	Fälldin, T.	Centre Party, Liberals
1982	Palme, O.	Social Democrats
1985	Palme, O.	Social Democrats
1986	Carlsson, I.	Social Democrats
1988	Carlsson, I.	Social Democrats
1990	Carlsson, I.	Social Democrats
1991	Bildt, C.	Conservatives, Centre Party, Liberals, Christian Democrats
1994	Carlsson, I.	Social Democrats
1996	Persson, G.	Social Democrats
1998	Persson, G.	Social Democrats
2002	Persson, G.	Social Democrats

Note: The party of the prime minister is listed first.

A brief survey of the Nordic countries

Denmark

Denmark is unique in the Nordic region in never having been ruled by any of its neighbours. On the contrary, it has ruled them. From 1397 to 1523, Denmark held sway over Norway and Sweden in the Kalmar Union. Gross misrule led to the revolt of the Swedes in 1523 under Gustav Vasa and to the emergence of Sweden as a major European power for a long period under the Vasa dynasty. Norway continued under Danish sovereignty until 1814, when the Danes were forced to relinquish control. Yet this long period of Danish ascendancy meant that the official Norwegian language – *riksmål* – was strongly influenced by Danish and that Copenhagen was the cultural centre for Norwegians seeking higher education until 1813, when the University of Christiania (later, Oslo) was founded. Iceland continued to be a Danish dependency until 1918, when it achieved home rule, and in 1944, when it became fully independent. Greenland and the Faroe Islands continue to be home rule territories whose foreign policy and defence are conducted from Copenhagen, although Greenland was permitted to opt out of the EC (1982) with a consequent reduction in the EC's surface area but a minimal drop in its population.

In 1863–64, Denmark lost a war against Prussia and Austria, and since then its foreign policy has been based on an acute awareness of military weakness and on a search for the option that represents the least of the evils. The country is geographically an extension of the north German plain and is hence virtually indefensible against an overland attack from the south. It was therefore occupied, almost without resistance, by German troops on 9 April 1940, although passive resistance, obstruction and sabotage became an increasing strain on the occupying power from 1943 onwards. Not surprisingly, in the immediate postwar period many Danes were apprehensive about closer contacts with Germany, hence the opposition to joining the EC campaigned in terms of this being a 'new 9 April'. The opposition failed. Yet it is no accident that, since joining the EC/EU, Denmark has been one of the members most reluctant to agree to proposals for closer political integration, as evidenced in particular in the Maastricht and Amsterdam Treaties. Equally, it is no accident that Denmark has perhaps the most stringent set of parliamentary controls of any member state over proposals emanating from Brussels.

The Danes finally settled almost a century of vexed disputes with the Germans over minorities on their southern border by treaty in March 1955, and in 1970 they reached agreement with the FRG on the division of the continental shelf. They may be described as being Scandinavian by instinct, European by necessity. Denmark does not regard its Scandinavianism and its Europeanism as mutually exclusive. On the contrary, it regards itself as the bridgehead between the two, as exemplified by its constant and eventually successful pressure to have a bridge built to Sweden across Öresund. This major engineering venture, agreed in 1991, opened to traffic in 2000. The impact in linking the Scandinavian economies more closely into Europe is likely to be considerable. But at the same time, the Danes are haunted by the fear of a gradual erosion of their national distinctiveness within a Europe dominated by the major EU states.

On the domestic front, Danish prime ministers since 1945 have more often than not been Social Democrats. However, the Social Democrats – or any other party, for that matter – were never strong enough to rule alone, so government in Denmark is overwhelmingly a matter of seeking coalitions, cross-party agreements and consensus. Nevertheless, in recent years, Danish politics has become more polarised with greater left–right division, as issues such as immigration and tax cuts have come to the fore of the Danish political agenda. Indeed, since the election (2001) and re-election (2005) of a Liberal–Conservative government led by Venstre Party leader Anders Fogh Rasmussen, the Danish government has introduced stringent new immigration laws that were highly controversial in Denmark.

Finland

Finland had never been a nation-state in its own right before achieving independence from Russia (1917). Once it did become independent, it had to manage its international affairs in the knowledge that it shared an 800-mile border with its increasingly formidable neighbour to the east, the Soviet Union. Its preferred course of action in the interwar years was to stay out of great power conflicts in Europe while if possible strengthening its ties with the Nordic states to the west, especially with Sweden. Unfortunately, however, Finland's strategic position, guarding the approaches to Leningrad (now St Petersburg) from the west and north, eventually exposed it to security demands from Stalin that it felt it could not concede. The upshot was the Winter War (November 1939 – March 1940), which Finland fought alone against the mighty Soviet Union. Then, in a vain attempt to recover the resultant losses of territory (ceded as a result of Finland's defeat), the country joined Germany in its attack on the Soviet Union in June 1941. Finland was a belligerent on a strictly limited front until forced to pull out in September 1944 and bloodily to expel all German forces on Finnish soil.

Plate 2.6 Finnish women MPs from different parties in November 1918. Finnish women were the first in the world to receive full political rights

Source: Parliamentary Office and Edita plc (2002).

The lengthy ensuing period of the Cold War between East and West thus saw Finland in the most exposed and vulnerable position of all the Nordic states. During this time, the term 'Finlandisation' came into use to signify a creeping erosion of the country's sovereignty through pressures exerted upon it by successive rulers in the Kremlin. The reality was more complex and subtle. The peace treaty signed by the Finns in Paris in February 1947 severely limited the size of the country's armed forces, levied heavy reparation payments and required the cession to the Soviet Union of 12 percent of Finland's territory. The April 1948 Treaty of Friendship, Cooperation and Mutual Assistance (FCMA) between Finland and the Soviet Union required the Finns to fight to repel any attack from Germany or any state allied to Germany and, furthermore, to consult with the Soviets whenever there was the threat of any such attack.

The crucial points in respect of Finno-Soviet relations throughout the entire period of the Cold War were therefore as follows:

- Finland, unlike other neighbours of the Soviet Union further to the south, notably Czechoslovakia, Hungary and Poland, was allowed to retain its liberal democratic system unscathed in all essentials.

- The country was aided in this respect because the most influential authors of the postwar foreign policy, Passikivi (president of Finland, 1946–56) and Kekkonen (president, 1956–81), were acutely aware of the basic needs of Soviet security policy.

- Finland became expert in the practice of 'trade-off' politics with the Soviet Union. For example, it renewed the FCMA treaty in 1955, long before its expiry date, and in return secured the withdrawal of Soviet troops from the Porkkala base, ten miles from the Finnish capital, Helsinki. Or again, Finland was allowed (partially) to join the European Free Trade Association (EFTA) through a special arrangement (FINEFTA) in 1961 because it agreed at the same time to equivalent parallel concessions for the USSR in respect of manufactured goods. Similarly, in 1973, it was permitted to sign a free-trade agreement with the EEC in return for the early renewal of the FCMA treaty.

The ending of the Cold War removed these constraints on Finnish foreign policy and eventually opened the way to EU membership (1995). A distinctive feature of the country's political system in the Nordic context, particularly until the Finnish constitutional reforms of 1999–2000, was the considerable amount of power and influence vested in the presidency (chosen by electoral college before 1994, now by direct election). Thus, the president was for a long time regarded as a leading player in questions of foreign policy and was also expected to play a crucial role in the complex business of government formation in a parliamentary system where many political parties have representation. President Kekkonen, for example, exploited the potentialities of his office to the full. As a Centre Party man, he was, more or less, at the balancing point of the parliamentary seesaw anyway, and on occasion, he used his 'clout' with Soviet leaders to influence domestic politics in the direction he desired, although never to the detriment of the basics of the liberal democratic parliamentary system. So, for example, he played a big part in bringing the 'Popular Front' wing of the Communist Party back to government in 1966 and at intervals again thereafter (a unique phenomenon in the Nordic lands). Since he left the scene through ill-health in 1981, however, the presidency has become an office whose powers have been exercised more modestly, and Finland has moved closer to the spirit of the political systems of its western neighbours. Indeed, the powers of the Finnish presidency in foreign policy matters have been curtailed under the Finnish constitutional reforms implemented in 2000, with some responsibilities transferred in practice to the prime minister.

Iceland

With a population of nearly 280,000 and an area of roughly 103,000 square kilometres, Iceland can be regarded as one of the smallest of the European 'small states' or as a very large 'micro-state'. Despite its geographical position – perched precariously astride the Mid-Atlantic Ridge – the fact that the island was first settled by the Vikings in the ninth century ensured that Iceland has been ensconced within the Nordic region.

While Icelanders have ethnic origins similar to their Scandinavian counterparts, it is problematic to apply many of the stereotypes associated with social democratic Scandinavia to Iceland. The Independence Party and the agrarian Progressives have been the key coalition partners in the formation of governments and substantial alternatives to the Social Democrats in the eyes of Icelandic voters. Part of the explanation for this lies in the fact that Icelandic traditions of nationalism include a substantial cultural element. Icelanders have stressed their Viking heritage and their Old Norse dialect, which enables them to read the centuries-old sagas at first hand and helps to set them apart culturally from the other Nordic peoples. Also, democratic principles were operational in the country well before the achievement of an independent Iceland. For instance, a separate consultative assembly, called the Althingi after its ancient predecessor, was inaugurated in 1845. The independence movement in this country was also well developed by the twentieth century, progressively achieving incremental home rule from the Danes in the period 1904–18. This helped to ensure that the (new) Independence Party became an active participant in electoral proceedings (by 1929), articulating a form of Icelandic nationalism that was essentially different from the Nordic mainstream.

Iceland clearly maintains an 'Atlanticist' orientation. The link with Denmark was finally broken by the April 1940 German invasion of Denmark, and the country's strategic location prompted the island's occupation by allied forces. Independence (1944) therefore took place at the time when the postwar international order was being laid and was associated with a close relationship with the Americans and not just the Europeans; a point not lost on the Icelanders ever since. To this day, the country maintains no armed forces of its own, having 'subcontracted' its defence to NATO through its membership of the organisation and relying on the presence of the US base at Keflavik.

Iceland is also singled out from its Nordic brethren by its unusual economic structure (see Table 2.8). Although fisheries are an important activity in some of the other Nordic countries (such as Norway), they are the primary economic activity in Iceland, accounting for three-quarters of the country's merchandise exports and 55 percent of foreign currency earnings. Not surprisingly, Iceland regards fisheries as central to the country's economic well-being, helping to ensure high standards of living (see Table 2.8). Fisheries issues have been the source of several key disputes with European neighbours (1952–56, 1958–61, 1972–73 and 1975–76 – the latter two known as the 'Cod Wars'). Indeed, fisheries have shaped Iceland's attitudes towards European integration and provided the main reason for Icelandic refusals to join the EC. Iceland objected to the Community's Common Fisheries Policy (CFP) and has been content with membership of EFTA (which it joined in 1970). Hence, Iceland has been a member of the family of European nations, but it prefers to be, on balance, on the periphery jealously guarding its cultural heritage and new-found political independence. Nevertheless, Iceland in more recent years has enjoyed good relations with the EU and has developed closer economic and political ties through participation in the European Economic Area (EEA) (see Thorhallsson 2004).

Table 2.8 Economic profile of the Nordic countries

	Denmark	Finland	Iceland	Norway	Sweden
GDP (US$ million)	172.9	131.5	8.4	190.5	240.3
Structure of economy (% of GDP)					
Agriculture	2.6	3.4	11.2	1.9	1.8
Industry	26.5	32.6	9.6	38.3	28.2
Services	70.9	64.0	79.2	59.9	70.0

Note: figures for 2002, except Iceland, for which GDP structure is for 2004.

(Sources: World Bank Group: http://www.worldbank.org/data/; CIA: http://www.cia.publications/factbook/goes.)

Norway

Norway is the only country so far to have rejected joining the EC/EU in a popular vote (1972 and 1994). The reasons have much to do with Norwegian geopolitical structure. Opposition to joining has continued to be especially strong in both the north and southwest of the country. These are regions of many small, scattered and fiercely independent local communities. From their perspective, even rule from Oslo has caused resentments, not to mention rule from Copenhagen (before 1814) or Stockholm (1814–1905). By the same token, rule from Brussels appears almost infinitely remote and potentially suffocatingly bureaucratic.

The primary sector of the Norwegian economy gradually declined by half (from 12 percent to 6 percent) between the two referenda, but its political clout continues to be disproportionate to its economic strength. So the country's fishermen, agitated by fears about the impact of the CFP on their livelihood if Norway acceded to the EU, have been resolutely determined to keep the country out. The same has been true of the farmers, fearing economic disadvantage from the impact of the Common Agricultural Policy (CAP). In addition, the country is more insulated than its neighbours from pressures to join the EU by virtue of its extensive, highly profitable, largely state-controlled North Sea oilfields and also because of its markedly more Atlanticist orientation than its immediate Nordic neighbours.

In this latter connection, the size and importance of the Norwegian mercantile marine is a weighty factor. During the Second World War, for instance, Norwegian merchant ships played a crucial part in bringing supplies to Britain during the anti-U-boat 'Battle of the Atlantic'. They constituted the fourth-largest merchant fleet at the disposal of the Allied powers. The continuing importance of trade in Norwegian merchant carriers has meant that the country has a global outlook and a particular interest in free-trade agreements on a worldwide scale.

This outlook eventually led Norway to decide to seek its security in NATO and to rely for its defence on the US nuclear shield rather than seek refuge in a Swedish-led Scandinavian Defence Pact. The bitter experience of occupation and Nazi repression during the Second World War set the Norwegians apart from the Swedes and made neutralism an unattractive foreign policy option. Indeed, the Norwegians remain ardent supporters of NATO and are cautious of any future association with the EU that could be perceived as compromising Norway's NATO credentials (Archer 2005).

The most important party on the Norwegian political scene since the severe depression years of the 1930s has been the Labour Party. Its early years were marked by an exceptional degree of radicalism, and for most of the 1920s its majority, alone among all its sister parties in Western Europe, attached itself to the Communist Third International. It first achieved real governmental strength in Oslo and in the northern part of Norway. Opposition to EU membership has, as mentioned, been persistently most marked in northern Norway and in the (predominantly non-Labour) territory of the mountainous southwest. The tilting of the balance against membership has owed much to the divisions on the issue within the Labour Party in the Oslo region. Objections to what was perceived as a conservatively oriented and capitalist edifice bulked large in 1972. In 1994, defence of the large Norwegian public sector against possible encroachment from Brussels tipped the scales.

Sweden

Sweden was not always pacifist. The Vikings from the Roslagen area, the Rus, perhaps gave Russia its name; and prison bars were known as 'Swedish curtains' in German-speaking Europe when Gustavus Adolphus ravaged the area during the Thirty Years War (1618–48). Yet the Swedes have not been involved (apart from international peacekeeping operations) in serious fighting since they lost the war of 1809 at the hands of the Russians and, with it, Finland and their Gustavian dynasty. With the exception of some skirmishes with the Norwegians, when the latter sought in vain to resist Swedish rule in 1814, the Swedes have enjoyed almost two centuries of peace. By the mid-twentieth century, their watchword in foreign policy was 'freedom from alliance in time of peace, neutrality in time of war'. Indeed, although Swedish non-alignment is now interpreted more flexibly since the 1989 political changes to Central and Eastern Europe brought an end to bipolar divisions within Europe, a foreign policy based on 'non-participation in military alliance' remains popular with the Swedish public.

Past Swedish neutrality, one cornerstone of their security policy for most of the postwar period, rested not on formal international recognition but on a careful calculation of the risks involved in the country's geographical position in Europe. The Swedes were primarily concerned with reducing ever-changing potential threats to their independence, namely:

- when Germany and the Soviet Union were heading towards conflict in the 1930s;
- when the Nazi Third Reich became temporarily dominant in Europe during 1940–43. During this period, when Norway and Denmark were both under Nazi occupation, Sweden walked the tightrope but used limited concessions (in respect of allowing German troop movements and supplying iron ore) to avert the threat to its independence;
- balancing the security interests of the superpowers in the Nordic region during the Cold War.

A second cornerstone of Swedish security policy was to maintain a modern and effective military capacity at considerable cost. The Social Democrats (SAP), who dominate the domestic political scene even today (after first achieving power in 1933), followed a different path from their Danish and Norwegian sister parties in this respect, Instead of securing NATO membership, Sweden's security was to be underpinned in the postwar years by the building of a 'total defence' capability, which would reinforce Sweden's claims of being a neutral state and deter superpower military intervention. The tradition of having an independent defence capability endured even in the 1990s, with Sweden's commitment to building its own modern multi-role fighter, the Gripen, and not to go for the cheaper option of purchasing arms from abroad. To join the EC was thus not an option for Sweden as long as the Cold War lasted because of the fear of losing control over security policy. By the same token, the ending of the Cold War opened up not just the possibility of EC/EU membership (secured in 1995) but also the way for serious consideration of cutting Sweden's expensive defence capabilities. Hence, since the late 1990s, the Swedish government has enacted major defence reforms that are cutting the size of Swedish military forces and are designed to make them more suitable for international peacekeeping rather than territorial defence roles.

Other, less crucial, factors have also coloured the Swedish attitude to Brussels. Perhaps most significant was the pride of the Social Democrats in the famous 'Swedish model' welfare state that they had painstakingly created, along with many ingenious innovations in economic management. It was feared that these would be put under threat by any close association with Brussels; these fears were voiced by the (then) prime minister, Tage Erlander, in his landmark speech to the powerful Metalworkers Union in 1961. Pride in the achievements of the welfare state was a central component in Swedish nationalism. The dominant party could not believe that its quasi-Keynesian reforms would have been possible in a predominantly conservative-oriented EC. Yet economic and political forces later clouded the picture. The severe recession of 1990–93 in Sweden and the consequent need for welfare cuts and tighter fiscal management by government went hand in hand with the changes in attitude towards joining the EC/EU as Swedish pride in its welfare state began to evaporate. At the same time, the parties of the moderate left became more powerful within the EU, so the force of the arguments against entry was greatly weakened.

A subsidiary objection to membership was the fear that Sweden would not be able to pursue its ambition to become a model power for the provision of aid to underdeveloped countries of the world within the confines of a policy made in Brussels. This was a genuinely idealistic strand of Swedish foreign policymaking not only among the supporters of the Social Democratic Party but also across a wider political spectrum.

In conclusion, the Social Democrats continue to be the largest and most influential party in the Swedish political system despite experiencing several spells out of office since 1976 (see Table 2.7). They have been greatly helped by divisions among the non-socialist parties and also by the support of the Left Party, to the left of them on the political spectrum. The only major exception to this is on EU-related issues, where the Left Party, along with the Greens, is openly against Sweden's continued membership of the EU. Long experience of office has in addition enabled the Social Democrats to establish a generally good working relationship with the leaders of industry and commerce in the country.

The Nordic countries and European integration

For a considerable time, the Nordic countries had a cautious attitude towards supranational European organisations and European integration. These countries, often for differing reasons, preferred more limited intergovernmental forms of European cooperation, all finding sanctuary in the Nordic Council (1952) and some of them (Denmark, Norway and Sweden) as founders of EFTA. Their official rationales for staying outside the more ambitious attempts at European integration by the EC6 are well documented. For Finland and Sweden, security policy considerations were paramount. The Swedes opposed any open-ended participation in security or defence matters and quite correctly argued that the EC's customs union would require the Swedish government to adopt the EC's Common Commercial Policy (CCP) on third countries, so indirectly compromising the country's neutrality. In addition, the governing Social Democrats disliked the 'capitalist', essentially Catholic and conservative basis of the EC. For Finland, it was the neutrality arguments that ruled out joining the EC. As long as Finnish foreign policy was restricted to the confines of the 1948 Treaty of Friendship, Cooperation and Mutual Assistance (FCMA) with the USSR, and the Soviets continued to regard the EC as little more than the 'economic arm' of NATO, then full membership of such an organisation was out of the question. For the Danes, Icelanders and Norwegians, membership of any international organisation that might compromise the 'Atlanticist' nature of their security policies was to be resisted.

However, there were also striking similarities in Nordic attitudes towards European integration. First, none of the Nordic countries subscribes to a federal Europe. Second, one of the main considerations of these countries (especially in terms of commercial policy) was the traditionally strong levels of international trade between themselves and with the UK. In the 1950s, the governments of these countries were unanimous in 'shadowing' the attitudes of the UK government and shared similar preferences for intergovernmental cooperation and limited trade liberalisation. So the Nordic countries were instrumental in the creation of EFTA, which brought together those nations (including the UK) that preferred more limited forms of European cooperation. This also enabled them to preserve the Nordic model of economic managment.

Key concept 2.3

The characteristics of the 'Nordic model'

- high degree of state involvement in welfare systems;
- largest sector of labour force employed in social and education sectors;
- highest proportion of public sector employees in social and education sectors;
- more uniform welfare systems;
- state enjoys high level of legitimacy;
- comprehensive welfare systems;
- social rights based on citizenship; not dependent on participation in labour market;
- welfare systems not class-based; generous and redistributive;
- welfare systems have strong concentration on provision of services;
- traditional goal of full employment (now less important);
- important to recognise that there is no common definition of a 'Nordic model';
- many aspects of the 'Nordic model' undergoing change since the early 1990s.

(Source: Petersson 1994.)

The sea-change in the UK's attitude towards joining the EC prompted some of the Nordic countries to consider EC membership more seriously from the 1960s. After the UK government's decision to apply for full membership in 1961, the Nordic countries adopted differing approaches to the EC. Denmark and Norway, for example, followed the UK and submitted full membership applications in 1961 (Denmark) and 1962 (Norway) and 1967 (Denmark and Norway), along with the UK. Little progress was made, for the Danes and the Norwegians were insistent that their applications were tied to the UK's and met a similar fate in both 1963 and 1967 due to French refusal to allow the UK to join the EC. The Swedish government, conscious of the costs of loosening ties with the UK but restricted by the policy of 'active neutrality', applied for associate EC status in 1961 and later even proposed an 'open' application in 1967 to consider new ways that might allow neutral Sweden to accede to the EC. Finland and Iceland remained 'non-candidates', choosing not to consider EC accession as a viable option.

The early 1970s marked an important watershed in Nordic relations with the EC. Once French objections to UK membership were removed in the early 1970s, the prospect of accession by some of the Nordic countries became a distinct reality.

Denmark joined the EC, while Norway nearly did so but ultimately 54 percent of those voting rejected the invitation in a 1972 referendum. For the first time, the Nordic region was split, with all save Denmark preferring not to join. Denmark assumed a significant leadership role as a bridge-builder between the EC and the Nordic countries that chose to remain outside. As an indirect outcome of the forthcoming UK and Danish accession, the remaining Nordic countries each signed bilateral free-trade agreements with the EC in 1972. In effect, the Nordic countries had, for the first time, secured formal, structured trading relationships with the EC and guaranteed access for their exports into EC markets.

The Norwegian rejection of full membership in 1972 followed a bitter campaign, and the issue of the EC was long taboo in Norwegian politics because of the deep schism that the referendum debates had created in Norwegian society. Yet, to a large degree, the Nordic countries (other than Denmark) were content to monitor their growing trading relations with the rest of Europe, principally through EFTA, which remained the main vehicle for trade liberalisation between the Nordic countries (Iceland finally joined in 1970 and Finland in 1986). In 1984, the Nordic countries participated through EFTA in the 'Luxembourg process', promoting closer cooperation with the EC.

However, the peripheral status of the Nordic countries was illustrated by the fact that changes in governmental attitudes towards European integration in the 1980s were prompted by external pressures. By 1985, the EC was beginning a more dynamic phase in its development and started in 1987 on the road towards completing the Single European Market (SEM). The Nordic governments, experiencing ever-growing levels of international trade with the EC, responded forcefully to the SEM programme, perceiving it as a challenge that needed to be met and contained. In particular, the Nordic governments were fearful that the SEM could turn into a 'Fortress Europe', excluding their exports and undermining the economic stability that was so essential to the continuation of their welfare states.

The economic challenge posed by the SEM was not exclusive to the Nordic countries, and along with their Alpine EFTA colleagues, they agreed a common EFTA reply. In response to the 1989 initiative by Jacques Delors, the president of the European Commission, all the Nordic governments were enthusiastic about developing a 'halfway house' arrangement that would allow them access to the SEM but did not require Finland, Iceland, Norway and Sweden to join the EC. For neutral Finland and Sweden, the proposed arrangement would theoretically allow them to maintain their non-aligned security policies while developing even closer economic relations with the EC. The outcome, the European Economic Area (EEA), proved to be a disappointment to the Nordic governments. On the one hand, the Nordic EFTA countries accepted a degree of supranationalism to allow for the SEM to be extended to the EFTA's territories. On the other, they failed to gain full decision-making input into the formulation of the EC's future SEM legislation, putting themselves at a disadvantage. Several of them therefore moved quickly to consider full membership, even before the EEA came into operation. Sweden, for example, grappling with a severe recession and heartened by the strategic changes affecting Eastern Europe, was actively considering the merits of a full membership application by 1990.

Once Sweden applied (1991), the floodgates opened to the rest of the Nordic flotilla. The Finnish government, led by Prime Minister Esko Aho, followed the Swedish lead, taking comfort in the fact that neutral Sweden now deemed non-alignment and EC membership as compatible and that the 1948 Finno-Soviet treaty had dissolved along with the Soviet Union. The Finns applied in March 1992. The Norwegian Labour government, led by Gro Harlem Brundtland, was confident that the return of the EC membership issue to the forefront of Norwegian politics would not lead to its electoral downfall and followed in quick succession (November 1992). It argued that if the rest of Scandinavia (and 80 percent of the Nordic population) would eventually be within the EC, full membership would be in the national interest. This left Iceland as the only country that still considered full membership to be unattractive. Iceland's obsession with the perceived negative impact of the CFSP meant that accession continued to be resisted.

The Nordic EC membership flotilla, like the arduous Arctic convoys of the Second World War, was susceptible to a few torpedo scares, dangerous rocks and unforeseen political icebergs. In particular, there remains a clear 'elite versus populace' divide on questions of European integration in nearly all the Nordic countries. Traditional north–south, urban–rural and liberal–conservative divisions in Nordic society have, to a large degree, been re-emphasised by domestic attitudes towards the EC/EU. In May 1992, for example, the domestic difficulties for Nordic governments in convincing their publics of the benefits of EC membership were only too apparent. The Danish government was placed in the embarrassing situation of seeing the country narrowly reject the Maastricht Treaty (see Table 2.9). The situation was only redressed after the Danish government secured numerous opt-outs and put the revised deal to another public referendum in June 1993 that approved the treaty by 57 percent. Danish enthusiasm for European integration remains less than wholehearted.

Similar difficulties were evident in the domestic debates on full membership undertaken in Finland, Norway and Sweden during the referendum campaigns of 1994. Although Finland approved full membership by 57 percent, this was only after vocal opposition from the northern provinces and farming communities had caused considerable discomfort for the Finnish government led by the agrarian Centre Party prime minister. Shortly after, the Swedes faced similar soul-searching on European questions. The final vote was very close, approving membership by only 52 percent. Norway once again rejected full membership in its referendum with a similar majority to that polled in 1972, illustrating how little the country's attitudes to the EC have changed (see Table 2.9).

It seems clear then that the peripheral status of the Nordic countries as small states on the northern frontiers of Europe will ensure that they continue to be cautious participants in closer European integration. High levels of domestic euro-scepticism, traditions of nationalism and attachments to Nordic identities will probably guarantee that it will be a considerable time before the Nordic region is united inside the boundaries of the EU. Only Finland (of the three Nordic EU members) has felt able to participate in Stage Three of the EMU timetable, which led to the establishment of the euro zone. Indeed, the single currency has remained a controversial issue in both Denmark and Sweden since full membership. In both

Table 2.9 Results of public referenda on EC/EU issues

Issue/Year	'Yes' (%)	'No' (%)	Turnout (%)
Denmark			
EC membership (1972)	63.4	37.6	90.4
Single European Act (1986)	56	44	75
Treaty on European Union (1992)	49.3	50.7	82.9
Treaty on European Union (1993)	56.8	43.2	86.5
Treaty of Amsterdam (1998)	55.1	44.9	74.8
Adopting the euro (2000)	46.8	53.2	87.6
Finland			
EU membership (1994)	57	43	74
Norway			
EC membership (1972)	46.5	53.5	79.2
EU membership	47.8	52.2	87.9
Sweden			
EU membership (1994)*	52.8	46.8	83.3
Adopting the euro (2003)**	42.1	55.9	82.6

Notes: *In the Swedish EU membership referendum, 0.9% of voters submitted blank protest ballots.
  ** In the Swedish euro referendum, 2% of voters submitted blank protest ballots.

countries, the ruling elite was given a bloody nose when their respective populations ignored governmental advice and rejected adopting the euro in public referenda (Denmark in 2000, Sweden in 2003).

Key fact 2.4

The Swedish euro referendum (14 September 2003)

The population's rejection of the euro in 2003 represents a key moment in the contemporary history of Sweden's relationship with the evolving EU. The plebiscite represented the first time since the start of Sweden's full membership status that the public had been 'consulted' on a key question of further integration (as opposed to just on EU membership). The referendum result, with a overwhelming margin of victory of nearly 14 percentage points (42 percent for; 56 percent against) for the 'no-sayers' on a high turnout of 82.6 percent of the electorate, can be regarded as being a definitive signal to the Swedish political elite. It represented a call for recognition that the Swedish public are wary of participation in further European integration without a more distinct idea of where the Union intends to go and what this implies for the country's traditions of a (relatively) open and consensual liberal democracy. Given the resounding result, the Persson government has a universally recognised 'fall-back' position for the first time since accession and the government is unlikely to return to the question of the euro for the foreseeable future. Sweden's political leaders now have a clearer idea of the domestic parameters under which 'popular' national EU policy will be conducted in the future (Miles 2004).

Conclusion: the challenges since the 1990s

Like the rest of Europe, the Nordic countries continue to take account of the changing post-1989 security environment in Europe. For Finland and Sweden, this means the continuing revision of their once strictly neutral status to incorporate ever more flexible definitions of non-alignment and facilitate closer cooperation with other Western powers. Sweden, for example, contributed forces to peacekeeping operations in Bosnia and Kosovo in the 1990s in spite of the fact that they were at times under NATO command, an act that would have been impossible in the heady days of 'active neutrality'. In similar fashion, the upheaval in Europe since 1989 has enabled Denmark, Iceland and Norway to re-examine their ties within NATO. In addition, the rather assertive US foreign policy under President George W. Bush has required the three NATO members, like others, to reconsider the importance of the Atlanticist ties with the USA. Denmark, for example, under the leadership of Prime Minister Anders Fogh Rasmussen, has adopted a more proactive foreign policy, and Denmark has even been a close supporter of the US-led invasion of Iraq in 2003.

These essentially strategic challenges to the Nordic countries have been accompanied by larger economic and political dynamics. The Nordic countries, once renowned for their stable, prosperous economies underpinning their social democratic welfare states, experienced greater volatility during the 1990s. Structural problems, such as declining productivity and spiralling labour costs, which were beginning to appear in the 1980s, were accelerated (in the Finnish and Swedish cases) by the onset of severe recession in 1990–93, estimated by the OECD to be the two hardest economic downturns to be experienced by any state in the developed world in the postwar period. Furthermore, the economic cycle of the Nordic region has become more diverse, asymmetrical and unpredictable since the discovery of large oil reserves by the Norwegians in the 1970s. Norway joined Iceland in operating on a more or less separate economic cycle from the rest of Scandinavia. Norway, buoyed by its large oil exports, was relatively immune from the economic problems experienced by Finland and Sweden in the early 1990s.

Certainly, elements of the economic and political 'model' associated with Scandinavia, the so-called 'middle way' (Key concept 2.3), have been abandoned in several of the Nordic countries. Centralised, collective bargaining of wage increases was, for example, terminated in Sweden from 1990. The once harmonious industrial relations are no longer always present in the Nordic countries. In Sweden, for example, relations between the governing Social Democrats and the blue-collar trade union congress (the LO) have been less cordial since the 1990s. Equally, the principles of universal entitlement and citizenship underpinning the social democratic welfare states have been selectively reinterpreted as Nordic governments have re-examined expensive welfare services to control public expenditure and consider the long-term implications of:

- demographic trends, such as ageing populations;
- shortfalls in pension contributions;
- stagnant birthrates;
- the impact of immigration.

Indeed, as the February 2005 general election in Denmark illustrates, questions of high taxation (deemed an essential prerequisite for supporting high levels of social services) have become more politically sensitive, while immigration issues have remained a continuing feature of Nordic political agendas since the late 1990s. Elsewhere, large Swedish firms (such as the telecommunications giant, Ericsson) intermittently threaten to continue to move production facilities outside the region unless lower taxes are introduced. To a degree, the social democratic-inspired consensus underpinning these 'consensual democracies' is under increasing threat.

One of the solutions that some of the countries adopted was to seek and attain full EU membership as a means of providing 'complementary medicine' for the process of economic restructuring, liberalisation and deregulation already taking place in some of the countries. Yet this solution has been fraught with political difficulties. Denmark, Finland and Sweden have secured full membership status, and public opposition to full membership has declined over time. However, substantial scepticism still remains, particularly in Denmark and Sweden, to participation in further European integration, as illustrated by public rejection of joining the euro zone in 2000 and 2003, respectively. Yet few alternatives remain open to these states, and even Iceland and Norway, which are not EU members, continue to foster closer relationships with the EU through the EEA arrangements (Archer 2005; Thorhallsson 2004). In addition, Nordic cooperation has to all intents and purposes been supplemented by a wider Baltic-based phenomenon; Baltic Sea cooperation has been intensified with the accession to the EU of Estonia, Latvia and Lithuania. Nevertheless, many areas remain where the Nordic EU members have enjoyed success in influencing the EU's agenda to reflect Nordic priorities, such as:

- aspects of EU environmental policy;
- questions of greater openness and transparency of EU decision making;
- the introduction of a civil crisis management role in the emerging European Security and Defence Policy (ESDP).

Most probably, the Nordic countries will continue to be seen as 'still peripheral Europeans'. Denmark, Finland and Sweden have joined the EU but have to a greater (Denmark and Sweden) or lesser (Finland) extent chosen selectively where and when to participate in EU developments. Iceland and Norway have chosen to remain outside the EU, but through the EEA they have close relations with the EU. With the possible exception of Finland, the Nordic countries continue to exhibit 'federo-scepticism' (Miles 2001) on the idea of a federal Europe. Hence their status as 'reluctant Europeans' may have moved into differing forums and venues and may at times be inappropriate as a label, yet their profiles as 'still peripheral Europeans' remains as constant as ever.

Further reading

We list the most useful recent sources comparing the countries considered in this section, together with a sample of good recent studies of the individual countries.

Andrén, N. (1967) 'Nordic integration', *Cooperation and Conflict*, 2(1).

Archer, C. (2005) *Norway Outside the European Union*, Routledge, London.

Archer, C. and Sogner, I. (1998) *Norway, European Integration and Atlantic Security*, Sage, London.

Arter, D. (1999) *Scandinavian Politics Today*, Manchester University Press, Manchester.

Einhorn, E.S. and Logue, J. (2003) *Modern Welfare States: Scandinavian Politics and Policy in the Global Age*, Praeger, Westport, CN.

Elder, N., Thomas, A.H. and Arter, D. (1988) *The Consensual Democracies?* Revised edn, Blackwell Basil, Oxford.

Gstöhl, S. (2002) *Reluctant Europeans: Norway, Sweden and Switzerland in the Process of Integration*, Lynne Rienner, Boulder, CO and London.

Hansen, L. and Wæver, O. (eds) (2002) *European Integration and National Identity: The Challenge of the Nordic States*, Routledge, London and New York.

Heclo, H. and Madsen, H. (1987) *Policy and Politics in Sweden*, Temple University Press, Philadelphia, PA.

Heidar, K. (ed.) (2004) *Nordic Politics*, Universitetsforlaget: Oslo.

Ingebritsen, C. (1998) *The Nordic States and European Unity*, Cornell University Press, Ithaca, NY.

Miljan, T. (1977) *The Reluctant Europeans*, Hurst, London.

Miles, L. (ed.) (1996) *The European Union and the Nordic Countries*, Routledge, London.

Miles, L. (1997) *Sweden and European Integration*, Ashgate, Aldershot.

Miles, L. (2001) 'Sweden in the European Union: changing expectations?' *Journal of European Integration*, 23(4).

Miles, L. (2004) 'Sweden: "hitchhiking" and the euro referendum', *Cooperation and Conflict*, 39(2).

Miles, L. (2005) *Fusing with Europe? Sweden in the European Union*, Ashgate, Aldershot.

Nordal, J. and Kristinsson, V. (1996) *Iceland – The Republic*, Central Bank of Iceland, Reykjavik.

Thorhallsson, B. (2004) *Iceland and European Integration*, Routledge, London.

Tiilikainen, T. (1998) *Europe and Finland*, Ashgate, Aldershot.

Section 2.4

Spain, Portugal and Greece

Introduction

During the mid-1970s Spain, Portugal and Greece emerged from periods of right-wing dictatorship. Spain and Portugal had been governed by authoritarian regimes since, respectively, the victory of General Francisco Franco in the Spanish Civil War in 1939 and the ascent to power of the Portuguese dictator Antonio de Oliveira Salazar in 1926; in Greece, a military dictatorship that seized power in 1967 had been preceded by almost two decades of quasi-democratic rule during which entrenched discrimination against left-wingers – the losers in the civil war of 1946–49 – was commonplace.

Although factors particular to each country were important in their respective democratic transitions, similar processes of social and economic change contributed to the dictatorships' downfall. Moreover, the fact that all three embarked upon the transition within a three-year period (1974–77) can scarcely be coincidental: the international context exerted an influence. The concept of southern Europe as a distinct regional subsystem has facilitated comparative analysis of the emergence and consolidation of new political systems. Aspects of this regional subsystem that have been highlighted include:

- relative economic underdevelopment;
- delayed political modernisation;
- cultural distinctiveness;
- particular exposure to international influences.

Relative economic underdevelopment is manifest in late and partial industrialisation, with the southern European countries remaining more rural and technologically backward than northern Europe. Some writers have argued that their economies are distorted by chronic unevenness and structural dependency.

At the political level, southern Europe was a latecomer to mass democracy: Spain's brief experience of democracy was stamped out by Franco's victory in 1939; Portugal and Greece only really achieved the status of functioning pluralist democracies after 1974. Moreover, all three countries have exhibited weak civil societies, with a relative lack of a participatory culture, the persistence of traditional elites and pre-modern forms of political organisation, and entrenched clientelism – the exchange of favours by politicians in return for the procurement of political support. Efforts at creating strong and autonomous interest groups and social movements have been patchy; and parties tend to remain relatively weak in terms of their roots in society and their effective articulation of societal interests. Moreover, the line between party and state is frequently traversed: for example, a party membership card often facilitates a job in parts of the public sector.

Culturally, southern Europe has continued to be more influenced by forms of traditional religion, although Spain, in particular, has recently undergone substantial secularisation. This point refers not simply to the fact that southern Europe tends to be Roman Catholic (or in the case of Greece, Orthodox) whereas northern Europe tends to be more Protestant; rather, it refers primarily to the traditional and more mystical forms that Catholicism takes in Portugal or Spain, as opposed to Catholicism in, say, France or Germany. Attention has also been paid to another cultural aspect with clear political implications: the greater importance of the family (including the extended family) in social life. Although rapid urbanisation in recent decades has disrupted traditional patterns of family life, the economic importance of the family as a buffer against unemployment and poverty in societies with relatively underdeveloped social welfare systems remains significant.

Finally, southern European countries are weaker powers that have been increasingly vulnerable to economic and cultural penetration in the latter half of the twentieth century and to the political influence of stronger powers. Throughout the immediate postwar decades, the USA exercised a clearly decisive influence over Greece, especially. Popular anti-US feeling remains strong throughout the region – largely as a result of mistrust of US foreign policy given US support for the old right-wing dictatorships in the three countries. More recently, the rest of Europe has probably replaced the USA as the primary external political influence throughout the region. External influences can crucially condition the options available to political and social forces.

Having embarked upon the transition to liberal democracy within a few years of each other and having joined the EU during the 1980s, these three countries can be seen as sharing a common path and facing similar challenges.

The crisis and downfall of the dictatorships

Portugal

The Portuguese dictatorship, overthrown in April 1974, had been in power since 1926. António Salazar was the regime's strongman until September 1968. He was succeeded by Marcelo Caetano, whose attempts to preserve power through controlled liberalisation ended in failure. The dictatorship came after a parliamentary, but not democratic, republican regime (1910–26).

Salazar's accession to power represented a triumph for the landowning class over more urban and modern strata. The regime attempted until the 1960s to preserve a conservative, Catholic Portugal based on the economic power of large landowners. Ideologically, it reinforced itself by reference to myths of rural purity,

Government 2.10

Government in Portugal

Portugal is a republic. Its president is directly elected for a five-year term. The parliament has one chamber, with 230 members, elected for a four-year term by proportional representation in multi-seat constituencies.

(Source: http://www.electionworld.org.)

anti-communism, Roman Catholic beliefs and morals, and Portuguese nationalism. It was opposed to modernity and reflected a curious blend of rural nostalgia and fundamentalist Catholicism.

Biography 2.14

António de Oliveira Salazar (1889–1970)

Portuguese right-wing (neo-fascist) dictator for 36 years. Born into a landowning family, Salazar took minor holy orders at a Catholic seminary before choosing to study economics at university. He became a professor of economics in 1918 and was elected to the Portuguese parliament as a Catholic deputy in 1921. He became finance minister in the military dictatorship that seized power in 1926, and prime minister in 1932, taking total control of the government. He was virtual dictator for the next 36 years until incapacitated by a stroke in 1968. (His dictatorship survived for another six years, under his successor Caetano, until swept aside by the army in a revolution in April 1974 that restored democracy.) As dictator, Salazar introduced a form of fascism, modified slightly by Catholic social teachings. The only legal party was the fascist Portuguese National Union. The repressive regime was ultimately unable to cope with economic modernisation, or with dissent in the army over a ruinously repressive policy in the African colonies.

Salazar did permit modest but important industrial growth, encouraged by tariff barriers, in the 1930s and 1940s. State investment in public works provided employment and laid the basis of an infrastructure that was to permit the economic U-turn of the 1950s and 1960s. During the 1950s, the economy gradually took advantage of favourable world conditions. In the 1960s an economic take-off, partially financed by inflows of foreign capital, transformed Portuguese society. As we shall see, urbanisation and modernisation rendered the regime ideologically bankrupt and politically isolated.

It has been argued that the attempt to create the so-called 'New State' (*Estado Novo*) came to an end in the early 1960s. At the start of the decade, Portugal was still a largely rural society with nearly half of its labour force employed in agriculture. Compared with northern Europe, high levels of illiteracy and low standards in healthcare and provision of basic sanitation prevailed. Political repression weighed heavily, with containment of dissent entrusted to the secret police. Throughout the

1960s, three developments contributed to worsening social tensions: increasing integration with the world economy (above all with northern Europe), the mounting burden of colonial wars in Africa, and a growing crisis of ideology and legitimacy.

The dictatorship had negotiated EFTA membership in 1959. This marked the beginning of a retreat from protectionism and isolation. It has been estimated that almost one million people – one-eighth of the total population – emigrated (mostly to northern Europe) during the 1960s. The outflow of people was matched by a huge increase in inflows of foreign capital; by 1970, foreign capital invested in Portugal had increased by nearly thirty-fold from 1959. Colonial wars added to the pressure for change. Liberation struggles against Portuguese imperialism began in Angola, Guinea-Bissau and Mozambique in the early 1960s. The dictatorship answered with a military build-up, resulting in a largely conscript force of almost 250,000 by the early 1970s. In relation to the country's population, this military machine was surpassed only by North and South Vietnam and by Israel. One in four men of military age ended up in an army that was increasingly enmeshed in futile and brutal colonial wars. The burden on the exchequer was vast. Spending on the military consumed half of total public expenditure by the late 1960s.

As the regime sought to improve living standards in order to maintain both its own legitimacy and support for the war effort, a programme of bringing in foreign capital became essential. The structural reorientation of the economy was radical. A small, protected home market gave way to emphasis on export-centred manufacturing industry, with foreign companies taking advantage of low wages and a union-free environment. Emigration and conscription soaked up potential unemployment, and emigrants' remittances helped with the balance of payments. The country was increasingly dependent on foreign capital and on northern Europe. By the 1970s employment in agriculture had dropped to one-third of the labour force.

Ideologically, the project of a rural, Catholic, anti-modern and isolated Portugal was dead by the late 1960s. However, the regime had no new vision to put in its place. A new urban working class had emerged. It was poorly paid and badly housed, its working conditions were harsh, and it was denied trade union rights. In a sense society was undergoing a profound identity crisis. Uncontrolled economic growth both raised expectations and created new problems of pollution, poor sanitation and housing conditions, and growing income inequality.

From September 1968 until April 1974, the regime veered shakily between controlled liberalisation and bouts of increased repression. Some exiles (including the future president, Mario Soares) were permitted to return home, and a 1972 trade agreement with the EC encouraged the regime's technocratic advisers to hope for full EC membership. Realisation that this would be facilitated by a transition to democracy increased pressure from within for further change. In 1973, Caetano resorted to repression in the face of industrial unrest. This coincided with discontent within the military, where younger officers had founded a radical Armed Forces Movement (MFA). War-weariness by now united broad sectors of society, including many conservatives. In April 1974 the MFA seized power, ending nearly 50 years of dictatorship. The new government ended the wars in Africa, granting independence to the colonies. On virtually every other issue, however, both army and society were divided. For the next two years, politics swung back and forth between left and right.

Biography 2.15

Mario Soares (1924–)

Portuguese socialist politician, prime minister (1976, 1976–78 and 1983–85) and president of Portugal (1986–96). Soares was born in Lisbon to liberal republican parents, studied law at the Sorbonne, Paris, and became a student activist against the Salazar dictatorship. In 1964, he helped to found the Portuguese Socialist Action, which had become the Socialist Party by 1974. He returned from exile in 1974, and in 1975 he became foreign minister, negotiating independence for Portugal's overseas colonies. In 1976 he became prime minister, serving on three occasions. In 1986, he became the first civilian president since 1926, ending 60 years of military domination. Although not noticeably charismatic, he proved to be a statesman of considerable integrity and gained the respect of his compatriots for his key role in democratic consolidation. A committed Europeanist, he has chaired the International European Movement since 1997 and has played an important role in the European Parliament since 1999.

Between April 1974 and the summer of 1975, the Portuguese Communist Party (PCP), the best-organised opposition force in the dying days of the old dictatorship, sought to capture the leadership of the revolution. It supported the appointment of a left-wing army officer, Vasco Goncalves, as prime minister in July 1974 and the formation of a Revolutionary Council in early 1975. This body nationalised banks and insurance companies, broke up the large landed estates and distributed land to the peasants. It was envisaged that the Revolutionary Council would guard against capitalist or fascist restoration.

However, from mid-1975 events moved against the left. While the majority of Portuguese had welcomed the demise of dictatorship, many – especially in the north, where Catholic strength is concentrated – remained conservative. Moreover, there was a widespread fear that the pro-Soviet PCP would simply replace one form of dictatorship with another. The PCP's tactics earned it the hostility of the Portuguese Socialist Party (PSP), led by Mario Soares. Pro-Western technocratic elements within the power structures, together with moderate army officers, began to regroup. Elections to a constituent assembly were held on 25 April 1975 and disappointed the Communists, who won just 12.5 percent of the vote. The PSP emerged as the only really national party with 37.9 percent; conservatives took 34 percent. In April 1976, the PSP won general elections, and in July the period of revolutionary turmoil ended when Mario Soares became prime minister.

Spain

In many ways, the path of the Spanish dictatorship is strikingly different. In power since 1939, Franco imposed a highly centralised and authoritarian regime. He shared with Salazar a hatred of socialism, communism and liberalism, and he was also concerned with repressing every sign of social or ethnic pluralism. Ethnic groups such as the Basques and Catalans bore the brunt of a repression that drove their languages and cultures largely underground. The Spanish dictatorship drew upon the support of rural landowners and the Catholic Church. It also appealed to the army's self-image as the protector of a unified and centralised Spain and its hatred of regional autonomy. The army was used to repress those who had supported the democratic government in the Spanish Civil War, and the divisions of that war were effectively institutionalised.

Government 2.11

Government in Spain

Spain is a monarchy. The parliament has two chambers. The Congress of Deputies has 350 members, elected by proportional representation in each province. The Senate has 248 members, 208 elected for a four-year term in four-member constituencies and 40 designated by regional legislatures.

(Source: http://www.electionworld.org.)

Franco's regime, although the most classically fascist of the three dictatorships, represented a coalition of forces which was riddled by contradictions. Monarchists, fascists (the Falange), rural landowners, technocrats, nationalist soldiers and Catholic clerics coexisted sometimes uneasily inside the National Movement, the regime's political party. Franco, proclaimed Caudillo (leader), presided over this coalition, mediating between its often warring components. It was the Falange that provided the fascist trappings – a uniformed mass movement complete with Roman salute, quasi-corporatist doctrines of social organisation and authoritarian nationalism. But the Falange was never more than one part of the movement.

Biography 2.16

General Francisco Franco (1892–1975)

Spanish general and right-wing dictator. Born in Galicia, Franco entered the army in 1910 and became a general in 1927, having served mainly in Morocco. He became chief of staff in 1935 and governor of the Canary Islands in 1936, the year in which he joined a military rebellion against the democratically elected government of the Second Republic. He quickly became the leader of the rebellion, which sparked the Spanish Civil War (1936–39). With the help of Nazi Germany and Fascist Italy, he emerged triumphant and declared himself 'Caudillo' (leader). He imposed a brutal dictatorship, which executed hundreds of thousands of supporters of the defeated democratic government. He suppressed all opposition. His fascist Falange, which he led from 1937, became the single political party. By keeping Spain out of the Second World War, he managed to prolong the life of his regime beyond the Nazi–Fascist defeat in 1945. In 1947, he proclaimed himself leader for life. In 1969, he nominated the young Prince Juan Carlos as his eventual successor. Franco's regime initially presided over a Spain marked by grinding poverty and hardship, but in the 1950s and 1960s, under the influence of technocratic advisers, he opened the country up to foreign investment. This eventually brought much-needed prosperity, but also desires for democratic change that his regime could not satisfy. Within weeks of his death in November 1975, his regime was unravelling and the transition to democracy had begun.

From 1939 until the mid-1950s, the regime pursued economic and social policies similar to those followed in Portugal. Trade unions were smashed and replaced by fascist corporations; political repression was employed to keep workers in line; low wages and high food prices meant that the spending power of most people was limited and little existed by way of demand-led growth. The power of the big landowners was reinforced, and agriculture remained notoriously inefficient. Marshall Aid was not offered in 1947, and Spain remained isolated internationally.

By the early 1950s, problems were mounting with shortages of food and technology necessitating imports. An economic debate divided the ruling party between opponents and advocates of the development of free-market capitalism. The latter won through; economic and military agreements with the USA in 1953 were followed by membership of the International Monetary Fund in 1958. A Stabilisation Plan in 1959 aimed at attracting foreign investment and modernising the economy while retaining political repression.

As in Portugal, the 1960s and early 1970s witnessed growing involvement with foreign markets, penetration by foreign capital and moves to draw closer to the EC. Spain requested associate EC membership in 1962. The regime hoped that full membership could eventually be achieved without democratisation. Growth rates rose dramatically in the 1960s, especially in the north. This rapid and uneven development generated social and economic problems – above all the uncontrolled growth of urban centres as people flocked from agriculture into industry, with consequent hardship for the newly urbanised workers.

Four important contradictions surfaced during the decade:

1. A growing urban working class began to find its voice. The illegal but active trade unions organised strikes from 1962. The regime's ability to keep workers passive depended on rising living standards. However, a reformist path was opposed by those who had reluctantly conceded the economic U-turn when assured of growing army representation in government and increased repression to avoid political change.

2. The balance of forces within the National Movement shifted away from the landowners and Falange towards an alliance of more internationally inclined forces – technocrats, bankers, and financiers.

3. Attempts at limited reform in the mid-1960s with a slightly relaxed press law simply encouraged the underground opposition forces to organise against repression.

4. As society secularised, with falling rates of church attendance in urban areas, the Catholic Church began to distance itself from the regime. Progressive priests and bishops condemned torture and repression of workers' rights. In 1971, the Church actually apologised to the Spanish people for the support hitherto given to Franco.

As the 1970s got under way, the regime's backers were split into two broad camps. Hard-line Falangists favoured continuing repression; reformists favoured controlled liberalisation and an opening to the opposition forces. This latter group included Adolfo Suárez, who was to preside over a new centre-right political formation in the mid-1970s, the Democratic Centre Union, and was to be prime minister of democratic Spain. Some of the regime's leading members veered between repression and reform. These included Manuel Fraga, who later emerged as founder of the Popular Party (PP), the main conservative party in present-day Spain.

In 1969, the ageing Franco appointed as his successor Prince Juan Carlos, son of King Juan in whose name Franco had ruled. Political instability and street protests increased in 1973, when the assassination of the regime's second-in-command, Admiral Luis Carrero Blanco, by Basque gunmen prompted reformists within the regime to move into dialogue with the (still illegal) opposition parties. Following Franco's death in November 1975, Juan Carlos was crowned king and the way was cleared for a democratic transition. Adolfo Suárez became prime minister in 1976, and despite opposition from hard-liners, political parties were legalised from February 1977. The moderate tactics of the opposition parties – including the communists – were decisive in enabling a transition to democracy without anything like the rupture that occurred in Portugal. Democratic elections in June 1977 gave victory to the centre-right UCD with 34 percent; the socialists led by Felipe González Márquez gained 28 percent; the communists led by Santiago Carrillo won 10 percent; and Fraga's conservatives won 8 percent.

Plate 2.7 Felipe González Márquez visiting prison to see members of his government convicted of illegal activities against ETA

Source: Woodworth (2001).

Biography 2.17

Felipe González Márquez (1942–)

Spanish politician and socialist prime minister (1982–96). An early opponent of Franco's dictatorship, González joined the Young Socialists in 1962 and the Spanish Socialist Workers' Party (PSOE) in 1964. Both were, at the time, suppressed and operating underground, their leaders in exile. He joined the party's Executive Commission in 1970, and in 1972 he represented those members still inside Spain at the XXV party congress, which was held in exile in Toulouse. With the support of European social democratic leaders such as the German Willy Brandt, González became party leader in 1974. In the first democratic elections in 1977, he established the PSOE as the country's second-biggest party, and in 1982 he became prime minister when the PSOE won a majority. In 1979, he had removed all references to Marxism from the party programme, and he continued to lead the socialists further towards the right, presiding over a moderate economic programme that embraced partial privatisations. The PSOE government carried out important reforms in women's rights and civil liberties and was credited with the modernisation of Spain. But it also became mired in controversy. González had initially opposed membership of NATO but, in the mid-1980s, he changed his stance and campaigned for a pro-NATO vote in a referendum that he held, to the dismay of left-wing supporters. He also led Spain into the EC. By the 1990s, his popularity was declining as the PSOE became implicated in corruption scandals and his government saw several of its members imprisoned for their part in an illegal and 'dirty' campaign of kidnappings and assassinations directed at supporters of the Basque group, ETA. PSOE finally lost elections in 1996, and González resigned the party leadership in 1997.

Greece

The short-lived Greek military dictatorship came to power at a time when the international climate was less tolerant towards such regimes than it had been in the 1920s and 1930s, and it had little time in which to consolidate its authority. Nevertheless, the Greek dictatorship enjoyed the support of the USA, which was more concerned with securing a solid anti-communist ally in an area judged vulnerable to Soviet influence than in defending democracy inside Greece.

Plate 2.8 The negative image of the Greek military dictatorship
Source: The Central Committee of AKEL, Nicosià (1978: 77).

In 1945, the allies had agreed that Greece should belong to the Western sphere of influence. Stalin did little to help the Greek Communist Party (KKE) when it attempted to seize power in 1946. The communists had played a leading role in the anti-Nazi resistance movement and resented signs of a conservative restoration under UK–US influence. UK military intervention helped to secure the defeat of the communists and the imposition of a conservative regime after a bitter and bloody civil war (1946–49) that left deep wounds on the body politic and helps to explain the highly partisan nature of political alignments ever since. From 1949, anti-communism was adopted as an instrument of state policy, and the KKE was banned.

Government 2.12

Government in Greece

Greece is a republic. The president is elected for five years by parliament, which has one chamber, with 300 members elected for a four-year term. The system is of proportional representation, with 51 multi-seat and five single-seat constituencies.

(Source: http://www.electionworld.org.)

Although Greece was formally a parliamentary regime, real power lay outside parliament. Despite a fairly liberal constitution, the army regarded itself as the guarantor of the established social order. Repressive laws were directed against those suspected of communist sympathies. The civil service and the teaching professions were purged. Suspected left-wingers could be deprived of a passport, a driving licence or a public sector job. In administering this system of discrimination, the police built up a huge network of spies.

Power was exercised by a triarchy of monarchy, army and the parliamentary right wing. Any attempt to open up politics to the centre-left risked jeopardising this balance and calling into question the role of the army as custodian of the *status quo*. (This is what happened in the mid-1960s, prompting the military coup in 1967.) After 1952, UK influence was superseded by US influence. The Greek economy was opened up to foreign (largely US) capital much earlier than the economies of Spain or Portugal. Greece joined NATO in 1952. Its vulnerability to outside influence was intensified by the situation in Cyprus, where extreme Greek nationalists were pushing for union with Greece and where violence exploded in the mid-1950s.

In the 1958 election, the left braved discrimination to poll 25 percent of the vote. More significant was the formation of a Centre Union in 1961 under the leadership of George Papandreou and his son, Andreas. The Centre Union combined elements of political liberalism, economic Keynesianism, radical popular nationalism and old-fashioned clientelism. It posed a real challenge to the dominance of the right, but elections in October 1961 returned the right, led by Constantine Karamanlis, to power. An association treaty with the EC in 1962 was intended to anchor Greece in the Western camp. In November 1963, elections returned a centrist government led by George Papandreou, and Karamanlis left for voluntary exile in Paris.

Biography 2.18

Konstantinos (Constantine) Karamanlis (1907–98)

Greek conservative politician and prime minister (1955–63 and 1974–80) and president (1980–85 and 1990–95). Karamanlis became a parliamentary deputy for the right-wing Populist Party in 1935 but left politics the following year after the dictator Metaxas closed parliament. He was re-elected to parliament after the war and between 1947 and 1955 he served successively as minister for transport, social welfare, national defence, public works, and communications. He became prime minister in 1955 at the head of the right-wing Greek Rally. He founded the National Radical Union in 1956. In 1963, he resigned as prime minister following disagreement with the monarchy. Between 1963 and 1974, he was in self-imposed exile in Paris. As a result, he escaped association with the corrupt and repressive right-wing military junta that ruled Greece from 1967 to 1974. Following the collapse of the junta, Karamanlis returned to Greece and became prime minister at the head of a government that restored democracy. He founded the conservative New Democracy Party and remained in power until 1980, when he became president of Greece. He left the presidency in 1985 after clashes with the socialist prime minister Andreas Papandreou, who announced plans to curb the president's powers. Karamanlis returned as president in 1990. His main achievements as prime minister include the restoration of democracy, the abolition of the monarchy and declaration of a Greek republic (1974) and the passage of a new democratic constitution (1975).

Further elections in February 1964 gave Papandreou a clear mandate for change. Social reforms followed, including raising the school-leaving age from 12 to 15 and launching a campaign against illiteracy. Keynesian intervention in the economy sought to raise wages and boost demand. Political prisoners were released. It seemed as if the centrists were moving towards full democracy by opening up the political system to the lower social classes and overcoming the civil war divisions. However, such changes alarmed the military and powerful business groups.

Biography 2.19

Andreas Papandreou (1919–96)

Greek socialist politician and prime minister (1981–89 and 1993–96). Papandreou was the son of George Papandreou, who served as prime minister of Greece at the helm of the mildly reformist Centre Union party in the early 1960s. As a young man, Andreas Papandreou had been arrested for political opposition to the Metaxas dictatorship (1939), and after release from prison he went into exile in the USA. He gained a PhD in economics from Harvard, became a US citizen and served in the US Navy during the Second World War. He returned to Greece in 1959 and became a parliamentary deputy for his father's Centre Union in 1964. He was arrested by the military after the 1967 coup and later sent into exile again. From 1968 to 1974, he organised oppositional activities. In 1974, with the fall of the military junta, he returned to Greece and founded the Pan-Hellenic Socialist Movement (PASOK). In 1981, PASOK won a landslide and Papandreou became prime minister. In 1989, he lost power after being indicted in a corruption scandal (he was cleared of wrongdoing in 1992). He bounced back in October 1993 and began a third term as prime minister. Ill-health forced his resignation shortly before his death in 1996. He was a charismatic and populist leader, a key player in Greece's democratic transition, but also a leader who was tainted by a whiff of corruption and by numerous dramatic policy U-turns, not least on EU membership, which he initially passionately opposed. In 2004, his son, also called George, became leader of PASOK.

In the summer of 1965, King Constantine II forced the government's resignation to appease the military. A right-wing cabinet was installed, presiding over mounting social unrest before agreeing to hold new elections in May 1967. To forestall these elections, the military seized power on 21 April 1967. A junta led by Colonel George Papadopoulos suspended human rights, banned political parties and strikes, proclaimed martial law, and sent thousands into internal exile.

Although ferocious anti-communist rhetoric was a hallmark of the junta, there is no doubt that its real target was the centrists; the military feared any threat to their privileged position. From 1967 to 1974, traditionalist values were extolled, but the corrupt lifestyle of the military leaders – soon enjoying the 'good life' on luxury yachts donated by grateful Greek shipping tycoons – belied their pious, moralistic propaganda.

The junta's contemptuous attitude towards all politicians alienated the traditional political establishment and even the king, who attempted an unsuccessful counter-coup in late 1967 before fleeing to Rome. Thereafter, all power was concentrated in military hands. The regime was isolated and discredited; it lacked internal unity or ideological coherence; and it was concerned with little more than its own privileges. It stumbled on with US support until 1974. Repression kept opposition contained until March 1973, when Athens students staged an uprising. A further uprising in November was brutally repressed; 34 students were killed and scores wounded. Soon afterwards, a hard-line coup inside the junta brought intensified repression.

In April and May 1974, the junta staged a military escapade in Cyprus, where its far-right sympathisers were pushing for the overthrow of President Makarios (whom they accused of being a left-wing stooge) and for immediate union with Greece. On 20 July, Turkey invaded Cyprus, allegedly to protect Turkish Cypriots, the island was divided into two zones, and the Greek army retreated in shambles. The junta lost US sympathy: Washington certainly had no desire to see two NATO allies at war. On 23 July, the junta withdrew from politics in disarray. Karamanlis, who created a new centre-right party called New Democracy (ND), returned from Paris to preside over a transition to democracy. This time, the measures that had enshrined military power in the 1950s were ended, the communists were legalised, and full parliamentary democracy under civilian rule was achieved.

Dynamics of the democratic transitions

None of the democratic transitions in southern Europe was the outcome of a spontaneous mass revolution. In all cases, the actions and interactions of key elite groups, social and political forces (including parties, trade unions and churches), and state institutions (especially the army) significantly determined the nature of the transition. It is essential, therefore, to study the social and political context that shaped these actors' perceptions of what was desirable and possible.

It is clear that sections of the old regime in Spain came to embrace the need to enter into dialogue with opposition forces and to abandon repression. By the early 1970s, technocratic and business elites were beginning to accept the need for a democratic transition, although they often disagreed on how far democratisation should go. The dictatorship in Greece isolated itself from traditional conservative elites, and apart from key business backers, such as the shipping tycoons, had a limited support base. In Portugal, the loss of military confidence in the dictatorship was decisive.

So why did the dictatorships disintegrate from within?

- Economic change since the 1950s involved greater dependence on foreign trade and foreign capital.
- Potential conflicts between manufacturers geared to supplying the restricted needs of a protected home market and multinational corporations and bankers and financiers had intensified.
- The suppression of trade unions and opposition parties alienated the workers, and the absence of channels of communication and negotiation dented support from business groups.
- The dictatorships did not permit real representation of diverse interests, even within the ranks of their own supporters.
- Conflicts intensified and industrial relations deteriorated.

A section of the dominant economic elites came to recognise the need for at least a limited pluralism. This was necessary both to achieve social and political stability and to allow renegotiation of the alliance between the component parts of the ruling bloc. But even a limited pluralism was thwarted by the elimination of genuinely representative parties and interest groups. Attempts at half-hearted reform floundered, as the regimes realised that they risked losing everything once reform got under way. This, in turn, helped to convince some elites that only a transition to liberal democracy could secure stability and economic growth.

External pressures were also important. The incentive of EC membership seemed to offer a guarantee of greater prosperity, less dependence on US capital and influence (especially in Greece), and political stability through anchorage in the family of established Western European democracies.

The relative weakness of mass opposition reduced the likelihood that the dismantling of the dictatorships might threaten the capitalist order and undermine the power of existing elites. Popular pressure from below for change certainly existed in all three countries – as was shown by strikes and demonstrations. Certain social groups in particular gave vent to this pressure – workers in Spain, students in Greece, young soldiers in Portugal – but there was never any real threat of left-wing revolution, except perhaps from sections of the Portuguese military. Pressure from below for change conditioned the actions of elites, but it rarely set the agenda.

Mass opposition was probably strongest in Spain, where the complex interactions of parties, trade unions, employers' organisations, political elites and the army were of critical importance. The moderate tactics adopted by the left-wing parties helped to reassure business groups and to facilitate a smooth transition to democracy. The Spanish Communist Party (PCE) found itself electorally and politically weakened by the dynamics of subsequent democratic consolidation, but its moderation and pragmatism were crucial in strengthening the hand of reformists such as Adolfo Suárez and in reducing military opposition to the transition. Similarly, the unions were prepared to demand sacrifices of their members and enter into agreements with the employers to guarantee the conditions for democratic stability.

The role of the military was decisive everywhere. The Spanish military had been interwoven into the fabric of the Franco dictatorship, enjoying a privileged position since the civil war and regarding itself as the defender of Spanish unity. In Portugal, the military's involvement in colonial wars was to prove the catalyst for the dictatorship's downfall. Only Greece approximated to a pure military dictatorship. Although the military possessed its own concerns, it also exhibited many of the tensions and contradictions present in society. Nowhere was the military to prove a monolithic bloc. In Portugal, internal divisions rendered the post-1974 army an unstable political instrument; the PCP for example found its attempts to use the Revolutionary Council to push for more radical transformations of society frustrated by the inability of the military to act cohesively. In Greece, military divisions forced the dictatorship to withdraw from the political stage. Even in Spain, many younger and better-educated officers perceived their role as a force for modernisation rather than crude repression. A Military Democratic Union was formed in 1974 to push for changes. The number of senior officers favouring legalisation of the PCE rose from 5 percent to 30 percent in 1975–76. The lesson from southern Europe seems to be that in times of rapid social and economic change precipitating a crisis of political legitimacy, the military can become a site of internal struggle. Much depends on the strength of civil society, the tactics and strategies of social and political forces, and external pressures.

The consolidation of new political institutions

Clearly, a distinction exists between transitions to democracy and the subsequent consolidation of new political systems. Admittedly, it is not always easy to state where transition ends and consolidation begins. Nor is it clear what time scale should be adopted. Moreover, the struggle to defend and reinvigorate democracy is a continuous one facing every generation. Bearing this in mind, it might still be argued that a qualitative step forward has been taken on the road away from authoritarian regimes when the values and ground rules of the new democratic political system gain widespread acceptance and new political institutions begin to function smoothly.

Democracy can be consolidated only through a number of processes. The powers and role of the state must be delineated, allowing an autonomous civil society to flourish. The new constitution must be accepted by a majority of citizens and political actors. The different interests and views in society must be represented effectively by parties that are autonomous from the state and accountable to citizens. Governments must be formed on the basis of a majority, and power must alternate peacefully between government and opposition. The party system must be stabilised, and anti-democratic parties must become marginal, preferably through lack of support. At the same time, opposition forces – including those that challenge the mainstream – must have reasonably fair and open access to media outlets. The armed forces must be subordinated to the democratic civilian authorities. Channels of communication and negotiation must be established between the state, parties and major interest groups. A civic culture must be established in which the concept of citizenship rights and obligations is accepted and understood.

Opinion 2.2

Consolidation of democracy – some questions to consider

- Is the state clearly based on the rule of law and the elimination of arbitrary repression?
- Has a civil society, autonomous from the state, begun to flourish?
- Has a democratic constitution been accepted by most citizens and political actors?
- Has there been a peaceful, democratic exchange of power between political parties, with the handover of power accepted by both winners and losers?
- Has a multi-party system been stabilised?
- Have anti-democratic parties, nostalgic for a return to authoritarianism, been marginalised?
- Have the army and security forces withdrawn from politics and accepted civilian rule and democratic accountability?
- Have opposition forces fair and open access to the main media networks?
- Is there a democratic civic culture, in which the rights of citizens are clearly recognised?
- Are interest groups and social movements able to have an input into politics through open channels of communications with the government and main parties?

Do you think the questions in this list are a good test of whether democracy is consolidated? Try applying them to a few countries.

Spain, Portugal and Greece have come a long way in achieving democratic consolidation. Civilian dominance over the military has been established. This happened relatively early in Greece, where the military discredited itself comprehensively; attempts to plot against the new government in 1974–75 floundered when a large majority of the officer corps remained loyal to the elected authorities. In Portugal, the military continued to play a significant role in politics into the 1980s; nevertheless, the Revolutionary Council was disbanded in 1982, and in February 1986 a civilian – Mario Soares – finally became head of state. In Spain, the civilian authorities had to make considerable concessions to secure the military's withdrawal from politics. These included increasing defence spending and soft peddling on regional reforms. An attempted military coup in February 1981 collapsed following the personal intervention of the king. As commander-in-chief of the armed forces, King Juan Carlos played a vital role in securing the triumph of democracy in Spain. Since February 1981, the military has stayed out of politics, although threats to Spanish unity can still provoke its unease.

Relatively stable party systems now function in all three countries. The only really 'anti-system' party in the region is the Basque Batasuna (political wing of the ETA terrorist organisation). Support for far-right or neo-fascist parties has not been significant to date. The communist parties all operate within the democratic system. In Portugal, a short-lived Democratic Renewal Party was founded by elements close to the military in 1985 but collapsed in 1987. Political competition since has been between three relatively stable forces: centre-right conservatives (PSD and CDS/PP), centre-left socialists (PSP), and communists (PCP). The latter now contest elections as part of a coalition with the Greens known as the United Democratic Coalition (CDU). In Spain, considerable turmoil in the mid-1970s has given way to a three-party system – socialists (PSOE), conservatives (PP), and communists and allies

Plate 2.9 Izaskun Ugarte, widow of an ETA member, touches her husband's ashes with one hand and with the other raises ETA's symbol, the axe (for strength) and serpent (for cunning) at his funeral ceremony in St-Jean-de-Luz in January 1984

Source: Woodworth (2001).

(United Left – IU). The remaining 20 percent of voters support regional parties, which mostly accept the Spanish constitution. In Greece, there is a similar three-party system of conservatives (ND), socialists (PASOK) and communists, although the communists are divided into two rival groupings. Signs of upheaval in the Greek party system appeared with a split within ND in spring 1993, leading to the formation of another right-of-centre party called Political Spring. Led by Antonis Samaras, it benefited from an upsurge in Greek nationalism following international recognition of the Former Yugoslav Republic of Macedonia (FYROM). It saw its support fade away by 2004 as ND reasserted itself on the right.

Survey evidence suggests that popular support for the new political systems is relatively high. Moreover, the recourse to referenda to abolish the monarchy and establish a republic (as in Greece in 1974), or to approve legalisation of parties (as in Spain in 1976), helped to confer legitimacy.

Nevertheless, a number of negative phenomena threatening the consolidation of democracy can be observed. The persistence of charisma as a key political asset is a double-edged sword. While the enormous popularity of certain leaders has helped to stabilise democracy, it may mean that some parties find it difficult to survive intact after the death or retirement of their leaders. The extreme factionalism within New Democracy after the retirement and subsequent death of Constantine Karamanlis is an example. The personalisation of politics can also accentuate rivalries and feed the tendency towards demagogic leadership and dynasties. The election in March 1997 of Kostas Karamanlis, nephew of the party founder, as leader of New Democracy in a bid to restore party unity is again an example, as was the election of George Papandreou, son of Andreas, as leader of PASOK at the start of 2004. Parliaments remain weak, and executives retain a considerable degree of autonomy from parliamentary supervision; however, this is a problem common to all European democracies. The weakness of civil society manifests itself in a number of ways:

- There are few genuinely mass parties, despite the use of state patronage.
- Trade unions remain numerically weak – only 10–15 percent of the labour force in Spain and Portugal – and plagued by political rivalries.
- Employers' organisations lack internal coherence.
- The relative weakness of channels of communication and negotiation between the state and the main interest groups has meant that industrial relations have recently been plagued by conflict.
- Evidence of corruption has come to light. The main parties in Spain and Greece on both left and right have been repeatedly embroiled in scandals involving allegations of embezzlement of state funds and massive use of patronage to reward their supporters. Repeatedly, elections in southern Europe have been won or lost on the basis of how corrupt the incumbent government party has become. Although the multifaceted crisis of parties is a feature of all Western democracies, the distinction between party and state has arguably been blurred to a greater extent in southern Europe than in northern Europe. Some writers detect a degeneration of political parties into little more than rival parasitical clans. Other writers argue that most examples of clientelism, as distinct from corruption, are fairly harmless and may even have helped to secure the new democratic systems.

Party competition since the transition to democracy

Party competition in southern Europe since the mid-1970s has been characterised by:

- the dominant role of conservative and socialist parties;
- the deradicalisation of the socialist parties;
- the struggle of the conservative parties to modernise;
- the decline of the communist parties, split everywhere between reformers and traditionalists.

The socialists

The socialist parties were the dominant force in Spain and Greece during the 1980s and part of the 1990s, and to a lesser extent in Portugal from the mid-1970s until the mid-1980s. By 2005, socialists had lost power to conservatives in Greece but had been returned to power in Portugal and Spain.

In Spain, the Socialist Workers' Party (PSOE) won elections in 1982, 1986 and 1989, polling between 40 and 48 percent of the vote. PSOE returned to power as a minority government with 39.1 percent in June 1993, despite losing seats and votes. It was finally ousted by the conservative PP in March 1996, when PSOE polled 37.5 percent, and again lost elections to the PP in 2000. Badly damaged by corruption scandals and revelations of the involvement of PSOE governments in a dirty war against Basque terrorists, the party entered the new century divided internally. It returned to power in extraordinary circumstances in 2004. Although it had not been expected to win the elections, a terrorist outrage in Madrid in March 2004, when Islamic extremists apparently protesting against the conservative Spanish government's involvement in the US-led war in Iraq exploded bombs on trains killing nearly 200 people, caused public opinion to turn against the conservative PP. The government was suspected of having lied about the nature of the terrorist attacks in order to deflect blame on to Basque extremists. Moreover, Spanish public opinion was strongly against Spain's involvement in the Iraq war. The Socialists, under their new and young leader José Luis Rodriguez Zapatero, snatched a surprise victory.

Table 2.10 Southern European socialist parties' electoral performance in the 1990s and beyond

	1991	1993	1995	1996	1999	2000	2002	2004	2005
Greece		46.9*		41.5*		43.8*		40.5	
Portugal	29.1		43.7*		44.1*		38.5		45.1*
Spain		39.1+		37.5		34.8		43.3+	

Notes: a. Figures refer to percentage of votes cast in elections to national parliaments.
   b. Socialist parties in question are PASOK (Greece), PSP (Portugal) and PSOE (Spain).
   c. The PSOE totals include votes for regional branches of PSOE that contested elections under slight variations on the party's national title.
   d. * indicates victory with absolute majority of seats. + indicates victory but minority government.

In Greece, the Pan-Hellenic Socialist Movement (PASOK) was founded by Andreas Papandreou in 1974 and won power in 1981 with 48 percent of the vote. PASOK held office until June 1989 and subsequently won elections in 1993, 1996 and 2000. Despite attempting to shake off its image as a party embroiled in public sector corruption and complacent with years in power by electing a new, young leader (George Papandreou) in early 2004, it lost power in March of that year.

In Portugal, the PSP has been less successful electorally, but it held the premiership in 1976–78 and 1983–85, has held the presidency since 1986, and won general elections in 1995 and 1999. It lost power in 2002 but, under a new leader, Ferro Rodrigues, polled better than most commentators had expected. In February 2005, the PSP benefited from mass popular disillusionment with the economic policies of the outgoing centre-right government and returned to power with its best ever electoral result.

The character of the socialist parties has changed enormously. Early radical aspirations have been abandoned in favour of moderate social democracy. PSOE dropped its commitment to Marxism in 1978, thereafter evolving steadily into a centrist party in terms of economic policy. During the 1980s, it was even accused of favouring Thatcherite economics. At the end of the 1980s, the trade unions accused PSOE of betraying the unemployed through its deflationary policies. Unemployment has remained the weak point of the party's record and, together with corruption scandals, probably helps to account for its 1990s electoral losses. The Spanish economy grew under PSOE direction, but monetarist policies brought about this growth. Even if the retention of the state's controlling share in many industries renders the charge of Thatcherism less than accurate, few would deny that the results achieved have little to do with socialism as the party once envisaged it. In foreign policy too, Felipe González abandoned former socialist policies in 1986 and secured NATO membership and entry into the EC. PSOE's most radical achievements in government involved reducing the Church's influence in education and introducing social reforms such as divorce and abortion legislation. By the mid-1990s, PSOE was embroiled in a series of damaging scandals and accusations of involvement in an illegal 'dirty war' against suspected Basque terrorists, which had seen some suspects abducted, tortured and murdered. It was perceived as having run out of ideas and as no longer the force for modernisation, attractive to young voters, that it once was. Its attempt to cling on to power in 1996, by branding the conservative PP as unreconstructed Francoists who would threaten both democracy and the social security system, failed and it went into opposition. In June 1997, González resigned as PSOE leader but refused to rule out a future comeback. His erstwhile protegé Joaquín Almunia was elected as leader, and other moderates dominated the party executive, routing supporters of Alfonso Guerra on the left and prompting Guerra's resignation as deputy party leader. Returned to power unexpectedly under the leadership of José Luis Rodriguez Zapatero in March 2004, PSOE again adopted the mantle of a liberal, secular reforming and modernising party – legislating for gay rights and secular control of education, for example.

In Greece, PASOK in opposition called for withdrawal from NATO and opposed EC membership. It advocated an independent foreign policy sympathetic to Third World causes, social reforms aimed at achieving gender equality, comprehensive health and education programmes, and widespread socialisation of industry and financial institutions. The first PASOK government attempted many reforms but was forced to moderate its foreign policy stance, especially with regard to the US military presence and membership of the EC. Papandreou made much of renegotiating the terms of EC membership so as to obtain a better deal for Greece, but he achieved little by doing so; moreover, EC aid probably created a dynamic of dependency. In the mid-1980s, PASOK adopted austerity measures that weakened trade unions and effectively shelved Keynesian-style spending plans. Back in government from 1993, its fate was tied up with Papandreou's declining health. From November 1995, PASOK was torn with factionalism between Papandreou's supporters and those of the technocrat, Kostas Simitis, who pledged to dismantle clientelism and introduce monetarist reforms to prepare Greece for European monetary union. Papandreou's highly personal and populist style and his refusal to allow the nomination of a potential successor had deepened party divisions. In January 1996, Papandreou was succeeded as prime minister by Simitis and in June he died.

Simitis became party leader after a bitter internal battle with Interior Minister Akis Tsokhatzopoulos, a Papandreou loyalist. Simitis was strengthened by success in elections held in September 1996, when he led PASOK to an unexpectedly comfortable victory. Although the election saw some PASOK voters transfer their support to the communists and other left-wing parties, Simitis could claim a mandate for his technocratic and pro-European policies, which were soon to provoke opposition from within both PASOK and the trade unions. PASOK retained power in 2000 but suffered a decline in popularity thereafter. Its 'capitalist' policies, deemed necessary to prepare Greece for entry to the euro zone, resulted in public sector cuts and alienated many traditional trade unionist and working-class supporters. At the same time, Simitis was still exhorting his supporters to 'clean up' corruption on the eve of the 2004 elections. His replacement by George (son of Andreas) Papandreou just in time for those elections was not enough to prevent the party's loss of office.

In Portugal, the PSP has sought to project itself as the party of EC-sponsored modernisation. In practice, this entailed reversing many of the nationalisations of the early revolutionary period and implementing measures to attract foreign investment. The party has been open to coalition with the centre-right PSD, which supported Soares' presidential re-election in 1991. When the PSP returned to power in 1995, under António Guterres, it was on a platform of modernisation and opposition to corruption, rather than radical social change. It narrowly lost its absolute majority in 1999; severe setbacks in local elections in 2001 caused Guterres to make way for Ferro Rodrigues. The party lost power to a resurgent centre-right in 2002 but regained office with an absolute majority in parliament in 2005. Its new leader, José Sócrates Carvalho Pinto de Sousa, became prime minister.

A number of factors explain the rightward move of the socialist parties. The 1980s saw the rise of New Right ideas internationally, and the vulnerable position of the southern European economies left the socialists exposed. There was a strong temptation to embrace the free-market modernisation promised by the EC as the only basis upon which to build for future prosperity. Moreover, there was a need to reassure dominant economic and social groups that democracy would not result in upheaval and revolution. Once the task of democratic consolidation was perceived as vital, a move away from radicalism was inevitable. The socialist parties all had fairly weak links to organised labour, which reduced internal organisational resistance to the rightward move. The parties were centralised machines in which a cult of leadership facilitated policy U-turns. Papandreou, for example, regularly purged the PASOK leadership almost at will and bequeathed it a legacy of personalised factionalism and bitterness. It is true that resistance in PSOE to González's policy changes has sometimes been forthcoming from a populist wing associated with Alfonso Guerra. Nevertheless, in March 1994, González was able to orchestrate a leadership reshuffle that reduced Guerra's influence; and in June 1997, even after his own resignation from the party leadership, González was able to marginalise Guerra and the PSOE left even further. Finally, socialists have faced weak competition on their left flank.

A balance sheet of the socialists' performance in southern Europe must record a number of substantial achievements: democratic consolidation, EU membership, extension of civil liberties and women's rights, and economic growth. But the socialists' loss of any clear radical or reforming commitment poses identity problems, as does their growing involvement in scandals and clientelist politics (although they are not unique in this).

The centre-right

The socialists' move towards the centre and embrace of market-led economics has compounded the identity problems of the right-wing or conservative forces. In both Spain and Greece, conservative parties played the dominant role in government during the 1970s but lost power in the early 1980s. The right was more successful electorally in Portugal during these years.

In Greece, ND, in power from 1974 to 1981, embraced welfare policies and a consensus approach to industrial relations; it enjoyed business backing while speaking of the need for social democracy. However, the moderate image was not accepted by all its members, and a backlash by right-wingers intensified after it lost power in 1981. During the 1980s, ND moved further to the right, calling for privatisation of state-owned industries and strict control of the money supply. Greece's crippling burden of debt, allegations of abuse of state funds by PASOK and the perceived need to meet EC conditions for aid all created a climate in which calls for fiscal rectitude gained a receptive audience. (Ironically, these themes were to be taken up by Simitis after he became leader of PASOK in 1996.) ND defeated PASOK in June 1989, but without gaining a majority in parliament. A year-long coalition with the communists – to tackle corruption – ended when ND gained a one-seat majority, ruling on its own until October 1993.

In the early 1990s, ND's economic policies provoked industrial and student unrest. The party backed down in 1991 in the face of opposition to its education reforms. It was forced to abandon plans to pardon the imprisoned leaders of the old military junta and was placed on the defensive by Greek insecurities over renewed instability in the Balkans. A split in 1993 showed how vulnerable it was to internal party conflict. Defeat by PASOK in October 1993 was followed by the election of a new leader, Miltiades Evert, a moderate who had previously clashed with the right wing of his own party. However, Evert found it increasingly difficult to compete with the pro-European policies of PASOK, especially after Simitis succeeded Papandreou as prime minister in January 1996. From September 1996, Evert's leadership was fatally undermined by electoral defeat and internal party feuding. His party had lost business support to PASOK in elections held in September. In March 1997, in a bid to restore unity, ND elected Kostas Karamanlis (nephew of its founder) as its new leader. It finally returned to power under Karamanlis in 2004, but arguably its victory owed more to the electorate's disillusionment with PASOK after eleven years of that party's rule.

In Spain, two main rightist formations emerged during the mid-1970s: the centre-right UCD (later renamed CDS), led by Suárez, and the more conservative PP, led until 1990 by Manuel Fraga. Political polarisation during the early 1980s badly squeezed the UCD and permitted the rise of the PP. Paradoxically, this may have sealed the electoral fate of the right throughout the 1980s, for many Spaniards were clearly unwilling to trust the PP, given some of its leaders' past associations with the dictatorship.

In the early 1990s, the PP suffered from factionalism, a failure to modernise its image and ideology, and difficulty in adapting to social change. It was unable to attract any significant working-class support and was thwarted by the fact that many conservative voters continued to favour regionalist parties. The election of Jose Maria Aznar as leader in 1990 heralded a serious attempt to address these concerns. Aznar pushed through reforms in February 1993 aimed at increasing the PP's appeal to women and young people, and he introduced mandatory dismissal for corrupt office-holders. A concerted drive in June 1993 to project the PP as a modernising, young and attractive alternative to a tired socialist government failed to produce immediate results but laid the foundations for future success. In 1993, the PP polled 34.6 percent of the vote, four points behind PSOE. However, the growing crisis of the socialist government through involvement in scandals allowed Aznar to fight elections in March 1996 on a platform promising renewal and moderation. The PP returned to office as a minority government, supported by regional parties. However, Aznar's cabinet was strongly conservative and Catholic. Although the PP reversed its opposition to regional reforms, it played to traditional conservative themes of austerity and privatisation. Budget cuts, to prepare Spain for the European single currency, resulted in renewed unrest and civil service strikes in 1996 and 1997. Nevertheless, Aznar's popularity, the Spanish economy's continuing good overall performance and PSOE's descent into internal strife facilitated a major electoral victory in 2000. Thereafter, Aznar's strongly pro-US foreign policy in defiance of Spanish public opinion would prove to be his undoing. The PP lost power in 2004 in circumstances described above.

In Portugal, the centre-right PSD dominated politics from the mid-1980s to the mid-1990s, balancing a neo-liberal, market-led approach to economics with the pursuit of consensus with the socialists. Led by Anibal Cavaco Silva, the PSD held power from 1987 to 1995. Nevertheless, it faced a challenge from the more right-wing CDS-PP. The PSD in power has not always been willing to push through the privatisation that its rhetoric had suggested. Critics have sometimes alleged that the patronage potential of the public sector is one reason why this is so; another may be an unwillingness to face deteriorating industrial relations. Indeed, corruption scandals and the perceived arrogance of Cavaco Silva both contributed to the PSD's defeat in elections in October 1995. In March 1996, the PSD elected Marcelo

Rebelo de Sousa as its leader in a bid to restore badly shaken party unity and morale. The party remained in opposition until 2002, when it returned to power (in coalition with the CDS-PP) under José Durão Barroso. As is so often the case in southern Europe, a pledge to clean up corruption featured prominently in its campaign pledges. Upon Barroso's election as president of the European Commission in 2004, his place at the helm of government was taken by Pedro Santana Lopes. In February 2005, the PSD and CDS-PP suffered electoral defeat, falling to just 28.7 percent and 7.3 percent, respectively.

Table 2.11 Southern European centre-right parties' electoral performance in the 1990s and beyond

	1991	1993	1995	1996	1999	2000	2002	2004	2005
Greece		39.3		38.1		42.7		45.4*	
Portugal	55.0		43.1		40.6		49.0*		36.0
Spain		34.6		38.7+		45.2*		37.8	

Notes: a. Figures refer to percentage of votes cast in elections to national parliaments.
    b. Centre-right parties in question are New Democracy (Greece), PSD and CDS-PP (Portugal) and PP and CDS (Spain).
    c. The Spanish totals include votes for regional branches of the PP that contested elections under slight variations on the party's national title.
    d. The Portuguese total is the combined vote for the two main conservative parties, PSD and CDS-PP. These two parties formed a coalition after the 2002 elections.
    e. * Indicates victory with absolute majority of seats. + indicates victory but minority government.

The record for the southern European conservatives is mixed. Nowhere has the right achieved real political dominance. In Spain, conservatives continued to suffer from association with the authoritarian past, although victory in 1996 and 2000 confirmed that this is easing as time passes. In Portugal and Greece, the right suffers internal divisions and factionalism. The dilemma everywhere is clear: should the right pursue consensus with the centre-left or aim for dominance, through conflict if necessary? Consensus may be a safer option, guaranteeing social stability and democratic consolidation. However, it threatens to erode the distinctive identity of both the socialist and conservative parties in southern Europe, given the similarity in their policies now, and to reward whichever can appear most competent at implementing a (largely) shared agenda. This in turn may increase the temptation to hurl accusations of corruption and incompetence at each other, exaggerating such differences as still exist.

The communists and ex-communists

The third main political force in the region has been the communists, although several such parties have now evolved into post-communist parties. The communist parties all resisted the old dictatorships, and the Iberian parties especially were important actors during the democratic transition. Since then, however, they have faced marginalisation. Two types of response have been characteristic. The first has involved a reformist strategy that prioritised democratic consolidation, isolation of the extreme right and establishment of the democratic credentials of the communists themselves. The second has involved an attempt to move the transition process along quickly, under communist leadership, in the direction of socialist revolution.

The majority of the Spanish communists chose the first response, contributing to democratic consolidation but paying an electoral price. Disappointing election results, the top-heavy leadership style of PCE boss Carrillo and direct interference from Moscow all contributed to a severe internal party crisis in the early 1980s. The PCE split into several factions, sank to around 3 percent of the vote and almost disintegrated in 1982–86. The Greek communists had split as far back as 1968 into a pro-Soviet hard-line KKE and a moderate minority faction that took a democratic line. The latter group was renamed Synaspismos (meaning 'coalition of the left and progress') in 1992. The Portuguese party remained wedded to Soviet orthodoxy.

Table 2.12 Southern European communist and ex-communist parties' electoral performance in the 1990s and beyond

	1991	1993	1995	1996	1999	2000	2002	2004	2005
Greece		7.4		10.7		8.7		9.2	
Portugal	8.8		8.6		9.0		7.0		7.6
Spain		9.3		10.7		6.0		3.2	

Notes: a. Figures refer to percentage of votes cast in elections to national parliaments.
  b. Communist and ex-communist parties in question are KKE (hard-line communist) and Synaspismos (ex-communist) (Greece), PCP (which contests elections with its Green allies under the banner of the United Democratic Coalition, or CDU) (Portugal) and IU (United Left, which includes the Communist Party and other small radical left groups) (Spain).
  c. The Spanish totals include votes for regional branches of IU that contested elections under slight variations on the party's national title.
  d. The Greek totals are for the KKE and Synaspismos combined.

Until the early 1990s, the PCP and the KKE maintained an electoral presence of around 10 percent, a strong trade union base and a loyal working-class following. However, since the collapse of the USSR, these parties have struggled to come to terms with the implosion of their ideology. Severe internal splits led to expulsions from both parties in the early 1990s. Not even the election of new leaders – Carlos Carvalhas (PCP) in 1992 and Aleka Papariga (KKE) in 1991 – has stemmed the haemorrhage of voters, members and influence. In October 1993, the KKE saw its share of the Greek vote fall to a humiliating 4.5 percent. The disillusionment of some left-wing voters with PASOK's policy of budget cuts allowed a modest revival in 1996, when the KKE polled 5.6 percent. Both the KKE and the PCP will struggle to maintain even their current diminished status in the future. Although they may well survive, it is likely to be as vehicles for the protest vote of those disillusioned by the socialists rather than as the proud and militant parties that they could once claim to be.

The PCE drew back from the brink of disaster in 1986 by joining with dissident socialists, pacifists, feminists and others to launch the United Left (IU) coalition. Conceived as a broad front of anti-Nato radicals, the IU was the third force in Spanish politics. In the 1990s, it polled around 10 percent. Since 2000, the IU has struggled to maintain its unity. Some perceived tactical blunders by its leadership, which allowed its opponents to accuse it of embracing Slobodan Milošević's regime in Serbia and backsliding on opposition to Basque extremism damaged the IU electorally. It failed to benefit from widespread Spanish opposition to the conservative government's support for the 'war on terror' from 2001 onwards; in 2004, the PSOE rode the crest of that tidal wave, while the IU fell back to under 4 percent. Perhaps with the PSOE back in government, the IU, if it can avoid splits, has a chance to occupy a position to the left of PSOE. The IU is now a post-Marxist movement that articulates the concerns of the green, feminist and peace movements.

The moderate Greek ex-communists who split from the hard-line KKE have evolved into a clearly post-communist party committed to gender equality and radical reforms rather than classical Marxism. Since the early 1990s *Synaspismos*, has hovered between 3 and 5 percent. It tends to represent intellectuals and white-collar public sector workers rather than a traditional working-class constituency. Alone among Greek parties, it rejects Greek nationalism and seeks to project a humanist and internationalist perspective. Both the Spanish IU and *Synaspismos* – rooted as they are in significant social movements and articulating concerns that many feel have been neglected or betrayed by the socialists – possess the potential to be dynamic if rather small political forces in the future. However, they have yet to develop a strategy that does not condemn them to merely reacting to a pace of events set by the socialists.

The impact of the European Union

Greece joined the EC in 1981, Spain and Portugal in 1986. There is no doubt that EC membership has had important economic, social, political and cultural effects. Those who supported membership enthusiastically – the centre-right parties and the Iberian socialists – argued that the EC would assist democratic consolidation, bring prosperity and achieve cultural reintegration into the European mainstream. EC aid would facilitate infrastructural improvements and industrial modernisation; and the discipline of membership would force the southern European economies to bring inflation and budget deficits firmly under control. In other words, a powerful external guarantee of both democratic consolidation and balanced growth would result. Those who opposed EC membership totally – chiefly the KKE and PCP – argued that the EC would accentuate uneven development and suck their countries into increased dependency upon northern European (and US) capital. Membership would erode national sovereignty and imperil the recently won democratic freedom by shifting real power away from national governments and parliaments to Brussels. A third group – comprising moderate Spanish and Greek communists – accepted EC membership as a guarantor of democracy and as a progressive development but opposed the free-market logic inherent in the EC and argued for a struggle to transform the Community from within. This would involve left-wing forces battling within a strengthened European Parliament to achieve a much stronger social Europe. PASOK, in Greece, has moved from outright hostility to warm support for EC/EU membership.

There can be little doubt that EC/EU membership has helped to stabilise democracy. On the other hand, southern Europe has found itself battling for a greater share of EU resources and for increases in social spending. Greece has benefited from the Integrated Mediterranean Programmes (IMPs), which had their origins in

PASOK's renegotiation of membership terms in 1982–83. Under the IMPs, southern Europe has picked up payments to assist with the readjustment of small businesses, agriculture and tourism to the requirements of participation in the European single market. Portugal has gained significantly from EU structural funds. Greece and Spain have benefited from agricultural subsidies.

Key fact 2.5

The Integrated Mediterranean Programmes

These were established in March 1985 in anticipation of the accession of Portugal and Spain to the EU in 1986. Their initial focus was on those parts of southern France, Greece and Italy that might be adversely affected by the special aid to be given to Portugal and Spain. They grew to be multi-annual coordinated development programmes embracing the Mediterranean areas of the EU. Latterly, they became part of the more general multi-regional development aid programme operated as part of the EU's structural funds programmes directed towards the 'Objective 1' regions – i.e. those with incomes per head well below the EU average.

Nevertheless, there have been difficulties in adjustment, and it remains unclear how the region will fare when the last of the special transitory protective arrangements for fruit and vegetables expires. Familiar problems remain: high foreign debt, high inflation (except in Portugal), very high unemployment and the threat of growing regional imbalances. Mass tourism has damaged the Mediterranean coastline and overloaded waste disposal and sewage systems; the Mediterranean is the dirtiest and most urbanised sea in the world, with few underdeveloped coastal areas left. This could endanger the tourist trade.

Although southern Europe is more prosperous now than it was prior to EU membership, its overall position as a poor and dependent region has not changed. Much now depends on the (unpredictable) nature of the EU's development. If a two-track or even three-track EU develops, then it seems certain that southern Europe will find itself more dependent than ever on decisions taken in the developed core. Moreover, the southern European countries are worried that the EU's expansion to Eastern and Central Europe means that a lot less money will be available to subsidise their modernisation programmes. The ability to tackle inflation and debt is hampered by political factors. Squeezing living standards and reducing real wages, or reducing expenditure on health and education provision, imposes heavy sacrifices. Dashing people's expectations about living standards could lead to political instability. Measures to raise revenue by widening the tax base and tackling fraud, evasion and corruption risk alienating farming and professional support for the ruling parties. Finally, such measures, and a more rational use of EU funds, require a change in political culture.

Conclusion

Spain, Portugal and Greece face a number of difficult challenges. Their democratic political systems are secure. Nevertheless, as in northern Europe, signs of political malaise are evident. Irredentist nationalism threatens to drift across the Balkans towards Greece, and the growing incidence of racially motivated attacks on immigrants in Spain and Portugal present a challenge to democratic leadership. Political elites have yet fully to face up to the task of carrying forward the modernisation of politics and political systems. This is not merely, or primarily, a generational question. The relative weakness of civil society, the persistence of clientelism and the tendency to resort to populist demagogy challenge the ability of political systems to express new socio-political cleavages as they arise through democratic channels.

Economically, southern Europe's fate is now firmly intertwined with that of the EU. Should the EU back away from the pursuit of a socially integrated political union, the region may suffer. Southern Europe now faces competition from Eastern and Central Europe, both in export markets and in the scramble for financial assistance from the EU. Finally, the Mediterranean region remains a potentially explosive area in the post-Cold War era, and the maintenance of political stability on Europe's southern flank is scarcely less crucial now than before.

Further reading

As with the previous sections, we list a variety of useful recent comparative studies and a few good up-to-date works on individual countries.

Bruneau, T. (1997) *Political Parties and Democracy in Portugal: Organizations, Elections and Public Opinion*, Westview Press, Boulder, CO.

Ethier, D. (1990) *Democratic Transition and Consolidation in Southern Europe, Latin America and South-East Asia*, Macmillan, Basingstoke.

Gillespie, R. (1996) *Mediterranean Politics*, Vol. 3 (Pinter, London).

Gillespie, R., Story, J. and Rodrigo, F. (1995) *Democratic Spain*, Routledge, London.

Gunther, R., Diamandouros, N. and Puhle, H.-J. (1995) *The Politics of Democratic Consolidation: Southern Europe in Comparative Perspective*, Johns Hopkins University Press, New York.

Gunther, R. *et al.* (2004) *Democracy in Modern Spain*, Yale University Press, Yale.

Heywood, P. (1998) *Spain: A European Democracy*, Frank Cass, London.

Lavdas, K. and Magone, J. (1997) *Politics and Governance in Southern Europe: The Political Systems of Italy, Greece, Spain and Portugal*, Westview Press, Boulder, CO.

Linz, J. and Stepan, A. (1996) *Problems of Democratic Transition and Consolidation: Southern Europe, South America and Post-Communist Europe*, Johns Hopkins University Press, Baltimore, MD.

Magone, J. (2004) *Contemporary Spanish Politics*, Routledge, London.

Maxwell, K. (1995) *The Making of Portuguese Democracy*, Cambridge University Press, Cambridge.

Pridham, G. and Lewis, P. (1995) *Stabilising Fragile Democracies*, Routledge, London.

Sapelli, G. (1995) *Southern Europe Since 1945*, Longman, London.

Veremis, T. (1997) *The Military in Greek Politics*, Hurst, New York.

Xenakis, D. and Chryssochoou, D. (2001) *The Emerging Euro-Mediterranean System*, Manchester University Press, Manchester.

Political and economic reforms in post-communist Russia

The Soviet Union: from crisis to collapse

Following an attempted coup in August 1991, Mikhail Gorbachev was forced to resign from his post as general secretary of the CPSU (Communist Party of the Soviet Union), and on 25 December 1991 he tendered his resignation as president of the USSR. In his six-year tenure as general secretary of the CPSU, Gorbachev had alienated all of the major institutions of the Soviet regime, and the vast majority of citizens had become increasingly dissatisfied with his key policies of *perestroika* (economic restructuring), *glasnost* (openness) and democratisation, which, by 1990, had led the country into economic and political crises.

For some sections of the Soviet political elite, Gorbachev's policies were far too radical, while for others they were not radical enough. Thus, by the time of the August 1991 coup, when a group of hard-liners attempted to oust him from power, Gorbachev had created enemies in both the reformist and reactionary wings of the CPSU. Fundamentally, Gorbachev had failed to control the scope and the pace of reform. Thus, for example, his calls for economic decentralisation and the injection of some elements of a market system into the ailing Soviet economy led to demands for full privatisation and a fully fledged market economy. His proposals for a limited democratisation of the political system, which would retain the leading role of the CPSU, fuelled radical grass-roots demands for a democratically elected parliament and multi-party system.

Gorbachev's policies of *glasnost* and democratisation also opened up a hornet's nest of nationalist demands in the country's 15 ethnic republics, and demands for secession were heightened after the collapse of communism in Central and Eastern Europe in 1989. By the end of 1990, all of the Soviet Union's 15 republics had declared their rights of sovereignty and secession. In April 1991, Gorbachev reluctantly signed a treaty (the '9+1 Treaty') with the republics, which sanctioned the

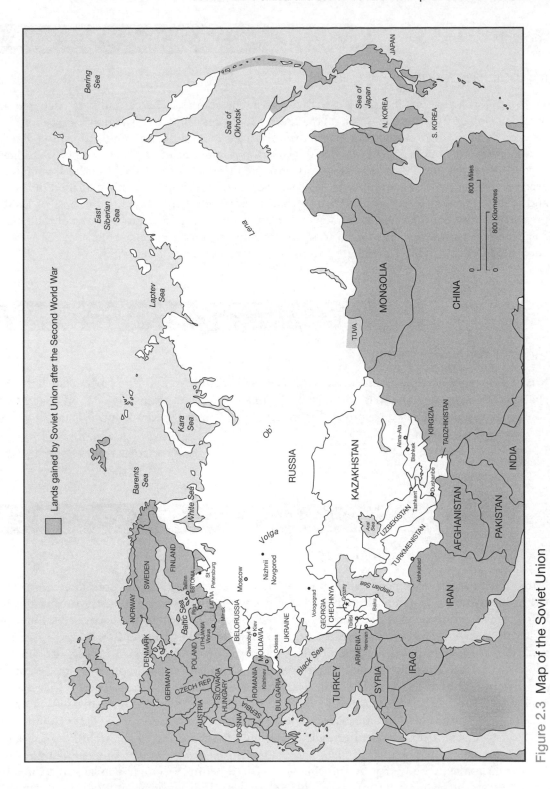

Figure 2.3 Map of the Soviet Union

Source: J. Debardeleben (1997) *Russian Politics in Transition*, 2nd ecn. Copyright© 1997 by Houghton Mifflin Company. Reprinted with permission.

Biography 2.20

Mikhail Sergeevich Gorbachev (1931–)

Mikhail Gorbachev was born in a small village in the south of Russia and was educated at Moscow University, where he studied law, 1950–55. On returning to his region (Stavropol') he worked for his local communist party organisation, eventually becoming the First Party Secretary of Stavropol' in 1966. In 1970, he was appointed head of the Stavropol' Regional Party Committee. In 1978, Gorbachev was promoted to the post of CPSU Central Committee Secretary in charge of agriculture. In 1980, he became a full voting member of the Politburo and in 1985 general secretary. In 1990, Gorbachev was indirectly elected to the post of USSR president by the USSR Congress of People's Deputies. In August 1991, in the wake of the failed August coup, Gorbachev was forced to resign from his post as General Secretary of the CPSU, and on 25 December 1991 he resigned from his post as president of the USSR.

Government 2.13

Government in Russia

Russia is a republic. The president is directly elected for four years. The parliament has two chambers. The State Duma has 450 members, elected for a four-year term, 225 in single-seat constituencies and 225 by proportional representation. The Federation Council has 178 members, two for each region.

(Source: http://www.electionworld.org.)

Biography 2.21

Boris Nikolaevich Yeltsin (1931–)

Boris Yeltsin was born in the Sverdlovsk region of Russia. In 1955, he graduated from the Urals Polytechnical Institute. Yeltsin started work in the construction industry in Sverdlovsk before moving to a career in the party. From 1968 to 1975, he headed the department for construction in the Sverdlovsk City party organisation. He was promoted to the post of first secretary of the Sverdlovsk Regional Party Committee in 1976. In 1985, he was brought to Moscow by Gorbachev, where he became the CPSU Central Committee secretary in charge of construction. From 1985 to 1987, he was the first secretary of the Moscow City Party Committee and from 1986 to 1987 a non-voting member of the Politburo. In 1987, Yeltsin was dismissed from the Politburo and appointed the first deputy chair of the State Committee for Construction, a post he held until 1989, when he was elected to the USSR Congress of People's Deputies. In March 1990, he won election to the newly formed Russian Congress of People's Deputies, a body that he subsequently chaired before becoming Russia's first directly elected president in June 1991. Yeltsin was re-elected Russian president in 1996. In December 1999, Yeltsin was forced to resign his post as president due to his chronic ill-health.

secession of six republics and gave sweeping powers to the remaining nine. The treaty was due to be ratified on 20 August, and the attempted coup took place on 19 August to try to prevent the treaty's ratification.

The coup failed in large part due to the efforts of Boris Yeltsin, who just a few months before had been elected president of the Russian Republic. Yeltsin rallied the country behind him, and crucially the armed forces took the side of the people rather than the plotters, who were finally forced to surrender on 21 August.

The failed coup was the catalyst for the collapse of the USSR. On returning from his holiday home in Foros, where he had been held under house arrest, Gorbachev faced a dramatically changed political landscape. Boris Yeltsin and members of the Russian Republic elite (*nomenklatura*) were now the dominant force in the country. Gorbachev was forced to resign his post as general secretary of the CPSU, and the party was made illegal. Yeltsin also spearheaded negotiations over the creation of a new loose alliance of Soviet republics, the Commonwealth of Independent States (CIS), which sounded the death knell of the Soviet Union. Gorbachev resigned as president of the USSR on Christmas Day, and on 1 January 1992 the new Russian Federation was born.

Russia's transition

The problems of creating a viable democracy in post-communist Russia were overwhelming. 'Whereas most countries in transition seek to change only their system of governance', Russia was faced with the momentous task of creating 'a new state, a new political system, and a new economic system simultaneously' (McFaul 1997: 65). Moreover, Russia's transition is a classic example of what we call a 'revolution from above', that is a revolution carried out by, and in the interests of, the ruling elite. 'Elite continuity', not 'elite circulation', was the major feature of the transition, as top members of the *nomenklatura* took over the reigns of power from Gorbachev.

A federal state

One of the most daunting tasks facing the Yeltsin regime was the creation of a new federal system. With a population of 142 million, the Russian state is one of the most populous and ethnically diverse states in the world. Within its vast territory, which encompasses one-eighth of the world's land surface, reside 128 officially recognised nations and ethnic groups (Sakwa 1996: 31).

The Federation comprises 89 federal subjects, 32 of which are based on ethnic criteria: namely, 21 republics, ten autonomous *okrugs* and one autonomous *oblast*, and 57 territorially defined subjects (see Figure 2.4). Since independence, there have been continual fears that Russia would follow the path of the USSR into ethnic secessionism and disintegration (Ross 2002).

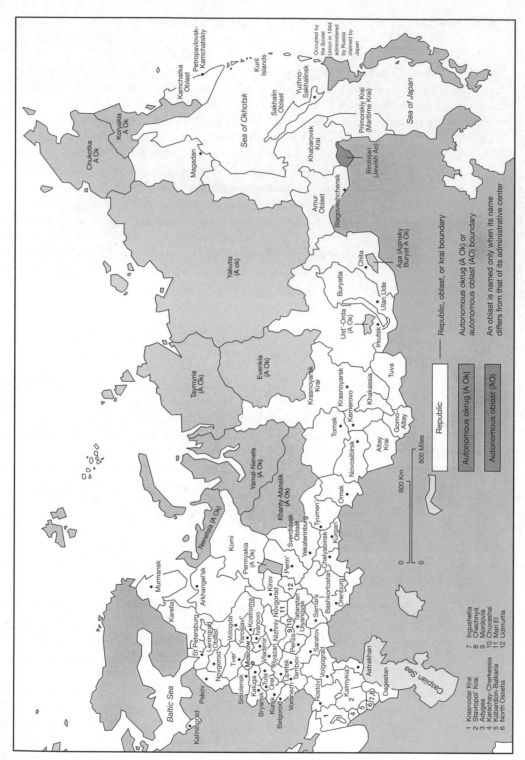

Figure 2.4 Administrative divisions of the Russian Federation

Source: J. Debardeleben (1997) *Russian Politics in Transition*, 2nd edn. Copyright© 1997 by Houghton Mifflin Company. Reprinted with permission.

Key fact 2.6

The Russian Federation

The Russian Federation comprises the following regions:

- **Northern Region**: Karelian Republic, Komi Republic, Arkhangel sk Oblast, Nenets Autonomous Okrug, Volgodsk Oblast, Marmansk Oblast.
- **Northwestern Region**: St Petersburg, Leningrad Oblast, Novgord Oblast, Pskov Oblast.
- **Central Region**: Bryansk Oblast, Vladimir Oblast, Ivanovo Oblast, Kaluzhska Oblast, Moscow, Moscow Oblast, Orlvo Oblast, Ryazan Oblast, Smolensk Oblast, Tvedr Oblast, Tula Oblast, Yaroslavi Oblast.
- **Volga Region**: Marii-El Republic, Mordoviya Republic, Chuvash Republic, Kirov Oblast, Nizhegorod Oblast.
- **Central–Chernozem Region**: Belgorod Oblast, Voronezh Oblast, Kursk Oblast, Lipetsk Oblast, Tambov Oblast.
- **Povolgski Region**: Kalmykiya Republic, Tatarstan Republic, Astrakhan Oblast, Volgograd Oblast, Penzensk Oblast, Samara Obalst, Saratov Oblast, Ulyanov Oblast.
- **North Kaukaz Region**: Adygeva Republic, Dagestan Republic, Ingush Republic, Kabardino-Balkar Republic, Karachaev-Circassian Republic, North Ossetian-Alaniya Republic, Chechen Republic, Krasnodarsk Krai, Stavropol Krai, Rostov Oblast.
- **Ural**: Bashkortostan Republic, Udmurt Republic, Kurgan Oblast, Orenburg Oblast, Perm Oblast, Komi-Permyatsk Autonomous Okrug, Sverdlovsk Oblast, Chelyabinsk Oblast.
- **West Siberia:** Altai Republic, Altai Krai, Kemerovo Oblast, Novosibirsk Oblast, Omsk Oblast, Tomsk Oblast, Tyumen Oblast, Khanti-mansi Autonomous Okrug, Yamalo-Nenetsk Autonomous Okrug.
- **East Siberia**: Buryat Republic, Tyva Republic, Khakasian Republic, Krasnoyarsk Krai, Taimyrsk Autonomous Okrug, Evenkisk Autonomous Okrug, Irkutsk Oblast, Ust-Ordinsk Buryat Autonomous Okrug, Chitinsk Oblast, Aginsk Buryat Autonomous Okrug.
- **Far East Region**: Sakha Republic (Yakutiya), Jewish Autonomous Oblast, Chukotsk Autonomous Okrug, Primorye Krai, Khabarovsk Krai, Amur Oblast, Kamchatka Oblast, Koryak Autonomous Okrug, Megadan Oblast, Sakhalin Oblast.
- **Kaliningrad Oblast**.

Over the period 1991–93, Russia's federal subjects, and particularly the ethnically defined republics, made vociferous demands for economic and political autonomy. In March 1992, in order to prevent the total collapse of the Federation, Yeltsin was forced to sign a federal treaty that gave sweeping powers to the 21 ethnic republics. Two republics refused to ratify the treaty, Chechnya and Tatarstan, and Tatarstan later declared that it was only an 'associate member' of the Federation. Chechnya later went even further, declaring its outright independence and provoking Yeltsin to order Russian troops into the republic in the first Chechen War of 1994–96.

After the ignominious withdrawal of Russian troops in 1996, Vladimir Putin launched a second Chechen offensive on the eve of the December 1999 parliamentary elections. Tens of thousands of combatants and civilians have been killed in the two Chechen wars, and Putin has used these wars to justify a clampdown on the powers of the federal subjects. Putin's strong and defiant stance against the Chechen insurgents has also been highly popular with Russian citizens and was a key factor in his presidential election victories of 2000 and 2004.

Post-communist Russia 1991–93: the battle of constitutions

In the wake of the August 1991 coup, Yeltsin was the most popular and powerful politician in Russia, but over the period 1991–3 he became embroiled in a massive struggle with the Russian parliament, which came to a tragic end when he sent in the army to dissolve the legislature forcibly in October 1993.

How had this dreadful scenario come to pass? How could such enmity arise between the executive and legislative branches? First, we should note the weakness of a democratic or legal political culture in Russia. Centuries of absolutism under the tsars and decades of communist totalitarian rule had created a society whose citizens had no experience of living under democratic rule and consensus politics. Only with the creation of the Congress of People's Deputies in 1989 did we see the creation of a full-time professional parliament in the USSR, and it was not until 1990 that a multi-party system was legalised. Second, the incomplete nature of the revolution in Russia in August 1991 meant that in all of the major institutions of Russian society there remained large contingents of communists who opposed Yeltsin's radical economic and political reforms. Third, we should stress the weakness of political parties, which had only been permitted to form with the repeal of Article 6 of the Soviet constitution in March 1990, after the conclusion of elections to the Russian parliament of the same month. This meant that the only party able to compete in the 1990 elections was the CPSU, which gained 86 percent of the seats, the rest going to independents. However, the Communist Party soon fragmented into a number of highly fluid and competing factions in the parliament, making it impossible for anyone to command a majority of the deputies.

In hindsight, a major mistake of Yeltsin was his failure to call for new elections to the Russian parliament in the immediate aftermath of the August coup. Left without a parliamentary majority to support his reforms, Yeltsin sought to consolidate his powers in the presidency and to rule by decree. These executive powers were challenged by the chairman of the parliament, Ruslan Khasbulatov, who moved from being a strong supporter of Yeltsin in August 1991 to his arch-enemy by 1993.

The final feature was the lack of a democratic constitution to regulate relations between the parliament and president. Yeltsin inherited the old Brezhnev Russian constitution of 1978, and by the end of 1993 more than 300 amendments had been enacted, each one entailing a fierce struggle in the parliament. Ruslan Khasbulatov sought a parliamentary system with a figurehead president, while Yeltsin favoured a presidential constitution with power firmly in the hands of the chief executive. The struggle for power between Yeltsin and Khasbulatov also had a policy dimension, with a majority of the deputies opposing Yeltsin's economic policies (Lane and Ross 1995).

By 1993, there was deadlock in the parliament, with neither Khasbulatov nor Yeltsin able to win enough support for their opposing policies or the two-thirds majority of votes to change the constitution in their favour. In April 1993, Yeltsin

won an important referendum on his leadership and his socio-economic programme. Armed with this new popular mandate, he quickly convened a
constitutional convention, which subsequently approved his draft constitution,
giving the president sweeping powers over the parliament.

The parliamentarians had lost the political battle, and they now saw the overthrow of Yeltsin as the only way forward. Yeltsin's vice-president, Aleksandr
Rutskoi, began to make contacts with disaffected military officers, and a shadow
'government in waiting' was formed in the parliament. Yeltsin now decided to go
on the offensive, arguing that no compromise could be reached with the parliamentarians. At the beginning of September 1993, he dismissed Rutskoi from his post as
vice-president, and on 21 September he passed a decree dissolving the Russian parliament. However, the next day the parliament passed legislation dismissing Yeltsin
from his post as president and appointed Rutskoi as the new president. A group of
deputies now came to the parliament (White House) and barricaded themselves in.
Yeltsin responded by cutting off the parliament's supplies of electricity and gas.
Huge crowds who supported the parliament came and surrounded the building,
and they were provided with weapons by the 'rebel' parliamentarians.

On 3 October 1993, Rutskoi and Khasbulatov called on their supporters to
storm the pro-Yeltsin Ostankino television station and the Moscow mayor's office.
Rutskoi was convinced that these actions would be supported by elements in the
armed forces that had earlier pledged their allegiance, but no such support materialised. In the early hours of 4 October, Yeltsin sent in the tanks against the rebels.
Russian citizens now witnessed the spectacle of Yeltsin attacking the very parliament he had so courageously defended against the coup plotters in August 1991.
By the afternoon order has been restored, but at the cost of 146 lives.

In the aftermath of the dissolution of the parliament, Yeltsin banned a number
of opposition parties that he declared had supported the parliamentarians, and he
called for snap elections to take place on 12 December 1993, the same day as the
referendum on his draft constitution. Yeltsin also quickly supervised the creation
of a new party, 'Russia's Choice', headed by Prime Minister Gaidar. This 'party of
power', which was created from above and whose members were drawn from
executive bodies of the state, won a plurality of the seats in Russia's first post-
communist elections in December 1993. In shock second place was Vladimir
Zhirinovsky's ill-named Liberal Democratic Party of Russia (LDPR) an ultra-right
nationalist party. The Communist Party of the Russian Federation (CPRF), which
had been re-legalised in February 1993, came third.

The Russian constitution

Official turnout for the constitutional referendum was 54.8 percent, and according
to official data the constitution was approved by 58.4 percent of those who voted.
However, in 42 of Russia's 89 republics and regions, the constitution was either
rejected outright or turnout was too low to ratify it. There has also been speculation that less than the required 50 percent of the electorate turned out to ratify the
constitution. Yeltsin had scored a pyrrhic victory over the legislature, and throughout his remaining tenure of office he had to contend with a hostile and

obstructionist parliament. Strong opposition to Yeltsin also came from the CPRF, which won the largest number (but not a majority) of seats in the 1995 and 1999 Duma elections.

Provisions of the constitution

Article 1 of the constitution defines Russia as a 'democratic federative rule of law state with a republican form of government'. Article 2 enshrines a number of key democratic and human rights, such as 'freedom of conscience, religion, thought and speech', and it also 'forbids censorship and guarantees freedom of the press'. Article 10 provides for a separation of legislative, executive and judicial powers, and Article 13 recognises 'political diversity and a multi-party system'.

The Russian parliament (the Federal Assembly), which is elected every four years, has two chambers: a lower house, the state Duma, comprising 450 deputies and an upper chamber, the Federation Council, with 178 deputies. Legislation passed by the Duma can be vetoed by the Federation Council and the president. A veto by the Federation Council can be overturned only by a two-thirds majority in the Duma. To overturn a veto by the president requires a two-thirds majority in the Duma and in the Federal Council.

The upper chamber is also charged with approving presidential nominations for the Constitutional, Supreme and Arbitration Courts and chief procurator, and presidential declarations of martial law and states of emergency. Until changes enacted by Putin in 2002, the Federation Council consisted of two representatives from each of the 89 components of the Russian Federation, one each from the representative and executive organs of state power. Since January 2002, regional representatives are no longer given direct *ex officio* membership of the upper chamber but instead nominate delegates to serve on their behalf. During the Yeltsin period, the Federation Council became a powerful advocate of regional interests, but Putin's removal of the regional governors and chairmen of regional assemblies has fundamentally weakened its status.

The president is elected every four years, and no individual may hold more than two consecutive terms in office. The constitutional powers of the president are immense. In his capacity as head of state and supreme commander-in-chief of the armed forces, the president is charged with 'determining the basic guidelines of the state's domestic and foreign policy'. The president has considerable powers of appointment. Thus, for example, the president, with the consent of the Duma, appoints the prime minister, the deputy prime ministers and director of the Central Bank. If the Duma rejects three candidates for prime minister, the president has the right to dissolve the Duma and schedule new elections. The president also has the right to chair sessions of the government and to dismiss the government.

As noted above, the president, with the approval of the Federation Council, also appoints the general prosecutor, and members of the Constitutional Court, Supreme Court of Arbitration and other federal courts. Moreover, the president forms and heads the Security Council, approves the military doctrine of the Russian Federation, and appoints and removes the high command of the armed forces and diplomatic representatives. The president has the right to introduce martial law and to declare a state of emergency with the approval of the Federation Council. The president also has the power to rule by decree.

Having engaged in a bloody battle to ratify his constitution, Yeltsin made sure that it would be extremely difficult to amend. Constitutional amendments require a two-thirds majority of the members of the Duma, the support of three-quarters of the members of the Federation Council and ratification by the legislatures of two-thirds of the 89 federal subjects. In sum, the 1993 constitution created a political system whereby the presidency totally dominates all of the other key political institutions of the state.

It is also extremely difficult to impeach the president; that requires a vote of two-thirds of the members of both chambers of the parliament and confirmation by rulings of both the Constitutional Court and the Supreme Court that the actions of the president are criminal or treasonable.

In the following sections, we turn to a detailed discussion of Russia's economic and political reforms.

Economic reform: all shock and no therapy?

When it came to the choice in 1991 between 'gradualism' and 'shock therapy', Russia opted for the latter. Shock therapy was strongly supported by Russian Prime Minister Yegor Gaidar, who favoured as rapid a move to the market as possible. Such a strategy he believed would make his economic reforms irreversible lest the communists were to return to power (Rutland 1994: 150–2). Rapid privatisation would also create a new middle class of entrepreneurs, which the new regime could look to for political support. Shock therapy was also actively promoted by the IMF and IBRD, which made any loans conditional on its implementation.

However, shock therapy did not lead to stability and prosperity but rather to a collapse in economic production, economic turmoil and biting poverty for large numbers of citizens, combined with fabulous wealth for others. Thus, for example, over the period 1991–98 GDP fell by a massive 40 percent, a greater fall than the 31 percent drop in GDP during the Depression of the 1930s in the USA (Goldman 2003b: 14). In 2002, industrial production was still only 67 percent of that achieved in 1991 (see Table 2.13). This massive fall in production almost bank-

Table 2.13 Russian economic and social indicators from Yeltsin to Putin

	1997	1998	1999	2000	2001	2002	2003
Real GDP growth %	1.4	−5.3	6.4	10.0	5.1	4.7	7.3
Industrial output (1991 = 100)	52.5	49.8	55.2	61.8	64.8	67.2	71.9
Consumer price inflation %	11.4	84.4	36.5	20.2	18.6	15.1	12.0
Average real wages % change	4.4	−10.0	−23.2	18.0	20.0	16.2	9.8
Exchange rate, roubles per US$, end of year	6.0	20.7	27.0	28.2	30.1	31.8	29.5

(Source: IMF 2004.)

rupted the government, which was soon unable to pay its civil servants, teachers, doctors and other state employees. Unemployment also rose sharply.

According to official figures, 15 percent of the population was unemployed in the late 1990s, but this figure does not include individuals who failed to register their unemployment. Nor does it include 'hidden employment', when workers are kept on the employment register of a factory but are given only part-time work or extended unpaid holidays. Taking these factors into consideration, it is reckoned that up to one-third of the workforce was out of work in the late 1990s, and in some regions it was as high as 50 percent.

During the Soviet era, many staple goods such as food and medicine were subsidised by the state. These subsidies were brought to an end with the introduction of price liberalisation in January 1992. Price liberalisation led to an immediate and sharp rise in prices, with an annual inflation rate of 2,600 percent in the first year. This hyperinflation continued right into the late 1990s. Thus, by December 1999, '1,602,658 roubles were required to buy the same basket of goods that theoretically only 100 roubles would have purchased in December 1990' (Goldman 2003b: 14). These massive price increases wiped out much of the general population's life savings. Hardest hit were those on fixed incomes, single mothers and pensioners. The situation became even worse after the August 1998 financial crisis, when the government was forced to devalue the rouble by 50 percent. Prices again rose sharply, food prices increased by 40 percent in September (White 2000b: 138–9), production slumped, and as Table 2.13 shows, incomes fell by about one-third.

In 1993, one-third of the population had been classified as living below the minimum subsistence level, and this rose to over 40 percent in early 1999. Citizens now also faced the reality of having to pay for a whole range of social services (e.g. health, education) that had been free during the Soviet period, and corruption in the state bureaucracy was rife.

Russia's economic reforms also led to fabulous wealth for some individuals. Russia now ranks second in the world in terms of the number of its billionaires, and Moscow is the billionaires' capital of the world. Moreover, wealth in Russia is highly concentrated, with the combined wealth of Russia's 36 richest people being equivalent to one-quarter of the country's annual GDP (Osborn 2004: 4).

Recovery under Putin

Bolstered by high oil prices, the economic situation has substantially improved since Putin came to power in March 2000. Thus, for example, GDP increased by around 5 to 10 percent in each year over the period 1999–2002 (see Table 2.13), and there was a further 7 percent increase in 2003. Putin's policies of doubling GDP by 2010 and bringing inflation down to 3 percent by 2008 may now be attainable. However, the most recent IMF mission to Russia (February 2005) expressed concerns about the slowing in real GDP growth and the persistence of inflation (IMF 2005). The sharp rise in GDP since 1999 has lifted a large number of people out of poverty, with the number of people classified as living below the subsistence level falling by one-third over the period 2000–04.

Nomenklatura privatisation

In the summer of 1992, Russia began the massive task of privatising its economy. Progress here was rapid, and by 1998 87 percent of all industrial enterprises had been placed under private ownership (White 2000b: 127). Gaidar had opted for a 'Czech-style voucher' privatisation scheme, which would give every citizen a stake in the system (Rutland 1994: 162). Thus, on 1 October 1992, privatisation vouchers, with a value of 10,000 roubles, were distributed to the population. However, voucher privatisation soon turned into what Breslauer has called the 'greatest case of insider trading in history' (2001: 45).

The privatisation process was captured by members of the Russian *nomenklatura*, who were able to use their privileged positions and political contacts to buy up the state's most choice assets. Moreover, in the 'shares for loans programme' of the mid-1990s, Yeltsin allowed state property to be auctioned off at ridiculously low prices. Priority bidding was granted to those bankers who were willing to give cash loans to the impoverished Russian government (Rutland 1994: 163). As Sergey Stepashin notes (2004: 2):

> It was a political decision, when 150,000 enterprises were handed over for a song, and the 9.7 billion roubles (320 million dollars) Russia received is a ridiculous figure.

Thus, for example, Mikhail Khodorkovsky paid approximately $300 million for Yukos Oil, which by 2003 was worth $20–$25 billion. Khodorkovsky's own bank, Menatep, conducted the auction. Similarly, Boris Berezovsky paid about $100 million for Sibneft Oil, which in 2003 was valued at $10 billion (Goldman 2003a: 324).

Moreover, members of Russia's new capitalist class were more interested in getting their money out of the country than in investing in Russia. Thus, for example, oil tycoon Roman Abramovich has spent millions of pounds on Chelsea Football Club. Indeed, capital flight from Russia is estimated to have reached the staggering sum of $14.1 billion per annum over the period 1994–98 (Lane 2004: 104). Russia's privatisation process should really be called 'piratisation' (Goldman 2003b: 92).

Putin and the Oligarchs

While Yeltsin sought to buy off the oligarchs and to reward them with political posts and tax concessions, Putin has taken a much firmer line. Although he has not sought to reverse the privatisation deals of the 1990s, he has nonetheless aggressively pursued the payment of back taxes, and he has made it clear that he will not tolerate any political opposition from the oligarchs. Thus, for example, two key supporters of Yeltsin who fell out of favour with Putin, Boris Berezovsky and Vladimir Gusinsky, have been hounded out of the country by the security forces (FSB) and the tax police. In October 2003, Russia's most powerful oligarch, Mikhail Khodorkovsky, head of the giant oil company Yukos, was arrested on charges of fraud and tax evasion. Khodorkovsky had stepped out of line by giving financial support to opposition parties in the run-up to the 2003 Duma elections (Kolmakov 2004: 10). By arresting Khodorkovsky, Putin was sending a message to all the other oligarchs that political opposition to the president is unacceptable. However, Putin's selective use of the law to attack political opponents is a major setback for the development of an independent legal system in Russia.

Political reforms: creating the institutions of democracy

A major problem as regards building democracy in Russia is the weakness of parties and the party system. Scholars of Russian politics have stressed the following key factors as major determinants of Russia's weak party system:

- the weakness of civil society and the legacy of an authoritarian political structure;
- the absence of strong and stable social and economic cleavages around which nationwide parties could coalesce;
- the specific nature of Russia's 'mixed electoral system';
- Russia's choice of a presidential rather than a parliamentary system; and
- the difficulties of creating strong nationwide parties in the largest multi-ethnic federation in the world.

The weakness of civil society and the legacy of an authoritarian political culture

Over 70 years of communist rule have left an authoritarian legacy, a very weak and inchoate civil society and massive citizen distrust in political institutions. In the Soviet Union, there was 'a virtual destruction of the space between the individual and the state, the space that in non-communist states is occupied by institutions of civil society – social networks, private business, public associations, clubs, church groups, labour unions, and so forth' (McFaul 2002: 111). Not surprisingly, then, given Russia's authoritarian history, most citizens today still tend to distrust political institutions. Only 9 percent of those in a poll conducted in 2001 expressed 'full or considerable confidence' in parties, compared with 49 percent for the army and 48 percent for the Church (White and McAllister 2004: 84).

Party identification is also extremely low in Russia. After only four rounds of free parliamentary elections (1993, 1995, 1999, 2003) and three rounds of presidential elections (1996, 2000, 2004), Russian citizens have had little time to develop strong political allegiances to parties. 'According to survey evidence, just 22 percent of Russians identified to some degree with a political party, compared with 87 percent of the electorate of the United States and more than 92 percent in the United Kingdom' (White 2000a: 82–3). Electoral volatility in Russia is six times higher than in Western Europe and twice as high as in Eastern Europe (Wyman 1999: 119).

In Russia's first elections in 1993, 13 parties and electoral blocs participated, but this rose to 43 parties in December 1995, and there were 26 in 1999 and 23 in 2003. It is also very confusing to the electorate when parties are named after their leaders and their names tell the voters nothing about their political orientation, as was the case with, for example, the 'Tikhonov–Tupolev–Tikhonov' bloc or the 'bloc of 30 words', which stood in the 1995 Duma elections.

Party identification is that much more difficult to inculcate where the party system is highly fluid. Only two parties, the CPRF and the LDPR, have successfully crossed the 5 percent threshold in all four Duma elections, and over half the parties registered for the 2003 elections were competing for the first time.

The absence of strong and stable social and economic cleavages

In the first years of Russia's reforms, we saw the formation of a multitude of parties that had very shallow roots in civil society. Strong programmatic parties that have the organisational and financial capability to compete in elections nationwide have been slow to emerge. With the exception of the Communist Party, only the so-called 'parties of power' created by successive Russian governments have had nationwide structures (see Key fact 2.7). Many parties are based around personal cliques and personalities rather than policies, and the traditional social and economic cleavages to be found in Western capitalist states are only slowly beginning to take shape. Thus, for example, we have witnessed a proliferation of right-of-centre political parties, founded long before there was any sizeable property-owning bourgeoisie to support them. Only recently have we seen the beginnings of the formation of an independent middle class of private entrepreneurs.

Key fact 2.7

Russia's 'parties of power'

- **Russia's Choice**, created by Yeltsin in 1993 and headed by former Prime Minister Yegor Gaidar.
- **Our Home is Russia**, formed in 1995 and headed by former Prime Minister Viktor Chernomyrdin.
- **Unity**, formed in 1999, ostensibly headed by a member of the government but really under the control of President Vladimir Putin.
- **Fatherland-All Russia** was initially a rival 'regional party of power' that stood against Unity in the 1999 elections. The party is headed by the mayor of Moscow, Yury Luzhkov, and former Prime Minister Yevgeny Primakov.
- **United Russia**, created in 2001 with the merger of the Unity and Fatherland-All Russia factions in the Duma. Formally headed by the speaker of the Duma, the party is in fact under the control of President Putin.

The specific nature of Russia's 'mixed electoral system'

Russia's choice of electoral system has impacted on party building. In the lower chamber (the Duma), a mixed electoral system is in operation. Half the members are elected by proportional representation using a party list system (with a 5 percent threshold) and half by a first-past-the-post system, in single-member districts. The 5 percent threshold was designed to reduce the number of small or frivolous parties that could win seats in the parliament, and at times it has been too successful. Thus, for example, in 1995 just four out of 43 parties crossed the threshold, and in 2003, four out of 23.

We should also note that most of the candidates competing in the single-member districts stand as independents. Independents won most of the seats in the 1993 elections, and they came second in 1995, 1999 and 2003.

Russia's choice of a presidential rather than a parliamentary system

Russia's choice of a hybrid presidential–parliamentary system at the national level has further weakened the development of strong cohesive parties. Where parliament is weak, as in Russia, then there is also a tendency for parties to decline in importance. Yeltsin repeatedly spoke out against joining any party, stating that his constituency was the Russian people, and likewise, Putin has steadfastly refused to join United Russia.

The difficulties of creating strong nationwide parties

The territorial distribution of national parties in the regions and republics is very low. With the exception of the CPRF and the 'parties of power', most parties have been based largely in Moscow and have very weak organisational ties with regional political structures. The sheer size of the Russian Federation makes it very difficult to create a nationwide organisation.

Putin's new law on parties

The new 'Law on Political Parties', which was ratified by the Duma in June 2001, does address some of the issues and problems of party building. In an attempt to reduce the overall number of parties and to discourage overtly frivolous parties from participating in the elections, the new law lays down strict criteria for party membership. Thus, before a party can be registered it must have a minimum of 10,000 members, with branches in over half of the 89 subjects of the Federation, and there must be a minimum of 100 members in each of the regional branches. Moreover, under the law, 'political blocs' and 'electoral associations' are prohibited.

In order to promote the development of strong nationwide parties, the law also contains provisions for the state funding of parties. Those parties that receive more than 3 percent of the party list vote will receive 0.2 roubles for each vote cast in their favour (Bacon 2004: 43). However, in a blow against the development of local democracy, the law also bans regional parties from competing in elections. Moreover, the law makes it relatively easy for the government to suspend the activity of a party. Thus, for example, 'if a party is banned for violation of the party law, it is also banned from holding public meetings and demonstrations'. Another worry concerns the state funding of parties. There are real fears 'that a state which pays the party piper will want to call the political tune' (*ibid.*).

Presidential power from Yeltsin to Putin

Yeltsin was a patriarchal ruler, and his presidential administration was more like a court than a cabinet. Like a sultanistic leader, he treated members of the government and the presidential administration as courtiers to be rewarded or dismissed for their loyalty. Yeltsin also believed that the state's assets were there to be disposed of as he thought fit. Thus, 'on a tour of Russia in 1992 he brought along hundreds of millions of roubles for gifts to the working people' (Breslauer 2001: 42). Yeltsin also turned a blind eye to corruption and abuses of power by regional governors as long as they delivered votes to the president, and he also made extensive use of his powers to rule by decree. Thus, for example, in his nine-year tenure Yeltsin issued over 1,500 'policy-relevant decrees', and no less than one-quarter of these related to pork-barrel politics (Willerton 2001: 29).

In his 1996 presidential campaign, Yeltsin struck a deal with the oligarchs, promising not to challenge the legality of their privatisation deals if they financed his election campaign. Yeltsin also used his control over the broadcast media and the financial resources of the state to promote his candidacy. Moreover, in the run-up to the elections, he toured the country doling out privileges and benefits to members of the regional elite in a blatant bid to buy votes. In Russia's presidential elections, if no candidate wins a majority of the votes in the first round the two highest-scoring candidates go on to compete in a second round. In the end, Yeltsin's generous distribution of the state's assets and his manipulation of the state media paid dividends, and he won the elections against all the odds in a second round run-off against the Communist Party leader, Gennady Zyuganov.

However, Yeltsin had been seriously ill with heart problems for much of his tenure in office, and he was finally forced to resign on New Year's Eve 1999. Under the constitution, when a president resigns the prime minister becomes acting president and elections must take place within three months. Thus, the presidential elections that were originally scheduled for June 2000 were brought forward to March 2000. Vladimir Putin, whom Yeltsin had appointed prime minister in August 1999, became the acting president. Yeltsin believed that Putin would be strong enough to protect him and his family from criminal investigations once he retired from office. As expected, soon after coming to power, Putin issued a decree guaranteeing Yeltsin and his family immunity from prosecution.

Biography 2.22

Vladimir Vladimirovich Putin (1952–)

Vladimir Putin was born in Leningrad (now named St Petersburg). After graduating with a degree in law from Leningrad State University in 1975, Putin spent 15 years working for the security services (KGB), predominantly in Dresden, East Germany. In 1991, after a short spell working as an assistant to the rector of Leningrad State University, Putin left the KGB to work for one of his former university teachers, Anatoly Sobchak, then mayor of Leningrad.

Under Sobchak, Putin rose to become the chairman of the city's foreign affairs committee, and by 1994 the first deputy mayor. Putin's primary role at this time was to attract foreign economic investment to the city and to oversee the implementation of Sobchak's privatisation programme.

After Sobchak's defeat in the mayoral elections of 1996, Putin was posted to Moscow to work in the Russian Presidential Administration. In March 1997, he was elevated to the post of deputy head of the Presidential Administration, and one year later he was appointed first deputy head.

In July 1998, Putin left his work in the presidency when he was appointed director of the Federal Security Service (FSB), the successor to the KGB. Yeltsin's trust in Putin was further demonstrated when in March 1999 he was appointed secretary of the Presidential Security Council. In August 1999, Putin was appointed prime minister, and in March 2000 he was elected Russian president at the age of 47.

Putin's first presidential campaign of 2000

During the 2000 presidential campaign Putin, like Yeltsin before him, made good use of the administrative resources of the state and his control over the broadcast media. Approximately half of all the television coverage of the elections was devoted to Putin. At times, the coverage was downright sycophantic. Thus, for example, during one television broadcast, a trade union official declared: 'All the Vladimirs that Russia has ever had have been great, from Saint Vladimir to Vladimir Lenin. But being Vladimir Vladimirovich, you are twice that great' (Wyman 2001: 64). Antisemitic and homophobic smear tactics were also used to try to discredit the campaign of Grigory Yavlinsky, the head of the centre-left party Yabloko. The campaign was also marred by corruption. Thus, there were serious cases of electoral manipulation in favour of Putin in Dagestan, where the local electoral commission simply manufactured the results, and in many other regions there were claims that 'stuffing of ballot boxes took place on a significant scale'.

Not surprisingly, Putin was able to win the presidency in the first round of elections with 53 percent of the vote. Communist Party leader Zyuganov was some way behind with 29 percent, followed by Yavlinsky (Yabloko) with 6 percent and Zhirinovsky (LDPR) with 3 percent (see Table 2.14). Putin's popularity had been strengthened by his decision to send troops back into Chechnya in 1999, and he was perceived by a majority of Russian citizens as strong, disciplined, and in sharp contrast to Yeltsin, untarnished by corruption.

Table 2.14 Russian presidential election of 26 March 2000

Candidate	Party	% of votes achieved
Putin, V.V.	Independent	52.9
Zyuganov, G.A.	CPRF (communist)	29.2
Yavlinsky, G.A.	Yabloko (social democratic)	5.8
Tuleev, A.M.	Independent	2.9
Zhirinovsky, V.V.	LDPR (extreme right)	2.7
Titov, K.A	Independent	1.5
Pamfilova, E.A	Independent	1.0
Govorukhin, S.S.	Independent	0.4
Skuratov, Yu.I.	Independent	0.4
Podberezky, A.I.	Independent	0.1
Dzhabrailov, U.A.	Independent	0.1
Votes Against All		1.9

(Source: http://www.russiavotes.org.)

The parliamentary and presidential elections of 2003–04

Of the 32 parties that submitted the relevant information to the Central Electoral Commission, 23 were permitted to take part in the December 2003 Duma elections. However, Putin was not content with just one 'party of power' (United Russia) entering the contest on his behalf. For these elections, the president sought the back-up of a number of 'reserve parties'. Thus, no fewer than four other parties closely associated with the president were registered:

1. the People's Party, a left-wing and nationalist group, headed by Gennady Raikov;
2. the Party of Life, chaired by the speaker of the Federation Council, Sergey Mironov;
3. the Party of Russian Resurrection, led by the Duma's speaker Gennadi Seleznev;

Table 2.15 Elections to State Duma, 7 December 2003 (turnout 55.6 percent)

Parties	% List vote	List seats	SMD seats	% Total seats
United Russia	37.57	120	102	49.3
Communist Party	12.61	40	12	11.6
Liberal Democrats	11.45	36	0	8.0
Motherland	9.02	29	8	8.2
People's Party	1.18	0	17	3.8
Yabloko	4.30	0	4	0.9
Union of Right Forces	3.97	0	3	0.7
Agrarian Party	3.64	0	2	0.4
Other parties	11.56	0	6	1.3
Independents	–	–	68	15.1
Against all	4.70	–	3*	0.7

* Repeat ballots held in three districts where the number of votes 'against all' exceeded votes for any single candidate.

(Source: http://www.russiavotes.org.)

4. Motherland–People's Patriotic Union (hereafter, Motherland) headed by Sergey Glaziev, a former leading member of the CPRF, and Dmitry Rogozin, chairman of the Duma Foreign Relations Committee. This latter party was set up specifically to attract the votes of the communist electorate (Michaleva 2003: 9).

Only four of the 23 parties crossed the 5 percent threshold (see Table 2.15). United Russia scored a landslide victory with 38 percent of the party list votes, and a total of 222 list and single-member district (SMD) seats. The CPRF suffered a humiliating defeat, with its share of the party list vote at 13 percent, almost half of that which it received in 1999. Overall, the CPRF won 52 seats in the parliament, a substantial drop from the 113 seats it won in 1999. The LDPR's 11 percent was almost double that of 1999, and its numbers rose from 17 to 36. Motherland came a surprising fourth with 9 percent and a total of 37 seats.

Perhaps the greatest tragedy for the future of parliamentary democracy in Russia was the failure of the two democratic opposition parties, Yabloko and the Union of Right Forces (SPS), to clear the 5 percent threshold. Yabloko won 4.3 percent and SPS 4.0 percent of the party list votes. In the SMD races, Yabloko won four seats and the SPS three. Remarkably, more citizens (4.7 percent or 2.85 million) chose to vote 'against all candidates' than for either Yabloko or SPS (see Table 2.15).

Once again, as in previous elections, a large group of independents (68 individuals) entered the parliament in the SMD races, and a large number of these later joined the United Russia faction in the Duma, as did members of other parties. Thus, United Russia by mid-2004 was able to command a constitutional majority of 306 seats. Among the defectors to United Russia were all three SPS deputies and one of Yabloko's four deputies (Hale 2004: 3–4).

The 2003 Duma campaign

The 2003 Duma elections were anything but free and fair. Thus, according to a report from the Organisation for Security and Cooperation in Europe (OSCE) election monitors, 'the extensive use of the state *apparat* and media favouritism to the benefit of United Russia' created 'an unfair environment for other parties and candidates' (OSCE 2003: 1–2). According to the report, there were also 'instances of police obstruction to campaigning and pressure on voters including intimidation'. For example, the police arrested campaign activists and impounded campaign materials in Moscow Region, Volgograd, Vladivostok and Bashkortostan.

Furthermore, regional leaders 'were required not only to deliver the vote for United Russia but to deliver voter turnout itself' (Michaleva 2003: 10). Thus, for example, during 'Soviet style agitprop door to door campaigning in Chuvashia, there were threats of sanctions if people did not come out to vote and vote in the proper way'. There were also cases of outright corruption. In Bashkortostan, tens of thousands of forged ballot papers were discovered that had been partially destroyed just days before the election (OSCE 2003: 5). Research carried out by Yabloko and SPS indicate that in 20 percent of cases, data on turnout from local election commissions do not tally with official data from the Central Electoral Commission. New information obtained by the CPRF in fact shows 'that *Yabloko* should have received 5.09 percent and SPS 4.52 percent of the vote' (Michaleva 2003: 10).

Media bias in favour of United Russia was also widespread. Thus, for example, the OSCE reports that, in their coverage, the state-owned TV channels exhibited clear bias in favour of United Russia and against the CPRF. There were also reports of regional administrative interference in the work of local media. For example, in Bashkortostan, the privately owned radio station 'Bulgar' was broken into and its antenna cut down (OSCE 2003: 6).

The campaign was also marred by a restrictive media law, which had been adopted in July 2002 with the aim of curbing negative campaigning. But some articles of the law were very vaguely worded and thus open to selective interpretation by the authorities. According to the provisions of the law, 'every party was to receive an equal amount of coverage; mass media sources were not permitted to take sides in their editorials and commentators were forbidden to express any opinions that could encourage support for one of the parties' (Nikonov 2003: 8). Any newspaper or television channel that infringed these rules could be closed down. As a result, until the repeal of the law in October 2003, the media engaged in an orgy of self-censorship, significantly reducing the amount of election coverage.

After United Russia's comprehensive victory in the December 2003 elections and the humiliating defeat of the CPRF, Yabloko and SPS, it was clear to everyone that the presidential elections would be a foregone conclusion and that no one stood a chance of defeating Putin. The hopelessness of the situation was graphically illustrated when the CPRF nominated the lacklustre Nikolai Kharitonov in place of party leader Zyuganov. Likewise, LDPR leader Zhirinovsky showed his contempt for the elections by nominating his bodyguard, Oleg Malyshkin. Yabloko and SPS, still reeling after their failure to win any party list seats in the Duma, declined to offer any candidates, although Irina Khakamada, one of the leaders of SPS, stood as an independent. Sergey Mironov, head of the pro-Putin Russian Party of Life, declared from the outset that he was entering the election to support Putin!

Sergey Glaziev, the former co-leader of Motherland, was considered the main challenger to Putin, but he now stood as an independent after an acrimonious split with his former coalition partner Dmitry Rogozin. Once again, Putin chose to run as a self-nominated candidate rather than as a representative of United Russia.

There were two ways of registering for the presidential elections. First, candidates nominated by parties that won party list seats in December 2003 were automatically registered. Second, self-nominated independent candidates, and those from parties that failed to win party list seats, were required to collect two million signatures by a deadline of 28 January, with no more than 50,000 of the signatures coming from any one region. Only candidates with access to substantial financial and/or administrative resources had any chance of fulfilling such stringent requirements (Michaleva 2004: 10).

Of the six individuals who finally registered for the elections (see Table 2.16), Putin, Glaziev and Khakamada stood as independents and thus had to collect the required signatures. Mironov also had to collect the signatures as his party (Russian Party of Life) did not cross the 5 percent threshold in the 2003 Duma elections. Kharitonov (CPRF) and Malyshkin (LDPR) gained automatic registration. As expected, Putin easily won the election in the first round, reaping 71 percent of the votes. Kharitonov came a distant second with 14 percent, a large fall from the 29 percent that the communists won in 2000. All of the remaining candidates won less than 5 percent of the votes.

Table 2.16 Russian presidential election of 14 March 2004 (turnout 64.3 percent)

Candidate	Party	% of votes achieved
Vladimir Putin	Independent	71.3
Nikolai Kharitonov	CPRF (Communist)	13.7
Sergey Glaziev	Independent	4.1
Irina Khakamada	Independent	3.8
Oleg Malyshkin	LDPR (extreme right)	2.0
Sergei Mironov	Russian Party of Life	0.7
Against all		3.4

(Source: http://www.russiavotes.org.)

The 2004 presidential campaign

Once again, there is strong evidence to suggest that the elections were marred by corruption and media bias. This time, Putin did not even try to conceal the blatant use of 'administrative resources' to support his campaign. State finances were used to gather the two million signatures required for Putin's registration. Once again, an OSCE report into the elections found clear evidence of media bias in favour of Putin, and it also gave a negative assessment of the count in one-quarter of the polling stations that were visited by its observers (OSCE 2004: 2). Sergey Glaziev and Irina Khakamada also made numerous complaints about local-level obstruction of their campaigns, citing numerous instances when the electricity supply was mysteriously cut off just as they were about to address the public.

With the results of the election a foregone conclusion, the main worry of the Putin camp was over the size of the turnout. In order for a presidential election to be declared valid, 50 percent of the electorate must turn out and vote. In light of the farcical nature of the election, Yabloko and Committee 2000 (a new alliance of liberal groups headed by chess player Gary Kasparov) called upon the public not to participate in the elections. However, the demands of these groups only led to higher levels of 'administrative pressure' on citizens to turn out to vote. Thus, for example, in St Petersburg a district housing administrator sent a letter to all his local managers instructing them to ensure a 70 percent turnout. In Khabarovsk, a hospital director demanded that before anyone could be admitted to hospital they would have to produce an absentee voting certificate (OSCE 2004).

The Putin presidency and the future of democracy

In his first speech as acting president, Putin was adamant that there would be 'no backsliding on any of the key political liberties gained in the past decade' and that, 'freedom of speech, freedom of conscience, freedom of the press, the right to private property – these basic principles of a civilised society will be protected' (Danks 2001: 326–7). In his address to the Federal Assembly in May 2004, Putin stated that the primary goal of his administration was 'to bring about a noticeable rise in our people's prosperity', and he also declared that he wanted to see the development of 'a mature democracy and a developed civil society' (Putin 2004: 1). However, the actual record of his regime puts these pronouncements in doubt. For many observers, Putin is recreating all the trappings of a fully fledged authoritarian state.

Throughout his presidency, Putin has sought to eliminate or emasculate alternative sources of political power. He has attacked or arrested oligarchs with political ambitions (Berezovsky, Gusinsky, Khodorkovsky), raising serious concerns about the independence of the judiciary. He has seized control of all national television networks and stifled the independence of the media. He has weakened the power of the Federation Council and 'tamed regional barons who once served as a powerful balance to former Boris Yeltsin's presidential rule' (McFaul 2003: 2).

As we have seen, Putin's control over the Duma is almost total. United Russia now commands a constitutional majority and the speaker and the two first deputy speakers are party members, as are all 29 chairmen of the Duma's standing committees. So weak is the parliament that it is now cynically referred to in some quarters as Putin's 'Ministry of Legislation'. As if this were not enough, plans are now under way in the Kremlin to raise the threshold for party list seats from 5 to 10 percent and to abolish the single-member seats altogether. By this method, Putin hopes to reduce the number of parties in the Duma to just two – United Russia and another bogus 'party of power' to be created before the next elections in 2007. There is also speculation that Putin will use his constitutional majority in the Duma to make amendments to the constitution that will allow him to stand for a third and perhaps even a fourth term of office.

A dictatorship of law

Shortly after assuming the presidency on 7 May 2000, Putin delivered a television address to the nation that called for a 'dictatorship of law'. For Putin, 'all policies both foreign and domestic must promote Russia's interests and strengthen the Russian state. … Human rights and democratic freedoms are of secondary importance to the maintenance of the Russian state' (Danks 2001: 328). Under Putin, we have also seen the worrying trend of the militarisation of politics, with over a quarter of the members of the national and regional elites coming from the military and security agencies (Kryshtanovskaya and White 2003: 294).

Putin has also carried out sweeping reforms of Russia's federal system, giving himself the right to dismiss popularly elected regional assemblies and regional governors from office and carving the country into seven super-federal districts, each headed by a personally appointed presidential representative. As we noted above, Putin has also fundamentally reshaped the composition of the upper chamber, reducing its status and its ability to act as an effective counterweight to the executive.

Civil society and freedom of speech

Putin has also launched an attack on Russia's inchoate and weak civil society. In his address to the Federal Assembly on 26 May 2004, he singled out non-governmental organisations (NGOs) for special criticism, accusing them of serving 'dubious group and commercial interests' and foreign masters. As the head of the human rights group Memorial, Arseny Roginsky, stated: 'The government has already taken under control the mass media, parliament and many other independent structures, and this is a step to attack our independence and a desire to take us under control'. For many activists, Putin's attack on the NGOs marked 'the beginning of a new campaign to punish groups that do not adhere to the government's line' (Glasser 2004).

Putin's idea of freedom of speech seems to be that which existed in the USSR – you are free to speak as long as you do not challenge the state. 'Putin's use of the term traitors to describe not just Chechen rebels but also journalists and environmentalists, implies a concept of patriotism that does not sit well with democratic pluralism and the rule of law' (Danks 2001: 328). According to what is thought to be a leaked document from the Presidential Administration, the opposition media should be driven to financial crisis, their licences and certificates withdrawn and conditions created where the work of every single opposition medium is either controllable or impossible.

Another worrying development is the widespread practice of media self-censorship, with editors of newspapers and television programmes too scared to publish criticism of the regime for fear that if they do Putin will use the tax police or the FSB to close them down. The number of journalists who have been murdered also continues to rise year by year.

'Russia's deviations from acceptable standards of democratic behaviour can no longer be attributed to the birth pains of a new democratic society. Rather it has become clear that the infant political system that was born ten years ago was congenitally deformed' (Rutland 2003: 9). After a decade of economic and political turmoil, Putin has undoubtedly brought much-needed economic and political stability to Russia's transition-weary citizens, but this stability has been achieved at a very high cost – at the sacrifice of democracy.

Further reading

There are many useful articles. However, in the following list, we concentrate on the most recent reasonably accessible books.

Bowker, M. and Ross, C. (eds) (1999) *Russia After the Cold War*, Longman, Harlow.

Danks, C. (2001) *Russian Politics and Society*, Longman, Harlow.

Goldman, M.I. (2003) *The Piratisation of Russia: Russia Reform Goes Awry*, Routledge, London.

Lane, D. (ed.) (1995) *Russia in Transition: Politics, Privatisation and Inequality*, Longman, Harlow.

Remmington, T. (1999, *Politics in Russia*, Longman, Harlow.

Ross, C. (2002) *Federalism and Democratisation in Russia*, Manchester University Press, Manchester.

Ross, C. (ed.) (2004) *Russian Politics Under Putin*, Manchester University Press, Manchester.

Rutland, P. (1994) 'The economy: the rocky road from plan to market' in S. White, A. Pravda and Z. Gitelman (eds), *Developments in Russian and Post-Soviet Politics*, Macmillan, London.

Sakwa, R. (2002) *Russian Politics and Society*, 3rd edn, Routledge, London (2nd edn is also useful).

White, S. (2000) *Russia's New Politics: The Management of a Postcommunist Society*, Cambridge University Press, Cambridge.

Section 2.6

Political and economic transitions in Eastern Europe

In this section, while our primary focus is on post-communist Poland and Romania, we also provide a more general survey of economic and political developments in Bulgaria, the Czech Republic, Hungary and Slovakia.

Government 2.14

Government in Poland

Poland is a republic. The president is directly elected for five years. The parliament has two chambers. The Sjem has 460 members, elected for a four-year term by proportional representation in multi-seat constituencies, with a threshold (5 percent generally, 8 percent for coalitions). The Senate has 100 members elected for a four-year term in multi-seat constituencies.

(Source: http://www.electionworld.org.)

Government 2.15

Government in Romania

Romania is a republic. The president is directly elected for four years. The parliament has two chambers. The Chamber of Deputies has 332 members, elected for a four-year term, 314 by proportional representation and 18 representing ethnic minorities. The Senate has 143 members, elected for a four-year term by proportional representation.

(Source: http://www.electionworld.org.)

Before the Second World War, this part of the world was usually divided by scholars into two distinct regions: Central Europe and the Balkans. Central Europe included Czechoslovakia, Hungary and Poland, while the Balkan states comprised Albania, Bulgaria, Romania and Yugoslavia. Each of these regions fell under the power of one or more of four 'great empires', the Habsburg, Ottoman, Prussian and Russian, before the First World War. Thus, for example, Central Europe was dominated by the Habsburg, Prussian and Russian empires, while the Balkans came primarily under the control of the Ottoman Empire. Each of these empires had a major impact on the domestic politics and economies of the states they ruled. The Ottomans imposed one of the most authoritarian systems, and the Balkan states were also more economically backward than those in Central Europe.

After gaining their independence with the collapse of the great empires in the First World War, the newly emergent states of Eastern Europe were soon captured by right-wing authoritarian dictatorships (Czechoslovakia was the only exception here) before succumbing to communism and Soviet hegemony following the Second World War. It was only with the imposition of communist rule during the Second World War that the region became known as Eastern (or Central and Eastern) Europe, which is a political definition rather than a geographical one. Thus, for example, Austria was considered part of Western Europe, even though its capital, Vienna, is situated to the east of the Czechoslovak capital, Prague.

While initially there was strong popular support for communist parties in some of these war-ravaged states (e.g. Czechoslovakia and Yugoslavia), communist parties were extremely weak in others (e.g. Poland and Romania), and communism there was primarily imposed by 'the barrel of the gun' as the Soviet army swept into the region during the Second World War. By the end of the 1940s, there were eight communist states in Eastern Europe: Albania, Bulgaria, Czechoslovakia, the German Democratic Republic, Hungary, Poland, Romania and Yugoslavia.

Under the dual processes of what Gati refers to as 'satellisation' and 'sovietisation', the states of Eastern Europe were 'closely integrated, politically, economically, and militarily' with the Soviet Union (Gati 1990: 9), and they became increasingly cut off from the rest of Europe, hidden behind what Churchill referred to as an 'iron curtain'. Six of the eight communist states were full members of the Soviet military alliance, the Warsaw Pact; the Soviet trading organisation, the Council for Mutual Economic Assistance (CMEA); and the Soviet transnational political organisation, the Communist Information Bureau (Cominform). The exceptions were Yugoslavia, which left the bloc in 1948–49, and Albania, which left the Warsaw Pact in 1961. The Soviet Union also attempted to impose political and economic blueprints that replicated its own domestic structures on each of these countries.

By the mid-1950s, there were four basic distinguishing features of communist states in Eastern Europe:

1. They all based themselves upon an official ideology of Marxism–Leninism.

2. They were all ruled by a single or at least a dominant communist party, within which power was typically highly centralised.

3. The economy in the communist states was largely or almost entirely under public rather than private ownership, and production was organised through a central planning apparatus and conducted by means of national economic plans.

4. The range of institutions that in Western societies are more or less independent of the political authorities (e.g. the press, trade unions, churches, courts) in communist states were effectively under the direct control of the party hierarchy (White *et al.* 1987: 3–4).

However, if we examine these states more closely, we discover that communism in fact took on markedly different forms across the region. There were, in practice, major variations in the degree of control that the Soviet Union was able to exercise over members of the bloc, and there were also important differences in their economic and political systems. Thus, for example, Albania, Romania and Yugoslavia were able to carve out significant degrees of autonomy in their foreign policies. Hungary and Yugoslavia were able to experiment with differing forms of economic decentralisation, and in Poland and Yugoslavia agriculture remained largely in private hands. Moreover, in Poland the Catholic Church was able to continue to function relatively free from state control, and civil society was more extensive there than in any other country in the bloc.

Sovietisation and satellitisation weakened the legitimacy of the communist governments in the region, and it was not long before there were a number of mass uprisings against Soviet hegemony. Thus, for example, in the German Democratic Republic (GDR) in 1953 and in Hungary in 1956 the Soviet army intervened to crush mass uprisings. In Poland, where regime legitimacy was especially low, there was a series of mass protests against the government in 1956, 1968, 1971, 1976 and 1980–81, all of which were violently suppressed. In 1981, the Polish government imposed martial law in order to forestall a Soviet invasion after the opposition movement, Solidarity, threatened to bring down the regime. This was in sharp contrast to the situation in the GDR (after 1953) and in the Balkans, where neo-Stalinist totalitarian systems were in operation and where civil society was weak or non-existent. In these countries, and in Czechoslovakia after the Soviet invasion of 1968, there were no such mass revolts.

In 1968, the Soviet Union adopted the Brezhnev Doctrine (named after the then Soviet leader, Leonid Brezhnev), which declared that each communist party was responsible not only to its own people but also to all socialist countries and to the entire communist movement. Through this doctrine, the Soviet Union claimed the right to intervene in any communist country that it considered threatened the interests of the communist bloc. It was only after Gorbachev came to power in 1985 that the Brezhnev Doctrine was finally brought to an end. Gorbachev realised that if he wanted to reform the Soviet system, he would have to gain the support of reformers in Eastern Europe.

Gorbachev also repeatedly made it clear that the Brezhnev Doctrine was dead and that the Soviet Union would no longer intervene in the internal affairs of these states. On a visit to Prague in 1987, Gorbachev stated: 'No one has the right to claim a special position in the socialist world. The independence of each party, its responsibility to its people, the right to resolve questions of a country's development in a sovereign way – for us these are indisputable principles' (Mason 1996: 49). This statement was widely interpreted as giving a green light to reformers in countries such as Hungary and Poland to press ahead with radical economic and political reforms, and it was also seen as a major blow against the hard-line regimes of Bulgaria, Czechoslovakia, the GDR and Romania, whose leaders were doing everything they could to block reforms. But Gorbachev's attempts to save some kind of reformed socialism failed, and his repudiation of the Brezhnev Doctrine was one of the key catalysts of the 1989 revolutions in Eastern Europe.

In the aftermath of the revolutions, the GDR was reunited with West Germany in October 1990, and Czechoslovakia split into separate Czech and Slovak republics in January 1993. Yugoslavia eventually disintegrated into five separate states, torn apart by ethnic and religious conflicts and a bloody civil war. The 1989 revolutions also played a major role in bringing about the collapse of the Soviet Union itself in 1991.

In addition to Gorbachev's repudiation of the Brezhnev Doctrine, economic decline and the erosion of communist ideology were key reasons for the 1989 revolutions and the collapse of communism. In Eastern Europe, 'economic performance came to play a peculiar role as a form of substitute politics: the people were offered high levels of consumption and welfare in exchange, as it were for the lack of political freedoms' (Batt 1993: 205). But when the economy collapsed so did support for the communist regimes, whose leaders could no longer buy legitimacy. As Table 2.17 shows, average annual rates of growth declined rapidly over the period 1951–88, with economic growth in the Soviet trading bloc (CMEA) dropping from 10.8 percent (1951–55) to just 3 percent (1986–88).

Moreover, as economic growth plummeted there was a massive increase in hard currency debts, which reached $88 billion by the end of 1990 (see Table 2.18). All

Table 2.17 Average annual rates of growth in Central and Eastern European countries, 1951–88 (percentages)

	1951–55	1955–60	1961–65	1966–70	1971–75	1976–80	1981–85	1986–88
Bulgaria	12.2	9.7	6.7	8.8	7.8	6.1	3.7	5.6
Hungary	5.7	5.9	4.1	6.8	6.3	2.8	1.3	1.7
GDR	13.1	7.1	3.5	5.2	5.4	4.1	4.5	3.5
Poland	8.6	6.6	6.2	6.0	9.8	1.2	–0.8	3.9
Romania	14.1	6.6	9.1	7.7	11.4	7.0	4.4	5.1
Czechoslovakia	8.2	7.0	1.9	7.0	5.5	3.7	1.7	2.4
CMEA	10.8	8.5	6.0	7.4	6.4	4.1	3.0	3.0

(Source: White 1993: 8.)

Table 2.18 Hard currency debt of Eastern European countries

	Net debt at end of 1990 ($ billion)
Poland	41
Yugoslavia	9
Romania	1
Czechoslovakia	6
Hungary	20
Bulgaria	11
Total	88

(Source: Mason 1996: 129.)

of the Eastern bloc countries with the exception of Romania (which refused to borrow from the West and suffered terrible economic hardship) had to suffer the humiliation of going cap in hand to Western banks to bale out their flagging economies. Poland had the highest debt of $41 billion, followed by Hungary with $20 billion.

With the decline in the economy there was a steady erosion of belief in communist ideology. Faith in communism had also suffered major blows with the Soviet invasions of Hungary and Czechoslovakia. Thus by the time Gorbachev came to power in 1985, the vast majority of citizens in Eastern Europe had long lost faith in communism, and the legitimacy of the ruling communist elites was weak or non-existent.

Revolutions from above and below

In Poland and Hungary, the 1989 revolutions were negotiated 'revolutions from above', that is revolutions carried out by, and initiated from within, the top party elites. In each of these countries, the communist leadership split into reformist and anti-reformist factions. The reformers, often backed by Gorbachev, emerged victorious and entered into round-table talks with the opposition.

In sharp contrast, the collapse of communism in the GDR and Czechoslovakia were primarily revolts initiated from below by the mass of the people, who were able to rise up and oust the communists from power. In Bulgaria and Romania, there was a mixture of revolutions from above and below. In these countries, there were few, or in the case of Romania, no opposition groups with which the leadership could engage, and in any case their rulers made it clear that they were not interested in pursuing reforms. Here, 'palace coups' orchestrated from within the top party echelons ousted the party leaders from power at the same time as there were mass uprisings on the streets. In the case of Romania, which was ruled by one of the most oppressive leaders in the bloc, Nicolae Ceauşescu, the revolution was very violent. The revolution eventually came to a bloody end with the execution of Ceauşescu and his wife on Christmas Day 1989.

Nicolae Ceauşescu (1918–89)

Nicolae Ceauşescu was born in Romania to a poor peasant family. He joined the illegal communist party in 1933 and became a leading activist in its youth movement. He was arrested and imprisoned numerous times both before and during the Second World War. In 1945, he was elected a candidate member of the Central Committee and secretary of the Union of Communist Youth. From 1948 to 1950 he was a member of the new communist government, where he held the post of deputy minister of agriculture. In 1953, he was promoted to the post of first deputy minister of the armed forces. In 1955, he became a full member of the Politburo and two years later he was appointed Central Committee secretary in charge of party organisation and cadres. In 1965, on the death of party leader Gheorghiu-Dej, Ceauşescu was

▶

appointed general secretary of the Romanian Communist Party, and in 1969 he was also appointed Romanian president. In the aftermath of the 1989 Romanian revolution, Ceauşescu and his wife (who was also a member of the Politburo and a government minister) were captured trying to flee the country. After a rather perfunctory trial, both Ceauşescu and his wife were sentenced to death, and they were executed on 25 December 1989.

The Eastern European transitions

In comparison with other transitions from authoritarianism in Latin America and Southern Europe, which involved a reform of the polity, the transitions in Eastern Europe necessitated a triple transformation of the polity, economy and foreign policy. Moreover, 'the reformers in Spain and Portugal in the 1970s and 1980s had the luxury of first shedding dictatorships and then tackling critical economic reforms' (Nagle and Mahr 1999: 100). In contrast, the post-communist countries of Eastern Europe were not able to consolidate their democracies before having to embark on radical economic reforms. In Eastern Europe, there was a real possibility that citizens undergoing the shock of economic transition would also reject democracy.

The ways in which the revolutions took place have also had an important impact on post-communist democratic transitions. In those countries where we have witnessed the clearest examples of 'revolutions from below' (e.g. Czechoslovakia and the GDR), we have also seen the most rapid economic and political transitions and the fastest turnover of communist political elites. In these countries, the communists had little or no say over the shape of the post-communist political and constitutional order. By contrast, in regimes where there were negotiated revolutions (Hungary and Poland), and mixtures of the two (Bulgaria and Romania), the pace of change has been much slower, and *nomenklatura* continuity has been far greater. Here, the communist parties were able to exert an important influence over the development of these regimes in the post-communist period, slowing the pace of economic and political reforms.

Thus, for example, in Poland's 'pacted revolution', the Communist Party was able to negotiate the election rules for the June 1989 parliamentary elections so as to limit the number of seats that Solidarity, the main opposition group, would be free to contest. Solidarity was permitted to compete in only 161 (35 percent) of the 460 seats in the lower chamber of the parliament (the Sejm). Nonetheless, Solidarity was able to snatch victory with the support of two other communist 'satellite parties', which jumped ship and sided with the opposition. However, Solidarity, in accordance with the terms of its pact, was forced to rule in coalition with the communists, and it was over two years before totally free and fair elections were eventually held in Poland in October 1991. Moreover, the round-table talks had also agreed that only the communist incumbent head of state, President Jaruzelski, would be allowed to stand as the single candidate in the presidential elections of July 1989. Jaruzelksi was subsequently elected president by members of both houses of the parliament. Solidarity leader Lech Walesa had to wait until

Lech Walesa (1943–)

Lech Walesa was born in Popowo, Poland. He trained as an electrician and worked as a car mechanic at a machine centre from 1961 to 1965. He served in the army for two years, rose to the rank of corporal, and in 1967 was employed in the Lenin shipyard in Gdansk as an electrician. In 1970, he was one of the leaders of the strike movement at the shipyard and for the next decade he played a leading role in creating an independent trade union movement. In 1976, he was fired from his post as shop steward and had to take on temporary jobs. In August 1980, he led the Gdansk shipyard strike and in September 1981 he was elected chairman of 'Solidarity', the first independent trade union in the Soviet bloc. In January 1981, Walesa, who is a devout Catholic, was received by Pope John Paul II in Rome. After the Polish government declared martial law in December 1981, Walesa was arrested and spent a year in jail before returning to his job at the Gdansk shipyards in 1982. In 1983, he was awarded the Nobel Peace Prize. In 1990, he became the first democratically elected president of Poland, a post he held until November 1995, when he was defeated in the presidential elections by Aleksandr Kwasniewski.

November 1990 before he was able to compete and win Poland's first free and fair presidential elections (see Millard 2003a).

In Romania, the revolution was hijacked by an anti-Ceauşescu clique in the Communist Party, which created a new political movement, the National Salvation Front (NSF). Under the leadership of Ion Iliescu, a former high-ranking communist leader in the Ceauşescu administration, the NSF went on to win the first two parliamentary and presidential elections in 1990 and 1992. It took until 1996 before there was any change of regime and political and economic reforms were begun in earnest. Moreover, the parliamentary victory of the Democratic Convention and the capture of the presidency by its leader, Emil Constantinescu, in 1996 proved to be short-lived. In the next round of elections in 2000, Iliescu won back the presidency, and the NSF returned to power under a new name and as part of a new coalition, the Democratic Social Pole.

Let us now turn to an examination of economic and political reforms in our six case studies, with a primary focus on Poland and Romania.

Ion Iliescu (1930–)

Ion Iliescu was born in March 1930 in Oltenita, Romania. He graduated with a degree in electrical engineering from Bucharest University and then was a foreign student at Moscow University. He joined the Union of Communist Youth in 1944 and was appointed secretary of the Central Committee of Communist Youth in 1956 and a member of the Central Committee of the Romanian Communist Party in 1965. He was a minister of youth affairs in 1967. In the early 1970s, Iliescu fell out of favour with Ceauşescu and he was demoted by Ceauşescu to the posts of party secretary in the cities of Timisoara (in 1971), and Iasi (in 1974). Between 1984 and 1989, he was director of the Technical Publishing House. After the 1989 revolution in Romania, Iliescu, as leader of the National Salvation Front, was elected president of Romania in the first post-communist elections (May 1990). In 1992, he won a second term in office before losing the 1996 presidential elections to Emil Constantinescu. However, Iliescu was able to return to power for a third time after winning the December 2000 presidential elections.

Economic reforms: from plan to market

All of the states faced the monumental task of transforming their state-planned economies into functioning market economies. Thus, they had to move from one price system – the distorted price system that prevailed under communism – to a market price system; they had to create markets and the institutional infrastructure that underlies them; and they had to privatise all the property that previously had belonged to the state (Stiglitz, 2002: 140). However, as Rutland notes: 'there were no blueprints or models explaining how to build capitalism out of the ruins of a centrally planned economy' (1994: 150). The problem was how to minimise the inevitable pain that would accompany the economic transition. Here, there were two fundamentally opposed philosophies, 'gradualism' and 'shock therapy'.

Key concept 2.4

Transition to the market system – gradualist or 'shock therapy'?

In the gradualist approach, economic reforms were to be introduced slowly over a period of between eight and ten years. The pain would be prolonged but not as painful as under 'shock therapy', and the welfare of the poorest members of society would be protected. In sharp contrast, under 'shock therapy', economic reform was to be rapid, and price liberalisation, privatisation and stabilisation policies were all to be implemented within a matter of just a few years.

The Czech Republic and Poland were the most vociferous supporters of 'shock therapy', while Hungary and Slovakia were early champions of gradualism. Indeed, the different approaches of the Czechs and Slovaks with regard to economic strategy was one of the factors that led to their split in 1993. Romania adopted radical reforms only in late 1996 after the election to power of the Democratic Convention.

However, in practice, no country fully limited itself to either of these competing models. The reality has been the adoption of a mixture of 'shock therapy' and 'gradualism' in all countries. Thus, for example, Poland chose to slow the pace of its economic reforms with the return of ex-communists (the Democratic Left Alliance) to power in 1993. Hungary, which adopted the gradualist path, slowed its economic reforms even further when its ex-communists returned to power in 1994. However, this new leftist coalition government was forced to adopt its own economic shock programme in 1995 in order to reduce a massive budget deficit inherited from the communist era. Romania pursued a gradualist path until 1996, and even with the return of Iliescu to power in 2000, the new leftist government was forced by international financial bodies to increase the pace of economic reforms. Indeed, all six of the countries studied in this section have at one time or another come under pressure from the IBRD and the IMF, which made it clear that loans would not be forthcoming unless specific economic policies were adopted. The EU's European Council has also exercised considerable leverage over the domestic policies of countries seeking EU membership (see discussion of Copenhagen criteria below).

The impact of economic reforms

The impact of economic reform was sudden and catastrophic. A sharp drop in GDP was accompanied by a sharp fall in the standard of living, high levels of unemployment and hyperinflation throughout the region. It was 1996 before this downward spiral began to be reversed and we witnessed the start of an economic recovery.

A universal feature of the economic reforms was a massive collapse in production. It took Poland until 1996 to regain its 1989 levels of GDP, and this was the fastest recovery in the region. Hungary and Slovakia reached this target only in 2000, and the Czech Republic in 2001. As Table 2.19 shows, GDP in Bulgaria and Romania in 2001 was still well below that of 1989.

Table 2.19 Post-communist economies: output performance (1989–2001)

Country	Output (real GDP) (1989 = 100)						
	1990	1992	1994	1996	1998	2000	2001
Bulgaria	92.9	64.7	63.0	71.3	78.1	80.7	84.2
Czech Republic	98.8	86.9	88.9	98.2	96.3	98.7	102.2
Hungary	96.5	82.4	84.4	86.8	95.1	104.3	108.3
Poland	88.4	84.4	92.1	104.5	117.1	126.7	128.1
Romania	94.4	75.0	79.2	88.2	78.8	79.3	83.5
Slovakia	97.5	77.9	78.7	89.3	98.7	102.8	106.2

(Source: Blazyca 2003: 219.)

Price liberalisation

One of the first tasks of the new governments was to bring an end to state subsidies and to allow the price of goods to be determined by the market. However, price liberalisation led to high levels of inflation, particularly in the early years of the transition, with hyperinflation in Bulgaria, Poland and Romania. It took until the mid-1990s before the rate of inflation began to drop to more manageable levels. Of our six countries (see Table 2.20), Romania has had the consistently highest rates of inflation and the Czech Republic the lowest.

Table 2.20 Post-communist economies: annual rate of inflation (percent)

	1990	1991	1992	1993	1994	1995	1996	1997	1998	2003
Bulgaria	26.0	338.5	91.3	72.9	96.2	62.0	–	–	–	2.3
Czech Republic	–	56.7	11.1	20.8	9.8	9.5	8.7	9.9	12.0	0.2
Hungary	28.9	35.0	23.0	22.5	18.8	28.2	20.0	18.4	14.2	4.9
Poland	586.0	70.3	43.0	35.3	32.2	27.8	18.7	13.2	12.1	0.7
Romania	4.0	223.0	199.0	296.0	62.0	30.0	56.8	151.7	55.3	15.4
Slovakia	–	61.2	10.0	23.2	19.8	9.9	–	–	–	8.5

(Sources: Agh 1998: 54; and the IBRD, Europe and Central Asia Region website http://www.worldbank.org.)

Unemployment

The sharp fall in production led to bankruptcies and a sharp increase in unemployment in all six countries. Thus, for example, over the period 1990–94, the size of the employed labour force fell by 26.1 percent in Hungary, 25.7 percent in Bulgaria, 15.7 percent in Slovakia, 14.9 percent in Poland, 9.6 percent in the Czech Republic and 8.5 percent in Romania (Cox 1998: 223). As Table 2.21 shows, Bulgaria and Slovakia have maintained relatively high levels of unemployment throughout the entire period. The Czech Republic has fared best, but even it showed a steep rise in unemployment, from 5.6 percent in 1998 to 10.0 percent in 2003. Poland, after a short recovery between 1998 and 2000, when unemployment fell below 10 percent for the first time, saw a marked rise to 17.6 percent by 2003. In Hungary, by contrast, there was a sharp rise over the period 1990–92 from 2.5 to 12.3 percent and then a continuous fall to 7.8 percent in 2003. In Romania, where privatisation has been much slower to get off the ground, levels of unemployment have been lower than in Hungary and Poland.

Table 2.21 Post-communist economies: actual unemployment percent, 1990–2003

	1990	1992	1994	1996	1998	2000	2003
Bulgaria	1.5	15.6	12.8	–	–	17.2	13.2
Czech Republic	0.8	2.6	3.2	3.5	5.6	8.4	10.0
Hungary	2.5	12.3	10.4	10.4	9.1	8.6	7.8
Poland	6.1	13.6	16.0	13.2	9.6	14.5	17.6
Romania	–	8.4	10.9	6.3	8.8	10.3	7.2
Slovakia	1.5	11.1	14.8	–	–	16.7	14.2

(Sources: Agh 1998: 56; and the IBRD, Europe and Central Asia Region website, http://ww.worldbank.org.)

Poverty

Rising levels of unemployment and inflation combined with a real cut in wages soon led to a massive increase in the number of citizens living in poverty. According to a 1994 study by the United Nations International Children's Emergency Fund (UNICEF), the economic reforms 'provoked a deterioration of unparalleled proportions in human welfare and a health crisis marked by rising incidences of infectious diseases, stress, malnutrition and alcoholism' (Mason 1996: 139). In Poland, the number of people living in poverty jumped from 25 percent in 1989 to 44 percent in 1992 before gradually falling to 18 percent in 2002. In the late 1990s, poverty increased sharply in Romania, doubling from 20 percent in 1996 to 41 percent in 1999, and it remains very high, with 28 percent still classified as living in poverty in 2002. Hungary, which originally opted for gradualism, has fared much better, with 8.6 percent classified as living below the subsistence level in 2002 (see Freedom House, *Nations in Transit* annual surveys for each country, and www.worldbank.org).

Privatisation

A key feature of the economic reforms has been the privatisation of industry. There have been two principal methods of privatisation: sale to private owners (auctions) and the redistribution of shares to the population, or what is known as voucher privatisation. While mixtures of each of these systems were adopted in each country, Bulgaria, the Czech Republic, Slovakia, Poland and Romania all championed voucher privatisation, while Hungary originally opted for the direct sale of state assets to private owners. The Czech Republic was the leader in the privatisation process, and its programme, which was begun in 1992, was completed in record time by 1995 (Blazyca 2003: 228). Voucher privatisation was attractive, as it promised the added benefit of bolstering support for the regimes by giving everyone a stake in the new capitalist economy. But far from enriching the people, privatisation soon became known as '*nomenklatura* piratisation', as members of the former communist elite (the *nomenklatura*) were able to use their contacts, positions and 'insider knowledge' to enrich themselves at the people's expense.

Let us examine privatisation in our two principal case studies, Poland and Romania.

Privatisation in Poland

In Poland, there was a massive commitment to shock therapy in the early 1990s followed by the return of the left in 1993 and a slowing down of the pace of privatisation until 1997, when a new right-of-centre coalition headed by Solidarity returned to power and pushed the process forward. Transformation of large companies was repeatedly set back, with only a quarter of Poland's 8,000 state-owned enterprises privatised by 1995 (Mason 1996: 132). In 1996, a new law on Commercialisation and Privatisation of State Owned Enterprises gave the green light to various privatisation methods, including voucher and direct sales. As of September 2001, out of 8,441 state-owned enterprises registered in July 1990, 1,494 had been transformed into joint stock companies owned by the treasury, 2,062 had been directly privatised, and 1,737 had been liquidated. By 1999, 61.3 percent of GDP was produced in the private sector, employing 71.4 percent of the labour force, while 92.3 percent of Poland's agriculture (which had remained largely private during the communist period) was in private hands (Freedom House, *Nations in Transit*, Poland 2003: 307–8).

Key fact 2.8

The Polish economy

In 2004, Poland was classified by the IBRD as an 'upper middle-income country', and it had a Gross National Income (GNI) per capita of $4,570 in 2002. After showing strong growth of around 5 percent per annum in the latter half of the 1990s, the economy slowed down with GDP growth falling to just 1 percent in 2001 and 1.4 percent in 2002. However, recovery resumed in 2003, with a predicted GDP growth of 4.7 percent in 2004. Inflation has also been brought under control, falling to 3 percent.

(Source: IBRD, Europe and Central Asia Region; website, http://www.worldbank.org, 2004.)

Privatisation in Romania

Romania started its post-communist transition in much worse economic shape than other Eastern European countries. By the late 1980s, the economy was on the verge of collapse 'after forty years of rigid central planning that had emphasised self reliance, an excessive focus on heavy industry and large, uneconomic infrastructure projects to glorify the Ceauşescu regime' (IBRD, Europe and Central Asia Region website, www.worldbank.org).

Economic reform and particularly large-scale privatisation of industry was continually delayed in the early years of the transition. Nonetheless, by the end of 1995, 55 percent of GDP was produced in the private sector, and a mass voucher privatisation scheme was completed on 31 March 1996. Privatisation was speeded up with the change of government in November 1996, and in 1999 a new privatisation law was adopted to accelerate the process and to create a more robust legal framework. 80 percent of Romania's farmland was privatised by 2000, accounting for 20 percent of GDP. However, as late as 2000 67 percent of industrial output was still being generated in the state sector (Freedom House, *Nations in Transit*, *Romania*, 2001: 307).

Key fact 2.9

The Romanian economy

According to an IBRD report of June 2004, Romania was classified as a lower middle-income country with GNI per capita of $1,850 in 2003. Growth in 2003 was expected to rise to 4.5–5 percent, and inflation fell from 55 percent in 1998 to 15 percent in 2003. The unemployment rate declined from 11.8 percent in 1998 to 7.8 percent in 2003. The prospect of EU accession in 2007 has undoubtedly played a positive role in Romania's recent economic recovery.

(Source: IBRD, Europe and Central Asia Region website, http://www.worldbank.org, 2004: 1.)

Political reforms: problems of democratisation

The collapse of communism created many new challenges for the new coalition governments. They were all faced with the task of 'establishing new multi-party systems; holding competitive elections for the first time in decades; transforming parliaments from puppet theatres in which the communists pulled the strings into working arenas for debate and legislation; and dismantling the pervasive networks of the political police' (Batt 2003: 6).

Political parties and democracy

Political scientists have long argued that strong parties and a stable party system are essential prerequisites for a strong democracy. However, the new parties in Eastern Europe had very shallow roots in society, and 'party identification' was very low. 'Instead of gradually incorporating the traditional cleavages of centre versus periphery, state versus church, and owner versus worker into a party system as in West Europe, East European voters tumbled into a confusing unfocused situation in which the only fixed pole was the old Communist regime, repudiated by most voters' (Roskin 1997: 157). The initial proto-parties that emerged in 1989 and 1990 tended to cover the entire left–right spectrum. Poland's Solidarity, for example, 'comprised some 10 million citizens from all walks of life' (Crawford 1996: 228). Likewise, Hungary's Democratic Forum, Czechoslovakia's Civic Forum and Public Against Violence, Bulgaria's Union of Democratic Forces, and the GDR's New Forum were all extremely broad 'catch-alls', united only in their opposition to the communist regimes. With the normalisation of politics in the post-communist period, these broad catch-alls began to fall apart. Thus, for example, as Crawford notes, Solidarity split into 15 different parliamentary groupings within 18 months of its electoral victory in June 1989.

Electoral systems and democracy

As Table 2.22 shows, all six countries adopted either proportional representation systems (PR) or a mixture of PR and first-past-the-post elections in single-member districts (SMD). In the first flush of political freedom, large numbers of parties and political movements emerged to contest the first post-communist elections. Thus, for example, 74 parties competed in Romania's elections in May 1990, and there were 67 parties in Poland's elections of October 1991. There were fears that with so many parties taking part in the elections the new parliaments would be politically fragmented and would produce weak and unstable coalition governments. Such fears were borne out in Poland's 1991 elections: 29 parties gained representation in the parliament, 11 of which won only one seat. In these elections, the leading party, the Democratic Union, won just 12.3 percent of the vote. Eventually, a seven-party coalition government was formed headed by Jan Olszewski

(Christian Democrat), but the parliament's extreme fragmentation led to the formation of three different unstable coalition governments between 1991 and 1993. Moreover, elections had to be brought forward to October 1993 after the success of a Solidarity vote of no confidence in Prime Minister Hanna Suchocka.

However, all six of our case studies have now adopted electoral thresholds (see Table 2.22) to reduce the number of parties gaining seats in parliament. Thus, for example, after Poland introduced its nationwide threshold of 5 percent for its 1993 elections (8 percent for coalitions) the number of parties represented in the parliament (Sejm) fell dramatically, from 29 to six. As Table 2.23 shows, the number of parties in Eastern European parliaments, five or six, is comparable with Western European assemblies. In addition, the number of 'effective parties' has fallen steadily across the region, dropping in Poland, for example, from 14.7 in 1992 to 2.9 in 1999 (Lewis 2003: 159).

Romania also adopted a new law on political parties in 1996, which had the effect of dramatically reducing the number of registered parties from 250 to 68. The law states that before a political party can register for elections it must have 10,000 members with representatives in at least 15 regions of the country. New higher thresholds of 5 percent for individual parties (8 percent for two-party coalitions, with an extra 1 percent for each coalition partner) were also introduced for the 2000 elections. Of the 68 parties and alliances that entered the 2000 race, only five gained seats in the parliament (Popescu 2003: 326, 329).

Table 2.22 Electoral systems in Central and Eastern Europe

	Type	Threshold (%)
Bulgaria	PR	4
Czech Republic	PR	5
Hungary	PR/SMD	4
Poland	PR	(0 1991 elections), 5% from 1993
Romania	PR	(3 1992 and 1996 elections), 5% from 2000
Slovakia	PR/SMD	5

PR = proportional representation; SMD = single member district.

(Source: Lewis 2000: 88; Roskin 1997: 151.)

Table 2.23 Parties in parliaments in Central and Eastern Europe, 1999

	Number of parties	Number of effective parties
Bulgaria	5	2.5
Czech Republic	5	3.7
Hungary	6	3.0
Poland	5	2.9
Romania	6	4.3
Slovakia	6	4.7

(Source: Lewis 2000: 88.)

Democratisation in Eastern Europe

All six countries have ratified democratic constitutions that enshrine key civil and political liberties. In addition, there has also been more than one democratic change of government in each country, which, according to Samuel Huntington, is a key prerequisite for the consolidation of democracy (1991: 263).

Four of the six, the Czech Republic, Hungary, Poland and Slovakia, were admitted to the EU in May 2004 after they were also judged by the European Union to have satisfied the so-called 'Copenhagen criteria' (see Part 1). Bulgaria and Romania have still not met these criteria but are considered to be on track for EU membership in 2007.

Rankings of democratic development

The Czech Republic, Hungary, Poland and Slovakia were also classified as consolidated democracies by the Freedom House, *Nations in Transit*, 2004 survey. As can be seen from Table 2.24 the survey ranks countries in terms of six categories. The ratings are based on a scale of 1 to 7 with 1 representing the highest level and 7, rep-

Key fact 2.10

Freedom House

Freedom House is an independent US-based organisation founded over 60 years ago to promote democratic values and to oppose dictatorships of the left or the right. Its trustees believe that US leadership in international affairs is essential to the cause of human rights and freedom. It is funded by charitable foundations but also by the US Department of State.

Table 2.24 Freedom House: nations in transit ratings 2004

Ratings	Bulgaria	Czech Republic	Hungary	Poland	Romania	Slovakia
Electoral process	1.75	2.00	1.25	1.50	2.75	1.50
Civil society	3.00	1.50	1.25	1.25	2.50	1.25
Independent media	3.50	2.25	2.25	1.75	3.75	2.25
Governance	3.75	2.25	2.50	2.00	3.75	2.25
Constitutional, legislative and judicial framework	3.25	2.50	1.75	1.50	4.25	2.00
Corruption	4.25	3.50	2.75	2.50	4.50	3.25
Combined average	3.25	2.33	1.96	1.75	3.58	2.08
Ratings	SCD	CD	CD	CD	SCD	CD

Key: CD = consolidated democracy; SCD = semi-consolidated democracy.

(Source: Freedom House 2004.)

resenting the lowest level of democratic development. Romania with a combined rating of 3.58 and Bulgaria with a score of 3.25 came out as the least democratic of our six case studies and were classified as semi-consolidated democracies.

Democratisation in Poland

According to Freedom House, Poland is one of the most successful of the post-communist states and 'since the collapse of communism has transformed itself into a stable democracy with a multiparty political system and free and fair elections and a well-developed civil society' (*Nations in Transit*, Poland, 2003, from which subsequent evidence derives). Poland's entry into the EU in May 2004 was a further confirmation of its democratic status. The country had voted to join the EU in a referendum in June 2003, with 77 percent voting in favour of membership.

Poland's thriving civil society is bolstered by a high degree of media freedom and independence. Article 14 of the 1997 constitution guarantees freedom of the press and other mass media. According to Freedom House, the environment for print journalism is the best among the post-communist countries. Poland also has a strong and independent judiciary, and a new Freedom of Information Law, enacted in July 2001, has played an important role in making the government more transparent and accountable.

New legislation in 2003 has also done much to improve the legal status of non-government organisations (NGOs), which are also very active, with over 50,000 foundations and associations in operation employing 100,000 citizens. Poland also has one of the strongest trade union movements in post-communist Europe, a factor that relates back to the leading role of Solidarity in the communist period.

While corruption remains of serious concern, and Poland ranked 45th out of 102 countries in 2002, systemic corruption, according to Freedom House, 'is not of a magnitude that it fundamentally distorts the political or legal environment'. In 2002, the government adopted an official anti-corruption strategy. The Freedom House rating for corruption at 2.50 is the best of our six case studies.

The 1997 constitution

It was not until 1997 that Poland was able to adopt a fully revised constitution. After the formation of its first freely elected parliament in 1991, an interim 'little constitution' was adopted in 1992 that created a semi-presidential system. However, the 'little constitution' failed to clarify relations between the legislative and executive branches of power, and a 'war of laws' ensued between the parliament and President Walesa. A Constitutional Commission, set up in 1992, finally placed a draft constitution before parliament in 1996. However, the debate over the constitution became a bitter battle that pitched the Catholic Church and the right-wing Solidarity successor parties against the liberal and leftist parties. One of the central problem areas was that of church–state relations. The Catholic Church opposed the 'liberalism', and the allegedly 'anti-national' and 'anti-Christian' character of the draft constitution (Batt and Wolczuk 1998: 90–3). The constitution was finally ratified in a referendum in May 1997, with just over half of those participating (53 percent) voting in its favour.

Political institutions and elections

Poland has both a president and a parliament. The parliament consists of two chambers, both of which are elected every four years: a 460-seat lower house (the Sejm), and an upper house (the Senate) with 100 members. After the semi-free elections of 1989, there have been four rounds of parliamentary elections: 1991, 1993, 1997 and 2001; and three rounds of presidential elections: 1990, 1995 and 2000. As noted above, in 1993 Poland adopted a party-list PR system with a 5 percent electoral threshold for individual parties and 8 percent for coalitions. In March 2001, further changes were made to the electoral system. The national list was abolished, and all members of the parliament are now elected by proportional representation in multi-seat constituencies. The system of counting votes was also changed to favour smaller parties. In addition, political parties were to be financed entirely by the state, each party receiving funds in accordance with the number of votes it wins in parliamentary elections.

Parties and elections

Post-communist elections in Poland have largely been dominated by the 'ex-Solidarity versus ex-communist cleavage' (Kubik 2003: 329), that is the struggle for power between the communist successor party, the Democratic Left Alliance (SLD), and various right-wing splinter groups that emerged from the break-up of Solidarity. Solidarity coalitions came to power in 1991 and 1997, and the Democratic Left Alliance was victorious in 1993 and 2001.

According to the rules for presidential elections, if no candidate wins a majority in the first round, then a second round is held as a run-off between the two top candidates. Elections are held once every five years. Lech Walesa won the 1990 election but was defeated by Alexander Kwasniewski of the SLD in the second round of the 1995 elections. Kwasniewski also won the 2000 election.

Biography 2.26

Aleksandr Kwasniewski (1954–)

Aleksandr Kwasniewski was born in Bialogard, Poland. He studied economics at Gdansk University (1973–77). While at university he became involved in politics and in 1976 became chairman of the University Council of the Socialist Union of Polish Students (SZSP). After leaving university, Kwasniewski worked as a journalist and was editor of the student weekly *ITD* (1981–84) and *Sztandar Mlodych* (1984–85). He was also the co-founder of the computer science periodical *Bajtek* in 1985. A member of the Polish United Workers' Party (PUWP), Kwasniewski entered the government of General Wojciech Jaruzelski and served as minister of youth affairs (1985–87) and chairman of the Committee for Youth and Physical Culture (1987–90). In January 1990, Kwasniewski helped to found the Social Democratic Party and became its first chairman. The following year, he played an important role in forming the Democratic Left Alliance. In November 1995, Kwasniewski was elected Polish president and in 2000 he was re-elected as president with 53.9 percent of the vote.

However, neither the Solidarity successor parties nor the SLD have been strong enough to govern on their own, and both have had to gain the support of other parties in the parliament. But while the SLD was able to forge a coherent and unified party structure by 1999, the Solidarity successor parties have always been more ideologically diverse and internally divided. Thus, for example, Solidarity Election Action (AWS), which swept to power in 1997 under the leadership of Marian Kerzaklewski, was an uneasy coalition made up of the rump of the old Solidarity trade union movement and more than two dozen right-of-centre political parties. Of the coalition's 201 parliamentary seats, 52 were won by members of the trade union wing, 45 by Catholic activists and the remainder by various conservative groups. It is not surprising therefore that this alliance eventually broke apart as the economy nosedived into a further recession, and there were sharp disputes over EU accession.

The victory of the Democratic Left Alliance in the parliamentary elections of 2001 certainly owed much to the weaknesses of the Solidarity alliance, but we should also stress that the SLD gained considerable popular support from its opposition to shock therapy and its promotion of welfare reforms.

In the parliamentary elections of September 2001, the SLD along with its electoral coalition partner, the Union of Labour (UP), captured 41 percent of the vote and 216 seats, just 24 short of a parliamentary majority (see Table 2.25). After entering into coalition with the much smaller Polish Peasant Party (PSL), a new left-wing government was formed under the leadership of Prime Minister Lezek Miller, a former high-ranking member of the Polish Communist Party. Some way behind, in second place, with just 13 percent of the vote and 65 seats, was the centre-right Civic Platform. The SLD–UP alliance also won 75 of the 100 senate seats.

For the first time in Poland's post-communist history, none of the right-of-centre Solidarity successor parties gained representation in the Sejm. Under its new name AWS-Right, Solidarity picked up just 5.6 percent of the votes, which was not enough to cross the 8 percent threshold required for coalitions. The pro-market Freedom Union, another Solidarity grouping, which had been part of the previous AWS governing coalition, also failed to win a single seat.

The implosion of AWS, whose support plummeted from 30 percent to less than 5 percent over the period 1999–2001, came in the wake of the party's disastrous

Table 2.25 Polish parliamentary election (lower house, the Sejm), 23 September 2001

Parties	Percent vote	Seats	Percent seats
Alliance of the Democratic Left (SLD) and the Labour Union (UP) SLD–UP	41.04	216	46.96
Civic Platform, PO	12.68	65	14.13
Self-Defence, SO	10.20	53	11.52
Law and Justice, PiS	9.50	44	9.56
Polish Peasant Party, PSL	8.98	42	9.13
League of Polish Families, LPR	7.87	38	8.26
Turnout 46.2 percent			

(Source: Millard 2003: 33.)

performance in the 2000 presidential elections. AWS presidential candidate, Marian Krzaklewski, had come in a very poor third, winning just 15.6 percent of the votes, failing even to beat the 17.3 percent of the vote won by an independent candidate, Andrzej Olechowski. The president, Alexander Kwasniewski (SLD), was returned to power, winning 53.9 percent of the vote in the first round (Millard 2003a: 368).

The stability of party representation in the Sejm was also brought to an end in these elections with the entry for the first time of two new parties into the parliament: the League of Polish Families and Farmers Self-Defence. Two new centre-right groupings were also formed out of the ruins of the AWS: Civic Platform (PO) with 12.7 percent of the votes and Law and Justice (PiS), which won 9.5 percent.

The League of Polish Families (which won 7.87 percent) and Farmers Self-Defence (10.3 percent) both stood on virulent anti-EU platforms. The latter was set up to protect the interests of Poland's farmers, who feared that EU membership would lead to unfair competition with the highly subsidised farmers of the West. The new party, which is notorious for its politics of direct action, was able to divert some votes from the traditional representative of the farming community, the PSL.

However, the popularity of the Democratic Left Alliance (SLD) was by 2003 on the wane as economic growth slowed, unemployment rose to over 17 percent and allegations of corruption were levelled at senior SLD officials. By the autumn of 2003, opinion polls gave a narrow lead to the centre-right opposition party, the Civic Platform (PO), which moved ahead of the other mainstream conservative opposition party, Law and Justice (PiS).

Problems for the SLD had intensified when on 1 March 2003 it split with its governing coalition partner, the Polish Peasant Party (PSL). The PSL had given the SLD only lukewarm support on key issues such as membership of the EU, but without the PSL's support the government was 19 votes short of a parliamentary majority, and quarrels over forging a new working majority in the parliament led to a number of senior politicians leaving the party in March 2003. Among those who defected was the speaker of the Sejm, Marek Borowski, who subsequently went on to create another left-wing party, Polish Social Democracy (SDLP).

All of these developments placed a great strain on Leszek Miller, the prime minister and SLD party leader, who was eventually forced to resign on 2 May 2004, just one day after Poland became a member of the European Union. The new SLD prime minister, Marek Belka (a former deputy prime minister and finance minister), after losing one confidence vote in the parliament on 14 May, was finally endorsed by the Sejm on 24 May with the support of Borowski's SDLP. New Parlimentary elections in September 2005 witnessed a crushing defeat for the Democratic Left Alliance and the formation of a new right-wing coalition government headed by the Law and Justice Party and Civic Platform.

Biography 2.27

Marek Belka (1952–)

Marek Belka was born in Lodz, Poland. He graduated from the Socio-Economic Department of the University of Lodz in 1972. He became a professor of economics in 1994. From 1990 until 1996, he worked as consultant for the Polish Ministry of Finance and the World Bank.

▶

He served as deputy prime minister (1997) and minister of finance in 1997 and 2001–02. He was an economic consultant to the president of Poland in 2002–3. He was nominated to the post of prime minister of Poland by President Aleksandr Kwasniewski on 29 March 2004 and sworn into office on 2 May 2004, one day after Polish accession to the EU. On 24 June 2004, his nomination as prime minister was finally ratified in the lower house of the Polish parliament (the Sejm).

Democratisation in Romania

As we noted above, the Ceauşescu era stifled the development of independent opposition groups and civil society, and the roots of democracy were very shallow. The new NSF government, which was dominated by former members of the Communist Party, called for new parliamentary and presidential elections to take place in May 1990, giving the myriad of new opposition political parties little time to organise. The NSF was also able to use all the powers of the state to fund and promote its campaign, and it swept the board in elections that were far from free and fair. The NSF won 66 percent of the vote in the parliamentary elections, and NSF party leader Ion Iliescu won 85 percent of the vote in the presidential election.

The 1991 constitution

Romania adopted a new constitution in 1991 that guaranteed political pluralism, freedom of expression, the rule of law and respect for human rights, and a free-market economic system. In 2003, extensive revisions to the constitution strengthened its democratic credentials.

However, as noted above, Freedom House classifies Romania as the least democratic of our six case studies. Civil society is still very weak, and freedom of the press is not as developed as in Poland. One of the major negative factors is the high degree of corruption, which 'is so widespread that it adversely affects the political and economic stability of the nation' (*Nations in Transit*, Romania, 2003, from which subsequent evidence derives). Indeed, former President Constantinescu cited corruption as one of the reasons why he retired from politics in 2000. In a television address to the nation in July 2000, he said: 'I can see the degradation of the political scene. There is a blind fight for personal interest. People buy and sell places in parliament, using lies and blackmail'.

Nonetheless, in 1997 the European Commission formally acknowledged that Romania had satisfied the Copenhagen criteria, and Romania expects to sign the accession treaty to the EU in 2005 and become a full member in 2007.

Elections

Romania has a bicameral parliamentary system. The Senate (the upper house) has 140 seats and the Chamber of Deputies (the lower house) 345. Both chambers, which have identical powers, are directly elected for a four-year term. For the presidential election, a two-round system applies similar to that in Poland.

There have been five rounds of parliamentary and presidential elections – 1990, 1992, 1996, 2000 and 2004 – and there have now been three turnovers of government, in 1996, 2000 and 2004. However, post-communist politics in Romania has been dominated by the communist successor party, the National Salvation Front, which has under various name changes won three of the five rounds of parliamentary and presidential elections (in 1990, 1992 and 2000). In 1992, the party split into two, with Iliescu heading one branch (the Democratic-NSF) and former Prime Minister Petra Roman heading the other branch, the Democratic Party. In 1996, Iliescu's Democratic-NSF was renamed the Romanian Party of Social Democracy (PDSR), and in 2001 it changed its name yet again to the Social Democratic Party (PSD).

It took six years before we witnessed the first turnover of government in Romania with the victory in 1996 of a coalition of liberal and democratic parties competing under the umbrella of the Democratic Convention (DC). The dominant party in the DC was the National Peasant Christian Party. Emil Constantinescu, who headed the DC, defeated Iliescu in the second round of the 1996 presidential election, winning 54.4 percent of the vote. The Democratic Convention (DC), which won 30 percent of the parliamentary vote, formed a coalition government with the Democratic Party and the Democratic Alliance of Hungarians in Romania (UDMR), a party set up to represent the interests of the Hungarian minority, which makes up 7 percent of the population.

Biography 2.28

Emil Constantinescu (1939–)

Emil Constantinescu was born in Tighina, which is currently part of the republic of Moldova. After graduating from the Faculty of Law of Bucharest University in 1960, he worked for only a year in the legal profession before embarking on a career as a geologist. After graduating from Bucharest University in 1966 with a second degree in geology, he rose from the post of lecturer to that of senior lecturer in 1990 and professor in 1991. In 1990, he was the founding member and vice president of the political movement Civic Alliance. In 1992, he was elected rector of Bucharest University. In June 1992, he stood as a candidate for the office of Romanian president, a representative of the democratic movement the Democratic Convention of Romania (DCR). He lost the presidential election in the second round to Ion Iliescu. In December 1992, he was elected president of the DCR. In 1996, Constantinescu won the presidential election this time defeating Ion Iliescu in the second round, a post he held until 2000, when he retired from politics.

However, the new government soon faced problems in holding its alliance together. Not only were there problems with its coalition partners but also bitter quarrels within the DC alliance itself. In 1999, so divided was the parliament that it was able to adopt only 59 out of 453 draft laws and ordinances (*Nations in Transit*, Romania 2002: 303). Finding it impossible to garner a majority of votes in the parliament, the government sought to bypass parliament altogether by adopting emergency ordinances that do not need parliamentary approval. In February 2000, the government even used an emergency ordinance to raise the electoral thresholds for entry to the Chamber of Deputies.

It was the DC that eventually adopted shock therapy and speeded up the privatisation programme after years of prevarication by the NSF. The Romanian population, which had been partially shielded from the worst aspects of shock therapy under Iliescu, now began to suffer even greater hardship under the DC, as the IMF and IBRD urged the new government to adopt ever more stringent economic programmes. Thus, by the time of the 2000 elections, the DC-led government was deeply divided and the majority of the population now blamed it for the deteriorating economic situation. In the 2000 parliamentary election, the DC paid the electoral price for its unpopular policies, gaining only 6 percent of the vote and failing to win a single seat. The most successful single group running in the 2000 elections was a leftist coalition of the PDSR, the Social Democratic Party and the PUR, the humanist party; this coalition formed a government with the support of other parties. The PSDR subsequently reorganised itself into the PSD by a merger of two similar social democratic parties.

2004 Parliamentary Elections

In the elections, the PSD competed again in coalition with the PUR, under the name of the National Union. Of the four parties that successfully crossed the electoral threshold (see Table 2.26), the National Union came first, winning 37 percent of the votes and 132 seats in the parliament. As in the 2000 elections, there was no overall majority. The National Union divided, with the PSD moving into opposition although it had the largest number of seats (113), and the government was formed by a coalition of the PD (with 48 seats), PNL (64 seats), PUR (19 seats) and UDMR (22 seats). The ultra-right-wing Greater Romania Party (PRM) had been led by Corneliu Tudor to a shock second place in the 2000 elections; in 2004, the PRM was beaten into third place by a new Justice and Truth Alliance. The new prime minister was Calin Popescu Tariceanu of the PD.

Table 2.26 Romanian parliamentary election results, 28 November 2004 (Chamber of Deputies)

Parties	Votes (%)	Seats
National Union (PSD + PUR)	36.8	132
Justice and Truth Alliance (PNL + PD)	31.5	112
Greater Romania Party (PRM)	13.0	48
Democratic Union of Hungarians in Romania (UDMR)	6.2	22
New Generation Party	2.2	–
Christian Democratic National Peasants' Party	1.8	–

The National Union was an alliance of the PSD, the Social Democratic Party and the humanist party, the PUR.
The Justice and Truth Alliance was an alliance of the National Liberal Party (PNL) and the Democratic Party (PD).

(Source: http://www.electionworld.org.)

Table 2.27 Romanian presidential election, 29 November (second round 13 December 2004)

Presidential candidates	Party/nominated by	First round votes (%)	Second round votes (%)
Adrian Nastase	Social Democratic Party (PSD)	40.9	48.8
Traian Basescu	Democratic Party (PD)	33.9	51.2
Corneliu Vadim Tudor	Greater Romania Party (PRM)	12.6	
Marko Bela	Democratic Union of Hungarians in Romania (UDMR)	5.1	
Gheorghe Corolian Ciuhandu	Christian Democratic National Peasants' Party	1.9	
George Becali	New Generation Party	1.8	
Petre Roman	Democratic Force	1.4	
Gheorghe Dinu	Independent	1.1	

(Source: http://www.electionworld.org.)

The 2004 presidential elections

In the first round of the 2004 presidential elections, Adrian Nastase, who like outgoing president Ion Illiescu represented the PSD, came first (see Table 2.27). Nastase had been prime minister in the previous parliament. Support for Tudor, who had come second in 2000, fell so far that he came only third and so was not involved in the run-off between the top two candidates. The candidate who did come second in the first round, Traian Basescu, picked up most of the support for the other candidates and so, surprisingly, emerged as victor in the second round.

Further reading

White, S., Batt, J. and Lewis, P.G. (eds), *Developments in Central and East European Politics,* Macmillan is the most useful single source, especially the second volume (1998) and the third volume (2003).

Other helpful sources are:

Agh, A. (1998) *The Politics of Central Europe*, Sage, London.

Crawford, K. (1996) *East Central European Politics Today*, Manchester University Press, Manchester.

Freedom House (2003/4) *Nations in Transit: Democratisation in East Central Europe and Eurasia* (see website for annual surveys: http://www.freedomhous.org/research/nattransit.htm).

Gati, C. (1990) *The Bloc That Failed*, I. B. Tauris, London.

Huntington, S. (1991) *The Third Wave: Democratisation in the Late Twentieth Century*, University of Oklahoma Press, Norman, OK.

Kubik, J. (2003) 'Cultural legacies of state socialism: history making and cultural-political entrepreneurship in post-communist Poland and Russia', in G. Eckiert and S.E. Hanson (eds), *Capitalism and Democracy in Central and Eastern Europe*, Cambridge University Press, Cambridge.

Lewis, P.G. (2000) *Political Parties in Post-Communist Eastern Europe*, Routledge, London.

Mason, D.S. (1996) *Revolution and Transition in East-Central Europe*, 2nd edn, Westview Press, Boulder, CO.

Nagle, J.D. and Mahr, A. (1999) *Democracy and Democratisation*, Sage, London.

Roskin, M.G. (1997) *The Rebirth of East Europe*, 3rd edn, Prentice Hall, Upper Saddle River, NJ.

Rutland, P. (1994) 'The economy: the rocky road from plan to market', in S. White, A. Pravda and Z. Gitelman (eds), *Developments in Russian and Post-Soviet Politics*, Macmillan, London.

Stiglitz, J. (2002) *Globalisation and Its Discontents*, Penguin Books, London.

White, S., Gardiner, J. and Schopflin, G. (1987) *Communist Political Systems: An Introduction*, St Martin's Press, London.

World Bank (2004) *Europe and Central Asia Region Website* (available at http://www.worldbank.org).

Section 2.7

Turkey and Cyprus

Turkey

Politics in Turkey: the quest for stability

The legacy of Atatürk

As we have seen in Part 1, the Republic of Turkey came into being in 1923 under the leadership of Kemal Atatürk, who had been declared the head of government of what remained of the Ottoman Empire in April 1920. He was fiercely nationalist in his policies, which led to him negotiating the return of much of the Ottoman territories in the Treaty of Lausanne in 1923. Even now, Kemalism continues to have a large impact on Turkish society and politics nearly 70 years after his death. Three areas of his legacy are particularly important for today's Turkey:

1. Secularism. As seen later in this section, Turkish political society remains secular, with the role of religion marginalised, although this has been challenged in the recent past.

2. The influence of the military in Turkish domestic politics. When he took power, Atatürk was an officer in the military and remained at the centre of a single-party government until his death. As explored later in this section, the military remain influential in Turkish politics.

3. Atatürk envisaged Turkey as a modern society that, in many areas, although not all, looked towards the West.

Government 3.1

Government in Turkey

Turkey is a republic. The president is elected by parliament for seven years. The parliament, the Grand (or Great) National Assembly, has one chamber, with 55 members, elected for a five-year term, by modified proportional representation (with a threshold of 10 percent of the vote).

(Source: http://www.electionworld.org.)

Party politics in Turkey

Until the 1950s, multi-party democracy in Turkey was a remote dream. Atatürk had attempted several times to introduce such a system, but he retreated from this when he realised that his party and policies would have been defeated in any election. Consequently, Turkey remained, in effect, a one-party dictatorship. This changed in the late 1940s with the emergence of the National Development Party in 1945 and the Democrat Party in 1950 as a challenge to the Kemalist Republican People's Party (CHP).

However, the development of a flourishing party political system did not stop the military from continuing to play a key role in Turkish politics. Traditionally, the Turkish military hierarchy has presented itself as the protector and guardian of the Kemalist legacy. Throughout the period 1950 to 1980, it continued to interfere in Turkish domestic politics, with the last coup taking place in 1980. The 1980 coup resulted in the writing in 1982 of the current Turkish constitution, one of the main purposes of which was to bring a new generation of politicians into the political arena as it tried to close down the political parties in existence before the 1980 coup and to prevent a number of major political figures from returning to political prominence. These measures did not succeed, and many of the pre-coup politicians returned to positions of political leadership after changes made to the law in 1987 (Mecham 2004). Since the reinstatement of democracy in 1983, the military has continued to be a major presence in Turkish politics, seen most notably in 1997, when it played a key role in bringing down the government of Erbakan. The role of the military, therefore, continues to be a controversial issue in Turkish politics and has contributed significantly to Turkish democratic instability.

Despite a rather rocky start to democracy, Turkey currently has a dynamic party political system. Party politics in Turkey has shown itself to be changeable, both in the numbers and format of parties; Turkish parties are prone to infighting and splits. Parties have also been willing to alter their policy stances: a series of policy shifts has taken place within the major parties several times since the 1950s. For example, in 1967 Bülent Ecevit moved the CHP, traditionally a Kemalist party, towards the left (Sapelli 1995). More recently, the moderate Islamist parties have radically changed their political approach, as we shall see. This change is reflected in the policies of the successful Justice and Development Party (AKP), which, though Islamist, is focused on secular rather than religious issues. The adoption of centrist, secular policies was one of the main factors that led the AKP to win a majority of seats in the Grand National Assembly in elections in November 2002. These elections were a turning point in several ways; for the previous decade and a half there had been a lack of stability in the assembly as no party managed to gain an overall majority, so parties had to form coalitions, which proved, largely, ineffective and unstable. There was also widespread dissatisfaction within the Turkish electorate with previous governments, which were tainted by allegations of corruption, economic instability and internal infighting.

Issues in contemporary Turkish politics: the rise and transformation of moderate Islamist political parties

The role of Islam has been one of the major debates in contemporary Turkish politics, the November 2002 election marking the culmination of a process of change and adaptation within the Islamist political sector. But how did this occur? Although the AKP was formed only in 2001 and was, therefore, a relatively new party when elected in 2002, its roots lie firmly in the wider Islamist political movement. The history of Islamist political parties in Turkey reflects the debates that have been present in Turkish politics since the introduction of multi-party democracy in the 1950s. These include:

• debates about the secular nature of Turkish politics;
• debates about the role of the military in Turkish politics;
• debates about whether Turkey should continue to be oriented towards Europe and the USA and, more specifically, whether Turkey should become a member of the EU;
• internal party disputes.

The election of the AKP in 2002 was not the first time that an Islamist party had been in government. Following elections in 1995, the Welfare Party became the largest party in the Grand National Assembly, and it eventually headed a coalition government in 1996 with Necmettin Erbakan as prime minister (Mecham 2004). However, the government headed by the Welfare Party was largely ineffective. It experienced problems with its main coalition partner, Tansu Çiller's True Path Party, and with the military. The problems that the Erbakan government experienced with the military came to a head on 28 February 1997, when the National Security Council, which was controlled by the military, issued a series of demands to be met by the government. This intervention by the military had been prompted by the increasing threat, as it saw it, that the Erbakan government posed to the secularism of Turkish politics. Erbakan eventually resigned in June 1997, with the Welfare Party being banned by the courts in January 1998 after being labelled as anti-secular (Taniyici 2003: 474–5; Mecham 2004: 344). The Welfare Party was effectively replaced by the Virtue Party, which was formed by former Prime Minister Erbakan in December 1997.

Table 2.28 Islamic parties in Turkey since 1971

Party	Leader	Year founded	Year banned
National Salvation Party (MSP)	Erbakan	1971	1980
Welfare Party (RP)	Erbakan	1983	1998
Virtue Party (FP)	Kutan	1998	2001
Felicity Party (SP)	Kutan	2001	–
Justice and Development Party (AKP)	Erdoğan	2001	–

(Source: Tanyici 2003: 464.)

It was with the formation of the Virtue Party that the nature of Islamic politics in Turkey changed radically and a series of transformations was set in place that eventually culminated in the election of the AKP in 2002. Although the membership of the Virtue Party was broadly united on the direction of policy, internal divisions emerged almost immediately after its formation. There were two main factions:

1. Reformists led by Tayyip Erdoğan (the mayor of Istanbul, who was imprisoned in 1999 for reading a section of a poem by a Turkish nationalist poet, Ziya Gökalp, during a political rally) and Abdullah Gül. One of the main calls of the reformists was to see greater internal democracy within the Virtue Party.

2. The old guard of the Welfare Party, which was loyal to Erbakan, and which eventually provided the leader of the party, Recaï Kutan (Mecham 2004: 345).

This division was seen throughout the life of the Virtue Party, which was finally banned in 2001.

However, the period 1997–2001 is key in understanding Islamist and contemporary politics in Turkey. During this period, the message of Islamist politicians changed. The Virtue Party no longer focused on its Islamic roots; instead, it advocated increased democracy in Turkey, along with support for human rights and political freedom for all. This was a sea-change and is particularly significant when looking at the November 2002 elections. It was the policy change of the Virtue Party that eventually set much of the agenda of the AKP, which was one of two parties that emerged with the banning of the Virtue Party. The other was the Felicity Party, which has not had much political success, as seen in Table 2.29.

It soon became clear that the leaders of the AKP had learned the lessons of the past. There was clear emphasis on democratic rather than religious issues, and the party also marketed itself as a centrist political party. By focusing itself in this way, the leadership of the AKP showed that they had accepted and were prepared to work within the constraints placed upon past moderate Islamist parties (Mecham 2004). In order to make the party more electable, the AKP leadership also recruited members of other centrist parties, which boosted its secularist, centrist credentials. This proved to be a successful policy, as the AKP gained a national spread of votes in the 2002 elections; its 34 percent of the vote gave it 363 Grand National Assembly seats, as can be seen in Table 2.29. The only other party to gain the required 10 percent of the vote to qualify for seats in the Grand National Assembly was the Republican People's Party (CHP), which with 19 percent of the vote was allocated 178 seats. Nine seats were allocated to independents.

Table 2.29 Results of November 2002 Grand National Assembly elections

Party	% of vote	Assembly seats
Justice and Development Party, AKP	34.3	363
Republican People's Party, CHP	19.4	178
True Path Party, DYP	9.6	0
Nationalist Action Party, MHP	9.3	0
Youth Party, GP	7.2	0
Democratic People's Party, Dehap	6.2	0
Motherland Party, ANAP	5.1	0
Felicity Party, SP	2.5	0
Democratic Left Party, DSP	1.1	0
New Turkey Party, YTP	1.0	0
Grand Unity Party, BBP	1.1	0
Independents	–	9

Note: Parties must gain 10 percent of the vote to be eligible for seats in the Grand National Assembly.

(Source: BBC, Elections in Turkey http://www.electionworld.org/turkey.)

The AKP has based its success on advocating a series of moderate, centrist policies that did not threaten the secular nature of Turkish politics. However, despite its overwhelming victory in the November 2002 elections, the past continued to affect the party as its leader, Erdoğan, continued to be prevented from taking political office. This ban was overturned, and Erdoğan was elected to the Grand National Assembly in March 2003. The AKP prime minister, Abdullah Gül, then resigned to allow Erdoğan to be become prime minister.

Turkish politics finally seems to have entered a phase of stability. The election of the AKP in November 2002 has shown that it is possible for a moderate Islamist party to hold power without threatening the general secular basis of Turkish politics and society, although the military continues to play a role in Turkish politics. When he founded Turkey, Kemal Atatürk envisaged the development of a secular, modern Turkey. If a stable democracy is a component of a modern society, then it seems, at last, that Turkey is finally achieving this goal.

Turkey and the EU

One of the major policy changes within the moderate Islamist political establishment in Turkey has been its attitude to the EU. The Welfare Party was not supportive of Turkish entry into the EU, which was regarded by many in the party as being a 'Christian club'. The attitude of the moderate Islamist parties changed with the policy shifts that followed the establishment of the Virtue Party in 1997. The leadership of the Virtue Party 'no longer viewed the EU as a "Christian Club", but as an institution embodying universal democratic values' (Taniyici 2003). On its formation, the AKP adopted the pro-EU stance of the Virtue Party and now carries out pro-EU policies. But just how close is Turkey to becoming a member of the EU?

Turkey's relationship with the EU is a long and complex one. In 1963, it signed an Association Agreement with the EEC, which came into force in 1964. Not only has Turkey's relationship with the EU been a long one, so too has its quest for membership; it formally applied for membership of the EC in April 1987 and, although a customs union with the EU came into force in 1996, Turkey is still awaiting a successful outcome.

The final outcome of the Turkish application for membership of the EU is important not just to Turkey but also to the EU. With Turkish membership, the EU could finally shake off the claim that it is a 'Christian club' and be seen to be more diverse in its membership. Turkish membership is also likely to strengthen European strategic policy, and it may also open up new opportunities for the EU due to Turkey's ties with the Middle East (Oguzlu 2004). For Turkey, EU membership may finally resolve some of the issues that have dominated Turkish politics and identity for much of the twentieth century. Not only would it confirm Turkey's alliance with the West, but it would help to resolve some of the struggles over identity in Turkish society and politics.

As discussed earlier, one of the defining factors in Turkish politics and society has been the legacy of Atatürk, and one of the features of this was Atatürk's vision of a fully modernised, Western-looking Turkey. For many in Turkey, the realisation of EU membership will be 'the crowning jewel of Turkish modernisation and integration with the West' (Çarkoğlu 2003a) and thus will be the ultimate fulfilment of the path laid out by Atatürk for his country. EU membership will also help to weaken one of the more negative legacies of Atatürk, the influence of the military in politics and society. Steps have been taken to try to reduce the role of the military in Turkish politics, but their success is still questionable (Hale 2003).

Why has it taken so long for Turkey to become a member of the EU? One of the main factors has been the time it has taken for it to meet the Copenhagen Criteria for membership of the EU. Meeting these criteria is an ongoing process for Turkey, but in 2001, it set out its programme for doing so (Erdemli 2003).

One of the main problem areas identified by the EU was human and minority rights. As part of its 2001 programme, Turkey started to take significant steps in these fields, including increasing the rights of minorities and abolishing the death penalty (Hale 2003; Erdemli 2003). A further review of Turkey's application was made at the EU Council meeting in December 2004; Turkey's continued progress was noted, and it was agreed that if Turkey continued to make satisfactory progress, particularly on abolishing torture and ill-treatment of prisoners, formal negotiations about Turkish membership should begin on 3 October 2005. However, there are some who feel that the EU has dragged its feet over Turkish membership and that, when the application process as applied to Turkey is compared with those of the new members from Eastern and Central Europe, Turkey has been unfairly treated (Arikan 2003). The truth of this claim is difficult to assess.

Figure 2.5 Cartoon of Turkish invasion of Cyprus. 'Why don't you rejoice? We're liberating you from the tyrants'
Source: The Central Committee of AKEL, Nicosia (1978).

The changes that have been made to Turkish social, economic and political policies have triggered debates within Turkey about the impact of EU membership on the country, not least on Turkish identity. Not everyone in Turkey supports membership of the EU, and there is a sizeable minority in Turkey that is euro-sceptical (Çarkoğlu 2003b). As we have seen, the moderate Islamist parties were against Turkey's EU membership until the late 1990s.

The question of whether Turkey will become a member of the EU is crucial both to the future of Turkey and to the resolution of a number of the debates that have hindered Turkish stability. It is also important to the EU. So far, Brussels has ruled that Turkey is not yet quite ready to join the EU, but in October 2005 the EU Council agreed to open formal negotiations with Turkey on its application for EU membership.

Cyprus

The contemporary history, politics and society of the island of Cyprus have been dominated by the effective division of the island in 1974. Since then, much of the international attention given to Cyprus has focused on reuniting the island, so far unsuccessfully. This subsection will briefly outline the recent political history of Cyprus and the role of the international community in attempting to resolve the Cyprus problem.

Cyprus: a brief history of division

Cyprus is currently divided between the Greek Cypriots, who control the south of the island, and the Turkish Cypriots, who currently control the northern part. Although the effective division of the island occurred in 1974, rivalry and dispute between the two communities had been a major factor in Cypriot politics and society for many years. On independence from the UK in 1960, the divisions in Cypriot society were reflected in the constitution of the new Republic of Cyprus. The constitution attempted to put in place a framework that would allow the Greek and Turkish Cypriot communities to live and work side by side. The Greek Cypriot community was, and continues to be, in population terms, by far the larger of the two communities. This was reflected in the 1960 constitution, under which the president was to be a Greek Cypriot and the vice president a Turkish Cypriot, each to be elected by their own constituencies. The 1960 constitution is a complex document, designed to prevent domination of one community by another, with certain types of legislation being subject to veto by either community. As later events showed, the 1960 constitution had little success in encouraging the two communities to live together in a united Cyprus.

One of the issues that remained unresolved by the 1960 constitution was the concept of *enosis* – the union of Cyprus with Greece. Those in the Greek Cypriot community who supported *enosis* looked towards Cyprus becoming politically united with Greece. *Enosis* had been present in Cypriot politics during UK rule, with EOKA, the main pro-independence guerrilla group, being supporters of *enosis*. The

Plate 2.10 Archbishop Makarios of Cyprus in
the ruins of his presidential palace in 1974
Source: The Central Committee of AKEL, Nicosia (1978: 77).

concept of *enosis* was opposed by the Turkish Cypriot community. The 1960 constitution, with its focus on both communities living together, did not further the case
for *enosis*, but interpretation of the constitution was the cause of much debate
between the Greek and Turkish Cypriot communities. These political debates eventually led to the outbreak of violence between the two communities towards the end of
1963. This was the start of the process that was to lead to the division of the island.

The problems experienced between the Turkish and Greek Cypriots culminated
in 1974. In July, an attempt was made by right-wing paramilitary elements in the
Greek Cypriot community, encouraged by the junta in Athens, to overthrow
Archbishop Makarios, who had been president of Cyprus since independence.
Their goal was *enosis*. However, the coup led to a Turkish military invasion of
northern Cyprus, necessary, according to Ankara, for the protection of the Turkish
Cypriot population. The presence of the Turkish military created further separation
within Cyprus through the encouragement of population movement, with the north
of the island being populated largely by the Turkish Cypriots and the south by the
Greek Cypriots. A Turkish Cypriot government was set up in the north following
the Turkish invasion, and northern Cyprus proclaimed itself independent as the so-
called Turkish Republic of Northern Cyprus (TRNC) in 1983. However, the TRNC
is recognised only by Turkey, and the Greek Cypriot government has continued to
be regarded as the official government of Cyprus by the rest of the world.

Government 3.2

Government in (Greek) Cyprus

Cyprus is a republic. The president is directly elected for five years. The parliament has one chamber, with 59 members, 56 of whom are elected for a five-year term by proportional representation (24 of these are allocated to the Turkish minority). The remaining three represent the Maronite, Roman Catholic and Goumenian minorities.

(Source: http://www.electionworld.org.)

Cyprus: the role of international organisations

Both the UN and EU have been engaged in efforts to resolve the problems of Cyprus. The UN, in particular, has been heavily involved in Cyprus for some time. It first deployed peacekeepers on the island in 1964, and since the division of the island in 1974 the UN has policed the 'Green Line' or buffer zone. The UN has also been one of the main initiators of negotiations aimed at a settlement of the Cypriot dispute. These efforts have sought to create a united island. However, the divisions between the two populations are deep, and efforts undertaken to reunify the island have so far failed.

The internationally recognised government of Cyprus applied for membership of the EU in 1990; this was regarded by the EU as being an application on behalf of all of the island. During the accession process, the EU placed pressure on both sides of the island to resolve their differences. At one stage, the EU hinted that only a united Cyprus would be able to become a member of the EU. However, this position changed as the 1 May 2004 accession date drew closer. Cyprus' Accession Treaty included provision that in the event of the island's remaining divided on that date then only the internationally recognised part of Cyprus would be admitted as an EU member (Europa 2004a). This, in fact, was what happened when the Republic of Cyprus became a member of the EU in May 2004.

The months that immediately preceded the entry of Cyprus into the EU were dominated by frantic diplomatic activity aimed at reuniting the island in time for 1 May. These efforts were led by the UN and its secretary-general, Kofi Annan. The 'Annan Plan' was agreed on 31 March 2004 and was supported not just by the UN and EU but also by the governments of Greece and Turkey. The plan centred on a united Cyprus becoming a federal state modelled on Switzerland. It also included

Table 2.30 Results of Cypriot referendum, 24 April 2004

	Yes votes (%)	No votes (%)	Turnout (%)
Greek south	24.2	75.8	88.0
Turkish north	64.9	35.1	87.0

(Source: BBC 2004a.)

measures for the demilitarisation of the island, along with territorial adjustment between the Greek and Turkish areas and proposals to resolve issues that arose for those who owned property they had left due to the division of the island (UN 2004). Despite the agreement of the Greek and Turkish governments, the plan could only be put in place with the agreement of both the Greek and Turkish Cypriot populations. Therefore a referendum was held in both parts of Cyprus on 24 April 2004.

Despite a vote for the plan by the Turkish north of the island, it was rejected by the south, so Cyprus remains divided, and only the Greek Cypriot south of the island became a member of the EU. Why did the south reject the agreement? Many of the parts of the Annan Plan were accepted by the Greek Cypriots; however, there were three main sticking points.

1. Provision permitting tens of thousands of Turkish troops to remain on Cyprus for many years to come was seen by many Greek Cypriots as constituting a security threat. Under the plan, the continued presence of Turkish troops on Cypriot soil is deemed justifiable in order to protect the rights of the Turkish Cypriots. However, the government of the Republic of Cyprus points out that this could have very broad (and threatening) application. For instance, if communal violence were to break out between Greek Cypriot and Turkish Cypriot neighbours in a town in the south of a reunited Cyprus, would this Turkish garrison consider itself justified in invoking the Annan Plan in order to sweep southwards, endangering the entire island's stability? Moreover, the Cypriot government considers the presence of these Turkish troops on the soil of a united and sovereign Cyprus a humiliation and a limitation of sovereignty.

2. The part of the agreement that dealt with property rights and the right to return to land in the north of the island were not deemed sufficient in the eyes of many Greek Cypriots (BBC 2004a).

3. Many in the Greek Cypriot community insist that the status of an estimated 120,000 settlers from mainland Turkey must be settled by negotiation. These are people who are not Turkish Cypriots and have no historic ties to the island at all, but are (mostly impoverished) Turks who have been encouraged by the Ankara government to move to Cyprus since the northern part of the island was seized by Turkish troops in 1974. 'Colonisation' has allegedly been used by Ankara as a way of easing social problems in Turkey itself. Many of these settlers have been given land, houses and property that belonged to the Greek Cypriots who were 'ethnically cleansed' from their historic lands after the Turkish invasion. (It should not be forgotten that Greek Cypriots were a majority in every part of the island, north and south, prior to the invasion.) Indeed, some Turkish Cypriots have also been vocal in criticising colonisation from Turkey, and the 'settler Turks' have been blamed for social problems, including crime and political extremism.

There have been some positive outcomes of the Annan Plan and the subsequent referenda. For Turkey, a positive outcome is that it has improved its chances of EU membership. The lack of resolution to the Cyprus problem has been one of the factors that have held back its application. Through Ankara's support for the Annan Plan, this obstacle has now been virtually removed.

For Greek Cypriots, too, the Annan Plan contained much that was positive. Many Greek Cypriots, especially the supporters of the left-wing AKEL party, which has around 30 percent of the vote and was the leading party in the Cypriot government when the referendum was held, strongly support a peace deal in principle. They wish to see a Cypriot confederation in which all Cypriots can live peacefully together. Other, more nationalistic, Greek Cypriots, especially on the right wing of politics, take a more hard-line approach. Although AKEL narrowly rejected the Annan Plan, because of the worries outlined above, it has stressed its commitment to achieving a new deal soon. The election of a new Turkish Cypriot leader in April 2005 greatly strengthens the hand of moderates and bridge builders in both communities. Mehmet Ali Talat, who replaced the intransigent Rauf Denktash as Turkish Cypriot leader, is a centre-left pro-reunification leader. His Turkish Republican Party (CTP) is actually AKEL's sister party.

Despite being the main losers of the referendum vote, there have been some positive outcomes for the Turkish Cypriots. Following the referendum, the EU undertook to provide 260 million euros (approximately £170 million) of economic aid to northern Cyprus (BBC 2004a). This will hopefully be the start of a process of reintegrating northern Cyprus into the global and European economy after years of isolation. The economic isolation of northern Cyprus has left it economically underdeveloped when compared to the south of the country.

It seems that Cyprus may continue to be dominated by the politics of division in the immediate future. There have been so many setbacks on the road to national reconciliation over the past three decades that it would be foolish to be overly optimistic. Nevertheless, there are certainly grounds for optimism in the years ahead. The Annan Plan held out hope that Cyprus would become reunited. In the short term the effort failed, and the divisions present in the Cypriot community have continued. In the longer term, however, the plan has given all interested parties the motivation to press towards reunification. The EU may well come to play a decisive role in this process.

Further reading

Arikan, H. (2003) *Turkey and the EU: An Awkward Candidate for EU Membership?*, Aldershot, Ashgate.

BBC (2004a) 'Cyprus "spurns historical chance"' (available at http://www.news.bbc.co.uk/go/pr/fr/1/hi/world/europe/3660171.stm).

BBC (2004b) 'EU pledges aid for Turkish Cyprus' (available at http://www.news.bbc.co.uk/go/pr/fr/1/hi/world/europe/3656753.dtm).

Çarkoğlu, A. and Rubin, B. (eds) (2003) *Turkey and the European Union: Domestic Politics, Economic Integration and International Dynamics*, London: Frank Cass.

Europa (2004b) 'Enlargement: candidate country: Cyprus' (available at http://www.europa.eu.int/comm/enlargement/cyprus/print-index.htm).

Mecham, R.Q. (2004) 'From the ashes of virtue, a promise of light: the transformation of political Islam in Turkey', *Third World Quarterly* 25 (2): 339–58.

Oguzlu, H.T. (2004) 'Changing dynamics of Turkey's US and EU Relations', *Middle East Policy* 11 (1): 98–105.

Xenakis, D. and Chryssochoou, D. (2001) *The Emerging Euro-Mediterranean System*, Manchester: Manchester University Press.

Part 3

The European Union

Plate 3.1: A group of European Studies students at the European Parliament. How important do you think field trips to Brussels are in helping you to understand the European Union?

Section 3.1

The evolution of the European Union

Introduction

Part 3 of the book focuses on the evolution, character, institutions, and current objectives and policies of the EU. It covers some of the different explanations and ways of making sense of the origins and development of the EU. Studies of the EU generally agree on the main stages in its 50-year history from a customs union to a single market to a currency zone. However, there are major disagreements over the nature, range, combination and importance of the factors responsible for this evolution. This is the topic we examine in this section, in which we concentrate on European integration and on the growth of the EU in the period since the end of the Second World War in 1945, starting with the history of the EU in its European Community (EC) phase during the period 1945–90.

We explore the dynamics of European integration in the light of the interests, policies and interactions of Western European states. We start with the states, because they were and still are responsible through their treaty-making powers for the formal construction of the EU. However, it should be noted that this is only one of several approaches to studying the subject. Early histories of the EC, for example, often gave pride of place to individuals and groups whose pan-European vision and idealism suggested that they were the prime movers in fashioning the EC. Such grand, heroic narratives frequently belittled the role and importance of the state and of national interests, rarely giving detailed attention to hard intergovernmental bargaining and power politics. Some of these accounts predicted the withering away of the nation-state and its replacement by a European superstate or federal system. In the past 20 years or so, however, studies of the emergence of the EC have challenged these earlier accounts, whether by portraying national interests as the motor of European integration (see, for example, the ground-breaking work of Milward (1984)) or by identifying economic interdependence as the driving force (see, for example, Moravicsik (1998)). Other studies have tended to offer multi-causal explanations that stress the changing blend and influence of a number of factors across time and space (see, for example, Dinan (2004), and for this type of analysis in explaining one episode in the history of the EU (see also Dyson and Featherstone (1999)).

Much of the debate about the making of the EC/EU in these accounts has centred on such matters as the relative importance of political and economic factors, the influence of sub-national, national, supranational and transnational pressures, the relationship between structural conditions and individual agents, and the impact of European and non-European conditions. In some respects, the contribution of historical study to this debate is limited due to the lack of access to primary source evidence relating to the past 30 years or so, especially government papers that would allow for a fuller study than is currently possible, for example of the relationship between policymakers' public representation of the EC/EU and their private assessments, calculations and priorities. An additional problem for the historian is that this subject is a matter of continuing controversy in that the public debate on European integration has taken a variety of forms, from fantasies demonising or defending the EC to using particular representations of the EC's past for current polemical purposes.

This opening section highlights some of the major landmarks and distinctive features of the EC in the period 1945–90. It identifies aspects of the historical legacy that are important in understanding current developments, and it also features some of the recurring issues, tensions and counter-integrative elements at the heart of the EC. The period is divided into three phases, each of which poses a question that has loomed large at various stages in the history of the EC.

Why Europe? Postwar reconstruction and the origins of the European Community, 1945–60

In the period 1945–60, the concept of Europe in Western European international relations and politics increasingly became a shorthand expression for the EC, the precursor of the EU. This section addresses two main questions:

1. Why did the EC come into being in the 1950s?
2. Why was the EC perceived by 1960 as the leading project in the field of European integration?

At the end of the Second World War in Europe in May 1945, the major European states experienced greatly reduced power and influence. Britain confronted the immediate price of victory in the form of the largest external debts (£4.7 billion) in its modern history. France had lost Great Power status as a result of military defeat by Germany in 1940. Defeated and occupied Germany was a mere object in the international system, losing land in the east amounting to 25 percent of its prewar territory. Italy was adjusting to the collapse of Mussolini's fascist state. The human cost of war was evident across Europe: 17 million Europeans (excluding the approximately 20 million war dead in the USSR) had been killed as a result of the war. Enforced population movements, including the expulsion of ten million Germans from Eastern Europe, compounded the problems of early peacetime reconstruction. There were acute shortages of food and energy as Europe's agricultural output and coal production (the chief source of energy) were still 25 percent below prewar levels by the end of 1946. Meanwhile, European countries wrestled with the problems of restoring political order; only six Western European states emerged from the war with their prewar political institutions intact.

It was against this background that the earliest postwar forms of cooperation between the Western European states arose out of their extreme economic and military weakness. All European states to a greater or lesser extent faced considerable difficulties in financing their recovery programmes and lacked dollars (the 'dollar gap') to pay for imports. US Secretary of State George Marshall offered American aid to assist the rebuilding of Europe (June 1947), and in the resulting four-year European Recovery Programme ('Marshall Aid/Plan'), $12,534 million was distributed.

Biography 3.1

George Marshall (1880–1959)

Marshall was a professional soldier who occupied a number of senior army posts before joining the General Staff in Washington in 1938. A year later, he was appointed head of US armed forces as chief of staff and was also made a general by President Roosevelt. He occupied this top post until shortly after the end of the Second World War. In January 1947, he returned to public life as secretary of state in the Democrat administration under President Truman. It was during his period of office as secretary of state (1947–49) that he was responsible for launching the four-year European Recovery Programme, which took effect through the Foreign Assistance Act (April 1948). He played a prominent role in encouraging the political and economic recovery of the Western occupation zones in Germany, which resulted in the formation of the FRG (1949). Marshall was awarded the Nobel Peace Prize (1953) for his contribution to the postwar recovery of Europe, the first professional soldier to receive this award. He resigned from the post of secretary of state in 1949 due to ill-health. He returned to public office a year later when he became secretary of defense and was responsible for organising US military efforts in the early stages of the Korean War. He finally retired from public service in September 1951.

Key fact 3.1

Marshall Aid

Extracts from a speech by US Secretary of State Marshall at Harvard University, 5 June 1947:

The truth of the matter is that Europe's requirements for the next three or four years of foreign food and other essential products principally from America are so much greater than her present ability to pay that she must have substantial additional help or face economic, social and political deterioration of a very grave character.

The remedy lies in breaking the vicious circle and restoring the confidence of the European people in the economic future of their own countries and of Europe as a whole.

… It is logical that the United States should do whatever it is able to do to assist in the return of normal economic health in the world, without which there can be no political stability and no assured peace. Our policy is directed not against any country or doctrine but against hunger, poverty, desperation, and chaos.

(Source: Department of State Bulletin, XVI.)

At American insistence, the 16 Western European states in receipt of this aid coordinated their efforts and formed the Organisation for European Economic Cooperation (OEEC), the first major effort at postwar economic cooperation between these states. This pump-priming exercise helped to lay the foundations of sustained economic recovery and growth in Western Europe over the next two decades. It also initiated longstanding American backing for European integration with a view to achieving the following objectives:

- to resist Soviet power and influence in Europe;
- to secure a revived Germany within a stable European framework (this and the above are often referred to in the literature as double containment);
- to facilitate the political and economic recovery of Western Europe;
- to create a more free, multilateral international economy;
- to reduce the need for American assistance to Western Europe;
- to devise a structure for managing relations between the USA and Western Europe;
- to export American ideas, practices and institutions.

The OEEC programme fell far short of some American plans at this time for a single European market and also for a federal Europe. The European states clearly preferred aid with no such strings attached and were disinclined to espouse the idea of federal Europe except as a rhetorical device to impress the US administration. Nevertheless, the OEEC took the first faltering steps towards the liberalisation of the international trade and payments system in Western Europe through the phased abolition of quotas (quantitative import restrictions) and the introduction of a trade-expanding credit system.

The rise of the two new superpowers, the USA and the USSR, also highlighted the precarious position of the weak states of a Balkanised Europe. The mutual hostility (Cold War) of the two superpowers resulted in the division of Europe and of Germany. The accompanying widespread fear of a Soviet threat to Western Europe, the reality of which has been hotly debated by historians ever since, further strengthened the case for some degree of cooperation between states in the area.

Key fact 3.2

The Iron Curtain

The division of Europe was commonly likened to an iron curtain in Western circles after a speech by Winston Churchill, the British Conservative Party leader, from which the following extract is taken:

From Stettin in the Baltic to Trieste in the Adriatic, an iron curtain has descended across the Continent. Behind that line lie all the capitals of the ancient states of Central and Eastern Europe. Warsaw, Berlin, Prague, Vienna, Budapest, Belgrade, Bucharest and Sofia, all these famous cities and the populations around them lie in what I must call the Soviet sphere, and all are subject in one form or another, not only to Soviet influence but to a very high and, in many cases, increasing measure of control from Moscow.

(Source: Speech: 'The sinews of peace', 5 March 1946, Fulton, Missouri, USA.)

International tension was particularly pronounced at the time of the first 'war scare' of the early postwar period, when the Soviet-imposed Berlin blockade (June 1948–May 1949) cut off all land routes between West Berlin and the West. In March 1948, Britain, France and the Benelux states (Belgium, the Netherlands and Luxembourg) formed the Brussels Treaty Organisation. This mutual security pact was born out of mounting Cold War tensions as the USSR rather than Germany was increasingly viewed in Western circles as the principal adversary.

Opinion 3.1

The origins of the Cold War

Explanations for the origins of the Cold War fall into three broad categories: traditional or orthodox, revisionist, and post-revisionist.

1. **Traditional** – the Soviet Union was primarily responsible for the onset of the Cold War largely due to its territorial ambitions in Eastern Europe, communist ideology, security concerns and Stalin's leadership. The response of the Western powers to Soviet expansionism came in the form of the policy of containment, which was exemplified by the Truman Doctrine of March 1947 and by the defensive character of the North Atlantic Treaty of 1949. According to this account, therefore, the Cold War was 'the brave and essential response of free men to communist aggression' (Schlesinger 1967). See also the memoirs of Western political leaders like Truman, Churchill and Acheson for classic statements of the same view.

2. **Revisionist** – the revisionist challenge to the traditional explanation emerged in the 1960s. It took the view that the USA was mainly responsible for starting the Cold War, particularly because it refused to accommodate the legitimate security requirements of the Soviet Union in Eastern Europe and also because it overturned the wartime allies' agreement to treat postwar, occupied Germany as a single economic entity. Furthermore, the Truman administration (1945–53) used the myth of Soviet expansionism to mask the true nature of American foreign policy, which included the creation of a global system to advance the interests of American capitalism. For an early and influential example of this view, see Williams (1962).

3. **Post-revisionist** – this view regards the name, blame and shame accounts of traditional and revisionist writers as misguided and simplistic. It aims to provide more balanced explanations and is strongly critical of the mono-causal explanations for the Cold War in traditional and revisionist accounts. Post-revisionist studies tend to emphasise the complex interplay of events and the contradictions, ambiguities, divided opinions and unintended consequences that characterised policymaking in Moscow, Washington and London. For an example of this view, see Yergin (1977).

(Sources: Williams 1962; Schlesinger 1967; and Yergin 1990.)

Which of these views do you find most plausible?

The Brussels Treaty Organisation served as a catalyst for the North Atlantic Treaty (April 1949), which was signed by the USA, Canada and ten Western European states and which assumed organisational form a year later with the emergence of the North Atlantic Treaty Organisation (NATO). NATO could be made to serve a number of purposes in Europe, and in the view of its first secretary-general it was designed 'to keep the Russians out, the Americans in and the Germans down'. The division of Europe at this time determined the geopolitical dimensions of Europe for the next 40 years and meant that European states played a largely subordinate part in the geopolitics of their own continent. The formation of NATO including the USA also had the longer-term implication that any type of European integration was unlikely to extend to defence and security in the absence of a fundamental change to the system of transatlantic relations established during this period. The evolution and significance of relations between the USA and Western Europe during this early postwar period has been much debated and has attracted different assessments, e.g.:

- The USA was from the outset an expansionist power intent on reshaping postwar Europe and on consolidating the US presence in Europe.

- The USA was a reluctant participant in immediate postwar European affairs and was drawn into making commitments to the postwar recovery and security of Western Europe by the European states and especially by the UK.

- The USA and Western European states shared a large number of fundamental common interests, including US leadership of the Atlantic Alliance and the development of the Western international economy.

While Western European states embarked on forms of cooperation as a result of weakness, a body of opinion emerged at the same time that put the case for European unity. The spectacle of a politically and economically exhausted Europe prompted a widespread reaction: 'Never again'. Europe's recent history of war, nationalism and economic rivalries offered no model for constructing a prosperous, peaceful and free continent. Radical programmes of political and economic reconstruction were based on a general desire to break with the disastrous past, as if 1945 represented 'year zero'. The idea of European unity gave rise to one such programme.

Much support for European unity was founded on the belief that a new European community would permanently contain the dangerous force of nationalism and accommodate defeated states that might otherwise succumb to a deep-seated sense of aggrieved isolation. The common European experience of wartime defeat, occupation and humiliation seriously called into question the traditional conduct of interstate relations in Europe. This second major conflagration on the European continent in less than a generation also fully exposed the inability of any single state to maintain peace or to protect its citizens in the event of war.

There was a marked contrast between such visions of a united Europe and the realities of an increasingly divided continent. Clarion calls for a federal Europe found expression at the unofficial Congress of Europe at the Hague (May 1948). By this time, however, the possibility of realising expansive schemes for pan-European unity was fast receding in the face of Cold War conditions. By this time, too, it was equally evident that any attempt at more intensive cooperation between Western European states might be assisted by advocates of European unity but would ultimately be determined by enfeebled states unable to achieve their security and welfare objectives by any other means – a recurring feature in the history of the EC/EU.

Early postwar Western European organisations operated on the principle of intergovernmental cooperation with no loss of national sovereignty. This arrangement suited some states more than others and gradually produced a basic, enduring division over the organisation of Western Europe. One set of states, led by the UK and including the Scandinavian countries, supported a limited intergovernmental approach that opposed any suggestion of federal political structures and proposals for a European customs union. UK understanding of the value of European unity was increasingly viewed in the context of the Cold War. The UK was reluctant to enter into any new, binding European commitments beyond those needed to organise Western European defence cooperation, to qualify for European Recovery Programme aid and to ensure US support against the USSR; the Empire and Commonwealth as well as the restoration of the 'special' UK–USA relationship took precedence over continental Europe in this order of external priorities. The Scandinavian countries were also disinclined to involve themselves too tightly. The modest functions of their own Nordic Council (established in 1952) and the failure to create a Nordic customs union in the 1950s demonstrated their restricted interest in political and economic integration.

A second set of states, led by France, advocated a more closely integrated European grouping for reasons often unrelated to the enveloping Cold War. France was particularly concerned to avert any future military threat from Germany in view of the German invasions of France in 1870, 1914 and 1940. After the defeat of the Nazi war machine in 1945, France initially aimed to maintain a weak, dismembered Germany. However, the onset of the Cold War resulted in the more limited partition of Germany into two states, one of which was the potentially powerful, partially sovereign Federal Republic of Germany (FRG, or West Germany), which was formed in 1949. France thus faced the unattractive prospect of FRG participation in the Western international system without any specifically European controls. It was against this background that Robert Schuman, the French foreign minister, presented a proposal drawn up by Jean Monnet (head of France's post-war modernisation programme), to place all Franco-German coal and steel production under a common authority in an organisation open to other European countries (May 1950).

Key fact 3.3

The ECSC and the federation of Europe

Extract from Robert Schuman's announcement of a plan for a coal and steel community, 9 May 1950 (subsequently known as Europe Day):

The pooling of coal and steel production should immediately provide for the setting up of common foundations for economic development as a first step in the federation of Europe, and will change the destinies of those regions which have long been devoted to the manufacture of munitions of war, of which they have been the most constant victims. The solidarity in production thus established will make it plain that any war between France and Germany becomes not merely unthinkable, but materially impossible.

(Source: European Communities 1990.)

Biography 3.2

Robert Schuman (1886–1963)

He was a leading political figure in France, especially in the first decade after the Second World War, when he served as prime minister (1947–48) and subsequently as foreign minister until 1953. A native of Luxembourg, he moved to France, where he was elected to the Chamber of Deputies in 1919. During the Second World War, he was a member of the French Resistance and of the Popular Republican Movement. As a strong supporter of European integration, Schuman was responsible for launching the idea of a European coal and steel community and for securing French government backing for this project, commonly known as the Schuman Plan. In 1958, he was elected president of the European Assembly (subsequently known as the European Parliament). Schuman's role in the formation of the first of the European Communities was formally acknowledged (1986) when the EC decided to recognise 9 May as Europe Day, the day on which Schuman had originally unveiled the plan for a European coal and steel community.

France, the Benelux states, the FRG and Italy supported this plan, signing the Treaty of Paris (April 1951) to establish the European Coal and Steel Community and thus as the 'Six' laying the first building block of the EC. A distinctive feature of the plan was the supranational High Authority with powers independent of the governments of the member states.

The adoption of the Schuman Plan reflected a wide range of national interests and concerns. In the case of France, Schuman declared (see Key fact 3.3) that the plan was designed to render war 'not merely unthinkable, but materially impossible'. Certainly, security against Germany was a major factor in seeking to anchor and control the FRG in a French-led European system that allayed fears of a revanchist Germany. The success of Schuman's initiative effectively started a process that was later described as Europeanising the Germans as opposed to Germanising Europe. The plan also enhanced France's status as a European power and challenged the prevailing notion of a UK-organised Western European bloc with France as the UK's junior partner. Besides protecting French access to German coal, the plan established a longer-term trend linking the modernisation and industrialisation of the French economy to the idea of an economically integrated Western Europe. FRG support was guaranteed by its first chancellor, Konrad Adenauer (1949–63), whose immediate concern was to advance FRG claims for full sovereignty and equality without arousing the bogey of German nationalism. In his support for a federal Europe, Adenauer established a connection between European integration and German interests that was to be maintained by his successors. Meanwhile, the Italian government aimed to restore the country's European credentials and to reinforce its as yet fragile authority in the face of a large Communist Party by acting as the cheerleader for European integration. The involvement of the Benelux states was predictable in view of their heavy dependence on the German economy and their support for close interstate economic ties, which had already led them to form the Benelux customs union in 1948.

Plate 3.2 Robert Schuman
Source: Audiovisual Library of the European Commission (2005).

Biography 3.3

Konrad Adenauer (1876–1967)

Adenauer was the first chancellor of the FRG and occupied this post in the period 1949–63. His political career commenced in the 1920s, when he was a member of the Catholic Centre Party and a leading figure in local (Cologne) and state (Prussia) politics. He strongly opposed Hitler and the Nazi Party, and was imprisoned (1934) and arrested by the Gestapo (1944). After the Second World War, he played a leading role in the formation of the Christian Democratic Union, which dominated FRG politics during the period of his chancellorship. Adenauer was particularly responsible for FRG foreign policy, first in ensuring that the FRG extracted from the Western occupying powers (France, UK, USA) the formal right to have a foreign policy and then in shaping that policy to align the FRG with the Western powers, especially with France and the USA. He was a strong opponent of Soviet policy in Europe and maintained that the Western powers should enter negotiations with the Soviet Union from a position of strength ('policy of strength'). He also insisted that the FRG alone had the exclusive right to represent the entire German nation (Hallstein doctrine), and his government refused diplomatic relations with any state, apart from the USSR, that recognised the German Democratic Republic (East Germany).

These responses to the Schuman Plan indicated how the idea of European integration could be used by national governments for a variety of purposes. The pursuit of national interests by European means was most evident in the case of French and FRG policies in this episode, lending substance to the view of Count Otto von Bismarck, the nineteenth-century German leader, that when politicians use the word 'Europe', they are making requests to other powers that they do not dare formulate in the name of their own country. In the years ahead, furthermore, Europe, or more precisely Brussels as the headquarters of the EC/EU, came to serve several latent functions in the internal politics of its member states, most notably as a safety valve or a panacea for deflecting attention away from internal weaknesses or the failure of national policies, as a bogeyman for governments and political parties under pressure on other fronts, and as a whipping boy of national governments wishing to escape blame for unpopular measures.

Key fact 3.4

The UK Foreign Office and European integration

A UK Foreign Office view (December 1951) of the main factors responsible for continental interest in European integration in the years immediately after the end of the Second World War:

> The experiences of the war years, Russian policy and American backing have thus given impetus to the movement for closer integration. This movement has supporters in every country in Western Europe. Their motives are varied and complex; some derive from idealism, others from self-interest … The idealistic motives, broadly speaking, spring from the belief that European culture and civilization have a vital contribution to make in the shaping of world affairs and that they can only effectively do so if the European idea supersedes the old national loyalties. The motives which derive from self-interest are those which see in the integration movement a means of gaining sectional or national advantage.

(Source: *Documents on British Policy Overseas*, series II, vol. I, no. 414.)

The process of European integration has been marked by setbacks from the outset. Shortly after the launching of the Schuman Plan, for example, a US proposal for a major Western European rearmament programme (September 1950), including the FRG, exposed the European states' deep-seated suspicions. France was determined to prevent the formation of a German national army and aimed to do so by proposing the creation of a European army including German troops (Pleven Plan, October 1950). This plan formed the basis of a supranational European Defence Community (EDC) treaty signed by the Six (1952), together with an accompanying plan for a European Political Community (EPC). In the event, France was unwilling to surrender its national sovereignty and refused to ratify the treaty (1954). This outcome exposed the limits of integration and the strength of counter-integrative forces in the form of right-wing (Gaullist) and left-wing communist opposition. (It was not until the 1990s that the EU states seriously reconsidered the sensitive issues raised by this episode, but they have so far failed to create anything resembling the original EDC/EPC. The EU still does not 'do' war, as the current German foreign minister, Joschka Fischer, expressed the matter.) The collapse of the EDC project confirmed UK doubts about the Six's unity of purpose and also provided an opportunity to reassert UK leadership in Western Europe. A British-inspired plan (1954) brought a sovereign, rearmed FRG into NATO and also an enlarged version of the Brussels Treaty Organisation known as the Western European Union (WEU).

In these seemingly unfavourable circumstances, the Six set in motion plans for what is commonly referred to as the 'relaunching of Europe'. The Messina conference of foreign ministers of the Six (June 1955) opened negotiations that resulted in the formation of the European Economic Community (EEC) and the European Atomic Energy Community (EAEC) through the Treaties of Rome (March 1957). The failure of the EDC proposal was partly responsible for this successful initiative. The community idea was no longer plagued by the issue of German rearmament, and attention was refocused on the economic track to integration. During the period 1953–58, intra-Six trade was already expanding by more than 10 percent per annum, suggesting that the common market project was an effect as well as a cause of trade growth and that it helped to reinforce the resumption of trading ties between the Six, which had been greatly damaged since the First World War. The regionalisation of EC trade continued apace thereafter, so that whereas in 1958 (immediately before the customs union came into effect) 30 percent of the total trade of the individual Six was carried on within the EC area, by 1970 this figure had increased to 48 percent. The birth of the common market was also assisted by the conventional wisdom of the time that there was a strong relationship between expanding international trade and high national economic growth rates, as most obviously demonstrated by the FRG's export-led economic growth rate (averaging approximately 8 percent per annum during the 1950s).

A distinct improvement in Franco-German relations was also an important factor in accounting for the success of the post-Messina intergovernmental negotiations. The formation of the WEU and UK military guarantees helped to reconcile France to a rearmed Germany and smoothed the path towards a new initiative. The Saar settlement (1956) removed a contentious issue from Franco-German relations as this territory, under French supervision since 1945, was now reunited with the FRG. The French government was less assured of achieving domestic support for the treaty than the other governments of the Six, so it was important that France succeeded in persuading the FRG to make concessions on such matters as the evolution of the customs union, the inclusion of agriculture, the association of the overseas territories of the EC states with the EC, and social policy. The common market also offered France an assured outlet for its mounting agricultural surpluses and assisted the burgeoning export-oriented industrial production of the FRG. The subsequent rapport between de Gaulle (first president of the French Fifth Republic, 1958–69) and Adenauer resulted in the Franco-German Treaty of Friendship (1963), which symbolised the postwar *rapprochement* between the two states and also set in place the infrastructure for close cooperation between them in EU affairs.

Key fact 3.5

The EEC

Article 2 of the Treaty of Rome establishing the European Economic Community, 25 March 1957:

It shall be the aim of the Community, by establishing a Common Market and progressively approximating the economic policies of Member States, to promote throughout the Community a harmonious development of economic activities, a continuous and balanced expansion, an increased stability, an accelerated raising of the standard of living and closer relations between its Member States.

Biography 3.4

Charles de Gaulle (1890–1970)

First president of the French Fifth Republic, 1958–69. After the defeat of France by Nazi Germany (June 1940), de Gaulle organised the Free French forces and continuing French resistance to Nazi Germany. He was head of the provisional government of France that was formed in June 1944. After the end of the Second World War, he became provisional president of France (November 1945) but resigned from this post two months later as the new constitution of the Fourth Republic made no provision for a strong executive. He returned to power in 1958 as the issue of Algerian independence engulfed the Fourth Republic and as he was regarded as the only political figure capable of achieving a settlement, which eventually emerged with Algerian independence in 1962. De Gaulle was primarily intent on restoring France's status and independence in the international system, as was evident, for example, in his determination to acquire an independent French nuclear deterrent, in his development of a Franco-German relationship with France as the senior partner, and in his pursuit of an independent French policy within the Western alliance. De Gaulle was re-elected president in 1965. His authority was severely challenged in May 1968, when Paris was rocked by strikes and demonstrations as students and workers revolted against what they regarded as an authoritarian political and educational system. In elections a month later, however, the Gaullists were returned to power on the back of a tide of opinion fearful of revolution. De Gaulle resigned from the presidency in 1969 following defeat in a referendum on constitutional reform.

The EEC was designed to form a common market with free movement of goods, capital, labour and services. Phased progression towards a customs union was a major goal. The introduction of the Common Agricultural Policy (CAP) also emerged as an immediate priority. However, descriptions of this policy as a basic deal between French agriculture and German industry are misleading. Such descriptions underestimate the role of the industrial modernisers in France, who aimed to galvanise French industry through the common market, and the influence of the agricultural lobby in the Christian Democrat governing party in the FRG. The underlying political purpose to create 'an ever closer union among the peoples of Europe' accommodated different views about integration and avoided any specific reference to the supranational principle contained in the ECSC treaty. The four main institutions of the EEC (see Section 3.2) collectively expressed an assortment of emphases:

1. The Commission as policy initiator represented the supranational dimension.
2. The Council of Ministers as the decision-making body was the organ of national governments.
3. The Court of Justice established a new legal order independent of the member states.
4. The Common Assembly (later European Parliament) was primarily a consultative body.

The successful negotiation of the Treaties of Rome sharpened and eventually formalised the division of Western Europe into two trading blocs. Fears of a widening gulf between the Six and the rest of Western Europe prompted a UK attempt to devise a European free-trade area including the Six. This proposal typified the strong tendency of UK policymakers at the time and later to underestimate the Six's seriousness of purpose and to overestimate UK influence on the continent. It offered too little, too late to accommodate the Six and was viewed by many of the EC's founders as an attempt to sabotage their project. At the same time, the UK was increasingly at odds with France and the FRG. UK handling of the Suez crisis (October–November 1956) angered the French, while UK support for negotiations with the USSR to reduce tensions in Europe conflicted with Adenauer's hard-edged Cold War policy.

The emergence of a more assertive political leadership in France under de Gaulle (May–June 1958) and a further tightening of Franco-German bonds sealed the fate of the UK proposal. France effectively strengthened its leadership of the Six while undermining UK influence in Europe by terminating the free-trade area negotiations (December 1958). The UK and six other states – Austria, Denmark, Norway, Portugal, Sweden and Switzerland – then established the European Free Trade Association (EFTA) in 1960 with no provisions for closer economic or political unification beyond a free-trade area in manufactured goods.

Western Europe thus entered the 1960s with a clearly institutionalised division between the EC and the EFTA. There was little doubt which organisation represented the core and which the periphery. In 1960, a major report commissioned by Harold Macmillan, the UK prime minister, concluded that 'There is already a belief that the Six are going to come out on top in Europe'. What immediately lent weight to this view was the fact that the EC accelerated its tariff-cutting programme (1960), launched political union negotiations (1961), attracted applications for membership from three EFTA states – the UK, Denmark and Norway – and Ireland (1961), and concluded the first agreements on the CAP (1962). This flurry of activity meant that the concept of Europe was fast becoming exclusively associated with the EC.

What is Europe? Crisis, renewal and recession 1961–79

During the 1960s and 1970s, the EC experienced a mixed record of achievements and failures. In the 1960s, the most notable developments were the completion of the customs union (1968), the full implementation of the CAP by the end of the decade and the emergence of the EC as a single actor in international trade negotiations in the Kennedy Round of GATT negotiations (1963–67). At the same time, however, a series of crises dashed hopes of political union (1962), blocked enlargement (1963) and even threatened the EC's survival. During the 1970s, moreover, ambitious plans for further integration were no sooner unveiled than they were swept aside by a major downturn in economic conditions. Throughout this period, many of the conflicts centred on the role and identity of the EC and the pace and direction of European integration. They invariably involved polarised views focusing on pairs of concepts, such as:

- intergovernmental cooperation and supranationalism;
- limited and expansive visions of the EC's global identity;
- political and economic integration;
- enlargement of EC membership and deepening of its functional integration.

In the 1960s, such concepts were very much to the fore in clashes between France under de Gaulle's leadership and the other EC member states, which ranged from the importance of national sovereignty to the conduct of national foreign policy within and beyond Europe. Gaullist emphasis on national independence and on intergovernmental cooperation in international affairs involved intransigent opposition to supranationalism. The French state, like the other EC member states, was by the mid-1960s stronger than it had been in the dark days of military defeat of 1940 or at the time of the collapse of the French Fourth Republic in 1958. In these circumstances, de Gaulle was particularly determined to attack the supranational plans and pretensions of the Commission, especially its plan for automatic funding of the EC. This confrontation resulted in a French boycott of all EC institutions (July 1965). The eventual settlement of this conflict, the Luxembourg Agreement (January 1966), amounted to an agreement to disagree between France and the other EC states about the right to exercise a national veto in the Council of Ministers. However, a further significant outcome of this trial of strength was that the economic benefits of European integration to France were such that not even de Gaulle could contemplate permanent exclusion from the enterprise or place at risk the value of the CAP to France's influential agricultural sector.

Other aspects of Gaullist foreign policy also clashed with the views of France's EC partners. De Gaulle's attempt to forge a political union of the Six collapsed as a result of irreconcilable differences between France and the other member states over NATO ties, which de Gaulle wished to weaken, and over the status of the EC relative to its member states. These differences, in turn, reflected contrasting views of the EC's role on the wider international stage. For his own part, de Gaulle presented an expansive vision of a French-led Europe 'from the Atlantic to the Urals' freed from superpower rivalries and able to act as a counterweight to the USA and to the UK–USA axis at the heart of NATO. This 'European Europe' opposed the prevailing view of an integrated Western Europe under the US-led NATO ('Atlanticist Europe'), and eventually resulted in France's withdrawal from NATO in 1966. A major US response to this challenge to US leadership in Western Europe came in the form of President Kennedy's 'Grand Design' speech of 4 July 1962, with its emphasis on cooperation between the USA and Europe. In de Gaulle's view, this US move was mere rhetoric designed to obscure the reality of US hegemony in

Europe. The dominant US role in the Western military and monetary system, as de Gaulle noted, remained untouched, especially as the Kennedy administration (1961–63) sought to confine possession of nuclear weapons in the Western alliance to the USA and refused to assist France's nuclear weapons programme or to accede to French demands for an enhanced leadership role within NATO. Part of the Kennedy 'Grand Design' initiative touching on transatlantic trade relations marked out one area where the emerging EC began to match US power and continues to do so. US/EC friction over trading relations was to be a recurring feature of transatlantic relations. It was first evident in the so-called 'chicken war' of 1962, when the emerging CAP resulted in a reduction of the proportion of US poultry in total EC imports of poultry.

During the 1960s, De Gaulle also raised in an early form questions concerning the relative importance of the deepening and enlargement processes at work in the EC. On coming to power in 1958 and contrary to some expectations, he accepted French membership of the EC and safeguarded the EC's unity and integrity by rejecting UK plans for a free-trade area (November 1958). He also strongly supported the implementation of the EC's common policies, especially the CAP, and feared that immediate enlargement of the EC to include the UK would jeopardise such policies. It was partly on these grounds and also because no French national interest was likely to be served at this stage by allowing UK membership that de Gaulle unilaterally vetoed UK applications for EC membership in 1963 and 1967.

Biography 3.5

Harold Macmillan (Earl of Stockton) (1894–1986)

UK politician and Conservative prime minister of the UK (1957–63), Macmillan first became an MP in 1924. He became secretary of state for air in 1945 and subsequently served as housing minister (1951–54), defence minister (1954–55), foreign secretary (1955) and chancellor of the Exchequer (1955–57). He restored good relations with the USA, damaged by the Suez policy of his predecessor, Anthony Eden. He advocated independence for UK colonies in Africa and elsewhere with his famous 'winds of change' speech. Macmillan's attempts to bring the UK into the EEC were frustrated by French president de Gaulle. Macmillan's premiership ended in controversy. A cabinet purge in 1962 earned him the sobriquet 'Mac the Knife', and his government was engulfed in scandal following the 'Profumo affair'. Citing ill-health, Macmillan resigned in 1963. He joined the House of Lords at the age of 90. A moderate, 'one nation' Conservative, he was critical of the policies of Margaret Thatcher towards the end of his life.

Biography 3.6

Harold Wilson (Baron Wilson) (1916–95)

UK politician and Labour prime minister of the UK (1964–70 and 1974–76), Wilson was first elected an MP in 1945 and served as president of the Board of Trade (1947–51). He succeeded Hugh Gaitskell as Labour Party leader in 1963 and became prime minister in 1964. His 'white heat of technological revolution' speech signified an attempt to project a modern and progressive economic outlook, but economic difficulties forced unpopular economic policies on Wilson, such as devaluation in 1967. By 1970, his personal popularity had revived and electoral defeat came as a surprise. He returned to power in 1974 and skilfully renegotiated UK membership of the EEC, calling a referendum to ratify membership and defuse tensions over the issue within the Labour Party. He resigned as prime minister in 1976 and joined the House of Lords in 1983.

Two further important and enduring elements were involved in this matter. First, the decisions of the UK governments under Macmillan (1961) and Wilson (1967) to apply for EC membership were greatly influenced by an acute awareness of national weakness and failed government policies, especially in the form of Britain's relatively slow economic growth rate, limited economic modernisation and sluggish industrial performance as compared with the EC and the accompanying recognition of the need for an external stimulus like membership of the large, competitive EC market. There was, too, strong, influential American backing for this move, which neither Macmillan nor Wilson could ignore without jeopardising what they perceived as the advantage of the 'special relationship' with Washington, which included:

- privileged contacts with the US government;
- preferential access to advanced American military technology;
- obscuring the UK's declining role and status in world affairs;
- concealing the imbalance of power between the USA and the UK;
- cultivating US support for sterling on money markets;
- securing US support for UK interests beyond Europe;
- occupying a pivotal role in relations between the USA and Europe.

Second, de Gaulle was convinced that there could be no place for Britain in the EC so long as its government was still wedded to the idea of a 'special relationship' with the USA and was thus unwilling to contemplate a European entity that assumed more responsibility for its own defence and was less dependent on the USA. During the Second World War, Winston Churchill, the British wartime leader, had told de Gaulle that if he was forced to choose between him and Roosevelt (the US president), he would always choose Roosevelt. Subsequent developments reinforced de Gaulle's view that the UK was a junior partner of the USA rather than a truly European state and that, if allowed to join the EC, it would serve as a Trojan horse, promoting and protecting US interests. The Nassau agreement between Kennedy and Macmillan (December 1962), whereby the UK obtained American-built Polaris missiles, simply confirmed for de Gaulle his view of UK dependence on the USA. The fact that the USA supported the UK application for EC membership was sufficient in itself for de Gaulle to exercise a veto.

Opinion 3.2

De Gaulle on the UK and the USA

At a meeting with Macmillan (15 December 1962), President de Gaulle of France informed Macmillan that he intended to veto the UK's application for EC membership, and he commented on UK relations with the USA:

... the organisation of Europe would be much easier when European countries were really independent. When European countries, and above all Britain, agreed to do their own things themselves, then the position would be different. Of course Europe must remain allied and friendly with the United States. It was difficult however to be both with the Americans and with Europe. Naturally Britain was reluctant to abandon her special link with the United States ... The President [de Gaulle] did not reproach Britain with her attitude which had been almost forced upon her. In her fine response during the war Britain had had to accept American partnership and eventual leadership in order to win. Then because of Britain's world position and the question of nuclear arms she had judged it more practical to stay linked to the United States ... So far, Britain had not taken the road to independence.

(Source: Public Record Office, PREM 11/4230.)

Is this opinion fair?

Changing international conditions by the late 1960s, including de Gaulle's retirement in 1969, gave renewed momentum to the EC. Georges Pompidou, de Gaulle's successor, broke the log jam on enlargement. This reversal of French policy was largely due to mounting anxieties about the FRG's economic power and strategic objectives, which in turn encouraged greater recognition of the value of UK membership as a counterweight to the FRG. While the FRG was still a 'political pygmy' (Willy Brandt) on the European diplomatic stage, it had emerged as Europe's economic superpower and as a model for other European economies in its sustained record of low inflation, high trade surpluses and competitive industries. It accounted for 20 percent of total world trade, possessed the strongest currency in Europe and acted as the EC's 'paymaster'. Changes in FRG policy towards Eastern Europe at this time particularly alarmed Paris. The *Ostpolitik* (policy towards the east) of the Brandt government (1969–74) abandoned the previous policy of non-recognition of the Eastern European states (Hallstein doctrine) and aimed for the normalisation of relations. This turn of events aroused French fears of a neutralist FRG drifting away from its Western ties, all the more so in view of the impact of superpower relations on Europe. The Soviet invasion of Czechoslovakia (1968) shattered de Gaulle's ambition to loosen the grip of the superpowers on Europe and also administered the last rites to the idea of a 'Third Force' Europe between the superpowers. Meanwhile, the quickening pace of *détente* at the superpower level threatened to exclude European governments from a bargaining system dealing with European issues.

In this new atmosphere, the Hague summit of EC heads of state and governments (December 1969) agreed to open negotiations with the applicant states (the UK, Denmark, Ireland and Norway), to develop new common policies, to proceed towards economic and monetary union (EMU) by 1980 and to explore the possibility of political cooperation. Shortly afterwards, in 1970, a process of continuing consultation, European Political Cooperation, sought to coordinate the foreign policies of the EC states. This process was further assisted by the emergence of the European Council (1975), which formalised the hitherto *ad hoc* meetings of EC heads of state and government. In some respects, the crises of the 1960s merely postponed agreements until the 1970s, as in the case of enlargement. The question of the EC's funding, for example, which had been to the fore in the crisis of 1965, was finally settled in 1970; all revenue from tariffs on manufactured goods and from levies on agricultural imports, together with up to 1 percent of value-added tax (VAT) collected by member states, became the EC's automatic revenue ('own resources'). In other respects, however, the EC emerged from this period resembling a conventional international organisation and in a different form from that envisaged by some of its federalist-minded founding fathers. The Commission, for example, was now overshadowed by the Council of Ministers, whose intergovernmental conduct of business resulted in paralysingly slow decision making often based on the lowest common denominator.

Plate 3.3 Prime Minister Edward Heath, flanked by Sir Alec Douglas-Home and Geoffrey Rippon, signing the Treaty of Accession for the UK to join the EC

Source: Audiovisual Library of the European Commission (2005).

More difficult economic conditions during the 1970s severely strained the European economies, blocked the more ambitious plans for integration emanating from the Hague summit and subjected the EC's decision-making system to new pressures. The 'golden age of prosperity' and high economic growth rates of the 1950s and 1960s ended in 1973–74 with the quadrupling of the price of oil by the Organisation of Petroleum Exporting Countries (OPEC); the average annual growth rate (in GDP) of the leading four Western European states slumped from 4.6 percent (1960–73) to 2.2 percent (1973–80). The consequent rise in inflation and unemployment undermined the economic aspects of the Hague programme. These worsening economic conditions also exposed problems of cohesion as the EC economies were very differently affected by recession; in 1975, for example, the rate of inflation in the FRG was 7 percent, while it rose to 25 percent in the UK and Italy. The economic and monetary union project (Werner Plan) was an early casualty of these new conditions, as the collapse of the dollar-based Bretton Woods fixed exchange rate system following the formal US abandonment of the dollar's convertibility into gold (1971) resulted in floating currencies.

Biography 3.7

Valéry Giscard d'Estaing (1926–)

President of France, 1974–81. He was elected to the French parliament in 1951 and held a number of government posts in the period 1959–66 and again in the period 1969–74, when he was economics and finance minister. He headed the pro-Gaullist conservatives from 1962 until 1974 and formed the Union for French Democracy in 1978. As finance minister and president he played a very active role in EC politics. He was particularly influential in institutionalising the summit meetings of EC heads of state and government in the form of the European Council (1975). He also played a prominent role in launching the European Monetary System (1979), and he had a close working relationship in this and other aspects of EC policymaking with Helmut Schmidt, the FRG chancellor (1974–82). Following defeat in the French presidential election of 1981, he remained a member of the French parliament until 1989, when he entered the European Parliament and eventually led the Liberal group. In 2002–03, he served as president of the Convention on the Future of Europe, whose report strongly influenced the content of the EU constitutional treaty. His views on some aspects of current EU affairs have attracted controversy, especially his opposition to the idea of Turkey's membership of the EU.

While economic and monetary union failed to materialise by 1980, a more modest project known as the European Monetary System (EMS) was introduced in 1979 and provided for closer cooperation in monetary policy. This Franco-German initiative developed out of a renewed emphasis on the Bonn/Paris axis at the centre of the EC; the French and West German leaders, Valéry Giscard d'Estaing and Helmut Schmidt, forged a close working relationship during the period 1974–81, in contrast to the preceding ten years of troubled relations. Schmidt was largely responsible for taking the initiative, although in this as in other episodes the FRG government was anxious to avoid the impression of an assertive Germany. The EMS aimed to create a zone of monetary stability in Western Europe and in particular to limit fluctuations between the currencies of the member states through the operation of the Exchange Rate Mechanism (ERM), the centrepiece of the EMS. While this scheme did not assign a special role to any currency, the deutschmark was effectively the leading, benchmark currency, and the Bundesbank was fast becoming a surrogate central bank for the EC. This highly visible German financial power and status eventually persuaded some influential bodies of opinion in the EC and especially in France that a fully fledged EC monetary union was preferable to German leadership of this halfway house. Meanwhile, the EMS survived to provide at least some of the foundations for the eventually successful scheme for economic and monetary union that was rolled out in the 1990s.

Biography 3.8

Helmut Schmidt (1918–)

Chancellor of the Federal Republic of Germany, 1974–82. He was elected to the lower chamber (Bundestag) of the FRG parliament as a member of the SPD in 1953. He occupied cabinet posts in the Brandt government of 1969–74, first as defence minister until 1972 and then as minister for economics and finance (1972) and finally as minister of finance (1972–74). He became chancellor in May 1974 following Brandt's resignation. Schmidt played an active role in developing close relations with France, especially in the management of EC affairs. While he was not an enthusiastic supporter of European integration, he was nevertheless prepared to take the lead as and when this served FRG interests, most notably in his advocacy of the case for introducing the European Monetary System, which largely materialised as a result of his personal backing. He was a strong supporter of NATO, incurring considerable opposition from elements within his own party for his pro-NATO policies. He lost the support of FDP ministers in his government in 1982 and later that year was forced to resign from the chancellorship as a result of a constructive vote of no confidence, the first post-1945 German chancellor to lose power by this device.

Plans for a European union during this period also met the same fate as the idea of full economic and monetary union. Following a European Council decision (February 1974) to set in motion a report on European union, Leo Tindemans, the Belgian prime minister, was invited to submit a report by the end of 1975. The content of this report anticipated many of the central features of the (Maastricht) Treaty on European Union (1992), especially with reference to economic and monetary union and the idea of a common foreign and security policy. In the circumstances of the 1970s, however, the Tindemans Report came to typify the way in which EC government leaders were willing to make pious professions about European union while steadfastly refusing to take action in view of political and economic difficulties.

The economic recession and the more protectionist climate of opinion limited EC progress on other fronts and contributed to what was often labelled 'eurosclerosis'. While the limited progress of the EC in these circumstances may have been overstated in some accounts, there was nonetheless a striking degree of inaction and failure of collective will. During the oil crisis of 1973–74, for example, the EC possessed neither the instruments nor the policy to present a collective approach. Its lack of solidarity was evident in its failure to give public support to one member

Leo Tindemans (1922–)

Prime minister of Belgium, 1974–79. Tindemans entered Belgian politics as a member of the Chamber of Deputies in 1961. His premiership ended in 1979 following a dispute with his coalition government partners over proposals for the restructuring of Belgium into a federal state. He served as foreign minister of Belgium in the period 1981–89, after which he became a member of the European Parliament. As Belgian prime minister, Tindemans was a very active supporter of European integration. His report of 1975 on European union, commonly called the Tindemans Report, reflected his interest in a federal Europe and in democratising the EC. There was very little official support for this report, while some of the advocates of a federal Europe were critical of its limited provisions. The report provided guidelines for the EC's future development, and many of its proposals, such as economic and monetary union, greater power for the European Parliament and foreign and security cooperation, were to receive more serious consideration in the 1990s.

state (the Netherlands) that was the target of an Arab oil boycott on account of its pro-Israeli sympathies, and also in the headlong rush of states like the UK and France to reach bilateral deals with individual Arab states. Meanwhile, on another front, the planned progression from 'negative' integration (the removal of existing restrictions) towards 'positive' integration (new common policies) ran into increasing difficulties. The absorption of 80 percent of the EC's budget by the CAP seriously impeded any new spending initiatives. An increasingly widespread government effort to curb public expenditure was also an obstacle, and governments looked to their own defences rather than to the EC for a collective approach to their problems. Some common policies were formulated, but they were either subject to severe funding limits, like the Regional Development Fund (1975), or delayed by lengthy negotiations, as in the case of the Common Fisheries Policy, which was first mooted in 1970 but did not materialise until 1983. The survival of the customs union was in itself something of an achievement in view of the harsh economic climate. The workings of the customs union continued to reinforce the regionalisation of EC trade (see Key fact 3.6). However, non-tariff or invisible barriers in the form of national regulations, arrangements and subsidies favouring the domestic producer continued to block the emergence of a common market.

The enlargement of the EC during this period also presented the prospect of a weaker organisation. The UK's protracted adjustment to membership underlined the extent to which the EC idea had continental European parentage. There were several reasons for the UK's difficult transition to EC membership, including:

- Some of the major EC policies (e.g. the CAP) reflected the interests of the founding member states rather than UK concerns.

- Conflicts within and between the Conservative and Labour Parties over the question of UK membership of the EC.

- Strong support for what were regarded as the superior merits of the UK model of European cooperation and a distaste for EU ideas about the divisibility of sovereignty.

- A greater proportion of the UK's trading and financial interests lay beyond Europe than was the case with other member states.

Key fact 3.6

Intra-EC trade

The value of the intra-European Community trade of each EC member state expressed as a percentage of each state's total exports in 1958 and 1980.

	1958	1980
Belgium/Luxembourg	35	71
Denmark	58	50
Germany	35	48
France	28	51
Ireland	83	74
Italy	32	48
Netherlands	57	73
United Kingdom	20	42

(Source: European Communities 1982.)

Some of the deeply rooted ambivalence of UK governments towards the EC and the often aphasic grasp of the mainsprings of European integration originated in the absence of a shared history between the UK and the founding member states of the EC. A major consequence of this in the 1970s, as indeed before and after, was that the historical foundations, language and rhythm of European integration were not easily assimilated into British political culture. This much was evident when the Wilson Labour government conducted a 'renegotiation' of the terms of entry (1974–75), which had been successfully negotiated by the Heath Conservative government of 1970–74. While eventually supporting continued membership of the EC, the Wilson government found itself facing hostile majorities against the renegotiated terms of entry at every level in the Labour Party and movement outside the Cabinet. A defensive semi-detached relationship between the UK and the EU thereafter became the norm under the Callaghan Labour government (1976–79). On the formation of the EMS, for example, the UK was the only EC state to withhold its currency from the operations of the Exchange Rate Mechanism (ERM), partly because of Labour Party antipathy towards this project and partly because many of Britain's industrial, commercial and financial interests were sceptical of the case for including sterling in the ERM. At the same time, the Callaghan government deliberately attempted to foster close relations with the USA, which had not been a priority of the Heath government, Heath himself being the most European and least pro-American or 'Atlanticist' of British prime ministers since 1945.

Biography 3.10

Sir Edward Heath (1916–2005)

UK politician and Conservative prime minister of the UK (1970–74), Heath became an MP in 1950 and served as minister of labour (1959–60), Lord Privy Seal (1960–63) and secretary of state for trade and industry (1963–64). He was elected Conservative Party leader in 1965 and became prime minister in 1970. His Industrial Relations Act (1971) brought him into conflict with the trade unions, and his premiership was marked by major industrial conflicts and fuel shortages, culminating in the infamous 'three-day week', when many people were restricted to working for three days only each week to conserve resources. A bitter miners' strike ultimately led to his downfall. A passionate pro-European, Heath's major achievement was to negotiate the UK's membership of the EEC in 1973. He was succeeded as Conservative leader by Margaret Thatcher, who had served as his education secretary but who became his most bitter rival and enemy. Heath remained an MP until 2001, frequently attacking Thatcher from the back benches throughout her time in office.

At best, mixed results emerged from attempts to develop an EC political identity on the international stage during this period. The US idea of a 'year of Europe', ostensibly intended to revive the Western alliance but primarily designed to reassert US leadership in the face of an enlarged and potentially stronger EC, met with limited European interest and exposed divisions between the EC states over transatlantic relations. US support for European unity by this time was far less in evidence than it had been in the 1950s and 1960s, and in some respects the absence of a single European voice assisted the USA in managing its Western European allies. Against such evidence of European disunity, however, the fluctuating state of East–West relations from *détente* in the first half of the 1970s to the 'second Cold War' (1979–85) did produce a common EC response. This was first evident in the Helsinki Conference on Security and Cooperation in Europe (1973–75), which resulted in East–West recognition of the territorial and political status quo in Europe. This development held out the possibility of peaceful change and growing links between the two halves of Europe.

As the 1970s drew to a close, however, the EC appeared to carry little clout in international affairs, especially as the second oil crisis of 1979–80 adversely impacted on EU economies and as relations between the superpowers deteriorated in the wake of developments in Poland and the Soviet invasion of Afghanistan (see Chronological Table) and a renewed arms race. The EC's combination of economic strength and military weakness suggested to some commentators at this time and later that it was a 'civilian power' rather than a 'superpower in the making', and that it was an economic giant but a political dwarf. In some quarters, moreover, by the early 1980s it seemed that not only the status and future direction of the EC were in doubt but that its viability was questionable in view of the way in which the project had stalled in the preceding decade.

Where next for Europe? The drive to closer union in the 1980s

The process of European integration in the 1980s involved a decisive shift from the immobilism of the 1970s towards a greater degree of dynamism. This was most evident in the making of the Single European Act (SEA; 1986) and in laying the foundations of the (Maastricht) Treaty on European Union (1992). During the same period, the seemingly immutable division of Europe and of Germany unexpectedly and dramatically dissolved in 1989–91 with the end of the Cold War, the unification of Germany, the disintegration of Soviet dominance in Eastern Europe, and the collapse of the Soviet Union (see Chronological Table). Meanwhile, the enlargement of the EC to include Greece (1981) and Spain and Portugal (1986), following the collapse of their dictatorships, meant that the EC became more representative of Western Europe and now comprised 90 percent of Western Europe's population and accounted for 88 percent of the area's GDP. Equally important, this enlargement of the EC was achieved at the same time as further moves towards deepening the process of integration through the SEA.

The SEA aimed to create a single market by the end of 1992 by eradicating all impediments to the free movement of capital, goods, services and persons. It resulted in the largest frontier-free market in the advanced industrial world, accounting for 22.5 percent of the world's GDP and 19.5 percent of world exports (1991). Part of the impetus behind this initiative lay in the accumulating evidence of the EC's relatively poor performance in the global economy and its declining economic growth rate. In the period 1973–85, when the EC's share of world trade in manufactured goods fell from 45 to 36 percent, the USA and Japan lengthened their technological lead over Europe in computing, robotics, telecommunications and other high-technology industries, while the new industrialising countries of the Far East posed a growing threat to large swathes of European industry. At one level, the EC response to this challenge was to embark upon a major programme of technological cooperation – the Eureka programme – which originated in a French initiative (1985). However, it was increasingly felt that more needed to be done to fashion the EC into a more effective economic and political unit by eradicating the remaining barriers to the free working of the internal market and by improving the decision-making procedures.

Favourable conditions within the EC were primarily responsible for the decision of the EC heads of government at the Milan European Council (June 1985) to convene an intergovernmental conference (IGC) on the EC's future, which paved the way for the SEA. A resolution of the issue of the UK contribution to the EC budget helped to clear the decks. On coming to power in 1979, the Thatcher government immediately sought to reduce the UK's net contribution to the EC budget (£1 billion in 1979). Britain was second only to the FRG as a net contributor to the EC budget by this time, while its GDP was much smaller than that of the FRG. There ensued over the next few years a rancorous, time-consuming set of negotiations over what the president of the Commission (Roy Jenkins) at the time described as the 'bloody British question'. One explanation for this lengthy saga, indicative of one of the functions of the EC for the governments of the member states, was that Thatcher deliberately exacerbated and prolonged the crisis as a way of boosting her flagging domestic popularity and of diverting attention from the devastating economic recession of 1978–81.

Biography 3.11

Roy Jenkins (1920–2003)

President of the European Commission, 1977–81. Jenkins held a number of posts as a UK government minister in the Wilson Labour governments of 1964–70, notably as home secretary (1965–67) and chancellor of the Exchequer (1967–70). He was elected deputy leader of the Labour Party when the party went into opposition following the election defeat of 1970. Jenkins was a strong supporter of British membership of the EC and led the minority support in the Labour Party for the application of the Conservative government for EC membership in 1971. He was regarded as the principal spokesman for social democratic opinion within the Labour Party. He was defeated in the contest for leadership of the Labour Party following the resignation of Harold Wilson (1976), after which he became president of the Commission. In this position, he played a prominent role in the introduction of the European Monetary System, which laid the foundations for the single currency. He returned to UK politics in 1981, left the Labour Party and helped to found the Social Democratic Party (SDP). He became leader of the SDP and returned to the House of Commons by winning the Glasgow Hillhead by-election (1982). He resigned as leader of the SDP after the general election of 1983 and was defeated in the general election of 1987, subsequently becoming leader of the Liberal Democrats in the House of Lords.

The settlement of the British demand for an EC budget rebate (June 1984), which still remains in being, contributed to a rare burst of positive interest in the EC by Thatcher. While the Thatcher government opposed the idea of convening an IGC (see Section 3.2), the single-market project chimed with its political ideology and definition of national self-interest. The elimination of commercial restrictions within the EC was in accord with the government's staunch adherence to free-market economics. It was also hoped that the UK's air transport and financial service industries, believed to be leaders in their field, would derive great benefits from the establishment of unfettered competition. This lifting of restrictions and emphasis on the freeing up of the market and neo-liberal economics were to remain enduring features of the UK's European policy under Conservative and Labour governments thereafter. Other EC member states were also keen to embark on closer forms of integration. Italy was characteristically determined to act as a pacemaker of further integration at the Milan European Council. Bettino Craxi, the Italian prime minister, was instrumental in obtaining a majority vote for an IGC to consider basic institutional reforms and a possible revision of the EC's founding treaties, the first occasion on which the Council had reached a decision by a show of hands. It was at this point that the idea of a 'multi-speed' approach to European integration first surfaced when the French president, François Mitterrand, suggested that some member states should be allowed to engage in new forms of integration while leaving others like the UK to catch up later. In the event, the outcome of the Milan European Council overrode the objections of the UK, Denmark and Greece to convening an IGC. By the early 1990s, the UK was in fact acting on the 'multi-speed' idea by opting out of provisions for the final stages of economic and monetary union (EMU) and also out of the Social Chapter (see below). The accompanying insistence by John Major, the UK prime minister, that the UK intended to be 'at the heart of Europe' suggested that the UK government wished to remain in the slow lane to integration while trying to direct traffic in the fast lane.

France and the FRG were the prime movers in rejuvenating the process of European integration via the SEA. Renewed French interest in the EC arose partly out of deep-seated fear of German detachment from the Western alliance as a result of widespread support for the anti-nuclear peace movement in Germany during the early 1980s. More importantly, the chastening experience of the 'socialist experiment' (1981–83) in the early years of the Mitterrand presidency in France and especially the massive fall in the value of the franc convinced Mitterrand that a strong franc (*franc fort*) necessitated a greater degree of monetary integration with the FRG. France accordingly took and maintained the lead in pressing the case for economic and monetary union. A principal calculation in French government circles was that a single European currency supervised by a central European bank was likely to be more susceptible to French influence than the German-dominated monetary regime of the EMS. Following the election of Helmut Kohl as chancellor in 1982, the FRG was also concerned to chart a new course for European integration. The FRG's main interest was to utilise the EC as a political entity and, as in the past, to advance German interests in a non-threatening way. There was a particular concern to protect the FRG's large investment in *détente* in the face of anatagonistic superpower relations during the 'second Cold War'. As superpower relations deteriorated in the early 1980s, there was widespread interest among EC states in maintaining improved relations with the communist Eastern bloc countries and in sealing off the process of *détente* in Europe from the global conflicts of the superpowers. Apart from the UK government, the EC states gave only qualified support to US toughness against the USSR, and they eschewed US President Ronald Reagan's depiction of the USSR as an 'evil empire'. This position lent weight to the case for a more distinctive 'European voice' in the security and foreign policy fields, which eventually found expression in the European Council's 'Solemn Declaration on European Union' (1983). By the mid-1980s, then, the leading EC member states were demonstrating a more pressing need to achieve some of their domestic and international objectives through the further development of the EC than they had done ten years earlier.

Biography 3.12

Ronald Reagan (1911–2004)

President of the USA, 1981–89. He was elected governor of California in 1966 and re-elected in 1970. In 1980, he won the Republican presidential nomination and also the subsequent presidential election. He took office in January 1981 and was re-elected in 1984. Reagan had a strong ideological commitment to free-market economic policies with a pronounced emphasis on cutting taxes and reducing government expenditure. US defence expenditure soared under his administrations by at least one-third and resulted in a large deficit in the federal budget. Reagan was a longstanding opponent of the Soviet Union and of communism, supporting anti-communist movements in Africa, Asia and Central America. His strident Cold War rhetoric included a description of the Soviet Union as the 'evil empire'. However, he did enter into negotiations with the new Soviet leadership of Gorbachev after 1985, resulting in such agreements as the treaty eliminating intermediate-range nuclear weapons.

The institutional provisions of the SEA established a key new principle in the decision-making procedure of the EC. The Council of Ministers was now empowered to take decisions by qualified majority voting, thus overcoming the use of the national veto and immediately expediting the passage of the large amount of legislation required to give effect to the SEA. The European Parliament, a directly elected body since 1979, acquired greater influence. The European Council and European Political Cooperation were formally incorporated into the EC. However, the EC retained its hybrid character, reserving substantial powers for the governments of the member states. For example, the European Parliament still lacked the legislative competence required to reduce the 'democratic deficit' in the conduct of EC affairs, while defence and security issues still remained outside the EC framework (see Section 3.2 for a discussion of more recent institutional changes).

Biography 3.13

Jacques Delors (1925–)

President of the European Commission, 1985–94. Delors started his career in banking, became active in the French trade union movement, and as a member of the French Socialist Party was elected to the European Parliament in 1979. He served as finance minister (1983–84) in the Socialist administration of President Mitterand. In 1985, he began the first of two terms as president of the European Commission. He was arguably the most influential of all holders of this post. Many of the key developments in EC/EU history during this period owed much to his vision, dynamism and strength of character. He played an important role in the making and implementation of the Single European Act (1986). He subsequently threw his weight behind the drive to economic and monetary union and was responsible for chairing the committee that considered EC monetary union and produced the Delors Report (April 1989). In addition, he played a leading role in drafting the Charter of Fundamental Rights (1989) and in the developments culminating in the Maastricht Treaty.

The significance of the SEA for the future development of the EC gave rise to a fierce debate that left its mark on the EC/EU in the 1990s. Some states, most notably the core or founding member states of the EC, saw the Act as a means of promoting further political, economic and monetary integration, and in particular of advancing policy harmonisation over such matters as taxation and border controls. This view was strongly championed by Jacques Delors, whose presidency of the Commission (1985–94) restored its role as a dynamic force in promoting new schemes, most notably a three-stage plan for full economic and monetary union (April 1989). Delors also proposed a social charter of workers' and citizens' rights (May 1989) with a view to popularising the EC or, as he expressed the view: 'You can't fall in love with a single market!' In July 1988, Delors further angered his critics when he told the European Parliament that in ten years' time 80 percent of economic, financial and social legislation affecting members of the EC would emanate from Brussels. The strongest counterblast to the Delors vision came from Margaret Thatcher. Her Bruges speech (September 1988) rejected the notion of a European superstate, poured scorn on many of the policies advocated by most EC governments and denounced Delors' plans as creeping backdoor socialism.

Plate 3.4 Jacques Delors
Source: Audiovisual Library of the European Commission (2005).

The Thatcher Bruges speech

Extracts from a speech by Margaret Thatcher in Bruges on 20 September 1988:

My first guiding principle is this: willing and active co-operation between independent sovereign states is the best way to build a successful European Community ... We have not successfully rolled back the frontiers of the state in Britain, only to see them reimposed at a European level, with a European superstate exercising a new dominance from Brussels. Certainly we want to see Europe more united and with a greater sense of common purpose. But it must be in a way which preserves the different traditions, Parliamentary powers and sense of national pride in one's own country; for these have been the source of Europe's vitality through the centuries.

(Source: Baroness Thatcher's Office.)

Is this a fair view?

By this time, however, Thatcher occupied a minority, often discounted position in EC councils and also within her own Cabinet, where her handling of European policy and in particular her deep scepticism about the ERM and monetary union eventually contributed to her downfall (November 1990). The fact that Thatcher agreed to sterling's entry into the ERM (October 1990), having resisted such a move since coming to power in 1979, was a further example of how the collapse of a government's economic strategy, in this case the Conservatives' counter-inflationary strategy, necessitated a more positive move towards the EC. This move also exemplified the UK's unpredictable trajectory as an EC member state often characterised by policy twists and turns, procrastination and unexpected decisions.

Key fact 3.7

Sterling and the ERM

The following extract is taken from UK Treasury papers (released January 2005) dealing with the ejection of sterling from the Exchange Rate Mechanism in September 1992. It offers some reflections on why the Thatcher government decided to join the ERM in the first place. The cut in interest rates from the historically high figure of 15 percent was made shortly before the Conservative Party annual conference:

> Personal recollection, as well as [deletion] record makes clear, that pre-entry preparations in 1989 and 1990 focused heavily on the domestic political handling of the entry decision, notably the persuasion of the Prime Minister herself. That Ministerial and senior official energies were focused on that aspect provided an unhelpful and distracting backcloth for our preparations. There is a wider issue here. The political consensus in favour of the ERM was fairly superficial. To some extent it [sterling's entry into the ERM] was regarded as a useful instrument for reducing interest rates. Indeed, from [deletion] account and from personal recollection, the Prime Minister seems to have accepted entry as a *quid pro quo* for a 1 percent cut in interest rates, a cut which many of us in the Treasury were intensely unhappy to see implemented before entry.

(Source: http://www.hm-treasury.gov.uk.)

Plate 3.5 9 November 1990: the unification of Germany

Source: Audiovisual Library of the European Commission (2005).

Questions concerning the EC's future beyond 1992 assumed even greater importance following the dramatic transformation of the Central and Eastern European political landscape in the period 1989–91 with the rapid collapse of communist governments in Eastern Europe and the fall of the Berlin Wall. The subsequent unification of the two Germanies in 1990 and the break-up of the Warsaw Pact Organisation (the Eastern bloc's counterpart to NATO) and of the Yugoslav and Soviet states in 1991 presented altogether unfamiliar conditions for determining the EC's future. In their response to these events, the EC states reflected their different historical experiences, strategic interests and divisions of opinion.

Opinion 3.4

Mitterrand on the transformation of Europe in 1989

Extract from a speech by President Mitterrand of France, 31 December 1989:

It is plain that Europe will no longer be the Europe that we have known for half a century. Yesterday she was dependent on two superpowers, now, as if coming home, she is going to return to her own history and geography. New questions are starting to be asked which can't be answered in a single day. But they are asked: the future of alliances, NATO and the Warsaw Pact; how fast should we proceed with disarmament; in what form and under what conditions will the German peoples reunite; what kind of co-operation between East and West; are existing frontiers inviolate and if so, how far; the reawakening of nationalities. Either the tendency towards busting apart, towards disintegration, will grow and we shall have again the Europe of 1919 and we know what happened then or else Europe will rebuild itself.

(Source: *Le Monde*, 2 January 1990.)

Is this a fair view?

The debate over the EC's future after the completion of the single-market project intensified when the European Council (April 1989) agreed to convene an IGC on economic and monetary union. The council subsequently decided (June 1990) to establish an IGC on political union. This last development was particularly assisted by a joint appeal for European union (April 1990) issued by François Mitterrand and Helmut Kohl in a further demonstration of the continuing importance of the Franco-German axis in the EC. These IGCs opened in December 1990 and culminated in the signing of the Treaty on European Union in Maastricht. The centrepiece of this treaty was the commitment to forge an economic and monetary union (EMU) by 1999 at the latest. The treaty also included provisions for a common foreign and security policy (CFSP) and thus held out the possibility of a more influential role for the EU in the international system. However, there were marked contrasts between the member states in their attitudes towards political union and the CFSP. For example, while France and Germany acted jointly in pressing for European union, each had very different views about such matters. The German government, in part influenced by the federal character of the FRG political system, had few qualms about extending the federal principle in the management of EC affairs and particularly advocated greater powers for some of the EC institutions, especially the European Parliament. By contrast, the French government, operating in accordance with what was historically a highly centralised state, was far more concerned to protect national sovereignty and was cautious about the case for granting more powers to EC institutions. The CFSP project also exposed divisions between France and Germany similar to those evident in the course of the abortive political union negotiations of the early 1960s. France was still outside NATO and was associated with the idea of reviving non-NATO bodies like the Western European Union to serve as a key forum for developing a CFSP. However, Germany was concerned to ensure that its NATO ties and relations with the USA were not imperilled by any exclusively European forum for foreign and security policy.

The relationship between the making of this treaty and the impact of fast-changing conditions in Europe at large in the period 1989–91 reflected several features of the dynamics of European integration at this time. In many respects, the treaty was born out of an unchanged European political landscape before the collapse of the Berlin Wall (9 November 1989) and the implosion of the East German state. The case for speedy progression from a single market to a single currency had already gained momentum as a result of relatively buoyant economic conditions in the late 1980s and as the EU states demonstrated a far greater degree of convergence in their economic performances than at the time of the earlier, ill-fated attempt at economic and monetary union in the 1970s. Events on the wider European stage and especially the unification of the two Germanies (October 1990) immediately reinforced and thereafter underpinned progress towards the completion of the treaty.

Franco-German relations were of decisive importance in the making and implementation of the treaty's provisions for EMU. The prospect of German unification was a devastating blow to the French government. It portended a shift in the balance of power in Europe that threatened France's status, demolished its longstanding interest in a divided Germany and gave rise to alarming visions of Berlin rather than Paris as Europe's centre of gravity. Mitterrand's initial opposition to the prospect of a united Germany was lifted only by his insistence on closer ties between a united Germany and the EC. The most bankable German assurance for France was Bonn's support for EMU. In the period before the first elections in a united Germany (December 1990), however, the EMU idea was not a top priority for the Kohl government. It was anxious to allay domestic fears about the possible loss of the deutschmark and the Bundesbank, key emblems of the FRG's economic success since 1945, or as Jacques Delors put it, 'Not all Germans believe in God, but all believe in the Bundesbank'. In the event, Bonn accepted the principle of EMU but insisted on the strict observance of a set of convergence criteria (see below). An integral part of France's longstanding rationale for European integration was thus reasserted in 1990.

Equally long-term considerations governed the reactions of the UK government. Thatcher, like Mitterrand, was also loath to concede the case for German unification and barely concealed her dislike for and suspicion of the Germans. Indications of her anti-German instincts came from leaked press accounts of a seminar held at Chequers in March 1990 at which she reportedly questioned experts on Germany about the German people's national failings. Unlike Mitterrand, however, Thatcher was no more disposed than other UK political leaders since 1945 to accept further European integration as a necessary price for controlling Germany. Instead of supporting further integration, therefore, the UK pressed the case for the enlargement of the EC as the top priority, first in respect of the remaining member states of EFTA (especially Austria, Finland, Norway and Sweden) and in the longer term with reference to the post-communist Eastern European states. This UK emphasis was a thinly disguised way of seeking to slow down the pace of integration. It was based on the assumption that an enlarged EC would be less capable of formulating and implementing any new far-reaching designs. In short, the EC would increasingly conform perhaps to the limited activities of a free-trade area and could become an updated version of the OEEC operating in accordance with the British preference for a loose, intergovernmental form of cooperation.

However, the prevailing view among the other EC states favoured the postponement of enlargement until the single market and European union were in place, thus accounting for the timing of the next enlargement (1995) to include Austria, Finland and Sweden. There was one important exception to this order of priorities, namely the integration of East Germany into the EC as German unification became a reality. East Germany had long enjoyed preferential access to the EC by virtue of its special trading links with the FRG. Trade between the two Germanies had effectively been subjected to the same regime as if it was trade between a pair of EC states. That apart, the setting up of the two IGCs in 1990 meant that the focus of attention was on deepening the process of political and economic integration and thus on the making of the (Maastricht) Treaty on European Union. What this treaty promised in terms of furthering closer integration and what actually materialised are among the questions discussed below.

By 1990, few doubted that Europe's political and economic space would be defined and shaped by the evolution of the EC and that the EC was now the principal European organisation within which or with which European states would organise their relations. Certainly, the immediate destination of the EC remained as ill-defined as it had ever been. At a comparable stage in the EC's development during the early 1970s, one commentator (Schonfield 1973) likened the EC member states to a bag of sticky yet individually identifiable marbles whose collective future suggested a journey to an unknown destination. In the intervening period, the member states had bound themselves more closely together by means of a slow incremental process and by shaping a very distinctive organisation that was neither quite a confederation of states acting in accordance with the principle of intergovernmental cooperation nor a federal or supranational organisation. What remained in question by 1990 was whether the member states could continue to benefit from the process of integration while retaining their existing powers and identities. Equally in doubt was whether national governments could command popular support for their European policies at a time when their latest project (EMU) reinforced the image of the EC/EU as an elitist, technocratic, top-down creation.

The EU since 1990

The Maastricht Treaty

The Maastricht Treaty represents a watershed in the history of European integration. Indeed, its opening provisions stated that the 'Treaty marks a new stage in the process of creating an ever closer union among the peoples of Europe'. The Maastricht Treaty coined a new name for the EC – the more federal-sounding 'European Union'. It was the first of the EU's four post-Cold War treaties. Many of its provisions, including the creation of a CFSP and new cooperation in fields like justice, policing and immigration, were symptoms of this new international environment. These new issues would also come to assume fundamental importance in EU politics for the next decade or so. The treaty set the basic institutional framework for today's EU. It reworked the supranational and intergovernmental balance of interests (see Key concept 3.2) with new powers and roles for existing institutions, new decision-making procedures and the new 'pillar' structure. Opt-outs from key policies on the part of some member states set the groundwork for future commitments to differentiated integration or variable geometry. The negative response of many citizens to these transformations also inaugurated a period of deep reflection among the EU elite about new forms of EU democracy and legitimisation, a process culminating in the negotiation of a new Constitutional Treaty in June 2004.

Plate 3.6 The Maastricht Treaty, surrounded by copies of the signatures
Source: Audiovisual Library of the European Commission (2005).

EU member states adopted the new Treaty on European Union (as the Maastricht Treaty is officially called) at the December 1991 European Council summit held in the Dutch city of Maastricht. One of its distinctive features was the creation of the new 'pillar' structure. The first or 'European Communities' pillar included treaty provisions and laws relating to the three existing European Communities, the ECSC, EEC and EAEC. It also included new provisions relating to EMU. To this core of existing activity member states added the second, or CFSP, pillar and a third, or Justice and Home Affairs, pillar. In the EC pillar, the supranational Commission, Parliament and Court of Justice (see Section 3.2 for descriptions of these bodies) retained considerable powers acquired in previous treaty provisions. In the new second and third pillars, however, these institutions had a limited role or no role at all. They were designed as 'intergovernmental' pillars, giving the Council of Ministers and (in CFSP decisions) the European Council a near decision-making monopoly. The term 'European Union' was an umbrella term that referred to joint activities in all three pillars.

Perhaps the most significant revision to the material incorporated into the EC pillar was the new legal framework for EMU. Important steps along the path to EMU had already been taken before the treaty came into force. However, treaty amendments were made to establish a three-stage timetable for EMU, a new European Central Bank (ECB) and to set out the so-called convergence criteria. The

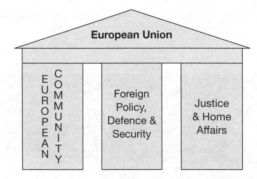

Figure 3.1 The pillars of the EU after Maastricht

Figure 3.2 The euro? (Cartoon by Royer, one of a series to introduce the euro to euro-zone members)

Source: Audiovisual Library of the European Commission (2005).

ECB was created to conduct the EU's monetary policy, together with the central banks of the states participating in EMU. The convergence criteria were tests requiring states wanting to join the euro zone to harmonise key aspects of their economies. The four convergence criteria effectively required all participating states to register low inflation, low interest rates, sound public finances (low budget deficits and low public debt) and stable exchange rates. The treaty also set a deadline of 1 January 1999 for the final stage of EMU. At this final stage, the new single currency, now called the euro, would replace national currencies for official transactions (although issuing of new notes and coins would take place at a later date) and the ECB would begin managing a single monetary policy for the euro zone.

Key concept 3.1

Subsidiarity

Subsidiarity required that the EU act only 'within the limits of the powers conferred upon it in the treaties' and that, where it had exclusive competences, to take action only 'insofar as the objectives of the proposed action cannot be sufficiently achieved by the member states'.

There were a number of other important changes to the operation of the old EC in the new treaty (Nugent 1999: 72–3). New policy areas were introduced in education, culture, public health, consumer protection, trans-European networks, improving industrial competitiveness and development cooperation. Some existing policy competences were extended, including research and technological development, environment, and regional policy. Decisions in many of these new and extended policy competences would involve qualified majority voting (QMV) in the Council of Ministers (see Section 3.2), thereby further extending the range of issues where member states lost their opportunity to veto EU decisions. As a counterpoint to the transfer of new policy areas to the EU level, the principle of 'subsidiarity', which sought to place limits on the scope of EU activities, was formally incorporated into the treaty. A series of important institutional changes were also made. 'Co-decision', a new legislative procedure, was introduced allowing the European Parliament the ultimate power to veto EU laws in some policy areas (see Section 3.2). The Court of Justice was given the power to fine member states. A new institution, the Committee of the Regions, was established to give the EU's regions and local authorities a formal chance to articulate their interests in the EU decision-making process.

Since the 1970s, when they inaugurated European Political Cooperation (EPC), member states had agreed to consult each other on, and coordinate, their separate foreign policies and to try to undertake common actions. The challenges of the new post-Cold War international environment, German unification and instability in neighbouring former communist states in the Balkans prompted member states to strengthen cooperation in this field. The Maastricht Treaty inaugurated a new CFSP to replace rather limited EPC cooperation. Its formal objectives were defined very widely and very generally to include:

- all areas of foreign and security policy;
- safeguarding the common values, fundamental interests and independence of the EU;
- preserving peace and strengthening international security;
- developing democracy and the rule of law, and respect for human rights and fundamental freedoms.

Member states could undertake joint actions, establishing concrete forms of cooperation such as setting up a special EU funding programme. They could also take common positions, where member states would agree to use national policies to implement a jointly defined EU position on an international issue. A prompt for possible further developments in defence cooperation was also included at a number of points. There was mention of an aspiration for 'progressive framing of a common defence policy, which might lead to common defence'. Furthermore, states simultaneously members of the EU and the WEU added a declaration to the treaty to the effect that the WEU would be developed as 'a defence component of the European Union'.

However, it is important, to remember that the CFSP was designed as an intergovernmental pillar. It was intended that the heads of state and government in the European Council and foreign affairs ministers in the council would dominate decision making. Despite some member states' preference for the use of qualified majority decisions, CFSP decisions were to be made by unanimity (or consensus) in almost every case. Essentially, each state could veto decisions it did not like. The only (partial) exception related to joint actions, where the council could decide, by unanimity, whether future decisions to implement a joint action could be taken by qualified majority vote.

Like the CFSP pillar, the Justice and Home Affairs (JHA) pillar sought to institutionalise and strengthen existing activities of the member states. Since the 1960s, and more intensively since the mid-1980s, *ad hoc*, informal networks of government ministers and officials working for state customs, police, immigration, asylum and internal security agencies met with counterparts from other EU member states to coordinate their activities. By creating the JHA pillar, the Maastricht Treaty institutionalised such cooperation in nine areas:

1. asylum policy;
2. the crossing of external borders;
3. immigration;
4. combating drug addiction;
5. combating international fraud;
6. judicial cooperation in civil matters;
7. judicial cooperation in criminal matters;
8. customs cooperation;
9. police cooperation.

New instruments, similar to those of CFSP, were created, allowing member states to define joint positions on relevant issues (such as on the nature of a refugee) and better coordinate cooperation through joint actions (such as programmes for improving cooperation between customs or police authorities). They could also draw up new conventions, or international treaties, that would be implemented independently by the member states. Like the CFSP, unanimity was the norm in these sensitive policy areas, with the same awkward exception allowing member states to decide unanimously if they wanted to take certain future decisions relating to implementation of a joint action by qualified majority vote.

One final innovation of the Maastricht Treaty that must be considered was the creation of EU citizenship. This is a legal status, associated with certain rights and duties, automatically and simultaneously held by anyone who is a national of an EU member state. Rights of EU citizens are:

- to move freely or live anywhere in the EU;
- to vote and stand for election in municipal and European elections in the member state where the citizen lives;
- to receive diplomatic and consular protection from another EU state in a country where the citizen's own state is not represented;
- to petition the European Parliament;
- to seek assistance from a newly created ombudsman, who is empowered to investigate EU citizens' complaints about EU authorities' administrative actions.

Maastricht and its aftermath

Although all of these new provisions were agreed in December 1991 and formally signed in February 1992, it was not until November 1993 that the treaty could be implemented. Quite unexpectedly, the Maastricht Treaty presented member state governments with an unprecedented level of public dissatisfaction. The treaty was rejected by 50.7 percent of Danes voting in June 1992. A few months later, in September 1992, the Maastricht Treaty was passed in a French referendum by only a narrow margin of 51.05 percent of those voting. In the UK, inter-party and intra-party disputes made Maastricht Treaty ratification in parliament a long and difficult process. In Germany, opponents asked the Constitutional Court to rule on the constitutionality of the treaty, which the court eventually affirmed in October 1993, albeit with certain reservations. Among the concerns prompting opposition to the Maastricht Treaty were issues as fundamental as the political implications of EMU, the implications of the CFSP and future defence cooperation, and challenges to national identities and democratic standards in the EU (Dinan 1999: 148–56). Various concessions were eventually offered to the Danes, notably the right to opt out of CFSP decisions with defence implications and the right to opt out of the single currency, and a second Danish referendum in May 1993 produced a rather narrow majority of 56.7 percent in favour. However, these policy 'opt-outs', together with 'opt-outs' secured by the UK on both the single currency and on a new social charter that would give the EU certain powers on labour-related issues, became key examples of a more pronounced differentiation, or variable geometry, in patterns of EU integration.

As the ratification crisis rumbled into late 1993, important decisions were made about what became one of the defining issues for the EU for the next ten years and more: the issue of enlargement. Between 1987 and 1996, no fewer than 19 states had applied for EU membership (see Key fact 3.8).

When in force, the Maastricht Treaty would formally assert the already established practice that 'Any European state may apply to become a member of the Union'. As we have seen in Section 1.1, further clarification of the criteria for membership was made at the June 1993 Copenhagen summit, producing the so-called Copenhagen criteria.

Key fact 3.8

Applicants for EC/EU membership, 1987–96

The applicants were:

1987	Morocco (soon rejected as a non-European applicant) and Turkey;
1989	Austria;
1990	Malta, Cyprus;
1991	Sweden;
1992	Finland, Switzerland, Norway;
1994	Hungary, Poland;
1995	Romania, Slovakia, Latvia, Estonia, Bulgaria, Lithuania;
1996	Czech Republic, Slovenia.

Accession negotiations with Austria, Finland, Norway and Sweden were relatively straightforward. These states were affluent, established market economies and long-standing democracies. Indeed, negotiations for their entry were achieved in a record 15 months, leading to formal accession on 1 January 1995 for all but Norway, where a majority of voters rejected membership in a referendum in November 1994. Accession negotiations for other applicant states were far more complex, particularly, as we have seen in Section 1.1, in relation to former communist Central and Eastern European applicant states. These states were not only fledgling democracies confronting the daunting task of converting communist command economies into market economies. They were also relatively poor in terms of GDP per capita compared with their Western European counterparts, which raised issues about the EU budget and the functioning of the CAP and the EU's Regional Policy. The sheer number of applicants and the prospect that membership could rise from 15 in 1995 to close to 30 in less than a decade raised fundamental questions about the functioning of the EU's institutions. These included questions about feasible numbers of European parliamentarians or European commissioners and the extended use of the less cumbersome qualified majority voting procedure for council decisions. Together with issues about the functioning of the new arrangements agreed at Maastricht, an increased sensitivity to issues of democratic accountability and EU legitimacy after the Maastricht ratification crisis, the challenges of eastward enlargement were to take centre stage in the EU's next two rounds of treaty reforms.

The Amsterdam and Nice Treaties

In June 1997, a new treaty was agreed by member states in Amsterdam, and in May 1999 the Amsterdam Treaty came into force. It was soon followed by another treaty, agreed in Nice in December 2000, which came into force as the Nice Treaty by February 2003. In many ways, these treaties can be considered 'follow-up' treaties. Provision had been made at Maastricht for an IGC in 1996 to review important institutional aspects of the treaty. The Amsterdam Treaty, in turn, included a protocol requiring another IGC to review treaty provisions relating to institutions at least one year before the EU enlarged to 21 member states. Each new treaty was influenced by new events and challenges emerging at the time of their negotiation. The Amsterdam Treaty, for instance, included measures addressing CFSP shortcomings revealed in the EU's failures in Bosnia and early concerns that only a small core of EU member states would be able to join EMU (Dinan 1999). Nice Treaty provisions were shaped by the experience of the 1999 Kosovo conflict and by a stronger commitment to large-scale enlargement (Phinnemore 2003: 55–7). However, given the character of these two treaties as 'review' treaties, at least in part, and the fact that they were negotiated within only a few years of a previous treaty, it is not surprising that many provisions were relatively modest reforms rather than radical innovations.

The EU's experience in the Balkans had been an eye-opener for member states (Smith 2003: 238). EU efforts to broker peace as Yugoslavia began to disintegrate in the early 1990s were eventually defeated by the individual member states themselves when they separately recognised the new breakaway republics as sovereign states. The EU was sidelined in international efforts to end ethnic conflict in Bosnia-Herzegovina, as the United Nations, NATO and the USA in particular led international intervention. Similarly, the 1999 international intervention on Kosovo was largely a NATO affair. Such events appeared to highlight the limits of joint EU foreign policy actions in their own backyard and highlighted what Hill (1993) called the 'expectations–capability gap' – that expectations about the EU's foreign policy did not match what EU instruments actually made it able to do. On the other hand, some commentators argued that it was misplaced to condemn the CFSP for these failures when the CFSP itself was so new. Others suggested that the EU could play a more prominent role in foreign policy actions relating to economic power, such as economic reconstruction in the Balkans, rather than foreign policy actions requiring military power or political coherence.

Figure 3.3 One view of the EU's Common Foreign and Security Policy

Source: P. Fontaine (1998).

From Amsterdam to Nice

Both the Amsterdam and Nice Treaties sought to respond to such lessons. At Amsterdam, member states agreed to set up a Policy Planning and Early Warning Unit to develop policies that are more forward-looking and less reactive. For similar reasons, they established a new type of CFSP decision (or instrument) called a 'common strategy'. As the name suggests, common strategies allow member states to articulate, in advance, a more coherent general framework for action on matters of common interest. They have so far been articulated for relations with Russia, Ukraine and the Mediterranean region. Following a French proposal, the Amsterdam Treaty also created a new leadership post, the High Representative for the CFSP. A high-profile figure, Javier Solana, a former Spanish foreign minister and NATO secretary-general, was appointed to this position in 1999. New decision rules extended the use of QMV in CFSP so that they could be used for decisions applying common strategies or implementing joint positions or joint actions. Given the political sensitivity of the CFSP, it is not surprising that some member states insisted on a safeguard clause, or an emergency break for these QMV decisions, allowing a member state to block majority voting for important reasons of national policy. New provisions for constructive abstention, pushed by the more integrationist states like Germany, Italy and the Benelux countries, provided another way around the unanimity rule, allowing a member state to abstain from a CFSP vote in the Council without blocking a unanimous decision (Dinan 1999: 179). The Nice Treaty also provided for enhanced cooperation, which

Plate 3.7 Diagram used to symbolise Nice Treaty as continuation of EU treaties

Source: Audiovisual Library of the European Commission (2005).

Biography 3.14

Javier Solana (1942–)

Secretary-general of the Council of the EU and EU High Representative for the CFSP. Solana joined the Spanish Socialist Party in 1964 and became a member of the Spanish parliament in 1977. Throughout the period 1982–1995 he was a Spanish cabinet minister, initially as minister of culture and finally as minister of foreign affairs. In 1995, he was appointed secretary-general of NATO. Four years later, he became secretary-general of the Council of the EU and EU High Representative for the Common Foreign and Security Policy, a five-year appointment that was renewed in July 2004. Solana will be appointed EU foreign minister if and when the EU Constitutional Treaty comes into force.

would allow some members to pursue closer cooperation, within certain limits, within the framework of the EU, without needing to involve every single EU member state – thus facilitating a multi-speed Europe.

Both the Amsterdam and Nice Treaties extended cooperation in defence matters to some extent. Defence cooperation has long been a difficult issue for EU member states. Concerns have been raised about the implications of EU defence cooperation for relations with NATO, an organisation involving many but not all EU member states (see Table 3.1). Most of the EU members that are not also NATO members are traditionally 'neutral' states, raising for them questions about the desirability of *any* EU defence cooperation. More fundamentally, EU defence cooperation raises concerns about the nature of the EU's relationship with the USA, particularly whether European states should develop a more autonomous defence policy, a position traditionally favoured by states like France, or retain close cooperation with the US defence establishment, a position traditionally associated with UK policy. Despite these differences, member states agreed to add certain 'soft' defence roles to the CFSP at Amsterdam. The so-called Petersberg tasks established an EU role, to be operationalised by the WEU, in:

- humanitarian and rescue tasks;
- peacekeeping tasks;
- tasks of combat forces in crisis management, including peacemaking.

Further defence cooperation received an important boost in 1998 when the UK's Tony Blair, prime minister of a state traditionally wary of EU defence initiatives, signalled a new willingness to cooperate in this field. This about-turn was an important step favouring development of an EU Rapid Reaction Force that would eventually be capable of deploying a 60,000-strong military force to implement the above-mentioned defence objectives. To complement this, the Nice Treaty created a permanent political and military structure responsible for political control and strategic management of crises.

Equally significant changes were made in the area of Justice and Home Affairs. Member states articulated a new EU objective to create an area of 'freedom, justice and security'. Its purpose was to ensure the free movement of persons within the

Table 3.1 Membership of the EU and NATO, 2005

Country	In EU?	In NATO?
Austria	Yes	No
Belgium	Yes	Yes
Bulgaria	No (applicant)	Yes
Canada	No	Yes
Cyprus	Yes	No
Czech Republic	Yes	Yes
Denmark	Yes	Yes
Estonia	Yes	Yes
Finland	Yes	No
France	Yes	Yes
Germany	Yes	Yes
Greece	Yes	Yes
Hungary	Yes	Yes
Iceland	No	Yes
Ireland	Yes	No
Italy	Yes	Yes
Latvia	Yes	Yes
Lithuania	Yes	Yes
Luxembourg	Yes	Yes
Malta	Yes	No
Netherlands	Yes	Yes
Norway	No	Yes
Poland	Yes	Yes
Portugal	Yes	Yes
Romania	No (applicant)	Yes
Slovakia	Yes	Yes
Slovenia	Yes	Yes
Spain	Yes	Yes
Sweden	Yes	No
Turkey	No (applicant)	Yes
UK	Yes	Yes
USA	No	Yes

EU, supported by common external border controls, while guaranteeing their security by combating crimes like:

- trafficking in human beings;
- sexual exploitation of children;
- vehicle trafficking;
- arms trafficking;
- drug trafficking;
- corruption;
- fraud;
- terrorism.

In order to achieve this objective, powers to regulate matters relating to visas, asylum, immigration, refugees, displaced persons and cooperation in civil matters were moved (with a transition period) from the rather cumbersome and ineffective intergovernmental JHA pillar to the supranational EC pillar. Member states also agreed to incorporate the so-called Schengen *acquis*, a pre-existing but non-EU set of agreements aiming to ease border controls between participating states. These agreements – the 1985 Schengen Agreement and the 1990 Schengen Convention – had been signed by all EU member states except the UK and Ireland, both of which were able to opt out of both the new EC pillar activities mentioned above and the newly incorporated Schengen agreements. Denmark also secured an opt-out from the incorporated Schengen activities. With the emptying of the JHA pillar, the EU's third pillar became 'Police and Judicial Cooperation in Criminal Matters'. Since it came into force, member states have made considerable progress in their aim to establish an area of freedom, justice and security. At a special European Council summit in Tampere in Finland (1999), they agreed an extensive action plan and published a 'scoreboard' against which progress could be monitored. Since '9/11', this area of EU activity has been used as part of the EU's attempts to combat terrorism. For example, a new European arrest warrant provides for simpler and faster extradition of terrorist (and other criminal) suspects between EU states.

As applications for EU membership began to accumulate in the early 1990s and member states agreed that large-scale enlargement should eventually take place, the complex question of institutional reform became increasingly pressing. Institutional reform became one of the most difficult issues of the treaty negotiations, so contentious in fact that member states postponed the main issues of Commission size and the redesign of QMV until they began negotiating the Nice Treaty. Two important divisions emerged in discussions (Duff 1997: xxxii):

1. differences between the more federalist states, such as Germany and the Benelux countries, and those, such as France and the UK, which were reluctant to empower EU institutions;
2. differences between the small states and the large states. Large states wanted to ensure that the allocation of votes in QMV decisions (see Section 3.2) would not allow the smaller member states to impose policies upon them. For their part, many smaller member states wanted to ensure some influence in the Commission with guarantees that at least one commissioner would come from each member state (Dinan 1999: 180).

At the time, this inability to finalise an institutional framework for an EU of 25 or 30 was seen as a major failure.

However, preparing the institutions for enlargement had to become the central point of discussion in the IGC negotiations leading to the Nice Treaty. By 1998, accession negotiations with six member states had already begun, and by 2000 negotiations had been initiated with another six. By late 2002, these negotiations were completed with eight Central and Eastern European countries (Poland, Hungary, Slovakia, Slovenia, Czech Republic, Latvia, Lithuania and Estonia), and the two Mediterranean islands (the Republic of Cyprus and Malta). After difficult negotiations over the budget, pitching net contributors (such as Germany, the

Netherlands, Sweden and Austria) against net recipients of EU agricultural and regional economic development (structural) funds (particularly Mediterranean states like Spain), the entry of new member states was set for 1 May 2004.

Despite intense criticism of the way in which the French hosts handled the Nice European Council summit, a compromise on the institutional question was eventually hammered out. In an example of a classical EU compromise, in which 'all member states could claim some success' (Gray and Stubb 2001: 15), the Nice Treaty established that there would be one commissioner per member state until the EU reached 27 members, followed by the introduction of an equitable rotation system. A new 'triple majority' decision-making procedure for Council of Ministers decisions required:

- a specific threshold of votes (as in the past);
- approval by a majority of member states;
- if a member state requested it, verification that the above majorities represented at least 62 percent of the total population of the EU.

The Amsterdam Treaty had set a limit of 700 members of the European Parliament, but the Nice Treaty revised this to 732. At both Amsterdam and Nice, more decisions previously requiring unanimity became QMV decisions in order that some of the real difficulties anticipated for unanimity decisions in a EU of 25 or 30 member states be minimised. In order to deal with increased diversity as a consequence of enlargement – and indeed to deal with differences between existing member states about the appropriate scope and speed of integration – member states also adopted important new innovations to facilitate differentiation and flexibility. The Amsterdam Treaty established, and the Nice Treaty modified, a new procedure for 'closer cooperation' or 'enhanced cooperation', which would allow, within certain limits, those member states that wanted, or were able, to deepen integration among themselves to do so using the EU institutional framework.

In addition to movement on enlargement, the launch of EMU also dominated EU politics during negotiation of the Amsterdam Treaty in particular. Even before the entry into force of EMU provisions in the Maastricht Treaty, there were strains and difficulties raising serious questions about whether all but a few member states would be able to join and even about the viability of the EMU project itself. In September 1992, EU recession and the difficulties of German unification caused a severe breakdown in the EMS, particularly the ERM.

Furthermore, EU recession through much of the mid-1990s made it difficult for many states to meet key convergence criteria like low inflation targets, reduced budget deficits and public debt (Dinan 2004: 300). Austerity measures introduced to meet the convergence criteria produced a public backlash in some member states. However, improved economic fortunes in 1996 and 1997, strong leadership on the part of Germany's Chancellor Helmut Kohl and French President Jacques Chirac, and a somewhat permissive interpretation of certain convergence criteria eventually brought agreement that all but four states would participate in the launch of EMU by January 1999 (*ibid.*: 300–1). Sweden, Denmark and the UK chose not to participate, while Greece failed to meet the convergence criteria and had to wait until January 2001 before it joined. New coins and notes for the single currency were introduced in January 2002.

In the post-Maastricht period, member states began to take increasing interest in questions about democracy in the EU and the related issue of EU legitimacy. For a long time, the legitimacy of EU governance appeared to rest on a permissive consensus, where relatively high levels of citizens' support for the EU were closely linked with outputs like peace in Europe and economic prosperity fostered by market integration (Chryssochoou 2003: 367). Negative public reactions to EU treaties was one important sign that this permissive consensus was ending, dissatisfaction highlighted in the Maastricht Treaty ratification crisis but also by the Irish electorate's rejection of the Nice Treaty in a referendum in June 2001 (a result later reversed in a second referendum). Other signs of dissatisfaction could be gleaned in opinion polls, such as a 2004 Eurobarometer survey (see Table 3.2).

The data show considerable variation among respondents from all EU member states on the question of whether EU membership is 'a good thing' or 'a bad thing'. In some member states, such as Luxembourg, Greece and Ireland, over 70 percent of respondents considered EU membership a good thing. In the UK, by contrast, only 29 percent of those surveyed considered EU membership a good thing and as

Table 3.2 Membership of the EU is/will be/would be ...

Member state	A good thing (%)	A bad thing (%)
Luxembourg	75	7
Ireland	71	8
Greece	71	7
Turkey	71	9
Romania	70	3
Bulgaria	65	6
Spain	64	10
Netherlands	64	12
Belgium	57	10
Portugal	56	13
Italy	54	13
Denmark	53	20
Lithuania	52	12
Malta	50	16
Finland	46	20
Slovakia	46	9
Hungary	45	15
Germany	45	14
France	43	18
Poland	42	18
Cyprus	42	16
Czech Republic	41	17
Slovenia	40	13
Sweden	37	33
Latvia	33	22
Estonia	31	21
Austria	30	29
United Kingdom	29	29

(Source: Eurobarometer, May 2004, EB61-CC-EB 2004: 1.)

many people actually considered it a bad thing. It is also notable that significant numbers of respondents from new member states (including Poland, the Czech Republic, Estonia, Latvia and Slovenia) showed very low levels of support for the statement that EU membership would be a good thing. Overall, only 47 percent of respondents from all EU member states considered EU membership a good thing. Other manifestations of dissatisfaction, or at best lack of interest, can be found in very low and declining levels of turnout in European Parliament elections and the increasing salience of euro-sceptical views in some member states.

Both the Amsterdam and Nice Treaties included measures that sought to respond to such signs of citizen dissatisfaction. Calls to strengthen the EU's democratic legitimacy led to progressive increases in the powers of the European Parliament, so that by the time the Amsterdam Treaty was in force, the European Parliament was officially, with the Council, a co-legislator in many policy areas (see Section 3.2 for more details). A Protocol on Subsidiarity, annexed to the Amsterdam Treaty, provided guidelines to improve application of this principle in order to 'ensure that decisions are taken as closely as possible to the citizens of the Union'. A new employment chapter was incorporated into the EU's first pillar activities, which, along with a strengthening of the EU's consumer and environmental protection powers, sought at least in part to 'assuage popular concerns that the EU didn't have citizens' interests at heart' (Phinnemore 2003: 54). Since the Amsterdam Treaty, there has also been a noticeable attempt to clarify and promote the 'values of the union'. The Amsterdam Treaty clarified that 'the Union is founded on the principles of liberty, democracy, respect for human rights and fundamental freedoms, and the rule of law'. It also provided that a member state's violation of those values could be punished, on the authorisation of the other member states, with the suspension of certain treaty rights, including the right to vote in the Council. This process of clarifying the union's values continued during negotiation of the Nice Treaty, culminating in the European Council's proclamation of a new declaratory (rather than legally binding) Charter of Fundamental Rights of the EU.

Future of the European Union: the Constitutional Treaty

It is now something of a truism that treaty making in the EU is a process rather than an event. The Nice Treaty, like the Maastricht and Amsterdam Treaties before it, reaffirmed this truism when it committed member states to holding another IGC in 2004. Unlike the Maastricht and Amsterdam Treaties before it, however, the Nice Treaty laid the foundations for radical innovation in both the mechanics of EU treaty making and, unwittingly, in the nature of the final document that would eventually be adopted. Annexed to the Nice Treaty was a 'Declaration on the Future of the Union' urging as a prelude to the planned 2004 IGC a deeper and wider debate, involving all interested parties, about the future of the Union. The declaration indicated that this debate, which would not hold up enlargement, should focus on four key issues:

1. how to establish and monitor a more precise delimitation of powers between the Union and the member states, reflecting the principle of subsidiarity;

2. the status of the Charter of Fundamental Rights of the European Union proclaimed at Nice;

3. a simplification of the treaties with a view to making them clearer and better understood without changing their meanings;

4. the role of national parliaments in the European architecture.

According to the declaration, addressing these issues would help the EU to 'improve and monitor the democratic legitimacy and transparency of the Union and its institutions, in order to bring them closer to the citizens of the Union'.

By December 2001, with the European Council's endorsement of the Laeken Declaration, it became clear exactly how member states would follow through on this commitment. For the first time ever, they would create a European Convention, composed of an unusually wide range of European political elites, to consider key issues, identify possible responses and make suggestions on a series of questions about the future of Europe. Moving beyond the agenda outlined in the Nice Declaration, the Laeken Declaration asked the convention to address three general issues and 50+ more specific questions relating to the future of the EU. One crucial theme was enhancement of the EU's international role, including questions about how to enhance the coherence of European foreign policy and extending external representation of the Union. Another important challenge was devising reforms to improve institutional structures for an EU of close to 30 member states, especially questions about whether the EU should extend QMV, simplify and speed up its decision-making procedures and replace the system whereby each state has a six-month turn at holding the EU presidency. A third and possibly the most important issue was improving the EU's democratic legitimacy and its ability to better match the expectations of citizens. The convention was asked to consider whether and how the national parliaments could help to legitimise the EU, whether the president of the Commission ought to be elected directly by the citizens and whether the European Parliament ought to be strengthened.

The usual method of treaty making, the IGC, is dominated by government ministers, their deputies and representatives and particularly, in the final stages, by heads of state and government (Nicholl and Salmon 2001: 162). The Commission does participate in IGC negotiations, but not as a signatory, while the European Parliament does not participate and makes its views known only in resolutions to member states (*ibid.*). However, in a bold change of method, the list of authorised members of the European Convention was much wider than the usual select group (see Key fact 3.9).

The European Council appointed three of its former head-of-government colleagues to lead and 'give impetus' to the Convention, namely former French president Valéry Giscard d'Estaing as chairman and former Italian and Belgian prime ministers, Giuliano Amato and Jean-Luc Dehaene, respectively, as vice-chairmen. The Convention, which worked from February 2002 to July 2003, was only advisory on the contents of a new treaty; its role was to pave the way for the planned 2004 IGC, where member states would decide which of the Convention's suggestions to adopt officially.

Membership of the European Convention

Presidency

Chairman (Valéry Giscard D'Estaing)
Vice-chairman (Giuliano Amato)
Vice-chairman (Jean-Luc Dehaene)

Convention members

28 Representatives of the heads of state or government of existing and applicant states
56 Representatives of the state parliaments of existing and applicant states
16 Representatives of the European Parliament
 2 Representatives of the European Commission

Observers

3 Representatives of the Economic and Social Committee
6 Representatives of the Committee of the Regions
3 Representatives of European social partners
The European ombudsman

What explains the rationale behind the initiation of this experimental method of treaty making and the content of its agenda? A number of factors can be emphasised. One is political leadership. A series of high-profile speeches by leading European politicians, such as German Foreign Minister Joschka Fischer, French President Jacques Chirac and UK Prime Minister Tony Blair, gave crucial political endorsement for the initiation of broader constitutional debates on the future of the EU. Another set of explanations is function-related, stemming from a need to respond to certain pressing issues and problems. These included the imminence of ten new states joining the EU and the challenges posed in the wake of the 11 September 2001 terrorist attacks and later divisions exposed by the Iraq crisis. As mentioned above, the salience of EU democratisation and legitimisation issues in the Convention agenda follows what has been, for member state governments, the unnerving experiences of the Maastricht and Nice Treaty ratification crises, low levels of public support for the EU and other manifestations of citizen dissatisfaction. Finally, one can identify some process-related explanations. One such explanation, articulated by both academics and politicians, points to an exhaustion of the IGC as a method for addressing certain fundamental issues, notably the failure of IGC (Amsterdam) after IGC (Nice) to resolve key institutional dilemmas. In contrast to the usual IGC method, the relative openness and consensual ethos that the Convention developed as a working method appeared to offer more opportunities for open-minded, creative and deliberative decision-making patterns, allowing participants to break old taboos.

What did the Convention achieve?

As just mentioned, the European Convention distinguished itself by its open, deliberative and consensual ethos. As one European parliamentarian and convention member, Andrew Duff (2003) commented: 'The consensus formed at the end of the life of the Convention was large, fresh and genuine. Nobody left triumphant. All had compromised. Most had refined if not realigned their positions'.

That recommendations had been agreed consensually added political weight to the draft constitution (Shaw *et al.* 2003), as did the participation, particularly during later stages, of some key figures from member state governments and the close contact that chairman Giscard d'Estaing kept with member state governments. At the same time, some complained about some of the seemingly heavy-handed decisions of Giscard d'Estaing, such as his decision to leave institutional questions, among the most contentious of all, until the end, when time was running short (Shaw 2003). Moreover, even though some hoped that the Convention itself might help to address citizen dissatisfaction with the EU by encouraging public engagement in constitutional debates, citizen engagement was limited. Convention participants came from a wider range of political actors, but it was nevertheless a wider range of political elite. Even though much documentation was publicly available, it was often impenetrable for the uninitiated and special events, Internet sites and attempts to involve representatives of civil society have often been criticised as inadequate (*ibid.*). This lack of citizen engagement may have significant consequences when it comes to ratification of the treaty, a step that must follow agreement by member state governments and that will take the form of public referenda in a number of member states.

Undoubtedly, the Convention's most important achievement was the negotiation of a 'Draft Treaty Establishing a Constitution for Europe', submitted to the president of the European Council in Rome on 18 July 2003. The follow-up IGC, beginning in October 2003, renegotiated many of its passages but nevertheless left large tracts and the overall structure of the Draft Constitutional Treaty intact. The IGC was a difficult affair, particularly the December 2003 European Council summit. This summit, overshadowed by deep divisions within the EU on the Iraq invasion, failed to break a deadlock between France and Germany on the one hand and Spain and Poland on the other over proposed new QMV rules. These and other disputes, including whether religion should have a place in the EU Constitutional Treaty, were settled some months later when in June 2004 member states finally endorsed the new 'Constitutional Treaty for Europe'. An easing of tensions over Iraq, a change of government in Spain following the 11 March 2004 Madrid terrorist atrocity and the skilful diplomacy of the Irish presidency were crucial factors contributing to the resolution of remaining issues.

How significant were the changes introduced by the Constitutional Treaty? Were they, as one politician remarked, merely a tidying-up exercise, or did the Constitutional Treaty introduce important reforms? The simple answer to this question is that it did both (Phinnemore 2004). One of the most important achievements of the Constitutional Treaty was to redesign and to a considerable extent simplify the EU's legal architecture. The complicated 'pillar structure' and distinctions between 'European Communities' and the 'European Union' were disbanded, being replaced by the single denomination, European Union. The multiplicity of EU treaties was also replaced by a single Constitutional Treaty incorporating the provisions of the Treaty of Rome and Maastricht Treaty as amended by the Single European Act, and the Amsterdam and Nice Treaties. The Constitutional Treaty is divided into four parts. The first sets out in brief and relatively easy-to-understand language the basics of the EU:

- the definition, values and objectives and symbols (see Key fact 3.10) of the Union; fundamental and citizenship rights;
- the Union's competences and the principles governing their exercise;
- rules for entry to, suspension from and withdrawal from the Union;
- the powers and composition of the Union's institutions;
- the main decision-making rules and legal instruments.

Key fact 3.10

Objectives, values and symbols of the EU (Part 1, Constitutional Treaty)

Values of the EU (article I-2)

The Union is founded on the values of respect for human dignity, freedom of democracy, equality, the rule of law and respect for human rights, including the rights of persons belonging to minorities. These values are common to the member states in a society in which pluralism, non-discrimination, tolerance, justice, solidarity and equality between women and men prevail.

Objectives of the EU (article I-3)

- Promote peace, its values and well-being of its peoples.
- Offer citizens an area of freedom, security and justice without internal frontiers, and an internal market where competition is free and undistorted.
- Work for the sustainable development of Europe based on balanced economic growth and price stability, a highly competitive social economy, aiming at full employment and social progress, and a high level of protection and improvement of the quality of the environment.
- Promote scientific and technological advance.
- Combat social exclusion and discrimination, promote social justice and protection, equality between women and men, solidarity between the generations and protection of the rights of the child.
- Promote economic, social and territorial cohesion, and solidarity among member states.
- Respect its rich cultural and linguistic diversity, and ensure that Europe's cultural heritage is safeguarded.
- In relations with the wider world, the Union shall uphold and promote its values and interests. It shall contribute to peace, security, the sustainable development of the Earth, solidarity and mutual respect among peoples, free and fair trade, eradication of poverty and the protection of human rights.

Symbols of the EU (article I-8)

- The flag of the Union shall be a circle of twelve golden stars on a blue background.
- The anthem of the Union shall be based on the 'Ode to Joy' from the Ninth Symphony by Ludwig van Beethoven.
- The motto of the Union shall be: 'Unity in diversity'.
- The currency of the Union shall be the euro.
- 9 May shall be celebrated throughout the Union as Europe Day.

Figure 3.4 The Constitutional Treaty runs to over 500 pages
Source: K.-D. Borehardt (2000).

This section, which in its simplicity and form is an innovation, both rewrites existing material from the EU treaties and introduces some important reforms.

The second part of the Constitutional Treaty incorporates as a legally binding text the Charter of Fundamental Rights of the EU proclaimed at Nice. The third section, by far the longest, fills out in much more detail the rules governing the functioning and policy competences of the EU that were only briefly set out in the first part. It is in this part that the description of a tidying-up exercise is most appropriate, given that all but a few provisions are inserted straight from the previous treaties (Phinnemore 2004: 9). The final part sets out some general provisions, such as the procedures for revision and ratification of the treaty.

A number of other changes are also noteworthy.

- *Institutional changes* (see Section 3.2 for more details): the creation of two new leadership posts; a 'Union minister for foreign affairs' to conduct the EU's foreign and security policy and a new president of the European Council to manage and lead this body. New powers for the Commission president and the European Parliament were added, and some changes in the size and composition of the Commission were made. The number of decisions taken by QMV was increased, and despite many initial differences between member states a new 'double majority' system for determining QMV was eventually adopted.

- *Competence catalogue*: largely as a response to calls by the powerful German regional governments (*Länder*), a new competence catalogue was added to the Constitutional Treaty. The competence catalogue spelt out more clearly which policy areas were exclusive EU powers, which were shared with member states and which were areas of supporting, coordinating or complementary action. Part of the rationale for developing this clear catalogue of competences was that a catalogue would, in theory, make it easier to enforce subsidiarity.

- *National parliaments and subsidiarity enforcement*: seen as one of the big winners of the new treaty settlement, national parliaments were given a new role in the enforcement of subsidiarity. National parliaments will review draft legislative proposals and if at least one-third of national parliaments (or their separate chambers) believe the proposal violates the subsidiarity principle, the Commission will be obliged to reconsider but not necessarily withdraw its proposal.

- *Enhanced cooperation*: the Constitutional Treaty makes it easier for those states that want to integrate further than others – possibly establishing a 'core Europe' – to do so within the EU framework. Further cooperation must further the objectives of the Union, protect its interests, reinforce the integration process, be open to all and involve a minimum of one-third of member states.

- *Common foreign, security and defence policy*: in addition to the creation of the Union minister for foreign affairs, the Constitutional Treaty increased scope for QMV in CFSP by making proposals by the Union foreign minister subject to this procedure. However, unanimity would still remain the default decision-making procedure, and safeguard mechanisms would allow a member state to veto decisions for 'vital and stated reasons of national policy'. The European Council was given authority to provide, with the approval of all member states, for a common defence policy, and a mutual assistance clause was added, obliging member states to help each other if one of their number became a victim of armed aggression. Provision was also made for 'permanent structured cooperation', a kind of enhanced cooperation that would allow those states that wanted to deepen defence cooperation among themselves to do so without being hindered by those states that did not.

Further reading

Dinan, D. (2004) *Europe Recast: A History of the European Union*, Palgrave Macmillan, London, is a good recent text.

Gowland, D. and Turner, A. (eds) (2000) *Britain and European Integration 1945–1998: A Documentary History*, Routledge, London, is a very useful source book.

Phinnemore, D. (2004) *Treaty Establishing a Constitution for Europe: An Overview*, Chatham House Briefing Note, provides a succinct account of the Constitutional Treaty.

Section 3.2

Institutions of the European Union

There are six main institutions of the European Union, the two 'intergovernmental' institutions, the European Council and the Council of Ministers, and four 'supranational' institutions, the Commission, the Parliament, the Court of Justice and the European Central Bank (see Key concept 3.2).

Key concept 3.2

Supranational and intergovernmental institutions

EU institutions are usually categorised as either 'supranational' or 'intergovernmental'. These are not technical terms, spelt out in any of the various EU treaties. They have developed to denote differences in the membership and representative functions of the different EU institutions. Intergovernmental institutions are those, like the European Council and Council of Ministers, composed of official representatives of the member states – heads of state or government, government ministers or member state civil servants. In theory, the members of intergovernmental institutions pursue the preferences of member state governments and represent the interests of the individual member states in the EU decision-making process. In contrast, supranational institutions are composed of people appointed to serve and represent the collective 'European' interest, whether it is directly elected members of the European Parliament, judges appointed to work in the ECJ, bankers appointed to make monetary policy in the ECB, or officials appointed to develop and oversee policies in the European Commission. The terms 'intergovernmental' and 'supranational' may also be used to describe different decision-making procedures used in the Council. Procedures that do not require member state governments to give up their right to veto unwanted decisions are often called intergovernmental procedures. Unanimity decision rules, which require agreement from all states, are thus intergovernmental. In contrast, 'supranational' decision rules, such as QMV, are procedures where member states accept surrendering their veto, ostensibly in the interests of improving the ease and quality of EU decisions.

Until the Treaty of Maastricht, the basic organisational relationship of the five major institutions (the European Central Bank did not exist until after the Treaty of Maastricht) could be stated quite simply. The Commission put forward the

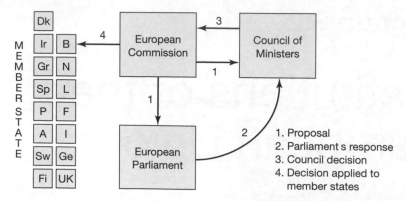

Figure 3.5 The European Union: the decision-making process

ideas, the European Parliament gave its opinion on the proposal, the Council of Ministers took the final decision and the Commission was responsible for putting the agreed policy into effect and monitoring its progress. The Court of Justice was not, and is not, directly involved in the decision-making circuit but is vital to its operation; without it, there would be no final and authoritative interpretation of the treaties and the powers of the institutions. This explanation is oversimplified, but it embodies an important basic fact – that this is a power-sharing structure in which each institution has particular powers and cannot, in the main, proceed without the others.

The European Council and the EU presidency

The European Council was founded in 1974 but not officially acknowledged in any EC treaty until 1986. It was founded to improve member states' control over the direction of EU policy, something that was more pressing after the initiation of new foreign policy initiatives such as European Political Cooperation and concerns about the ability of existing EU institutions to offer effective leadership. Over time, the European Council has come to sit at the apex of the EU's decision-making structure, a position dictated both by the authoritative positions held by its members and its particular functions in the EU decision-making system. European Council meetings, which attract a great deal of media attention, take place at least twice a year.

The European Council is composed of the heads of state and government of all EU member states, assisted by their foreign affairs ministers, plus the president of the Commission (see below) and another Commission member. According to the Maastricht Treaty, this body is responsible for providing impetus for the development of the EU and its general political guidelines. Although the EU treaties do not provide much further guidance on this role, in practice the European Council takes many of the most important and politically sensitive decisions in the EU. Increasingly, the final texts of new EC/EU treaties are negotiated in the European Council. Key decisions about the scope, scale and conditions for EU accession have been made in the European Council, as were decisions about membership of economic and monetary union, compromises unravelling budgetary disputes and the launch of the EU's military 'rapid reaction force'. The European Council also has an important role in the EU's CFSP, defining its principles and general guidelines and expressing the EU's common views on international affairs. Since the launch of EMU, it is involved in discussions on economic policy issues, including the broad guidelines of the economic policies of the member states and the EU as a whole. In line with its more general role as a forum for the resolution of politically sensitive problems, treaty provisions allowing closer cooperation or enhanced cooperation (see Section 3.1) among some (but not all) EU member states within the EU institutional framework also give the European Council an important dispute-resolving role.

Closely associated with the European Council is the presidency of the European Union. Unlike the president of the United States of America, or even the president of the European Commission, the presidency of the European Union is not held by an individual. Rather, it is held by single member states in turn for a six-month period. The state holding the presidency of the EU performs functions on behalf of the European Council and the Council of Ministers (see below), including chairing meetings, establishing the agenda of EU business for its term in office and facilitating bargaining and compromises among the member states. The state holding the EU presidency speaks for the EU as a whole in certain international matters, including some dealings with third countries and in some international organisations. It also speaks for the Council in its formal dealings with other EU bodies like the European Parliament. A number of problems have been identified with this system, including the excessive administrative demands it can create for smaller member states and the inefficiency of so frequent a change in leadership (George and Bache 2001: 254–5). In the context of the May 2004 EU enlargement, which dramatically increased the number of small member states in the EU, the European Convention and the new Constitutional Treaty dismantled the rotating presidency system and replaced it, for the European Council, with a single appointed president of the European Council.

Key fact 3.11

Changes to the European Council in the Constitutional Treaty

- *An EU institution*: the Constitutional Treaty clarifies the previously rather ambiguous position of the European Council as a separate EU institution.

- *President of the European Council*: a new post of European Council president or European Council chair was created, replacing the old rotating presidency system for the European Council (but not the Council of Ministers, see below). The new president will be appointed by the European Council, by qualified majority, for a term of two and a half years, renewable once. Responsibilities include chairing and 'driving forward' the work of the European Council, facilitating cohesion and consensus in the European Council, enhancing the European Council's cooperation with the Commission and the Council of Ministers, reporting to the European Parliament after European Council meetings and playing a role in the external representation of the Union (alongside the new Union foreign minister).

- *New European Council participants*: the European Council president and the Union foreign minister (see below) have the right to participate in European Council meetings.

Council of Ministers (Council of the European Union)

The Council of Ministers (also known as the Council of the European Union) is one of the original institutions of the EC/EU, tracing its history to the founding of the ECSC in the 1950s. Although it is often seen as the 'bastion of member state interests', many analysts argue that the Council of Ministers is in reality more complex. As an archetypal 'intergovernmental' institution, its members are made up of representatives of member state governments, of varying ranks, who are expected to pursue the interests of the individual member states in Council of Ministers decision making. Government ministers negotiate and formally vote for their state in one of the nine policy-specific Council of Ministers formations:

1. General Affairs and External Relations;
2. Economic and Financial Affairs ('ECOFIN');
3. Justice and Home Affairs;
4. Employment, Social Policy, Health and Consumer Affairs;
5. Competitiveness (Internal Market, Industry and Research);
6. Transport, Telecommunications and Energy;
7. Agriculture and Fisheries;
8. Environment;
9. Education, Youth and Culture.

Membership of the different Council of Ministers formations is determined by policy speciality, so that, for example, member state environmental ministers vote in the Environment Council and agricultural and fisheries ministers vote in the Agricultural

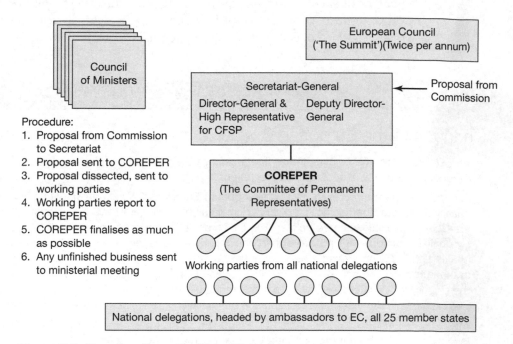

Figure 3.6 How the Council of the EU works

and Fisheries Council. Ministers are assisted by a whole series of other state officials, including permanent ambassadors, who prepare most of the work of the Council of Ministers in weekly meetings of the Council's Permanent Representatives Committee (or COREPER). (Member state agricultural officials meet separately in the Special Committee for Agriculture (SCA).) COREPER is itself assisted by 250 working groups and committees made up of other member state governmental officials. One recent estimate of the numbers of national officials involved in the Council of Ministers' multifaceted organisational structure was as high as 25,000 (Wessels and Rometsch 1996: 331, cited in Lewis 2003: 150). In practice, most Council business is agreed between officials in working groups, committees and in COREPER, with only formal ratification of decisions and negotiation of the most sensitive issues left to the government ministers (Nugent 1999: 157).

In terms of membership, the Council of Ministers may be easy to identify as an intergovernmental institution. However, Council of Ministers voting procedures are increasingly supranational. Initially, most EU decisions were made by unanimity, which gave each member state a chance to veto a decision of which it disapproved. Indeed, as their Luxembourg Compromise of 1966 showed (see Section 3.1), member states were reluctant to make decisions by QMV for decades, even though provisions had been made for QMV in the treaties. Following the EC/EU 'relaunch' of the mid-1980s and revisions in all treaties since the SEA, QMV has become the normal voting procedure in the Council of Ministers, now being used for most types of decision in the EC pillar, some CFSP decisions and some Police and Judicial Cooperation matters (Nugent 1999: 166).

From 1 November 2004, the QMV procedure works as follows: each state is allocated a number of votes, roughly in proportion to their population (Table 3.3). This distribution of votes was carefully balanced to ensure that majorities included a mix of large and small states. Nevertheless, treaty negotiations affecting the allocation of votes are contentious, as wrangles at the December 2001 Nice summit and disputes between Poland and Spain on the one hand and France and Germany on the other during negotiation of the Constitutional Treaty demonstrate.

From November 2004, a qualified majority is reached:

- If a majority of member states (in some cases a two-thirds majority) approves.

- If a minimum of 232 (of a total of 321 possible votes), equivalent to 72.3 percent of votes, is in favour.

Table 3.3 Distribution of votes among member states (from 1 November 2004)

Germany, France, Italy, United Kingdom	29
Spain, Poland	27
Netherlands	13
Belgium, Czech Republic, Greece, Hungary, Portugal	12
Austria, Sweden	10
Denmark, Ireland, Lithuania, Slovakia, Finland	7
Cyprus, Estonia, Latvia, Luxembourg, Slovenia	4
Malta	3
TOTAL	321

(Source: Council of Ministers web pages, http://www.europa.eu.int.)

- A member state can also invoke a third type of majority requirement. It can ask for confirmation that votes in favour represent at least 62 percent of the total population of the Union. If not, the decision will not be adopted.

Most Council of Ministers decisions are made by QMV. For some important decisions, such as amending the treaties or launching a new common policy, unanimity is still required, and for a few decisions there are different voting rules – e.g. for cases where a member state is regarded as violating the rules of EMU.

The Council of Ministers' most important powers are legislative. Although it has increasingly come to share its powers with the European Parliament (EP), it is still the case that all EU laws must be passed by the Council of Ministers before they can be enacted. The Council of Ministers also shares some budgetary powers with the EP, with the Council of Ministers having final say over types of expenditure known as 'compulsory expenditure' (mainly agriculture), but the European Parliament is responsible for approving the budget overall. The Council of Ministers is the principal body for decision making in CFSP matters, where it defines and implements policy, based on European Council guidelines. For Police and Judicial Cooperation in criminal matters, the Council of Ministers adopts measures and coordinates the actions of the member states. Other responsibilities are coordinating the broad economic policy of the member states and concluding international agreements with international organisations and other states on behalf of the EU as a whole.

Key fact 3.12

Changes in the Constitutional Treaty affecting the Council of Ministers

The Union minister for foreign affairs

The Constitutional Treaty creates a new post of Union minister for foreign affairs. The new post merges and replaces the High Representative for CFSP (see Section 3.1) and the Commissioner responsible for external relations.

- *Responsibilities*: to conduct the Union's CFSP. To ensure the consistency of the Union's external action. The Union's foreign minister will also be a vice-president of the Commission.
- *Powers*: can make proposals developing the EU's CFSP and its Common Security and Defence Policy. Presides over the Foreign Affairs Council. Carries out policies mandated by the Council of Ministers.
- *Appointment*: appointed by the European Council, deciding by qualified majority vote, with the agreement of Commission president. The European Parliament has an indirect vote, given that it must give a vote of approval for the whole Commission, which includes the Union foreign minister.
- *The European External Action Service*: the Union foreign minister will be assisted by the new European External Action Service, comprising staff seconded from member state diplomatic services, the Council General Secretariat and the Commission.

Council of Ministers Formations

A draft constitution proposal to replace the previously existing nine Council of Ministers formations with a single legislative council was rejected. The Constitutional Treaty establishes that the Council of Ministers will meet in different configurations, including a General Affairs Council and a Foreign Affairs Council, and others to be determined by the European Council

Presidency of the Council of Ministers

Unlike the presidency of the European Council, which will be given to a single individual, all Council of Ministers configurations except the Foreign Affairs Council would still continue to be presided over by member states on the basis of equal rotation. The Union foreign minister will preside over the Foreign Affairs Council. However, Council of Ministers presidencies will be 'team presidencies' jointly held by three member states for 18 months, although each member state will have a six-month turn at chairing all Council of Ministers configurations (except Foreign Affairs).

Qualified Majority Voting procedures

The system of weighted votes is replaced by a new 'double majority' system requiring:

* support of at least 15 member states and of at least 55 percent of the member states (at present, with 25 member states the support required is 60 percent of the members, but the proposal is written to allow for further enlargement);
* support from states representing 65 percent of the EU's population.

There are two additional conditions regarding blocking minorities:

* A blocking minority needs to comprise at least four states.
* It is possible to postpone a QMV decision for a reasonable time to allow further discussion, if at least three-quarters of a blocking minority so demand. The 'three-quarters' could refer to either three-quarters of member states or three-quarters of the EU's population.

The European Parliament

While the European Parliament was initially a rather powerless, 'multilingual talking shop', it has benefited more than any other EU institution from a cumulative increase in power and influence. The European Parliament began life as the Common Assembly of the ECSC, only taking the name of European Parliament in 1962. Its representative function was circumscribed, with members selected from state parliaments rather than directly elected. Its powers were also limited to formulating non-binding opinions on ECSC policies and laws and the right to scrutinise the actions of, and under certain conditions to dismiss, the ECSC's High Authority (the forebear of the European Commission). The Treaties of Rome extended the Common Assembly's field of activity, but its powers remained fundamentally weak. However, the Treaties of Rome did open the way for the direct election of members of the European Parliament (MEPs), even if it took them 20-odd years to implement!

The first direct elections were held in 1979, and elections have taken place every five years since. This makes the European Parliament the EU's only directly elected body. Each state is allocated a share of seats roughly in proportion to its population, although the populations of smaller states (like Cyprus, Luxembourg and Malta) are overrepresented (Table 3.4).

Successive enlargements have seen total MEPs increase from 78 in 1952 to 732 in 2004. Current arrangements for elections are different in each state, with wide differences in electoral practices resulting. Polling may even occur on different days:

Table 3.4 Distribution of European Parliament seats per member state

Country	1999–2004	2004–2007	Population (millions)
Germany	99	99	83
France	87	78	60
UK	87	78	60
Italy	87	78	59
Spain	64	54	42
Poland	–	54	39
Netherlands	31	27	16
Greece	25	24	11
Belgium	25	24	10
Czech Republic	–	24	10
Hungary	–	24	10
Portugal	25	24	10
Sweden	22	19	9
Austria	21	18	8
Denmark	16	14	5
Finland	16	14	5
Slovakia	–	14	5
Ireland	15	13	4
Lithuania	–	13	3
Latvia	–	9	2.3
Slovenia	–	7	1.9
Estonia	–	6	1.3
Cyprus	–	6	0.95
Luxembourg	6	6	0.45
Malta	–	5	0.38
Total	626	732	

the 2004 European Parliament elections were held on the 10, 11, 12 and 13 of June, depending on the member state. Voter turnout has been notoriously low and falling, challenging claims that the European Parliament is an effective democratic representative of EU citizens. After the 2004 elections, turnout figures were 45.7 percent compared with 49.8 percent in 1999 and 56.8 percent in 1994 (European Parliament, http://www.europa.eu.int). Although European Parliament election issues tend to be national rather then European in focus – with many voters issuing judgement on state government performance – MEPs organise along European lines once they are elected. As Table 3.5 shows, there are Europe-wide party groups, reflecting a broad range of ideological positions.

As Scully argues, the reluctance of member state governments to allow direct elections to the European Parliament was motivated by a fear that a democratically elected European Parliament would be in a stronger position to claim more powers for itself (Scully 2003: 169). This fear was well founded. MEPs continually called for new powers and jealously guarded those they already had. Indeed, in the well-known 1981 Isoglucose case, the European Parliament initiated a suit against the Council of Ministers when it failed to consult the European Parliament as the treaties required (Shackleton 2002: 98). The European Court of Justice ruling that the European Parliament must be consulted as the treaties required annulled the

Table 3.5 Party groups in the European Parliament (April 2005)

European People's Party (Christian Democrats) and European Democrats: 268 MEPs from all member states, with largest delegations from Germany (49), the UK (28), Spain (24) and Italy (24)

Socialist Group of the European Parliament: 202 MEPs from all member states except Latvia and Cyprus. Largest delegations from France (31), Spain (24) and Germany (23)

Alliance of Liberals and Democrats for Europe: 88 MEPs from all but six member states. Largest delegations from the UK (12), Italy (12) and France (11)

Greens and European Free Alliance: 42 MEPs from just over half of all member states. Largest group is from Germany (13). This grouping includes members of European Green and minority nationalist parties

European United Left and Nordic Green Left: 41 MEPs from just over half of all member states. Largest delegations from Germany (7), Italy (7) and Czech Republic (6)

Independence and Democracy Group: 36 MEPs from ten member states. Largest delegations from Poland (10) and UK (10). This party includes members from euro-sceptical parties, like the UK Independence Party

Union for Europe of the Nations: 27 MEPs from six member states. Largest delegations from Italy (9) and Poland (7)

Non-attached: 28 MEPs from eight member states

Council of Ministers' law and effectively gave the European Parliament the power to demand concessions under threat of a delay in issuing its opinion. In addition to informal influence, the European Parliament has accumulated additional formal powers in three key areas:

1. *Budgetary matters*: treaty revisions in 1970 and 1975 gave the European Parliament important powers of co-decision in budgetary matters. It can now propose modifications for budget items in areas such as agriculture, including increases in expenditure, and it could impose amendments for so-called non-compulsory expenditure (most areas other than agriculture). The European Parliament can also reject the budget if it is not satisfied with it and ask for a new one, action it felt justified in taking in 1979 and 1984. European Parliament approval has also been sought for successive multi-year EU budgets (Nugent 1999: 213–15).

2. *Democratic control over EU institutions*: the scrutiny powers of the ECSC's Common Assembly have also grown. Its powers of scrutiny are strongest in rela-tion to the Commission. The European Parliament has a say over the appointment of commissioners, including the Commission president. Member state nominees are questioned and must be approved by MEPs before they can take office. The Commission is also accountable to the European Parliament in the sense that the European Parliament can pass a motion of censure calling for the resignation of the whole Commission. In 1999, the European Parliament came close to exercising these powers when it forced the Commission led by Jacques Santer to resign *en masse* in the face of serious financial mismanagement allegations. The European Parliament also monitors the work of the Commission

and Council of Ministers by presenting them with written and oral questions, examining reports, examining petitions from EU citizens and setting up temporary committees of inquiry.

3. *EU legislation*: initially, the EP's legislative powers were testimonial. It was merely 'consulted' for its views, and the Council of Ministers was not obliged to take them into account. Since the mid-1980s, however, the EP's powers in the legislative process have increased significantly, so that it is now joint legislator with the Council in many important areas of EU policymaking. Increases in European Parliament powers took place with the introduction of the cooperation and assent procedures introduced in the SEA and co-decision in the Maastricht Treaty, but subsequent treaty changes have meant that co-decision has superseded these other procedures in importance. Co-decision has become the normal, template EU legislative procedure, covering 43 areas of EC pillar competence since the coming into force of the Nice Treaty and covering all EC pillar policies except agriculture, fisheries, taxation, EMU, competition, trade and most international agreements (Shackleton 2002: 104). The co-decision procedure is complex, allowing input from various EU bodies and institutions, including the Commission, the European Parliament and the Council at as many as three different stages or readings. The intricacies of the procedure are set out in Figure 3.7. However, it is worth pointing out that the European Parliament can propose amendments to draft legislation, and if the Council refuses to accept those amendments, a special Conciliation Committee comprising European Parliament and Council representatives is to hammer out a deal acceptable to majorities in both institutions. If no deal is found, the legislation cannot be passed, effectively giving the European Parliament a veto over EU legislation.

Key fact 3.13

Changes to the European Parliament in the Constitutional Treaty

- *MEP numbers*: raised to 750. Each state to have at least six MEPs. No state to have more than 96 MEPs.

- *Democratic terminology*: in the Constitutional Treaty, the European Parliament is composed of 'representatives of the Union's citizens' rather than of the 'peoples of the States brought into the Community'. Similarly, the candidate for Commission president will be 'elected' by the EP. Previously, the nominee was merely 'approved' by the EP.

- *Election of Commission president*: clarification that if the European Parliament fails to elect a European Council nominee for Commission president, the European Council would re-nominate candidates until the European Parliament approves. Previously, most assumed that this would be the practice adopted. However, a declaration annexed to the Constitutional Treaty states that the European Parliament and European Council would consult with each other prior to the selection of Commission president nominee, focusing on the background of the nominees and the results of European Parliament elections.

- *Legislative powers and co-decision*: the co-decision procedure will become the ordinary or default decision-making procedure, being used for 95 percent of European laws. In this procedure, the European Parliament has veto powers.

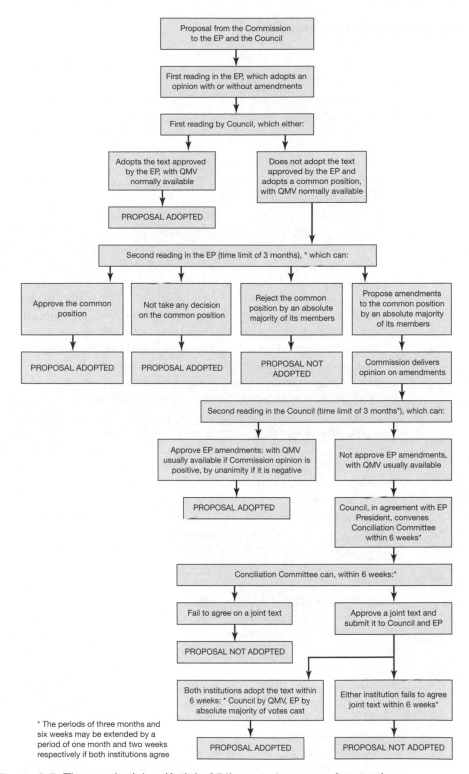

Figure 3.7 The co-decision (Article 251) procedure post-Amsterdam

Source: Nugent (1999).

The European Commission

The European Commission, the EU's executive and administrative body, has been eulogised as both a carrier and a symbol of the 'European project' and the servant of the collective 'European interest'. It has also been demonised as the corrupt, unaccountable sovereignty-devouring, bloated bureaucracy. The Commission's role in the EU policymaking process and the question of whether it is influential or weak, a promoter or destroyer of integration has been the subject of intense and detailed study by academics (see Section 3.3). Whatever one may conclude on these various issues, it is hard to deny that the Commission has important powers that set it apart from the secretariats of most other international organisations.

The European Commission currently employs about 24,000 people from all EU member states. At the top of the Commission hierarchy sit around two dozen commissioners, collectively known as the 'College of Commissioners'. Each commissioner holds their own policy portfolio, or areas of policy responsibility, and heads one of the directorates-general, equivalent to a government department, related to their portfolio responsibilities. The most influential and prestigious member of the College of Commissioners is the Commission president, who is expected to give 'political guidance' to the Commission as a whole and oversee its day-to-day operations. The importance of the office is signalled by the calibre of its nominees, which have included former prime ministers like Romano Prodi (Italy) and Jacques Santer (Luxembourg) and senior government ministers such as former French finance minister Jacques Delors. The commissioners are assisted by tens of thousands of administrative officials, experts, translators and secretarial staff, many of whom are selected through highly competitive examinations. Although it is often accused of supporting a 'bloated' and 'inefficient' bureaucracy, the number of Commission employees is 'fewer than that of many national ministries and indeed many large city councils' (Nugent 1999: 108).

The number of commissioners has fluctuated in recent years to accommodate enlargements, but the Nice Treaty established that the numbers would settle at 25 for 2004–09, with one commissioner from each member state. However, with the prospect of member states numbers rising to 27 or more, the Nice Treaty set a limit of 'less than 27' commissioners for the future, with a system of equitable rotation determining the nationality of commissioners. The procedure by which commissioners are appointed has also changed over time, largely in an attempt to increase the Commission's accountability to the European Parliament and counteract the charge that commissioners are unaccountable 'faceless bureaucrats'. Initially, commissioners were appointed by the collective agreement of the member states, but amendments in the Maastricht, Amsterdam and Nice Treaties increased the influence of the Commission president and the European Parliament in the appointment procedure. Since Nice, the Commission president must agree, in conjunction with member governments, to the other Commission appointees and can decide which portfolios are allocated to each commissioner. He or she can also sack an individual commissioner, if the rest of the college agrees. The member state governments' nominees for Commission president and the College of Commissioners as a whole must receive the approval of the European Parliament. Only then can they officially be appointed. While member states still have an important say over which

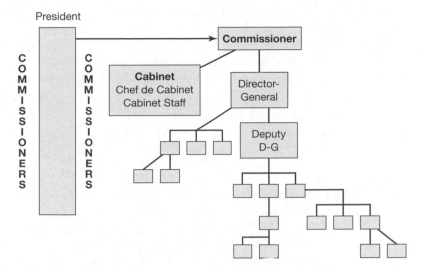

Each commissioner is responsible for one or more Directorates-General. Commissioners do NOT represent the country of origin, or anything else. Their oath of loyalty is to the Community alone. There is one commissioner (including the president) from each member state.

Figure 3.8 The European Commission

commissioners are selected, it must be remembered that the Commission is a supranational body. According to article 213 of the EU Treaty:

> Members of the commission shall, in the general interest of the community, be completely independent in the performance of their duties ... they shall neither seek nor take instructions from any government or from any other body.

The Commission has four main powers:

1. *Guardian of the Treaties*: the Commission is responsible for ensuring that member states correctly apply EU legislation. If it thinks a member state has failed to meet its obligations, the Commission will initiate an 'infringement procedure' notifying the member state of its breach and allowing the member state to present its own view on the issue or to rectify the situation. If the Commission is not satisfied with the member state's response, the Commission will initiate proceedings in the ECJ, which can deliver binding decisions and impose penalties on the member state.

2. *Implementing EU policies*: in many EU policy areas, member state authorities, including central, regional and local government authorities and agencies, are responsible for implementing EU decisions. However, in many of these areas the Commission may adopt administrative or secondary laws to spell out in more detail how the EU laws should work in practice. The Commission has much greater implementing powers in fields like competition policy, including responsibility for monitoring cartels and mergers and state subsidies to industries and investigating and fining businesses involved in anti-competitive practices. The Commission also has some other management or administrative functions, including administering the CAP budget and managing Structural Fund programmes.

3. *External representation*: in some matters, the Commission speaks for the EU as a whole. Under the watchful eye of the Council, which approves EU negotiating positions, the Commission represents and speaks on behalf of the EU in the WTO. It also negotiates trade and cooperation agreements with third countries and the terms of accession with applicant member states.

4. *Legislative role*: arguably, the Commission's most important power is its exclusive right to initiate legislation within the first, or EC, pillar. The importance of this right of initiation lies in the agenda-setting, or agenda-defining, powers it places in the hands of the Commission. Essentially, while ideas for new first-pillar legislation may follow pressure or lobbying by other EU institutions, member states and other political and social actors as well as from the Commission's own initiatives, first-pillar legislation cannot be passed unless it is first presented as a proposal by the Commission. Moreover, in decision-making procedures such as co-decision, the Commission also has the power to make it difficult for the Council or the European Parliament to change a proposal in the course of the legislative procedure, making it, with these two bodies, a key partner in the legislative process. In Common Foreign and Security Policy (second pillar) and Police and Judicial Cooperation (third pillar) matters, the Commission shares the power of initiation with the member states.

Key fact 3.14

Changes in the Constitutional Treaty relating to the Commission

* *Appointment of Commission president*: when appointing a Commission president, the European Council will take into account the results of a prior European Parliament election.

* *Appointment of commissioners*: the draft constitution gave the Commission president powers to select commissioners from a list of member state nominees. This was rejected in favour of the existing system.

* *Composition of Commission*: until 2014, there will still be one commissioner per member state. After that, the total number of commissioners will equal two-thirds of the total number of member states, with nationalities chosen on a basis of equal rotation. Commission composition should also reflect the demographic and geographical range of all member states.

* *Union foreign minister*: the Union foreign minister will simultaneously hold the post of Commission vice-president and thereby personify a new link between the Commission and the Council. The Union foreign minister will also hold responsibility for external affairs in the Commission. The Commission president helps to select the Union foreign minister.

* *Dismissal of commissioner*: the Commission president now has the power to dismiss a commissioner.

European Court of Justice

The European Court of Justice (ECJ) must not be confused with the European Court of Human Rights, which we will discuss in Part 4 – the latter is not an EU institution and has a quite different remit.

The ECJ is the final main EU supranational institution discussed in this section. Its members are judges, rather than politicians or civil servants, and they must be highly qualified judges or legal experts of recognised competence 'whose independence is beyond doubt'. There is a total of 25 judges, one from each member state, appointed by the common accord of the member states for a six-year period. Eight advocates-general assist the ECJ judges by preparing reasoned legal opinions on cases that will later be presented and decided by the ECJ judges. Advocates must also be independent of member state influence, be highly qualified legal professionals and meet the approval of all member states.

As the number of member states and areas of EU activity has grown, the ECJ has seen its caseload grow. According to EU statistics, the ECJ was presented with an average of 20 cases a year during the 1950s and made an average of around seven judgements a year (*Annual Report of the European Court of Justice*: 2003, http://www.curia.eu.int). By the 1980s, however, there was an average of around 350 new cases a year and an average of 178 judgements. This increase in the level of activity prompted the creation, in 1989, of a new tribunal, the Court of First Instance, to take some of ECJ's caseload. More recently, the Nice Treaty made provision for the creation of 'judicial panels', which are special courts established to make rulings on specific types of case or proceedings in specific areas (such as disputes involving the civil service or disputes relating to Community patents). Like the ECJ, Court of First Instance and judicial panel judges must be independent and highly qualified members of the legal profession. The caseload in 2003 for both the ECJ and Court of First Instance was still very high at 556 new cases for the ECJ and 465 for the Court of First Instance.

These judicial institutions form the centrepiece of a functioning and, in international affairs at least, unique legal system. That is, the EC/EU has established mechanisms to ensure that member states implement certain kinds of important decision made at the EU level. The role of the EU's judicial institutions in this system is to ensure that the EC/EU treaties and the laws applying them are

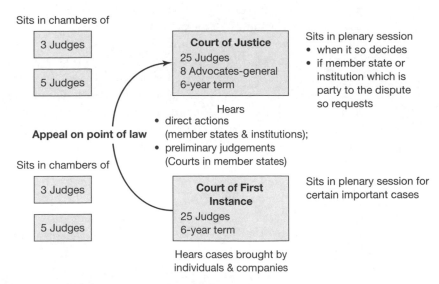

Figure 3.9 The European Court of Justice

observed both by member states and the EU institutions and to interpret the treaties if there is some ambiguity or dispute about their meaning. Court decisions are binding and, since the Maastricht Treaty, the ECJ has been able to impose fines on member states in some circumstances. The main areas of the ECJ's jurisdiction are:

- *Determining whether a member state has fulfilled its obligations under Community law*: such cases may be brought by the European Commission or another member state.

- *Determining whether a measure adopted by EU institutions should be annulled*: such an action can be brought by a member state, one of the Community institutions (Parliament, European Council, Council of Ministers or Commission) or by individuals directly affected by such a measure.

- *Determining whether a Community institution has failed to act when according to EU law it should have acted.*

- *Making a preliminary ruling on a case referred to it by the national courts of an EU member state*: national courts play an important role in the EU legal system, particularly as they have responsibility for addressing cases where individuals seek remedy for a breach of an EU law affecting them. However, to ensure the effective and uniform application of EU law, the national courts may turn to the ECJ to ask for clarification on a point involved in their cases – that is a preliminary ruling – relating to aspects of EC law. The national court is bound to apply the opinion of the ECJ.

In its rulings, the ECJ has made a number of decisions that have deeply influenced the nature of the legal order and politics of the EU. In one of its most important rulings, in the 1964 case of *Costa* v. *ENEL*, the ECJ declared that where there is a conflict between EC law and national law, EC law must prevail. This was not explicitly spelled out in the treaties, but the ECJ reasoned that because member states had created a permanent organisation, with its own institutions and 'real powers stemming from limitation of sovereignty or a transfer of powers from the states to the Community', member states created a system of law that was binding on them and their citizens. In other words, they had *intended* that EC law would be supreme in the field of the application of the EC treaties. A year earlier, in the 1963 *Van Gend en Loos* case, the ECJ ruled that EC law applied not only to member states, which is the usual case in international law, but to individuals as well. It thereby established the principle of 'direct effect', which like the 'primacy' or 'supremacy' of EC law was not explicitly conferred in the treaties (George and Bache 2001: 279). The ECJ rulings have also played a role in the resolution of disputes between member states and between different EU institutions and have, as one author commented, 'proved decisive in helping achieve the EU's economic and social goals' (Dinan 1999: 308). One area where ECJ judgements have had a significant social impact is in the area of equal pay for men and women, a treaty requirement that the ECJ ruled, in the 1971 *Defrenne* case, should be applied in all EC member states.

Key fact 3.15

Changes in the Constitutional Treaty relating to the EU legal system

* *The General Court*: the name of the Court of First Instance has been changed to the General Court.
* *Legal instruments*: the multiplicity of EU legal instruments has been reduced. The main types of legal instrument will be European laws, European framework laws, European regulations, European decisions, recommendations and opinions.
* *Primacy of EU law*: the legal principle articulated by the ECJ that where there is a conflict between member state and EU law that EU law would prevail was formally inserted into the first part of the treaty.
* *European Public Prosecutor's Office*: the Council has been mandated to create a new body responsible for investigating, prosecuting and bringing to judgement 'those who commit offences against the Union's financial Interests'.
* *Charter of Fundamental Rights of the Union*: this charter was proclaimed at Nice (a political act) but will become legally binding under the Constitutional Treaty. It binds all EU institutions and the member states when they are implementing EU law.

Other EU bodies

There are a number of other EU bodies that are not officially denominated EU institutions but that play a role in EU decision making. Some of these bodies, like the ECB, play a very important role.

European Central Bank

The ECB is the centrepiece of the overarching European System of Central Banks (ESCB), composed of the ECB itself and the central banks of the states participating in the EU's single currency. Created by the Maastricht Treaty, the ECB, with the national central banks, is responsible for formulating and implementing the EU's monetary policy. In pursuit of its guiding objective of promoting economic (especially price) stability, the ECB's and the ESCB's responsibilities include setting interest rates for the euro zone, executing exchange market operations, managing official reserves and promoting the smooth operation of payment systems (McNamara 2002: 171). We discuss the ECB more fully in Part 5.

Committee of the Regions

Established in 1994 on the basis of Maastricht Treaty provisions, the Committee of the Regions (CoR) provides a voice for the EU's regions and local authorities in EU decision making. It has 317 full members, comprised of representatives of regional and local authorities from each of the member states. The Commission and the Council are obliged to consult the CoR in EU policy matters relevant to regions and local authorities, many of which play an important role in the implementation of EU legislation. Policy areas where it is consulted include economic and social cohesion, trans-European infrastructure networks, health, education and culture, employment policy, social policy, the environment, vocational training, and transport. Like the European Economic and Social Committee, the CoR is an advisory body, whose opinions are non-binding.

European Economic and Social Committee

The European Economic and Social Committee (EESC) is one of the oldest EC/EU bodies. It was established by the Treaty of Rome in 1957 to represent social and economic interests in EU policymaking. Now, 222 representatives of groups such as employers, workers, farmers, small businesses, the professions, scientists, and consumer and environmental groups are represented on the EESC. Their main task is to create their own study groups and issue non-binding opinions on EU decisions relating to the internal market, education, consumer protection, the environment, regional development, social affairs, employment, public health and equal opportunities.

Further reading

George, S. and Bache, I. (2001) *Politics of the European Union*, Oxford University Press, Oxford, is a good and still reasonably up-to-date overview.

Cini, M. (ed.) (2003) *European Union Politics*, Oxford University Press, Oxford, contains several very useful chapters.

Peterson, J. and Shackleton, M. (eds) (2002) *The Institutions of the European Union*, Oxford University Press, Oxford, also contains several very useful chapters.

Section 3.3

Theories of political integration and the EU

Theories of political integration

European integration theories, like social theory more generally, involve competing narratives, explanations and sometimes contrasting political projects. In the 1970s, one analyst unflatteringly compared integration studies to the fate of blind men discovering an elephant: each blind man touched a different part of the large animal, and each concluded that the elephant had the appearance of the part that he touched. While no man arrived at a very accurate description of the elephant, a lively debate ensued about the nature of the beast because each man disbelieved his fellows (paraphrased from Puchala 1972: 267).

Before going on to review current theoretical work on European integration, it is worth pausing to consider the more abstract question of why theories are necessary. At first glance, the moral of the blind men and the elephant fable – the fruitlessness of theorists apparently working at cross-purposes – might be conceived as an argument against theory. However, such a conclusion is problematic for a number of reasons. In the first place, it is probably impossible to formulate any statement about social activity without invoking theory at some level. As Rosamond puts it: 'we are all informed by theoretical perspectives' because any statement about the world is 'always grounded in a particular set of assumptions about how the world operates' (Rosamond 2000: 5). Theories are indispensable tools that help the observer to make sense of, attribute meaning to and identify what is significant about a complex reality (*ibid.*). Second, theories perform many useful functions, including defining and classifying social phenomena; explaining, elucidating and predicting social processes and events; and offering critiques of existing or proposing alternative social practices and institutions (Diez and Wiener 2004: 17; Landman 2000: 5–10). Finally, trends in European integration theory (and the social sciences more generally) have shown that 'trans-paradigm mavericks' do eventually tend to emerge 'to establish constructive dialogues and to accomplish theoretical syntheses' (Rosamond 2000: 7; see also O'Neill 1996).

The development of theories of European integration can be divided into three, somewhat overlapping phases. The first phase is dominated by what are often called the classical theories of integration: neo-functionalism and intergovernmentalism. These two theories tended to dominate analysis in the 1960s, 1970s and early 1980s, although intergovernmentalism in particular is still an influential theory today. A second phase of integration theory begins in the late 1980s and is characterised by a concern with understanding the EU as a system of governance. More and more of those conducting research on the EU began to take an interest in how the EU might be considered a political system with policy inputs and outputs similar to (but not the same as) those of state-based political systems. In this phase, terms like 'policy networks', 'multi-level governance' and 'institutionalism' also became common currency. As we come closer to our own time, it is more difficult to characterise the features of theorising. Some have characterised it as a period in which researchers are much more concerned with understanding how the EU is and should be constructed. In other words, there is a marked concern to understand 'how and with which social and political consequences integration develops' (Diez and Wiener 2004: 7). In addition to constructivism, democratic deficit and legitimacy, this is also a period in which Europeanisation has emerged as a key focus of analytical attention.

Classical theories of European integration: neo-functionalism and intergovernmentalism

Neo-functionalism is a pioneering theory of regional integration developed from the 1950s, largely by US-based scholars Haas (1961, 1968a, 1968b, 1970), Schmitter (1970, 2004), Lindberg (1963) and Lindberg and Scheingold (1970). It essentially aims to explain and predict change in the international relations of states produced by regional integration. Initially, neo-functionalists defined regional integration in a way that reflected their interest in investigating how the integration of states might produce a new form of political community. Haas, the founding father of neo-functionalism, famously defined regional integration as:

> the process whereby political actors in several distinct national settings are persuaded to shift their loyalties, expectations and political activities towards a new and larger centre, whose institutions demand jurisdiction over the pre-existing national states.
>
> (Haas 1961: 366–7.)

Conflict resolution was an important sub-theme in early neo-functionalist work as well, particularly the question of whether integration and new methods of cooperation between states might contribute to international peace. However, as neo-functionalist research developed in response to critique and new information, neo-functionalists adopted a broader conception of integration. Their focus of study became:

explaining how and why states cease to be wholly sovereign, how and why they voluntarily mingle, merge and mix with their neighbours so as to lose the factual attributes of sovereignty while acquiring new techniques for resolving conflict.

(Haas 1970: 610).

Neo-functionalists tended to be less interested in explaining the reasons why states decided to integrate in the first place than in explaining the processes of community building it was expected to unleash. Nevertheless, an account of why states integrate does underpin the theory. Haas rejected explanations focusing on purported linguistic, cultural or religious similarities in Western Europe and the unifying impulse that 'fear of the Soviet Union' or 'envy of the United States' may have provided (Haas 1961: 319 and 322). He argued that the gloomy 'national situation' of many Western European states in the 1950s – when many were still recovering from the truama of war and economic devastation – discredited the state and state nationalism to the degree that alternative supranational means to achieve security, welfare and peace were contemplated (*ibid.*: 316). However, a more fundamental explanation for the initiation of regional integration was a convergence of economic goals. He argued that Western Europe's advanced industrial capitalist states depended on foreign trade if they wished to maintain minimum standards of economic welfare for their citizens (Haas 1961: 322; Haas 1968b: 155–9). In Europe, regional integration was, paradoxically, 'a conservative impulse' that 'sought to innovate in order to preserve something already existing' (Haas 1961: 321).

Although there were attempts at regional integration outside Europe, it is widely acknowledged that integration in Europe has been deeper and more advanced than elsewhere. Some neo-functionalists sought to understand why integration in Europe had gone so much further. In so doing, they developed additional arguments about how the internal characteristics of Europe's integrating states favoured integration. Haas argued that there were crucial economic, social and political similarities among the founding members of the ECSC, EEC and EAEC that set them apart from states forming regional organisations in places like Latin America, the Middle East or Soviet-dominated Europe (Haas 1961, 1968b). Unlike counterparts in other regions, integrating Western European states were all advanced industrial capitalist economies, committed to welfare provision and reliant on international trade. In part as a consequence of these socio-economic conditions, decision making in the Western European integrating states was bureaucratised and pluralistic: their civil services typically stressed high professional competence and technical expertise. They routinely consulted and worked with major voluntary groups like trade unions, industrial associations, bankers and farmers. According to Haas, this similarity in training and outlook among Europe's civil servants smoothed the process of negotiation and decision making at the European level (Haas 1961: 320). Furthermore, similar socio-economic factors helped to produce similar ideological divisions, political parties and interest group goals within the Western European integrating states. This not only created similar feelings and expectations among major group elites, it also made it easy for political actors to identify, ally with, meet and formulate common cause with their counterparts in other states (*ibid.*).

Spillover

The most fundamental and indeed emblematic theme of neo-functionalism was analysis of what happens after states make an initial agreement to surrender or transfer sovereignty to institutions like the EC/EU. Initially, neo-functionalists argued that limited integration, such as that in the areas of coal and steel, set in motion a logic of change that would, step by step, unite previously autonomous states into some form of new supranational political community. Central to the logic of change was the concept of 'spillover', or the idea that even limited integration had an expansive logic that would inevitably create new pressures for further integration regardless of the initial intentions of integrating states. Contemporary commentators generally identify three main types of spillover in neo-functionalist writing: 'functional (or technical) spillover', 'political spillover' and 'cultivated spillover' (see Key concept 3.3).

Key concept 3.3

Forms of 'spillover'

1. *Functional spillover* is the process whereby integration in one sector of the economy creates pressure for integration in other connected sectors of the economy. However, actions to respond to this pressure for further integration are expected to create yet more pressure for integration in other areas, eventually creating a snowballing of pressures for the fuller integration of economies (Lindberg 1963: 10). The initial expansion of integration from the coal and steel sectors (ECSC) to integration in the related field of nuclear energy (EAEC) and the creation of a general common market (EEC) to extend the common market in the sectors of coal and steel (ECSC) were seen as prime examples of functional spillover. Expansion of activity to these sectors was seen as necessary to achieve the original objectives of the ECSC and to overcome certain initially unforeseen problems (Haas 1968b: 297–301).

2. *Political spillover* could take a number of forms. New areas of responsibility could be transferred to the supranational level as a consequence of 'package deals', a negotiating practice where states agreed to integrate in one issue area in exchange for integration, or some other form of concession, in another issue area. Another form of political spillover involved the build-up of further pressures for European integration in the integrating states (George and Bache 2001: 11). Neo-functionalists expected national elites intimately involved in regional-level decision-making eventually to transfer loyalties to these regional institutions and to press national governments to take further integrative steps. Pressures for further integration could also come from formerly state-based interest groups and political parties that had responded to incentives to reorganise into new regional-level units as more decisions were taken at the regional level.

3. *Cultivated spillover* captures the role that officials in supranational institutions like the European Commission were expected to play in promoting further integration. They could perform the role of 'institutional conciliators' (Haas 1968b: 153) or, as Schmitter put it, 'reform mongers' (2004). Supranational officials could help member states to 'upgrade their common interests' and in so doing steer them towards further integration and increasing the powers of regional-level institutions at the expense of member states. They may even 'invent and promote new symbols of regional identity' to further their integration goals (*ibid.*).

The very early history of European integration provided some promise that neo-functionalist predictions might bear fruit. As mentioned above, integration in the coal and steel sectors seemed to 'spill over' into nuclear energy integration and the creation of a general common market. According to neo-functionalists like Lindberg (1963), there was further evidence of spillover in the early history of the EEC. Key interest groups began to reorient some of their activities to the European level, forming by 1963 over 200 EEC-level interest groups. Evidence that key business groups had pressured national governments for further integration was uncovered. For instance, they were seen to have been influential in bringing about before-schedule implementation of treaty commitments on the removal of internal barriers to trade. An activist Commission, led by former German foreign secretary Walter Hallstein, played an important brokerage role in these 'acceleration' negotiations and also encouraged member states to make further progress in the field of agricultural policy.

However, it was not long before the tide of European integration history turned against the neo-functionalists. The series of anti-integration moves orchestrated by French President Charles de Gaulle, which we have discussed in Section 3.1, showed how a resurgence of state nationalism and indeed individual leaders could obstruct further integration. Moreover, failure to follow through on key 1969 Hague summit commitments – like economic and monetary union by 1980 – the lethargy of economic slowdown and the 1970s mood of 'eurosclerosis' seemed to indicate that neo-functionalists had mispredicted the trajectory and dynamics of European integration. In light of these setbacks, neo-functionalists revised their theories, removing assumptions that integration was somehow 'automatic' or 'inevitable' and acknowledging the possibility that disintegration ('spill-back') or stasis could also occur.

Despite its predominance during the early decades of the postwar period, contemporary interest in the neo-functionalist approach as a whole tends to be of an archaeological kind – more an interest in the origins of the field of EU studies than in a set of convincing theoretical propositions. This is not to say that neo-functionalist vocabulary, and some of its research questions about the role of supranational institutions, interest groups politics and identification patterns, no longer find a place in European integration theories. Indeed, as later discussions of theory will show, such questions are still crucial. There was also an attempt to resurrect the theory – under the unwieldy label of 'neo-neo-functionalism' – in the wake of the EU's single-market-led revival in the mid-1980s (see, for example, Tranholm-Mikkelsen 1991; Sandholtz and Zysman 1989). Nevertheless, it is a telling sign of the status of this theory in contemporary European studies that, as one former neo-functionalist lamented in 2004, 'virtually no one currently working on European integration openly admits to being a neo-functionalist. Its own creator has even declared it obsolescent' (Schmitter 2004: 45). Some of the reasons for this can be seen in the critiques and counter-arguments developed by other theoretical approaches, especially those associated with intergovernmentalism.

Intergovernmentalism

In the conventional narrative of European integration theory, intergovernmentalism – particularly the work of writers like Hoffman (1966, 1995), Milward (1992, 2000) and Moravcsik (1998) – developed as a challenge to neo-functionalism.

Indeed, for a number of decades following the 1960s, debate among scholars of European integration was presented as one deeply divided by a neo-functionalist–intergovernmentalist schism proposing stark alternatives (Rosamond 2000: 2). The main difference between the two is their views on relevant actors. Neo-functionalists consider a wide range of potential contributors to the integration process, including state governments, supranational institutions and transnational interest groups. Intergovernmentalists, on the other hand, see only state central governments pursuing a form of national interest as the key actors. For this reason, intergovermentalism, with its emphasis on relations between member state governments, is often referred to as a state-centric approach.

Hoffman was the most influential early intergovernmentalist. He criticised neo-functionalism for its overly narrow focus on the process of integration at the expense of a sufficiently developed understanding of the international context in which it took place (Hoffman 1968: 198). He argued that key properties of the international system preserved existing nation-states and their diversity. In so doing, the international system limited the scope of regional integration and the likelihood that states would integrate themselves into obsolescence. In the first place, existing nation-states – with their differing geo-historical positions, interests, values, prejudices and traditions – were legitimised and sustained by the emotive pull and moral justifications of nationalist ideology. This was reinforced at the international level by widespread acceptance of the principle of national self-determination. Furthermore, the global nature of international politics, and particularly the global impact of the Cold War, meant that members of regional organisations like the EC/EU had to make decisions reflecting both their regional and their international interests. Integrating states had different 'national situations', comprising internal differences and 'positions in the world' and would, consequently, continue to define their 'national interests' rather differently.

This 'logic of diversity' meant that member states ultimately launched the EC/EU for different reasons and that integration took place only when there was a convergence of national interests. Among these, Hoffman noted:

> for Germany, integration meant a leap from opprobrium and impotence, to respectability and equal rights; for the smaller powers, it meant exchanging a very modest dose of autonomy for participation in a potentially strong and rich grouping. France could not help being much more ambivalent, for integration meant on the one hand an avenue for leadership and the shaping of a powerful bloc, but it also meant on the other hand the acceptance of permanent restrictions to ... autonomy.

> (Source: Hoffman 1966: 211.)

However, the logic of diversity could also put the brakes on further integration. It could explain how a surge of nationalism on the part of one member state – such as Gaullist France – could plunge the EC/EU into deep crisis. More fundamentally, different national interests could 'rule out agreement on the shape' or end-point of the integration enterprise, or agreement on fundamental issues like the 'world role of the new, supranational whole' (*ibid.*: 182). Differing national interests, shaped by the different national situations of EC/EU member states, for instance, meant there was no common vision on the crucial issue of the EC/EU's world role *vis-à-vis* the USA. In France, the EC/EU was seen in some quarters as an instrument for eliminating Europe's dependence on US security, a policy shaped by the memories of Europe's former power, suspicion of US hegemony and the hope that the Soviet Union, a former wartime ally, might be wooed to moderation (*ibid.*: 191). In Germany, on the other hand, where dependence on the USA was accepted as a strategic necessity, the EC/EU was 'merely a way to make [US] dependence more comfortable' (*ibid.*: 189). As a front-line Cold War state, divided by the Iron Curtain, with a staunchly anti-communist leadership, the more pro-US German elite's preferences on the role of the EC/EU *vis-à-vis* the USA would be difficult to square with those of its French partners. Such differences would make it very difficult for member states to develop the coherent and effective foreign policy of the kind that state-like units invariably need.

Such differences, according to Hoffman, set limits on the scope of integration. Initially, there was sufficient ambiguity about the integration process – including about whether it would preserve or diminish dependence on the USA – that the diversity of state preferences was not a serious block to the integration process. Hoffman also conceded that spillover could drive integration in areas of 'low politics', essentially areas related to economic integration and welfare provision. However, as soon as integration strayed into the area of what he called 'high politics', or political integration, or when some of the early ambiguities about the consequences of integration became clearer, then integration would hit its ceiling. It was no surprise for Hoffman, then, that no powers in key areas of national importance like foreign and defence policies had been transferred to the EC/EU level. While such arguments may have appeared appropriate in the wake of the failure of the European Defence Community in the 1950s, by the 1970s, the development of (albeit limited) foreign policy coordination in the context of European Political Cooperation hinted that integration in areas of high politics would soon be on the agenda (Rosamond 2000: 78). Since the Maastricht Treaty, CFSP and later defence cooperation has developed considerably. Other fields of political integration in areas such as immigration, policing and justice have also opened up, and together with the very politically significant decision to create a single currency they provide clear instances of when 'member states willingly surrendered control over issues of central importance to national interest' (*ibid.*: 78).

Moravcsik is the best-known contemporary intergovernmentalist. His book *Choice for Europe* (1998) analyses EU treaty decisions from Rome to Maastricht. He argues that

> European integration resulted from a series of rational choices made by national leaders who consistently pursued economic interests – primarily the commercial interests of powerful economic producers and secondarily the macroeconomic preferences of ruling governmental coalitions – that evolved slowly in response to structural incentives in the global economy.

> (Source: Moravcsik 1998: 3.)

Supporting this argument was his theory of liberal intergovernmentalism, a more explicit and rigorous set of proposals than his intergovernmental predecessors. This theory holds on to the basic intergovernmentalist premise that member state central government bargains determine outcomes and that supranational institutions are agents of the member states rather than autonomous political actors. However, it builds on Hoffman's underdeveloped arguments about the role of domestic politics (George and Bache 2001: 14).

Liberal intergovernmentalism models EU decision making as a two-level game. The first game takes place in the domestic arena and mostly involves economic interests pressuring the government to take account of their views. These views are moulded into the national preferences, or the position that state representatives bring with them to the negotiating table in EU bodies. EU-level negotiations represent the second game or phase in the EU decision-making process and involves the reconciliation of different state interests. Decisions are reached when there is a convergence of national preferences. However, as Moravcsik explains:

> These interstate conflicts are resolved only through hard interstate bargaining, in which credible threats to veto proposals, to withhold financial side-payments, and to form alternative alliances excluding recalcitrant governments carried the day. The outcomes reflect relative power of states – more precisely patterns of asymmetrical interdependence. [That is] those who gain the most economically from integration compromised the most on the margin to realize it, whereas those who gained the least or for whom the costs of adaptation were highest imposed conditions.

> (Source: Moravcsik 1998: 3.)

In contrast to the neo-functionalist vision of supranational institutions, Moravcsik envisioned the role of supranational institutions as auxiliary.

> To secure the substantive bargains they had made ... governments delegated and pooled sovereignty in international institutions for the express purpose of committing one another to co-operation.

> (Source: *ibid*.: 4.)

The role of supranational bodies like the Commission in the CAP or the ECB in EMU, for instance, was to make sure that individual member states kept to the rules and were not tempted to defect from agreements.

Understanding the Euro-polity: comparative politics, governance and institutionalism

In the mid-1980s and early 1990s, the EU underwent a process of profound institutional change. The Single European Act and the Maastricht Treaty consolidated a commitment to deepen economic integration in the form of the single-market project and eventually EMU. The EU was also given wider powers in areas related to the operation of the single market – such as environmental, regional and consumer policy – and areas like immigration, asylum, and police and judicial cooperation, areas that cut to the heart of traditional areas of state sovereignty. This expansion of the field of EU activity would also affect and involve a much wider range of domestic policy actors in EU decisions, not only those who might want to mobilise and lobby EU decision makers to influence the content of EU laws and regulations but also those who might be required to implement EU laws at home. Additionally, new powers were given to EU institutions, particularly to supranational institutions like the European Parliament and the European Commission.

For theorists, these changes had some important consequences. In particular, they invited theorists to consider what kind of political system the EU was becoming and how it could be described (Diez and Wiener 2004: 7). Scholars also became more interested in studying the day-to-day politics of the EU in its own right, rather than just the history-making decisions such as major policy changes and the treaty-making process. Hix's work (1999) is a good example of this new kind of approach. He argued that it would be helpful to analyse the EU as a political system and to use the tools of comparative politics to understand it. Hix acknowledges that the EU is not a state in the traditional understanding of the term, because it lacks a 'monopoly on the legitimate use of coercion' (*ibid*.: 4). That is, the EU does not have police and security forces that can be used to enforce its laws and decisions. These powers remain with the member states and, indeed, the EU relies on the member states to 'administer coercion and other forms of state power on its behalf' (*ibid*.: 5). However, just like other democratic political systems, he argues, the EU has four key characteristics:

1. There is a stable and clearly defined set of institutions for collective decision making and rules governing relations between and within these institutions. (Moreover, successive institutional reforms have given these institutions an ever-wider range of executive, legislative and judicial powers.)

2. Citizens and social groups seek to achieve their political desires through the political system, either directly or through intermediary organisations like interest groups and political parties.

3. Collective decisions in the political system have a significant impact on the distribution of economic resources and the allocation of social and political values across the whole system.

4. There is a continuous interaction ('feedback') between these political outputs, new demands on the system, new decisions and so on (*ibid*.: 2–3).

Hix shows that we can usefully study the EU using tools and concepts that we might use to study politics in democratic states, including looking at 'public opinion, party competition, interest group mobilization, executive and political discretion, legislative bargaining, economic policymaking, citizen–state relations and international political and economic relations' (*ibid*.: 2).

For similar reasons, many authors began to study different EU policy areas as discrete fields of inquiry. This provided an opportunity to understand the nature of the EU from the bottom up and to undertake detail-rich empirical studies of EU politics on the ground. The field of policy analysis provided a series of useful concepts that could be applied to the study of the EU, as did other fields, such as international relations (Richardson 2001). Researchers looked at agenda setting and the role of policy entrepreneurs in order to understand why the EU made some decisions but not others. They looked at how knowledge professionals (epistemic communities) could shape the way decision-makers understood the problems they had to deal with and which solutions would be more successful. They looked at how the configuration of policy networks or the activity of advocacy coalitions might shape particular decisions (see key concept 3.4 for definitions of these policy concepts).

Key concept 3.4

Policy concepts in the study of the EU

- *Agenda setting* 'is an initial crucial "veto point" in the policy process at which political and administrative leaders can exercise their power, either to have a policy intervention considered, or to prevent anything from happening that would diminish the well being of their constituent group' (Peters 2001: 78).
- *Policy entrepreneurs* 'are policy actors who are able to set or manipulate the political marketplace' (Cini 2003: 421).
- *Epistemic communities* 'are transnational groups united by their shared beliefs and conceptions of scientific validity. They supply knowledge, usually about technical policy matters, and thereby help to frame the interests and preferences of policy actors (notably states)' (Rosamond 2000: 199).
- *Advocacy coalitions*: 'An approach … that identifies (a) the significance of knowledge in the policy process and (b) the role of like-minded activists united by common belief systems who seek to influence policy agendas' (*ibid.*: 198).
- *Policy networks*: 'a metaphor for a cluster of actors, each of which has an interest or "stake" in a given EU policy sector and the capacity to help determine success or failure. EU policy networks usually bring together a diverse variety of institutional actors and other stakeholders: private and public, national and supranational, political and administrative. Actors in policy networks are dependent on each other for scarce resources, such as information expertise or legitimacy' source (Peterson and Bomberg 1999: 8).

Those analysing the EU as a political system are often grouped together as governance approaches to the study of the EU. Like other fashionable terms, 'governance' has been defined in a variety of ways. Some define it as more or less equivalent to policymaking. Another, more sophisticated formulation contrasts governance with government. In this formulation, government refers to more traditional forms of governing, characterised by the dominance of the formal institutions of the state, such as parliaments, courts, governments, presidents and prime ministers. Governance, on the other hand, reflects a change in the style or process of governing in which the state's institutions are still important but become brokers rather than protagonists in policymaking (Stoker 1998; Kohler Koch 1996). This means that rather than controlling decision making themselves, public institutions, sometimes from multiple levels of government – local, regional, state and EU level – bring together networks of actors relevant to social and political matters and enable them to negotiate mutually acceptable solutions to particular policy problems.

The work of Marks and Hooghe (2001) on multi-level governance has been one of the most influential examples of this governance approach. According to these authors, 'multilevel governance describes the dispersal of authoritative decision-making across multiple territorial levels' (Marks and Hooghe 2001: 1). They argue that such a process has taken place in Europe as a consequence of two developments. One is the effect of European integration, which has shifted authority in several key areas of policymaking from the state to the EU level. The other is regionalisation (or the process by which state authority has shifted from state to sub-state (or regional) levels of government in some member states). A consequence of these developments is that the EU has become transformed into a multi-level polity where state-level bodies no longer have a monopoly on political authority. Marks and Hooghe propose a model of the EU very different from the liberal intergovernmental view of an EU dominated by the preferences pursued by member state governments. In the multi-level governance model, regions, states and supranational actors 'share control over many activities that take place in their respective territories' (Marks *et al.* 1996: 346–7). The EU becomes a polity in which there are transnational linkages between actors located in and representing different political arenas and where the 'complex relationships in domestic politics do not stop at the nation state but extend to the European level' (*ibid.*: 346–7). The idea of policy networks (see key concept 3.4) has been an important concept used by multi-level governance theorists to model the relationship between these different levels of government.

Analysis of the special effects that institutions may have on EU politics – often called institutionalism or new institutionalism – also emerged as an area of interest for scholars of European integration in the late 1980s and early 1990s. The study of institutions is a rather abstract object of study. However, because institutions are always created by people, they provide many interesting insights into how cooperation is managed and how power is exercised. Institutions can be defined in a very broad way as 'a stable, recurring pattern of behaviour' (Goddin 1996). Distinctions are often made between specific and social institutions. Specific institutions are organisations, for example states, international organisations, firms, universities or government departments. Social institutions are more generalised and less concrete patterns of activity and include practices as diverse as religious ritual, marriage and handshakes, and political principles like state sovereignty and respect for elders (Keohane 1989). Scholars often distinguish between different kinds of institutionalism, distinctions drawn to identify different arguments about the nature of institutional effects (Hall and Taylor 1996).

Rational institutionalism is founded on a particular theory of social action that assumes that individuals are rational, purposive agents who deliberately pursue a set of interests through the most efficient and cost-effective means. Rational institutionalists argue that institutions can act as restraints on the way that political actors pursue their interests. For example, political actors (such as EU member states) may develop institutions (such as the European Commission or the ECJ) to help member states to monitor each other's compliance with the agreements they reach in the EU (Garret and Weingast 1993). Such functions are particularly crucial in situations like European market integration, where the cost of obtaining information on whether all other states are following all of the hundreds of laws regulating the common market is too high for individual member states. By delegating the task of monitoring compliance to supranational institutions, integration can be strengthened because the obstacle of uncertainty about each other's behaviour is reduced, as is the temptation to defect from agreements.

A second approach, sociological institutionalism, begins with quite different founding assumptions about the nature of social action. Those associated with this approach assert that people's behaviour is guided by a concern to behave appropriately. From this perspective, the logic of appropriateness is quite different from behaviour that follows the logic of purposeful, rational calculation of an individual's best interests. Action following the logic of appropriateness is action in accordance with socially derived rules about what is a normal, natural, right or good way for an individual to behave in particular circumstances (March and Olsen 1989). These socially derived rules are considered institutions insofar as they become chronically repeated actions sustained by a set of social rewards and sanctions. Insofar as they become internalised and taken-for-granted guides to individual behaviour, they may also become part of people's identities. Anderson (1997), for instance, understands the German state's orientation towards the EU in this way. He argues that the redefinition of Germany's postwar interests and particularly its deprioritisation of material goals and the pursuit of 'exaggerated multilateralism' can be related to an identity-driven German concern to express its non-predatory, liberal democratic credentials and meet 'foreign expectations about acceptable German behavior' (Anderson 1997: 83–5).

A third institutionalist approach is historical institutionalism, which is particularly concerned about the effect that institutions have on choices and outcomes over time. These effects include a locking in, or protection, of particular sets of interests and policy agendas within a set of institutional rules and procedures. These become difficult to change, even if new challenges or circumstances seem to require it. The locking in of such interests and agendas in institutions may also produce path-dependent processes of change. This means that decisions taken in the past become embedded or reinforced in a set of institutional rules and procedures in a way that makes some particular policy options appear more feasible than others.

Recent developments in EU theory

Constructivism, Europeanisation and Normative Theories

Like the innovations of the single-market project and the Maastricht Treaty, recent EU developments have influenced the kinds of problem and aspects of the EU that many have chosen to study. The constitutionalisation of EU treaty making – particularly through the work of the European Convention and agreement of the Constitutional Treaty – have provided a context in which normative theories of the EU have become more prevalent. Normative theories are reasoned arguments about how the EU ought to be shaped in order to achieve certain objectives, such as democratic principles or legitimate government. In the post-Maastricht period, the pace of change and particularly increasing evidence of the impact of EU policies, such as EMU, on domestic politics has created a marked interest among scholars in the idea of Europeanisation (Ladrech 2004). In recent years, constructivism, an approach with many similarities to sociological institutionalism, has also become an important framework for analysing EU politics.

Plate 3.8 Jean Monnet
Source: Audiovisual Library of the European Commission (2005).

Normative theories of European integration are as old as the EU itself. Federalism, or the belief that the EU should be constituted as a federal system of government (like the USA or Germany) has informed the ideas of many current and former EU leaders (Spinelli 1972; Monnet 1963). While in some member states the prospect of creating a federal Europe is seen as an undue incursion on state sovereignty and a challenge to national identities, in others, major political parties and currents of opinion consider federal government as an important way to balance self-rule and shared rule or unity in diversity (Burgess 2003: 70). More recent normative theories have looked at questions about the nature of and possible responses to what some have called the EU's democratic deficit and legitimacy crisis. Problems with the ratification of the Maastricht Treaty and more recently the Irish rejection of the Nice Treaty in the first of two referenda, declining turnout in European Parliament elections and the rise of euro-scepticism have made the EU elite more concerned about 'bringing the EU closer to the citizen'.

Biography 3.15

Altiero Spinelli (1907–86)

Italian statesman, European federalist thinker and leader, EC Commissioner and MEP. Born into an anti-fascist family, Spinelli was arrested by the fascist regime in 1927 and sentenced to ten years' imprisonment and a further six years in internal exile. A communist in his youth, he was expelled from the party in 1937 for criticising Stalin's purges. In 1941, with a group of young anti-fascist intellectuals, he issued a call for a federal United States of Europe as the only secure future for European democracy after fascism's defeat. The Manifesto of Ventotene (named after their place of exile) was to become a key document in the history of European integrationist thought; it embodied the idealism of the left wing of the European federalist movement. After 1945, Spinelli emerged as a key federalist thinker, generating ideas and providing intellectual stimulus for the movement towards European unity. He was disappointed by the slow progress made, and by the triumph of more mundane (but perhaps realistic) functionalist approaches over his more idealist vision of what a united Europe could achieve. In the 1950s and 1960s, he influenced Italian politicians of all parties. In the 1970s, he gravitated back towards the Italian Communist Party (PCI), which he saw as having become a social democratic party in all but name and which he sought to convert to the cause of European federalism. In this, he was largely successful and the PCI became a firm exponent of European integration. Spinelli served as a European Commissioner (1970–76), gaining a reputation as one of Europe's few visionaries who was ahead of his time in fighting for vital EC reforms. He resigned from the Commission to take a seat in the Italian parliament as an independent elected on the PCI's lists. He served in the European Parliament from 1977 until his death. As an MEP, he launched the Crocodile Club of pro-integrationists to push for fundamental reforms of the EC's institutions and a strengthening of the European Parliament. He drafted the Parliament's Draft Treaty on European Union (adopted by the Parliament in February 1984). He was severely disappointed with the Single European Act, which contained little of his federalist idealism. He is remembered as an authentic voice of the most idealistic and visionary strand in European federalist thought in the late twentieth century.

The democratic deficit

One of the most important achievements of those working on questions about democracy and legitimacy in the EU has been to challenge the notion of democratic deficit. Often, when people decry the existence of a democratic deficit in the EU, they are judging the EU by the standards of Western liberal democratic states. On these standards, they argue, the EU cannot be considered democratic, because EU elections and the European Parliament, European-level political parties and the media do not perform the same functions as they do within states. In particular, they do not serve as instruments for holding EU decision makers to account or to channel the preferences of the European public (if such a thing can be said to exist) into the EU decision-making process. Many of those trying to understand the nature of and prospects for democracy in the EU reject this approach on the grounds that the EU is not a state and lacks some of the essential features of state-based democracy, not least a relatively cohesive democratic community. This insight has encouraged authors to invent new ways of judging the EU's democratic credentials (see Lord 2001).

One interesting example of this is consideration of the EU as a 'post-parliamentary' form of network governance (Anderson and Burns 1996). These authors argue that the EU is an instance of 'post-parliamentary governance, where the direct "influence of the people" through formal representative democracy has a marginal place' (*ibid*.: 227). They further argue that parliaments are 'undergoing systematic erosion' and that modern governance is increasingly taking place in thousands of specialised technical and often scientific expertise ... groups with special concern or interest in the particular specialised policy matter ... [where] the democracy of individual citizens tends to be replaced by *de facto* democracy of organised interests, lobbies and representatives of organisations (and movements) that engage in policy areas and issues that are of particular concern to them.

(Source: ibid.: 229.)

This is a form of direct participatory democracy rather than parliamentary democracy, the authors contend. Some authors have also subjected ideas about the legitimacy of the EU to similar scrutiny (Scharpf 1999; Lord and Magnette 2004). An argument often made in this literature is that democratic principles may be only a part of what makes people consent to EU rule and that certain outputs, such as common policies more efficient or effective than those of individual states, may also underpin consent.

Social constructivism

Social constructivism has also become an important part of the theoretical vocabulary of integration studies in recent years, although key arguments, methods and philosophical positions can be observed in earlier work from sociology, linguistics, philosophy and elsewhere. Risse helpfully identifies a series of fundamental features of constructivism, the first of which is that it is an approach to or way of studying the EU (or other social phenomena) rather than a theory making specific claims about the nature or evolution of the EU (Risse 2004: 160; see also Christiansen *et al.*: 1999). Risse also notes that it is founded on the basic truism that 'social reality does not fall from heaven, but that human agents construct and reproduce it through their daily lives and practices' (Risse 2004: 161). According to this view, individuals are subject to the behaviour-shaping influence of social structures (like ideologies, social role constructions, norms and values) but also play an important role, often unconsciously, in the creation of those structures. This is the central constructivist contention, that structures and agents are mutually constitutive:

> The social environment in which we find ourselves, defines ('constitutes') who we are, our identities as social beings. 'We' are social beings, embedded in various relevant social communities. At the same time, human agency creates, reproduces and changes culture through our daily practices.

(Source: *ibid.*: 161.)

A number of propositions follow from this position and have been subject to serious study by constructivists. It suggests that the preferences and interests of participants in the integration process are not just the result of material factors such as what an actor (or state) owns or wants to own, or their relative power or weakness in the international system. Preferences and interests may also have a social component, derived from the way 'social norms not only regulate behaviour ... [but] also constitute the identity of actors in the sense of defining who "we" are as members of a social community' (*ibid.*: 163). Constructivists thus study and investigate the social identities of actors in order to understand why they may pursue one set of preferences rather than others. Furthermore, if the EU is considered a kind of social structure – with its rules, laws, institutions, norms and prevalent discourses – then it too may affect the way members define their interests and identities. In other words, constructivists emphasise that the EU affects discursive and behavioural practices and that it has become part of the social furniture with which social and political actors have to deal on a daily basis (*ibid.*: 164).

Europeanisation

'Europeanisation' has become another important buzzword in EU studies in recent years. Like many fashionable concepts, it has come to have a variety of meanings. Olsen (2003) identifies five conceptions of this term:

1. Europeanisation as changes in external territorial boundaries (such as in the case of enlargement);

2. Europeanisation as the development of institutions of governance at the European level;

3. Europeanisation as the export of European forms of political organisation and governance beyond Europe;

4. Europeanisation as a political project in support of the construction of a unified and politically strong Europe;

5. Europeanisation as the penetration of European-level institutions into national and subnational systems of governance.

As Olsen further notes, in all these definitions it is clear that Europeanisation is about change or transformation of some sort (2003: 335). However, those working on Europeanisation are not the first to be interested in processes of change. To some extent, understanding change has interested all theorists of European integration, whether it be why states voluntarily transferred sovereignty to the EU level or why some policy outcomes were more likely than others. What is innovative about work on Europeanisation is that it often focuses on types of change that have not received much attention – such as the impact of the EU on the domestic arena – or it tries to identify new ways of understanding processes of change.

Some of the most interesting work has looked at Europeanisation and domestic change. Green Cowles *et al.*, for example, put together an ambitious research project that sought to understand

> whether and how the ongoing process of European integration has changed nation states, their domestic institutions, and their political cultures ... [how the EU affected] formal structures such as national legal systems and national as well as regional administrations ... [and] the ability of the EU to shape informal structures such as business–government relations, public discourses, nation-state identities, and collective understandings of citizenship norms.

(Source: Green Cowles *et al.* 2001: 1.)

They found evidence of domestic institutional changes produced as a need to adapt to European integration in every member state studied. Nevertheless, the authors also found that changes did not take place in the same way in different member states. Policy processes and domestic institutions could be organised very differently in different states; they could have different constitutional traditions and different ways of understanding or responding to pressures to change; and different kinds of actor could be powerful overseers of change. All of these factors could mediate or affect the way that member states responded to EU pressures to adapt, creating 'domestic adaptation with national colours' (*ibid.*: 1).

The EU's regions and stateless nations

As we have seen, our conceptualisation of the EU has varied over time. In the run-up to the Maastricht Treaty, the EU's regions and stateless nations demanded that they too should be formally incorporated into the EU's decision-making processes. Although the outcome was for the most part only a partial success, it helped to fuel the impression, briefly, that the time might come when the member states would simply wither away and we would have a 'Europe of the regions' instead. That failed to come to fruition – for the moment at least we have a 'Europe with regions' (Borrás-Alomar *et al.* 1994).

Nonetheless, it had long been apparent that the regions had mobilised – one stimulus was the Single European Act (SEA) in 1986. Another stimulus was the EU's structural funds (Keating and Jones 1985). The funds' 1988 reform was significant not merely because a good deal more EU aid would be distributed to underperforming regions, as a result of the Delors I package, but also because from then the actual implementation of EU aid was supposed to be partially bottom-up; those regions that were involved in the funding process would be partners. With EU aid set to increase and EU policies impacting directly on their competences, the regions, especially the more powerful ones, had little option but to respond. Over time, therefore, a number of regional governments cultivated their own channels with the EU's institutions in Brussels, unmediated by their own government (Keating 1995). In sum, these developments helped to fuel the impression that the regions, or more precisely certain regions, were semi-autonomous actors in their own right. Accordingly, the regions' engagement with the EU had to be taken into account – both in terms of their mobilisation from the bottom up and their participation in the EU's arena as semi-autonomous actors in their own right. These various factors contributed to the concept of multi-level governance – in effect, the regional or 'third level' of government had to be taken into account as well.

Marks, one of the earliest advocates of this model, observed:

I suggest we are seeing the emergence of multi-level governance, a system of continuous negotiation among nested governments at several territorial tiers – supranational, national, regional and local – as the result of a broad process of institutional creation and decisional reallocation that has pulled some previously centralized functions of the state up to the supranational level and some down to the local/regional level.

(Source: Marks 1993: 392.)

Superficially, multi-level governance was seductive because it coincided with a period in the EU's evolution when the regions had apparently secured a degree of influence within the EU. In practice, however, it was of greater salience to those regions that are situated in federal polities such as Belgium or Germany (see, for example, Jeffery 1997a: 201). It was also apparent that to no small extent the governments of the member states could still act as gatekeepers, so far as the regions' involvement in the EU's funding processes was concerned (Bache 1998: 155–6). Consequently, multi-level governance is of questionable general applicability, not least because the EU's regions are so diverse not just in terms of the functions of their governments but also in relation to the latter's autonomy *vis-à-vis* their state. That said, as suggested above, as more and more competence has been assigned to the EU in successive treaties, European matters have increasingly had a direct effect on the regions – they have been 'Europeanised'.

We have already seen that Europeanisation is something of a multifaceted term. From one perspective, it is indicative of the premise that the regions no longer merely reacted to EU policymaking. By the early 1990s, they had become more proactive – they joined or formed transnational networks such as the Conference of the Peripheral and Maritime Regions or the Association of European Regions of Industrial Technology, so that they could mount joint lobbies in the EU. They opened their own bureaux in Brussels in order to gather intelligence, and more generally they sought to influence the EU's agenda (John 1994, 1997). Another aspect of Europeanisation was the extent to which the EU had encroached on areas that hitherto had fallen either exclusively within the competence of the more powerful regions (e.g. the German *Länder* and the Belgian sub-national entities (SNEs)) or that they shared with their state government. In effect, as far as the regions were concerned, especially those with the most autonomy (i.e. those in federal polities), domestic policy had been Europeanised (Jeffery 1997b, 1997c). As such, the regions could be portrayed as being the 'victims' of European integration on the basis that for the most part, prior to the Maastricht Treaty, representatives from their state government took decisions in the Council of Ministers alongside colleagues from the other member states. There was therefore a challenge to the regions as to how best they could regain (in the case of regions in federal polities) or secure (in the case of more centralised polities) greater influence over European affairs. The underlying issue was whether this could best be attained through their collective mobilisation or whether, on an individual basis, they should focus on intra-governmental mechanisms within their own state.

Consequently, the 'third level' mobilised in the run-up to the Maastricht Treaty. At the same time, the German *Länder* and Belgian SNEs sought to secure more formal entitlements over their state government's handling of European affairs first in relation to those areas of policy that fell within their exclusive competence or that they shared with their state government, and second, in relation to further transfers of authority to the EU. This was something of an incremental process (the origins of which can be traced to the SEA) in as much as both the *Länder* and the Belgian SNEs did eventually enjoy certain rights over their government with regard to the EU (Gerstenlauer 1985; Kerremans and Beyers 1997; Kerremans 2000). More particularly, aside from securing these rights they stood at the vanguard of third-level mobilisation, the culmination of which was the Committee of the Regions (CoR), the principle of subsidiarity (see key concept 3.1) and the entitlement of regional ministers to vote in the Council of Ministers, where their country's constitution so allowed. However, to date the CoR has been a somewhat toothless body, not least because it lacks decision-making powers; it can only issue opinions in relation to those areas of policy where the treaties so allow. The principle of subsidiarity so far has related primarily to the EU–member state nexus (although that may change somewhat if the new constitution is adopted – see below). The entitlement to vote in the Council of Ministers has been primarily of benefit to those regions in federal polities. In practice, therefore, their influence over EU matters was enhanced by upgrading intra-governmental mechanisms rather than by securing greater influence over EU policymaking more generally. As a result, the EU has continued to threaten the autonomy of many of its regions.

In the period after Maastricht, the third level has continued to lobby for a greater say over European affairs – albeit that for the most part the German *Länder*, having secured their own internal intra-governmental mechanisms, took something of a back seat. During 2000, a group of regions with constitutional powers met in Flanders with a view to formulating a common position in advance of the Treaty of Nice. They subsequently requested that the CoR should be assigned more power, that they should have access to the ECJ, where their competences stood to be affected by EU policies, and that the principle of subsidiarity should be applied to the regions rather than to the EU–member state nexus. In the run-up to the draft Constitutional Treaty in 2004, the more powerful regions (since renamed RegLeg) continued to demand more influence within the EU. In part, the intention was to prevent the EU from encroaching further into their competences. In addition, it was based on the growing appreciation that homogenised EU policymaking could be wholly disproportionate at the regional level. A one-size-fits-all approach was less appropriate for the regions of the EU due to their very diversity. In effect, the new constitution offered them an opportunity to rein in the EU (Wright 2005).

The draft treaty has acknowledged that the EU is comprised of not only its member states but also its regions. A Protocol on Subsidiarity and Proportionality may potentially be of worth to the regions. Equally, the entitlement of national parliaments to object to a legislative proposal emanating from the Commission may have a resonance for regional legislatures such as the Scottish Parliament. On the other hand, the Protocol does not appear to relate to individual regions *per se* but to the competences of the CoR. While national parliaments can object to an EU proposal, in practice it would seem that this would not be tantamount to a veto. Moreover, given the timeframe for the EU legislative process, it might prove difficult for the regional and state-level parliaments to agree a common position before it is too late. More particularly, the Constitutional Treaty does not provide any additional 'extra-state' channels of influence for the regions (Bourne 2003). In sum, therefore, for the moment at least, the Maastricht Treaty can be regarded as the high point of regionalism in the EU. In the meantime, some regions have secured a fair modicum of influence on European matters thanks to internal mechanisms within their own states. Others, such as Scotland, continue to demand a greater say over EU policymaking.

Further reading

If you are looking in the first instance for a general introduction to give you more depth, try the following:

Haas, E. (1968b) *The Uniting of Europe*, Stanford: Stanford University Press, CA.

Monnet, J. (1963) 'A ferment of change', *Journal of Common Market Studies* 1.

Moravcsik, A. (1998) *The Choice for Europe: Social Purpose and State Power from Messina to Maastricht*, University College Press, London.

Rosamond, B. (2000) *Theories of European Integration*, Houndsmill, Palgrave.

If you are interested in reading more about one or more of the various theories described in this section, follow up the detailed references in the text.

Section 3.4

The policies of the European Union

In Section 3.1 and 3.3, we looked at the historical and political considerations that underlie the EU's policies. To complete our understanding of the concepts that have influenced the policies, we need briefly to consider the economic background.

There are two relevant sets of background analysis – macro-economic (to do with the economy as a whole) and micro-economic (to do with the efficiency of markets). Macro-economic considerations are important principally when we are concerned with topics such as the management of the euro and overall growth rates and unemployment levels. These topics will mainly be discussed in Part 5, when we will examine the euro zone, so we will defer full treatment of them till there. Until the completion of EMU for those member countries that chose to join the euro zone, the policies of the EU were driven almost exclusively by micro-economic considerations, which we will focus on here.

The basic thrust of EU economic policy is to try to promote internal competition while protecting EU producers from 'unfair' competition from non-EU countries. We can see this right from the Treaty of Rome and in much subsequent EU legislation. The belief behind this is that competition is in the interest of consumers, because it keeps prices as low as possible, and in the interest of EU producers, because it makes them competitive in world trade. As we have seen in Part 1, the ancestry of this is the efficiency of markets, relative to other forms of economic organisation, in solving the economic problem. Our starting point here will be the existence and implications of international trade.

Why does international trade occur?

In Part 1, we examined the production possibility curve representing the combinations of goods that a Stone Age family could produce and found that its position depended on the technology available to the family and on the resources it could command. Even in Stone Age society, the mix of resources available would differ from one family to another – for example, one family might be living on flat land that is good for growing corn, whereas another might be living fairly high up a mountain, whose rock is ideal for making axes. In these circumstances, it would obviously make sense for the family on the flat land to bake more bread than it needs and exchange some of its surplus bread for axes, while the family on the higher ground makes more axes than it needs and exchanges its surplus axes for bread. This is the principle of the division of labour, where each family makes the products for which its resources are best suited, and surpluses are exchanged. When we consider not Stone Age families but modern countries, there will usually be quite big differences between countries in the kind of resources available, and these differences are the basic reason why trade is mutually advantageous.

To see why, let us look at the example of Tayside, in Scotland, and Bordeaux, in France. The climate and the soil conditions in Tayside are such that the only way to grow grapes is to do so in a greenhouse, but raspberries grow very well in the fields. In Bordeaux, raspberries grow quite well, but grapes flourish in the vineyards and hence wine can readily be produced. We can illustrate the options for each region in a stylised way in Figure 3.10, where on diagram (a) TT represents the production possibility curve for Tayside and on diagram (b) BB that for Bordeaux.

If there were no trade between Tayside and Bordeaux, each region would at most be able to choose some combination of raspberries and wine on its curve, like for Tayside point T_1 (with R_1 raspberries and W_1 wine) and for Bordeaux point B_1. However, both regions can probably do better for themselves if they trade. Look at diagram (c) in Figure 3.10, in which curves TT and BB are repeated from diagrams (a) and (b). Suppose, to simplify the analysis, consumers in both regions would like the combination of wine and raspberries represented by point A where each region would have R_A raspberries and W_A wine. This point is not available to either region without trade, because it lies outside the range of possible combinations on both TT and BB, but point A can be reached by trade. We can reach A if Tayside grows R_2 and Bordeaux R_3 raspberries, Bordeaux makes W_2 and Tayside W_3 wine, and Tayside sells to Bordeaux R_A–R_2 raspberries in exchange for W_A–W_2 wine. As common sense would suggest, Tayside grows more raspberries, the product in which it has an advantage over Bordeaux, than it wants to consume, and exports the surplus to Bordeaux. At the same time, Bordeaux makes more wine than it wants to consume and exports the surplus to Tayside for raspberries.

Although Figure 3.10 portrays a very simplified analysis, its results generalise into the real world of many products and many countries. Provided countries differ from each other at all in the mixes in their basic factor endowments, trade can always make available combinations of goods that are otherwise unattainable. If these new combinations are what the citizens of participating countries want, trade will be mutually beneficial by making more goods available to everybody. This can happen because trade lets each country specialise in making the products at which its resources give it a relative advantage: countries, like our Stone Age households, adopt the principle of division of labour.

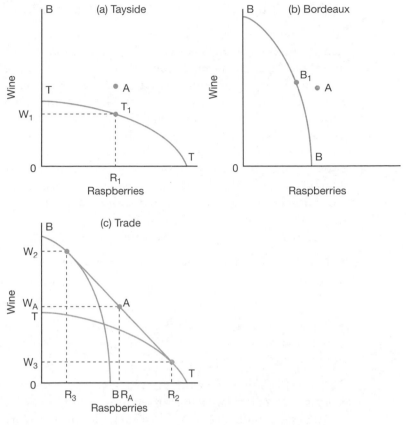

Figure 3.10 Production possibility curves for (a) Tayside, (b) Bordeaux and (c) both regions

Once the division of labour has occurred, its advantages may be compounded by economies of scale, which occur if the average cost of production declines as output grows. Economies of scale do not exist for all products (indeed, in some cases average costs may actually rise as output grows) but they are a common phenomenon and hence frequently add to the benefits available from trade.

In advanced modern economies, trade can take sophisticated forms, including that of intra-industry trade, in which what is in some sense the same product is both imported and exported. All Western European countries both import and export cars, exporting those they produce themselves (perhaps under licence arrangements from another European country or Japan) and importing different models. Intra-industry trade seems paradoxical; if France is relatively good at producing Renault cars, why is it not also relatively good at producing Audi cars? However, it is readily explicable by a mixture of accidents of history (which determine where goods were made in the first instance), economies of scale (which perpetuate the accident of initial location) and the extent to which the citizens of prosperous countries demand a wide range of goods (so that some Germans want Audis and some want Renaults).

What are the economic objectives of the EU?

After these preliminaries, we can return to our basic question. As we shall show, many aspects of the EU's current industrial and social policy are driven by concerns about the EU's long-term economic prospects in the face of increasing global competition. However, the underlying rationale is that markets provide an efficient solution to the economic problem, and they can adapt flexibly and quickly to new products. International trade enables all the advantages of the market system to operate across national boundaries. But, as we shall see, markets have limitations. The aim of the EU's economic policy is to foster markets, at least internally within the EU, while protecting consumers and workers from some of their limitations. Thus the main context of much EU policy is one of international trade within the EU, but increasingly it is concerned with harmonisation of policies of governments of member states.

The main limitations of markets are:

- Big firms can exercise undue influence over consumers.
- Employers can exercise undue influence over workers.
- Markets do not consider third party interests – such as environmental impacts.
- There is no guarantee that market solutions will be equitable – chance factors of inheritance or inborn talent have a significant influence on an individual's power in the marketplace.

The undue influence of big firms is what is called the power of monopolists. Hence, the EU has a raft of legislation to try to enforce competition, which we will discuss later.

The undue influence of employers can mean that workers are confronted with poor wages or bad working conditions. As we shall see, EU industrial and, especially, social policy tries to improve the rights of workers in a wide range of circumstances.

Environmental issues typically have international ramifications – the major environmental problems are global. As we shall see, the EU has developed policies to address some of the environmental problems within the EU, but it is also a protagonist in worldwide approaches – the EU is an active player in the Kyoto agreement.

Issues of equity are typically addressed by a range of measures. One example might be a system of taxation so that the rich pay proportionately more tax than the poor. Another is a method of supporting the incomes of the poorest members of society by social security payments. Variants of these measures typically operate at national level within the EU countries, but the EU also has a range of relevant social and regional policies.

So the EU has policies to try to address the major limitations of markets. However, its fundamental economic position is that it should promote freely working markets as the best way of ensuring that production in the EU is globally competitive. This leads the EU into various policies to ensure 'level playing fields' for internal competition. Such policies can lead to tension with the governments of member states, where EU policy prevents the governments from taking action that they believe to be in the best interest of their country or may lead them to use policy instruments that they think are not the best for their country. An example is regional policy, discussed in Opinion 3.5.

Opinion 3.5

Regional policy

Countries take various steps to try to address the problems of regions suffering from industrial decline. For example, these can consist of subsidies towards the cost of building new factories and installing new machinery required by firms setting up production in depressed regions. EU regional policy tries to ensure that regions with similar needs enjoy broadly similar assistance. From the EU's perspective, regions are regions within the EU, not within countries, and a fairly working EU regional policy must work with common rules across the different countries. So if one member country offers a more generous package of assistance than another, national policy conflicts with EU policy. However, some member countries may have chosen to attach relatively high degrees of importance to solving regional problems, so they may not be happy to work within common EU rules.

To identify whether there is such a conflict, EU rules require that regional assistance be 'transparent' – that it can be measured in monetary terms. Certain sorts of assistance that countries want to offer are therefore ruled out because they are not transparent.

Recent reforms of regional policy complicate matters further. In an attempt to ensure that EU regional policy is sensitive to local needs, EU policy works through partnerships with national governments and with representatives of the region. Particularly where there is some formal political devolution to regions, this opens up the potential for conflict between three parties – the EU, the national government and the regional government – all trying to achieve the same broad objective but not necessarily agreeing on the best means to do so.

How might these interests be reconciled?

One of the clearest examples of EU policy to promote fair internal competition is the Single European Act. While it is relatively easy to identify tariffs and quotas on trade in goods and arrange to eliminate them between EU countries, there are more subtle barriers that can similarly inhibit trade. For example, to protect people from financial fraud, countries have various regulations to control companies offering life insurance. These regulations differ from one country to another, and that makes it difficult for companies set up to meet the legal requirements of one country to sell their services in another country. One of the specific measures in the Single European Act was that, if a company meets the financial regulations required by any member state, it can then sell its services in any other member state. The rationale of this was to promote competition and make life insurance, for example, cheaper in most EU countries.

EU economic policy consists not just of policies to alleviate the limitations of markets, as discussed above, but also of policies to try to shelter EU production as a whole from worldwide competition. The most obvious examples of this are its policies on agriculture and on fisheries, but we will see that elements of the EU's competition policy are to enable EU producers to move into new markets at the expense of non-EU producers. Many of these measures sit uneasily with the fundamental view that freely working markets are best for both producers and consumers. The balance that should be struck is a matter of important current debate.

Also important in current debates is the whole question of harmonisation of monetary and tax policy. The issues here, too, spring from the belief that internal competition is the fundamental economic policy objective.

If there are no exchange rate transactions, it is cheaper for customers in one country to buy from another, because they do not have to pay the costs of exchanging from one currency to another. Similarly, it is much easier for producers to sell in another country – not only do they not have to pay the costs of exchanging currency, they also do not have to worry about the risk that exchange rates will change between their making a product and selling it. So if exchange rates are fixed, trade is easier and cheaper for both consumers and producers. If exchange rates are not just fixed but there is a single currency, it is much easier for producers and consumers to compare prices, and hence to buy and sell in the market most advantageous for them. As we shall see, these are the basic arguments used to support the decision by the EU to press ahead with economic and monetary union by introducing the euro as a single currency.

When neighbouring EU countries have different rates of tax on goods, consumers will, if they can, buy goods in the country with a lower rate. We can, for example, see this where households in the southeast of England go on shopping trips to France to buy alcohol and tobacco for their own consumption, because the tax rate in the UK is so high that they can save money even after paying for the trip to France. Where the differences become sufficiently large, governments (perhaps encouraged by the EU Commission!) may feel the need to take action to bring tax rates closer. An example of this is the tax levied on new cars, which has been reduced in many EU countries simply because it was so much cheaper for drivers to import cars that significant numbers of drivers stopped buying cars in the more heavily taxed countries. The arguments in favour of early tax harmonisation within the EU spring principally from an attempt to forestall what it is believed market forces will eventually bring about. Since these market forces will lead to more purchases in the countries with the lower tax rates and fewer in the countries with higher tax rates, the overall effect will be to reduce tax rates. If tax rates on goods fall, governments lose revenue, so unless they can raise revenue from somewhere else they have to cut their spending. EU member states that fear that their tax income will be eroded therefore have an interest in pressing for early harmonisation, so that their tax rates are not forced down to the lowest level. EU member states that think they have little to fear, either because their tax rates are already low or because they are physically remote from most of the EU, will resist harmonisation because they will be long-term gainers from the competitive forces.

Environmental policy

A list of the most well-known environmental issues, such as climate change, ozone depletion and biodiversity loss, makes it readily apparent that such issues are inherently regional, and very often global, in scope. The EU has since the early 1970s developed as an important environmental policymaker within its own regional orbit, in many cases imposing upon its member states laws designed to ameliorate some aspect of their regional environment – see Key fact 3.16 for an outline of the policies, and Key concept 3.5 for a statement of the underlying principles. On the global stage, the EU has also been emerging since the 1970s as an important participator in the development of international agreements to tackle global environmental issues. However, given the jealousy with which the constituent states of the EU guard their independence in the sphere of foreign policy, the role of the EU as a distinct international actor has often been less than clear-cut.

Key fact 3.16

Environmental Action Programmes of the EEC/EU

First: 1973–76

Not a comprehensive policy or legally binding but began to outline principles and objectives, which were reaffirmed and developed in subsequent EAPs.

Second: 1977–81

Core principles established, including the preventive principle, 'polluter pays' principle and importance of participation in international environmental organisations.

Third: 1982–86

Introduced the idea that environmental policy needed to be integrated into other appropriate policy areas. Priorities established, such as use of environmental impact assessments, reduction of pollution at source, development of clean technologies and cooperation with developing countries on environmental matters.

Fourth: 1987–92

Established the need for standards of environmental quality and the importance of implementation of EU environmental laws.

Fifth: 1993–2000

Began development of a more anticipatory, long-term, strategic approach to EU environmental policy, emphasising the concept of sustainable development. Focused specifically on trans-European environmental problems, such as climate change and water pollution, and picked out five sectors for specific concern: industry, energy, transport, agriculture and tourism. Emphasises the centrality of ecological modernisation to the EU's conception of sustainable development.

Sixth: 2002–12

Focuses on four main areas for action: climate change, health and environment, nature and biodiversity, and natural resource management. Emphasises again the need for a strategic approach, the implementation of EU directives, and the stronger 'ownership' of environmental objectives by stakeholders. Commission to pressure states by publicising implementation failures. Emphasis on the 'greening' of the market, with environmentally friendly forms of production and consumption. New instruments mooted, such as Integrated Product Policy, fiscal measures and better information for citizens. New member states to be encouraged to apply existing legislation. 'Broader dialogue' with stakeholders to be emphasised, on the basis of sound scientific and economic assessments, in the provision of which the European Environment Agency will play a key role.

Key concept 3.5

Basic principles governing EU environmental policy, established by the first Environmental Action Programme (1973)

1. Prevention is better than cure.
2. Environmental impacts should be considered at the earliest possible stage in decision making.
3. Exploitation of nature that causes significant damage to the ecological balance must be avoided.
4. Scientific knowledge should be improved to enable action to be taken.
5. The polluter pays principle: the polluter should bear the cost of preventing and repairing environmental damage.
6. Activities in one member state should not have detrimental effects on the environment in another.
7. Environmental policy in the member states must take into account the interests of the developing countries.
8. The EU and its member states should promote international and worldwide environmental protection through international organisations.
9. Environmental protection is everyone's responsibility and therefore education is necessary.
10. Environmental protection measures should be taken at the most appropriate level taking into account the type of pollution, the action needed and the geographical zone to be protected.
11. National environmental programmes should be coordinated on the basis of a common long-term concept, and national policies should be harmonised within the Community.

As McCormick explains, in a historic ruling (*Commission v. Council* (AETR)) in 1971, the European Court of Justice determined that

> whenever the Community adopted common rules in a particular area, the member states no longer had the right – individually or collectively – to enter into agreements with third parties that affected those rules ... In policy areas within which the EU has a large measure of competence, or even sole competence, it is possible for it to sign an international agreement without the member states also signing.

(Source: McCormick 2001: 265.)

Thus the EU casts a single vote in such areas of international debate that thereby bind all the EU member states. But, since the 'sole/main competence' criterion is inherently somewhat vague, it is also possible for the EU and the member states together to take part in discussions to produce an international agreement, in which case both the EU and the individual states sign the agreement. However, when that occurs, it is normally the case that the individual states first reach a consensus among themselves before the EU can also add its signature (*ibid*.: 268).

However, ever since the 1990 Dublin European Council meeting, the intent of the Council of Ministers has been expressed in various places to the effect that the EU should promote measures at regional and international levels to deal with environmental problems. This has meant that where a consensus has developed among the member states, the EU has been able to head international negotiations on their behalf. This happened with respect to the Ozone Depletion Protocol signed in Montreal in 1987. At the Rio Earth Summit (the UN Conference on Environment and Development) in 1992, the EU was a full participant, with many of the rights of an independent state (Bretherton and Vogler 1999: 91). It was at this conference that the EU committed itself to undertaking the goal of sustainable development. Ten years later, in Johannesburg, the EU was a leading participant in an international conference – the World Summit on Sustainable Development – which aimed to review what had been achieved in this area and to point the way ahead to further developments.

In one area during that ten-year period, namely that of climate change, the EU could plausibly claim a global leadership role. This claim would be justified on the basis of the EU's support for the process initiated at the Kyoto Conference in 1997 designed to reduce the emissions of greenhouse gases by industrialised states, and its intense lobbying to keep other industrialised states committed to the process. However, this has not stopped key players, such as the USA and Australia, from refusing to ratify the Kyoto process. Nor has the EU been pressing for a further international conference to try to give the Kyoto process some new impetus (Burchill and Lightfoot 2004: 178). Hence the plausibility of the claim that, as Burchill and Lightfoot put it, the EU's leadership on the issue of climate change stems from the fact that in this area there is a 'lack of serious competition' (*ibid*.: 184).

To return to the issue of who negotiates on behalf of the EU, this is not just a matter of resolving the tension between the EU and member states over the areas of EU's exclusive competence. As Burchill and Lightfoot argue, a significant difference is made to EU success in international negotiations depending on which member state holds the EU presidency at the point at which the EU's position is being prepared. For example, an environmental 'laggard' state, Spain, provided the presidency during the Bali Preparatory Committee (PrepCom) meeting for the Johannesburg conference, and the result was, according to some observers, disappointing (*ibid*.: 181).

A further ongoing complication is the internal rivalry between different Directorates-General within the EU Commission. As Burchill and Lightfoot point out, environmental critics of the EU's Johannesburg position claim that its pro-business position stems from the neo-liberal character of the Trade Directorate-General. The latter is able to influence the Commission as a whole much more strongly than can the Directorates-General for Environment and Development, which push rather ineffectually for ecological perspectives and social conscience, respectively, not just business ones (*ibid*.: 181–2).

Thus, the relationship between the EU and international bodies and processes is not a straightforward one. There is the issue of the rights of the EU *vis-à-vis* the member states to be the key player in such international forums, and there is the crucial question of who are the key players on behalf of the EU in such relationships, and of how the power games within the EU Commission are worked out in any given instance.

However, in one area of international environmental importance, namely fisheries policy, the EU has, since the development of the Common Fisheries Policy in 1983, been overseeing an activity that is conceived as the management of a 'common resource'. This has made it easier to act on behalf of the Community as a whole. Fish move beyond the regional waters of the EU, and move around within them *ad lib*. The need for the conservation of valuable fish stocks wherever they may roam has led to the EU entering into many agreements with third parties. It has reached more than two dozen agreements with non-EU states on fishery conservation, and it participates in the conservation efforts of many international fisheries organisations, such as the Northwest Atlantic Fisheries Organization and the North Atlantic Salmon Conservation Organization (McCormick 2001: 250–1).

Fisheries and agricultural policy

Fisheries policy

Although the Treaty of Rome contained provisions for a Common Fisheries Policy (CFP), it was not until the early 1970s that the state of marine fisheries became of sufficient concern for the EU to begin to develop such a policy. In 1970, coastal states extended their protected fishing zones from 12 to 200 miles offshore as a measure to cope with dwindling stocks and catches of commercial species. In addition, in 1973 three major fishing nations, the UK, Ireland and Denmark, joined the EEC (McCormick 2001: 249).

The economic value of fisheries to the EU as a whole is slight. According to the EU's official website, fishing contributes less than 1 percent to member states' gross national product (Europa 2004c). It employs only 0.2 percent of the EU's workforce (McCormick 2001: 250), amounting to about a quarter of a million fishermen (Europa 2004c). However, this still makes the EU a major fishing region, coming third in the world after China and Peru. It is in the nature of fishing that the activity is concentrated in specific coastal regions, and in those areas it is a major source of employment. Given that those regions are often hard put to find alternatives, they also tend to be among the least prosperous parts of the EU. Hence fishing policy is an area of often acrimonious dispute between the member states, as the claim can often be made that a state's 'whole industry' is under threat, and that in an economically underprivileged region too. Right from the start, therefore, as well as being an aspect of food security for the EU, the CFP was viewed as a key element in helping with the project of economic and social cohesion, which is the label given to the economic development of poorer regions.

The establishment of the CFP took a decade of hard bargaining. When it emerged in 1983, the policy recognised that the key issue was that of conservation, for without the existence of the commercially important fish species no fishing industry is possible. As a wild animal resource, fish are free to go where they choose, and as the seas and coastal waters cannot be physically compartmentalised as the land can, the only way fish can be viewed for the purposes of policymaking is as a 'common resource' and part of the EU states' 'common heritage' (Europa 2004c). Hence the paramount need is to prevent any one state overfishing – taking more fish than can be replaced by the natural breeding cycle, which eventually leads to the extinction of the species in question, to the detriment of the fishing industries of other states.

However, although the issue of conservation clearly requires a sound under-standing of how fish relate to their marine ecosystems, it was only in the late 1990s that the EU bodies responsible for the CFP, especially the Fisheries Directorate-General (formerly Directorate-General XIV), began to adopt an inte-grated ecosystem approach to fisheries conservation (McCormick 2001: 251). This now means that it is recognised that fishing has important effects not simply on the fish species targeted, but also

> on their predators ... competing stocks and prey stocks (on which the target stocks feed). These changes may, in turn, affect the reproduction of birds and marine mammals, if the reduction in food available to them is too severe.

> (Source: Europa 2004c).

Such considerations also apply to the increasingly important activity of fish farm-ing, or aquaculture, which is one popular response to the declining stocks of wild fish. As the official website puts it:

> Aquaculture can represent a potential risk to the environment, whether through the pollution which can result from the discharge of waste or the risk of infec-tion of wild fish by diseases in farmed fishstocks.

> (Source: *ibid*.)

In fairness, it has to be said that although a full ecological approach has only recently been developing in the CFP, the precautionary principle did structure the CFP from the beginning. Hence, there has always been an emphasis on the need to acquire reliable scientific information on the state of species in order to anticipate overfishing and prevent it.

In the attempt to balance conservation with fairness in obtaining access to the 'common resource', the CFP opened up all the waters within the EU's 200-mile limit to the fishing boats of all member states while allowing the states to restrict access to fisheries within 12 miles of their coast (McCormick 2001: 250). Given these ground rules, the prevention of overfishing depends upon the use of various technical measures. All EU fishing boats have to be licensed; a system of satellite surveillance of fishing activities has been established; and an EU inspectorate is empowered to oversee all the stages of fishing from catching to selling (*ibid*.: 250).

In addition, a quota system (TACs, or total allowable catches) operates in the North Sea and North Atlantic. The EU Commission's Scientific, Technical and Economic Committee for Fisheries supplies the annual estimated stock levels upon which quotas are based. These limit the total catches of particular species in spe-cific marine areas, and this total is then divided up among the member states with fishing industries on the basis of a formula that includes each member state's past catch record. The final decision concerning TACs is determined at the Council of Ministers level, by the fisheries ministers of the member states at their December meeting. It is then a matter for such states to allocate the quotas among their local fisheries. However, further measures to help with conservation, such as minimum mesh sizes and weight of fish caught, are established at the EU level (*ibid*.: 250). Finally, since fish roam beyond the territorial waters of the EU, an important ele-ment in the conduct of EU fisheries policy involves negotiations with states outside the EU over matters of conservation.

The CFP remains a matter of considerable controversy, at least in member states with fishing industries. In particular, its conservation policies have been castigated as ineffective, with a poor quality of monitoring. A testament to the justice of such criticisms can be found in the crisis that has been developing over one species in particular – cod. As a European Commission press release explained in May 2003: 'Despite measures that have been put in place over the past two years, more cod continue to be removed from stocks than are replaced by reproduction' (Europa 2004c). The proposed recovery plan will require a long-term effort lasting between five and ten years, and it will require severe restrictions on fishing with respect to this species. This emphasis on the long term was a more general development of the CFP as part of the reforms endorsed in December 2002. One might well ask why it took so long for a policy directed towards the management of populations of wild animals to adopt such a long-term approach.

Table 3.6 Principal economic dimensions of the EU fishing sector

Sector	Production value (ecu million)	Number employed (full-time equivalent)
Marine fishing	6,287	234,003
Fish processing	11,351	86,625
Marine aquaculture	1,385	36,975
Inland aquaculture	632	9,720
Inland fishing	258	6,814
Totals	19,913	374,137

(Source: European Communities 2000.)

Agricultural policy

Why should the EU have an agricultural policy? Nearly all countries have some form of support for farming, for two basic economic reasons.

1. *Some agricultural commodities are subject to wide supply fluctuations due to weather, so farmers' incomes fluctuate a lot.* The demand for most agricultural products is not very sensitive to price, so weather-induced changes in supply have a big effect on farmers' incomes. Furthermore, the problem that farmers experience if they have a bad harvest is worsened if food can be imported from other countries not affected by the bad harvest (because farmers do not have much to sell and cannot get high prices if imports are cheaper). The volatility in their income can drive farmers out of business, or lead to worse problems if they react to unusually high (low) prices by planting more (less) area with the relevant crop the following year.

2. *Food prices are important.* In a poor country, if food prices are high people may be short of food, so as a matter of social policy governments are sensitive to the price of food. Food prices feature in the cost of living and thus in the measured rate of inflation; if a government is worried about the rate of inflation, it does not want to see great volatility in food prices.

In addition to these economic reasons, in many countries there is a political reason – farmers are an important political lobby, so they can exercise political pressure greater than their numbers in the population would suggest.

To understand the importance of agricultural policy to the EU, one also needs to appreciate a little history. At the end of the Second World War, there were severe food shortages in many Western European countries, and starvation would have been widespread but for food aid, especially from North America. The founders of what is now the EU were determined that there would be no more food shortages in Europe and so attached high priority to increasing the production of food in Europe so as to make Europe self-sufficient. They realised that one of the problems of European agriculture was that in many countries farm holdings were too small, so they tried to devise a scheme to encourage the merging of small farms and help people displaced from farming to find alternative occupations. They also tried to encourage European farmers to adopt new technology in production.

For many years, the main element in the CAP was a system of price guarantees. Key fact 3.17 outlines how such a system works.

Key fact 3.17

Price guarantees

- In a price guarantee system, farmers are promised that they will get at least the guaranteed price for their produce.
- Since not all that they produce might be wanted by consumers at the guarantee price, this means that the government may have to buy up excess production, so it needs tax revenue to buy and store excess production (which it may be able to sell in future years of poor production).
- To prevent imports undercutting the guarantee price, there may also have to be special taxes (tariffs) on imports.
- Less has to be raised in tax (probably) than with a scheme of direct subsidy payments to farmers for the food they produce, but food prices are higher than with a subsidy scheme.
- To enable exports from a price guarantee system regime, farmers have to be subsidised for the difference between the world price and the guarantee price.

The price guarantee system worked well initially, achieving its objectives of increased output and more stable income for farmers, but it gradually fell into disrepute. The price set in the system was chosen as a market-clearing price in a relatively high-price area, so usually there was a little excess production to be bought up and sold off when harvests were poor. Gradually, however, excess production became endemic. This was mainly because of substantial improvements in agricultural production per hectare brought about by

- more intensive farming – bigger fields, less waste ground, etc. – especially as small farmers left the industry;
- better seeds, with improved germination and yield;
- selective breeding of cattle, etc. – so milk and beef yields were much higher;
- much more intensive use of chemicals in agriculture – to fortify animal feedstuffs, to fertilise fields and to kill weeds and crop pests.

The consequence was the notorious beef, butter and grain mountains and wine lakes, because guarantee prices were not reduced in step with productivity improvements, so more and more surplus was bought up and stored.

From a variety of motivations, momentum was built up for a major reform of the CAP:

- *Cost of the policy*: EU member governments, except those benefiting substantially from the CAP, were concerned about the growing bill to pay for the price guarantees. The CAP price guarantee scheme alone absorbed about half of the total EU budget, and there were many demands for new activities, such as more spending on regional policy, which could not be financed.

- *Wastage of food*: the waste of the mountains of unsold food revolted public conscience in EU countries, because there was no simple method of disposing of the surplus without causing damage elsewhere. For example, if it was given in food aid to Third World countries, it damaged the interests of farmers there. So much of it was simply destroyed.

- *Environmental worries*: the increased use of agrichemicals led to public concern about the environmental implications and pressure (reflected in elections, particularly in Germany) for a 'greener' approach in European agriculture.

- *Enlargement*: as we have seen, enlargement of the EU meant that it would contain more counties with large agricultural output.

- *External pressure*: pressure from outside the EU – especially from the USA, Australia, New Zealand and Canada – led to the WTO investigating the tariff barriers and export subsidies needed to operate the guaranteed price system.

Initial steps of reform were principally to impose quotas to restrict production and so get rid of the mountains and lakes. However, the more radical reform has been to reduce guaranteed prices towards world levels, and to substitute from 1992 more direct support of farmers' incomes regardless of how much they produce. A second recent focus of the reform has been the encouragement to adopt more environmentally friendly farming methods. There has in consequence been a dramatic change in the patterns of CAP expenditure. In 1991, two-thirds of total CAP expenditure was on guaranteed prices, with the remainder on export subsidies. By 2002, export subsidies and guaranteed prices together were well under a quarter of CAP expenditure, three-quarters of which was in the form of direct income support. However, the changes have not been cost-free to farmers, who experienced, and continue to experience, income volatility in the shift from one scheme to the other.

Industrial and social policies

Introduction – the Lisbon strategy

Until 2000, the EU had a range of policies on industrial and social matters that, while containing many useful elements, lacked clear overall aims. A new urgency, and a new focus, was given to such policy at the European Council meeting in Lisbon in March 2000.

We outlined some of the background to the Lisbon strategy in Part 1. The strategy's main motivator was growing concern about the performance of the EU's economies. Unemployment was persistent and high. Growth was slow in comparison with the well-established industrial economies, especially Japan and the USA; with the new industrialised countries of the Far East, such as Korea and Taiwan; and with the countries with huge industrialisation potential, such as China and India. The combination within Europe of slow growth rates and an ageing population contained the potential for great economic difficulties, as a smaller workforce was going to be asked to support a steadily growing economically inactive population. The problem of persistently high unemployment rates was first addressed systematically at EU level in 1997 by the launch of the European Employment Strategy to coordinate the employment policies of the member states; the European Employment Strategy was placed in a more general context by the Lisbon strategy.

The Lisbon strategy identified an ambitious method of creating jobs in the EU. The EU could not compete in basic manufacturing and services with the low-wage economies of India and the Far East, so it had to find a field in which it could enjoy a competitive advantage. The objective was therefore to make the EU by 2010

the most competitive and dynamic knowledge-based economy in the world, capable of sustainable economic growth with more and better jobs and greater social cohesion.

(Source: European Council 2000.)

How was this to be achieved? A strategy for doing so was set out with three main elements, each divided into a number of subheadings (see Key fact 3.18).

Key fact 3.18

The structure of the Lisbon strategy

The strategy consisted of three main elements, with a set of subsidiary objectives:

1. preparing the transition to a knowledge-based economy and society by better policies for the information society and for R&D (research and development), as well as by stepping up the process of structural reform for competitiveness and innovation and by completing the internal market;

2. modernising the European social model, investing in people and combating social exclusion;

3. sustaining a healthy economic outlook and favourable growth prospects by applying an appropriate macro-economic policy mix.

(European Council 2000.)

Important within this were:

- an information society for all (including facilitating e-commerce, simplifying the regulatory framework for telecommunications, making the Internet cheaper, developing multimedia education and resources in schools, and opening basic public services to Internet access);

- establishing a European area of research and innovation (including various measures to improve research cooperation within the EU by academic and private sector institutions, to use tax policies etc. to promote private research investment, and to create a simple EU-wide patenting system);

▶

- helping innovative businesses, especially small businesses, to start up and develop (mainly in the first instance by coordinating information, but also by promoting venture capital funding for them);
- completing the Single European Market (especially in the services sector);
- improving the workings of financial markets (by reducing various barriers);
- coordinating macro-economic policies (to reduce the tax burden on individuals and to divert more government expenditure towards investment projects);
- improving education and training (especially of young people and the unemployed, particularly in entrepreneurship, IT, language and social skills, but also by promoting lifelong learning, all with a view to raising overall employment rates from an EU average of 61 percent in 2000 to 70 percent in 2010 (from 51 percent to 60 percent for women), with a particular focus on raising the employment rate of older people (those aged 55–64));
- 'modernising' social protection (particularly to solve the potential problem of the future pensions bill);
- promoting social inclusion (to try to reduce the numbers living below the poverty line, and more generally to address the problems of the growing 'underclass' that successful pursuit of the rest of the policies was likely to generate).

The most specific targets were on the employment rate – the proportion of the population in the age group 15–64 in work – overall, for women, and for older workers (those in the age group 55–64). Associated with the overall strategy was a large number of specific targets (represented in 117 indicators), each with a detailed timetable for implementation within the ten-year period. Progress was revisited at the European Council meetings held in June and December 2000, with some refinement of the details and, at the latter meeting, the agreement of a detailed social policy agenda, particularly to create what was described as a new balance between flexibility and security in labour markets.

However, it soon became apparent that the targets were being missed, and an employment taskforce, chaired by Wim Kok (former Netherlands prime minister) was established in March 2003 to review progress. The Kok Report (November 2003) was significantly entitled *Jobs, Jobs, Jobs; Creating More Employment in Europe*, and it underlies current EU industrial and social policy.

The Kok Report

The Kok Report started by reaffirming the importance of achieving something like the Lisbon targets. In 2000, there were 71 million people in the EU25 over the age of 65; this was expected to rise to 110 million by 2030. The working-age population (those aged 15–64) was expected to fall from 303 million to 280 million. In consequence, the proportion of those aged over 65 to the working-age population was expected to rise from 23 percent in 2000 to 39 percent in 2030. Even if the Lisbon targets of increasing the economic activity rate of those in the working-age population are met, there is still a problem in ensuring adequate living standards for the ageing population. Failure to meet the targets simply makes the problem worse.

The report's review of progress identified clear problems. On the key objective of increasing the overall employment rate, the 2005 intermediate target of 67 percent for the EU15 was very unlikely to be achieved. The rate had risen to over 64 percent in 2002, well on target, but rose no further in 2003 and looked likely to reach only 65 percent in 2005. To get back to the 2010 target, there would therefore have to be a very rapid increase from 2006, with the number in work growing at about 1.5 percent per annum. Achieving this would require:

- a return to increasing rates of labour force participation overall;
- particularly, increased economic activity rates among women (especially in Greece, Italy and Spain, where employment rates for women were about 30 percent below those for men) and among older workers (especially in Austria, Belgium, France, Italy and Luxembourg, where under 33 percent of people aged 55–64 were economically active);
- an improvement in skills levels (in the EU15, the employment rate of the low-skilled was about 49 percent, mainly because they are more likely to experience long-term unemployment; in contrast, 83 percent of the highly skilled were economically active);
- the creation of enough jobs – since the ambition was that these would be in knowledge-based industries, in which the productivity of labour is high, this in turn implies a fast growth rate of output.

The Kok Report noted in particular worrying evidence about the productivity of labour in the EU15. The report's evidence is summarised in Table 3.7. The 'apparent labour productivity' simply compares the growth of output and employment and calculates the implied growth of output per worker. Hourly labour productivity, which corrects for differences in the length of the working week and in holiday entitlement, is a more meaningful measure. The level of productivity of labour per hour was 15 percent lower in the EU15 than in the USA, and the gap seemed to be increasing after 1996.

Table 3.7 GDP, employment and productivity, EU15 and USA, annual average change, percent

	1991–96 EU15	1991–96 USA	1997–2002 EU15	1997–2002 USA
GDP	1.5	3.2	2.4	3.0
Employment	–0.3	1.7	1.4	1.0
Apparent labour productivity	1.9	1.4	1.0	1.9
Hourly labour productivity	2.2	1.4	1.5	2.2

(Source: Kok 2003: Chart 13.)

The Kok Report thus revisited the specific points and targets set out in the Lisbon strategy and reaffirmed most of the general objectives. Thus its recommendations and policy suggestions about:

- the need to foster new business and keep the cost of job creation low;
- the need to develop and disseminate innovation and research;

- the need to develop labour market policies to help the unemployed into work;
- the need to increase the labour force participation of women;
- the need to achieve the integration into the labour force of minorities and immigrants; and
- the need to improve education and skills training, including lifelong learning;

were quite similar to the Lisbon strategy, although the Kok Report made much more reference to examples of good practice and examples where improvements could be made.

However, the Kok Report was much more explicit than the Lisbon strategy in two areas of potential conflict between industrial and social policy – how to combine flexibility and security in the labour market and how to raise the participation rate of older workers.

Potential tensions between industrial and social policy

Industrial policy in any market-driven capitalist economy is led by considerations of helping firms to be competitive, and therefore of removing unnecessary costs (both financial and regulatory) that impede their progress. Even before the endorsement of the Lisbon strategy, EU industrial policy was very much in this mould. EU social policy, like that in other Western countries, is mainly concerned with helping those who cannot thrive in the labour market (e.g. because they are too young, or too old, or too infirm) to achieve a reasonable standard of living, by offering them various forms of social security assistance, in money or in kind. Social policy also addresses the working conditions offered to those in employment, e.g. by specifying a minimum wage, by stating various health and safety requirements, or by specifying maximum working hours. The two sets of policies potentially come into conflict most dramatically where changes are made to try to force more people into the labour market and away from social security support, or to make labour markets more flexible. The Kok Report identified these tensions in discussing how to raise the labour force participation rate both in general and specifically among older workers.

In discussing the need for flexibility in labour markets, the Kok Report argued that

While promoting flexibility on the labour market, it is also important to foster new forms of security. Security in today's labour markets is not a matter of preserving a job for life. In a more dynamic perspective, security is about building and preserving people's ability to remain and progress in the labour market. It is related to decent pay, access to lifelong learning, working conditions, protection against discrimination or unfair dismissal, support in the case of job loss and the right to transfer acquired social rights when moving jobs ... Employers must be able to adapt the size of their workforces by interrupting contracts without excessive delays or costs when other measures, such as working time flexibility or re-training of workers, have reached their limits. Overly protective terms and conditions under standard employment contracts can deter employers from hiring in economic upturns or encourage them to resort to other forms of contracts, which can have a negative impact on the ability of less advantaged workers – notably young people, women and the unemployed – to access jobs. While not losing sight of the positive features of employment protection – such as fostering employee commitment and encouraging employers to invest in the training of their workforce – Member States should assess and where necessary alter the level of flexibility provided in standard contracts ... In pursuing such reforms, it is important to take into account the interplay between the contractual framework and the many other factors that impact on the levels of flexibility and security in the labour market, such as the social protection system.

(Source: Kok 2003: 28.)

Similarly, the report recognised that one of the central issues in raising the average retirement age of workers was to make early retirement less attractive. It was estimated that in 2001 the average age of workers leaving the labour market in the EU15 was just under 60; it had been determined that this would have to rise to about 65 to meet the overall Lisbon strategy target. The report acknowledged that a potentially difficult change was required here:

Raising the employment rate for older workers and postponing the average exit age from the labour market is a major challenge for Europe. In most Member States, this requires a radical shift in policy measures, away from a culture of early retirement, towards comprehensive active ageing strategies ... Reforming pension rules to encourage longer working lives is a priority. As part of pensions reforms, it is important to remove incentives for early retirement, which has too often been used as an expedient for people to leave the labour market and for enterprises to rejuvenate their staff and reduce labour costs ... Such reforms are difficult and often imply a radical culture shift for enterprises, workers and public authorities.

(Source: *ibid.*: 42.)

The implications of these arguments – that it was necessary to consider reducing job security in the pursuit of labour market flexibility, and that it was necessary to tighten up on pension rules to make older workers stay in the labour force – together with earlier Lisbon strategy ideas, such as making it tougher for young people and the unemployed to opt out of the labour market and putting pressure on women with young families to return to work, was a radical revision of thinking in the EU's social policy. Classic EU social policy before the Lisbon strategy can conveniently be represented by the Social Chapter of the Maastricht Treaty, with its emphasis on concepts such as improvements in living and working conditions, fair remuneration, social protection and worker participation (see Dearden 2005: 205 for a convenient summary). While the adoption of the Lisbon strategy and the translation into action of the Kok Report conclusions have not implied an abandonment of the aspirations of the EU's older social policy, they have nevertheless brought about a radical change of emphasis.

Current EU industrial and social policy

The Kok Report was part of the background to a general review of progress on the Lisbon strategy. The European Council meeting in March 2005 endorsed a mid-term revision of the Lisbon strategy, which the European Council agreed required amendment because of the very limited progress. It was agreed to concentrate on the coordination of national policy of member states in three policy areas:

1. making Europe a more attractive place to invest and work;
2. promoting knowledge and innovation for growth;
3. creating more and better jobs.

All this was to be achieved by the pursuit of 23 'integrated guidelines', the first six of which set the macro-economic context, the next nine were concerned with market conditions, and the last eight specifically considered employment policies (see Key fact 3.19 for details).

Key fact 3.19

Integrated guidelines for growth and jobs (2005–08)

Macro-economic guidelines

1. to secure economic stability;
2. to safeguard economic sustainability;
3. to promote the efficient allocation of resources;
4. to promote greater coherence between macro-economic and structural policies;
5. to ensure that wage developments contribute to macro-economic stability and growth;
6. to contribute to a dynamic and well-functioning EMU.

Micro-economic guidelines

7. to extend and deepen the internal market;
8. to ensure open and competitive markets;
9. to create a more attractive business environment;
10. to promote a more entrepreneurial culture and create a supportive environment for small and medium-sized enterprises;
11. to expand and improve European infrastructure and complete agreed priority cross-border projects;
12. to increase and improve investment in research and development;
13. to facilitate innovation and the take-up of information and communications technology;
14. to encourage the sustainable use of resources and strengthen the synergies between environmental protection and growth;
15. to contribute to a strong industrial base.

Employment guidelines

16. to implement employment policies aimed at achieving full employment, improving quality and productivity at work, and strengthening social and territorial cohesion;
17. to promote a lifecycle approach to work;

18. to ensure inclusive labour markets for job seekers and disadvantaged people;

19. to improve matching of labour market needs;

20. to promote flexibility combined with employment security and reduce labour market segmentation (i.e. make it easier for people to move from one job to another or from unemployment into work);

21. to ensure employment-friendly wage and other labour cost developments;

22. to expand and improve investment in human capital (i.e. education and training);

23. to adapt education and training systems in response to new competence requirements.

(Source: European Commission, 2005c.)

The Commission's new Social Agenda, launched in February 2005 for the European Council meeting, contains what it describes as a two-pronged strategy (for details, see European Commission 2005b). The first prong is to build confidence, espccially among young people, in their capacity to thrive in the dynamic, knowledge-driven Europe envisaged in the Lisbon strategy. The second is to deal with two priority areas: moving towards full employment and creating a more cohesive society. For full employment, the emphasis, as in the Kok Report, is on increasing the adaptability of workers and enterprises, attracting more people to enter and remain in the labour market, investing more, and more effectively, in education and training, and ensuring the implementation of reforms through better governance. For greater cohesion, the emphasis is on reforming national systems of social security, to change incentives and direct aid to where it is more strongly needed.

Following the European Council meeting, the Commission prepared a new document spelling out in more detail the rationale of the 23 'integrated guidelines'. As is obvious from the list, they represent an ambitious attempt to bring together a whole range of EU policies – macro-economic policy (especially guidelines 1, 2 and 6), industrial policy (especially guidelines 7–13 and 15), cnvironmental policy (guideline 14), employment policy (especially guidelines 16–21), social policy (especially guidelines 16, 20, 22 and 23) and education policy (guidelines 22 and 23). How achievable all this will prove to be depends on the attitudes of the governments of member states. Evidence from the first five years of the Lisbon strategy is not encouraging, but there does seem to be evidence that some governments are beginning to take at least some of the guidelines seriously. For example, since the beginning of 2005 the rates of tax on business have been cut in Austria, Estonia, Germany and Poland.

Commercial, monetary and economic integration

Commercial integration

As we have seen, a basic objective of the EU is to ensure fair competition between its members – and so to abolish barriers to such competition – while protecting them as necessary from competition from the rest of the world. Hence there are many elements in EU law, from the Treaty of Rome onwards, to try to combat the powers of monopolies. Where EU producers are genuinely competitive in world terms, there is no conflict even in the short term between promoting competition within the EU and promoting the competitiveness of the EU in world terms. But where EU producers are not competitive, it may not be in the interests of the EU to support trade liberalisation.

Competition policy within the EU is therefore rather ambivalent. The initial focus of EU competition policy was firmly on intra-EU international trade; each country had its own legislation on restrictive practices by companies within its boundaries, and the idea of the EU policy was to prevent cartels and restrictive agreements from distorting international trade within the EU.

The role of the EU's own competition policy was therefore to deal with anti-competitive practices pursued by multinational companies, some of which are truly major players on the world stage. Multinational companies – such as Shell or Coca-Cola – make output or provide services in more than one country and are important as a source of jobs and exports in the countries in which they locate overseas operations. The 1995 Census of Industrial Production in Ireland, for example, found that 47 percent of the employment and 77 percent of the net output of Irish manufacturing was in multinational companies, which represented 83 percent of all Irish manufacturing exports. Most of the multinational companies are from the USA, with Japan a fairly close second, but France, Germany and the UK are all sources of big multinational operations; nearly a third of the biggest multinationals (the top 500 by revenue and the top 100 by foreign assets) are European in origin.

The role of multinationals is controversial. On the positive side, they provide jobs in the countries in which they locate, pay taxes, contribute to output and exports, and frequently introduce new methods that 'spill over' into technological improvements in other firms in the host countries. They increase profits for their shareholders by choosing the most favourable locations in which to operate. On the negative side, they are accused of exploiting labour, damaging the environment and using their economic power to wring favourable tax and legal treatment from host governments. When economic conditions are difficult, they may well meet the demands of their shareholders by withdrawing from the host countries to concentrate activities at their home base, thus creating problems in the host country. In recent years, protests about the activities of multinationals have led to the blockading of international economic meetings, especially the WTO, because the protesters believe that the WTO is biased in favour of the multinationals (consider the role of the multinationals in the 'banana wars' case discussed in Part 1).

It was to deal with multinational companies that the EU Commission was given special powers. These powers were extended from 1989 by giving the Commission the authority to examine, and if thought appropriate, prevent proposed company mergers and takeovers that crossed national boundaries. The Maastricht Treaty includes provisions to prevent aid from EU national governments to companies, including state-owned concerns, unless this aid is consistent with EU objectives. All of these measures are designed to ensure fair competition within the EU and to prevent dominant producers from exploiting consumers. But what if some proposed restrictive practice damages the interests of EU consumers in the short run but is designed in the long run to enable EU producers to meet foreign competition or to exploit global market opportunities?

A good example of these tensions can be seen in the EU competition policy on telecommunications, a big, profitable and still rapidly growing industry of literally global scale. Opinion 3.6 illustrates the dilemma.

Opinion 3.6

Competition and competitiveness in telecommunications

Writing in the spring 1996 edition of the European Commission's *Competition Policy Newsletter*, Alexander Schaub, the director-general responsible for the policy, explained:

> We cannot risk that such markets as digital interactive TV, or global mobile satellite systems, are sewn up by defensive commercial moves before they are even opened up to competition.

> (Source: Schaub 1996: 2.)

It was clear that digital interactive media facilitated by global satellite communication systems was a rapidly developing market with huge growth potential. The major EU firms in this field, such as British Telecom, were relatively small in world terms, and unless they were sheltered would not be able to develop activities on a big enough scale to be viable in competition with the established US and Far Eastern multinational operators. This would lead to the conclusion that, if the EU wanted a significant local presence in providing these technologically advanced services, support should be given to suitable EU providers. However, the snag was that the only EU firms with any immediate prospect of success were, like British Telecom, already very dominant in related national communication services, so supporting such firms would be anti-competitive in national markets, because it is hard for new producers to be competitive in the more conventional communications markets unless the big firms are curbed. Schaub therefore concludes:

> Real synergies between telecoms and broadcasting, and really global service offerings are benefits which should be promoted. But this will always be weighted against the risks of extending dominance and harming competition.

> (Source: *ibid*.: 5.)

What do you think the policy should be?

Underlying many of the recent deliberations of the EU, including some of the provisions of the Treaty of Amsterdam and much of the Lisbon strategy, is concern not only about competition within the EU but also about the competitiveness of EU producers *vis-à-vis* those in other countries. As we have just seen, there is a complicated relationship between these two considerations. We can see these complications reflected in the Lisbon strategy, which seeks to encourage competition within the EU but also seeks to promote the development of knowledge-based enterprises within the EU to form the basis of output and employment growth. As we have seen, the modified Lisbon strategy, which is current EU policy, includes specific priorities to promote research and development and to make social protection systems more employment-friendly. Research and development matters are clearly key in the case we have just examined.

Monetary and economic integration

To understand EU policies about monetary integration, we must first consider what exchange rates are and how they are determined.

What are exchange rates?

We noted earlier that barter is complicated, so in practice international trade usually entails financial transactions rather than direct swaps of goods. The financial arrangements for international trade are one step more complicated than those for the purchase of goods and services in any one country. Consider, for example, a group of Tayside farmers selling raspberries. They will want payment in sterling. Households in Bordeaux buying the raspberries will want to pay in euros. So the farmers (or an agent acting for them) must convert the euros into sterling. Each time any item is sold from one country to another, if the two countries have different currencies, there is a foreign exchange transaction as well as the transaction of selling the good or service. If the foreign exchange rate is determined by the operation of market forces, the price of any currency in terms of any other depends on the interaction of supply and demand like any other price.

What determines exchange rates?

Let us think through carefully what demand and supply mean here. Consider the exchange rate between the £ sterling and the euro as a market for the euro, where the quantities are quantities of euros and the price is the price of euros in sterling.

Earlier in Part 3, we talked about Tayside raspberry farmers selling their products to Bordeaux in exchange for wine from Bordeaux. We can now look at the effect on the exchange rate between sterling and euros of the sale by our raspberry farmers to Bordeaux. Let us suppose that we start with one euro being worth 60p, so the price of a euro is £0.60.

When the raspberry farmers make their sale in Bordeaux, they receive payment in euros. They want sterling, so they sell euros and buy sterling – they are *supplying* euros to the exchange market in exchange for sterling. Because more euros are being supplied, the supply curve moves to the right, so the equilibrium price of euros falls to, say, £0.50. A euro is now worth 50p instead of 60p. Figure 3.11 illustrates the analysis.

Start again with the price of a euro at £0.60. When the Bordeaux wine producers sell their wine to Tayside, they receive payment in sterling and want to convert it to euros, so they are *demanding* euros in this exchange market between euros and sterling. Because more euros are being demanded, the demand curve moves to the right, so the equilibrium price of euros rises to, say, £0.70, making a euro worth 70p.

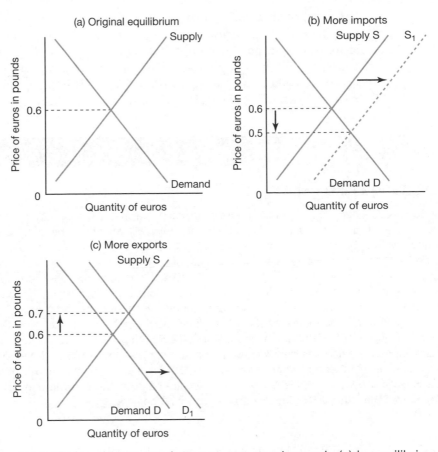

Figure 3.11 The exchange rate between euros and pounds (a) in equilibrium, (b) after an increase in imports to France and (c) after an increase in exports from France

In reality, many exchange transactions are taking place in any one day, and the value of transactions from euros into sterling is normally nearly equal in any day to the value of transactions from sterling into euros. The difference between the two flows is what causes the exchange rate to change, so normally there is very little movement from day to day in the exchange rate. Where dramatic changes do take place, as for the Russian rouble in August and September 1998, it is because the small changes resulting from trading flows are swamped by speculative transactions. To understand speculation in currency markets, we have to consider what activities, besides trade, produce foreign exchange transactions.

Besides importing and exporting goods, firms and households can also import and export factor services. For example, Irishmen might work in Norway on a major construction project. If they do, this is an export from Ireland to Norway – instead of providing goods to Norway, Ireland is providing labour. The Irishmen will be paid in Norwegian currency and will want to convert some of it to euros, perhaps to send money home when they are working in Norway and to take their savings home at the end of the contract. However, imports and exports of labour are small in volume in comparison with the international flow of financial capital.

When a British company issues shares, some of the shares may well be bought by people in other countries, e.g. Spain. The initial transaction – the purchase of the share – is an 'export' from Britain to Spain, and money has to be converted from euros to sterling to pay for the share. When dividends are paid on the share, the flow is the other way (an export from Spain to Britain because the dividend is payment for a service provided by Spain), with sterling being converted to euros.

Key concept 3.6

Exchange rate risks

Suppose a Spanish household has some spare cash, which it is prepared to lend for a year for a fixed interest rate. It does not want to risk that the borrower will default on the loan, so it decides to lend to a government. Suppose the best interest rate available to it for any government savings in the euro zone is 10 percent per annum and that it therefore decides to lend it to the British government for a fixed period of a year by buying some savings certificates, which offer interest of 15 percent per annum – for £100 the household lends, it will get £115 in a year's time. Provided the rate of exchange between the euro and sterling is constant, the family will obtain a return of 15 percent in terms of euros. However, if the exchange rate alters, it will do better or worse than this. Suppose that when it made the loan £100 = 150 euros, and it lent 150 euros to buy £100 worth of certificates. If, when the loan matures, sterling has depreciated against the euro, so that £100 = 100 euros, the £115 will give the family only 115 euros, whereas it invested 150 euros and so incurs a loss of about 25 percent on the investment. However, if sterling has appreciated against the euro, to, say, £100 = 200 euros, the £115 gives the family 230 euros, a return of about 50 percent.

Some of the financial flows are very volatile, because they represent surplus cash that is being lent out for short periods (often a matter of days) to whoever gives the highest return. The return on money is the rate of interest, so if it wants to attract more of these volatile financial flows a country should offer a rate of interest a little higher than that prevailing elsewhere. But this may not be enough, because there is also the question of what is happening to the exchange rate. Key concept 3.6 uses an example to explain the principle of exchange rate risk.

To simplify the arithmetic of the illustration in the example, we have assumed 50 percent depreciation and 33 percent appreciation, which are quite high figures even for a year, but it is not unrealistic for currency movements to swamp interest differentials. To see why, we must remember that the really volatile financial flows are lent for periods of days, not years, so the interest they expect to attract is normally measured in fractions of a percent and can easily be outweighed by quite small exchange rate changes. That is why in currency crises, when a country is trying to stave off a devaluation, it is not uncommon for interest to have to be offered for one-day loans at 100 percent or more, because 100 percent per annum is under a third of a percent per day, not much of a return if the currency is expected to depreciate tomorrow.

Exchange markets exist, then, to facilitate trade in both products and factors. Because of the extra risks (of unfavourable exchange rate movements) implied by foreign trade, various arrangements have been developed to insure traders against the risk. If the raspberry farmers are worried that, by the time they are paid, the pound will have appreciated against the euro (so that the euros they expect to be paid will give them less sterling than they expected to receive), they can obtain protection against that risk by operating in a futures market, today buying sterling for euros that they promise to deliver in, say, three months' time. Then, when the farmers are paid in euros for the raspberries, they use the euros to pay for the sterling they have agreed to buy. Thus the farmers know now how much sterling they will get for the euros they have not yet received, whatever the exchange rate becomes. Of course, the farmers have to pay for avoiding the risk of devaluation, because the extra transaction will involve extra brokerage fees, and the future price they are quoted may not be attractive, but if the currencies are volatile the protection may be thought to be worth the payment.

Futures markets were thus created to facilitate trade, but once they exist their nature changes, with agents buying and selling foreign currency as a commodity in its own right and not because of trade flows. Such agents are speculators, who make their living by anticipating movements of the exchange rate. If, for example, a speculator thinks that sterling will depreciate against the euro, he or she will buy euros for sterling now and then sell the euros for what he or she expects will be more sterling in the future. Thanks to the existence of futures markets, the speculator does not have to pay for the euros now and so can operate in terms of a set of contracts to buy and sell large amounts of currency that he or she does not in fact have, because all that will have to be paid for is any net loss on the contracts. Speculators can have a powerful destabilising effect in the short run on currency markets whenever they share opinions that therefore become self-fulfilling. Suppose that most speculators expect sterling to depreciate against the euro. They therefore sell sterling and buy euros. As they do this, the price of sterling in terms of euros falls – i.e. the 'market sentiment' has produced exactly the outcome the speculators expected. Such speculative activities have been important in the recent history of monetary union in Europe. However, market sentiment is unlikely to hold strongly to some opinion without its having some underlying basis in the economic or political realities, so most of the time speculation simply hastens the inevitable.

Why might governments want to intervene in exchange markets?

Volatility in exchange markets is not welcome to those who are trying to trade products or factor services, because of the uncertainty it causes for them. It is not welcome either to governments, which are sensitive both about the country's trade and about its international capital markets, and which also attach prestige to the strength of the currency. For these reasons, it is not uncommon for countries to intervene in the operation of currency markets. This intervention can take many forms. It can consist simply of *ad hoc* action in particular circumstances to nudge the exchange rate in the desired direction (operated usually by the government or the central bank – for the euro zone the ECB – using foreign exchange reserves to buy the country's own currency to push the exchange rate up). It can involve bilateral or multilateral international agreement to fix exchange rates at some particular level and to use appropriate instruments to ensure that the level does not change. It can be the outright prevention of any official free market in a currency by the use of various exchange controls such as preventing citizens and visitors from taking more than a minimal amount of currency out of the country and by conducting foreign trade in barter terms. Until the end of the 1980s, nearly all the internal trade, and a high proportion of the external trade, of the former Soviet bloc was based on swapping commodities because the USSR rouble, Polish zloty, etc. were either not convertible at all to other currencies or were convertible only at official rates that bore very little relationship to reality.

What is the current state of play on European monetary and economic integration?

Monetary union within the EU has been achieved by the 12 countries that are members of the euro zone. They have a single currency, the euro, and common interest rates determined by the ECB. For various reasons, Denmark, Sweden and the UK regarded it as not in their national interest to join the euro zone. The ten countries that joined the EU in 2004 are not yet members of the euro zone.

Economic integration would involve the further step of full harmonisation of tax and public expenditure policy. For reasons explained earlier, some elements of tax harmonisation (affecting taxes levied on goods and services) are under discussion. There is currently no proposal for significant harmonisation of income or company taxation, let alone for any unification of policy on public expenditure. However, monetary union does include some matters, such as overall public borrowing levels, that restrict the extent to which euro-zone members can finance public expenditure by borrowing.

Plate 3.9 Large mock-up of a euro coin on top of notes of the currencies it replaced

Source: Audiovisual Library of the European Commission (2005).

There have been various stages in the evolution of monetary integration in the EU, and it is instructive to consider briefly some of the background before we look at the euro. In a monetary union, countries do not necessarily have to have a single currency, but if there are different currencies the exchange rates between them must be fixed. This can be achieved only if monetary policies are harmonised, so that the different countries follow agreed plans about the rate of expansion of their money supply and operate, and maintain, agreed interest rate differentials.

The history of the EC's Exchange Rate Mechanism (ERM) in late 1992 and early 1993 gives ample illustration of the problems that occur if these conditions are not met. One of the problems was that the exchange rates were not quite fixed: each currency could move up and down within a prescribed range (usually 2.25 percent) against the ecu (a weighted average of all EU member currencies). The fact that movement was permitted at all enabled the market to read signals into the extent to which currencies persisted at the top or bottom of the permitted range, because if there is a big underlying problem it can be predictable what the monetary authorities will do, and speculators will continue to push the currency to the limit until either they see the action they expect or they are forced to make losses by powerful countervailing action by the monetary authorities. An example of this, sterling's exit from the ERM, is outlined as Key fact 3.20.

Key fact 3.20

Sterling and the ERM

In early September 1992, when sterling was in the ERM:

* Sterling was at the bottom of the range for some time partly because of market belief that the UK economy was weak, and partly because UK interest rates were low relative to those in Germany.
* Germany had a stronger currency, with no danger of devaluation, but high interest rates for domestic macro-economic reasons related to German unification.
* In the UK, interest rates had been cut, for macro-economic reasons, to try to stimulate economic growth.
* Market sentiment was that sterling was overvalued, so speculators sold it.
* By the rules of the ERM, when sterling reached the critical level, the governments of the UK and the other member countries had to act. They tried to support sterling by buying it in exchange for other currencies, but the reserves available were small relative to the strength of speculative selling. The UK government raised interest rates in one day from 10 to 12 and then to 15 percent to try to strengthen sterling by encouraging financial inflows.
* But by then it was too late for the move to be credible to the markets, so later that day sterling had to be devalued (in fact by leaving the ERM rather than changing its parity within it).

However, depreciation of the French franc in 1992 was averted because in that case the monetary authorities' support for the currency was stronger than speculators' determination to sell it, but when the French franc came under renewed pressure in August 1993, the only economically and politically possible solution was a radical review of the ERM, widening the bands of permissible movement of currencies to ±15 percent – bands so broad as to be almost useless in achieving the exchange rate stability that was the whole objective of the ERM. A successful monetary union requires a degree of policy harmonisation that was evidently lacking overall in the ERM in its successive crises in 1992 and 1993.

The tests for euro membership were carefully chosen to assess how far in economic policy and economic performance potential euro members really are like each other and both capable and willing to be governed by a common monetary policy. A common monetary policy can work only if the participants have broad agreement on how to react to internal pressures – for example, the aspirations of their trade unions for increased real pay levels, and of their citizens for more jobs and improved public services – and to external shocks, such as the abrupt downturn in many formerly rapidly growing Asian economies.

The tests were set out in the Maastricht Treaty. As already outlined, they set 'convergence criteria' that countries had to meet in order to join the single currency. The criterion about stability of exchange rates – that countries had to be members of the ERM for the preceding two years and not devalue in that period – is obviously a direct measure of similarity of economic performance. However, the others deserve a little elaboration.

They enjoin euro members to achieve low inflation, low interest rates and sound public finances (defined by reference to the current level of state borrowing and to overall state debt). Why were they defined in this way rather than the achievement of some sort of average performance? Aspirant euro members were required to aim towards macro-economic performance similar to that achieved by Germany, which had in the 1950s and 1960s been the economic engine of the EU on the basis of its low inflation, low public debt and strongly market-led economy. There are two fundamental reasons for this ambition.

1. If Germany were to give up its well-regarded currency for the euro, it had to be satisfied that the euro would be as strong a currency as the deutschmark had proved to be. Other countries would be more willing to abandon their own currencies if they thought the substitute would be stronger. No country with ambitions to join the euro wanted the euro to be a failure. If as a result some countries with weaker currencies could not satisfy the criteria (as was the case initially with Greece), that was regarded by most countries as acceptable.

2. As already explained, the main drivers behind the criteria were representatives of national central banks. Central bankers place a high value on monetary stability and prudence and are perhaps less concerned than elected politicians about implications for unemployment.

Members of the euro zone are expected to run their economies in accordance with criteria set out in the Stability and Growth Pact. This pact requires them to keep their government borrowing within strict limits and to control their inflation rates. However, experience is currently showing that the borrowing limits seem rather too tight, and in practice Germany and France in particular are being allowed to ignore the pact's requirements. It is ironic that Germany and France are the first euro-zone members to have experienced significant problems in meeting the pact's rules. Germany was the prime mover in pressing for tight rules. France was right from the start concerned that the rules were insufficiently responsive to the needs for governments in some circumstances to borrow more to maintain employment levels.

The Stability and Growth Pact tests are not – and do not profess to be – all that is needed for full economic union. Even if their governments were in complete agreement on matters such as the relative importance of inflation and unemployment, different countries do tend to react to common external shocks in a different way because they affect their economies differently – as we have seen in Part 1. If countries in the euro zone are indeed affected in different ways by some shock, there would almost certainly be a greater effect on output and employment in their economies than if they were not in the euro zone. Economic union cannot make economic volatility go away, and a careful set of policies, including appropriate transitional assistance through regional policy, is needed to ensure that harmonisation elsewhere does not produce unbearably severe pressures in the face of unexpected shocks. We will return to this theme in Part 5.

European foreign, security and defence policy

The EU increasingly regards itself as a global actor concerned with a wide range of issues. For the EU to fulfil this role successfully, it is essential that it has a workable foreign and security policy. A major part of developing a successful EU foreign and security policy will be the realisation of a defence policy that matches in capability the EU's ambition to be an influential global actor.

The question of whether the EU should have a foreign and defence policy is not a new one. Cooperation over areas of foreign policy has been taking place for many years. This was first institutionalised under European Political Cooperation (EPC), and the Common Foreign and Security Policy (CFSP) is one of the pillars of the EU under the Maastricht Treaty. Since Maastricht, the CFSP has developed and become increasingly effective in some areas, such as the Middle East. However, despite these successes the CFSP is often regarded as being weak and ineffectual. Thus there are areas of serious concern that need to be addressed in order for the CFSP to be truly effective. As shown earlier, distinctively European defence cooperation first surfaced in 1950, when the formation of a European Defence Community (EDC) was explored. These efforts proved unsuccessful. The arguments and debates first seen with the EDC have continued over the years and persist today. These discussions concern whether the EU should actually have some sort of military capability, the relationship between any EU military capability and NATO, and, most significantly, whether the EU is, in fact, capable of being a regional, or global, military actor.

It is essential from the outset to realise what is meant by a common European foreign and security policy. It does not mean that the EU is going to develop a view on every foreign and security policy issue that would then be binding on all member states. This would currently be impossible and unworkable. What the CFSP does try to do is to produce a united stance on areas of concern to all or most member states. It has also attempted to ensure that EU member states have a joint concept and understanding of what is meant by security within the context of the EU and how this should be applied by member states. It is important for the EU to have a joint concept and a view on what it means in practical terms. Internal movement has become easier within the borders of the EU, and the EU has also become increasingly concerned with potential security threats along its external borders. Also, although NATO remains the primary security organisation in Europe, the membership of the two organisations differs (see Table 3.1). This again shows the need for an EU security policy and identity.

Many of the contemporary debates surrounding European foreign and defence policy have arisen since the conflicts in the former Yugoslavia, especially those seen in Bosnia. These took place in the mid-1990s. At the start of the break-up of Yugoslavia, the EU took the chance to try to prove itself on the global stage. With Bosnia, the Europeans bit off more than they could chew. The situation was highly complex, with not one conflict taking place, but three. Resolution of the conflicts proved to be beyond the capabilities of the EU. It had already proved difficult for the EU to come up with a viable, united policy over the break-up of Yugoslavia, especially as major member states had historic sympathies with the parties involved (Germany with the Croats and France with Serbia). These difficulties were seen during the Bosnian War, which made policy formation difficult and led to the CFSP generally being regarded as a failure in Bosnia.

Some of the main problems with the CFSP that were exposed in Bosnia are those of decision making, stability and leadership. These may seem easy issues to resolve, but the questions raised here go right to the heart of the debates about the CFSP and what place it should have in the EU today and in the future.

Currently, the member state that is the president of the European Council plays a key leadership role in the conduct of the CFSP. The presidency rotates every six months, and this can lead to an inconsistent policy. When member states come into the presidency, they have their own set of concerns in the foreign and security arena. These may differ from both the previous holder of the presidency and the next holder of the post. This not only has the potential to affect policy in the short term but can also create problems with consistency of approach to long-term issues.

An option for increasing the consistency and effectiveness of the CFSP would be to give a greater role to the High Representative (HR) for foreign and security policy. This has been advocated by writers such as Crowe, who sees a greater leadership role for the HR as being an essential part of giving the CFSP greater stability. The current HR is Javier Solana, who has managed to undertake the role with some success (Crowe 2003). It looks likely that reforms will be made to the CFSP along the lines suggested by Crowe. As part of the Constitutional Treaty, the role of EU foreign minister will be created. This will be similar to the position of the HR, as it will represent the EU in areas where there is an agreed common policy. However, as the post also replaces the external affairs commissioner, it is probable that the EU foreign minister will have a greater public role than Solana currently has. For example, the foreign minister will lead a range of international negotiations on behalf of the EU, giving them a larger public profile, and, as mentioned earlier, will be vice-president of the European Council.

A second major limitation of the CFSP is the intergovernmental nature of decision making. This not only makes the process complex, but decisions are made through consensus. This means that the resulting policy is often of the lowest common denominator; with 25 views from 25 member states, formulating anything other than a basic policy has proved to be difficult. Therefore, on contentious issues it is virtually impossible for there to be a common, coherent EU foreign policy. Some of the most notable examples have been the conflicts in Bosnia and, more recently, Iraq. It is likely that decision making within the CFSP is going to remain on a consensus basis, as under the Constitutional Treaty the CFSP is one area where the power of veto will remain.

It is important that these weaknesses are overcome, so that the EU can project itself as a major global player. Some progress has been made under the Constitutional Treaty at strengthening the CFSP. However, until policymaking becomes stronger it is unlikely that the CFSP will be truly effective. A key area that remains to be resolved is defence policy. Events have shown that without an agreed position on defence and on a EU military capability, the CFSP may remain a policy without real bite.

European defence policy

It is unlikely that there will be a single military force in the EU in the near future; some of the reasons for this will be outlined later in this section. But what became clear following the debacle of Bosnia was that defence policy would have to play a major role in the creation of an effective and workable EU common foreign, security and military policy.

The conflicts in Bosnia are often seen as being important to the development of contemporary European defence policy. One of the major impacts is that Bosnia, and the later Kosovo conflict, showed the ineffectiveness of EU foreign, security and defence policy. The EU was incapable of undertaking any effective military intervention. The EU depended on the US-led NATO for military intervention in both conflicts. The failure of the EU in Bosnia contributed to the decision of the Blair government in 1999 to support the principle of a EU military force. The UK had always opposed the formation of a specifically EU military force, preferring to conduct any operations through NATO. However, Bosnia had caused the UK to think again, and this new policy was announced at the UK–French summit at St Malo in 1999.

This was an important moment for European defence policy. It led to the commitments made at the Helsinki summit, later in 1999, to form a European Rapid Reaction Force (ERRF). By 2003, EU member states agreed that the ERRF should be able to deploy 60,000 military personnel in 60 days for a period of a year. This is known as the 'headline goal'. The ERRF was, as we have seen, designed to be a humanitarian force, with it adopting the Petersberg Tasks as its *modus operandi*. These are 'humanitarian and rescue tasks; peacekeeping tasks; tasks of combat forces in crisis management, including peacekeeping' (**http://www.weu.int/eng/ comm.92-petersberg.htm**). However, the problems that surround the creation of an effective European defence policy have been highlighted by the moves towards achieving the headline goal, as, in reality, it has yet to be achieved.

It is important to understand that the ERRF is not a 'euro-army', as it is not a standing force as such and will be drawn together on an *ad hoc* basis. It is unrealistic, certainly in the short term, for there to be any type of permanent EU-wide army. There are too many areas of debate and hindrance, not least the problems that this may bring in states that do not favour a politically integrated Europe.

However, despite the promise of closer EU defence cooperation, it has proved to be difficult to achieve and has become caught up in debates about the nature and future of EU defence cooperation.

One of the main areas of discussion concerns the relationship between an EU-based military defence force and NATO. France, along with several other EU member states, has long been a supporter of an independent European military force. However, France has, so far, been unable to separate European defence and security from NATO. The UK has led opposition to this approach and argues that it is more efficient economically and militarily to have close links between an EU military force and NATO. There are also serious military capability questions to be asked about the viability of an EU-based military force that is independent of NATO. The USA, for its part, is supportive of the development of the ERRF. However, Washington would not back a separation of EU and NATO defence policy.

Plate 3.10 Dutch Police officer holds EU flag during handover ceremony in Sarajevo. Dutch police officer Maria Donk holds the European Union flag next to the flags of the United Nations and Bosnia and Herzegovina during the handover ceremony in Sarajevo on 1 January 2003, to launch the Euopean Union Police Mission (EUPM). It took over the training and monitoring of Bosnia's police forces from the UN's International Police Task Force, which had done the work after the 1992–95 war. The EU's first ever defence and security operation ended the UN's decade-long peacekeeping involvement in Bosnia

Source: European Communities (2003). Reuters/Danilo Kirstanovic 01/01/2003.

NATO continues to remain the dominant military and defence force in Europe. Within NATO, the USA is the principal contributor, and this is a major problem for European defence policy. European capabilities in key areas are inadequate and are dependent on the USA through the US contribution to NATO. A good example of this is heavy strategic lift capability. The closing of the capabilities gap with the USA is possible for the EU and is an essential part of ensuring that Europe has an effective defence policy. But it will take time, money and political will. All too often the last two of these have been absent when it comes to decision making and implementation. Since the end of the Cold War, defence spending within the EU has decreased. Without either some increase or, at the very least, stability in EU defence budgets, it will prove very difficult to overcome these capability problems and, therefore, for any EU defence policy to operate effectively and successfully.

The weaknesses in EU foreign, security and defence policy have been an area of limitation in its global relationships. The development of an effective CFSP and supporting defence policy is essential for the EU to become a major global political player. However, at present, it seems that the EU is a long way from being able to undertake this role successfully.

Further reading

To analyse EU policy, you must be up to date with your information and be aware of its context. The references in the text guide you to the most important sources for the context. You will find the latest information on the EU website, particularly the Commission's section (http://www.europa.eu.int/comm/), in which the topics are discussed by policy area. The coverage of new EU policy initiatives in on-line sites such as BBC news (http://www.news.bbc.co.uk/) is usually useful; most serious newspapers are quite useful sources, as are some weekly publications such as *The Economist* (the CD version of which, available in most university libraries, has a good index).

Part 4

Society, culture and politics in contemporary Europe

Plate 4.1 The Jewish Museum in Berlin, opened in 2001, celebrates the history of the Jewish people since Roman times. In light of the Nazi Holocaust, is Berlin a suitable location for such a museum?

Source: Copyright Jewish Museum Berlin; photo: Jens Ziehe, Berlin.

Section 4.1

Social structure and social change in Europe

European society has been transformed over the last two centuries by a series of changes that have revolutionised the way in which we live and think. A largely rural society based on agriculture has become urbanised and industrialised and is now entering a new phase of de-industrialisation as manufacturing jobs disappear in Western Europe and reappear in less developed countries. Europe today finds itself part of a new global economy, specialising in the provision of services for domestic and foreign consumption: banking, insurance, research, communications, education, health and welfare, tourism, and arts and entertainment.

In this section, we start by examining the changes that occurred in the initial transition to industrial society, especially the influence of economic development on social inequality and politics. We then explore the ways in which patterns of inequality, including social class and gender, have developed since the middle of the twentieth century.

The rise of modern society

With the Industrial Revolution and the French Revolution (1789), a number of optimistic forecasters began to herald the arrival of a new society. In France, for example, Henri de Saint-Simon (1760–1825) and his acolyte Auguste Comte (1798–1857) proclaimed that science was replacing religion as the dominant thought pattern of the modern world. Advances in technology were solving the problems of production, but the new economy would require a shake-up in our thinking about politics and society. The *ancien régime* of monarchy and aristocracy had been supported by the established Church, but as science became the new currency of intellectual debate, both the Church and the class structure it supported would have to be replaced. They predicted that a new generation of scientifically trained leaders, drawn from the rising middle classes in commerce and industry, would assume power. By applying their science to the problems of society, they would usher in a secular world in which old disputes about religion or nationalism would fade away.

Although these 'prophets of Paris' were overoptimistic about the prospect of avoiding social and political conflict, modern social scientists support many of their original claims. They were right to spot the revolutionary nature of the economic and intellectual transformations taking place. Modern societies are quite different from the traditional societies that preceded them. Table 4.1 summarises the contrasts often drawn between the two types of society.

Table 4.1 Traditional and modern societies

	Traditional	Modern
Economic basis	Rural population mainly engaged in subsistence agriculture	Urban population mainly engaged in commerce and industry
	State and municipal regulation of economic life	Free trade based on market forces; supply and demand balanced by price mechanism
	Traditional technology based on water and animal power	Advanced technology using mechanisation and fossil fuels
	Informal domestic units of production	Large-scale formal work organisations and wage labour
Social system	Closed communities, isolated by poor communications	Urban cosmopolitan climate induced by improved transport and communications
	Status ascribed at birth; authority inherited	Status achieved by ability and education
Political system	Rule by monarchy, aristocracy and landed gentry	Democracy led by professional experts
Belief system	State religion legitimises traditional rule of landed elite	Freedom of belief; scientific explanations of nature and society
	War and military domination the base of state policy	Free trade and peace replace war and civil insurrection
	Nationalism	Internationalism

Religion in modern Europe

Saint-Simon and Comte believed that, with the rise of science, churches would go out of fashion. They proposed to replace them by temples to Newton, where ordinary people would be exposed to the wonders of gravitational theory instead of the mysteries of religion! Although one could argue that the mass media and the modern educational system (apart from the minority of schools still run by churches) tend to indoctrinate us with a scientific viewpoint, it is hard to conclude that religion has simply faded away. Indeed, in societies as far apart culturally as the USA and Iran, religious fundamentalism is challenging the status of established scientific theories, such as Darwin's theory of evolution.

The French Revolution had attempted to abolish the Catholic Church, but subsequent generations saw it restored despite fierce opposition from secularists. The religion that developed in the new industrial societies of Europe tended to become more fragmented than hitherto. Ruling classes tended to support their established national religion, although that differed from one country to another. The wars of religion that had preceded the modern period had broken up Western Christianity into Catholic and Protestant states, as some monarchs declared national independence from Rome during the Reformation. The map of religious allegiance has remained fairly stable since (see Figure 4.1).

.... The divide between the Eastern Orthodox and the Western Latin Church

——— The Reformation divide between the Protestant and the Roman Catholic Churches

– – – The divide between the former communist and the non-communist regimes

▨ Long-established Islamic populations

Figure 4.1 The religious map of Europe

Source: Spybey (1997: 243, Figure 12.1).

However, established state churches could not retain their hold over an urban industrial population that had escaped the traditional social controls of rural village life. In the rapidly growing industrial cities, there was little provision for the material needs and still less for the spiritual needs of the newly forming working class, which began to build its own community organisations for self-help, trade unions and cooperative movements, and sometimes to join anti-establishment religious sects associated with reformist movements.

In Catholic countries, the Church was regarded by radicals and socialists as a counter-revolutionary force, the opiate of the masses. Church control over education was strongly resisted by campaigners for secular education and freedom of belief. In countries such as England and Scotland, where the state Church was Protestant, its opponents might include Catholic minorities (such as Irish immigrants) and Protestant dissenters such as the Quakers, Methodists and Baptists, as well as non-believers supporting socialism and other radical beliefs.

Thus nineteenth-century religion was associated with social divisions and political conflict between those who supported the official state religion and those who opposed it, often for quite different reasons, yet could unite in a call for freedom of belief and the extension of full rights of citizenship to all. Some countries retained a plurality of beliefs and lifestyles; for example, in the Netherlands a complex division appeared, with supporters of the official Dutch Reformed Church opposed by more radical groups of Calvinists and by Roman Catholics and socialists. Each of these communities developed its own separate social institutions: trade unions, political parties, schools and universities, sports and social clubs, even including a Catholic Goat Breeders' Association (McLeod 1997: 18).

Religion thus served to divide society, creating separate subcultures in local communities within the new industrial cities. While religion appealed more to the upper and middle classes than to the workers, and to women more than to men, it remained an important source of identification, complicating the economic and political struggles of modern society. It sometimes played an important part in rallying nationalist opposition to foreign domination, for example in the fight for Irish independence from UK rule, and more recently in the emancipation of Central and Eastern European nations from the Soviet bloc. It has shown its uglier face in the subsequent ethnic conflicts in Yugoslavia and elsewhere.

As new waves of immigrants have added to the social mix of Europe (see the later sections in Part 4), new religious communities have continued to form, for example Muslim groups of Turks in Germany, Algerians in France, and Pakistanis in the UK. These have to be distinguished from the older Muslim communities left behind in the Balkans by the receding Ottoman Empire.

Contemporary surveys reveal that religious observance has declined, even among the formerly more religious middle and upper classes. Fewer people now belong to any church, established or not, and some churches are having trouble maintaining their buildings and recruiting clergy, men or women. But religious beliefs seem to persist without regular church attendance. Science may have improved our understanding of the natural world, and social science may have dispelled some of the mysteries of social and political life, but secular explanations can provide little spiritual comfort. Most people still seem to need something more to believe in, and some ritual celebration of the great turning points in their lives, such as marriage, the birth of a child, and the loss of a loved one. Sociologists of religion suggest that this search may lead them in new directions as new minority cults and exotic religions take root in Europe, for example the more exciting brands of evangelical Christianity introduced by West Indian immigrants into the UK or Asian mystic religions introduced into European cities by other immigrant groups. In a new society based on mass consumption, religions may compete for customers with differing tastes, and religious toleration may grow to reflect our greater respect for individualism over conformity to community traditions. However, such a free market in religious belief is not universally supported, and even supporters of individual rights have drawn the line at allowing public recognition of minority religions. The French government has objected to Muslim girls wearing religious clothing or headscarves in school, and in Hampstead, a middle-class suburb of London with a large Jewish population, a violent row broke out when a group of more orthodox Jews sought planning permission to mark off a public space as a sacred area. More radical libertarians have even tried to have church bells silenced or traditional religious processions banned, as well as objecting to the privileged place given to religious representatives in some government bodies. It is difficult to arbitrate between those who wish to celebrate their belief publicly and those who feel their public space is being invaded by zealots whose beliefs they reject. In the UK, there is hot dispute about the government's intention to introduce a new criminal offence of religious abuse, on a par with racist and sexist abuse, with opponents claiming that this will make frank expressions of atheism or agnosticism illegal.

Theories of class and inequality in modern society

The development of modern society, involving a change from a fairly rigid traditional status system to one related more to people's changing economic roles, gave rise to two main interpretations, the liberal and the socialist views.

The liberal view was promoted by the rising middle classes, which first challenged the agrarian elites that ruled Europe before the Industrial Revolution. Fighting against inherited wealth and power, liberals tended to champion the idea of equality of opportunity. In the capitalist economy that was sweeping across Europe, from the north and west towards the east and south, they saw the prospect of opportunity for all to compete on equal terms. A free labour market would allow workers to sell their talents to the highest bidder rather than be tied to a particular landlord. Although trade and manufacturing would create fortunes for some and penury for others, the rewards would be fairly distributed on merit.

The socialist view was most potently expressed by Karl Marx (1818–83), who appreciated the material progress made possible by the development of modern industry. Eventually, he believed, the new methods of production would be harnessed for the benefit of all, but not under the system of capitalism that had ushered them in. Although capitalism was a necessary stage in human progress, it would have to be replaced by a socialist system before the full democratic potential of modern industrialism could be realised.

Marx thought that liberal capitalism was almost as oppressive as the feudal regimes it had replaced. In the past, a minority ruling class exploited the mainly agricultural workforce by various forms of compulsion. When workers moved from the domination of their local landlord to make an apparently free contract to work for the factory owner, they were, Marx claimed, entering a new form of wage slavery from which they had little possibility of escape. Forced to accept whatever pay and conditions were on offer, they could not really be said to share in the new freedom enjoyed by their middle-class employers.

Under capitalism, Marx predicted that, although overall living standards might rise, the gap between the wealthy owners of capital and their workers would increase. Wealth would become concentrated in a plutocratic elite, and small businessmen or independent craftsmen would be unable to compete with large monopoly companies. Skilled workers would be replaced by machinery, and the working class would become a mass of unskilled and alienated drudges, struggling to survive on minimum wages.

However, Marx thought that the horrors of the capitalist labour market would force workers to organise, initially into trade unions and then into their own political parties, to fight for reform, but reform would be blocked by the capitalist class, who would dominate the state. Social inequality would be intensified by periodic booms and slumps. Social protests would escalate until the labour movement was strong enough to lead a revolution to sweep away capitalism and replace it by a socialist system based on common ownership.

Liberals and Marxists both recognised the international dimension of modern society. Marx lived long enough to see large-scale capitalist organisations encircling the globe, employing new means of communication to link together producers and consumers in many countries. Given such a powerful enemy, he argued that workers could not defeat it at local or national level. The socialist revolution might start in one country, probably in one of the most advanced capitalist societies, like the UK or the USA, but it would have to spread throughout the world. Workers of the world would have to unite as effectively as the capitalists had done on an international scale. As one later sympathiser put it, capitalism was a tiger and it was impossible to tame it claw by claw!

Modern social scientists, particularly in the USA, tend to enshrine liberal beliefs in their criticisms of Marx. They fall into two groups, functionalist and pluralist.

The functionalists argue that a complex industrial society is bound to develop inequalities, because there will always be a need for leadership. Qualified experts in positions of authority have to be rewarded for exercising their talents and are bound to become the new elite. They point to what happened under the Soviet brand of state socialism, where getting rid of capitalism did not prevent senior party members awarding themselves all sorts of special privileges.

The pluralists accuse Marx of oversimplifying the link between economic wealth, social status and political power. They prefer to follow Max Weber (1864–1920), who accepted that, while social class was a major cleavage in modern society, it was not the only one. They point to conflicts within classes, between one trade and another, or between rival regional, national, ethnic or religious groups, as in Northern Ireland, Italy, Spain and various parts of Eastern Europe today. While not believing in the classical liberal model of a society of competing individuals, they reject the two-class model and stress the plurality of social conflicts. Politics is not a simple football match between two sides, capital and labour. Political parties are seen as shifting coalitions representing constellations of interests, all seeking a share of power. The parties have even been likened to firms competing for customers.

These rival theories of industrial democracy continue to offer different interpretations of the same facts. In the next subsection, we will see how well the theories fit the available facts about social inequality in modern Europe.

Class and capitalism since the Second World War

The two world wars and the unsettled economic and political circumstances of the period between them did not stop the process of modernisation. The whole of Europe continued along the path of industrialisation, although some regions followed generations behind the leaders. As modernisation proceeded, people moved from rural areas and agricultural jobs into urban and industrial occupations, both manufacturing and services.

It is not easy to translate these sectoral shifts in employment into changes in class structure. Broadly speaking, the increase in the service sector means more non-manual office jobs. But as manufacturing has become more technologically

Figure 4.2 The nineteenth-century image of the ruthless capitalist.
This Dutch cartoon of *c*.1900 portrays Nathan Rothschild (1777–1836) in top hat rubbing his kid-gloved hands in glee as in the background workers are apparently being whipped into work in the factories
Source: Vaizey (1971: 38).

sophisticated, it too employs many administrative workers and technicians who are classed as non-manual. The service sector also includes many back-breaking jobs, such as nursing, furniture moving and refuse collection, not to mention ballet dancing and all-in wrestling. However, on balance, the shift from manufacturing to services increases the number of people who work with their heads rather than their hands.

These changes have tended to erode traditional class distinctions between the labouring classes and the more genteel occupations. The entry of women into formerly male-only occupations has also upset the pecking order. Because women have traditionally received lower pay than men, the influx of women into office work has somewhat lowered its status. The traditional male 'white-collar' worker has been increasingly replaced by a lower-paid 'white-blouse' worker.

Marxists focused on the male factory worker as the typical member of the working class, exploited by his class enemy, the ruthless capitalist (see Figure 4.2). They expected class inequality and conflict to escalate to the point of revolution. However, instead of the class structure polarising into a small elite dominating a mass of unskilled labourers, the middle ranks of the occupation structure have expanded. The mature industrial workforce is usually represented by a pyramid-shaped hierarchy of occupations graded by skill and responsibility and rewarded by appropriate pay and social status (see Figure 4.3).

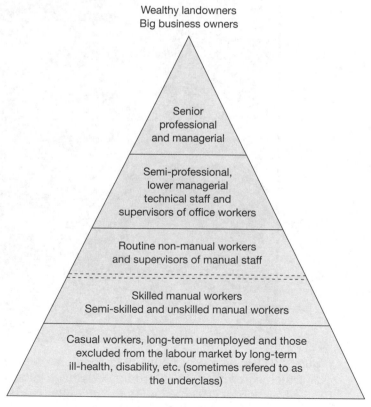

Figure 4.3 The modern hierarchy of occupations
Source: John Berridge.

This pyramid model is misleading in several ways:

- The base is too broad. Unskilled jobs began to be eliminated by labour-saving machinery. The pyramid ought to be redrawn as a diamond or a pear. Indeed, unskilled jobs are harder to come by in the more prosperous Western European countries as manufacturers have moved jobs into countries with cheaper labour.

- There has always been some overlap in pay and status, with skilled manual workers, the 'aristocracy of labour', earning more than the lowest level of white-collar workers.

- Such a diagram tends to imply that everyone is an employee. It leaves out self-employed professionals or craftsmen, and the owners of corner shops or small businesses. In the closing decades of the twentieth century, there was considerable corporate downsizing, with former employees of large corporations being helped to set up in business as independent consultants.

- It also ignores a significant minority, the idle rich, who could live off unearned dividends from large fortunes, generally inherited. However, many of these hold well-paid directorships or even managerial posts in their own or other companies, so they tend to merge into the managerial class.

However, the pyramid model does convey well enough the large part played in modern society by white-collar workers at all levels, from junior clerical workers to senior managers and professionals. Non-manual employment increased during the twentieth century to meet the growth in the scale of organisations in the private and public sectors of all European countries. White-collar work grew from about a fifth of the workforce or less in the 1930s to around two-fifths or more in the 1980s, and has grown since then (Spybey *et al.* 1997).

Figures on the occupational structure of employment have to be read with some caution, as there are regional variations within countries and different proportions of women workers in each country. For example, how does one categorise the social class of families where the husband is a manual worker and the wife or daughter an office worker? However, these complications apart, it is clear that the polarisation of society into two distinct classes has not occurred.

Many managers and professionals have savings and investments to supplement their considerable salaries and fringe benefits, and they clearly have a stake in the continuation of a system that rewards them so well. In the economic boom that lasted roughly from 1950 to the mid-1970s, living standards improved for most classes, and a wider group, including most white-collar workers and some of the higher-paid manual workers, began to acquire middle-class living standards. With savings and investments, company pension cover, houses of their own, cars and other consumer durables, not to mention holidays abroad, these new beneficiaries of the postwar boom were hardly likely to be pining for a proletarian revolution. However, research on the so-called affluent manual workers revealed a continuing awareness of class differences and a willingness to support trade unions to defend their own interests. Their voting behaviour tended to favour centre-left parties but responded pragmatically to government performance: they would support any party that offered them a better deal, providing that they thought it could deliver. Although broadly supportive of state welfare, they were resistant to paying for it via heavier tax deductions from their own pay packets and opposed to 'welfare scroungers'. Their behaviour fitted the pluralist model of competing interest groups better than the Marxist theory of class conflict.

Social mobility and equality of opportunity

One result of the expansion in the numbers of white-collar jobs was to make it more likely that the children of manual workers would end up in occupations considered to be superior in social status. With a shrinking demand for manual work in general, and unskilled work in particular, many children would need to acquire a more extended education to qualify for technical, supervisory and managerial posts. Modernisation triggered off an explosion of educational provision at all levels. Do we then have equality of opportunity?

Surveys conducted in the 1970s showed between a quarter and a third of the sons of manual workers obtaining white-collar jobs. In addition, especially in the newly industrialising countries, there was a considerable movement from agricultural families into both manual and non-manual jobs in industry, commerce and public services. However, children from middle-class families continued to have much better prospects than those from the lower classes, and boys in every class had a slight edge over girls. There was some variation, with the most open society being Sweden, with its long history of Labour governments, and the more closed being France, Germany, Italy and Spain, possibly as a result of their histories of more right-wing governments.

Study of entry into the very top elites of societies, as opposed to movement between lower- and middle-class occupations, revealed a much greater degree of social closure. Although there was more room at the top in all societies and some sons (and, more rarely, daughters) of peasants or factory hands could find their way into comfortable managerial or professional occupations, there was not such easy access to the boardroom or to very senior government posts. Wealth, private education and family influence still counted in the 'corridors of power' in capitalist societies. Studies of the class structure in communist countries revealed an uncanny similarity (Hamilton and Hirszowicz 1993), with the party elite using what might be called their political capital to secure good careers for their children.

The end of the postwar boom

The postwar boom from about 1950 to the early 1970s encouraged optimism among the aspiring lower classes that they or their children could 'get ahead'. Even for those who remained manual workers, most could look forward to full employment, improved living standards and the security of living in a welfare state. The prewar curse of mass unemployment seemed to have been lifted.

Prospects after the mid-1970s were less rosy. With slower growth but continuing advances in productivity, unemployment returned to prewar levels of around 10 percent, even in the prosperous countries of north and west Europe. Young people's expectations were lowered, and resentment built up as more and more education and training was demanded for relatively humble career openings. Among those who failed to secure education or training, a pool of long-term unemployed was being created, some of whom never had secure jobs. It was suggested that this deterioration in job prospects was a factor in rising rates of violence, crime and drug abuse.

Those lucky enough to find permanent jobs would continue to rise on merit thereafter, but the struggle to find work was fiercer. As we shall see later in Part 4, added competition from migrants from other parts of Europe and beyond intensified ethnic and racial conflicts. Demographic factors eased the problem a little, as birthrates dipped in the more advanced countries following the postwar baby boom, but employment prospects will continue to decline in the peripheral countries of Europe, particularly in the former Soviet countries, unless they can improve educational provision and attract more inward investment. Within the EU15 countries, Greece, the former East Germany, the southern parts of Italy, Portugal and Spain have much higher rates of youth unemployment than the rest, with regional rates sometimes topping 50 percent. These rates are matched in the worst urban ghettoes of large cities throughout Europe, where immigrants are usually twice as likely to be unemployed as others.

In northern Europe, there is still a stronger tradition than in the south of continuing education or training beyond the age of 20. For example, the Eurostat labour force survey for 2002 shows that in Belgium, Denmark, Finland, Netherlands, Sweden and the UK at least a quarter of the population had completed tertiary education, whereas the corresponding figure was 10 percent or less in Italy and Portugal (even among the age group 30–39, completion of tertiary education was much lower in Italy and Portugal than in the rest of the EU15). Although state educational provision has expanded in most countries over the last couple of generations, the rate of take-up is still strongly influenced by home background, so that in most countries the working-class taxpayer effectively subsidises the further education of the middle classes. Even if access to education can be improved so that all able pupils gain their maximum level of qualification, in a tight labour market family influence may continue to tip the scales of justice in the allocation of jobs. Children of disadvantaged groups may have more chance of success in small business and other careers where formal qualifications are less important.

Gender and inequality

Formal political inequality between women and men was eroded by the move to universal adult suffrage, completed as early as 1907 in Finland but not until after the Second World War in Belgium, France, Italy and Switzerland (see Table 4.2). However, it took some time before women's new electoral strength was translated into a greater measure of social equality. Traditional gender roles tended to persist, especially in late industrialising countries or those with strong religious and legal support for male supremacy. In most countries, women worked on the land and young unmarried women worked in industry, especially textiles, but at the start of this century most women would be expected, unless they were very poor, to devote their adult lives to motherhood and housework.

Table 4.2 Introduction of universal suffrage in Europe

	Universal male suffrage	Universal adult suffrage
Austria	1907	1919
Belgium	1894	1948
Denmark	1849*	1918
Finland	1907	1907
France	1848	1945
Germany	1871	1919
Ireland	1918	1923
Italy	1913	1946
Netherlands	1918	1922
Norway	1900	1915
Sweden	1909	1921
Switzerland	1848	1971
UK	1918	1928

* With significant restrictions.

(Source: extracted from Pierson 1998: 106, Table 4.3.)

The cause of women's emancipation was taken up by a radical minority, often led by middle-class women who had struggled to enter the professions, but it was wartime experience that helped to loosen stereotypes considerably, as women took on formerly male occupations. Longer-term demographic trends towards smaller families, reinforced by the legalisation of abortion and advances in contraception, probably had a greater effect, freeing women at an earlier age from the burdens of child rearing and opening up prospects for a return to full-time employment. The spread of household equipment such as washing machines and vacuum cleaners may have helped, but standards of housekeeping often kept pace, offsetting possible reductions in hours of housework. Changes in family law improved women's property rights and made separation and divorce easier. The growth of state welfare benefits and services also made it more feasible, although still not easy, for a woman to exit from an intolerable marriage, although there was still strong economic pressure to marry or remarry until recent generations, when cohabitation and single parenthood have become more common.

The postwar period saw a general rise in the rate of economic participation in paid work by women, especially married women (Spybey 1997: 137). By 2004, women's employment had increased markedly throughout the EU, but with considerable variation between countries: within the EU25, the activity rate for all women in the third quarter of 2004 was just over 62 percent, but this ranged from 37 percent in Malta, through just over 50 percent in Italy to over 70 percent in Denmark, Finland and Sweden. The sectoral distribution of employment, too, differed between men and women. There is much variation in women's employment between and within countries according to the stage of industrial development and the state of the labour market. However, a common feature is for women to be concentrated in particular industries and occupations that echo their traditional caring roles: nursing, primary school teaching and social work, catering and cleaning, textiles, clothing, and hairdressing, for example. Even when employed in general office work, they tend to be confined to junior posts serving the needs of male bosses. These jobs are identified as 'women's jobs' and consequently carry poorer pay and promotion prospects. Even where women compete on equal terms with men, their domestic ties and male prejudice may prevent their getting top jobs. Women are also more likely than men to work part-time, a particularly pronounced tendency in the UK, and this often entails poorer pay and conditions and less chance of continuous employment and an occupational pension. However, the European Court of Justice has built upon the Treaty of Rome principle of equal pay for equal work, to exert some pressure against such gender discrimination in employment and other spheres.

The impact of marriage on women's working lives can be seen in Figure 4.4, which also shows the contrasting pace of change in Italy, the FRG, Poland and Sweden between 1950 and 1982. Whereas in Sweden in 1950 most women left the labour force on marriage, by 1982 they continued in work with participation rates almost as high as men's. The generous provisions of the Swedish welfare state no doubt support this trend: better education and child care, and a tax and benefit regime that encourages both parents to work full-time and provides parental leave entitlement for fathers as well as mothers.

Women in communist countries were encouraged to perform paid work, but the 'emancipation' of Soviet woman was not accompanied by the domestication of Soviet man, who expected his wife to combine a full-time job with all the duties of the traditional wife, made worse by the shortage of consumer goods in the shops

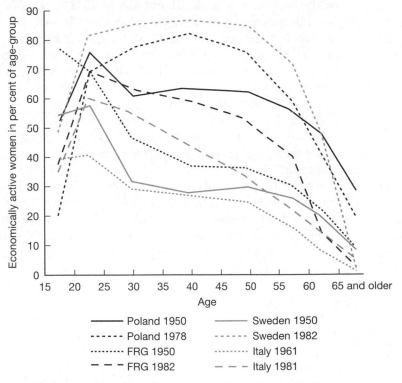

Figure 4.4 Age-specific female participation rates for various countries, 1950–82 (percent economically active persons in age-group)

Source: Ambrosius and Hubbard (1989: 51, Figure 2.2).

and the need to spend hours in queues. State child care was provided, with East Germany and Hungary providing the best services, but provision often lagged behind demand, and the collapse of the Soviet system has seen savage cutbacks as state spending is slashed. The revival of religion in some countries has tended to reverse some of the changes made under communism, such as more liberal provision of contraception and abortion facilities. There may be a tendency, for those who can afford it, to go back to more traditional wifely roles. However, the prolonged economic crises in the East have thrown many out of work, with women more affected than men. Economic dislocation has resulted in a high divorce rate, and some women have been driven into prostitution as their only means of support. It remains to be seen how long it will take for economic reorganisation to provide new jobs for all.

In the long term, Europe will have to come to a new social consensus on the role of women, and men, in modern economic circumstances. If Europe recovers fully from the prolonged recessions of recent years, a real alternative to the male breadwinner/female housewife tradition could open up, one in which both husband and wife worked, full-time or part-time according to the needs of the family. The burden of care for young children and elderly relatives or other dependants could be shared equally between the sexes. However, we seem to be stuck halfway to this new regime, with women more involved in paid work outside the home but men not yet reciprocating by taking more responsibility for housework and caring tasks, which are still regarded as 'women's work'. As we shall see, the Commission has tried to lead change in social attitudes in the EU, but change is slow to implement. It is still true for many career men that they feel uncomfortable phoning the boss to tell him (or her) that they must take the day off because the children are ill, or that they have to attend to a sick parent while their partner is on a business trip abroad!

The dual-career household is, in any case, unlikely to be a universal phenomenon. Surveys of work patterns suggest that couples in which both partners have secure jobs constitute a fortunate group, to be contrasted with other cases in which both partners are unemployed. Moreover, the children of couples in work are more likely to find employment themselves. Employment and unemployment seem to run in families, leading to a greater polarisation of the workforce into the 'haves' and 'have nots'.

An egalitarian family structure requires considerable changes in social policy, which are being introduced rather slowly. The state has to introduce new patterns of taxes, welfare benefits and social services at affordable cost to support two-earner families as well as single parents who wish to work. It also has to monitor occupational training, recruitment, promotion, pay and pensions to ensure equality of opportunity between the sexes. As most of our existing welfare states were built in the 1940s, when the male breadwinner was the norm, there is still much rethinking to be done.

Practice varies across Europe in terms of the proportion of women who work part-time. Discussion revolves around whether some women prefer part-time work to combine with caring roles in the home or whether many are forced to do so because their government fails to deliver sufficient child-care facilities to allow them to compete with men on fair terms for full-time careers. However, social attitudes and practice vary considerably throughout Europe (see Opinion 4.1). The only consistent feature was that women were generally underrepresented in positions of power, in politics as well as at the workplace.

Opinion 4.1

Cross-national comparisons of rates of full-time and part-time work

Catherine Hakim, a tireless researcher of women's employment trends, produced a summary of figures for the EU15 countries and a few Eastern European countries. She reports that in 1995 half of EU15 women were employed, nearly a third of them part-time. By contrast, more than seven out of ten men were employed, only 5 percent of them part-time.

There seemed to be large variations between countries: in Sweden, the female employment rate matched the EU15 average for men at 72 percent, but nearly four out of ten worked part-time (despite Sweden's reputation for good child-care services). Other countries in rank order:

Country	Female employment rate (%)	Of which part-time (%)	Full-time equivalent rate (%)
Above 50 percent of women employed			
Sweden	72	43	57
Denmark	68	36	56
UK	63	44	49
Austria	61	27	53
Finland	60	16	55
Luxembourg	56	21	50
Portugal	56	12	53
Germany	54	34	45
France	53	29	45
Netherlands	53	67	35
Below 50 percent of women employed:			
Belgium	46	30	39
Ireland	42	23	37
Greece	39	8	37
Italy	36	13	34
Spain	32	17	29
EU15	**50**	**31**	**42**
Eastern European comparisons:			
Hungary	77	2	76
Slovenia	58	2	57
Poland	52	13	49

Note: full-time equivalent rates (FTE) of women's employment were estimated on the basis of counting every part-time worker as half a full-time worker.

Can you find any consistent patterns in the above figures?
What factors influence the rate of part-time working for women?
What policies should governments follow to improve women's opportunities for employment?
What factors militate against women working full-time?

(Source: Hakim (1998: 105, Table 5.1.)

There is a protracted debate among feminists about where private enterprise stands on the gender-equality issue. Some maintain that capitalist employers are gender blind and will hire whatever labour is cheapest, most flexible and adequately skilled. Others argue that capitalism takes advantage of older patriarchal traditions, continuing to pay women less than men and using them as a pool of reserve labour that can be drawn on in a boom and expelled in a recession. The role of trade unions is somewhat ambiguous. They have a long history of male domination, which has sometimes caused them to see women as unwelcome competition for skilled jobs. More recently, especially as unions have fought hard against declining membership, they have taken a more progressive attitude. However, because women are more likely to work part-time, and often for small employers, they are harder to recruit into trade unions. Their domestic commitments make it harder to attend union meetings or hold office, even if they are bold enough to outface male prejudice.

More women will be needed in government, industry and trade unions before their needs are fully embodied in social policy. The EC has accepted the principle of equal opportunities for men and women, but it remains to be seen how effectively such a principle can be implemented, given the competing pressures of legislation, public opinion and market forces.

Further reading

Ambrosius, G. and Hubbard, W.H. (1989) *A Social and Economic History of Twentieth-century Europe*, Harvard University Press, Cambridge, MA.

Bailey, J. (ed.) (1997) *Social Europe*, Longman, Harlow, has chapters on social stratification, gender, race, trade unions, religion and other topics.

Breen, R. and Rottman, D.B. (1995) *Class Stratification: A Comparative Perspective*, Harvester Wheatsheaf, Hemel Hempstead.

Hamilton, M. and Hirszowicz, M. (1993) *Class and Inequality: Comparative Perspectives*, Harvester Wheatsheaf, Hemel Hempstead.

McLeod, H. (1997) *Religion and the People of Western Europe, 1789–1989*, Oxford University Press, Oxford.

Spybey, T. (ed.) (1997) *Britain in Europe: An Introduction to Sociology*, Routledge, London – an excellent introduction to sociological theories and facts about European society.

Theobald, R. (1994) *Understanding Industrial Society: A Sociological Guide*, Macmillan, Basingstoke.

Section 4.2

Visions of Europe

External images of Europe: economic and commercial

With an economy of more than $9 trillion in 2002 (larger than the USA) and a population in its home market of 454 million in 2004, the EU is a major market for goods, a major competitor in world trade and a major player in world financial markets; and for many people in other rich economies, Europe will be thought of primarily in this perspective. Correspondingly, in very many poor countries, Europe (along with the USA and Japan) will often be the object of envy, desire or resentment; people may imagine Europe through a stereotype that exaggerates its wealth and the luxuriousness of the lives of its inhabitants, and they may also see these 'complacent rich' as racist. But for those in rich countries who can afford tourism, Europe is thought of, rather, as a location for the cultural riches of the past, while many Australians, Canadians, South Africans and US citizens think of Europe with special affection as the home of their ancestors. Partly for these reasons, they may think of Europe as out of date (as in Donald Rumsfeld's label 'Old Europe'). Thus technological development and spectacular technological achievement are especially important for Europe in combating this out-of-date image.

External images of Europe: geopolitical

In geopolitical terms, it makes a great difference whether Europe is thought of as a single power in the world, or as a congeries of states like Germany, France, Italy and the UK. These nation-states are certainly important, but they do not have the significance of major players in the world, like the USA, or potentially China, Russia and Japan. But as a united structure incorporating these states, and projecting power in economic or financial form or as cultural influence ('soft power'), or projecting the threat of serious trade sanctions or military power ('hard power'), Europe has the potential to be one of three or four superpowers in the world. This possibility arouses alarm in some people in the USA, who fear a potential rival with even more power to obstruct US policies than Germany or France (whose opposition to the Iraq War so annoyed the Bush administration in the USA). Russian and Chinese observers are more likely to view the possibility of effective European power favourably (although cautiously) as providing a partial counter to currently dominant US power. Thus those who dislike or fear this possibility (mainly those in the USA) are likely to pour scorn on the prospects of effective unity or coordination of the policies of the European states, especially in foreign and defence policy and intelligence gathering. At the time of writing, it seems too early to say whether these sceptics are right, but it is clear that the widespread unpopularity in Europe of US policies since 2001 (especially in the Middle East) may encourage European governments to seek at least more effective European cooperation. And Russians and many people in the Caucasus, Ukraine and Central Asia may favour some kind of alliance or joint policy directions with European states (or with the EU). This may help them to find a less abrasive way of living with and relating to the Muslim states of the Middle East than US policies seem to offer.

Europeans' ideas of Europe

For the Europeans themselves, attitudes to 'Europe' are largely swallowed up in attitudes to the EU on the one hand and attitudes to the separate nations of Europe on the other. Attitudes to the EU vary greatly, but considerable cynicism about it is widespread. This arises mainly from the typical attitudes towards government of any modern person; for such a person, discontent with the unsatisfactory outcomes of government action, with the compromises that political action involves, and with the remoteness of officials. Such attitudes may be counterbalanced, in the case of national governments, by the knowledge that at least the politicians who determine policies are directly elected by one's fellow citizens, and by loyalty to the nation. In the case of the EU there is – at first glance – no such counterbalancing of popular discontent with government, and indeed the fact that EU policies may frustrate or oppose, in some cases, the policies of one's own elected national government causes particular resentment. Thus a main source of the low level of loyalty to the EU and its institutions is supposed to be the 'democratic deficit', the fact that EU policy is not determined mainly by directly elected politicians. But this is unavoidable if Europe is not to become a single superstate. If the EU is formed from its component nation-states, then it must be representatives of these states who, negotiating with each other within the framework of EU institutions, determine policy. They are helped by a civil service (the European Commission), which has significant influence and has important powers of initiative to make up for the slowness of the manoeuvrings in the European Council. Thus the widespread cynicism about the EU within Europe is not surprising, and is not easily dissolved.

The value of the framework of the EU

Nevertheless, there are factors underlying public opinion in Europe that tend towards support for the EU. Many people are aware of factors such as:

- the support provided by the underlying framework of the euro;
- the importance of the open European market for commercial development supported by EU competition policy;

- the defence of European trade interests in the WTO by EU negotiators;
- the need for policies to protect the environment to be articulated at European level, through the EU;
- the freedom of movement within the EU that it makes possible.

These factors tend to relate to the general framework of the EU rather than particular policies; it is often particular policies that (rightly or wrongly) arouse resentment.

Europe as a cosmopolitan structure

For some – more politically aware – Europeans (and also for non-European observers) there is also an important positive factor. In today's globalised world, the nation-state (unless perhaps one of superstate size, like the USA) is too small to promote its citizens' interests effectively. For example:

- The environment needs protection on at least a continental scale.
- Commercial interests, their protection and control, must operate on the scale of the multinational corporations.
- Military alliances must be effective over global regions much larger than nation-states.
- Police measures against terrorists, drug cartels, and money-laundering operations must be fully coordinated on a global scale.
- Even taxation and social security provisions impinge on supranational commercial competition and so may need to be negotiated internationally.

But that does not mean that nation-states should be replaced altogether by political units of some larger size. Rather, there has to be a network of negotiating and cooperative relationships between political units, and much of what matters in the world must be determined through loosely coordinated structures that fix these networks in effective institutions. Thus the EU's structure, even though it eludes classification in terms of constitutional theories based on past institutions, may be the very kind of politico-economic structure that the world will increasingly come to need. Against the background of the terrible history of wars in Europe, wars whose renewal now seems inconceivable thanks to this structure, the maintenance of differences within loose overall structures seems to be a way of responding to the global situation adequately and so coming out from the grip of some of the pervasive vicious circles of bitterness that have engulfed Europe in the past. Ulrich Beck calls this loose unity a 'cosmopolitan' structure, in which difference (between nations or other interest groups) is not overridden but is managed in networks of relationships. For some Europeans, as for some non-European people, the EU may stand as a kind of example – not of course a completed and fully worked-out example, but one in constant adjustment and movement – of the political structure that is also now appropriate for other regions of the world.

Key concept 4.1

Cosmopolitan Europe

Cosmopolitan Europe is a Europe that struggles morally, politically, economically and historically for *reconciliation* ... It is to be realised quite profanely as a creation of interdependencies in the political spheres of security, the economy, science and culture. The adjective 'cosmopolitan' refers to this openness, constrained by the critique of ethno-nationalism, which argues for recognition of cultural difference and diversity.

(Source: Beck 2003.)

Further reading

Beck, U. (2003) 'Cosmopolitan Europe: a confederation of states, a federal state, or something altogether new?' in S. Stern and E. Seligman (eds) *Desperately Seeking Europe*, Archetype Publications, London.

Gowan, P. and Anderson, P. (1997) *The Question of Europe*, Verso, London.

Haseler, S. (2004) *Superstate: the New Europe and its Challenge to America*, I.B. Tauris, London and New York.

Jenkins, B. and Sofos, S. (eds) (1996) *Nation and Identity in Contemporary Europe*, Routledge, London and New York.

Stern, S. and Seligman, E. (eds) (2003) *Desperately Seeking Europe*, Archetype Publications, London.

Thomas, N. and Le Saux, F. (1998) *Unity and Difference in European Culture*, University of Durham Press, Durham.

Section 4.3

The state of European democracy

In a very real sense, the past 15 years or so have seen major advances for multi-party liberal democracy in Europe. Many of the former communist states of Central and Eastern Europe – which, although self-proclaimed as 'people's democracies' were in reality one-party authoritarian regimes – have embraced the transition to multi-party liberal democracy. Nowadays, although problems of democratic consolidation (and indeed state consolidation) remain in a few European countries such as Albania, it is really only the former Soviet republic of Belarus that remains outside the democratic family, so to speak. Moreover, the accession of ten new member states to the EU in May 2004, including eight former communist states, was held by many people to be an important step in democratic consolidation.

In several crucial respects, however, the state of democracy in Europe is far from enjoying a clean bill of health. Real worries and concerns have, if anything, grown in recent years. In this section, we focus on four interrelated developments – three causes for concern about European democracy and one undoubtedly positive development. The topics we shall examine are:

1. the state of democracy at the level of the EU;

2. the functioning of democratic institutions at national and EU levels;

3. the growth of right-wing extremism;

4. the growth in non-governmental organisations.

First, we discuss some concerns that have been expressed about the state of democracy at the level of the EU. In an era of globalisation, corporate power seems to be growing ever stronger, and democratic control over that corporate muscle ever more difficult to establish. Huge business and media conglomerates now exercise unprecedented power. The ability of nation-states to hold these conglomerates to any sort of democratic accountability is questionable. Whether the EU has either the ability or the will to do so, at a pan-European level, is hotly contested. Thus the issue of the 'democratic deficit' within the EU goes beyond the questions we have already raised (in Part 3) about the powers of the European Parliament and embraces the ways in which EU institutions function, the decision-making processes at work, and the political culture that drives the EU forward.

Second, public disenchantment with the functioning of democratic institutions at both the national and EU levels is visible in many parts of Europe. This disenchantment can manifest itself in the growing crisis of political parties, which, almost everywhere, suffer from falling membership, ageing memberships, falling levels of activism and a perceived inability to offer voters clear-cut choices and alternatives. The exceptions to this 'rule' are often smaller and more extremist parties. There is also evidence of falling voter turnout in elections – also, now, a marked phenomenon in the new liberal democracies of Central and Eastern Europe. We also see growing disillusionment with the EU as a project.

Third, there is evidence of a marked growth in right-wing extremism over the past 15 years with growing electoral support for neo-fascist and racist parties in many European countries. Such parties often benefit from, and help to create, a climate of increasing xenophobia, Islamophobia, anti-Semitism and violent intolerance of immigrants and of ethnic and racial or religious minorities. Their growing success threatens the solidity of European democracy and, in some people's eyes, even calls into question the extent to which the values of the European Enlightenment – such as the values of reason (against superstition), of tolerance (against bigotry) and of acceptance of diversity (against suppression of non-conformity) – are now under threat.

Finally, one positive development has been the growth of non-governmental organisations (NGOs) and other social movements that seek to act as new channels of popular participation in politics and linkage institutions (between citizens and the state). Although this in itself does not offer a solution to the serious challenges to democracy we consider, it is nevertheless a clear sign of democratic health.

The democratic critique of the EU

Our reflection on the problems and challenges facing European democracy begins with a brief summary of some of the ways in which the EU itself has been criticised as contributing to a weakening of mechanisms of democratic control and accountability. Many writers and commentators argue that the way in which the EU project has developed to date has been dangerously elitist, out of touch with European public opinion, and it has compounded the difficulty facing those who would try to convince Europeans that European unity is a desirable end. For example, Larry Siedentop, in his critically acclaimed *Democracy in Europe* (2000: 216–17), argues that 'European elites today are in danger of creating a profound moral and institutional crisis – a crisis of democracy – which may even call into question the identity of Europe'. This is so because they have become obsessed with the goals of market economics, expressed in technocratic language, and have not paid sufficient attention to political values, such as the dispersal of power and strong democratic accountability. Indeed, Siedentop sees a weakening of democratic accountability at the heart of the EU:

In the absence of a shared language and a Europe-wide public opinion, the appeal to democracy often becomes self-serving. Decisions taken in Brussels are opaque, the result of bureaucratic in-fighting and a lobbying process which puts a premium on special access and money. National identities and the civic traditions associated with them are being held of little account compared to the advantages of economic integration and rationalisation. In that way, alas, the market has begun to usurp its function.

(Source: Siedentop 2000.)

Over-rapid integration, for Siedentop, risks discrediting the mainstream parties of the centre-left and centre-right as the European public turns against a project that seems to serve the interests of big corporations and economic and political elites rather than ordinary people. The failure of EU policymakers to carry public opinion with them, and to make the EU a model of democratic accountability – of democracy in action – means that the EU itself may inadvertently contribute to a growth in support for extremist parties, some of which may reject democracy. Although Siedentop remains a supporter of the goal of a federal Europe, he argues that it

has to be approached gradually. For one of the pre-conditions of successful federalism is a consensus on which areas of decision-making belong to the centre and which ought to be reserved for the periphery. **Today in Europe there is no consensus** ... it cannot be created overnight. Nor can a Europe-wide political class, able to defend such a consensus and make the exercise of governmental power accountable, spring up suddenly.

(Source: Siedentop 2000: 231; emphasis in original.)

Critics of the EU on both the right and the left have highlighted some of the aspects of its democratic deficit that Siedentop discusses. On the right, various euro-sceptical parties and movements have attacked the EU's erosion of national sovereignty and of the powers of national parliaments – its tendency to override 'national identities and the civic traditions associated with them'. While some of these parties belong to the extreme right and do themselves advocate values and policies that are of dubious democratic pedigree, others are defenders of democracy (at the level of the nation-state), which they see as being threatened by bureaucratic 'big government' from Brussels. This latter group would, for example, include many UK Conservatives as well as the United Kingdom Independence Party, which shocked commentators by polling more than 16 percent in the 2004 European Parliament elections.

On the left, critics of the EU have focused on the extent to which it is dominated by big corporations and powerful interest groups, denying access to the public at large. Steve McGiffen, who works in the European Parliament as an official of the Confederal Group of the European United Left/Nordic Green Left, argues in his *The EU: a Critical Guide* (2001: 23) that the lobbying and corruption of MEPs by big business is so blatant that 'some would get marks for honesty if, like footballers, they wore the names of their corporate sponsors on their shirts'. Another left-wing critic of the undemocratic nature of the EU highlights the extent to which the 'democratic deficit' goes beyond the weakness of the European Parliament and encompasses the ability of big business to shape the agenda pursued by both the European Commission and the Council of Ministers (Carchedi 2001: 34).

All of these points help to explain why many people, on both left and right, and including some who remain fundamentally sympathetic to the cause of European integration, are becoming increasingly alarmed. Their concern is that the *nature, direction and speed* of integration at present, combined with a *profound lack of democracy and transparency* at the heart of EU policymaking, may be contributing to growing disillusionment across Europe, not only with the EU but possibly even with the efficacy of democratic politics itself.

Electoral alienation, low turnouts and the crisis of traditional parties

For many observers of the state of European democracy, electoral alienation is a cause for increasing concern. There seems to be an increasing reluctance among European electorates to engage in even that most rudimentary of democratic activities – the casting of one's vote. Low turnouts have always been a marked feature of local elections in any state that has such things. Given the focus of local elections on fairly low-level issues that seldom set any pulses racing, and given that such elections are often seen as poor substitutes for the national elections, where matters of high politics – the economy, war and security, issues of national prestige and so on – are decided, it is not surprising that this should be so. Also, local politics are often dominated by only one party or grouping, making the business of casting one's vote, at least in first-past-the post systems, seem rather pointless.

At the other end of the spectrum, casting one's vote in the elections for the European Parliament, given the latter's remoteness from the voter and its lack of much genuine power, is also something that one might predict that voters will see to be of limited point – unless one wishes to express a protest against a domestic party by using the election as a proxy for the national elections (see Table 4.3).

Table 4.3 EU average percentage turnout of voters at elections for the European Parliament

1979	63
1984	61
1989	58.6
1994	56.8
1999	49.8
2004	45.7

(Source: Eurobarometer: Post European election 2004 survey.)

From the point of view of democratic theory, low turnouts and apathy towards the issues in local and EU elections, while regrettable, need not cause too much heart-searching about the state of democracy in Europe. At least, this is true while the European Parliament continues to lack the powers and status of a genuine legislature.

It is the declining turnouts and perhaps increasing apathy of the electorate in national elections across Europe, and elsewhere in the liberal democratic world (except where voting is required by law), that has led to the claim that the state of contemporary democracy gives cause for grave concern. However, such declines in Europe, although marked, are perhaps not yet too dramatic compared with the situation in the USA, where even for presidential elections an electoral turnout around the 50 percent level has become the norm (Table 4.4 shows that EU voters achieved a turnout of 71 percent in the most recent national elections).

Table 4.4 Percentages of EU voters who voted in the European Parliament election of 2004 and in their last national election

Voted in both	40
Voted only in national	31
(= 71 in last national election)	
Abstained in both	23
Voted only in European	5

(Source: Eurobarometer: Post European Election 2004 survey.)

However, insofar as declining turnout is noticeable, various explanations are available for this phenomenon. First, it may be that it is a sign of voter contentment. Where there are no burning issues on which society is strongly divided, and where governments, of whatever complexion, are seen to be doing a reasonably good job, the cost of voting outweighs the benefits of doing so for many voters. Then there is the 'Tweedledum and Tweedledee' explanation, that voters cannot see any real difference between the major parties and so see no point in wasting time voting. This 'interchangeability of parties' view may in turn be explained on the basis of the emergence of ideological consensus across society (the 'end of ideology' thesis), or it may be the result of the adoption by a major party of the tactic of 'stealing their opponents' clothes' (sometimes called 'triangulation') so as to leave them no room to make a distinctive policy choice to offer to the electorate. This

Figure 4.5 NGOs trying to make their voices heard
Source: K.-D. Borchardt (2002).

tactic will tempt politicians, particularly on the left of politics, who emphasise the need to acquire power in order to do anything worthwhile. It involves acceptance of the implication that one may only be able to achieve a limited amount of what one really stands for. This is the 'half a loaf is better than none' phenomenon.

Then there are rather more mechanistic explanations, such as the nature of the voting system. First-past-the-post gives major parties what many see as an unfair advantage, provided the support for those parties is not spread too evenly around the country, and leads to a sense on the part of those who wish to support minor parties that there is no point in voting. At best it might lead to tactical voting, if people feel sufficiently motivated to try to keep one major party from gaining power, even though their first preference would be some party other than the one likely to win if the tactical voting strategy works. Even when the system allows for proportional representation, and so some prospect of your preferred party's having at least a share in power via its membership of a coalition government, this can lead to disillusionment if too many of your favoured party's election promises have to be set aside as the cost of gaining a share in power.

Whatever the explanation may be of declining turnouts in national elections, and there may be different explanations in different states, it is perhaps a long stretch to the idea that this betokens some deep-seated unhappiness with the democratic system as a whole. As we will see, participation in NGOs and protest politics shows that citizens of European states are not indifferent to politics or to policy outcomes. There is no evidence of a desire among large numbers of the electorate to return to pre-democratic forms, or to the one-party systems of the 'people's democracies' of the former Soviet bloc. Nor does there seem to be any great desire to extend democratic forms of decision making beyond the customary bounds, into the workplace, for example. Oscar Wilde's comment, that the trouble with social-ism is that one never has enough free evenings, still seems to resonate with many people. That said, the recent rise of extremist and anti-democratic parties in a number of countries shows that there is also no room for complacency about the state of European democracy.

The extreme right and the challenge to democracy

Extreme right-wing parties have been on the rise in a number of European coun-tries throughout the past 15 years or so. Whereas, a generation ago, the presence of the Soviet Union and its allies on the other side of the 'iron curtain' that divided the European continent generated widespread fears of a communist threat to European democracy, there is no doubt today that the primary threat to democracy comes not from the extreme left but from the extreme right. Those European communist par-ties that remain as significant political forces in the post-Soviet era have mostly been fully reconciled to democracy. Some – such as the Spanish and Italian commu-nists – had already become enthusiastic defenders of multi-party parliamentary democracy long before Gorbachev came to the leadership of the Soviet Union in 1985. By contrast, many of the extreme right parties that have seen their support grow dramatically in recent years have preached a message that challenges democ-racy's core values. That message emphasises such anti-democratic themes as extreme nationalism, xenophobia, racism, hostility to pluralist democracy, and support for repressive state power (Mudde 2000: 11).

Table 4.5 shows that in a number of European countries in recent general (national) elections, extreme right parties have polled between 10 and 20 percent of the total votes cast. Indeed, this by no means reflects the full picture. Some of these parties have shown an ability to poll much higher than these figures. In 1999, for example, the extreme right in Austria polled an astonishing 27 percent, and in 2002, the French extreme right leader, Jean-Marie Le Pen, shocked democratic France by overtaking the Socialist candidate in the first round of that country's presidential elections with almost 17 percent – allowing him to enter a second round run-off with President Jacques Chirac.

Table 4.5 Electoral support for the extreme right in a number of European countries in recent national elections

Country	Parties	% of total vote	Year
Austria	Freedom Party (FPÖ)	10.0	2002
Belgium	Flemish Block (VB)	11.6	2003
	National Front (FN)	2.0	
Denmark	Danish People's Party (DF)	12.0	2001
France	National Front (FN)	11.3	2002
	Republican National Movement (MNR)	1.1	
Italy	National Alliance (AN)	12.0	2001
	Northern Leagues (LN)	3.9	
	splinter groups	0.4	
Romania	Greater Romania Party (PMR)	19.5	2000

(Source: derived from Elections around the World website, http://www.electionworld.org.)

There are many reasons why extreme right-wing parties have performed so well electorally in Europe in recent years. These parties have sought to exploit growing fears over mass unemployment and deindustrialisation by focusing anger on immigrant workers, asylum seekers or simply anyone whose skin colour is different from that of the white majority and targeting these people as scapegoats for economic and social problems. For example, the French National Front has sought to draw a simple, and entirely bogus, correlation between high unemployment and immigration. Popular fears over immigration have been heightened by irresponsible newspaper reporting, including exaggeration of the figures, and the extreme right has played this theme repeatedly. Such parties have also drawn on a longstanding tradition of racism towards indigenous minorities, such as Jews and Roma (Gypsy) people, in many European countries. In addition, they have benefited from a backlash in some quarters over rapidly changing moral, social and cultural values by attacking homosexuals, single parents, feminists, secularists and liberals. Thus, Umberto Bossi, the Italian Northern Leagues leader, sought to project a 'macho' image for his party by ordering the expulsion of any party members who were found to be homosexual and calling for mass expulsion from Italy of immigrants; and Jean-Marie Le Pen, the French National Front leader, tried to win tacit Vatican approval by attacking the legalisation of abortion.

But the extreme right has also benefited from a number of other issues that European policymakers have failed to address properly. The elitist nature of the EU – its failure to connect with ordinary people (discussed above) – has allowed the extreme right to attack the EU in the name of nationalism. Many of these parties advocate withdrawal from, or partial dismantling of, the EU, portraying themselves as champions of the nation-state against 'Brussels'. They have also frequently taken up the cudgels against globalisation, offering a heady mixture of nationalism (accusing globalisation of undermining national cultures and calling for economic protectionism), racism and xenophobia (accusing globalisation of 'threatening the white race' by facilitating labour migration into Europe, and from Eastern to Western Europe), and economic populism (portraying themselves as champions of the 'small man' against the big global corporations). The extreme right has also sought to exploit the growing sense that both centre-left and centre-right parties offer basically the same sort of policies nowadays to attack all mainstream parties as out-of-date and 'corrupt' and to put themselves forward as 'new'. In one sense, the growing success of the extreme right reflects the failure of democratic parties to connect with the mass of voters. Centre-right parties have not always come up with solutions to the social problems and damage to communities that can spring from rampant free-market neo-liberalism. Left and centre-left parties have struggled – and often failed – to explain convincingly how their traditional values of equality and solidarity can still be translated into concrete policies in a world where any alternative to neo-liberalism seems at times Utopian. Thus the extreme right has sought – albeit in a shallow and demagogic way – to fill a real political vacuum that has grown in recent years in much of Europe.

There are many variants of extreme right parties. Not all follow the same policies, above all in the economic field, where their policy positions can range from enthusiastic free-market neo-liberalism to support for strong state intervention in the economy. Nevertheless, it is possible to identify a number of core values that almost all of these parties share, which are summarised in Key concept 4.2.

Key concept 4.2

Core ideological features and themes of extreme right-wing parties

- *Nationalism (usually ethnic)*: belief in a strong state that is congruent with the dominant ethnic community. Only people deemed as belonging to the dominant ethnic community have the right to live within the borders of the state. Foreigners are accepted, if at all, only as guest workers without political rights and entitlements.

- *Exclusionism*: a distinction is drawn between (for example) ethnic or religious groups whereby one group ('us') is included and other groups ('them') are excluded. This is often accompanied by racism, anti-semitism, etc.

- *Xenophobia*: fear, hate or hostility towards foreigners, immigrants or asylum seekers. Anything 'alien' is branded as 'threatening'.

- *Anti-democratic features*: criticism of democracy as a political system. Opposition to the core values of democracy, such as pluralism, political equality, parliamentary government. Espousal of elitism, intolerance, authoritarianism, strict hierarchy.

- *Populism*: demagogic appeals to 'the common man'. Manipulation of popular prejudice.

- *Anti-party sentiments*: manipulation of popular disenchantment with politics, or alienation from the political process, in order to launch virulent attacks on mainstream political parties. Sometimes involves rejection of multi-party democracy altogether and advocacy of one-party state.

- *The strong state*: emphasis on law and order policies, hard punishments, support for state repression. Militarism – sometimes including support for aggressive foreign policies.

- *Traditional values*: claim to have a strong ethical outlook by espousing traditional moral and religious values (opposition to abortion rights, support for discrimination against non-heterosexuals, opposition to secular and liberal values). Hostility towards feminism and towards non-traditional families (such as single parents). Attempts to use traditional religious views to advocate a moral backlash against modern, pluralist society.

- *Socio-economic policies*: these vary greatly between extreme right parties, but almost all emphasise what is sometimes called 'welfare chauvinism' – the belief that jobs and social benefits should be reserved primarily for members of the dominant ethnic group ('our own people'). They typically also believe that the state should protect 'national' industry against 'foreign' competition.

(Source: Adapted from Mudde 2000: 187–9.)

It will be readily apparent from this summary that many of the extreme right's core values at best sit uneasily alongside the traditions of European democracy and at worst are reminiscent of the dark days of Nazism and fascism during the 1930s and 1940s. Yet democratic politicians of both right and left, and political commentators, have been divided on how to react to the extreme right-wing challenge to democracy. There was outrage across Europe when the Austrian extremist Freedom Party (FPÖ), led by Jörg Haider, a man who has praised the Waffen SS and whose supporters have sometimes been seen giving the Hitler salute at rallies, polled 27 percent of the vote in November 1999 and entered coalition government with the Christian Democrats. EU leaders imposed temporary (and largely symbolic) sanctions against Austria. Yet few European leaders demurred when Silvio Berlusconi formed his second Italian coalition government in 2001, bringing two extremist parties – the neo-fascist (now self-styled as 'post-fascist') National Alliance (AN) and the racist Northern Leagues (LN) – into government. Europe, it seems, was becoming accustomed to the presence of the extreme right in government. Some commentators have argued that the presence of the extreme right in coalition governments will have a moderating effect on them. They believe that by bringing the extreme right in from the cold, and exposing them to the constraints and responsibilities of government, the extreme right will:

- be forced to abandon 'irresponsible' rhetoric;
- play by the democratic ground rules;
- lose their 'novelty' value;
- lose their ability to rant against governing parties.

They argue that the wings of the extreme right may be clipped and their support reduced. There is some evidence in support of this. The Austrian FPÖ, at the time of writing, remains in government but has seen its support drop from 27 percent to 10 percent. And both the AN and LN in Italy have suffered electoral setbacks recently.

However, other commentators argue that to bring the extremists into the orbit of government – or to seek to win back those who vote for them by adopting hard-line policies on immigration or citizens' rights that pander to racial prejudice – is to play with fire. It risks undermining core democratic values and shifting the centre of gravity of European politics dangerously towards the extreme. As Angus Roxburgh (2002: 17) argues: 'the risk of infection by far-right ideas is as danger-ous, at least, as the extremists themselves'.

One thing appears certain: as Europeans, in 2005, marked the sixtieth anniver-sary of the liberation of the Nazi extermination camps where millions of innocent people were brutally murdered, the need for vigilance against the simplistic propa-ganda of those who are indifferent to the pain and suffering (and human rights) of their fellow human beings whom they have branded as 'alien', 'inferior', or even 'subhuman' is as great as ever.

Non-governmental organisations and the democracy of interest and protest

The conventional analysis of democratic processes in liberal democracies uses the concept of 'linkage mechanisms' to refer to the ways in which citizens' policy pref-erences are converted into policy initiatives and legislative outcomes at the level of government. Elections, referenda and parties are examples of such linkage institu-tions, built into the formal structures of the political system, but there are also vitally important linkage institutions that are located within the civil society of democratic polities.

The media constitute one such linkage institution, at least considered in their role as conduits of public opinion (as well as being important shapers of such opin-ion). In a political culture in which, for the purposes of creating election-winning strategies, political parties increasingly turn to focus groups to discover how their policy lines are playing out in the minds of the public, media-focused expressions of discontent can have an important impact upon the ways in which elected govern-ments conduct their business. This may be at a relatively superficial level, of 'spin' and management of political news, in which timing and presentation of policy ini-tiatives and outcomes become all-important. It may be at a more fundamental level, where a government postpones, greatly modifies or abandons one of its policy com-mitments in the light of a campaign of criticism and dissent conducted via, and thus with the considerable help of, some influential elements of the mass media.

Such campaigns conducted via, and with the aid of, some part of the mass media rarely emerge without the efforts of the other important kind of linkage institution to be found in the civil society of a liberal democratic polity – the non-governmental organisation (NGO). This term has begun to supersede older notions prevalent in political science – those of the interest group, pressure group and protest group. NGOs encompass all those organised and semi-organised groups of citizens that lie outside the formal structure of government and that possess the latent or actual ability to mobilise their members and supporters in pursuit of some policy aim that they all, or mostly, support. The term 'NGO' therefore encompasses such entities as corporations and groups of them (within manufacturers' organisations, for example), trades unions, consumer protection groups, think tanks, charities and humanitarian organisations, philanthropic foundations, local protest groups, and churches.

Many such NGOs were not formed to pursue a specific political purpose but were designed to foster and support some shared set of values or purposes. Even charities, which are often very restricted in their political roles by legislation, can nevertheless play an important role in political campaigns with other NGOs in pursuit of some shared aim.

The most important distinction between NGOs is between those that appeal primarily to their members' legitimate self-interest and those that ask of their members some commitment to a shared ideal, the pursuit of which may involve some sacrifice of self-interest – even if this is only in the form of the sacrifice of time, money and effort. In other words, some NGOs rely upon idealism of some sort. Others rely upon their reputation for efficacy in protecting and enhancing their members' self-interest. As is well known, the latter kind of NGO is at an advantage over the former kind, for the latter is better placed to cope with the free-rider problem, which involves individuals accepting benefits conferred as the result of the efforts of others without themselves contributing to those efforts. An interest-serving NGO can more easily identify which members are benefiting without contributing and can more easily bring pressure to bear upon them to take a proper share of the effort. Such NGOs are less prone to free-riding in the first place, because individual members can more easily see that a successful effort to protect their interests does require a contribution from all the members, and the amount of interest protection they receive will usually be large enough for individuals to feel justified in making the effort to participate.

Idealist groups, such as environmental protection groups, are, by contrast, seeking to obtain benefits, such as reduced environmental pollution, that affect any given individual only slightly and that may be obtained if sufficient, but not most, members participate in trying to secure it. In such a situation, the temptation to free-ride is rather high unless individuals feel sufficiently strongly in favour of the aim. In other words, they must be idealistic about the issue to some degree. What is perhaps remarkable is that idealistic NGOs should exist at all in such circumstances. But they do, and they have sufficient success often enough to be an important part of the political landscape of liberal democracies.

The range of NGOs operating within the EU can be gauged from the contents of the directory of EU-level interest groups produced in March 2000 by the Secretariat-General of the European Commission (see Table 4.6).

The final dimension of linkage institutions to be aware of is that of the social movement, in which constellations of linkage institutions – parties, media sources and NGOs (some interest-pursuing, some idealistic) – form alliances in the pursuit of some broad political aim. Examples abound from the history of democratic polities, in Europe and elsewhere – the labour movement, the feminist movement, the environmental movement, the nuclear disarmament movement, and so forth. In

Table 4.6 European NGOs classified by issue area, March 2000

Religious	10
Consumers, social and welfare policy	37
Development aid and human rights	30
Animal, nature and environmental protection	23
Trade unions	16
Regions and cities	15
Small and medium-sized firms	10
Services	313
Industry	289
Agriculture	129
Various diffuse interests	30
Total	**902**

(Source: Cini 2003: 198.)

contemporary Europe as elsewhere, a notable example is the (perhaps misnamed) anti-globalisation movement.

In considering the importance for the working of democracy of NGOs and social movements in contemporary Europe, it will be important to consider three main foci:

1. the internal politics of the longer-standing European liberal democracies, such as the UK and France;

2. those states that until the collapse of communism operated a version of democracy in which the state/civil society distinction was not (fully) operable and that have been developing civil societies on the liberal democratic model (or re-establishing them) only in the last decade and a half. In addition to Russia itself, within this group it may be useful to distinguish between new states that were once independent polities, at least to some degree (the Czech Republic and Poland, say) and those that were incorporated in the former Soviet Union (e.g. Belarus, Ukraine);

3. there is also the issue of how far the EU can be said to accommodate the impact and importance of NGOs and social movements.

In the longer-standing European states, NGOs and social movements are highly active and can on occasion involve large numbers of people in campaigns, demonstrations and even forms of direct action that take them into conflict with the law. It is remarkable how quickly such forms of action can bubble up to confront even very recently undertaken governmental action, such as the huge numbers of protesters in Italy, Spain and the UK against their governments' planned involvement in the invasion of Iraq in 2002–03. The protests in the UK against high fuel taxes in September 2000, which involved well-organised forms of direct action, are another example, as is the Countryside Alliance's many rallies since 2001 in protest against the UK government's policies for the countryside, especially in connection with the foxhunting issue. The latter two examples are, arguably, illustrations of interest-serving activity by NGOs and their allies in the media and elsewhere. However, the first is even more impressive as an example of idealism – individuals spending non-negligible amounts of time, money and effort in the attempt to dissuade their government from pursuing a policy that is unlikely to have much direct impact on the personal interests of many of the individuals concerned.

In the older liberal democracies, the phenomenon of NGO protest and lobbying activity has long been accepted as part of the legitimate scope of citizens' involvement in the political system, although it is inherently a rather hit-and-miss affair. None of the three examples mentioned resulted in victory for the campaigners, although the fuel protesters had some limited impact upon the UK government's policy on fuel taxes. But in some of the older European democracies, NGOs have used direct action to significant effect, the French farmers' protests over recent decades being only the most obvious example. If the existence and effectiveness of NGO activity is a measure of the health of a liberal democracy, then there appears to be no reason yet to suppose that the older European democracies are showing any marked lack of vitality.

With respect to social movements, there is also evidence of ongoing activity and occasional effectiveness in the achievement of aims. The environmental movement, for example, has campaigned with some effect against the introduction of genetically modified food into the European marketplace. This has involved a many-pronged strategy, ranging from direct (if largely symbolic) action against crop trials to political lobbying, participation of environmental NGOs in public inquiries, and the provision of arguments and evidence in at least some sections of the media. The targets of this activity, as so often, are not just governmental institutions but also other NGOs – in this case, the biotechnology multinationals, such as Monsanto, which have been trying to market their products in Europe.

The anti-globalisation movement has lost some of the high profile it had established prior to '9/11', but the various NGOs involved in its activities remain committed to fighting the various elements of globalisation that they see as pernicious. Given its highly idealistic and non-specific set of aims, it is unlikely ever to attract large amounts of support within the mainstream of European public opinion. However, its environmentalist tone and its concern with the injustices of developing countries' debt and the manifest unfairness of 'free trade' as it currently operates give its concerns at least some resonance for many other political actors in Europe and elsewhere (see Soborski 2004).

With respect to the states of the former Soviet bloc, it is possible to see much evidence of a vibrant NGO and protest sector of politics. Indeed, for all that the countries behind the Iron Curtain were supposed to have been subjected to a form of totalitarian rule that had extinguished anything resembling a civil society in the Western European mould, there has been no more impressive example of the power of popular protest and mass action on the streets than the various episodes that constituted the revolutions in the late 1980s and early 1990s in many of those states, leading to the overturn of their communist regimes.

This tradition of mass popular protest has carried on in some of the parts of former Yugoslavia and the Soviet Union that have become independent states during the last 15 years, such as Belarus, Georgia and Serbia. Here the issue has often turned on the attempt by politicians to corrupt the democratic process in order to secure power in the face of popular rejection. This has led to mass demonstrations, defection of elements of the governing security apparatus to the side of the protesters and the ejection from office of the offending figures. It is becoming apparent that the protesters, for example in Ukraine, have had some powerful allies, notably the USA, which has provided expertise, funds and other sources of aid to mount successful protests (see Traynor 2004).

On the one hand, the need for such demonstrations might lead to a pessimistic view of the prospects for democracy in those states. On the other hand, the readiness of large numbers of citizens of those states to take the risks involved in mass demonstration to eject powerful political figures might well be taken as the most optimistic sign that such democratic practices are in safe hands.

Finally, what of the EU and its relation to the politics of interest and protest? An examination of the relation of the European Commission to the environmental movement highlights two important points. The first is that the Commission's Environment Directorate has made some concerted attempts to ensure that as many NGOs as possible have been consulted in the course of preparing environmental legislation. The second is that some NGOs have been better able to take up those opportunities than others. The corporate sector has been more influential on matters of environmental legislation than have the environmental NGOs. This is not surprising, because the corporate sector does not have the problems of free-riding to contend with, given its interest-protection focus, possesses copious amounts of cash and expertise and, in virtue of its undeniable economic importance, is always going to receive the careful consideration of government at all levels. It is not really possible to speak of a European environmental movement (Rootes 2004). The styles of political activity and the issues and priorities of environmental NGOs across the EU have been too disjointed to produce anything resembling such a movement. With the accession to the EU of states from Central and Eastern Europe, where issues of development and catching up with the West may be expected to predominate in the near future, it seems unlikely that NGOs dedicated to protecting the environment will be more successful.

The prospects for the creation of effective EU-wide NGOs and effective protest activities do not seem very promising for the same kinds of reason as apply to the environmental case. NGO activity seems to be most effective in domestic political settings. It has its most effective outcomes when national politicians use the appropriate intergovernmental institutions, such as the European Council, to give voice to views that their own electorates, often operating via NGOs, have shown to be important to them.

In conclusion, then, it can be said that the aspect of democratic activity that centres on the formation of NGOs and their pursuit of political aims and policies via all the forms of legitimate action available to them appears to be in reasonably good shape wherever one looks in contemporary Europe.

Further reading

Barry, J., Baxter, B. and Dunphy, R. (eds) (2004) *Europe, Globalization and Sustainable Development*, Routledge, London, contains several very useful chapters.

Carchedi, G. (2001) *For Another Europe: A Class Analysis of European Economic Integration* , Verso, London.

Cini, M. (2003) *EU Politics*, Oxford University Press, Oxford.

Dunphy, R. (2004) *Contesting Capitalism? Left Parties and European Integration*, Manchester University Press, Manchester.

Fraser, N. (2000) *The Voice of Modern Hatred: Encounters with Europe's New Right*, Picador, London.

McGiffen, S.P. (2001) *The EU: A Critical Guide*, Pluto Press, London.

Mudde, C. (2000) *The Ideology of the Extreme Right*, Manchester University Press, Manchester.

Roxburgh, A. (2002) *Preachers of Hate: The Rise of the Far Right*, Gibson Square Books, London.

Section 4.4

Citizenship, human rights and migration

The Treaty of Amsterdam, signed on 2 October 1997, states that European integration is to be developed as a 'European area of freedom, security and justice'. A specific agenda for this field, known in the EU as 'Justice and Home Affairs', was established at the summit meeting in Tampere (Finland) in October 1999 and covers four key areas of action:

1. rights and citizenship;
2. migration, asylum and border controls;
3. judicial and legal cooperation;
4. improved cooperation in policing and crime prevention with action to combat cross-border crime such as terrorism and drugs (European Commission 2004a).

Following some rather slow progress, the European Council meeting (November 2004) established the Hague Programme, or, confusingly, also 'Tampere II', with targets for achieving a common European policy on migration and asylum by 2010. It also proposed that decisions on these issues would be taken by qualified majority voting rather than requiring unanimity (http://www.uropa.eu.int/comm./justice_home).

The wider context here is tensions throughout Europe, and for individual European states, between on the one hand moves towards increasingly open borders to facilitate the free movement of people, capital and services and on the other hand attempts to regulate these flows (Xanthaki 2002). Over the last few decades, border controls within the EU have been reduced, specifically within the Schengen area (see Key fact 4.1), in which EU citizens can travel without showing passports. However, open borders bring other challenges, such as the need for cross-border cooperation on policing. Increased attention is being paid to the need to develop the policing and control of the external borders of the EU in relation to crime and terrorism but also in respect of different forms of immigration: 'while freedom and justice, democracy, respect for human rights and the rule of law' are foundations of the EU, 'they can be enjoyed fully only in an environment of security' (European Communities 2004: 4). At the same time, the EU and European states have adopted policies to make more effective the experience of this common European space for its citizens, expanding on the nature of EU citizenship and on the rights of those living in the EU. Action is also being taken to ensure that the diverse population groups within the EU (who may or may not be EU citizens) are integrated effectively into the moves towards economic and social cohesion in Europe and are not subjected to discrimination.

Key fact 4.1

The Schengen area

Two agreements (1985 and 1990), the first signed in the Luxembourg town of Schengen, established the principles of an area in which there would be no internal border controls, the common external border being controlled in accordance with agreed principles. The Schengen area came into existence in 1995. All of the EU15 countries except Ireland and the UK have more or less abolished internal border controls, although Denmark, France and Germany have retained some controls. In addition, the non-EU countries of Iceland and Norway are participants in the Schengen area.

Concomitant with the reduction in border controls was increasing international cooperation between customs, police and judicial systems. All the EU15 countries plus Iceland and Norway participate in this, which includes, for example, Eurodac, an arrangement for the exchange of fingerprint records.

(Source: http://www.europa.eu.int/scadplus/leg.)

These are challenging issues for Europe, raising questions about the relative importance of the EU and nation-states in decision making on matters of central importance to national sovereignty. As the European Commission recognises: 'it has not always been possible [thus far] to reach agreement at European level for the adoption of certain sensitive measures relating to policies which remain at the core of national sovereignty' (European Commission 2004a: 4). This has already been demonstrated by initial failure to achieve the first deadline of the Tampere programme in 2004. Progress depends in part on the extent to which decision making around issues of justice and home affairs move from the 'third pillar' of intergovernmental decision making (established in the Maastricht Treaty and using unanimous voting) to the EU's normal 'community method' (as proposed in the Constitutional Treaty). Agreement is difficult, and the European Parliament has expressed concern about the lack of democratic legitimacy for this policy area, since it has had only a consultative role thus far. Nevertheless, there has been progress on a range of measures, and all new member states are required to meet these obligations as part of the criteria for membership. This has been facilitated by EU funding of the preparation of candidate countries for their duties in justice and home affairs as well as in the economic and political spheres.

It is in this context, then, that the themes of citizenship, human rights and migration are discussed in turn below. Key questions informing this discussion involve the relative significance of EU policy and that of nation-states in these areas, the balance between issues of security and encouraging mobility and freedom, and the wider issue of how such processes create new forms of belonging and new spaces of exclusion and inequality in Europe.

Citizenship and rights in Europe

> Citizenship of the Union is hereby established. Every person holding the nationality of a Member State shall be a citizen of the Union. Citizenship of the Union shall complement and not replace national citizenship.

(Source: Article 17 of Maastricht Treaty.)

When the Maastricht Treaty came into force on 1 November 1993, every citizen of a member state of the EU became a citizen of the EU too. EU citizenship does not replace national citizenship, bringing with it instead additional rights and responsibilities. Citizens of new member states automatically become EU citizens with their country's accession to the EU. These rights and duties are constantly being incorporated more explicitly into the EU's treaties, although key elements have remained central over the years and are considered below in relation to freedom of movement and residence, civil and political rights, human and fundamental rights, and anti-discrimination measures.

Freedom of movement and residence

Article 18 of the Maastricht Treaty defines the right to free movement and residence as a citizen's right within the EU. Perhaps the most obvious manifestation of EU citizenship for most Europeans is their maroon-coloured EU-style passport and the ease with which they can pass border controls. Freedom of movement, that is the right to travel freely within the EU, is enshrined in the various treaties of the EU, starting with the commitment to the free movement of labour in 1951, when the movement of 'citizen-workers' (Castles and Davidson 2000) was incorporated as part of the broader project of realising a common market with the free movement of capital, goods and services. Rights of movement and residence developed over time and were extended by three directives in 1990 to those not in work (pensioners, students and the economically inactive), subject to them having sufficient resources and health and social insurance cover for themselves and their family. These rights of movement and residence were confirmed with the establishment of EU citizenship in 1993 and further underpinned in the Treaty of Amsterdam so that every EU citizen has the right to move and live where she or he wants, without reference to economic activity, so long as the criteria for social insurance and sufficient resources are fulfilled. In addition to such rights for EU citizens, visitors from non-EU countries may enter the Schengen area with an appropriate visa and travel freely within it for up to three months, and non-EU nationals with a valid residence permit issued by a Schengen country may travel for short periods to other Schengen countries without a visa. However, all rights of movement and residence for EU citizens and non-EU citizens are explicitly subject to limitations on grounds of either public policy, public security or public health.

EU citizens not only have the right to travel freely within the EU (subject to some important variations on border controls between the Schengen area and non-Schengen area countries), but they also have the right to settle anywhere within the

EU's territory. This right of residence is currently used by around five million EU citizens, while many others commute daily across national borders, travel as long-term tourists or move to study. However, there are transitional restrictions on some of these rights in relation to citizens of the new member states following enlargement (see opinion 4.2).

Opinion 4.2

Restrictions on freedom of movement for workers from the new member states after enlargement

In response to worries from member states about the possibility of a large number of workers arriving from the new member states following enlargement on 1 May 2004, transitional arrangements restrict the freedom of movement of workers from these states (with the exception of Cyprus and Malta). The EU15 states may allow 'total or partial freedom of movement of workers' during a maximum period of seven years. At a minimum, the EU15 states may not make their pre-existing arrangements more restrictive, and new member states may institute reciprocal requirements for permits. 2006 will see an interim assessment of the policy, after which full freedom of movement can be implemented or the transitional arrangements extended to 2009. Thereafter, individual states may apply to extend the arrangements for a maximum of two more years if 'major disruption to their labour markets' is observed. Thereafter, complete freedom of movement of workers will apply.

Oddly, perhaps, this policy arrangement restricts the movement of workers (due to concerns about their impacts on labour markets) but does not restrict movement for non-employment reasons (e.g. students or pensioners). Workers who are nevertheless accepted into the labour market of an EU15 member state are entitled to normal rights such as the right to residence, non-discrimination and protection of workers.

A similar initial restriction was introduced in the 1980s when Portugal and Spain joined the EU. However, contrary to worries about a huge influx of workers, experience there suggested that emigration decreased after enlargement and the transition period was shortened. A Eurobarometer survey suggests that in the present situation only around 1 percent of those of working age in the new member states are considering moving. Furthermore, the concern should arguably be rather that those most likely to move are the young and highly skilled and qualified, the loss of whom through brain-drain to the EU15 states would be detrimental to the economies of the new member states.

(Source: http://www.europa.eu.int/comm/employment_social/.)

What do you think the policy should be?

Despite long-term moves to make residence in other EU states possible for EU citizens, fewer EU citizens currently live and work elsewhere in the EU than live and work outside the EU altogether. Since the development of mobility and the right of residence are seen as key means by which European identity can be consolidated further, a recent EU directive has sought to simplify the right of every EU citizen to move and reside freely within the EU along with their family (whether or not their family members, defined as spouse or registered partner, dependent children and dependent older people, are EU citizens themselves). The directive, to be put into effect by 2006, simplifies the need for registration in the country of residence and also introduces a permanent right of residence for EU citizens and their families after a period of five years. It also gives greater protection to family members who are non-EU citizens in the event of the death of, or divorce from, the EU citizen on whom they depend. In addition, there is provision in the directive to require member states to facilitate the entry and residence of partners who are not legally married but with whom the EU citizen has a 'durable relationship duly attested'. Other measures to improve the experience of residence elsewhere in the EU include moves towards mutual recognition of legal and financial decisions in other member states (such as divorce settlements or reclamation of debts owed), rights to certain minimum standards in access to justice (including when accused of an offence), with the services of an interpreter if necessary. A directive on the mutual recognition of qualifications also seeks to facilitate the mobility of labour. The long-term aim is to create a system where EU citizens can in principle move between member states in a similar way to moving within a nation-state. See Opinion 4.3 for a discussion of the ways in which many people already use these rights to develop new forms of transnational belonging in Europe.

Opinion 4.3

Mobile Europe: new forms of belonging within Europe

For many EU citizens, their practical experience of 'being European' comes from forms of mobility, from business travel to traditional package holidays, from retirement and second home migration to cheap weekend jaunts facilitated by low-cost airlines and high-speed transport networks, from student exchanges to school trips (McNeil 2004). Increasing numbers of northern Europeans have taken advantage of the rights of residence offered by EU citizenship to relocate either periodically or permanently to southern Europe for their 'place in the sun'. Moving mostly for quality of life reasons rather than economic factors, key pull factors include the desire for a more relaxed way of life, escape from the cold and rain of northern Europe and the possibility of a more sociable retirement.

Evidence of the extent to which such migrants develop a more 'European' consciousness is mixed. In one study of UK expatriate (expat) residents on the Costa del Sol in Spain, for example, Karen O'Reilly (2000) shows that many migrants move in search of a particular version of 'Spanish' life, one very much associated with the landscapes and practices of the areas already dominated by mass tourism from the UK. Many do not learn much Spanish, and they tend to socialise with other expats. As such, the expats do not necessarily develop a more 'European' outlook. They may in fact have a strongly 'British' identity, reinforced by the experience of expat life. At the same time, there is evidence of their developing a sense of being part of a spatially extended set of social networks, part of a 'transnational community' between the UK and Spain. In contrast, Buller and Hoggart (1994) found that UK people relocating to rural France seemed more integrated with their local communities, learning French and generally not wishing to socialise with other expats. Whether this constituted a new 'post-national' European identity is not clear, although there is evidence of a clear sense of identity of being British in France. However, not all French communities have welcomed the British arrivals – *The Guardian* (24 February 2005) described protests in the Breton village of Bourbiac; one of the village residents was reported as saying 'We are not anti-British ourselves, but anti-British feeling is growing in Brittany and we are tapping into that. Unless something is done, the British will be targets. In small villages, the British come and almost take the village over. The local people feel overwhelmed'. The Bretons are reported as feeling that the British need to integrate more, learn French and make an effort to appreciate the local culture.

These examples suggest that while mobility and the right to residence within the EU is welcomed by many, the assumption that such moves will lead to new forms of post-national European consciousness are perhaps exaggerated. Migration can as easily serve to reinforce stereotypes, with migrants seeking a fixed or romanticised version of the region to which they have moved, or drawing on an essentialised notion of their home identity.

What do you think? What is your experience?

Civic and political rights

EU citizenship also entails civil and political rights. EU citizens have the right to vote for candidates and to stand for election to the European Parliament in either their country of residence or their home state, if that is different, although they may not vote in both. They also have the right to vote for and stand as candidates at municipal elections in whichever member state they are resident. In local elections, member states may stipulate that only their own national citizens may hold leadership posts (such as a local mayor). There is also scope for a member state to derogate from these arrangements if more than 20 percent of the eligible electorate are non-national EU citizens. This is the case in Luxembourg, for example, where the government may require a longer minimum period of residence for participation in local elections.

Citizens also have a right to access documents of the Parliament, Commission and Council of Ministers under certain conditions, and to contact and receive a response from any EU institution in any one of the EU's official languages. They have a right to petition the European Parliament and to complain to the European ombudsman. Citizens also have access to the diplomatic and consular protection of another member state when outside the EU. Further proposals include addressing the loss of the right to take part in certain national elections that affects some EU citizens while resident elsewhere in the EU.

In recognition of the limited access to these wider rights (of political voice, as well as of movement and residence across the EU) for those who are not EU citizens, but have a legal right to live or work in one of the EU member states (known as 'third country nationals'), there have been proposals for a limited form of 'civic citizenship'. This would give legal immigrants core rights and obligations, including the right to live and work in another EU member state, rights that they might acquire incrementally over a number of years. Other policies in this area include those on family reunification. Overall, these proposals are particularly aimed at facilitating the participation of skilled migrants in the EU economy and at countering discrimination against non-EU citizens currently working in the EU. These non-EU citizens also have some levels of protection under the Council of Europe human rights legislation.

Human rights and fundamental rights

Rights of EU citizenship sit alongside the increasingly important issue of human rights, central to which is the European Convention on Human Rights (ECHR), established in 1950 by the Council of Europe and with over 40 European countries as signatories, including all member states of the EU. The ECHR is upheld by the European Court of Human Rights, which is based in Strasbourg, and which acts as a court of last resort for claims not resolved at national level. Although its member states are signatories to the ECHR, the EU itself is not as yet a signatory to the convention. However, over the years in its rulings on the activities of EU institutions and in respect of member states and their implementation of EU policies, the European Court of Justice (ECJ) has recognised the importance of such fundamental rights as human dignity and the principle of non-discrimination. The EEC Treaty of Rome and the Maastricht Treaty do not list such fundamental rights, with the exception of the principle of equal pay for men and women, which was in the Treaty of Rome (article 119). However, the Single European Act (1986) and the Maastricht Treaty (1992) do formally require the EU to respect the rights laid out in the ECHR. This was further underpinned by the Treaty of Amsterdam's commitment to a number of fundamental principles (such as 'liberty', 'freedom', 'respect for human rights', 'the rule of law' and 'fundamental freedoms'). The Treaty of Amsterdam gave power to the ECJ to ensure that such principles are respected by EU institutions and, for the first time, allowed for sanctions against any member state in breach of these principles (including suspension of membership and voting rights). Specifically, the Treaty of Amsterdam extended the general principle of non-discrimination on grounds of nationality to allow the EU to take action 'to combat discrimination based on sex, racial or ethnic origin, religion or belief, disability, age or sexual orientation' (articles 12 and 13).

Over the years, therefore, the issue of human rights and fundamental rights has become more prominent in the politics of Europe, including the EU, yet the EU was in a slightly anomalous position of having the ECJ ruling on issues of human rights but with no specified legally enforceable set of rights. The ECJ in particular was keen to see a clearly defined set of rights, rather than the mix of case law, national traditions and treaty articles that had emerged and that had to be reconciled with the ECHR (Meehan 2002). The Cologne European Council meeting (June 1999) decided to draft the 'Charter of Fundamental Rights', which would set out clearly the 'personal, civil, political, economic and social rights of the peoples of the EU' (European Communities 2004b: 4).

The charter, drafted by a convention of representatives of national governments, the EU institutions and the European Parliament, was 'solemnly proclaimed' at the Nice European Council (December 1999) (see Key fact 4.2). The charter has been incorporated into the Constitutional Treaty, and future changes to the legal status of the EU would allow the EU itself to accede to the ECHR. The charter contains a mix of generally applicable human rights that apply to all persons living in the EU and some rights guaranteed only to EU citizens (as outlined above). It also goes beyond the scope of the ECHR to include reference to social rights, to the right to good administration and to the rights of workers. There is also an attempt to create a framework in which contemporary issues such as bio-ethics, protection of personal data and the right to asylum can be addressed.

However, it is fair to say that although all EU member states are signatories to the ECHR, the status of the charter in relation to the EU is not without its tensions (Meehan 2002). Is the charter's main purpose primarily to make more obvious the rights that EU citizens and those resident in Europe already enjoy in what one UK politician described as a 'shop window' for human rights (*ibid.*: 250)? The charter may address some issues of the democratic deficit of EU institutions and processes, and its very existence may make the rights discourse more prominent in European politics. On the other hand, is the purpose of the charter to improve and legitimate the rulings of the ECJ and to subject to more effective scrutiny the actions of EU institutions and member states in implementing EU agendas? If so, how will this affect the balance between the rights of individual citizens and the collective interests of member states, for example? This is also important since at the moment the ECJ and the charter rule on only those elements that are part of the 'first pillar' of EU competences. It will be interesting to see whether the existence of the charter allows in future for increased scrutiny of the other European agencies and institutions that are being developed in the intergovernmental elements of European integration, particularly around issues of policing and judicial cooperation (*ibid.*).

The drafting of the charter in advance of EU enlargement was particularly important. It was necessary to have clear statements of human and fundamental rights that should underpin the growing EU and to which both existing and future member states should subscribe. Given the difficulties facing the ratification of the Constitutional Treaty, the status of the charter in future is as yet unclear. Nevertheless, its existence does at least mark the foundation of rights that might be built on in the future.

Key fact 4.2

Charter of Fundamental Rights

The charter covers the following chapters and articles:

Preamble

1. Common values of the people of Europe
2. Indivisible and universal values that, along with the principles of democracy and the rule of law, are the foundation of the Union
3. Union respects cultures and traditions of the peoples of Europe
4. Need to make rights visible
5. Rights protected by various constitutional traditions and international obligations reaffirmed in accordance with the principle of subsidiarity
6. Responsibilities and duties to come with these rights

▶

Chapter I: Dignity

Human dignity
Right to life
Right to the integrity of the person
Prohibition of torture and inhuman or degrading treatment of punishment
Prohibition of slavery and forced labour

Chapter II: Freedoms

Right to liberty and security
Respect for private and family life
Protection of personal data
Right to marry and right to found a family
Freedom of thought, conscience and religion
Freedom of expression and information
Freedom of assembly and of association
Freedom of the arts and sciences
Right to education
Freedom to choose an occupation and right to engage in work
Freedom to conduct a business
Right to property
Right to asylum
Protection in the event of removal, expulsion or extradition

Chapter III: Equality

Equality before the law
Non-discrimination
Cultural, religious and linguistic diversity
Equality between men and women
The rights of the child
The rights of the elderly
Integration of persons with disabilities

Chapter IV: Solidarity

Workers' rights to information and consultation within the undertaking
Right of collective bargaining and action
Right of access to placement services
Protection in the event of unjustified dismissal
Fair and just working conditions
Prohibition of child labour and protection of young people at work
Family and professional life
Social security and social assistance
Healthcare
Access to services of general economic interest
Environmental protection
Consumer protection

Chapter V: Citizens' rights

Right to vote and to stand as a candidate at elections to the EP
Right to vote and to stand as a candidate at municipal elections

Right to good administration
Right of access to documents
Ombudsman
Right to petition
Freedom of movement and of residence
Diplomatic and consular protection

Chapter VI: Justice

Right to an effective remedy and to a fair trial
Presumption of innocence and right of defence
Principles of legality and proportionality of criminal offences and penalties
Right not to be tried or punished twice in criminal proceedings for the same criminal offence

General provisions

a. Scope of charter rights
b. Scope of limitation of charter rights
c. Level of protection
d. Prohibition of abuse of rights

With its concern for the adherence of member states and EU institutions and policies to the charter, the EP, through its Committee on Citizens' Freedoms and Rights, Justice and Home Affairs, adopts and publishes an annual report on respect for human rights across the Union, supported by a network of independent experts.

(Sources: http://www.europarl.eu.int/comparl/libe/elsj/news/default_en.htm and
http://www.europa.eu.int/comm/justice_home.)

Anti-discrimination measures

While being an EU citizen involves access to a number of rights and responsibilities, it is also necessary to consider critically the extent to which such citizenship is experienced effectively by EU citizens and reasonably equitably between different population groups within the EU. In response to this concern, action is being taken across the EU to counteract different forms of discrimination, either towards EU citizens or towards others resident in different European countries. While action on anti-discrimination is included in the Charter of Fundamental Rights and addressed in article III-124 of the Constitutional Treaty, legal grounds for EU action in this area already exist with the Treaty of Amsterdam (articles 12 and 13). These measures are designed to improve the economic and social cohesion of the EU in recognition both of the uneven experience of national and EU citizenship in Europe and of the challenges of integrating non-EU nationals living in European countries, and particularly issues of discrimination around race and ethnicity, although the directives also cover other forms of discrimination. As the *Commission Communication on Immigration, Integration and Employment* (3 June 2003) argues: 'the creation of a society with a social and cultural environment where immigrants can take active part and interact with the host population is a very important step to increase tolerance and respect and to counteract discrimination'. It calls for 'strong political leadership and clear commitment to promote pluralistic societies and condemn racism' (European Commission 2003a).

Indeed, in 2000 the EU introduced the Racial Equality Directive and the Employment Equality Directive, affording a minimum level of protection against discrimination, and, importantly, putting the burden of proof on the employer or other respondent to prove fair treatment. Member states are obliged to incorporate these directives into national law, with formal monitoring and eventually referral to the ECJ, which can impose fines on states that fail to do so. By 2005, Germany, Greece, Luxembourg, Austria and Finland had all been referred to the ECJ for such failings (European Communities 2005). The Commission also monitors progress more widely in these areas (European Commission 2004c).

The Treaty of Amsterdam also required the EU to take measures actively to counteract discrimination, resulting in the EC Action Programme (2001–06) to combat discrimination alongside these directives. Its aims are:

- to improve the understanding of issues related to discrimination by evaluating the effectiveness of policies and laws;
- to develop the capacity to tackle discrimination effectively through exchange of examples of good practice and creating European networks on these issues;
- to promote the values underlying the fight against discrimination.

The Action Programme funds activities such as a five-year public awareness campaign, media awareness and media training. Other areas of EU action involve legal cooperation, including legal training in anti-discrimination and developing a common list of actions constituting racist or xenophobic actions so that those committing such acts cannot simply move across borders to avoid prosecution. This also involves outlawing such activities on the Internet. There is also a directive on compensation for victims of such crimes. All of these moves are underpinned by the establishment of the European Monitoring Centre on Racism and Xenophobia, in Vienna in 1997, and a current proposal to develop out of this a 'Human Rights Agency' for the EU (European Commission 2004a: 8).

The programme is regarded as particularly important in view of the enlargement of the EU, and efforts are being made to expand its influence beyond the EU with the EEA countries of Iceland, Liechtenstein and Norway and the three EU applicant countries of Bulgaria, Romania and Turkey all participating (European Commission 2005). Enlargement has also expanded the focus of the programme. For example, a key topic for 2005 is discrimination against the Roma population, a stateless population group who face considerable discrimination across the EU (see Part 1). Consideration is also being given to the position of 'kin-minorities', that is ethnic-cultural minorities living outside their notional kin-state, such as ethnic Hungarians who live outside Hungary, for example in Romania, but who are not Hungarian national citizens. Overall, the EU is adopting a process of attempting to 'mainstream' anti-discrimination into its policies, laws and institutional practices, and a further action programme for 2007–13, the EU Progress programme, takes this agenda forward.

Such EU actions serve to complement the concern of the Council of Europe with the rights of minority populations, and issues such as the cultural, human, economic and civic rights of minority populations. For example, the Council of Europe worked to encourage Latvia and Estonia in the 1990s to extend greater rights to the Russian minority populations in these states after their independence from the

Soviet Union in 1990. Despite such moves, many of these populations, although long-term residents in these states, do not have full national citizenship and therefore do not have access to EU citizenship post-enlargement. Instead they carry a 'grey passport' entitling them to move across the borders between Russia and either Latvia or Estonia. Expressions of concern from the Council of Europe and from the EU prior to enlargement have encouraged these states to offer citizenship, at least to those actually born there (Smith 1999). Issues of borders, citizenship and the rights of minorities and migrants are also integrally linked to the development of policy towards migration in Europe, which represents a key focus of the Tampere/ Hague programmes.

The reality and the politics of migration

Table 4.7 Inflows of foreign populations into selected European countries, 1991–2000 (thousands)

	1991	1992	1993	1994	1995	1996	1997	1998	1999	2000
Austria	–	–	–	–	–	–	–	59.2	72.4	66.0
Belgium	54.1	55.1	53.0	56.0	53.1	51.9	49.2	50.7	68.5	68.6
Czech Republic	–	–	–	–	5.9	7.4	9.9	7.9	6.8	4.2
Denmark	17.5	16.9	15.4	15.6	33.0	24.7	20.4	21.3	20.3	–
Finland	12.4	10.4	10.9	7.6	7.3	7.5	8.1	8.3	7.9	9.1
France	109.9	116.6	99.2	91.5	77.0	75.5	102.4	139.5	108.1	119.3
Germany	920.5	1207.6	986.9	774.0	788.3	708.0	615.3	605.5	673.9	648.8
Greece	–	–	–	–	–	–	–	38.2	–	–
Hungary	23.0	15.1	16.4	12.8	13.2	12.8	12.2	12.3	15.0	–
Ireland	–	–	–	13.3	13.6	21.5	23.5	20.8	21.6	24.1
Italy	–	–	–	–	–	–	–	111.0	268.0	271.5
Luxembourg	10.0	9.8	9.2	9.2	9.6	9.2	9.4	10.6	11.8	10.8
Netherlands	84.3	83.0	87.6	68.4	67.0	77.2	76.7	81.7	78.4	91.4
Norway	16.1	17.2	22.3	17.9	16.5	17.2	22.0	26.7	32.2	27.8
Portugal	–	13.7	9.9	5.7	5.0	3.6	3.3	6.5	10.5	15.9
Sweden	43.9	39.5	54.8	74.7	36.1	29.3	33.4	35.7	34.6	33.8
Switzerland	109.8	112.1	104.0	91.7	87.9	74.3	72.8	74.9	85.8	86.4
United Kingdom	–	203.9	190.3	193.6	206.3	216.4	236.9	258.0	276.9	288.8

Note: Data are gathered differently in different countries. Counts for the Netherlands, Norway and especially Germany include substantial numbers of registered asylum seekers. In other countries these are not included. Data often do not register other EU citizens living temporarily in a country either.

(Source: OECD SOPEMI Report 2003.)

The politics and processes of migration are a key feature of contemporary Europe. As Table 4.7 demonstrates, European countries experience in-migration of populations to rather varying degrees. Furthermore, these patterns can vary substantially even in a relatively short timeframe. However, before considering current policies, it is important to place the contemporary period in a wider context. It is helpful to distinguish three main periods of migration in Europe since the Second World War (Geddes 2003):

1. *Primary labour migration* between the 1950s and the early 1970s. Two strategies of labour recruitment developed to address the major labour shortages affecting Western Europe in the early postwar period. The first was recruitment of labour from colonies and former colonies by countries such as France, the Netherlands and the UK. The second was the so-called 'guest worker' or '*Gastarbeiter*' system, named after the German term for the process that developed from a series of bilateral labour recruitment agreements between Western European states and sending countries, mostly in southern Europe and North Africa. In parallel with the focus on labour mobility in the emerging EC of the time, the focus was on migration of workers. Most were men, although many women were also recruited. In general, policy tended to consider those migrating primarily as workers, rather than as people with wider social needs, and these 'birds of passage' (Piore 1979) were viewed as temporary residents who would one day return 'home'. Similar types of labour recruitment, but on a much smaller scale, existed between some Eastern European states and other communist states elsewhere. This period was marked by only very limited asylum migration, with some migration from Eastern Europe to the West via Berlin prior to the building of the Berlin Wall in 1961. After its height in the 1960s, labour migration in Western Europe came to an end with the recruitment stop of 1973–74. This reflected on the one hand economic changes in the demand for and supply of labour – the oil crisis of 1973 and its effects on Western European economies, the improved position of some sending countries' economies, such as Italy, and the wider shifts of the Western European economy away from Fordist forms of mass production to a period of restructuring towards post-industrial economies. On the other hand, the increasing politicisation of migration and its links to the politics of race meant that reductions in migration were politically timely.

2. *Secondary or family migration* increased in significance from the mid-1970s onwards. Once labour recruitment migration had fallen, family migration became the dominant form of immigration. This involved both the reunion of families (for example, with spouse or children of existing migrants joining them) and the immigration of marriage partners for settled migrants. Together these produced a feminisation of migration (Castles and Miller 1998). These levels of such migration and the extent to which (for example from the FRG) those who had settled were encouraged to return to their countries of origin varied cyclically over the years with the relative economic performance of these economies and their changing need for labour. This period also saw second and even third generations of migrant families, who were 'often caught between the home country affiliations of their parents and the need to build lives for themselves' (Geddes 2003: 17). This gave rise to a new politics of national belonging around issues of race and ethnicity. These issues tended to vary between those states where the children of migrants had citizenship status, at least formally (such as France and the UK), and where migrant children remained 'foreigners' (such as was the case in the FRG and Germany until recently; Giesen 2001). Labour migration into Europe did not cease entirely in this period, narrowing instead to recruitment of highly skilled labour, a focus that continues to the present day. This period also saw some forms of asylum migration, but these were generally

managed by European states through a quota system offering to accept specific numbers of refugees, such as the Vietnamese 'boat people' in the 1970s, although there were also increases throughout the 1980s in unplanned forms of asylum migration, particularly to the FRG, which had a very liberal constitutional position on asylum. Overall, however, the political focus for this period up to the late 1980s was very much on the implications for European countries of permanent settlement by migrants and their families.

3. The so-called *'third wave' of migration*, which accelerated after the end of the Cold War in 1989–91, is characterised by an increasing bifurcation between the continued migration of highly skilled migrants necessary for Europe's economic growth and global competitiveness and the increased significance of asylum-seeking migration and migration defined by states as illegal. This 'third wave' of migration reflects what Castles and Miller (1998) call the 'age of migration' where Europe, just as much as other parts of the world, is affected by the globalisation of migration, the acceleration of the rate of migration, and increasing differentiation of the forms of migration and of the countries of origin of migrants. Furthermore, these trends have also affected countries, such as those in southern Europe, that were traditionally countries of net out-migration and that have needed to develop new policies to deal with the arrival of new population groups (King 2001). Similar challenges also now face many countries in Eastern Europe.

Figure 4.6 The fortress of the rich

Source: *The Guardian* (14 February 1994). Copyright David Simonds 1994.

While the migration in all three of these periods affects Europe's populations today, it is noticeable that the current 'third wave' migrations form the focus for much recent EU and national government policy on migration issues.

The Europeanisation of migration?

Geddes (2003) considers how 'Europeanised' migration policies and politics have become in recent years. The origins of EU cooperation in relation to migration lie in the focus on the freedom of movement of labour in the Treaty of Rome in 1957. The EU has over time sought to facilitate the movement and residence of EU citizens in other EU countries. Of increasing importance, however, are measures being developed for increased cooperation within the EU over the management of non-EU migration into Europe. The Tampere programme set out a timeframe of five years to 2004 for development of common policies across the EU on migration issues and a framework for sharing the burdens of such measures. However, this process has been more difficult than anticipated, and the Hague programme (or Tampere II), agreed in November 2004, sets a new timetable with 2010 as the deadline for this cooperation. Furthermore, Denmark, Ireland and the UK continue to exercise an opt-out from cooperation in these measures. Outlined below is a critical assessment of the development of policies towards legal migration and the integration of migrants, migration defined by states as illegal, and asylum migration and refugees.

Legal migration and the integration of migrants

EU policy on legal migration is based on two key factors: a desire to allow those living and working legally in European states to participate more fully in the economic competitiveness and social cohesion of the EU; and the argument that the EU as a whole benefits from the migration of skilled workers to address its skills gap (Moraes 2003). This latter point is underpinned by arguments that long-term demographic shifts, which are leading to the ageing of the EU's populations, will, in the near future, mean that migration is required once again to maintain the EU's labour force (European Commission 2004f). For example, the UN estimates that the EU will need around 80 million immigrants in the period to 2050 to maintain its labour force. So in parallel with continuing efforts to encourage and enable the mobility of EU citizens within the EU, the Tampere programme includes moves to develop a common policy on legal migration of non-EU citizens and the integration of migrants within the EU (see Key fact 4.3).

The development of this common policy agenda has proceeded under a process of 'open coordination', allowing for considerable flexibility. However, there is evidence that member states have used this process to stall more rapid integration on these issues, which go to the very heart of debates about national sovereignty. The diverse traditions and situations in different European countries make it difficult to

Key fact 4.3

Common policy on legal immigration

1. *Coordinated management of migratory flows*: harmonisation of grounds for entry for family reunification, economic factors, access to professional studies and training, humanitarian grounds; member states are still to be responsible for determining the volume of admission open to third-country nationals coming for work purposes; harmonised procedures on visas and residence permits.

2. *The fair treatment of third-country nationals*: coordination of national policies on residency, including introduction of a uniform long-term residence permit after five years of uninterrupted legal residence, and the possibility of a scheme to develop 'civil citizenship'; right to free movement across the EU of those with residence permits and their families; actions to integrate foreigners, including language courses and anti-discrimination actions.

(Sources: http://www.europarl.eu.int/comparl/libe/elsj/news/default_en.htm and http://www.europa.eu.int/comm/justice_home.)

identify universal policies (Moraes 2003). Furthermore, there are in-built limitations on the extent of coordination in this model, since nation-states still set the parameters for legal immigration into their individual states. The uneven and problematic implementation of the policy is exacerbated by the political influence of right-wing populist and anti-immigration parties at local, national and EU elections, raising the political temperature on migration issues still further for national governments working towards some forms of coordination (Lloyd 2003).

There is also concern about the strongly economic focus of the policy. Economic globalisation is intensely tied in with the circulation of highly skilled professionals between countries and within the transnational networks of global companies. Competing in the global economy for particular skilled workers who are in shortage, European states already have schemes for particular groups, such as IT professionals (Germany) and medical staff (UK). While such recruitment may benefit the European economies, there is a potential danger of 'brain drain' in the countries of origin, which train key staff and then lose the benefit to their economies. Given that many of the countries of origin are developing and newly industrialising countries, such loss of key personnel may be counterproductive. In addition, the focus on highly skilled labour migrants in the policy does little to provide alternatives to illegal or asylum forms of migration for those with lower skills levels or who cannot obtain the requisite legal papers.

Interestingly, the EU has learned to some extent from the problems of early national policies on labour migration, which failed to address the wider social and cultural needs of migrants. Its focus on improved integration of migrants is welcomed by many migrant groups. However, EU policy can still be rather focused on the benefits of migration for the EU's economies, so moves to wider considerations of integration are being welcomed. Nevertheless, the anti-discrimination measures supported by the EU (outlined in earlier sections) still stop short of moves towards encouraging member states to integrate migrants as full citizens. Thus a distinction remains between EU citizens on the one hand and non-EU citizens on the other.

Table 4.8 Numbers of foreign population resident in selected European countries, 1991–2000 (thousands and percentages of total population)

	1991	1992	1993	1994	1995	1996	1997	1998	1999	2000
Austria	532.7	623.0	689.6	713.5	723.5	728.2	732.7	737.7	748.2	757.9
% of total population	6.8	7.9	8.6	8.9	9.0	9.0	9.1	9.1	9.2	9.3
Belgium	922.5	909.3	920.6	922.3	909.8	911.9	903.2	892.0	897.1	861.7
% of total population	9.2	9.0	9.1	9.1	9.0	9.0	8.9	8.7	8.8	8.4
Czech Republic	–	41.2	77.7	103.7	158.6	198.6	209.8	219.8	228.9	201.0
% of total population	–	0.4	0.8	1.0	1.5	1.9	2.0	2.1	2.2	2.0
Denmark	169.5	180.1	189.0	196.7	222.7	237.7	249.6	256.3	259.4	258.6
% of total population	3.3	3.5	3.6	3.8	4.2	4.7	4.7	4.8	4.9	4.8
Finland	37.6	46.3	55.6	62.0	68.6	73.8	80.6	85.1	87.7	91.1
% of total population	0.8	0.9	1.1	1.2	1.3	1.4	1.6	1.6	1.7	1.8
France	–	–	–	–	–	–	–	–	3263.2	–
% of total population	–	–	–	–	–	–	–	–	5.6	–
Germany	5882.3	6495.8	6878.1	6990.5	7173.9	7314.0	7365.8	7319.5	7343.6	7296.8
% of total population	7.3	8.0	8.5	8.6	8.8	8.9	9.0	8.9	8.9	8.9
Hungary	–	–	–	137.9	139.9	142.2	143.8	–	127.0	–
% of total population	–	–	–	1.3	1.4	1.4	1.4	–	1.3	–
Ireland	87.7	94.9	89.9	91.1	96.1	117.0	114.4	111.0	117.8	126.5
% of total population	2.5	2.7	2.7	2.7	2.7	3.2	3.1	3.0	3.2	3.3
Italy	863.0	925.2	987.4	922.7	991.4	1095.6	1240.7	1250.2	1252.0	1388.2
% of total population	1.5	1.6	1.7	1.6	1.7	2.0	2.1	2.1	2.2	2.4
Luxembourg	117.8	122.7	127.6	132.5	138.1	142.8	147.7	152.9	159.4	164.7
% of total population	30.2	31.0	31.8	32.6	33.4	34.1	34.9	35.6	36.0	37.3
Netherlands	732.9	757.4	779.8	757.1	725.4	679.9	678.1	662.4	651.5	667.8
% of total population	4.8	5.0	5.1	5.0	4.7	4.4	4.3	4.2	4.1	4.2
Norway	147.8	154.0	162.3	164.0	160.8	157.5	158.0	165.0	178.7	184.3
% of total population	3.5	3.6	3.8	3.8	3.7	3.6	3.6	3.7	4.0	4.1
Spain	360.7	393.1	430.4	461.4	499.8	539.0	609.8	719.6	801.3	895.7
% of total population	0.9	1.0	1.1	1.2	1.3	1.4	1.6	1.8	2.0	2.2
Sweden	493.8	499.1	507.5	537.4	531.8	526.6	522.0	499.9	487.2	477.2
% of total population	5.7	5.7	5.8	6.1	5.2	6.0	6.0	5.6	5.5	5.4
Switzerland	1163.2	1213.5	1260.3	1300.1	1330.6	1337.6	1340.8	1347.9	1368.7	1384.4
% of total population	17.0	17.6	18.1	18.6	18.9	18.9	19.0	19.0	19.2	19.3
United Kingdom	1750.0	1985.0	2001.0	3032.0	1948.0	1934.0	2066.0	2207.0	2208.0	2342.0
% of total population	3.1	3.5	3.5	3.6	3.4	3.4	3.6	3.8	3.8	4.0

Note: data are gathered differently in different countries, and opportunities for 'foreign' populations to achieve citizenship vary substantially.

(Source: OECD SOPEMI Report 2003.)

There is also concern from ethnic and racial minority groups that the focus of policy on immigrants misses the issues affecting ethnic and racial minority populations who are already citizens of EU member states. Table 4.8 shows considerable variation in levels of registered foreign populations across EU member states. This reflects in part their different approaches to citizenship and nationality for migrants. The UK and France, for example, have allowed dual nationality, and achievement of citizenship for migrants has long been possible, although the specific conditions have changed over time. Germany, in contrast, did not permit dual nationality, and the achievement of German citizenship for migrants and even for their children born in Germany was almost impossible until very recently (Giesen 2001). Given these facts, the numbers here do not reflect the existence of ethnic minority populations who are full citizens of the member states but whose interests are often sidelined in current policy, with the focus on new migrants, and who are often affected negatively by the rise of the politics of race in many European countries.

Policies on illegal immigration

Finding reliable figures on forms of migration that are deemed 'illegal' by European states is difficult, since by definition many migrants whose position is not completely regularised seek to keep their status and location hidden from the state. Forms of illegal or irregular migration can include:

- entering legally on a tourist or student visa, for example, but overstaying the visa;
- crossing state borders without proper authorisation or documentation;
- those legally resident who may work in the semi-legal informal economy or illegal underground economy;
- being someone who entered legally but who finds themselves made 'illegal' by changes in national legislation (Geddes 2003).

National and EU policy developments increasingly regulate such forms of movement and are part of what Hollifield (2000) calls the 'liberal paradox' of modern advanced capitalist states, which on the one hand have become increasingly open to the movement of goods, capital and services but 'at the same time make quite stringent efforts to filter the movement of people and to distinguish between wanted and unwanted forms of migration' (Geddes 2003: 20; see also Lahav 2004). Such distinctions can be seen in figures cited by Geddes (2003: 19) for 2000 showing that of the 89 million people arriving at UK points of entry, 29 million were not UK citizens. However, among this number were family members of UK citizens, EU citizens with free right of entry, citizens of other countries covered by agreements, and workers with highly prized skills with work permits. Most were tourists passing through on the increasingly globalised networks of travel and leisure. In contrast, fewer than 100,000 of these arrivals were seeking asylum (see below).

Geddes argues that rather than Europe's borders being 'soft' or uncontrolled, European states have a formidable range of measures in place to control entry and regulate the flows of population across their borders. However, a number of reasons can be seen for the increased perception that Europe's borders need further protection in relation to immigration.

1. It is a reaction to the shift in geographical locus during the 'third wave' migration whereby countries in Southern Europe and in Central and Eastern Europe are dealing with forms of illegal or irregular immigration in the context of having been in the past emigration countries (in Southern Europe) or countries little affected by international migration (in Central and Eastern Europe) (Papademetriou 2003).

2. The expansion of the EU through enlargement has produced worries about the effectiveness of the EU's external border controls and the Europe-wide policing of crime (concerns addressed more generally in the Tampere programme).

3. Rises in the levels of those claiming asylum in the 1990s in particular, and concerns that large numbers of those doing so were not 'genuine' refugees, led to the conflation generally of concerns about 'bogus asylum seekers', refugees and illegal immigration, which have fuelled public concerns and become part of the mainstream political process.

A Europeanised response to the issue of illegal migration has been developed in response to these wider issues, but also under the heading of 'burden sharing' and 'solidarity'. Thus EU policies seek to address the concerns of states about the security of EU borders and about the reduction of criminal activities in a way that shares the costs of such policing between the member states and creates a framework for cross-national cooperation (see Key fact 4.4).

Key fact 4.4

Common policy on illegal immigration

1. Increased exchange of information between states on illegal immigration; system of monitoring and sharing of data on illegal immigration between member states (CIREFI); introduction of 'early warning system' to share information between states about illegal immigration and 'facilitator networks' (i.e. traffickers); system of 'immigration liaison officers' stationed with the immigration services of potential source or transit countries; Eurodac database, in operation since 2003, containing fingerprints of all foreigners apprehended when crossing the external border of the Union in an irregular manner (also designed to facilitate monitoring of claims to asylum across the EU).

2. Development of an integrated border management system and visa policy at the external borders of the EU: harmonising visa requirements, creating a harmonised visa information system, and the new Schengen Information System (SIS II); coordinated policing of borders, including cooperation with states bordering on the EU; initiatives to train police and border forces, particularly in the new member states; directive requiring carriers (e.g. airlines) to return third country nationals to their home country if refused entry to the EU (supplements the Schengen Implementing Convention, or Dublin Convention (1990), with its system of fines for carriers (e.g. airlines) bringing migrants without suitable documentation).

3. Coordinated policy on return of those caught entering illegally, and on their possible readmission to the EU.

4. Coordinated measures to counteract criminal activities in human trafficking, particularly of women and children: coordinated policing and supply of information to Europol and support from Europol in fighting such crimes as document forgery and theft; policy on the exchange of criminal and security intelligence; development of the single European arrest warrant to avoid the need for

lengthy procedures on extradition; granting short-term residence permits to victims of traffickers who cooperate with national authorities, giving access to the labour market, education, healthcare and psychological assistance; development of a system of fines and other penalties for those engaged in trafficking, including a bar on professional activity in the EU, deportation or confiscation of the transport used.

(Sources: http://www.europarl.eu.int/comparl/libe/elsj/news/default_en.htm and http://www.europa.eu.int/comm/justice_home.)

Discussion of these policies centres on the balance between regulating illegal immigration and recognising the likelihood of its continued existence. It is widely argued that the rise in illegal and irregular migration in Europe is part of the wider global development of migration. Migration in semi-legal or illegal forms marks the flipside of the narrowed focus within labour recruitment on skilled migrants. Semi-legal or illegal migrants tend to occupy the margins of the labour market in Europe's post-industrial societies, often in jobs with low pay, poor conditions and little security, and sometimes in conditions of forced or degrading and dangerous work. However, these are arguably also jobs on which post-industrial societies tend to depend – in catering, hotels, construction, agriculture and so on. The question is then whether it is better to adopt the EU focus of tighter border controls, policing and prevention or to accept that the development gradient between Europe and other parts of the world is such that migration to Europe will remain something that people are prepared to pay a high price to achieve and to seek instead to regularise and regulate such migrations. Experiences in Spain and Italy, for example, have demonstrated benefits from periods where amnesties have been offered to those who are there illegally. Such regularisation can move migrants into formal registration, paying taxes and being entitled to some level of job protection.

Plate 4.2 Controls of Spain's Mediterranean border to prevent illegal immigration from Africa

Source: http://www.bbc.co.uk/1/hi/world/europe/4242411.stm

However, this is not to suggest that either Spain or Italy has an open border policy, as both states make extensive attempts to patrol their Mediterranean borders. A strong clampdown on illegal migration can potentially make these processes more dangerous for illegal migrants, because they have to pay high prices to those helping their migration, thus leaving them in vulnerable positions as forced labour, for example. The balance between these elements of policy varies between member states and also over time, particularly in relation to national politics. For example, recent policy changes in Italy include creating 'holding' centres for potential migrants in North Africa.

Asylum migration and refugees

Table 4.9 shows the changing pattern of applications for asylum in the EU over the 1990s. Concerns emerged about the steep rise in asylum applications in 1990–93 that followed the opening of borders to Eastern Europe after the Cold War and were also a direct result of the humanitarian crisis of the wars in the Balkans following the break-up of Yugoslavia. Conflicts and humanitarian crises in the Middle East, Somalia and Rwanda all added to the stream of applicants for refugee status. In addition, there was evidence that use of the asylum route was growing among those denied access to Europe following the closure of primary labour migration.

This newly prominent form of migration was very unevenly distributed between different states, with Germany taking the largest numbers for a number of historical reasons. Furthermore, the level of recognition of refugee status among applicants for asylum varied substantially. In some states it was higher, while in other states (Italy, for example), levels of recognition were very low. Such variations suggested the need for some level of European coordination in responses to asylum, particularly as there was some evidence that tightening of regulations in some countries, such as Germany, merely led to the displacement of migrants to southern European countries, which had less fully developed policies and practices. Given the open borders within the Schengen area, such shifts did not give any guarantees of lower overall asylum applications. Table 4.10 shows the numbers of people granted nationality in selected European countries – some, but not all, of these represent successful asylum seekers.

Overall, the United Nations High Commission for Refugees (UNHCR) estimated that around half of applicants in the EU were 'genuine refugees'. However, for a variety of reasons, around three-quarters of applicants tend to be granted leave to stay. These figures lead to growing suspicion among governments and in public debate that a large number of economic migrants are using the asylum route to gain access to Europe, giving rise to the term 'bogus asylum seekers'. However, all of this must be put into the wider context of global patterns of refugee migration and displaced persons, where the major concentrations of refugee populations are in some of the poorest countries, such as Pakistan, Mozambique or Sudan, with the global split in the number of refugees between developed countries and developing countries being around 20:80.

Moves towards a Common European Asylum System (CEAS) have developed over a number of years. It is important to note that the power to grant refugee

Table 4.9 Inflows of asylum seekers into selected European countries, 1992–2001 (thousands)

	1992	1993	1994	1995	1996	1997	1998	1999	2000	2001
Austria	16.2	4.7	5.1	5.9	7.0	6.7	12.8	20.1	18.3	30.1
Belgium	17.5	26.4	14.6	11/6	12.4	11.8	22.1	35.8	42.7	24.5
Bulgaria	0.2	–	–	0.5	0.3	0.4	0.8	1.3	1.8	2.4
Czech Republic	0.9	2.2	1.2	1.4	2.2	2.1	4.1	7.2	8.8	18.0
Denmark	12.9	14.3	6.7	5.1	5.9	5.1	5.7	6.5	10.3	12.4
Finland	3.6	2.0	0.8	0.8	0.7	1.0	1.3	3.1	3.2	1.7
France	28.9	27.6	26.0	20.4	17.4	21.4	22.4	30.9	38.7	47.3
Germany	438.2	322.6	127.2	127.9	116.4	104.4	98.6	95.1	78.6	88.4
Greece	2.0	0.8	1.3	1.4	1.6	4.4	2.6	1.5	3.1	5.5
Hungary	0.9	0.9	0.4	0.6	0.7	1.1	7.4	11.5	7.8	9.6
Ireland	–	0.1	0.4	0.4	1.2	3.9	4.6	7.7	10.9	10.3
Italy	2.6	1.3	1.8	1.7	0.7	1.9	11.1	33.4	24.5	9.8
Luxembourg	0.1	0.2	0.2	0.2	0.3	0.4	1.6	2.9	0.6	0.7
Netherlands	20.3	35.4	52.6	29.3	22.9	34.4	45.2	42.7	43.9	32.6
Norway	5.2	12.9	3.4	1.5	1.8	2.3	8.5	10.2	10.8	14.8
Portugal	0.5	1.7	0.6	0.3	0.2	0.3	0.3	0.3	0.2	0.2
Romania	0.8	–	–	–	0.6	1.4	1.2	1.7	1.4	2.4
Slovak Republic	0.1	0.1	0.1	0.4	0.4	0.7	0.5	0.9	1.5	8.2
Spain	11.7	12.6	12.0	5.7	4.7	5.0	6.8	8.4	7.9	9.2
Sweden	84.0	37.6	18.6	9.0	5.8	9.6	12.5	11.2	16.3	23.5
Switzerland	18.0	24.7	42.2	55.0	37.0	41.5	58.0	91.2	98.9	92.0
United Kingdom	145.5	200.4	202.4	208.2	150.0	73.1	50.3	45.8	57.0	8.4

(Source: OECD SOPEMI Report 2003.)

Table 4.10 Acquisition of nationality in selected European countries, 1991–2000 (thousands)

	1991	1992	1993	1994	1995	1996	1997	1998	1999	2000
Austria	11.4	11.9	14.4	16.3	15.3	16.2	16.3	18.3	25.0	24.6
Belgium	8.5	46.4	16.4	25.8	26.1	24.6	31.7	34.0	24.3	62.1
Denmark	5.5	5.1	5.0	5.7	5.3	7.3	5.5	10.3	12.4	18.8
Finland	1.2	0.9	0.8	0.7	0.7	1.0	1.4	4.0	4.7	3.0
France	95.5	95.3	95.5	126.3	92.4	109.8	116.2	122.3	145.4	150.0
Germany*	141.6	179.9	199.4	259.2	313.6	302.8	271.8	236.1	64.3	186.7
Hungary	5.9	21.9	11.8	9.9	10.0	12.3	8.7	6.4	6.1	7.5
Italy	4.5	4.4	6.5	6.6	7.4	8.9	11.6	10.8	13.6	11.6
Luxembourg	0.6	0.6	0.7	0.7	0.8	0.8	0.7	0.6	0.5	0.6
Netherlands	29.1	36.2	43.1	49.5	71.4	82.7	59.8	59.2	62.1	50.0
Norway	5.1	5.1	5.5	8.8	118.	12.2	12.0	9.2	8.0	9.5
Portugal	–	–	–	–	1.4	1.2	1.4	0.5	0.9	0.7
Spain	3.8	5.3	8.4	7.8	6.8	8.4	10.3	13.2	16.4	12.0
Sweden	27.7	29.3	42.7	35.1	32.0	25.6	28.9	46.5	37.8	43.5
Switzerland	8.8	11.2	12.9	13.8	16.8	19.4	19.2	21.3	30.4	28.7
United Kingdom	58.6	42.2	45.8	44.0	40.5	43.1	37.0	53.9	54.9	82.2

* Note figures for Germany includes large numbers of ethnic Germans from Russia and elsewhere in Eastern Europe, who have automatic right to German citizenship.

(Source: OECD SOPEMI Report 2003.)

status or leave to remain rests with member states. However, moves have been made towards a common set of policies across the EU, and these have intensified since the Tampere programme. As with policies on illegal migration, these are designed to create a degree of equality in the process across Europe and to create a system of some level of burden sharing, while strengthening the capacity of states to develop forms of cross-national regulation of asylum (see Key fact 4.5).

Key fact 4.5

Common European Asylum System (CEAS)

1. *Common definition of asylum and refugee status*
Common definition of refugee status based on the Geneva Convention on Refugees and the European Convention on Human Rights – 'any third country national or stateless person who is outside their country of origin and is unwilling to return to it owing to a fear of being persecuted for reasons of race, religion, nationality or political opinion'.
Proposal for 'subsidiary protection' where people 'cannot return to their country owing to a well-founded fear of being subjected to serious and unjustified harm, such as torture or inhuman or degrading treatment or punishment; violation of a human right that is sufficiently severe to engage the Member State's international obligations; a threat to life, safety or freedom as a result of indiscriminate violence in situations of armed conflict or of systematic or generalised violations of human rights'.

2. *Common procedures in implementing these definitions*
Creating a common procedure for granting and withdrawing this status and a common system of temporary protection.
Integrated approaches to administrative decision making on returns, reintegration schemes and entry procedures.

3. *Definition of minimum common standards for reception of asylum applicants and refugees* (reception directive adopted January 2003).

4. *Developing systems of burden sharing*
European Fund for Refugees established in 2003 to fund emergency measures (e.g. Balkan crisis), integration of refugees and voluntary return.
Proposals for a status of 'temporary protection' for up to two years in the case of a mass influx.

5. *Regulating asylum applications within Europe*
Dublin convention and Schengen agreement fines carriers (e.g. airlines) that fail to ensure travellers have requisite documents.
Dublin II regulation aims to avoid 'asylum shopping' and 'asylum-seeker-in-orbit' situations, where applications are made in a number of EU countries until status is achieved. It defines instead a single point of application for asylum, usually the first country of arrival within the EU.

6. *Cooperation on policing and management of asylum migration*
Eurodac database to fingerprint all registered asylum seekers in EU, including those whose applications have been refused elsewhere in EU.
Links to increased policing of external borders and crackdown on human trafficking under the policy on illegal migration.
Preventing the need for asylum migration by supporting measures on human rights and development to improve 'home' environments.

(Sources: http://www.europarl.eu.int/comparl/libe/elsj/news/default_en.htm and http://www.europa.eu.int/comm/justice_home.)

EU policies aim first to create a baseline of shared minimum standards for treatment of those making an application for asylum, and second to develop practices of uniform status and treatment. Although there are some positive elements to the policy (including attempts at fair treatment of applicants and those granted refugee status or subsidiary protection, and rights of family reunification for those granted official status), the policies have been criticised on a number of points. The minimum standards for reception do not require states to maintain the standards they already provide, still permit countries to restrict the freedom of movement of those awaiting the outcome of their application, and allow states to withdraw support. The system of single point of entry and application presumes equality of justice between different states, but member states have very different recognition rates and vary in their approaches to the right of appeal. Measures to streamline procedures may also lead to fast-tracking of applications in order to reduce waiting times, with only limited safeguards on the rights of the applicant, and detention of applicants continues to be permitted.

There is also considerable debate as to the effectiveness of various policies, in part due to the variability of their implementation across member states of the EU. Prior to the implementation of these policies, it is arguable that the major fears of the early 1990s about steep rises in asylum applications do not appear to have been realised: 1992–93 seem to have been exceptional years, but while overall levels of applications for asylum per annum are historically high, they have by and large fluctuated at between 200,000 and 400,000 across the EU15 (Zetter *et al.*, 2004). Further evidence from 2003 shows a 22 percent fall compared with the 2000–01 figures. There also seems to have been a shift to a more equal distribution of applications between member states (see Table 4.9). However, whether these changes are due to EU and national policies or to external factors is not clear. Zetter *et al.* (*ibid.*) found considerable variation at national and indeed local level in the implementation of asylum policies, as well as reluctance by a number of states to implement agreed EU policy. There was also little clear evidence of any assumed link between the overall levels of applications and the levels of welfare available to asylum seekers or their access to housing or employment.

Far more significant in terms of the variation in the levels of asylum applications between countries and over time were the legacies of past connections between source and destination country (through earlier migrations, for example) and the conditions within the home country, including the impact of 'complex emergencies' such as civil war and state collapse, as well as persecution of citizens, vulnerability to warlord economies and absence of protection of minorities. There was also evidence that more restrictive policies resulted in increased levels of trafficking and illegal entry, both for *bona fide* asylum seekers and for economic migrants (*ibid.*: 123). These findings suggest that there is some danger that attempts to regulate asylum migration in the EU, including policies adopted by member states on such measures as deportation, detention and dispersal (Schuster 2004), do not necessarily deal with the causes of asylum migration. Such attempts may be focused too strongly on the 'protection' of European states against unpredictable demands. It is argued, for example, that the designation of a range of states around the EU as 'safe' states to create a geopolitical 'buffer zone' through which asylum seekers will be less easily able to pass is effectively seeking to keep the problem at arm's length from the new 'fortress' of the ever more integrated Europe and fails to address the deeper causes of such largely unpredictable population moves.

Citizenship, rights and migration – new forms of (un)belonging in Europe?

In considering overall developments in citizenship, rights and migration in Europe, this section poses two key questions:

1. How 'Europeanised' are these processes?
2. How equal are these processes in creating new spaces of belonging in Europe?

How 'Europeanised' are citizenship, rights and migration issues?

To many people, European citizenship seems a distant, mainly administrative issue. The European Commission argues that justice and home affairs are at the heart of efforts to forge a real concept of European citizenship. The Commission believes that until people are aware of their rights and freedoms as Europeans and of the benefits they get from the EU in being able to live, work and travel in safety anywhere in the EU, the EU will remain a somewhat vague and distant concept for many individuals. This fear is reflected in a survey, by the European Commission on the tenth anniversary of the introduction of EU citizenship, which showed a lack of knowledge about these rights among the population of Europe, with only one-fifth feeling well informed about their rights and one-third knowing what EU citizenship meant. Significantly, despite efforts at an open process in its drafting, only 8 percent knew what the Charter of Fundamental Rights was. This suggests that one of the limitations of the current moves towards the 'constitutionalisation' of the EU is that it can often be a rather remote, technocratic process that engages only in a limited fashion with public debates and civil society across the EU (Meehan 2002).

However, when it came to more practical elements of the rights of citizenship, knowledge was considerably higher, with 60 percent knowing that they achieved EU citizenship automatically by having the nationality of a member state and 89 percent knowing that EU citizens could work in any EU country. This suggests that it is the practical experience of the benefits of citizenship that tend to be valued most (**http://www.europa.eu.int/comm/justice_home**) (see also Opinion 4.3).

Nevertheless, there is no escape from the fact that the civil and political rights of EU citizenship are in many ways limited compared with those in a democratic nation-state. There is, as yet, no right to vote in national elections in other EU member states, even for long-term residents. The right to settle in another state is dependent on access to financial support, and the right to stand for senior political office is also restricted. EU citizenship might be regarded as a kind of 'quasi-citizenship', which confers significant rights but does not equate to full citizenship of a nation-state, for example. So in some ways 'EU citizenship does not separate citizenship from national belonging; instead, it creates a two-level model in which supra-national rights (at the EU level) are dependent on national belonging (at the member state level)' (Castles and Davidson 2000: 98). It is not possible to be only an EU citizen without also being the citizen of one of its member states.

Crucially, developments in issues of citizenship, rights and migration all impinge on difficult questions about the nature of the EU and its relation to its member states. For example, Eder and Giesen (2001) consider the possibilities of EU citizenship as an avenue for social integration in the EU. On the one hand, developments may indicate the future of the EU as lying between the realm of international law and an intergovernmental area of cooperation, implying no major change in national citizenship or the existence of a polity of shared values. On the other hand, the development, whether intentionally or not, of strong supranational institutions with claims to a distinctively EU citizenship with a new relationship to diverse national citizenships suggests changed relations between member states and the EU.

Despite the emergence of a variety of shared European approaches to such issues, it is important to remember the extent to which these general principles vary substantially in their application within member states, particularly between those in the Schengen area and those that have opted out, and the existence of transitional arrangements for new member states. 'Most commentators expect that justice and home affairs will continue to offer examples of applied integration of variable speeds for the foreseeable future' (Xanthika 2002: 241). Furthermore, it remains obvious that the politics of race and migration vary substantially between European states despite efforts at common policies on the integration of migrants and anti-discrimination measures. This brings us to the second main question in this discussion.

How equal are these processes in creating new spaces of belonging in Europe?

A key question raised by Geddes (2003), Kofman (2002), Castles and Davidson (2000) and others is whether the EU is on its way to creating a space for a new form of post-national citizenship, and if so, how inclusive this new form of belonging is. What forms of inclusion and exclusion does it create? Although EU citizenship does not replace national citizenship, it might be argued that the impacts of EU directives, ECJ rulings and the rights in the ECHR and the Charter of Fundamental Rights all have some impact in promoting some kind of shared civic space across the EU, particularly in relation to social and political rights. For example, Meehan (2002) argues that the development of social rights around employment and European Court of Human Rights rulings spill over into what were previously national competences. So for Meehan the current situation could be read as a stage in the move from rights given to citizens as workers to rights achieved by citizens as human beings (discussed in Castles and Davidson 2000: 99). Arguably, too, recent proposals on civic citizenship for non-EU nationals after a longer period, and the access of these denizens to wider sets of human rights within the ECHR and the Charter of Fundamental Rights, as well as the provisions of the Amsterdam Treaty on anti-discrimination, already move beyond the strictly national basis of EU citizenship.

Nevertheless, full participation in EU citizenship or national citizenship still remains stratified into what Kofman (2002) argues is an increasingly diverse set of entitlements and rights divided between a disparate range of population groups.

This occurs as the EU and member states seek to address the existence of multi-ethnic populations and the presence of many non-national citizens in their borders by creating ever more diverse categories of belonging, from full citizenship to temporary leave to remain to those most marginalised, who are either asylum seekers awaiting processing of their claims or undocumented migrants (Schuster 2004). One example of this 'civic stratification' (Kofman 2002) is that the Charter of Fundamental Rights includes both universally applicable rights and a set of eight rights available only to EU citizens. Geddes (2003) also asks why, for example, the EU focuses on broad approaches such as anti-discrimination measures but is not pushing for a system of full political rights and citizenship for the range of resident foreign populations in the EU, including many who were born in the EU as second- or third-generation descendants of migrants but who may have very limited citizenship rights.

These new forms of belonging created in the EU's policies produce new forms of exclusion, new delineation of who is inside and who is outside the categories of 'European' belonging, and a stronger definition of Europe versus non-Europe (Eder and Giesen 2001). This then raises fundamental questions about the nature of being European. EU policies have so far trod a fine line between achieving the benefits of integration and cooperation in a wider Europe, the interests of nation-states and overall interests in security. However, the rise of right-wing and anti-immigration politics and sentiments in many European states at the very time when Europe's cultures are increasingly internationally interconnected and culturally diverse suggests that these issues will remain high on the political agenda for some time.

Further reading

Castles, S. and Davidson, A. (2000) *Citizenship and Migration: Globalization and the Politics of Belonging*, Macmillan, Houndmills, a very useful general introduction.

Eder, K. and Giesen, B. (eds) (2001) *European Citizenship between National Legacies and Postnational Projects*, Oxford University Press, Oxford.

Geddes, A. (2003) *The Politics of Migration and Immigration in Europe*, Sage, London.

Gower, J. (ed.) (2002) *The European Union Handbook*, 2nd edn, Fitzroy Dearborn, London, contains a number of good papers.

Lahav, G. (2004) *Immigration and Politics in the New Europe*, Cambridge University Press, Cambridge.

McNeil, D. (2004) *The New Europe: Imagined Spaces*, Edward Arnold, London.

Spencer, S. (ed.) (2003) *The Politics of Migration*, Basil Blackwell, Oxford, contains several useful studies.

Section 4.5

Living with diversity? Nation-states and national identities in contemporary Europe

All human beings in modern political systems possess multiple political identities, which go far beyond the immediate communities, rooted in family, locality, or workplace, to which they belong. National identities are often among the most significant of these. Both nationalism and a universalised sense of national identity are essentially modern phenomena, although a sense of national identity does not automatically make one a nationalist. Nor does a shared national identity necessarily evoke the same response in different individuals. Two people may both feel German or British; but whereas one may take pride in a perception of past or present national greatness, the other may feel shame and even pain in a perception of past or present injustices perpetrated in the country's name. National identity, after all, is a complex phenomenon, the product of complex interactions between social, economic, political and cultural histories. Moreover, national identity is rarely a person's only politically significant identity, even when it is of prime importance to the individual: national identity coexists with identities rooted in attributes such as region, class, religion, gender and sexuality.

Identification with a nation need not be identification with only one such group. For example, one might be proud to be Welsh as well as British. One might identify oneself as a supporter of Juventus football club, a citizen of Turin, a Roman Catholic and an Italian, all together; as well as a European perhaps. So these group identifications about which people feel so strongly can and do overlap, in multiple identities. Sometimes these multiple identities reinforce each other, and at other times they challenge each other. For example, a Catholic citizen of the Irish Republic – until recently a devoutly Catholic society – may feel that his or her religious and national identities reinforce each other; on the other hand, an Irish Protestant, Jew or atheist may feel compelled to reject attempts to conflate Irish national identity with Catholicism and to argue for a more inclusive and pluralist definition of 'Irishness'. Above all, group identifications change as societies change. Nowhere does a sense of national identity remain static. As with all identities, national identity is constantly reinterpreted and reconstructed, even if some nationalist political movements, appealing to myths of racial or cultural 'purity', seek to obscure this.

Many of the more powerful group identifications are associated with institutions such as the Church or the state. These institutions build up their strength by doing all they can to promote a sense of identification and loyalty in their supporters. The state in modern times takes extensive measures to build up a sense of nationhood in its citizens and to disseminate the belief that it is the state that embodies the sense of nationhood shared by at least a majority of those living within its boundaries. The success, or otherwise, of the state in disseminating this belief will critically affect the extent to which ruling elites enjoy political legitimacy (that is, a widespread acceptance, active or passive, of their right to exercise state power in the name of the collective group).

This relates to another characteristic of the modern era: the fact that most modern states tend to be nation-states, the territorial limits of which are justified by reference to the perceived common national characteristics of a majority of those inhabiting the state's territory. Insofar as features of physical geography – such as oceans, seas or mountain ranges – may contribute to cultural differentiation between peoples, the myth of 'natural state frontiers' may be deployed by those engaged in the process of nation-state building. However, the reality is that – geography notwithstanding – few, if any, states in modern Europe are ethnically or nationally homogeneous. There are few universally or even commonly perceived 'natural' frontiers. Furthermore, European history has been marked – and looks set to be marked for some time to come – by disputes between the rival aspirations of peoples and ambitions of their rulers, on the one hand, and by the increasingly necessary search for a means of defusing potentially violent conflicts and accommodating clashing identities within a 'common European home', on the other.

National feeling can arise in people even if they are not already united in a state. Often (but not always) demands may be made for some degree of national self-government, or even outright independence from an existing state. A group of people who have come to regard themselves as distinct may seek the institutional structure of a state to uphold and to maintain their own special features – language and culture, for instance, or a commonly shared religion, or sufficient respect for people who share their (perceived) national characteristics. Frequently, the belief that economic prosperity and advancement will be facilitated by a degree of self-government or independence adds powerful stimulus to the emergence of a movement seeking to articulate a sense of national identity in terms of 'self-determination', that is, a nationalist movement.

Although many states have come into existence as a result of such nationalist movements, they are almost never ethnically uniform; there are nearly always different ethnic groups within the state, and often some of these groups identify themselves as being of different 'nations'. So a modern nation-state is a paradox. It is supposed to be a state that is the institutional organisation of one nation on a definite territory whose borders it protects, but frequently it is also a state that holds together as

Plate 4.3 Medieval mosaic from Monreale Cathedral in Sicily depicting the building of the Tower of Babel

citizens people of different ethnic groups, some of whom may well think of themselves as separate nations. Thus Spain holds together the Castilians of the centre, the Basques of the northeast, the Catalans of the east, the Galicians of the west and the Andalusians of the south; Switzerland holds together the people of the different cantons, speaking four different languages and of two different major religious groupings; the UK holds together England, Wales, Scotland and Northern Ireland; Russia holds together many different semi-autonomous nations and ethnic groups; Belgium holds together French speakers (Walloons) and Flemish speakers (Flemings), and so on. It is therefore normal for a state to have to operate with some potential for political danger arising from these separate national groupings within it.

How dangerous such tensions can be was shown in a terrible fashion when Yugoslavia broke up from 1991. Many people identified themselves as Albanians, Bosnians, Croats, Macedonians, Montenegrins, Serbs, Slovenes, etc., and among several of these peoples aspirations and demands for separate states – or, in the case of the Serbs, for dominance within the Yugoslav state – were manipulated and exacerbated by ambitious and sometimes ruthless political leaders. In practice, many people were of mixed ethnicity, and at the start of the 1980s more than one million people (5.4 percent of the total population of Yugoslavia) refused all 'divisive' national categories and simply defined themselves as 'Yugoslav' (Kellas 1998: 21). Moreover, even where people defined themselves as Serbs, Croats and so on, they were frequently intermingled in adjoining villages and in the same villages and towns throughout the southern Balkans. Thus it was never completely obvious where the boundaries of new states should be. Extreme nationalist forces fought each other to try to secure territory that could be regarded as, for example, Croatia, or Serbia. In such tragic situations, even individuals who have no desire to participate in wars, and whose sense of belonging to a common humanity transcends the narrow confines of nationalism (or, in the case of Yugoslavia, thought of themselves as Yugoslavs) are often forced to identify with one group or another. Only in that way can they obtain protection, by being regarded as potential citizens of one or another incipient or possible nation-state.

The origins of these identities are various. They can lie in language, although most states have substantial minorities speaking different languages from the majority. It can, in any case, be just a matter of decision when two people are regarded as speaking a different language rather than just variant forms or dialects of one language. Or the criterion can be religious; for example, when by the Treaty of Lausanne of 1923 it was agreed to end the Greek–Turkish War by resettling a million 'Greeks' in the territories designated as part of Greece and a million 'Turks' in the territories designated as part of Turkey, the criterion that determined whether a person was Greek or Turkish was whether they were Christian or Muslim. As a result, many Turkish-speaking Christians found themselves labelled Greek and removed to Greece. In the eastern parts of Poland, the criterion determining whether someone was Polish or Ukrainian was partly linguistic and partly whether the person was Roman Catholic or Orthodox (at least by family tradition). And in Bosnia, the group whose ancestors had once favoured a Christian heresy and who had subsequently largely adopted Islam became identified as the 'nation' of Muslim Bosnians who later suffered such losses in the Bosnian War of the 1990s.

It has also often been supposed that another criterion for classifying peoples as belonging to one national group or another might be 'racial'. The use of this idea is nearly always dangerous. Europe in the twentieth century has been scarred indelibly by the murder of millions of men, women and children on the grounds of alleged 'racial impurity'. And in fact this notion of determinate characteristics of a race is an illusion or a myth. People do differ in their physical appearance, and this is to a large extent determined by their genetic inheritance. But every human being inherits a very mixed set of genes, and people's appearance (colour of skin, etc.), intelligence and moral character vary very greatly, so there are no coherent groups in which people can all be said to be of the same 'race' in the sense of physical, intellectual or moral characteristics. Indeed, the latest scientific research shows that gene differences between individual members of the same ethnic group or race are much more significant than differences between actual ethnic groups or races, thus undermining any scientific basis to the concept of race. Racism is therefore a myth, though a powerful one. It differentiates human beings from one another by constructing an entirely spurious hierarchy of 'superior' and 'inferior' peoples on the basis of what are supposed to be inherited genetic features, both physical and (in association with these physical features) behavioural qualities of 'character'. This view – allied to nationalism – has been symptomatic of the far right of the European political spectrum, especially its Nazi and fascist variants.

Over and above these criteria of nationhood, everything depends on what people feel themselves to be. It is important to pay attention to the idea of a nation in which people believe, and to bear in mind that such ideas are obviously subject to historical change. Benedict Anderson (1983) calls a nation an 'imagined community', imagined, that is, by people who go along with the idea of the nation. Its basis is a sort of vision of collective identity, history and so on, but on this basis the community can become very real indeed. To establish such an idea, which can grip people's imagination, it is necessary to have a history, a tradition, or at least to believe in such a history or tradition even though many national traditions are in fact invented, exaggerated or distorted. Examples of inventions, exaggerations or distortions based on literature or music are:

- the Spanish history of El Cid, the medieval warrior who fought the Moors;
- the Hungarian tradition of the horsemen of the Milky Way, who will return to aid the Hungarians in their hour of need;
- the Finnish independence movement of the nineteenth century involved the collection of fragmentary ancient stories and myths and putting them together as a coherent set of stories, the Kalevala, to play the role of the national tradition of the Finns;
- the folk-musical traditions of Finns were raised by the great composer Sibelius to the status of the national music;
- the music of Frederic Chopin became a powerful symbol of the Polish nationalist movement.

Nationalist movements

It is clear that movements that make loyalty to a nation central to their purpose will have a very different character depending on whether they direct their appeal to the dominant national group in an existing nation-state or to a minority that seeks separation to form its own state. The former might be called a *status quo movement*; its purpose will tend to be the assertion of the unity of the existing nation-state, and therefore it will tend to play down other loyalties and other divisions within the state (notably class divisions and the status of ethnic minorities). The latter is a *disruptive movement*, which seeks to limit or break the power of the existing state in order to detach part of its territory. It is also possible that an ethnic nationalist movement might seek the advancement or protection of its own ethnic group within a (reformed or decentralised) nation-state without seeking actual separation. Or that such a movement might be pushed to a separatist or 'disruptive' stance only by the intransigence of the existing state. *Status quo* nationalist movements do not necessarily want to leave everything as it is. They may be opposed to progressive forces in the state, which emphasise how the *status quo* benefits the rich and powerful, like movements for radical social change or parties that represent the poorer classes. The Franco regime in Spain (1939–75), the Salazar regime in Portugal (1926–74), and the regime of the Greek colonels (1967–74) are examples of authoritarian regimes that invoked defence of the *status quo* and preservation of the existing nation-state in attempted justification of their repression.

The most dangerous *status quo* nationalist movements (from the point of view of democracy and stability) are those that add to their promotion of national unity in their state (1) hostility to particular minority groups within the state and (2) aggressive hostility towards other nations in other states. European history can show many examples of nationalism of this kind, and there is ground for serious concern that manifestations of reaction and resentment against immigrants, now widespread in Europe, might develop into much more extreme forms of anti-democratic, aggressive and minority-persecuting nationalism. The risks of such movements in contemporary Europe will be considered shortly, but it is important to remember that not all *status quo* nationalist movements, either on the right or the left, reach these extreme forms.

Disruptive nationalism – since it is based on the discontent of its supporters with their place within existing states – is sometimes apt to be more populist, invoking the loyalty of ordinary people while attacking the existing social, political, economic or cultural hierarchy. Like *status quo* nationalism, such movements have milder and more extreme forms. In their mild form, they shade off into cultural movements promoting minority culture in the form of language and literature, folk music, and so on. They assume a more disruptive form (in the sense of demanding political change) when they seek some kinds of special rights for the minority (such as teaching in the minority language in schools), which can easily develop into demands for a degree of local self-government. Sometimes, perhaps in response to state repression or due to frustration with their inability to command sufficient support through democratic channels, such movements can produce a wing that is prepared to use violence to secure total independence. The IRA (Irish Republican Army) in Northern Ireland and ETA (Euskadi Ta Askatsuna) in the Basque lands of Spain are examples of such groups. By the end of the 1990s, both these movements were seeking ways of advancing their causes through less violent methods, having apparently learned that states that enjoy a high degree of democratic legitimacy cannot easily be brought to their knees through terrorism. In the 1990s, the Corsican nationalist movement, although it has an extreme wing seeking separation from France through armed force, mostly operates as a movement seeking only a degree of local autonomy and recognition of the Corsican language.

On the other hand, the nationalist movements in Estonia, Latvia and Lithuania applied peaceful mass pressure to obtain total independence from the state that had previously exercised sovereignty over them (the Soviet Union) in 1990. Such movements (insofar as they use peaceful methods) may be tolerated by the existing state structure, and their demands to some degree conceded, as they have been by Spain and Belgium, which have tried in this way to defuse the potential danger from the separatist movements of the Basques, the Catalans and the Flemings.

Alternatively, the state may resist the demands of ethnic groups and find itself in this way confronted with demands for total secession backed by the threat of force. Such a situation may develop into one of endemic terrorism and state repression, as in Russia with the Chechens, in Turkey in its relations with its Kurdish minority, or in the UK during the 1916–21 period in its relations with Irish nationalists.

Disruptive or revolutionary nationalist movements are often led and inspired by middle-class people who feel that their social, political or economic ambitions are being thwarted within the existing state, and that they are being excluded because of their nationality from the important positions in society to which they feel entitled. To understand why this is so, we need to realise that the modern nation-state is (among other things) a way of organising the job opportunities and career paths of people in a complex modern economy, in which many jobs require expertise so that candidates for them have to be found through some open competitive system. The state's institutional framework for this system of competition always favours the official culture and the official language, and in this way talented people with energy and organisational capacity may feel themselves to be held back by this power structure and so come to support movements that give some kind of recognition to their own different culture; they may even reach the point of supporting revolutionary nationalism. This may happen, above all, when the state practises institutionalised discrimination on grounds such as religion or language.

We can ask, then, how such movements will relate to social issues and class conflict. This is a question that has perplexed and confounded the European left throughout its history. Many socialists have argued that nationalist movements are regressive, opposed to socialist internationalism and to workers' interests. This may be because they have the effect of dividing workers along national or ethnic lines or because, in the name of what they claim is the 'national interest', they submerge or suppress issues pertaining to social injustice and class inequality. But other socialists have argued that they may represent the interests of workers because of their perceived anti-imperialist and democratic character, and that the class structure of modern states often operates by suppressing both minority cultures and the workers who share it.

State strategies for dealing with national or ethnic minorities

The paradox of the nation-state, described above, implies that virtually every state will have a more or less serious problem with minorities. How can they try to deal with it in contemporary Europe? Various strategies can be distinguished.

Melting-pot assimilation

This strategy involves submerging by every possible means any separate national feeling within the state so as to strengthen as much as possible the new nation that is to be formed on the basis of the sense of identification with a new state. The classic example of this strategy in the nineteenth and twentieth centuries is the USA, which had such a large and various influx of immigrants that this seemed the only tactic that could build any sense of 'American-ness'. In Europe, there is no real example of this since new states have always been based on one existing ethnic group. Lenin and the early Bolsheviks certainly envisaged in the immediate post-1917 period that the new Soviet Union would solve the problem of national and ethnic tensions through a process of 'melting-pot assimilation', the end-product being a new Soviet national identity. Bukharin, one of the Bolshevik leaders, argued that French should be the state language in the Soviet Union because he wished to avoid Russian cultural dominance of the other nationalities. But under Stalin especially, such ideals were all but reduced to empty rhetoric as Russian nationalism and Russian domination of other national groups took centre stage again under the guise of Soviet patriotism.

One-nation dominance

The end goal of this strategy is apparently very similar; but the sense of national identity that the state seeks to promote is that of an existing nation or ethnic group, already present as the most powerful (and usually the majority) element in the state. In fact, the two strategies operate very differently, since the dominance strategy places citizens on an unequal footing depending on whether they are, to start with, already members of the dominant ethnic group or members of a minority group that it is the state's policy to extinguish as a separate group. It is thus more likely to arouse resentment.

Such a strategy has been applied by, for example, Poland, which after the end of the Second World War transferred great numbers of its citizens of Ukrainian background and language to a part of Poland (the northwest) remote from their former homes and from other Ukrainians and dispersed them in isolated pockets while giving them purely Polish education. The idea was that in a generation or two they would feel themselves to be simply Polish and so become loyal members of the Polish nation. Several of the states that emerged from the break-up of Yugoslavia in the early 1990s – notably Serbia and Croatia – applied similar strategies under the slogan of 'ethnic cleansing'. Indeed, the brutal imposition of one-nation dominance by the Serbs upon the overwhelmingly Albanian population of the region of Kosovo in the late 1990s provoked a new civil conflict as Serb forces attacked Albanian civilians, and the newly formed Albanian Kosovo Liberation Army (KLA) retaliated with attacks on Serbs. There was a massive escalation of this conflict in 1999 as the Serb-dominated Yugoslav army, assisted by paramilitary terrorists, drove almost one million Albanian civilians from their homes into refugee camps in neighbouring countries. Thousands of Albanian men were kidnapped and feared murdered, and NATO responded with massive air strikes upon targets in Yugoslavia. NATO's goal was implementation of an agreement that would end one-nation dominance in Kosovo while leaving Kosovo as a semi-autonomous region of Serbia.

A less bloody variant of the strategy of one-nation dominance was attempted in some of the Baltic states to discourage their large Russian minorities from exerting an unwelcome influence in states that were founded precisely to get away from the power of Russia. While Lithuania offered automatic citizenship to its Russian speakers, Estonia and, especially, Latvia imposed a second-class status upon their Russian-speaking populations after independence. Latvia's denial of citizenship to Russian speakers and their descendants unless they officially 'naturalised' after passing stringent language tests meant that around one-third of the country's population of 2.6 million people had no right to vote, had their housing and social benefits removed or reduced, and were branded as 'aliens'. A combination of pressure and threats of economic sanctions from Russia, and dire warnings from the EU that such discriminatory policies would jeopardise Latvia's chances of greater integration with the EU, forced a retreat in October 1998. In a referendum, 53 percent of Latvians voted to give passports to all children of Russian speakers born in Latvia since independence and to make it easier for older Russian speakers to gain passports also. EU pressure also resulted in an easing of the situation of Russian speakers in Estonia in the late 1990s and early 2000s.

The national character of most European states, based on the dominant ethnic group, has been established for a long time, with usually one official language and an education system and broadcasting system that favours that group and its traditions. For such long-established states, a one-nation dominance strategy is unnecessary. For any state, such a strategy is a high-risk option because it involves an active suppression of the special characteristics of the minority groups it seeks to merge into the dominant nation, for example by a suppression of their language, their religion, even sometimes their national dress (as in the suppression of Highland dress in Scotland in the late eighteenth century). If, in their resentment at this, they resist by founding nationalist movements, it involves active suppression of these movements, which as we have seen can lead to a vicious spiral of violence. Quite apart from the undemocratic nature of such policies, the implications for both long-term political stability and human rights are usually pretty grim.

An extreme form of one-nation dominance strategy is the attempt to eliminate a minority (or all minorities) altogether from the territory of a state by forced mass emigration or by genocide. The most recent large-scale European examples of mass expulsions at the time of writing are the expulsions of Germans from east of the Oder–Neisse line (the new Polish border) and from Czechoslovakia in 1945–46, and the refugee exodus from former Yugoslavia, which had reached more than 800,000 by the end of 1998, with a further 4.5 million persons left displaced or homeless within the former state. Genocide as a policy of one-nation dominance has cast its infamous shadow over European history in the Nazi Holocaust of the Second World War, in which six million Jews, about a million Poles, and at least a quarter of a million Roma (not to mention trade unionists and socialists, homosexuals, and others who failed to fit the Nazi image of being a true German) were exterminated. But although the Holocaust is unique in its scale (so far), the strategy has been applied by other racially motivated nationalists, as by the Turks in 1915–23 against the Armenians and by the Serbs in the 1990s ('ethnic cleansing') against the Muslim Bosnians and Kosovan Albanians. There is a continuing risk that any extreme nationalism could use the tactic; from the extremist's point of view, it has the great attraction of seeming to be a 'final solution' of the problem of minorities (although it is never really a final solution).

One-nation hegemony with tolerance

This strategy is different from the dominance strategy because it does not seek the legal or violent suppression of minority cultures. Instead, it seeks to use state power to 'discourage' them in the hope that they will fade away, being gradually displaced by the officially backed culture of the dominant nation. For instance, the language of the law courts, of government and of the education system is the language of the dominant ethnic group; the best job opportunities in practice go to those with the right language (or dialect) and culture; the history and traditions taught in schools and favoured in the official broadcasting system are those of the dominant group. Such a policy relies on the minority group's language, traditions and so on gradually disappearing as the style of an older generation, without arousing too active a resentment. There are many processes at work in the modern world that tend to favour such a strategy, by undermining minority languages and cultures within a state. Compulsory public education, mass culture and the advent of television and radio all tend to 'universalise' knowledge of the dominant language and culture within a state. Military conscription may also function to socialise young men from minority cultural groups into the dominant language of the state. Divisions may emerge within a minority group between, for example, rural areas, where folklore, old traditions and the group's language or dialects live on, albeit in an ever-threatened way, and urban areas, where the upwardly mobile and professionally ambitious may cast off as 'backward' the language and traditions of their forefathers and embrace those of the dominant nation within the state. Indeed, the spread of the language, culture and, ultimately, the national identity of the dominant nation may appear as progressive and liberating to some members of the minority group even as others see these same developments as repressive and imperialist (Drysdale 2001: 380–3).

The 'one-nation hegemony with tolerance' strategy is the sort of policy followed by France and the UK, and with some success (although the degree of tolerance shown towards minority languages and culture has varied over time). But one should remember that the UK's attempt to apply such a policy in Ireland in the period 1800 to 1916 ultimately failed. Although the Irish language suffered irreparable damage as the spoken language of most Irish people, great resentments were aroused, and discontent took a nationalist form, so that active nationalism arose and – after bloody conflict – led to the secession of most of Ireland from the UK in 1921. Italy has had a longstanding problem of a similar kind in the Austrian national feeling of many people in the Italian Tyrol (Südtirol). Attempts to assimilate these people led to bomb outrages in protest at Italianisation, but the situation was defused by the retreat of the Italian government from an assimilation policy to the strategy of regional pluralism.

Regional pluralism

Not all minorities occupy definite regions within a state. Indeed, many of Central Europe's Roma follow a wandering life all over the countryside, and most Jews in prewar Europe were scattered over Central and Eastern Europe, usually living in towns. The problem of immigrant groups is also not one for which there could be a regional solution. But where a minority *does* occupy a particular region, one possible strategy for the state is to grant the region a substantial degree of self-government. Under such a system, the regional government will support the culture and language of the ethnic group dominant in the region, but in the framework of the state that holds sovereignty over it. This solution has been applied quite widely in postwar Europe, and especially since 1980. Switzerland has long had a federal structure giving local power to its separate cantons, and it is in this way that a state containing four language groups and two main religions has been able to hold together. Similarly, in 1948–49 the representatives of the *Länder* who set up the constitution of the FRG reserved a great deal of power to the separate *Länder*.

Belgium has responded to growing tensions between its two language groups by devolving power in the state to three regions, a Walloon region, a Flemish region and a Brussels central region. Spain, after the death of Franco, decided on a strongly devolved structure, in which the strong sense of regional loyalties, especially in Catalonia, in the Basque region and in Galicia could be satisfied. But such policies are also risky. They can encourage the sense of separateness of regional ethnic groups as distinct nationalities and so lead to the break-up of the state or to substantial clashes between separatists and the state (arguably, something like this happened in Slovakia's separation from the Czech Republic). Alternatively, the sovereignty of the state can exert itself to make sure that the concessions to minority identity are just tokens and that the real power still rests with the dominant group. To succeed, the strategy of regional pluralism would seem to require a fairly well-developed civil society with wide acceptance by both the state and the political movements representing various national groupings of the values of democratic tolerance and constitutional rule.

The Soviet Union – in which these conditions were absent – landed itself with the worst of both worlds. In the 1920s, it encouraged the sense of separateness of its component nations, so that they came to feel more of a sense of separate nationhood as a result, while from the 1930s the separate nations were in fact suppressed, thus arousing resentments that ultimately contributed to the break-up of the state.

Cultural pluralism

This strategy tries to accommodate the policy of the state to the reality of the pluralist, multi-ethnic character of all states, and especially (perhaps) of modern European states. The aim is to acknowledge this reality and use the state as a legal framework holding together many different kinds of people with different cultures, which should all – so far as possible – be recognised and encouraged. This leads to the idea that national identity is not ethnic – does not depend on particular cultural characteristics or possessions like language – but is simply that of a citizen of the state. This inclusive nationalism fits well with the ideology of liberalism, which conceives of the state as a neutral legal framework within which people can each pursue their own lifestyles. But in practice application of the strategy meets with severe difficulties. For one thing, the role of the state in a modern economy, as explained above, favours a single official language and a reasonably uniform education system to ensure reliable qualifications acceptable throughout the state. For another, the sense of identity on which modern states build the loyalty of their citizens tends to need more content than just the idea of a state with a particular name and flag. People associate the state with the dominant culture within it, and this tends to be thought of as the identity of the nation. Moreover, even apart from the direct influence of the state, minority languages have difficulty in maintaining more than a peripheral status in a modern economy, since most parents want their

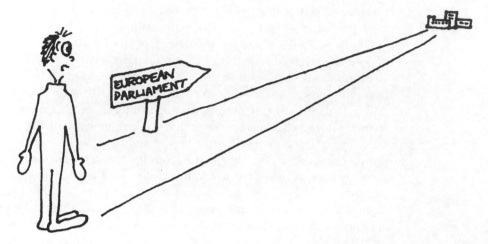

Figure 4.7 Remoteness from the European Parliament
Source: Katy Jones.

children to learn and use the language that will enable them to succeed in the job market, and time spent on minority languages is time not spent on chemistry, or geography, or some other 'useful' subject.

Sometimes a policy of cultural pluralism is legally entrenched as a system of minority rights; sometimes, indeed, such a system of legal minority rights is demanded by international pressure or treaty obligations. The League of Nations in the 1920s tried to protect Europe's minorities by requiring member states to grant specific rights to minorities. The policy failed, but it may be that it did so mainly because of the more general failure of the League of Nations. The most disastrous problems were those of German minorities in Czechoslovakia and Poland, and Nazi Germany was not interested in protection of Germans by the League, of which in any case it had ceased to be a member in 1934. Perhaps the prospects for protection of minority rights are better since 1945, but the policy is still fraught with dangers and difficulties. Since 1975, the human rights clauses of the Helsinki Final Act have contained some provision for protection for minority groups, but these have not so far been very effective. The reason for this is not only lack of will; to implement any *general* form of protection for minorities is very difficult, since entrenched positions for special groups cannot be made available to every group, and it seems nearly impossible to formulate criteria for how big or how different or how vulnerable a group needs to be to deserve protection. Nevertheless, the prospect of possible future admission to, or association with, the EU (with all its economic advantages) is sufficiently attractive for many states of Eastern Europe that the EU is able to exert a considerable influence in favour of tolerance and liberal democratic standards.

Finally, it may be noted that many of the economic, social and cultural processes that have for some time militated against cultural pluralism by undermining minority languages and cultures have, if anything, accelerated considerably in recent years with the phenomenon of globalisation. Nowadays, it is not only minority languages – such as Breton and Corsican in France, or Sardinian in Italy – that are under threat. French and Italian and many other European languages that have hitherto been dominant languages within their nation-states are increasingly chal-

Key concept 4.3

State strategies for dealing with national or ethnic minorities

- *Melting-pot assimilation* attempts to create a new national identity and forge loyalty to a new state by merging and integrating by every possible means the pre-existing national identities of all the groups that live within that state.

- *One-nation dominance* attempts to impose the national identity of the dominant national group within a state upon hapless minorities whose cultures and identities may be denied or suppressed, and whose very existence may be threatened.

- *One-nation hegemony with tolerance* attempts to use state power – in education, for example – to promote the language, culture and national identity of the dominant national group, universalising this as the basis upon which all citizens give loyalty to the state. Minority languages, cultures and identities are discouraged but not brutally suppressed.

- *Regional pluralism* attempts to accommodate diversity within a state by granting regions a substantial degree of self-government. This may involve minority languages and cultures being accorded equal status with the official or dominant state language and culture in particular regions.

- *Cultural pluralism* attempts to accommodate the multinational character of many modern European states by according as wide a recognition as is feasible to different languages, cultures and identities, and by accepting that loyalty to the liberal democratic state does not demand that citizens all speak the same language or belong to the same ethnic or national group.

lenged by the spread of English as the language of global communications. French commentators and public opinion, especially, seem increasingly concerned by the challenge that English poses to the international standing of their language and culture – a process that is intensified by EU expansion, as many of the new member states that joined the EU in 2004 have opted for English over French or German as their principal second language. Some commentators fear that relentless pressure towards a sort of global 'monoculture' may result in the death of more human languages in the next century than in any other period in world history. For example, it is estimated that around half of the 6,000 or so languages that were spoken by the human race at the start of the twenty-first century may have disappeared by the end of the century and that only 10 percent (600 or so languages) can be regarded as safe (Abley 2003: 4, 276–7). Some commentators accept this aspect of globalisation as inevitable or even celebrate it as facilitating better global communications and understanding. Others argue that what it really facilitates is a dangerous concentration of media and economic power and an irreversible impoverishment of human experience and culture.

The main problems of ethnic feeling in contemporary Europe

Regional self-government and inter-regional disputes

As we shall show, these problems manifest themselves in very different ways in Central and Eastern Europe, on the one hand, and in Western Europe on the other.

Central and Eastern Europe

The removal of the old structures of authority with the fall of the communist governments led to a situation in which people were uncertain what political authority might ultimately be established. In some cases, the fragility of state structures and political institutions in the post-communist period, combined with uncertainty about the future, made many people afraid that their own national group or region might lose out unless as much local control as possible was established. This was especially true, perhaps, of many of the semi-autonomous regions and republics of Russia – rich in natural resources and anxious to bypass central control from Moscow. In addition, economic instability, poverty and high unemployment fuelled fear and discontent. The situation was ripe for ambitious and often unscrupulous political leaders – many of them recycled from the old communist ruling *nomenklatura* – to whip up prejudice and ultimately aggression against vulnerable minorities who could be made the scapegoats for society's problems by being portrayed as undermining the cohesion of the nation, or seeking to attack it or gain advantages over it.

Both Russia and Central and Eastern Europe are ethnically very mixed; every state contains substantial minorities, and the concept of ethnically 'natural' boundaries between one state and another is potentially a very dangerous myth. To add to the instability, the area has a confused and destructive history of national and ethnic conflicts, so that many families retain sad and bitter memories of past injustices, which can easily give rise to present-day hatreds. It is precisely these 'historical experiences of national humiliation' that can be whipped up into 'ethnic paranoia' (Caplan and Feffer 1996: 219) by political elites seeking to advance their own careers on the back of national chauvinism. Against this, the main force preventing the descent of the whole area into conflict is the people's own awareness of how futile, destructive and terrible such conflicts are. Moreover, common economic interests were beginning to pull countries of Central and Eastern Europe together into an array of regional organisations from the 1990s. There is a surprising number of possible conflicts in the area that have not (so far) got out of hand; examples are the peaceful separation of the Czech Republic and Slovakia in 1992 and the avoidance of serious conflicts arising from the presence of sizeable ethnic minorities in Bulgaria, Romania, Slovakia and the Baltic republics. That said, the prevalence of 'narratives of victimisation and of threat, linking the present with the past and projecting onto the future' (Brubaker 1996: 74) remains a frightening danger.

Just how dangerous such narratives can be is illustrated by the terrible examples of the war between Serbia and Croatia and the Bosnian War, which began in 1992, and the war between Serbia and the Kosovan Albanians, which began in earnest in 1998 (following almost a decade of Serb attempts to impose their domination in Kosovo). It is possible that eventually a counter-movement of unification may set in, because of the substantial economic ties connecting the different regions and states making them mutually dependent on each other, but it seems very likely that the pattern for any such overarching structure will not be a reunification of separate states into one larger state but looser arrangements of economic connection.

Western Europe

In Western Europe, the people of richer regions may feel that poorer regions of the same state are living off their backs and holding them back, while the people of poorer regions may feel trapped in a relationship of underdevelopment, exploitation and worsening dependency. For the richer regions, there are two possible tactics in this situation: to get control of the central government and make it reduce its subventions to the poorer regions by free-market policies, or to split off the richer region from the state. The Northern Leagues in Italy is a movement that veers between these two approaches, combining a neo-liberal assault on central government's public spending with occasional calls for the rich north to secede from the rest of Italy so as to stop having to 'subsidise' the south.

One possible development is that Europe may ultimately operate with the EU as its overarching structure (corresponding to the effective economic unit, the European market as a whole) while within it the units representing territorial interests could be of the size of (present-day) regions like Lombardy or Alsace or Jutland, while existing large states cease to exist or to be significant. Such a structure might be utilised either in the interests of the richer regions, entrenching their position, or as a structure to enable redistribution of wealth and resources from the richer to the poorer regions. Such a 'Europe of the regions', embodying the 'principle of subsidiarity', would require very drastic changes in the present structure of the EU itself as well as to the entrenched political structures, which depend on the existing states.

Most of the larger European states, and some of the smaller ones, have already progressed some way on the road of regionalisation, following the model of Germany. Spain has devolved a great deal of power to its regions, while Italy has devolved quite a lot of power; and Belgium, the Netherlands and Switzerland have long-established entrenched rights for their regions. Under Conservative governments (1979–97), the UK continued to centralise power in London, and for much of the period it was the only large-scale centralised state in the EU. However, following the election of a Labour government in May 1997, constitutional reform – including directly elected regional assemblies for Scotland, Wales and Northern Ireland – sought to change this anomaly. If a devolved structure in the EU as a whole is to serve as a basis for a redistributive polity, the control over its operation exercised by EU institutions themselves – especially distribution of the Social and Regional Funds – would have to be much stronger than it is at present. These considerations provide part of the reason for the strong opposition of sections of the political right to enlargement of the powers of the EU.

Contemporary racism in Europe

Since the latter half of the 1980s, there has been a perceptible growth in manifestations of racism and especially anti-Semitism in many European countries. In the early years of the twenty-first century, many European countries have witnessed a growth in racist hostility directed against Muslims. In the aftermath of '9/11' and the US-led war in Iraq beginning in 2003, many Muslim citizens of European countries have felt that they are the target of suspicion and are treated as a sort of cultural 'enemy within'. With increased immigration into Europe, violent attacks on racial minorities have also increased. For example, anti-racist groups in Spain – which accepted 600,000 immigrants in 2003, a third of the EU's total – estimated in 2004 that more than 1,000 violent racist incidents occurred each year and that the problem was growing steadily worse. Regrettably this is nothing new; racism has a long history in European culture, and 'the dark side of Europe' is as much part of Europe's political legacy as the Enlightenment ethos. How far Europe will outgrow this, and how far it is likely to become caught in a vicious spiral of racism and ethnic conflict, is one of the most important issues facing us today.

It is not so difficult, though, to discern some causes of the current wave of racism. Continuing economic recession seems to have condemned many millions to long-term unemployment and has compounded social problems. The policies pursued by governments show little sign of being able to improve the situation greatly, and many people give up hope in democratic politics, identify closely with a narrow group of their own people and take out their frustrations in hatred of outsiders.

The extent of racism is notoriously difficult to measure. For example, there are problems in determining how far verbal or physical attacks are motivated principally by racism rather than other causes such as general aggressiveness. There are therefore few reliable statistics. Nor is it easy to find conclusive evidence relating the incidence of such attacks to the ethnic origin of either victims or perpetrators. However, it seems clear that the vast majority of such attacks in Europe are inflicted by the majority population on minorities. Not all racial offences are of this nature, however – some racist convictions come from one minority population discriminating unlawfully against another, and in a few cases citizens from the minority population have been convicted of racist offences (including murder) against the majority population.

Racism may appeal to those who feel their material security, or their sense of identity, or both, to be threatened by processes of change that are too complex to grasp or to control easily.

Racist ideology focuses on difference as constituting a threat. Those who are defined as different – the outsider, the stranger – are targeted as scapegoats for the resentments and frustrations of ordinary people. In fact, even the physical presence of minority groups is not always necessary for such 'scapegoat' hatreds to become established. It has been noted, for example, that strong anti-Semitism has persisted in Poland, despite the fact that the Holocaust, followed by decades of discrimination at the hands of the Polish communist regime, effectively reduced that country's Jewish community to a tiny handful (less than 5,000 by 1989, although thereafter rising somewhat to an estimated 12,000, partly as a result of some young Polish Catholics converting to Judaism). Throughout the continent, the Jewish community has once again been exposed to insult (manifested in the daubing of Nazi slogans on Jewish graves and synagogues and in attacks on Jews). However, the main targets of racist attacks in recent years have been immigrants, and these attacks have often been associated with prejudices about those with different skin colour, those who are simply desperately poor, and those from predominantly Muslim cultures – not just North African societies, but also Bosnia and Albania, for example.

Immigration and immigrants

The recent upsurge in racism is manifest in rising support for far right political parties and in a sharp increase in physical (often murderous) attacks upon refugees and immigrants in many Western European countries. Far right parties that openly advocated policies against immigrants made substantial gains in elections in France, Germany, Italy, Austria, Belgium, Switzerland and Denmark in the 1990s and early 2000s, leading to the inclusion of these parties in governing coalitions in Italy, Austria and Switzerland. And the policies of many European parties on the 'respectable' right moved sharply in a racist direction in anti-immigrant policies adopted by, for example, French Interior Minister Charles Pasqua in 1993.

As we have seen, in January 1994 the European Commission tried to promote a constructive European policy on immigration by issuing a 'Green Paper'. As a result, the member states of the EU agreed to allow easier movement of immigrants between member states without the need for visas, to guarantee security of residence for immigrants and their families, and to outlaw racial discrimination at work. At the same time, tough moves against illegal immigrants were contemplated. A controversial development was the decision by the EU in 1995 to fund a barrier on the North African coast to keep illegal immigrants out of Europe. Classified as a military project, this high-tech 8.5-kilometre wall was to be constructed on the border between the Spanish enclave of Ceuta and Morocco at a cost of $29 million. Comparisons with the former Berlin Wall and accusations of institutionalised racism in a new 'Fortress Europe' were inevitable.

Some European governments have attempted to tackle racism by granting their immigrant communities new rights and seeking to integrate them more fully. For example, this approach characterised the Social Democrat–Green coalition government in Germany that was elected in October 1998. Germany had long operated one of the most restrictive nationality and citizenship laws, denying even the right to vote to millions of German-born children of immigrants. The new government of Chancellor Gerhard Schröder promised a radical overhaul of the antiquated 'blood and soil' citizenship law, dating from 1913, to make where a person was born rather than who their mother was the key criterion in deciding citizenship. The new law – vigorously opposed by the centre-right Christian Democrats as well as the far right neo-Nazis – was aimed at conferring full citizenship rights on three million immigrant children born in Germany, making it easier for several million others to acquire German citizenship (by reducing the length of the residence requirement), and challenging racism head-on by countering an exclusive, blood-based view of what constitutes the national community with an inclusive and democratic view. In some other countries, a vigorous, if not always balanced, debate on how best culturally to integrate members of the Muslim minority community was under way by 2004. In France, this was hastened by the decision of the French government in 2004 to outlaw the display of religious symbols – including the Muslim headscarf – in French schools in the name of upholding the secular nature of the French Republic. And in the Netherlands, the murder in November 2004 by an Islamic extremist of Theo van Gogh, a controversial film director whose work had offended some Muslims, gave rise to a heated debate about the perceived threat to Dutch liberal values. Right across Europe, as far right organisations sought to exploit widespread feelings of insecurity after September 2001 by focusing their attacks on the presence of Muslim communities, and as the possible admission to EU membership of Turkey, with its large Muslim population, gained new momentum, questions of human rights protection, cultural pluralism and the meaning of European identity loomed large.

Further reading

Abley, M. (2003) *Spoken Here: Travels Among Threatened Languages*, William Heinemann, London.

Anderson, B. (1983) *Imagined Communities: Reflections on the Origin and Spread of Nationalism*, Verso, London.

Brubaker, R. (1996) *Nationalism Reframed: Nationhood and the National Question in the New Europe*, Cambridge University Press, Cambridge.

Caplan, R. and Feffer, J. (eds) (1996) *Europe's New Nationalism: States and Minorities in Conflict*, Oxford University Press, Oxford.

Drysdale, H. (2001) *Mother Tongues: Travels Through Tribal Europe*, Picador, London.

Kellas, J. (1998) *The Politics of Nationalism and Ethnicity*, 2nd edn, Macmillan, Basingstoke.

Part 5

Main issues and challenges

Plate 5.1 The Mostar Bridge, in Bosnia, was built in the sixteenth century. It was destroyed in 1993 during the fighting between Muslims and Croats. The rebuilt bridge was opened in July 2004. The rebuilding of this bridge was regarded by many as an important symbol of the need for reconciliation of communities. What else might be done to help achieve a lasting peace?

Source: Old Mostar bridge: Nicolas Janberg's *Structurae*, international database and gallery of structures, photographer Sheldon Breiner (1959); rebuilt Mostar bridge, *Structurae*, photographer Alexandra Henriques (2005).

Section 5.1

Introduction

In Part 5, we revisit rather more comprehensively some of the important current topics we raised earlier in the book. Our focus is on issues that provide challenges to the EU or to a wider Europe.

We start by reviewing in a general way the cultural fault lines that divide contemporary Europe. We then look at the most striking example in recent European history of the problems of such cultural differences by a brief examination of the troubled story of Yugoslavia and pose the question whether there are other potential Yugoslavias in Europe.

We then change perspective by looking at one of the manifestations of 'multi-speed' or 'variable-geometry' Europe, the euro zone. We discuss the causes of both the euro zone's successes and its worryingly persistent high unemployment rates. From this, we proceed to think again about the 2004 EU enlargement, which we introduced in Part 1, and discuss the prospects for further enlargement of the EU; is it likely that in the near future all European countries will be members of some kind of multi-speed EU?

Key concept 5.1

Multi-speed and variable-geometry Europe

'Multi-speed Europe' is the term used when a group of member states is able and willing to integrate in a particular way and does so in the expectation that the other member states will in due course follow them – so in due course they will all have the same degree of integration.

'Variable-geometry Europe' is the term used when a group of member states is able and willing to integrate in a particular way and does so but is fully aware that other member states have no intention of following them – so there will be a permanent difference in the degree of integration.

What kind of multi-speed or variable-geometry EU might be on offer depends, among other things, on the fortunes of the proposed Constitutional Treaty. We looked at the Treaty in some detail in Part 3, but here we will lead to a more fundamental question by asking what real difference, if any, its ratification might make to the future structure of Europe.

Cultural divisions in society and hostility to minority groups

Every society of any size contains cultural differences. If they are sufficiently significant and have sufficiently wide-ranging consequences for people's ways of life or their moral attitudes, they can be regarded as making divisions between different groups of people, especially if several different kinds of cultural difference coincide in the same groups. Such differences might be rooted in religion, or language, or social attitude, e.g. to consumption of alcohol or drugs. Other differences (which are usually – but not always – regarded more lightly) include support for different football teams, or liking for different kinds of music and dance, or levels of formal education. Sometimes differences of physical appearance coincide with such cultural differences – most notably, colour of skin. Since every society contains many such differences, there is no reason in general to think that they have to prevent social interaction or cooperative and friendly relations within that society. But it can happen that different groups that such cultural differences set up become hostile to each other; they may even fight each other, or one may try to exterminate the other (genocide). Usually, this happens because there are real or perceived clashes of interest between them. Before 1945, Europe had a long and unhappy history of hostilities between such culturally determined groups, although also many examples of untroubled coexistence.

Religion

In the sixteenth and seventeenth centuries, differences of religion led to ferocious wars in Europe. But the hostility between different religious groups was especially fierce and intractable because people then assumed that everyone in the same state ought to practise the same religion. Partly this was because people thought that if they were right about God (and their faith compelled them to think that they were), then everyone who thought differently must be wrong; and partly it was because religion was thought to express loyalty to the ruler and to the law, so that people thought a society would disintegrate if there were different religious beliefs in it. In other words, religion was felt to have an overriding importance and significance. When in the eighteenth century most people came to accept that different religious beliefs could be held in a society so long as everyone accepted the law (religious toleration), much of the hostility between different religious groups faded away to a level short of outright persecution or fighting. However, religion remains a source of possible jealousy and dislike, especially because people still feel that it has an overriding status. Consequently, it still sometimes degenerates into hostility, especially if it is combined with other cultural differences. For example, the difference between Roman Catholics and Protestants in Northern Ireland has given rise to long-lasting hostility and violence. Why was this? Partly it arose from a 400-year-old history of conflict and oppression, and partly from continuing assumptions about giving jobs, local authority houses and other bases for success in life only to those of one's own religion, reinforced by discrimination in civil rights. Thus a person's prospects in life depended on his or her religion, and some people (mainly Roman Catholics) felt unfairly disadvantaged just because of their religion. Jealousies and dislikes based on cultural difference were exacerbated into hostility by discrimination, which seriously disadvantaged members of one group.

This way in which cultural difference may be exacerbated into hostility is rather common. This is why many people hope that a modern open capitalist society, in which jobs are competed for fairly in a labour market in which all discrimination is illegal, will cause hostility between different cultural groups to disappear. No doubt that is a tendency of such a modern society, but it is easy to see that in practice such neutrality may not be attained and discrimination may continue even if not officially sanctioned (and Northern Ireland is a striking example of this). This is particularly likely to happen if a state is founded on the basis of the religion of its majority group, so that religion defines the national identity. This was the origin of the separate province (within the UK) of Northern Ireland (set up for Protestants), and of the state of Israel (set up for Jews). If Christianity comes to be understood as the defining condition of the identity of the EU, as some Europeans wish, the EU, too, will be based on religion, and discrimination against Muslims and perhaps Jews will be encouraged. It is these two religious groups that are already somewhat discriminated against, Muslims particularly because they may be associated with terrorism (however unjustly in general) and may be resented as major immigrant groups, and Jews because the deep historical roots of traditional anti-Semitism keep reviving, especially when they are exacerbated by opposition to the policies of the state of Israel and sympathy for Palestinians. In both cases, it is events whose origins are external to the society that might tend to raise a minor sense of difference to the level of serious hostility. An official endorsement of the idea that the EU is essentially Christian Europe (associated perhaps with refusing Turkey admission to the EU) would probably greatly strengthen such hostility. But in the case of Muslims, there is also a widespread suspicion that traditional Muslim attitudes to women entrench male dominance and block the full participation of women in social and political life; and many Europeans (of both sexes) oppose and dislike Islam for this reason. In fact, although these traditional attitudes are undoubtedly strong, Islam also contains traditions of special respect for women that fit very well with the democratic requirement of gender equality. Nevertheless, the perception among many non-Muslim Europeans of Islam as a male-dominated ideology is a potential source of hostility.

Language

Groups that speak different languages usually have many other differences as well, because they often have separate histories and because language affects so many other aspects of culture. Also, there is a strong tendency for language to affect favourably or adversely a person's prospects in life; e.g. one's chances of a good job may depend on speaking the dominant language in a given society fluently, partly because one could do the job better with that linguistic skill, partly because employers may have a prejudice in favour of the language they themselves understand best. This is part of the reason why most nation-states have tried to instil linguistic competence in one language as the official language of the state (and to define its rules and vocabulary, establishing in this way what the language is); everything in the state works best if all adult citizens speak the same language.

Nevertheless (as pointed out in Part 4), linguistic minorities within a state are virtually universal. In Europe, for example, they occur in:

- Switzerland (where three main languages – German, French and Italian – are found in different cantons, but the society works very well);
- Belgium (where the Flemish speakers so much resented the second-class status left to them by the relative dominance of the French speakers that they have converted Belgium into a federal state with separate semi-autonomous departments with different official languages);
- in Germany (where Turkish immigration has established a large Turkish-speaking population with Turkic lifestyles, generally poorly placed for social success compared with the German speakers).

Where such minorities occur in a definite region, it is common for some spokesmen for the region to demand autonomy or even independence, as the Basques have demanded autonomy or independence in Spain, or the Slovaks (successfully) within what had been (until their secession in 1993) Czechoslovakia. Sometimes the state will resist such pressures in order to retain control over its territory, if necessary by using decisive force if it can, as Yugoslavia opposed the secession of Slovenia and Croatia in 1991–95, Spain continues to resist the demands for Basque independence, and France continues to resist the (rather small-scale) demands for Corsican independence. Such a state will tend to regard any speaker of the minority language (or minority culture) as a potential recruit to a subversive organisation, a suspicion that tends to increase hostility on both sides and leave members of the minority disadvantaged and aggrieved, so that a spiral of increasing violence can be generated. Yet Europe in the twentieth century had quite a good record of states permitting secession or autonomy for culturally different regions, as in Norway's secession from Denmark (1905), Finland's from Russia (1917), Slovakia's from Czechoslovakia

(1993), or the Flemish regions of Belgium or the largely German-speaking Alto Adige (South Tirol) in Italy establishing some sort of accepted autonomy within their states. The worst recent example of a state using violent force to maintain its grip on a disaffected region is Russia's resistance to Chechen separatism, where the cultural difference is as much religious (Islam is the main religious tradition in Chechnya, whereas Orthodox Christianity is the main religion in most of the rest of the Russian Federation) as linguistic, and where violence on both sides has reached a terrible level. The framework of community law and of respect for human rights established by the EU is likely to be a major restraining influence on member states, leading to compromises and concessions to avoid the spiral of violence, an influence lacking in the case of Russia.

Linguistic minorities that do not occupy a definite region (such as nearly all immigrant groups) cannot sensibly seek autonomy or independence, and members of these groups who hope for social and economic advancement must gradually adapt themselves to the dominant language and lifestyle (at least insofar as this is grounded in the law). But respect for their human rights as culturally defined peoples requires that their state tries so far as is possible to enable them to preserve their way of life and language in addition to expecting that they become competent in the official language of the state.

Differences in languages of member states of the EU

A quite different problem of linguistic diversity arises from the different languages of the member states of the EU. Since there is (or is supposed to be) a unified labour market across the EU, and there are many kinds of legal and administrative interconnection through it, there would be the same advantage as for any nation-state in having all citizens speaking the same language. But in the case of the EU this is wholly impracticable; the many languages of Europe are essential to it, and since all members are of equal status, it is essential in principle that every such

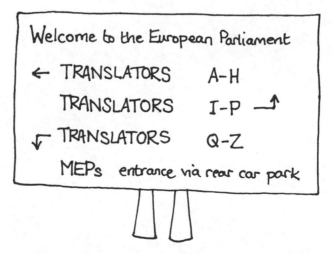

Figure 5.1 A comment on the number of official languages in the EU
Source: Katy Jones.

language is given equal status. This principle would require huge expenditure on translation within EU institutions, and since the expansion of the EU in the 1990s and the twenty-first century, the laudable but impractical aim of equal status for all EU languages has been tacitly abandoned except, for example, in the proceedings of the European Parliament. English and French are the effective languages of EU communication, and English especially tends to be the language of commerce throughout Europe (and indeed throughout the world). The widespread use of English is a great advantage for the operation of the EU as a unified labour market, but the EU also operates a general policy of promoting linguistic education for all citizens so as to encourage effective communication among Europe's citizens without treating any language as second class. The aspiration is that each child should preferably learn at least two foreign European languages at school; this seems in practice to enable a fairly good level of communication within the EU.

Further reading

Campbell, D. (1998) *National Deconstruction and Violence: Identity and Justice in Bosnia*, Minnesota University Press, Minneapolis, MN and London.

Castles, S. (2000) *Ethnicity and Globalization*, Sage, London.

Eickelman, D.F. and Piscatori, J. (1996) *Muslim Politics*, Princeton University Press, Princeton, NJ.

European Commission on the Press and Communication (2004) *Many Tongues, One Family: Languages in the European Union*, European Office of Official Publications of the European Communities, Luxembourg.

Hutchinson, J. and Smith, A.D. (1996) *Ethnicity*, Oxford University Press, Oxford.

Section 5.3

Yugoslavia

We have at various times in this book mentioned the recent conflicts in what used to be Yugoslavia. Here, we will put them into context so that we can understand their origins and identify whether similar conflicts might arise elsewhere in Europe.

Yugoslavia lay in the Balkans, which for centuries was disputed particularly between the Habsburg and Ottoman Empires. The various peoples who were brought together to make up Yugoslavia had very different histories, particularly as the Ottoman Empire started to decline in the nineteenth century and the major European powers started to try to increase their influence in the area. Yugoslavia came into existence in the aftermath of the collapse of the Habsburg Empire at the end of the First World War, when Croat, Serbian and Slovenian leaders formed a federation to protect themselves against what they thought was the threat from an expansion of Italian interest in the area (Italy had been promised various Balkan territories by the Allied powers during the First World War).

But right from the start this federation, which became the Kingdom of Yugoslavia, was rent by internal divisions. The Croats, Serbs and Slovenes had different political and cultural traditions. To make matters worse, the kingdom also contained sizeable non-Slav minorities, such as Albanians, Germans, Hungarians, Romanians and Turks, as well as smaller groups of other peoples such as Greeks and Italians. Cutting across ethnic lines were religious divisions, with Christian (mainly Roman Catholic and Orthodox), Islamic and Jewish faiths all well established.

During the Second World War, Bulgaria, Germany, Hungary and Italy divided Yugoslavia between themselves:

- Bulgaria took Macedonia and part of Serbia;

- Germany created a puppet Croatian state (Nezavisna drzava Hrvatska, NDH), embracing Bosnia-Herzegovina and most of Croatia, and occupied parts of Serbia and Slovenia;

- Hungary took parts of Croatia and Slovenia;

- Italy took the rest of Slovenia and Montenegro and ran a puppet state in Albania that included Kosovo.

NDH, with Italian support, started to massacre Jews, Roma and Serbs within its area. Two resistance groups developed. One, developed mainly from the remains of the Yugoslav army and from Serbs fleeing genocide, was known as the Chetniks. The second resistance group, the communist Partisans, led by Josip Broz Tito, became the more important. Infighting between the two groups led eventually to the Chetniks switching sides to try to prevent a communist victory; but such a victory was assured when the Soviet army reached Yugoslavia. During the Second World War, Yugoslavia lost about 11 percent of its prewar population, mostly to Yugoslavs killing other Yugoslavs.

At the end of the Second World War, Tito, who was of Croatian-Slovenian descent, was firmly established in power. The monarchy was abolished and a Soviet-style federal state established. The new federation consisted of six republics: Bosnia-Herzegovina, Croatia, Macedonia, Montenegro, Serbia and Slovenia. Macedonia and Montenegro were made separate republics to try to prevent Serbian domination of the country, and Kosovo and Vojvodina were established as autonomous regions within Serbia. From 1949, with Western aid, Tito established the independence of Yugoslavia from the rest of the Soviet bloc, and Yugoslavia pursued an increasingly independent approach, particularly in its unique mixture of a market system with state ownership of the means of production.

Tito's policy was of strong central leadership, and he put down various outbursts of unrest by a mixture of minor concessions and purges of the rebel leadership – such incidents occurred, for example, when Albanians demanded (1968–69) that Kosovo should have the full status of a republic, when a nationalist movement developed in Croatia (1967–71) and when in 1972 there was a series of local pressures in Macedonia, Serbia and Slovenia for economic and political reform. When Tito died, in 1980, many commentators expected the early collapse of Yugoslavia into its constituent parts, but in fact it was another ten years before the tensions became too much and a decade of violent conflict ensued. We have discussed some of the details of this conflict earlier in the book – e.g. in Part 4 – but the next few paragraphs summarise events. The tangled history of the wars in Yugoslavia, 1991–99, is summarised very well in the article 'Yugoslav Succession, Wars of' in Microsoft Encarta Online Encyclopedia (at http://www.encarta.msn.com), from which much of the following is drawn. See also the Chronological Table for further information.

The crisis was started by the desire of Serbia, under Slobodan Milošević, its president in 1989, to reassert Serb dominance of Yugoslavia, but events were precipitated into war by the actions of Croatia and Slovenia. In 1988 and 1989, Serbia denied autonomy to Kosovo and Vojvodina, and the Albanians, who were the majority population in Kosovo, were repressed. A round of elections in 1990 brought nationalist parties to power in all six Yugoslav republics, some communist and some anti-communist. The new governments in Croatia and Slovenia wanted a looser federation (envisaging the break-up of the country), but the Montenegrins and Serbs wanted a centralised structure (which the Serbs expected to dominate). Bosnia-Herzegovina and Macedonia tried to find a compromise. In a referendum in December 1990, the Slovenes voted for independence if agreement on their proposal could not be reached in six months. In May 1991, the Croatians also voted for independence, and Croatia and Slovenia declared their independence on 25 June 1991.

A brief war in Slovenia in June–July 1991 ended with the permanent withdrawal of the Yugoslav army from that country. The conflict in Croatia was rather more severe because its causes were more deep-rooted, stretching back to the Great Schism of 1054. The anti-communist Croatian government elected in 1990 (under Franjo Tudjman) had started to deny rights to Serbs living in Croatia, and the Serbs in Croatia feared that the new government was in effect a restoration of the wartime German puppet state NDH. The Serbian government encouraged these fears and invited Bosnian Serbs and Croatian Serbs to secede from those countries and join a greater Serbia; the Serbs in one region in Croatia, Krajina, accepted this invitation and in effect declared in March 1991 that they were no longer in Croatia but that their region was part of Serbia. The main battlefields between the Yugoslav forces and Croatians were in the sieges of Dubrovnic and Vukovar. By the time of the ceasefire negotiated under US pressure in December 1991, Serb forces controlled about a third of Croatia, including Krajina. In January 1992, all these territories were transferred into the control of a UN peacekeeping army. By 1998, Croatia had regained them all, by a mixture of military intervention and international agreement – but as it did so most of the remaining Serbian population in these areas fled. Croatia and Slovenia were internationally recognised as independent states from January 1992, first by the EC in response to strong German pressure (Germany had retained a strong interest in Croatia).

Bosnia-Herzegovina fell victim particularly to the worsening relationship between Croatia and Serbia in 1991. At that time, Bosnia-Herzegovina was very mixed ethnically – about 44 percent of its population were Muslim Slavs, about 31 percent Serbs and about 17 percent Croats. The Serbs and Croats started to organise themselves into separate autonomous regions. When Croatia and Slovenia applied for EC recognition as independent states, the Bosnia-Herzegovina government also decided to do so, despite protests from Bosnian Serbs. A referendum on independence was boycotted by the Bosnian Serbs but gave the government the basis for declaring independence and having this recognised in April 1992 by the EC and the USA. This precipitated war, with the Bosnian Serbs being supported by Serbia, the Bosnian Croats by Croatia and the Bosnian Muslims (much the least well armed) by volunteers from Islamic countries. The Bosnian Croats started by supporting the Bosnian Muslims but latterly worked for the expansion of Croatia into the country. The war ran from 1992 to 1995. Various international peacekeeping attempts, mainly directed against the Serbs, failed to protect civilians from mass murder and captured combatants from death in concentration camps. The international community was eventually provoked into more decisive action after UN peacekeepers were unable to prevent a massacre in what was a supposedly safe enclave in Srebrenica. NATO intervention and military success by the Croat army against the Bosnian Serbs finally brought about the Dayton Peace Accord at the end of 1995. The Dayton agreement nominally divided Bosnia into a Muslim–Croat federation, with 51 percent of the territory, and a Serb republic, with the remainder. In fact, Bosnia-Herzegovina was, and still is, run by the EU, NATO and the UN, but with a steady reduction in the size of the forces based there.

The last episode of armed conflict in the region was the Kosovo war, conducted by NATO in 1999 to protect the Kosovan Albanians from Serbian persecution.

Now, Bosnia-Herzegovina, Croatia, Slovenia and the Former Yugoslav Republic of Macedonia (FYROM) are fully independent countries in their own right, and Serbia and Montenegro have formed a federal union. (FYROM has its cumbersome name because of a continuing dispute with Greece over the use of the name 'Macedonia' (see Key concept 5.2). Kosovo is formally in Serbia but in practice a separate region administered by the UN. Slovenia, as we have seen, joined the EU in 2004, and Croatia and FYROM are currently applicants to join the EU.

Key concept 5.2

Macedonia

The name 'Macedonia' historically belonged to territory now partly in Greece and partly in FYROM. The ancient Greek city-states were in the southern part of what is now Greece, and Macedonia lay to their north. In the first half of the fourth century BC, the Persian Empire was very powerful and expanding rapidly westwards towards Greece. Two successive kings of Macedonia, Philip II and Alexander the Great, repelled the threat. The Greek city-states, led by Athens and Thebes, first fought unsuccessfully against Macedonia but were then led by Macedonia into the Corinthian League, which conquered the Persian Empire. Not only did Alexander's armies conquer the Persians, they also crossed the Indus and defeated the rulers of the Punjab in India. When Alexander died, in 323 BC, the Corinthian League controlled the whole swathe of territory from Greece eastwards into India. By about 300 BC, these lands had become fragmented. The memory of the achievements of Philip II and Alexander lived on, however, in legends throughout Greece, the Middle East and northern India. Northern Greece and southern Yugoslavia derived great pride from their association with the name 'Macedonia'. Thus, claims by FYROM to the name simply of Macedonia offend Greek sensibilities, since the Greek region of Macedonia has equal claim to the title.

Yugoslavia was, as we have seen, a country created by a federation of interests with many internal cultural, ethnic and religious fissures. Crucial factors in holding the country together for so long after 1945 were Tito's choice of a federal structure and his own personality. But the internal pressures, particularly Serbia's frustration at being denied the dominance its population numbers would imply (see Table 5.1) and Croat nationalism, were too great, and international intervention was necessary to protect the interests particularly of the Albanian and Bosnian minorities. Partition, such as that of Bosnia by the Dayton Peace Accord of 1995, can rarely produce a satisfactory solution. Partition may involve large-scale movements of people ('ethnic cleansing'), with all the resentment thereby aroused. If there is no 'ethnic cleansing', partition leaves behind significant minorities who remain cut off from their cultural or ethnic or religious fellows, thus creating a cause for more tension in the future. The problems of the former country of Yugoslavia clearly cannot be over until the problem of Bosnia-Herzegovina is fully solved, by formal partition or by a peaceful cooperation for which history offers little hope.

Table 5.1 Population of former Yugoslavia (millions)

	1991	2004 (estimate)
Bosnia-Herzegovina	4.4	4.0
Croatia	4.8	4.5
FYROM	2.0	2.1
Montenegro	0.6	(in figure for Serbia)
Serbia	9.8	10.8
Slovenia	1.7	2.0

(Source of 2004 estimates: CIA, 2005, http://www.cia.gov/cia/publications/factbook/geos.)

What of the rest of Europe? Are there other potential Yugoslavias? The actions by most Western European governments in regional devolution of power seem to have taken the steam out of most separatist movements there. In Central and Eastern Europe, however, and especially in Russia and Turkey, there are many minorities who feel deprived of their rights and who may well be the majority in specific areas. The countries that are applicants to be members of the EU are required to address problems of their treatment of minorities as a condition of entry. For the rest, however, there is no obvious external force to lead them away from potential problems. Indeed, when Russia can portray its treatment of Chechnya as part of the 'war on terror', the constraints may be very few.

Further reading

Much useful information on the history of Yugoslavia until December 1990 is available on the (US) Library of Congress Country Studies website: (http://www.cweb2.loc.gov/cgi-bin/query).

For recent information, the BBC News country profiles are helpful – the website is (http://www.newsvote.bbc.co.uk).

'Yugoslav Succession, Wars of' in *Microsoft Encarta Online Encyclopedia* (available at http://www.encarta. msn.com).

CIA, *The World Factbook*, February 2005 (http://www.cia.gov/cia/publications/factbook/geos).

Section 5.4

The economic policy of the euro zone

Signing up to membership of the euro zone (as is the case for any monetary union) implies more than simply giving up your own currency and adopting the euro. There are also questions of economic and political gains and losses. To weigh these up, we must first briefly consider the objectives and, especially, the instruments of macro-economic policy.

The boxes look at these topics in a little more detail. Key fact 5.1 outlines the main objectives of macro-economic policy – policy about the level of output in the economy as a whole – and explains that modern macro-economic policy requires a delicate balancing of demand and supply. Macro-economic policy is policy about the running of the economy as a whole, including the financing of government and its level of expenditure. The total of expenditure in the economy is conventionally considered in the broad headings of consumption (mainly by households), investment (mainly by firms on new buildings and other capital equipment), government expenditure, exports and imports.

Policy to try to influence the total of all this expenditure is called demand management. Although the very earliest works in economics – such as Adam Smith's *An Inquiry into the Nature and Causes of the Wealth of Nations* (1776) – tried to analyse the scope for macro-economic management, the focus of most of the work in economics in the nineteenth and early twentieth centuries was on the operations of markets, with the general approach being that little could or should be done about the overall level of economic activity. The revolution in economic policy brought about by the work of John Maynard Keynes, particularly in his *The General Theory of Employment, Interest and Money* (1936), was to introduce the idea that it was possible for governments to undertake demand management. Keynes was writing against the background of the severe interwar depression, conventional policy towards which was to help the poorest through charitable endeavour but otherwise that little could be done to alleviate unemployment. Keynes argued that the government could reduce unemployment by raising its own expenditure and by policies such as interest rate cuts to try to stimulate investment. Keynesian policies of demand management were generally adopted in Western countries from the late 1930s until the 1960s.

The very success of demand management policies in the 1950s and early 1960s produced its own problems. Governments realised that if they ran their economies with very low levels of unemployment there was a danger of inflation, but it was thought that there was for each country a very similar menu of choices between inflation and unemployment, portrayed in what was known as the Phillips curve (after its discoverer, A.W. Phillips). According to the Phillips curve, unless unemployment fell to very low levels, there was a fairly small price to be paid in inflation for reducing unemployment, so Western European governments typically chose what appeared to be the fairly modest inflation (around 2 or 3 percent per annum) that combined with about 2 percent unemployment. In the 1960s, a new economic problem became very apparent – there was systemic inflation, represented by higher and higher levels of inflation being associated with any particular level of unemployment. It was evident that the hitherto stable Phillips curves were shifting, because all the decision makers in the economy – especially firms and households – expected prices to rise and acted accordingly. The 'fine tuning' of total demand by upward or downward adjustment of government income and expenditure and of interest rates could not solve these new problems of inflation.

A monetarist approach to economic policy, associated particularly with the US economist Milton Friedman, argued that the inflation was being caused by lack of control of the money supply (much as in the German hyperinflation we looked at in Part 2). The monetarist approach required a different set of policy instruments, focusing on control of the money supply. However, these proved in fact to be rather difficult to operate, because as soon as one definition of 'money supply' was picked for the purpose, its nature changed. The other major problem with monetarism is that the policy works only after quite a long lag – about 18 months, but the exact lag seems to be variable.

A third approach to economic policy proved to be more effective in tackling inflation. This was supply-side economics. It argued that the problem with Keynesian policy was that it looked only at the total of demand in the economy and ignored total supply. Just as in any individual market, if quantity demanded does not equal quantity supplied prices will change, so the same is true at the macro-economic level. If total demand is greater than total supply, overall prices will rise – the process of inflation – and the long period of pursuit of demand management policies had built inflation into the economy. Once everyone expects inflation to occur, it takes drastic measures to drive out these inflationary expectations. So the way to get rid of inflation is to adopt two sets of policies. In the short run, total demand must fall; longer-term policy should also increase total supply, by making the capacity of the economy grow faster. The implication is that in the short run there is a trade-off between employment and inflation, but the trade-off is not as gentle as the Phillips curve analysis suggested: to get rid of inflation, employment must fall (so unemployment must rise), and if employment is not cut quite sharply inflationary expectations cannot be driven out of the economy. Supply-side economists advocated, as their longer-term policies to increase total supply, measures such as:

- increasing the efficiency of the use of resources in the economy (so they advocated reducing the size of the government sector – believing that the private sector was more efficient than the public sector – by measures such as the privatisation of state assets and other transfers of hitherto public sector activity to the private sector);

- increasing the efficiency of labour markets (so they advocated reducing the power of trade unions, reducing regulations affecting the labour market and reducing state benefits to the unemployed);

- reducing the tax burden on firms and individuals (because they believed that high taxes were a disincentive to effort, so with lower taxes firms and people would work harder because they would keep more of what they earned).

Supply-side economics lies behind the economic policies pursued by many European governments – such as the Thatcher government in the UK – in the 1980s. From the 1990s, a more balanced approach, with elements of both demand management and supply-side policies, has been generally adopted, with relatively left-wing governments being more tempted by demand management to address unemployment problems and relatively right-wing governments following more supply-side approaches.

Key fact 5.1

The objectives of macro-economic policy

Macro-economic policy aims to achieve the following objectives:

- *Low unemployment*: this is achieved if total demand is high; supply-side policies in particular also stress the importance of freely working labour markets.

- *Low inflation*: this is achieved if total demand is not too high, but even with fairly low total demand there may be problems if inflationary expectations are built into the economy

- *Steady growth*: demand management policies interpret this as simply being to try to mitigate the effects of the trade cycle, but for supply-side policies this is crucial, because growth in the potential supply in the economy is the only way to have any permanent effect on the levels of unemployment or inflation.

- *A healthy foreign trading position*: in a more or less fixed exchange rate system, such as that operated by the IMF or the EC's Exchange Rate Mechanism, failure to balance exports and imports means pressure on the exchange rate, covered in the very short term by movements into or out of reserves but in the longer term by adjustments to aggregate demand; in a floating exchange rate system, such as that of the Danish or Polish currencies, failure to balance imports and exports means that the value of the currency drifts up or down, causing some instability to inflation and/or to output in the country's economy.

It may well not be possible for an economy to achieve all these objectives at once. The achievement of low unemployment may cause inflation. If the economy hits what the government thinks is the right balance between unemployment and inflation, this level of economic activity may not be consistent with the desired foreign trading position.

For some European economies, especially the UK, rising inflation was not the only macro-economic headache from the 1960s – their governments were also worried about the balance of payments. If incomes are relatively high, people consume more goods and services, including imports, so there is a tendency towards balance of payments problems. Where exchange rates were fixed (as in the IMF-run system from 1945 to 1973), this meant that measures had to be taken to reduce excessive imports, which in turn meant a reduction in demand and possibly a rise in unemployment.

The instruments in principle available to adjust total demand and supply are discussed in Key fact 5.2, the most important being government expenditure, tax rates, interest rates and exchange rates.

A country that chooses to join the euro zone automatically gives up independent control of interest rates and exchange rates. It has no independent money supply, so the interest rates prevailing in its economy are determined by the European Central Bank (ECB), over which it has limited control. It has no exchange rate of its own – when it joined the euro zone the exchange rate of its hitherto independent currency was permanently fixed against the euro, and now that it is in the euro zone its exchange rate against other currencies is that of the euro. That leaves it with independent control only of its government expenditure and tax rates, and as we shall see there are limits to its independence there, too.

Key fact 5.2

The instruments of macro-economic policy

To achieve the objectives of macro-economic policy, a range of instruments is available.

- *Government expenditure*: the government can raise or lower total demand by raising or lowering its own expenditure. This can take the form of the government spending more or less on the goods and services it pays for – such as education or defence – or of its paying more or less in 'transfer payments' to individuals, such as pensions. One of the problems in manipulating government expenditure in this way is that if the economy is running at near capacity (up against the restraints of total supply), its expenditure may 'crowd out' expenditure by the private sector in the economy, such as investment by firms in new production capacity. Policy on government expenditure is part of what is known as fiscal policy.

- *Taxes*: the government can raise or lower total demand by lowering or raising its tax take. If, for example, it reduces the income tax rate, that leaves more income available for households to spend on consumer goods, so total consumption will rise and with it total demand. Low tax rates on companies are desirable for supply-side policies, because if companies can keep more of their profits they will grow faster; similarly low personal tax rates encourage people to work harder and/or longer. Policy on taxes is the other part of fiscal policy.

- *Interest rates*: the government can raise or lower total demand by lowering or raising interest rates. If, for example, it cuts interest rates, households and firms have to spend less to borrow money, so there will be a rise in both consumption and investment. When governments were trying to pursue monetarist policies, their focus was on the total supply of money rather than the interest rate, but the two are connected. To cut interest rates, governments increase the money supply. So when governments were trying to follow monetarist policies, they lost the use of the interest rate as a policy instrument. Low interest rates are desirable for supply-side purposes, because the encouragement

▶

they give to investment promotes the long-term growth of the economy. As we have seen, interest rate changes also have implications for exchange rates – if interest rates rise, the country attracts foreign funds, and this tends to raise the value of the country's currency. There is also a connection between interest rates and the balance between taxes and government expenditure; if a government chooses, for example, to spend more than it raises in taxes, it has to finance the difference by borrowing, and if it wants to borrow more it will probably have to raise the rate of interest. Policy on interest rates or on money supply is known as monetary policy.

- *Exchange rates*: the government can raise or lower total demand by causing the value of its currency to rise or fall. If, for example, the value of the Danish currency rises against other currencies, imports into Denmark seem more expensive, so in the short run Danish households and firms will be more likely to buy home-produced rather than imported goods, so raising total demand for Danish-made goods. In the longer run, the effect may be minimal (or even negative), because the imports that still have to be made to Denmark will cost more, so there will be a tendency to inflation as firms pass on the higher costs they experience, and Danish exports may fall as a result.

- *Other policy instruments*: governments also have available a battery of other instruments, such as prices and income policies (restricting the rises in prices and incomes) or exchange controls (limiting the flow of foreign exchange) that can be used for macro-economic policy. Although some of these are still in principle available, in practice they have not been used by Western European governments since the 1960s, because their operation is cumbersome and their effects of very limited duration.

So we can see the source of the costs to countries of joining the euro zone: loss of control over macro-economic policy. If governments have no independent money supply, they cannot adjust their money supply or interest rates in the way their domestic economy requires but have to rely on the institutions of the euro zone, particularly the ECB, to act in a manner appropriate for them.

This does not matter so much if the euro-zone member states experience cyclical swings at about the same time and of the same intensity, because in that case the monetary policy actions appropriate for any one euro-zone member are likely to be appropriate for them all – one size does indeed fit all. But if their cycles are not fully synchronised, then a policy by the ECB, say to expand output because some countries are in cyclical decline, may be quite wrong for a country whose main problem is inflation. There is perhaps some risk that the very process of economic integration, by encouraging specialisation of output, will make the euro-zone economies less similar and so increase the risk that some random occurrence affects some of them differently from others (Healey 2005: 110–11). As we have seen, concern principally over cyclical harmonisation lies behind the UK government's refusal so far to join the euro zone.

Another important condition for one size of monetary policy to fit all is that labour markets are flexible and labour is mobile. If these conditions are not met, it is harder for those thrown out of work by some random shock affecting a euro-zone country to find work either in another industry in their own country or by moving to another country in the euro zone; and unless all euro-zone countries are affected alike by that shock, it is unlikely that the ECB's policies will be sensitive to their plight. It is clear that language and cultural differences within the euro zone limit the freedom of movement of labour between countries.

In general, if governments retain control over their fiscal policies, they may feel they still have enough scope to manage their own economies without any independence of monetary policy. It may therefore well be the case that the countries that have happily joined the euro zone will find tax harmonisation policies a step too far and so will want to resist movements towards closer economic integration. As we shall see, the rules of the Stability and Growth Pact, designed to achieve some harmonisation of fiscal policy within the euro zone, have recently been relaxed.

Let us now look briefly at the benefits to countries of joining the euro zone. Many of these are obvious to anyone who has travelled within the zone. You do not have to change currencies as you move from one euro-zone country to another – this saves transactions costs, because financial institutions do not have to make arrangements to let you sell one currency and buy another – so it is cheaper for you and similarly for businesses making transactions within the euro zone. It is easy to compare prices when they are expressed in the same currency, so consumers can decide whether it is worth their while to travel from one country to another to buy particular goods, and similarly firms can easily source their materials in the cheapest market. Producers particularly benefit from the elimination of uncertainty about exchange rates when they are doing business in the euro zone; a firm in Germany doing business with a firm in the UK has to take into account the possibility that the exchange rate between the euro and sterling will change part way through the transaction, whereas if the German firm is doing business with a French firm it has no such worries.

The final reason why countries have chosen to join the euro zone is a little less obvious – they believe it will generate low and stable inflation. This is partly because the factors we have just discussed – the absence of transaction costs, easy price comparisons and reduced uncertainty – in themselves tend to lower prices, or at least cause them to rise less quickly. However, the main consideration is that, as we shall see, the rules of the Stability and Growth Pact and the guidance given to the ECB place heavy weight on combating inflation. Insofar as governments wish to give priority to attacking inflation rather than, say, attacking unemployment, euro-zone membership is appealing because it lets them achieve what they want while being able to tell their electorate that unpopular measures are not their doing but are the fault of the ECB or the EU. As we shall suggest, it may be significant that the rules for macro-economic policy in the euro zone were agreed in 1989, when many EU member states had centre-right governments.

Even when countries are not in the euro zone, they may wish to behave as if they are to try to maintain stability of the exchange rate with the euro to help their exporters. This is much more difficult than if they are in the euro zone because, as we shall see, the operations of the euro zone enable the ECB to act in the foreign exchange markets using the pooled reserves of euro-zone member states. Thus non-member countries trading heavily with the euro zone may find that it is in their best interests for their exchange rate to 'shadow' the euro, but they have to bear the burden of administering this on their own and thus at greater cost than if they were members. So, for such countries, full membership might in fact actually give more, not less, scope for independence of macro-economic policy than they have by staying out.

In conclusion, let us pull together the considerations that might make countries want to join the euro zone rather than stopping at some earlier stage in the process of economic integration. The answer lies in the extent to which a successful economic integration leads to a desire for closer and closer links. If the countries of the

EU become increasingly interdependent in trade, it is more and more in the interests of their producers and consumers to cut out avoidable costs in transactions between member countries. This means first dismantling the internal barriers to trade. Once this has been done, exchange costs are the obvious next barrier to remove, together with impediments such as different systems of taxing goods and different tax rates on goods. Governments may worry about the loss of sovereignty over economic matters, but they are in practice gradually ceding sovereignty to the EU by the extent to which achieving exchange rate stability requires them to make their monetary and fiscal policies coherent with those of their EU partners. If economic linkages are working well, it takes major national political events, like the need to ratify treaties, or major externally induced problems, like the partial collapse of the ERM in late 1992, to occasion serious questioning of this gradual apparent inevitability of monetary union.

How not to arrange a monetary union

Before we look at how the euro zone actually works, let us look at another monetary union in Europe. The full monetary and economic union of Germany in 1990 is interesting in its own right, but also because important lessons were learned from it when the final details of the euro-zone operations were worked out. Because the GDR was much the smaller party in German unification, the effects there were greater than in the FRG, but even in western Germany, unemployment has risen at least partly as a consequence of the economic dislocation caused by the unification.

In looking at what was, in hindsight, clearly a badly managed monetary union, it is important to remember that, as we saw in Part 2, there was little time for the two German governments to get it right. Even before the Berlin Wall fell (November 1989), the GDR was losing population to the FRG through various roundabout routes, and after the wall fell the movement of population became a flood. The FRG could not find houses or jobs for all the new arrivals, and the GDR could not sustain the population loss. It was clear that something had to be done quickly to try to persuade GDR citizens to stay in the GDR, and unification was therefore implemented very quickly.

One of the first questions when countries decide to enter a monetary union is at what exchange rate they are going to merge their money supplies. In the case of German monetary union on 1 July 1990, political considerations led to a decision to use what, on all economic criteria, was at best a compromise rate.

- If we think about exchange rates in terms of what currencies can buy, in principle, exchange rates in the long term should reflect what is known as purchasing power parity – a representative collection of goods is identified, and the exchange rates should be such that the amount of one currency needed to buy it is equal to the amount of the other currency needed to buy it. Various German economic institutes tried in early 1990 to estimate what purchasing power parity would imply and concluded that a rate of about 1 GDR ostmark (M) to 1 FRG deutschmark (DM) was about right.

- However, another way of looking at it was to work from supply considerations, by comparing the productivity of resources used in export industries in the two

Germanys and set a rate at which GDR exporters could compete with those in the FRG. On this basis, the right rate was thought to be about 4.4 M to 1 DM.

- More generally, the productivity of resources in all activities was thought at the time to suggest a rate of about 2 M to 1 DM.

- To add to the confusion, while the (pegged) official exchange rate was 1 M to 1 DM, the unofficial market rate in early 1990 was between 7 and 11 M to 1 DM (the unofficial market was heavily influenced by political uncertainties, and a rather more normal value was about 6 M to 1 DM).

The choice confronting the two German governments was, then, basically whether to try to protect GDR exporters (by going for a rate of 4 or 5 M to 1 DM), to protect GDR production generally (by a rate of about 2 M to 1 DM) or to protect the savings of GDR consumers (by a rate of about 1 M to 1 DM). In fact, it opted for a rate between these solutions. For current transactions (prices, wages, etc.) the conversion rate used was 1 M to 1 DM. Most financial assets and liabilities were converted at the rate 2 M to 1 DM, but up to a certain limit household savings by GDR families were converted at 1 M to 1 DM. The overall average for all financial assets and liabilities was 1.8 M to 1 DM. The compromise created problems for producers and both gains and losses for consumers in eastern Germany (the former GDR).

The problems for producers are predictable – industrial production in eastern Germany fell in the last six months of 1990 by about 50 percent (overall output fell a bit less – by about 30 percent – and employment also fell by about 30 percent). Part of the fall in industrial production was due to the switch from a planned to a market economy and the consequential drastic relative price changes; a reasonable estimate is that these effects account for about half the fall in industrial output. The remaining 25 percent fall is attributable to two factors. One is eastern German loss of trade with its former CMEA partners (on which it relied for 65 percent of its foreign trade) because of their economic difficulties. The other is the combination of the initial overvaluation of eastern German production (implied by the failure of the exchange rate to reflect productivity) with rapid rises in costs for eastern German producers from wage inflation.

In deciding at what rate to convert GDR ostmarks into deutschmarks for general current payments purposes, such as calculating prices and wages, the two German governments tried to balance issues of labour productivity against the need to make sure that wages in eastern Germany would be high enough to prevent any further outflow of labour from eastern into western Germany. Wages were initially converted at 1 M to 1 DM, which, since GDR money wages were about a third of the FRG levels, would have been consistent with GDR labour productivity being a third of that of FRG. However, what is important for wage inflation is not so much the initial figure but the expectations of both workers and employers. The two German governments had promised to reduce the gap in living standards between the FRG and the GDR, so it was reasonable for the workers and employers in eastern Germany to expect subsidies from the new German government (i.e. in practice from western German taxpayers) to cover the period until their capital equipment and their labour training were brought up to previous FRG levels. When these subsidies were not forthcoming on the scale expected, labour unrest resulted.

Money wages in eastern Germany rose by about a third in 1990. However, the consequence of the rise in eastern German wages was that labour productivity had to rise in step with wages, and this meant that new capital equipment was even more urgently needed. The difficulty of upgrading capital equipment quickly across the whole economy meant that eastern Germany simply could not make output competitively, even with generous subsidies.

Unemployment hit some households, but those in work benefited from the wage rises. Average income rose by 5 percent in 1990. Living standards also improved because Western European and especially western German goods were much more readily available and could be substituted for inferior eastern German or Soviet bloc products – e.g. people bought second-hand Volkswagen cars instead of new Trabants. But the real income of many households fell because of the loss of free or heavily subsidised services the GDR government had provided, e.g. help for newly wed couples to set up house and for families with young children to use creches and kindergartens.

The other major impact on eastern German households was on their wealth. The average rate of 1.8 M to 1 DM reduced the wealth of eastern German households by about a third (the effect varied from family to family, with the wealthier families losing more). The effects of this wealth loss are more widespread than might at first sight be expected, because in the GDR, as in the other planned economies, the economic problems of the late 1980s meant that households had accumulated savings. There had been shortages of goods to buy and, in a communist country, they could not spend their money savings to buy other financial assets (like company shares) or many real assets (such as houses). The economic and monetary unification of Germany therefore reduced household wealth in eastern Germany and thereby the willingness of eastern German households to buy goods and services. The effect of all these considerations is that the experience of eastern German households was very diverse, some clearly gaining and others losing from the monetary union.

As far as western Germany is concerned, the impact of the poor post-unification performance of eastern Germany meant that there was a much bigger, and much more protracted, drain on the western German taxpayer than expected. The German government was worried about the potential inflationary effects of the wage rises in eastern Germany and so squeezed the whole German economy. This had the effect of deepening and prolonging economic recession in unified Germany and thus, indirectly, in many EU countries throughout the 1990s.

The creation of the euro zone and the role of the European Central Bank

German economic and monetary union is obviously a very special case, because of its abruptness and because it combined a planned and a market economy. However, some of the lessons apply to any monetary union, such as the creation of the euro zone. In particular, the choice of the exchange rates at which to fix conversions in the monetary union is important. The obvious technique seems to be to try gradually to reduce the volatility of rates over time in order to head towards stability at some exchange rate sanctioned by the market. This was the method adopted by the

EU in its progress towards the euro but, as we saw in Part 3 when we discussed the fortunes of the EC's Exchange Rate Mechanism (ERM) in 1992–93, gradualist approaches do not always work. Indeed, some commentators expressed serious worries about the method used to pave the transition to the creation of the euro, but their fears proved to be misplaced.

One of the problems of the ERM was that the exchange rates were not quite fixed: each currency could move up and down within a prescribed range (usually 2.25 percent) against the ecu (the European currency unit, a weighted average of all EU member currencies). The fact that movement was permitted at all enabled the market to read signals into the extent to which currencies persisted at the top or bottom of the permitted range, because if there is a big underlying problem it can be predictable what the monetary authorities will do, and speculators will continue to push the currency to the limit until either they see the action they expect or they are forced to make losses by powerful countervailing action by the monetary authorities. So the first lesson that was learned in setting up the euro was that in the period running up to the introduction of the euro as a physical currency, there should be completely fixed exchange rates between national currencies and the euro.

The second lesson was that a successful monetary union requires a degree of policy harmonisation, which was evidently lacking overall in the ERM in its successive crises in 1992 and 1993. Accordingly, the tests for euro-zone membership were carefully chosen to assess how far in economic policy and economic performance potential euro members really are like each other and both capable and willing to be governed by a common monetary policy. A common monetary policy can work only if the participants have broad agreement on how to react to internal pressures – for example, the aspirations of their trade unions for increased real pay levels and of their citizens for more jobs and for improved public services – and to external shocks, such as the abrupt downturn in many formerly rapidly growing Asian economies.

The tests are not – and do not profess to be – all that is needed for full economic union. Even if their governments were in complete agreement on matters such as the relative importance of inflation and unemployment, different countries do tend to react to common external shocks in a different way because they affect their economies differently – we have already considered the example of the different impacts on different European countries of an abrupt change in the world price of petroleum and derivatives. Economic union cannot make economic volatility go away, and a careful set of policies, including appropriate transitional assistance through regional policy, is needed to ensure that harmonisation elsewhere does not produce unbearably severe pressures in the face of unexpected shocks.

The route to the introduction of the euro was set out in Delors (1988) – a report prepared for the European Commission by a committee chaired by Jacques Delors, the Commission's president – and adopted as EC policy in 1989. There was to be a three-stage process:

1. Stage 1 set up the conditions that countries had to meet to enter the euro zone.

2. Stage 2 identified which countries could join the euro zone, at what exchange rates, and what the rules for the zone would be.

3. Stage 3, which the Delors Report envisaged as starting not later than January 1999, culminated in the introduction of the euro in place of national currencies in the euro-zone countries.

The most important part of Stage 1 (1990–93) was the agreement of criteria for membership of the euro zone – these were the Maastricht convergence criteria, discussed in Part 1. They required that interest and inflation rates converged towards those of the three lowest-inflation countries over a test run-up period, that government debt and current borrowing did not exceed a target proportion of GDP, and that the countries had been in the Exchange Rate Mechanism, and had not devalued their currency, for at least two years.

Stage 2 (1994–98) established the forerunner of the ECB to strengthen central bank cooperation within the EC. It set up what is now the Eurosystem – the ECB and the national central banks of the euro-zone countries. It was during Stage 2 that the Stability and Growth Pact was agreed (June 1997). France wished the Eurosystem to be supportive of growth. However, Germany was more concerned that the strength of the euro might be undermined by inflationary policies pursued by some other potential euro members (particularly Greece and Italy). The Stability and Growth Pact required that member governments could not run budget deficits of more than 3 percent of GDP, save in really exceptional circumstances, or overall debt of more than 60 percent of GDP. It provided that all the governments of all EU member states, whether or not in the euro zone, had to report annually on whether they had satisfied these limits, and it stated that governments of euro-zone member states that had overshot the criteria were liable to be fined, with the ECJ acting as arbiter. It seemed rather paradoxical to envisage levying a fine, the payment of which would increase government expenditure, on countries because their government expenditure was already too high! In fact, this provision has not been used, even though France and Germany have both breached the 3 percent limit.

Figure 5.2 The Strong Euro (cartoon by Royer, one of a series to introduce the euro to citizens of euro-zone countries)

Source: Audiovisual Library of the European Commission (2005).

Also in June 1997, decisions were made about which of the countries that wished to join the euro zone had met the criteria. For various reasons, Denmark, Sweden and the UK did not wish to join. Of the remaining twelve countries that were members of the EU at that stage, only Greece was found not to have met the criteria (Greece was subsequently permitted to join the euro zone, from 1 January 2001). For each of the eleven countries that were to enter Stage 3 in 1999, a fixed exchange rate between their currency and the euro was calculated, based on the recent actual exchange rates.

Stage 3 ran from January 1999 to February 2002. On 1 January 1999, the euro was introduced as a unit of account, used for interbank and intergovernmental transactions and internal activities of the EU; euro notes and coins were not introduced until January 2002 and then ran in parallel with national currencies for euro-zone members until February, when national currencies were withdrawn. Some commentators feared that the last six months of Stage 2 and all of Stage 3 would cause the euro zone troubles similar to those afflicting the ERM in 1992–93, but in practice the fixed exchange rates did not come under pressure, so there was no need for ECB intervention, and the transition to the general introduction of euro notes and coins was very smooth and trouble-free, even seeming to cope well with a sudden flush of national currencies as people disgorged cash savings in January 2002 to change them into euros.

The role of the ECB (which is central to the whole Eurosystem) was clearly specified in the Maastricht Treaty. Its primary objective was stated there as being to maintain price stability. Only secondarily could it support other EU policy objectives such as reducing unemployment or promoting growth. It is perhaps not coincidental that centre-right governments were in power in many EU countries when the treaty was signed, and that the rules for the ECB were drafted by a committee of central bankers! As we shall see shortly, there is evidence that in practice the ECB has been a little more concerned about unemployment than its stated objectives suggest. Further evidence of a less inflation-centred stance in the euro zone is the March 2005 modification of the Stability and Growth Pact.

The specific tasks of the ECB are very like those for any independent national central bank:

- to define and implement monetary policy for the euro zone;
- to conduct foreign exchange operations;
- to hold and manage the euro zone's official foreign exchange reserves (which, because national reserves were pooled, gives it substantial potential weight in the foreign exchange markets);
- to promote the smooth operations of payment systems;
- to issue banknotes for the euro zone;
- to collect and publish relevant statistics;
- to supervise commercial banks and other financial institutions within the euro zone;
- to maintain working relations with relevant institutions within and beyond the EU. (**http://www.ecb.int/ecb/orga/tasks**).

The performance of the euro and the ECB

The most obvious measure of how the euro has fared is to look at its exchange rate. The difficulty in analysing exchange rates is that they are the ratio of the value of two currencies, so when the rate changes it is not clear whether the underlying cause is something to do with the currency you are interested in or with the comparator. Much use is therefore made of synthetic measures, such as trade-weighted exchange rates, but for the period we are going to examine we can form a fair impression by looking at the exchange rates between the euro and the two other major world currencies, the US dollar and the Japanese yen. In the figures in Table 5.2, the measures used are how many units of the foreign currency a euro is worth, so if the figure rises the euro is getting stronger against the other currency, and if it falls the euro is getting weaker.

Table 5.2 Exchange rates: the euro against the Japanese yen and US dollar, annual averages, 1997–2004

Year	Japanese yen	US dollar
1997	137.08	1.1340
1998	146.41	1.1211
1999	121.32	1.0658
2000	99.47	0.9236
2001	108.68	0.8956
2002	118.06	0.9456
2003	130.97	1.1312
2004	134.44	1.2439

(Source: ECB 2005: Table 4.7.)

Table 5.2 shows that the euro fell steadily in value from 1997 to 2000 against the yen and to 2001 against the dollar but has subsequently recovered to its 1997 level. The longer fall against the US dollar was because the dollar was abnormally strong in 2001 because the US economy was performing very well. The implication of Table 5.2 is that firms in the euro zone trading outside the zone (not just to countries like Japan and the USA but also to EU countries not in the euro zone, like Denmark and the UK) have experienced volatility in exchange rates. So a firm in, for example, France will have found the profitability of its trade with Germany much more predicable than the profitability of its trade with Sweden. However, what the data also show is that there is no evidence so far, contrary to the fears of many commentators, that the euro is destined to be an endemically weak currency.

To assess how well the ECB has been doing, we should start with its primary objective, price stability. It seems clear that the ECB, with the agreement of the euro-zone member governments, has interpreted price stability as the achievement of a rate of inflation of not more than 2 percent per annum (Healey 2005: 118). We can see from Table 5.3 that it has missed the target, albeit narrowly, in each year since 2001. The reason why the euro zone member governments have been content to condone these failures becomes obvious when we look at Table 5.4 – data on unem-

Table 5.3 Rates of consumer price inflation (HICP) in the euro zone, 1991–2004

Year	Inflation rate (% per annum)
1991–95	3.2
1996–00	1.6
2001–04	2.2
2001	2.3
2002	2.3
2003	2.1
2004	2.1

(Source: ECR 2005: Table 5.1.)

ployment rates since 1992 in the euro zone eleven (the original 11 euro-zone countries), in the EU15 (i.e. the EU before the 2004 enlargement), in Japan and in the USA. We can see that unemployment rates in the euro zone have consistently been quite significantly higher since 1994 than those in the rest of the EU15 as well as those in Japan and the USA. Typically, unemployment rates in the euro zone have been in the range 8–10 percent; in the same period in Japan, they have been typically between 2 and 5 percent and in the USA between 4 and 7 percent.

Table 5.4 Harmonised unemployment rates, euro zone 11, EU15, Japan and the USA, 1992–2004 (percent)

Year	Euro zone 11	EU 15	Japan	USA
1992	8.2	8.4	2.2	7.4
1993	10.1	10.0	2.5	6.8
1994	10.8	10.4	2.9	6.1
1995	10.5	10.0	3.1	5.6
1996	10.7	10.1	3.4	5.4
1997	10.6	9.8	3.4	4.9
1998	10.0	9.3	4.1	4.5
1999	9.1	8.5	4.7	4.2
2000	8.1	7.6	4.7	4.0
2001	7.7	7.2	5.0	4.8
2002	8.2	7.6	5.4	5.8
2003	8.7	7.9	5.3	6.0
2004	8.8	8.0	4.7	5.5

(Source: Eurostat data from http://www.europa.eu.int/comm./eurostat/newcronos.)

Why has the euro zone experienced such stubbornly high rates of unemployment? There are two main reasons:

1. special problems for the German economy;
2. the actions of euro-zone governments in preparing for euro-zone entry and in trying to observe the rules of the Stability and Growth Pact.

During the 1950s to 1970s in particular, economic growth in the EU countries was driven by the German 'economic miracle' – fast, non-inflationary growth. There were many sources for the economic miracle in the FRG, including;

- Destruction towards the end of the Second World War, together with postwar occupation controls and reparations, meant that the German economy started from a very low base.

- The FRG benefited from substantial international aid for economic reconstruction.

- A beneficial export-led Western international economy in the 1950s, which assisted the growth of the FRG's capital goods industries.

- It was a matter of national pride for the FRG to reassert its economic might, since the country had abandoned any militaristic aims.

- The FRG achieved non-inflationary growth by its policy towards immigration, welcoming in 'guest workers' but denying them citizenship rights, so it suffered no significant employment bottlenecks.

- Generally harmonious labour relations were achieved by incorporating trade union representatives as members of the management boards of companies and by the relatively simple trade union structure.

However, by the 1980s the performance of the FRG economy was becoming noticeably less miraculous, and, as we have seen, German unification created real problems, from which the unified German economy has still not recovered.

The second important factor was that, to prepare their economies for entry to the euro zone, many countries pursued too restrictive policies. We have seen that one of the Maastricht criteria required that potential euro-zone members had to keep their current government borrowing to not more than 3 percent of GDP. If the economies had been booming, that might not have been a problem, but they were in a cyclical depression, so the policies that governments adopted were inappropriate.

When an economy is in the low point of the trade cycle (see Key concept 5.3), GDP is lower than normal and unemployment is higher than normal. Because GDP is lower than normal, the government receives less tax income than normal. Because unemployment is higher than normal, the government has to spend more than normal on unemployment and other social security benefits. Since its income is less than normal and its expenditure is more than normal, the usual behaviour of a government when its economy is in a cyclical depression is to borrow, following what is known as counter-cyclical policy. Government borrowing as part of counter-cyclical policy is not necessarily a problem, because when the economy recovers, government tax income will rise and expenditure will fall, so the borrowing can be repaid. However, the Maastricht criteria specified an upper limit on government borrowing, and to meet the criteria potential euro-zone entrants therefore could not borrow – indeed, if anything they had to cut public expenditure. The result was that, far from using fiscal policy to counteract the trade cycle, the fiscal policy they followed made the depression worse – they were reducing economic activity when it was already too low, or pursuing what is known as a pro-cyclical policy.

Key concept 5.3

The trade (or business) cycle

All economies experience some fairly regular fluctuations in GDP. This phenomenon – the trade cycle – goes back well into the nineteenth century. Nineteenth- and early twentieth-century economists put much effort into trying to understand the basic causes of the trade cycle, but they are still a little unclear. What seems to happen is that, when the economy is growing relatively quickly, different parts of the economy grow at different rates, so the economic system gets out of balance; this lack of balance causes growth to slow down, so a cycle of faster and slower growth comes about. Once such a cycle is established, it tends to reinforce itself through echoes of the original cycle. In the nineteenth century and the early years of the twentieth century, most countries experienced very large trade cycles, with periods of decline in output and falling prices. Demand management policies in the latter half of the twentieth century seemed to be successful in moderating the extent of the cycle but not in getting rid of it altogether.

Pro-cyclical fiscal policies continued to be followed by most euro-zone countries after their entry to the zone, because the Stability and Growth Pact specified exactly the same limits on current government borrowing as the Maastricht criteria and so were equally inappropriate to economies with high unemployment.

If unemployment rates are high for several years running, the problems tend to get worse. People who have been out of work for a long time find it especially hard to obtain jobs, and they lose self-belief. Any average unemployment rate will conceal pockets of relatively high unemployment – areas where very few people are in work. In such high-unemployment areas, the motivation even of young people is low because they know of so few people actually in work, so they see little point in education or in acquiring work-related skills; but the increasing mechanisation of production even in services means that there are few decent jobs for the low-skilled. Really persistent high unemployment can lead to a whole raft of social problems – unemployed youngsters turn to crime or to drugs (or both) – and to growing disillusionment with the political process and intolerance of strangers.

Particularly as more centre-left governments came to power in the EU member states, persistent unemployment in the EU generally, and the euro zone particularly, was regarded with growing anxiety. Concerns were expressed in the Amsterdam Treaty, but no very concrete suggestions were made about the solutions. The first attempt at EU level to offer systematic solutions was in the Lisbon agenda, with its aspirations to make the EU a fast-growing dynamic economy. The measures here – which we discussed in Part 3 – may well have very beneficial long-term effects. They are classic supply-side measures, which should eventually bring about a permanent improvement in the growth rate of the EU and hence of the euro zone, but do little to solve the current unemployment problems.

However, there may be a more immediate solution in the March 2005 review of the operation of the Stability and Growth Pact. Although the Council of Ministers presented their recommendations as being to endorse, and reinforce the workings of, the pact, in practice they allow some relaxation precisely to meet the need for demand management suitable for depressed economies. The key change is the suggestion that it would improve the pact if it were possible to 'use more effectively periods when economies are growing above trend for budgetary consolidation in order to avoid pro-cyclical policies' (Council 2005: 19) – i.e. to allow for the borrowing limit of 3 percent of GDP to be interpreted over the whole cycle, with less borrowed in cyclical booms and more in cyclical slumps. This marks a return to conventional demand management policy.

Further reading

Council (2005) *Presidency Conclusions of the Brussels European Council* (22/23 March 2005) Council of the European Union, Brussels, 7619/05.

Delors, J. (1988) *Report on Economic and Monetary Union in the European Community* (available on the EU website: http://www.europa.eu.int).

ECB (http://www.ecb.int/ecb).

ECB (2005) *Statistics Pocket Book*, March 2005 (available on ECB website).

EMU (http://www.europa.eu.int/pol/emu).

Eurostat (2005) (http://www.europa.eu.int/comm./eurostat/newcronos).

Healey, N. (2005) 'Economic and Monetary Union', in F. McDonald and S. Dearden (eds) *European Economic Integration,* 4th edn, Prentice Hall, Harlow.

Section 5.5

Enlargement of the European Union

We shall divide this section into three parts. First, we will look very quickly at how the countries that joined the EU in 2004 are faring in economic terms. Then we will review the list of countries that are currently applicants to join the EU and discuss the current state of their applications. Lastly, we will speculate on which other countries might want to join the EU, and whether, indeed, the EU and Europe will become synonymous.

The 2004 accession countries

Of the countries that joined the EU in 2004, we looked in depth in Part 2 only at Cyprus and Poland. We examined Cyprus because of its complicated relationship with Turkey, and we made a special case study of Poland because it is much the biggest and most important of the new members.

Since we have seen that persistent and high employment rates are a problem in the euro zone, let us start by looking at some more data about unemployment. Data for the overall (seasonally adjusted) unemployment rate in the EU15 and in each of the ten new member countries are presented in Table 5.5; we quote figures just for February 2004 and February 2005, but the figures for the intervening months show a quite smooth pattern in all cases.

This information confirms the general impression from Table 1.1 that unemployment rates in the ten countries that joined the EU in 2004 are in general not far from the EU15 average, with the striking exception of very high rates in Poland and Slovakia, where unemployment is twice the EU average. In both countries, however, our new table shows that the unemployment rate was falling. This is not surprising when we remember from Table 1.1 that GDP in Poland was growing at a rate of 6.1 percent per annum in 2004, and in Slovakia at 5.4 percent. In nearly all the new member states, unemployment fell over the year from February 2004, whereas it was constant in the EU15. Except for Malta, all the new member countries were experiencing growth rates at least as high as those in the EU15 countries.

Table 5.5 Seasonally adjusted unemployment rates in the EU15 and in the ten new member countries, February 2004 and February 2005 (percent)

	February 2004	February 2005
EU15	8.1	8.1
Cyprus	5.0	5.6
Czech Republic	8.4	8.3
Estonia	9.9	8.0
Hungary	5.8	6.3
Latvia	9.9	9.6
Lithuania	11.6	8.9
Malta	7.8	6.8
Poland	19.1	18.1
Slovakia	18.5	16.2
Slovenia	6.2	5.8 (January 2005)

(Source: Eurostat.)

Most of the new member countries have to grow a great deal to catch up on the EU15 in terms of GDP per head, but rapid growth will help them to do it and at the same time reduce their unemployment problems.

The current applicants

In our country studies in Part 2, we have already looked in some depth at Romania and Turkey. The other countries that were in one or other of the stages of formal application for membership of the EU in mid-2005 were Bulgaria, Croatia and the FYROM.

The process of accession is multi-stage. A country indicates its interest in joining. Unless its application is ruled invalid (e.g. because it is not in Europe), what can sometimes be a long process of negotiation starts. The Commission undertakes extensive investigations as to whether it satisfies the criteria for admission; these are summarised in annual reports, to both the Council of Ministers and the government of the applicant country. The applicant country's government is invited to take steps to meet any critical comments. After what can be (in Turkey's case, was) many years of effort to meet the criteria, the country moves to the status of being a 'candidate state' and, if it appears that the accession criteria are being met, is invited to open formal accession negotiations. Once these have been successfully completed, representatives of the EU and of the applicant country sign an accession treaty, which includes a date for membership. At each stage, including those after the accession treaty is signed, the EU can put continued pressure on the applicant country to meet certain specific requirements, with the prospect of membership being refused if this does not happen, but in practice it is hard for the EU to impose any more than minimal conditions after the treaty is signed.

Bulgaria and Romania are the only countries in this group that have been offered a firm date for accession to the EU. In the case of both countries, all the outstanding issues in the accession negotiations had been wrapped up in December 2004, and both have been offered membership from January 2007, provided a few final issues are tidied up. For both countries, the outstanding matters are on human rights, but in addition Romania has to address questions about competition and the environment. Both Bulgaria and Romania were invited to sign accession treaties in April 2005.

Opinion 5.1

President Chirac on Turkey

In a TV interview on 15 April 2005, President Chirac of France commented on Turkey's application to join the EU:

All we have to say to Turkey is that it is your responsibility to make the necessary efforts to become totally European.

(Source: *Le Figaro*, 17 April 2005.)

Is Chirac right?

Turkey has reached the stage of entering formal accession negotiations. It is expected that negotiations will start in October 2005. As we saw in Part 2, the main focus of negotiations will be how far Turkey is prepared to proceed on important matters of human rights.

Croatia has started these processes. The country applied for membership in February 2003. The Commission's 2004 report suggested that there was a prospect of Croatia's meeting most of the criteria for membership, but that a great deal had to be done on the *acquis*, particularly on environmental legislation. In March 2005, EU foreign ministers delayed the start of Croatia's membership bid on the grounds that Croatia's government had not been pursuing suspected war criminals with sufficient vigour.

The FYROM applied for membership in March 2004. There has not, at the time of writing, been any formal report in response to this application.

Possible future applicants

The EU has nurtured a set of relationships with other countries, including some not in Europe. Probably the most likely to give rise to early new applications for membership are those with Balkan countries. These were inaugurated by the EU's Stabilisation and Association process in the wake of the wars in the Balkans; Albania, Bosnia-Herzegovina, Croatia and the FYROM have all made progress with the EU under this process, and, as we have just seen, Croatia and FYROM have now proceeded to formal membership applications. The EU also has a system of Partnership and Cooperation Agreements with Central and East European (and some ex-USSR Asian) countries:

- Armenia (agreed 1999);
- Belarus (agreed 1995 but did not come into force because of the deteriorating situation);
- Georgia (agreed 1999, Georgia has made it plain that it wishes to join the EU, but not at the cost of antagonising Russia);
- Kazakhstan (agreed 1999);
- Kyrgyzstan (agreed 1999);
- Moldova (agreed 1994);
- Russia (agreed 1997);
- Tajikistan (agreed 2004);
- Turkmenistan (agreed 1998);
- Ukraine (agreed 1998; Ukraine is also a 'priority partnership country' under the European Neighbourhood Policy);
- Uzbekistan (agreed 1999).

The EU's relationships with other countries are also governed by the European Neighbourhood Policy, which embraces:

- Algeria;
- Armenia;
- Azerbaijan;
- Belarus;
- Egypt;
- Georgia;
- Israel;
- Jordan;
- Lebanon;
- Libya;
- Moldova;
- Morocco;
- the Palestinian Authority;
- Syria;
- Tunisia;
- Ukraine.

This 2004 structure replaces a complicated set of bilateral arrangements but will involve detailed negotiation with each country about its relations with the EU; in some cases, these may become the prelude to full membership.

From this large list of countries in Central and Eastern Europe, Western Asia and North Africa, and this plethora of agreements, it is easy to identify potential new EU member countries at some stage – those in the Balkans, and, subject to the attitude taken by Russia, Georgia and the Ukraine seem likely early future applicants. We have argued in Part 2 that Russia is unlikely to wish to join (or, perhaps, even to be acceptable, simply because of its size).

What of Western European countries? We have explained in Part 2 why Iceland and Norway are 'reluctant Europeans', although it is possible that a future Norwegian government might wish to try again if it believes public opinion would support membership. The only significant remaining gap is Switzerland. Ireland and Sweden have chosen to join the EU despite their long traditions of neutrality, so why not Switzerland? Perhaps part of the answer might lie in the Swiss banking system; Swiss banks have been famed for respecting client confidentiality in a way not consistent with the relatively open banking systems favoured in EU countries, and in this respect Switzerland was nearly as good a home for tax-avoiding money as the anomalous mini-states in Europe (Andorra, the Channel Islands, the Isle of Man, Liechtenstein, Monaco, San Marino, the Vatican City), which are also formally outside the EU. However, recent changes to international banking practice, designed to make money laundering more difficult, have reduced the secrecy of Swiss bank accounts. Nevertheless there are probably other advantages to Switzerland of staying out of the EU – its status as a major location of UN activities, for example, might be compromised – and probably very little to be gained by joining rather than settling for its EEA status.

Further reading

To keep up to date on the enlargement and association processes, visit the 'EU in the world' section of the EU website (available at http://www.europa.eu.int/comm/world).

Section 5.6

The Constitutional Treaty

In Part 3, we examined some of the details of the Constitutional Treaty. Our concern here is not to repeat that discussion but to ask two questions:

1. What difference, if any, will it really make if the treaty is ratified?
2. What is the state of play on ratification?

What difference would the treaty make?

We commented earlier that treaty making in the EU is a process rather than an event. It would be a fundamental mistake to see the Constitutional Treaty either as the definitive final EU treaty, designed to shape the EU for all time, or as something quite different from the existing treaty structure of the EU. It is a bit more than the simple tidying-up process that some commentators claim it to be, but it is not a drastic alteration of the institutions and workings of the EU. Europhiles are wrong to see in it the makings of a United States of Europe. Euro-sceptics are wrong to see in it a fundamental loss of national sovereignty. All EU citizens will be disappointed if they expect it to make a big contribution to solving the democratic deficit.

We can highlight the important changes that would occur if the treaty is ratified:

- The treaty would simplify the EU's legal framework – it proposes the abolition of all the existing treaties and their replacement by the single new treaty.

- It would, as we explained in Part 3, modify the existing 'pillar' framework of the EU, which means that matters of foreign and security policy and of police and judicial cooperation would cease to be intergovernmental matters and would instead be dealt with at EU level by the European Council in conjunction with the European Parliament and the European Commission.

- The common foreign and security policy approach would be signalled by the appointment of the EU's own minister for foreign affairs; however, member states would still have a right of veto over important foreign and security policy areas.

- The common approach to police and judicial cooperation would lead to the creation of a European Public Prosecutor's Office, which might be particularly concerned with new areas of judicial cooperation such as money laundering and organised crime.

- The European Council would have a full-time president; the current arrangement is that the presidency moves round member states in a six-month rotation, but the new president would be appointed for two and a half years and could be reappointed once.

- There would be some minor alterations to the areas in which member states can act only if the EU does not do so – the 'shared competences' – to include in these energy policy and space exploration.

- It would be clear that the EU can only act to support member states in some new areas, including sport and tourism.

- There would be some increase in the areas in which the European Council decisions cannot come into operation without the agreement of the European Parliament, but these areas would still exclude anything to do with the common foreign and security policy.

- There would be some increase in the areas in which the European Council makes decisions by qualified majority rather than by unanimity, but there would continue to be many topics, mainly concerned with commercial policy, with foreign security and defence and with further constitutional amendments that would still require unanimity; the rules for qualified majority voting would be changed from 2009.

- The EU would be identified as founded on values (rather than 'principles' in previous treaties) of liberty, democracy, respect for human rights (including those of minorities), the rule of law, human dignity and equality, and society in the EU would be described as being one in which 'pluralism, non-discrimination, tolerance, justice, solidarity and equality between men and women prevail';

- There would be provision for a member state that violated these values to be denied voting and other rights.

- There would be provision for a member state that so wished to withdraw altogether from the EU.

For more detail, see Phinnemore (2004).

While the appointment of a president of the European Council and of the EU's minister for foreign affairs look innovative, they do not amount to very important changes in the way the EU would operate. The Commission (whose composition would be modified from 2014, as we showed in Part 3) would continue to be responsible for initiating new policies and for acting as the EU's executive, the European Council (and the Council of Ministers) for taking decisions and the European Parliament for endorsing policy.

Figure 5.3 A wry illustration of changing French attitudes to the Constitutional Treaty
Source: *L'Express* (14 March 2005).

Opinion 5.2

A common European foreign policy

The idea of a common European foreign policy has been sceptically described by one participant as designed to create 'a single voice, but silent; a single chair, but empty'. European governments have found it easier to set up new institutional mechanisms than to agree on common policies, let alone to shoulder the implications of implementing what has been agreed.

(Source: Wallace 2003: 222.)

Do you agree?

There is little to address the remoteness of the EU from most people in the EU. The Constitutional Treaty does create a European Citizen's Initiative, allowing citizens to approach the Commission with their own ideas, but since any such proposal requires one million signatures spread across a range of member states, it is likely to have limited impact. Similarly, while the treaty does include references to the role of national parliaments, this, too, is in practice unlikely to be very significant; national parliaments can indicate cases where they feel the principle of subsidiarity is not being observed in a proposed new law, and if enough of them protest, their views have to be considered (although there is no compulsion to change the draft law).

In summary, if the Constitutional Treaty is ratified:

- EU law will be a little simpler to understand, but changed very little.
- The EU institutions will work rather more efficiently, but there may be increased tensions between the European Parliament and the Commission or the European Council (or both).
- The EU's foreign, security and defence policy will be higher-profile (but still formulated only by unanimity).

If the Constitutional Treaty is not ratified:

- Existing EU law (Treaty of Nice and earlier treaties) will continue.
- The existing institutions will continue, but decisions in the European Council may be a little harder to achieve.
- Foreign, security and defence policy will be more a matter of intergovernmental cooperation.

What is the state of play on ratification?

Each member state has its own constitutional arrangements. Some require a referendum on constitutional matters, others require approval by parliament alone, some require both, and some do not specify how constitutional decisions are to be taken. Where a referendum is held, it may be simply consultative, or it may be binding. It is therefore not surprising that there is great diversity in how the EU member states are going about obtaining national ratification of the Constitutional Treaty. We summarise the picture in Table 5.6.

It is evident from the table that ten of the eleven countries that have so far ratified the treaty have done so by parliamentary processes alone. The only favourable referendum held so far, that in Spain in February 2005, produced a clear majority in favour of the treaty, but the turnout was low. The other two referendum votes, in France on 29 May 2005 and in the Netherlands three days later, had respectable turnouts and produced clear majorities that, to the dismay of their governments, were against ratification. Key fact 5.3 discusses in some detail the referendum campaign in France.

Table 5.6 Ratification of the EU Constitutional Treaty

Member state	Procedure	Date scheduled	Status
Austria	Parliament	25 May 2005	Ratified
Belgium	Parliament	19 May 2005	Ratified
Cyprus	Parliament	30 June 2005	–
Czech Republic	Not decided	? June 2006	–
Denmark	Referendum	27 September 2005	–
Estonia	Parliament	Not decided	–
Finland	Parliament	? early 2006	–
France	Referendum	Referendum 29 May 2005: in favour 45.1%, against 54.9%, turnout 60.7%	Rejected
Germany	Parliament	27 May 2005	Ratified
Greece	Parliament	19 April 2005	Ratified
Hungary	Parliament	20 December 2004	Ratified
Ireland	Parliament + referendum	October–November 2006	–
Italy	Parliament	6 April 2005	Ratified
Latvia	Parliament	2 June 2005	Ratified
Lithuania	Parliament	11 November 2004	Ratified
Luxembourg	Parliament + consultative referendum	Referendum 10 July 2005	–
Malta	Parliament	July 2005	–
Netherlands	Parliament + consultative referendum	Referendum 1 June 2005: in favour 38%, against 62%, turnout 63% (provisional figures)	Rejected
Poland	? Referendum	? 25 September 2005	–
Portugal	Referendum	? October 2005	–
Slovakia	Parliament	11 May 2005	Ratified
Slovenia	Parliament	1 February 2005	Ratified
Spain	Parliament + consultative referendum	Referendum 20 Febuary 2005: in favour 76.7%, turnout 42.3%	Ratified
Sweden	Parliament	December 2005	–
UK	Parliament + consultative referendum	? early 2006	–

(Source: http://www.europa/eu.int/constitution/ratification, news.bbc.co.uk.)

Key fact 5.3

French referendum on the EU Constitutional Treaty, 29 May 2005

On 29 May 2005, French voters delivered what most commentators assumed was a 'knockout blow' to the proposed EU Constitutional Treaty when they rejected it by a decisive margin. On a turnout of 69.7 percent, the 'no' campaign secured 54.87 percent, with 45.13 percent voting 'yes'. The campaign revealed that France remained a bitterly divided society. However, the intensity of political passion and heat that was generated by the national debate also revealed that politics matters greatly to the French. Although much of the debate did indeed focus on 'Europe', inevitably very few voters read – and even fewer, we can safely assume, understood – the complex and often turgid document of several hundred pages that ostensibly was the object of the referendum. Instead, voters seem to have used the occasion to express their deep sense of malaise and unhappiness at the direction in which France and Europe are moving. With unemployment at over 10 percent (a five-year high), many voters also wished to pass their judgement on President Chirac and the French political elite. Indeed, the key figure associated with the drafting of the EU Constitutional Treaty – former French President Valéry Giscard d'Estaing – is almost synonymous with that elite.

The referendum campaign cut across the usual left–right divide in French society. On the right, the National Front and other extremist groups campaigned for a 'no' vote, as did nationalist leaders such as Philippe de Villiers of the Movement for France. A minority of centre-right voters backed the 'no' cause. On the left, the Communist Party, far left groups and a strong section of the Socialist Party campaigned for a 'no' vote. The Greens were split. The 'yes' campaign was backed by President Chirac, the leadership of the Gaullist UMP party, the centre-right UDF and the majority of the Socialist Party leadership.

Exit polls showed how divided France was. Paris voted strongly 'yes', as did more affluent cities such as Lyons, Strasbourg and Bordeaux. More working-class cities such as Marseilles and Lille voted 'no', as did working-class districts in other cities. Rural France also tended to vote 'no'. Younger people voted 'no' heavily (59 percent), as, to a lesser extent, did the 35–49 age group. Only the over-65s, those with long memories of how the EU consolidated Franco-German friendship and cooperation, voted decisively 'yes' (56 per cent). Blue-collar workers and the unemployed overwhelmingly voted 'no' (75 percent) but managers and professionals and university graduates voted 'yes' by clear margins (62 percent and 57 percent respectively).

On the right, some of the 'no' campaigners used nationalist arguments about 'protecting traditional French values'. Sometimes xenophobic arguments – attacking immigration from Eastern and Central Europe – were utilised. A Gaullist 'no' campaigner, Nicolas Dupont-Aignan, expressed popular fears over possible Turkish EU membership by calling for a 'no' vote in the name of 'a Europe that will not extend its frontiers as far as Turkey'.

There is little doubt, though, that the core of the 'no' vote was a left-wing vote. Here it was not xenophobic arguments but worries over unemployment, declining social welfare provision and the threat of the EU imposing Anglo-American neo-liberal-style attacks on workers' rights that provoked the most passion – that, and a desire to punish the French political elite for its perceived incompetence.

An exit poll showed that voters who rejected the EU Constitutional Treaty gave three main reasons for doing so:

1. fears that the EU Constitutional Treaty would increase the unemployment rate in France (cited by 46 percent of all respondents and 51 percent of blue-collar workers);

2. a general 'feeling of dissatisfaction with the present situation in France' (cited by 40 percent of all respondents and 48 percent of blue-collar workers);

3. a belief that the text of the Constitutional Treaty itself was too neo-liberal and pro-market (cited by 34 percent of all respondents).

Opposition to Turkish EU membership did not feature as being of any real significance to respondents.

(Source: TNS-Sofres opinion poll for *Le Monde* and FTI television, cited in *The Guardian*, 31 May 2005.)

The veteran French political analyst Pascal Perrineau commented that 'the strength of the no camp is that it is so heterogeneous that it is having no trouble simply hoovering up all the fear, worries, concerns and angers of a majority of the French population at the start of the 21st century' (cited in *The Guardian*, 23 May 2005). This comment highlights how the question of the EU can become a lightning rod for popular discontent over the failings of modern politics.

In the Netherlands, the reasons for the 'no' majority appear to have been similar to but not identical to those in France. As in France, the 'yes' camp was broadly the political centre – the unpopular Christian Democrat government and its coalition partners, together with the opposition Labour Party and the Green Left – with the 'no' camp combining the extreme right with socialist and various Christian parties. The 'no' campaign rap song's theme was 'if you want a social Europe and a Europe for the people, not for business and money, then say "no" to the constitutional treaty' – a theme very much endorsed by the socialist opposition to the Constitutional Treaty. The extreme right-wing part of the 'no' camp, as in France, played on fears of immigration and opposition to Turkish membership of the EU. What seemed to be distinctive about the 'no' support in the Netherlands was the worry that the EU was now simply too big and not sufficiently sensitive to the concerns of small countries – the EU had grown too fast and that it was necessary to have a period of consolidation before any new developments. However, it is likely that in the Netherlands as in France many voters used the referendum as an opportunity to voice their opinion on their government and its economic policies.

We are therefore in the position that some EU member states have ratified the Constitutional Treaty, and others have not. What happens now? The treaty was signed in October 2004. The European Council agreed that if two years after signature in October 2004 80 percent of member states have completed ratification, and one or more 'encountered difficulties' in doing so, it will consider the matter. So far, out of thirteen countries that have made their decision eleven have ratified and two have not, so at present the 80 percent threshold is satisfied and there is some rationale for the European Commission's view that the remaining countries should make their own decisions on the Constitutional Treaty, with the ratification timetable continuing as if nothing had happened. What options are open to the European Council are far from clear; the treaty itself requires ratification by all 25 member states, so all the Council would be likely to do, if the 80 percent threshold is reached, would be to put pressure on the member states who had not obtained ratification to try again.

However, decisive rejection of the Treaty by two of the original six member states must cast the whole process into considerable doubt. The European Council meeting in mid-June 2005 represented the first opportunity for member state governments to take stock. The UK assumed the presidency of the Council in July 2005, and the six-month UK presidency period is likely to prove crucial in determining what can be done. The UK government will probably be reluctant to hold an early referendum in the UK, which it would almost certainly lose, and so might support some delaying measures. It is very unlikely that the Constitutional Treaty as it stands can go ahead, and the question is likely to be what bits, if any, can be rescued from it.

One unexpected consequence may be to put the brake on enlargement. If the governments of the EU member states take seriously some of the views expressed by 'no' voters, Turkey's admission is likely to be postponed even further, and there may be delays to the timetable for Bulgaria and Romania. Ironically, if enlargement is postponed, some of the problems that the Constitutional Treaty was designed to address will themselves be less pressing.

Further reading

http://www.europa/eu.int/constitution/ratification is the crucial website to enable you to stay abreast of developments.

Hussain, N. (2004) *Referendums on the EU Constitutional Treaty: The State of Play*, Chatham House European Programme EP BP 04-01, is useful background.

Phinnemore, D. (2004) *The Treaty Estabishing a Constitution for Europe: An Overview*, Royal Institute of International Affairs European Programme EP BN 04-01v2, is an excellent summary of the main features of the Constitiutional Treaty.

Chronological table

1917   Lenin and the Bolsheviks seized power in Petrograd (November).
Finland declared independence from Russia on the outbreak of the Bolshevik Revolution and was recognised by the Bolshevik government (November–December).

1918   Finnish Civil War between the Whites and Reds won by Whites under General Mannerheim (January–May).
Civil war began in Russia and continued until the Bolshevik victory in March 1921 (May).
Armistice ended the First World War (November).

1919   Completion of Treaty of Versailles under which Germany surrendered Alsace and Lorraine to France and made other concessions over territory, reparations and armaments (June).

1920   Treaties of St Germain (with Austria) and Trianon (with Hungary) completed break-up of the Austro-Hungarian Empire (June and September).

1921   Treaty of Riga confirmed new Russo-Polish borders (March).
'Vivovdan constitution' adopted in Yugoslavia, ensuring Serb dominance in interwar period (June).

1922   Mussolini and Fascists came to power in Italy (October).

1923   *Coup d'état* in Bulgaria toppled Alexander Stamboliski and ended democratic government (June).

1924   Death of Lenin (January). Stalin finally prevailed in ensuing five-year power struggle and from 1929 embarked upon a drastic transformation of Russian economy at huge cost in lives.

1926   Pilsudski seized power in Poland, ending Polish democracy.
Beginning of Sanacja regime in Poland (May).
In Portugal, right-wing dictatorship came to power. From 1928, its leader and strongman was Antonio de Oliveira Salazar.

1929   Start of the Great Depression.
King Alexander of Yugoslavia began dictatorship, trying to suppress local nationalism and create a 'Yugoslav nationalism' (January).

1930   King Carol II of Romania began more personal regime, ending with his dictatorship by 1938 (June).

1932   Gyula Gömbös became prime minister in Hungary and pushed Hungary to the right over next four years (October).

1933   Hitler became chancellor of Germany (January).

1935   Germany repudiated military clauses of Treaty of Versailles (March).
        King Boris *coup d'état* in Bulgaria began period of 'benevolent dictatorship' until 1943 (April).
        Elections in Czechoslovakia resulted in Sudeten German Party becoming largest party in Czech Parliament (May).
        Italy invaded Abyssinia (October).

1936   Germany remilitarised the Rhineland (March).
        Spanish Civil War began and continued until April 1939 (July).

1938   *Anschluss*: Austria incorporated into Germany (March).
        The question of the future of the Germans in the Sudetenland (in Czechoslovakia) came to a head, reaching its climax at the Munich Conference, at which Hitler's demands were largely satisfied by Britain and France (August–September).

1939   German troops occupied Prague, followed by German annexation of Czech areas with Slovakia becoming a German satellite state (March).
        At end of March, Britain and France guaranteed Polish independence, already under threat from Germany.
        Spanish Civil War ended with defeat of the democratically elected Spanish government; Franco's dictatorship began (April).
        In Yugoslavia, central government made a special agreement (*Sporazum*) with Croatia granting the Croats wide autonomy (August).
        Germany and USSR signed Nazi–Soviet Pact, settling division of Poland and their future spheres of influence in Eastern Europe.
        Germany attacked Poland on 1st, UK and France declared war on Germany on 3rd (September).
        USSR attacked Finland without declaration of war (November).

1940   The 'Winter War' between Finland and USSR ended. Finland lost some eastern territories (March).
        In series of lightning campaigns, Germany defeated Denmark, Norway, the Low Countries and France. UK struggled to survive in the following 12 months, although with some moral and economic support from USA (April–June).
        Britain and USA occupied Iceland. USA established airbase at Keflavik (May).
        Fall of King Carol of Romania; period of brutal rule by 'Iron Guard' (1940–41) and regime of Marshal Antonescu (1941–44) (September).

1941   Germany invaded Yugoslavia and Greece. Independent Croatian state set up under Ustasha regime, which began genocide of Serbs (April).
        Germany invaded USSR (June).

Finland joined Germany in attacking USSR though on a restricted front and with limited objectives.

Reinhard Heydrich began 'regime of terror' in the Czech lands. Heydrich assassinated May 1942 (September).

German declaration of war on USA (December).

1943 German surrender at Stalingrad followed by defeat during summer in battle of Kursk. Soviet forces advanced steadily westward thereafter (January).

Outbreak of civil war between factions of Greek anti-Nazi resistance movement (September).

Tehran Conference between Churchill, Roosevelt and Stalin, which did much to shape future (November–December).

1944 US and UK forces landed in France and began their drive to victory from the west (June).

Bretton Woods Conference – 44 countries led by UK and USA devised plans for the postwar international financial system, including the establishment of the International Monetary Fund (IMF) and International Bank for Reconstruction and Development (World Bank) (July).

Warsaw uprising put down brutally by Nazis (August–September).

Germany's ally, Finland, concluded an armistice with the USSR (September).

Germans began to withdraw from Greece. Stalin agreed to assign country to UK sphere of influence (October).

Fall of Admiral Horthy in Hungary; brutal rule of fascist 'Arrow Cross movement' until April 1945.

British forces began to take action against the communists in Greece (December).

1945 Moscow recognised Lublin Committee as the provisional government of Poland (January).

Yalta Conference on future of Europe attended by Churchill, Roosevelt and Stalin (February).

Italy finally liberated from Fascism. Benito Mussolini executed by partisans (April).

Suicide of Adolf Hitler (30 April).

Allied forces met in heart of Germany and war in Europe ended (8 May).

Labour Party, led by Clement Attlee, won UK general election (July).

Allied leaders met at Potsdam, and USA tested and then used atomic bombs against Japan (July–August).

Potsdam: agreement on conditions for signing peace treaties with Bulgaria, Hungary and Romania (August).

Alcide de Gasperi became Christian Democrat prime minister of Italy (December).

1946 Forced merger of Social Democrats (SPD) with Communists (KPD) in Soviet Occupation Zone in Germany to form Socialist Unity Party (SED) (April).

Peace treaties negotiated with all former enemy states except Germany and Austria (April–December).

Italians rejected monarchy and voted in a referendum for establishment of a republic (June).

Constitution of French Fourth Republic promulgated (October).

Greek Civil War began when communist resistance fighters, organised as the Democratic Army of Greece, refused to accept a right-wing royalist government under British tutelage.

1947 Economic merger of UK and US occupation zones in Germany to form Bizonia (January).

Peace treaties signed with Bulgaria, Finland, Hungary, Italy and Romania (former allies of Germany) (February).

France and UK signed a 50-year friendship treaty (March).

Benelux states agreed to establish a customs union, commencing in January 1948.

Truman Doctrine formulated in general terms to assist 'free peoples in the struggle against communism'. It was prompted by UK warning that it could not continue to back Greek government and by fear of communist gains in Greece and Turkey (March).

Communists expelled from French and Italian governments with American encouragement (May).

First steps taken in the creation of the Marshall Plan, which, after departure of Soviet delegation, was directed at economic recovery of Western Europe (June–July).

Cominform set up by USSR in response to Truman Doctrine and Marshall Plan (September).

Establishment of General Agreement on Tariffs and Trade (GATT) (October).

1948 Political crisis in Czechoslovakia left communists as dominant political force (February).

Brussels Treaty signed by Benelux states, France and UK providing for military cooperation (March).

USA granted massive economic and military assistance to right-wing forces in Greece.

Organisation for European Economic Cooperation (OEEC) set up in Paris (April).

Finland signed Treaty of Friendship, Cooperation and Mutual Assistance (FCMA) with USSR.

Congress of Europe called for political and economic union of European nations (May).

US Senate approved Vandenberg Resolution, which opened way to US defence cooperation with Western European states (June).

East–West differences over German questions led to interruption of Western supply lines to West Berlin (the Berlin blockade). West responded with airlift.

Cominform expelled Yugoslav Communist Party and approved Soviet model of industrialisation and agricultural collectivisation for the 'people's democracies' (July).

UK Labour government implemented major health and social security reforms, establishing National Health Service.

1949   Comecon set up by USSR and its partners (January).

North Atlantic Treaty (NATO) signed by Belgium, Canada, Denmark, France, Iceland, Italy, Luxembourg, Netherlands, Norway, Portugal, UK and USA (April).

Southern Ireland became completely independent of British Commonwealth when Irish parliament promulgated Republic of Ireland Act.

Federal Republic of Germany (FRG – West Germany) adopted its post-war constitution (May).

Berlin blockade ended.

'Show trials' began in Eastern Europe.

Statute of Council of Europe signed in Strasbourg by ten states.

First Soviet nuclear test (August)

Konrad Adenauer became first chancellor of the FRG (September).

Greek Civil War ended with defeat of communist forces (October).

German Democratic Republic (East Germany – GDR) established.

Cominform denounced Yugoslav regime. Soviet bloc countries broke off diplomatic relations with Yugoslavia (November).

1950   France proposed European Coal and Steel Community (Schuman Plan) (May).

Outbreak of Korean War (June).

Start of Western talks on West German rearmament (September).

France proposed Pleven Plan, resulting in attempt to establish the European Defence Community (EDC) (October).

Growing East–West tension led to major increases in defence spending by NATO and a larger and firmer commitment by USA to defence of Europe (December).

1951   Benelux states, FRG, France and Italy signed treaty establishing European Coal and Steel Community (ECSC), which operated from July 1952 (April).

Conservatives returned to power under Winston Churchill in UK (October).

1952   New constitution promulgated in Greece (January).

Greece and Turkey entered NATO (February).

USSR proposed German peace treaty based on withdrawal of foreign troops and neutralisation of Germany (March).

Benelux states, FRG, France and Italy signed treaty to create EDC (May).

Yugoslav Communist Party renamed League of Communists of Yugoslavia (LCY) (November).

Right-wing forces won elections in Greece.

1953   First US thermonuclear test (first deliverable bomb tested in March 1954) (February).

First session of Nordic Council comprising Denmark, Iceland, Norway and Sweden (Finland joined in October 1955).

Death of Stalin (March).

Soviet intervention put down demonstrations in East Berlin and other cities in East Germany (June).

Korean armistice signed.

Soviet–Yugoslav diplomatic relations resumed.

Recently appointed Prime Minister Imre Nagy introduced 'new course' in Hungary (July).

First Soviet thermonuclear test (August).

1954   French National Assembly refused to ratify EDC treaty (August).

London and Paris conferences opened way to creation of Western European Union (WEU), rearmament of the FRG, its membership of NATO and achievement of full sovereign status (September–October).

1955   Leadership struggle in USSR: Malenkov replaced by Bulganin (February) with Nikita Khrushchev (CPSU general secretary) increasingly influential, taking over premiership in 1958.

Nagy replaced as prime minister in Hungary (March).

Churchill succeeded as UK prime minister by Anthony Eden (Conservative) (April).

Austrian Peace Treaty provided for withdrawal of occupation forces and establishment of a neutral Austria. The Warsaw Pact between USSR and its Eastern European allies concluded in same month (May).

Khrushchev's *rapprochement* with Tito.

The FRG became a sovereign state.

Messina Conference of foreign ministers of the six ECSC states discussed further integration (June).

A four-power summit in Geneva failed to reach any substantive agreements but reflected a temporary easing of Cold War in Europe (July).

Introduction of so-called 'Hallstein Doctrine' in the FRG (December).

1956   Khrushchev denounced Stalin at 20th Party Congress (February).

Cominform dissolved (April).

Strains developed in Poland. Poznan riots. Władysław Gomulka restored to leadership in October (June).

Rakosi removed from Hungarian party general secretaryship after visit of high-level Soviet delegation (July).

Nagy restored as prime minister in Hungary. Uprising ended with heavy bloodshed after Soviet military intervention occasioned by USSR's refusal to accept end of one-party rule and Hungary's departure from WTO (October–November).

Anglo-French action at Suez led to temporary crisis in Anglo-American relations, and deeper rift between Paris and Washington (November).

1957   Harold Macmillan (Conservative) succeeded Eden as UK prime minister (January).

Treaties of Rome signed, establishing the European Economic Community (EEC) and the European Atomic Energy Community (EAEC) (March).

1958   Treaties of Rome came into force (January).

USSR agreed to withdraw troops from Romania (May).

Long-running crisis in French Fourth Republic came to a head with army coup in Algeria; Charles de Gaulle returned to power in France, promising end to colonial war in Algeria and return of political stability at home (May–June).

French referendum approved constitution of Fifth Republic (September).
A Soviet note on future status of Berlin led to period of intermittent and at times serious tension between East and West over Berlin (and Germany) until end of 1961 (November).
De Gaulle elected president of France (December).

1960   European Free Trade Association (EFTA) convention signed in Stockholm by Austria, Denmark, Norway, Portugal, Sweden, Switzerland and UK (January).
Four-Power summit in Paris a dismal failure (May).
Growing evidence of a rift between communist China and USSR (June).
Cyprus became independent republic within British Commonwealth (August).
OEEC reorganised into Organisation for Economic Cooperation and Development (OECD) (December).

1961   USSR cancelled aid to Albania (April).
Denmark, Ireland and UK applied for EC membership.
Berlin Wall erected to stop growing numbers of East Germans going to the West (August).
22nd Congress of CPSU – Khrushchev renewed de-Stalinisation (October).
Move to 'goulash communism' in Hungary (December).

1962   French colonial war in Algeria ended. Algeria became an independent republic in July (March).
Norway applied for EC membership (April).
A Soviet attempt to deploy nuclear missiles in Cuba followed by most serious crisis in the Cold War (October–November).
De-Stalinisation began in Czechoslovakia (December).

1963   De Gaulle vetoed UK bid to enter EC. Franco–West German Treaty of Friendship and Cooperation signed (January).
Sino-Soviet rift made public (June).
Yaoundé Convention between the EEC and 18 African states and Madagascar (July).
The FRG opened a trade mission in Poland (September).
The GDR adopted New Economic System.
Alec Douglas-Home became Conservative prime minister of UK (October).
Ludwig Erhard succeeded his fellow Christian Democrat Konrad Adenauer as chancellor of FRG.
In Greece, Centre Union, led by George Papandreou and his son, Andreas, won office (November).
New crisis in Cyprus: clashes between Greeks and Turks (December).

1964   Constantine II succeeded to throne of Greece (March).
Central Committee in Romania issued declaration asserting independence of all communist parties (April).
The FRG opened trade mission in Hungary (July).
Hungarian Socialist Workers' Party Central Committee accepted principles of New Economic Mechanism.

UK elections returned Labour government under Harold Wilson (October). Khrushchev relieved of all his posts in USSR. Leonid Brezhnev shared power with Alexei Kosygin but steadily became the more influential figure.

1965   Signing of treaty (Merger Treaty) establishing a single Council and a single Commission of the EC. Treaty took effect in July 1967 (April).
France began a boycott of EC institutions to register its opposition to various proposed supranational developments (July).
Constitutional crisis in Greece ended in defeat for elected government of George Papandreou when King Constantine forced its resignation to appease army.

1966   Luxembourg Compromise ended French boycott of EC institutions (January).
De Gaulle announced French withdrawal from military participation in NATO (March).
Grand Coalition government formed in the FRG with Social Democrat Willy Brandt as foreign minister (December).
Kurt Georg Kiesinger became third postwar Christian Democrat chancellor of the FRG.

1967   The FRG established diplomatic relations with Romania (January).
Military coup in Greece led to establishment of 'dictatorship of the colonels'. In December, King Constantine left for exile in Rome having failed to remove colonels (April).
EC Merger Treaty came into force (July).
De Gaulle vetoed UK entry to EC again (November).

1968   Alexander Dubček elected first secretary of Czech Communist Party. A wide variety of reforms followed, but 'Prague Spring' ended by Warsaw Pact invasion in August, the USSR once again fearing that matters were drifting out of control. In November, so-called 'Brezhnev Doctrine' laid down that a socialist state was bound to intervene if socialism was threatened in another socialist state (January–November).
Paris rocked by strikes and demonstrations as students and workers revolted against the perceived authoritarian and paternalistic nature of de Gaulle's regime. Benefiting from fears of revolution, French right wing won a parliamentary majority in general elections in June. Similar student protests elsewhere in Europe (May).
Completion of EEC Customs Union (July).
Marcello Caetano succeeded ailing Salazar as dictator of Portugal (September).

1969   De Gaulle resigned French presidency following defeat in referendum on constitutional reforms (April).
Georges Pompidou became president of France (June).
UK troops arrived in Northern Ireland, ostensibly to keep peace between the province's Protestants and Catholics. A split in paramilitary Irish Republican Army (IRA) produced hard-line 'Provisional' IRA in August–December, which began serious campaign of violence against British presence in Northern Ireland (August).

Massive labour unrest in Italy led to trade union reforms and to forms of collective bargaining that increased strength of labour movement. An extreme right-wing backlash saw neo-fascist terrorist groups carry out some bombings.

Brandt became FRG chancellor heading an SPD–FDP coalition. In October, he made overtures to the USSR and Poland and showed his desire to open a dialogue with the GDR (September).

The Hague summit of EC leaders (December).

1970 First FRG–USSR agreement on supply of Soviet natural gas to the FRG by pipeline (February).

Brandt's *Ostpolitik* led to first conference of FRG and GDR leaders (March).

Conservatives returned to power in UK led by Edward Heath (June).

EC membership negotiations reopened with Denmark, Ireland, Norway and UK.

FRG–USSR treaty of non-aggression (August).

FRG–Poland treaty of non-aggression (November).

Riots occurred in Gdansk in Poland. Edward Gierek replaced Gomulka as first secretary (December).

1971 Erich Honecker replaced Walter Ulbricht as general secretary of GDR Communist Party (SED) (May).

Quadripartite Agreement on Berlin (September).

UK parliament approved EC membership (October).

1972 Enrico Berlinguer became leader of Italian Communist Party. Over the next four years, he articulated the ideology of Eurocommunism and sharply criticised the USSR (January).

President Richard Nixon visited Moscow and signed first Strategic Arms Limitation Treaty (SALT I) and Declaration on Basic Principles of Soviet–American relations (May).

The FRG and GDR signed 'Basic Treaty' on mutual relations (December).

1973 Ireland, Denmark and UK joined EC (January).

Conference on Security and Cooperation in Europe (CSCE) opened in Helsinki, including representatives of all European states (except Albania), Canada, USA and USSR (July).

The FRG concluded a treaty with Czechoslovakia and established diplomatic relations with Bulgaria and Hungary (December).

1974 British Labour Party regained office; Wilson prime minister again (March).

Radical Portuguese army officers overthrew right-wing dictatorship of Salazar–Caetano, initiating a period of revolutionary upheaval and ultimately consolidation of multi-party democracy. First free elections for 50 years held in 1976 (April).

UK government demanded renegotiation of terms of accession to EC.

French President Georges Pompidou died; succeeded by Valéry Giscard d'Estaing (April–May).

Helmut Schmidt (Social Democrat) succeeded Willy Brandt as chancellor of the FRG (May).

Greek military intervened in Cyprus; driven back by the Turks.

Cyprus divided into Greek and Turkish zones. Greek military regime collapsed (July).

In Greece, democratic elections returned centre-right New Democracy Party led by Constantine Karamanalis to power (November).

Greeks voted by huge majority to abolish monarchy and declare a republic (December).

EC heads of state and government decided to meet regularly as European Council.

1975   First Lomé Convention between EC and 46 African, Caribbean and Pacific states (ACP states) (February).

Elections to a new constituent assembly in Portugal established Socialists as biggest party (April).

UK referendum; two-to-one majority in favour of remaining in EC (June).

Greece promulgated a new constitution and applied for EC membership.

Final Act signed at Helsinki Conference on Security and Cooperation in Europe (August).

General Franco died and transition to democracy began in Spain under King Juan Carlos. Free elections held in June 1977 (November).

1976   James Callaghan succeeded Harold Wilson as Labour prime minister in UK (April).

Portuguese general elections won by Socialists.

Italian elections. So-called govenment of 'national solidarity', 1976–79, sought communist support in parliament in return for consultation. However, Communists denied cabinet seats (June).

Socialist leader, Mario Soares, became prime minister of Portugal (July).

The Committee for the Defence of Workers (KOR) set up in Poland (September).

1977   Charter 77 formed in Czechoslovakia (January)

Legalisation of political parties began in Spain (February).

Portugal applied for EC membership.

A NATO summit agreed to increase defence spending by 3 percent a year in real terms as confidence in *détente* weakened (May).

Spain's first free elections for more than 40 years (June).

Spain applied for EC membership (July).

1978   China cut off aid to Albania (July).

Polish archbishop Karol Woytila elected as Pope John Paul II (October).

1979   European Monetary System (EMS) came into operation (March).

Margaret Thatcher led British Conservatives to election victory and became first female prime minister of UK (May).

SALT II was signed but not subsequently ratified by USA (June).

First direct elections to European Parliament.

Second Lomé Convention between EEC and 58 ACP states (October).

NATO took twin-track decision to negotiate with USSR on intermediate-range nuclear systems and, if Soviet SS-20s not removed by 1983, to deploy Pershing and cruise missiles in Europe (December).

Soviet invasion of Afghanistan.

1980   Karamanlis became president of Greece (May).
          Death of President Tito of Yugoslavia.
          Price increases in Poland led to establishment of the Solidarity free trade union under leadership of Lech Walesa (August).
          Turkish government toppled by military coup (September).

1981   Start of Ronald Reagan's presidency of USA (January).
          Greece joined EC.
          Attempted military coup in Spain failed (February).
          Nationalist disturbances in Kosovo (March–April).
          François Mitterrand became first socialist president of French Fifth Republic, defeating Giscard d'Estaing. In June, Mitterrand's Socialist Party also won general elections. A left-wing government formed that included four cabinet ministers from French Communist Party (May).
          Giovanni Spadolini, a Republican, became Italy's first non-Christian Democrat prime minister since 1945 (July).
          Elections in Greece returned Socialist Party, PASOK, to power. Andreas Papandreou became prime minister (October).
          Further FRG–USSR gas pipeline agreement (November).
          Martial law declared in Poland by Jaruzelski. Solidarity leadership arrested. American sanctions against Poland and USSR followed. In 1982, this led to serious controversy between USA and its European allies over handling of issue (December).

1982   Greenland referendum voted in favour of withdrawal from EC (February).
          Argentina invaded Falkland Islands. Hostilities continued until UK victory in July (April).
          Spain joined NATO (May).
          FRG Chancellor Schmidt lost vote of confidence and was succeeded by Helmut Kohl, who led a CDU/CSU–FDP coalition government (September).
          Brezhnev died. He was succeeded briefly by Yuri Andropov (1982–84) and Konstantin Chernenko (1984–85) (November).

1983   Reagan announced intention to proceed with Strategic Defence Initiative (SDI). The anti-nuclear movement became increasingly active in Western Europe (March).
          Conservatives under Thatcher returned to power in UK elections (June).
          Martial law lifted in Poland (July).
          Anti-communist Bettino Craxi, leader of Italian Socialist Party, headed CD-dominated government (August).
          NATO began to deploy Persching and cruise missiles. USSR broke off East–West arms talks (November).

1984   Free-trade area established between EC and EFTA (January).
          Mitterrand shifted France to more pro-federalist position, implicitly recognising failure of 1982–83 'socialist experiment' largely due to pressure of world economic trends; in July, French communists left government in protest (June).
          The FRG granted DM950 million loan to the GDR in return for further relaxation of travel restrictions. By August, there was a growing USSR–

GDR rift over *détente* and relations with the FRG (July).

Third Lomé Convention between EC and 65 ACP states (December).

1985   USA and USSR took first steps towards renewal of arms talks (January).

Mikhail Gorbachev became general secretary of Central Committee of Communist Party of Soviet Union. USA–USSR arms talks renewed in Geneva (March).

Karamanlis resigned as Greek president (May).

Greek Socialists, led by Papandreou, returned to power in elections (June).

Geneva summit between Reagan and Gorbachev marked beginning of end of 'Second Cold War' (usually dated as starting with Soviet intervention in Afghanistan in December 1979) (November).

Anglo-Irish Agreement gave Irish government a consultative role in Northern Ireland.

European Council agreed principles of Single European Act (SEA) (December).

1986   Spain and Portugal joined EC (January)

SEA signed in Luxembourg, fixing end of 1992 as completion date of Internal Market.

Assassination of Swedish prime minister Olaf Palme (February).

Mario Soares replaced General Eanes as president of Portugal.

Right-wing parties won parliamentary majority in France, forcing a period of 'cohabitation' between Jacques Chirac as prime minister and Mitterrand as Socialist president. This continued until May 1988 (March).

Major accident at nuclear power plant in Chernobyl, Ukraine (April).

Gorbachev proposed 30 percent cut in strategic nuclear arms (June).

Stockholm Security Conference: agreements on observers and on notice of military movements (September).

Reagan and Gorbachev met in Reykjavik. Western Europeans alarmed by USA's unilateral (though unsuccessful) proposals on strategic nuclear arms cuts (October).

1987   FRG coalition government (CDU/CSU–FDP) returned to power in elections (January).

USSR proposed Intermediate-range Nuclear Forces (INF) agreement (March).

Turkey formally applied for EC membership.

Gorbachev, in a Prague speech on a 'common European home', emphasised the shared history and culture of Europeans (April).

Italian prime ministership passed from Bettino Craxi to the Christian Democrat Amintore Fanfani.

Slobodan Milošević, who became Communist Party leader in Serbia in 1986, exploited unrest in Kosovo.

Conservatives won third term of office in UK (June).

Single European Act came into effect (July).

Milošević became general secretary of the League of Communists of Serbia (October).

Proposed economic reforms in Poland failed to win support of 50 percent of the people. Strikes followed in spring and summer of 1988 (November).
INF treaty provided for elimination of all INF weapon systems in Europe within three years (Decemeber).
Milošević removed Ivan Stamboli as president of Serbia.

1988 Janos Kadar, Hungarian leader, replaced; radical reforms promised (May).
Mitterand won second presidential mandate in France. Socialist Party also won general elections. Michel Rocard became prime minister.
Rallies in former Baltic states calling for autonomy (August).
Lech Walesa invited to help to end strikes in Poland.

1989 Independent opposition political parties legalised in Hungary (January).
Talks began between Polish Communists and Solidarity; agreement reached in April on trade union, economic and political reforms.
Solidarity won all but one of the seats it was allowed to contest in June elections (February).
Serbia removed autonomy of Kosovo (March).
The Delors Report proposed three-stage progression to economic and monetary union (EMU) (April).
Hungary opened its borders to allow East German 'tourists' to cross to the West (May).
European Council of the EC agreed to begin Stage I of programme for EMU on 1 July 1990 (June).
Greek elections resulted in stalemate. A short-lived and unprecedented Communist–Conservative coalition took office to 'clean up' alleged corruption of outgoing Socialist administration.
Milošević celebrated 600th anniversary of Battle of Kosovo.
Franjo Tudjman founded new political party: Croatian Democratic Union (HDZ).
Human chain across Lithuania, Latvia and Estonia marked 50th anniversary of Molotov–Ribbentrop pact (August).
Solidarity-led government formed in Poland.
Hungarian government agreed to hold multi-party elections.
Hungarian Socialist Workers' Party became simply Socialist Party. Party's leading role dropped from constitution (October).
Serbia removed autonomy of Vojvodina.
Pro-Milošević regime installed in Montenegro.
Soviet statement effectively ended the 'Brezhnev Doctrine'.
Massive demonstrations in East German cities (November).
GDR government promised free elections and free exit on 8 November. Within hours, Berlin Wall breached.
Zhivkov replaced in Bulgaria.
All-party government formed in Greece.
Coalition government formed in Czechoslovakia (December).
European Council of the EC agreed to convene an intergovernmental conference (IGC) on EMU and subsequently (June 1990) to establish an IGC on political union.

Union of Democratic Forces formed in Bulgaria.

Romanian communist leader, Nicolae Ceaușescu, and his wife Elena executed.

Communist Party of Lithuania left CPSU.

1990   GDR government proposed unification of Germany (January).

Extraordinary Communist Party conference in Belgrade: Slovene and Croatian communists left the organisation.

Balcerowicz plan for economic shock therapy adopted in Poland.

First free general election in the GDR. Christian Democrats won almost 50 percent of vote, paving way for unification (March).

Lithuania declared its independence from USSR.

Free elections in Hungary produced right-of-centre coalition government led by Josef Antall's Hungarian Democratic Forum.

Centre-right New Democracy won one-seat majority in Greek elections. In May, Karamanlis returned as president (April).

Milošević changed Serbian constitution to ensure his position.

Franco-German proposal for IGC on political union.

Free elections in Croatia won by Democratic Union (April–May).

Free elections in Romania won by Iliescu's National Salvation Front (May).

Communists defeated in free elections in Slovenia and Croatia. Parties of Milan Kucan and Tudman took power.

FRG–GDR treaty on monetary, economic and social union.

Boris Yeltsin elected president of Russian Republic.

Free elections in Czechoslovakia won by Civic Forum and its Slovak counterpart Public Against Violence (June).

Free elections in Bulgaria won by Socialist (ex-Communist) Party.

Germany adopted single currency (July).

NATO summit in London began to consider implications of post-Cold War era.

Group of seven states (G7) discussed integration of Eastern Europe into world economy.

First stage of EC plan for EMU came into effect.

28th CPSU Congress. Yeltsin and others left party.

State treaty on German unification signed by the FRG and the GDR (August).

Treaty on Final Settlement on Germany signed by the two German states and France, UK, USA and USSR ('2+4' Treaty) (September).

Albanians of Kosovo organised referendum for independence.

Formal declaration of suspension of Four-Power rights in Germany (October).

Croatia and Slovenia proposed 'confederal' model for Yugoslavia, which was rejected by Serbia.

Germany became a single state once again. Helmut Kohl (FRG chancellor) elected chancellor of reconstituted state in December and led a CDU/CSU–FDP coalition.

Margaret Thatcher forced from office in UK due to internal Conservative Party coup. John Major became party leader and prime minister (November).

CSCE summit – Charter of Paris declared that the Cold War was over.
Lech Walesa elected president of Poland (December).
Bulgarian government resigned following widespread strikes.
Elections in Serbia and Montenegro won by ex-Communists.
Elections produced a weak coalition government in Bosnia-Herzegovina and a nationalist one in Macedonia.
Central Committee plenum removed hard-liners from Albanian Party of Labour as anti-government demonstrations mounted.
Opening sessions of the two intergovernmental conferences on economic and monetary union and political union.

1991   Harder line by Gorbachev reflected in OMON (paramilitary force) attacks in Vilnius and Riga. Yeltsin recognised sovereignty of Baltic states (January).
Italian Communist Party (PCI), under leadership of Achille Occhetto, voted to dissolve itself and to give birth to the Democratic Party of the Left (PDS). A minority seceded to form rival Party of Communist Refoundation (PRC) (February).
Growing crisis in Yugoslavia. Kucan and Tudjman agreed that Yugoslavia could only survive as a voluntary league of sovereign republics.
Milošević and Tudjman discussed partition of Bosnia between Serbia and Croatia (March).
Albanian Party of Labour (APL) won Albania's first free elections (April).
In France, President Mitterrand appointed a new Socialist prime minister – Edith Cresson (May).
Albanian government replaced by coalition following widespread strikes.
APL became Socialist Party of Albania (June).
Declarations of independence by Croatia and Slovenia.
Yugoslav army invaded Slovenia but was forced to retreat. Serbia accepted Slovenian independence.
Comecon dissolved.
Bundestag voted Berlin capital of united Germany.
Warsaw Treaty Organisation dissolved (July).
Serbo-Croat war began in Croatia.
Attempted putsch failed in USSR. Gorbachev lost all credibility on return to Moscow. He resigned his post as general secretary of the CPSU. CPs banned and much of their property taken over by republican governments following Yeltsin's lead in Russia. Estonia, Latvia and Lithuania declared independence, and Yeltsin urged world to recognise them (August).
Romanian government forced to resign. Coalition government formed (September).
Social Democrats defeated in Swedish elections; right-wing government came to power.
Indecisive Polish elections resulted in formation of weak coalition government under Olszewski in December (October).
Union of Democratic Forces narrowly defeated Socialists in Bulgarian elections.

Bosnian parliament debated motion to declare Bosnia a sovereign republic: Serbs walked out of session.

Start of EC sanctions against Serbia (November)

NATO Rome summit announced the new strategic concept. Alliance to have a wider security role.

Fall of Vukovar to the Serbs.

Caretaker government formed in Albania (December).

EC association agreements with Czechoslovakia, Hungary and Poland provided for free trade within ten years and possibility of eventual EC membership.

EC heads of state and government meeting in Maastricht agreed on a treaty framework for European Union incorporating agreements on economic and monetary union and political union, and introducing a new security/defence dimension to EC cooperation.

Gorbachev tendered his resignation as president of the USSR. USSR replaced by Commonwealth of Independent States (CIS).

1992	EC recognised independence of Croatia and Slovenia (January).

EC recognised independence of Croatia and Slovenia (January).

Ceasefire in Serbia–Croatia war signed in Sarajevo.

Zhelyu Zhelev re-elected president of Bulgaria.

Broadly effective ceasefire in Croatia.

Treaty on European Union signed in Maastricht (February).

Democratic Party decisively won Albanian elections. Its chairman Salih Berisha was elected executive president in April (March).

Proclamation of independence by Bosnia-Herzegovina. War started in Bosnia: siege of Sarajevo until 1994.

Italian general elections confirmed crisis within corruption-tainted Christian Democrats and their Socialist allies. But the former Communists also polled poorly. New parties did well, especially right-wing secessionist Northern Leagues (April).

Serbia and Montenegro created 'Federal Republic of Yugoslavia'.

Conservatives returned to power in the UK, but with a much reduced majority (May).

EC and EFTA signed treaty establishing the European Economic Area (EEA).

Yeltsin won Russian presidential election.

UN imposed sanctions on Serbia and Montenegro.

Leningraders voted to restore name of St Petersburg (June).

Olszewski government fell in Poland. In July, Hanna Suchocka formed a seven-party coalition government, which survived until May 1993.

General elections in Czechoslovakia. Strong performance of Meciar's Movement for a Democratic Slovakia made early dissolution of federation inevitable.

Danish voters rejected Maastricht Treaty.

Tudjman's Croatian Democratic Union consolidated its grip on power after lower house and presidential elections (August).

UK hosted London conference on Bosnia.

Horrors of Serb concentration camp at Omarska made public to world media.

Iliescu re-elected president of Romania, but general election results forced his Democratic NSF into a government coalition with three hard-line nationalist parties (September).

French referendum narrowly approved Maastricht Treaty.

Brazauskas' Democratic Labour Party (former Communist Party of Lithuania) won general election (October/November).

Czechoslovakia, Hungary and Poland (Visegrad group) signed free-trade agreement (December).

'Non-party government of experts' led by Lyuben Berov installed in Bulgaria.

Dissolution of Czechoslovakia into Czech Republic and Slovakia at midnight on 31 December.

1993	EC formally became a single market (January).

EC formally became a single market (January).

EC opened negotiations with Austria, Finland and Sweden (and Norway – April 1993) on their applications for membership (February).

Attempt to impeach Yeltsin failed (March).

French general elections returned a parliamentary landslide for right-wing parties. Edouard Balladur became the new Gaullist prime minister, heralding new period of cohabitation with Mitterrand.

Russian referendum; 59 percent backed Yeltsin (April).

Danish referendum voted in favour of Maastricht Treaty (May).

Athens summit: Bosnian Serbs forced to sign Vance–Owen Plan. War crimes tribunal began to be set up.

Spanish general elections returned a minority Socialist government, dependent on Catalan nationalist support (June).

Copenhagen European Council meeting approved membership of former communist Central and Eastern European states if they met the economic and political conditions of the 'Copenhagen criteria'.

EC finance ministers agreed to alterations in EMS following turmoil in financial markets (August).

Polish elections. Ex-Communists of Democratic Left Alliance returned to power in coalition government with old allies in Polish Peasant Party. Solidarity and Church-backed parties did poorly. Pawlak became prime minister (September).

Yeltsin dissolved Russian Republic Supreme Soviet, intending to rule by presidential and governmental decree until elections to new State Duma on 12 December. Vice-president Rutskoi announced he had taken over presidency and was supported by Supreme Soviet, which also attempted to replace Defence Minister Grachëv by hard-liner Achalov. Deputies, led by Rutskoi and Speaker Khasbulatov, occupied White House.

Army units stormed White House. Rutskoi, Khasbulatov and other leaders arrested (October).

Socialists, led by Andreas Papandreou, returned to power in Greece, inflicting a heavy electoral defeat on New Democracy. The latter elected a new leader, Miltiades Evert.

Maastricht Treaty on European Union formally came into effect (November).

Elections to Russia's State Duma and Federation Council. Disarray among pro-Yeltsin parties and public apathy and disillusionment boosted Zhirinovsky's inappropriately named Liberal Democratic Party and also Communist Party of Russia. New constitution approved in referendum (December).

Elections increased majority of Milošević's Serbian Socialist Party.

114 countries agreed on treaty for liberalisation of world trade following seven years of GATT negotiations (Uruguay Round) (December).

1994   Second stage of EMU came into effect with establishment in Frankfurt of European Monetary Institute (EMI) as a precursor to European Central Bank (January).

NATO Brussels summit announced intention of the alliance to enlarge its membership.

European Economic Area (EEA) came into existence creating a free-trade zone comprising all EU member countries and six of the seven EFTA countries, Switzerland having voted against participation in December 1992.

Russia's State Duma granted amnesty to leaders of parliamentary resistance to President Yeltsin in October 1993 (February).

Shelling of Sarajevo marketplace resulted in death of 69 people and led to Serb forces pulling back heavy artillery from siege of the city.

Croatia agreed ceasefire with self-declared Republic of Serbian Krajina (March).

Austria, Finland, Norway and Sweden agreed terms for joining European Union in January 1995.

Italian general elections confirmed collapse of old discredited Christian Democrat and Socialist Parties. The main beneficiaries of the crisis of the old party system were the neo-fascists, the right-wing Northern Leagues, and a new right-wing, pro-free market movement, Forza Italia, led by media mogul and billionaire Silvio Berlusconi.

Slovak Prime Minister Meciar lost no-confidence vote and was replaced by Jozef Moravcik, leading a five-party coalition government.

Hungary and Poland became first former communist states to apply for membership of EU (April).

Silvio Berlusconi became Italian prime minister. His government included five neo-fascist cabinet ministers, raising concern in many European capitals (May).

Hungarian Socialist Party (ex-Communists) won overall parliamentary majority in elections.

Austrian referendum voted in favour of EU membership (June).

Russia joined NATO's Partnership for Peace and signed a 'partnership and cooperation' agreement with the EU, which stopped short of setting full EU membership as the final goal. After being accepted as a full political partner at G7 summit, Russia also seemed about to apply for admission to the Paris club (of government creditors).

The supreme NATO commander in Europe and the Russian defence minister agreed to set up working groups to draft a programme of joint activities. NATO missions to be established in Russia and Russian military missions at NATO's European headquarters.

Jacques Santer appointed to succeed Jacques Delors as president of European Commission (July).

Tony Blair elected leader of the UK Labour Party.

Withdrawal of all American military forces from West Berlin after five decades of presence in the city.

Italian anti-corruption judges resigned in protest at bail for prisoners on remand accused of corruption. Berlusconi's brother accused of corruption.

Norway rejected EU membership in a referendum (November).

1995   Austria, Finland and Sweden joined the EU (January).

Kostas Stephanopoulos, a veteran centre-right (ND) politician, became president of Greece (March).

Bosnian Serb forces took Srebrenica.

Chirac succeeded Mitterrand as president of France (May).

Croatia drove Serb forces out of western Slavonia.

Cannes European Council meeting agreed that the introduction of a single currency by 1997 was unrealistic (June).

Croatian 'Operation Storm' retook Krajina area of Croatia (August)

Latvia and Slovakia applied to join the EU.

Socialists won Portuguese general elections; António Guterres became prime minister (October).

Estonia applied to join the EU (November).

Dayton Accord, supported by NATO forces under UN mandate, brought end of hostilities in Bosnia.

Andreas Papandreou found it increasingly difficult to discharge his duties as Greek prime minister due to recurrent ill-health; power struggle developed within PASOK.

Lech Walesa defeated by SLD leader Aleksander Kwasniewski in Poland's presidential elections.

Bulgaria and Lithuania applied to join the EU (December).

Dayton Accord provided for a bipartite state of Bosnia and Herzegovina and for a NATO-led Implementation Force to supervise the implementation of the accords.

Madrid European Council meeting confirmed introduction of the single currency for 1 January 1999.

1996   Jorge Sampaio of the Socialist Party was elected president of Portugal (January).

Deployment of NATO forces in Bosnia to implement Dayton Accord.

The Czech Republic and Slovenia applied to join the EU.

Andreas Papandreou was forced by ill-health to relinquish the post of prime minister of Greece to Kostas Simitis.

Basque terrorists attempted to destabilise Spain's general election campaign by murdering several political leaders from the ruling Socialist Party. One million people protested against ETA's violence in Madrid (February).

Jorge Sampaio formally succeeded Mario Soares as president of Portugal (March).

IGC convened in Turin to review the Treaty on European Union (Maastricht Treaty).

Portuguese Conservatives (PSD) elected Marcelo Rebelo de Sousa as their leader in a bid to restore party unity and morale after recent defeats and divisions.

Spanish socialists (PSOE) lost power to a minority conservative (PP) government that was led by José María Aznar and relied on Catalan nationalist support.

Death of Andreas Papandreou. He was succeeded as leader of PASOK by Kostas Simitis (June).

Spanish Conservative government, despite its hard-line anti-ETA stance, hinted at negotiations with ETA in return for a permanent ceasefire.

Greek general elections returned PASOK under Kostas Simitis to power (September).

Czech Republic and Germany signed a treaty of reconciliation in which Germany expressed regrets for Nazi atrocities and the Czech Republic for Czechoslovakia's expulsion of the Sudeten Germans (November).

Tough austerity budget introduced by Greek government saw huge farmers' protests, which threatened to paralyse the country (November–December).

Dublin European Council meeting agreed a single currency Stability Pact (December).

1997   Renewal of trade union protests in Greece against government cuts in order to qualify for euro (January).

Kostas Karamanlis replaced Miltiades Evert as leader of ND party in Greece (March).

Spanish government secured PSOE support for an economic stabilisation plan that aimed to secure Spain's entry into the European single currency through 'drastic' government spending curbs (April).

Election of Labour government in UK (May).

French general elections – called a year early – saw the rout of Chirac's right-wing allies and the return of a left-wing coalition government under Lionel Jospin (June).

Felipe González resigned as leader of PSOE, to be succeeded by Joaquín Almunia, who was regarded as a González supporter (June).

Amsterdam European Council meeting agreed the Treaty of Amsterdam following the IGC review of the Treaty on European Union (Maastricht Treaty).

NATO invited the Czech Republic, Hungary and Poland to start membership negotiations (July).

NATO Madrid summit agreed to admit the Czech Republic, Hungary and Poland as new alliance members in 1999.

After parliamentary elections in Albania (June/July), a Socialist-led coalition government took office under Fatos Nano. Rexhep Meidani succeeded Sali Berisha as president (August).

Scottish and Welsh voters approved proposals for national assemblies in Scotland and Wales in referenda (September).

Parliamentary elections in Poland brought to power a coalition government comprising Solidarity Electoral Action (AWS) and the Freedom Union (UW).

Gordon Brown, British chancellor of the Exchequer, specified five economic tests for UK entry into the euro zone and indicated that the UK would not be ready for entry before the end of the current parliament (October).

Greek government unveiled tough budget that imposed effective freeze on wages in public sector and abolished some tax perks for the better-off; measures were declared necessary if Greece was to qualify for euro in 2001 (November).

Serbian operations intensified in Drenica region of Kosovo following clashes with the ethnic Albanian Kosova Liberation Army (KLA) (November).

Luxembourg European Council meeting invited Cyprus, the Czech Republic, Estonia, Hungary, Poland and Slovenia to start membership talks in March 1998 with a view to entry to the EU early in the next century (December).

Entire leadership of Herri Batasuna was imprisoned in Spain for collaborating with ETA.

Partnership and Cooperation Agreement (PCA) between the EU and Russia ratified.

1998   Serbian operations against Kosovar Albanians killed hundreds of civilians, many the result of deliberate or indiscriminate attacks. 60,000 Kosovars fled their homes (February–June).

UN Security Council Resolution 1160 urged Yugoslavia and Kosovar Albanians to reach a political solution, with wide autonomy for Kosovo (March).

Greek PASOK government adopted austerity package that reduced rights of workers in the public sector by giving managers new powers to curb overtime, reduce collective bargaining rights and reduce benefits (February).

Greek government devalued the drachma by 14 percent and rejoined the exchange rate mechanism (March).

European Commission ruled out Greek entry into the euro in 1999, saying that Greece had yet to meet any of the criteria contained in the Maastricht Treaty.

Good Friday peace settlement between Irish and UK governments, parties in Northern Ireland, and parliamentary representatives was signed and approved in simultaneous referenda in both parts of Ireland (April–May).

Eleven of the 15 EU states agreed to proceed to the third and final stage of EMU (scheduled for 1 January 1999) with provision for the establishment of the European Central Bank, the fixing of exchange rates and the introduction of a single currency – the euro. Denmark, Sweden and the UK had previously obtained opt-outs from this timetable, while Greece was deemed to have failed to qualify (May).

After parliamentary elections in Hungary, the Alliance of Young Democrats (FIDESz) formed a centre-right coalition government with the Smallholders Party.

Unemployment in Spain stood at 19.63 percent – the first time it had fallen below 20 percent since 1982.

Referendum in Portugal on easing the country's abortion law; narrow majority voted against, but the result was not binding because of a turn-out of only 32 per cent (June).

NATO threatened military intervention if Milošević did not withdraw troops from Kosovo. Milošević and Yeltsin agreed that Serbia would resolve the Kosovo situation by political and peaceful means (June).

Elections to new Northern Ireland Assembly saw pro-agreement forces triumph, but by a very narrow majority on the Ulster Unionist side.

In the Czech Republic, the Czech Social Democratic Party formed a minority government.

ETA announced an 'indefinite and total' unilateral truce in Spain; moderate Basque parties welcomed this as a breakthrough; Spanish prime minister Aznar, who had followed a policy of harsh repression of ETA since 1996, gave first indication of willingness to make concessions to secure peace (September).

UN Security Council Resolution 1199 expressed concern at the 'excessive and indiscriminate use of force by the Serbian security forces' in Kosovo (September).

Serbia agreed to peace agreement negotiated by US Balkan envoy Richard Holbrooke; OSCE to put 2,000 unarmed monitors into Kosovo (October). 700 monitors were sent in, but by the end of 1998 Yugoslav military action against the KLA was escalating.

After parliamentary elections in Slovakia, Mikulas Dzurinda, leader of the Slovak Democratic Coalition (SDK), formed a coalition government.

Renegade IRA terrorists tried to sabotage Northern Ireland peace process by exploding huge bomb in Omagh, County Tyrone, which killed 29 people and injured over 300.

Election of SPD–Green government in Germany.

Gerhard Schröder became federal chancellor in Germany, with Oskar Lafontaine as finance minister and Joschka Fischer as foreign minister (October–November).

EU agreed in principle to lift the ban on the export of British beef (November).

British and French governments agreed principles of a defence policy for the EU (December).

1999   The euro, the new EU single currency, was formally launched with eleven of the 15 EU states participating (January). In the following six months, its international value declined considerably.

Massacre of Kosovar Albanians at Recak lent greater publicity to Serbian oppression in Kosovo. Officials of War Crimes Tribunal were refused access to massacre sites (January).

Blair announced a 'national changeover plan' for the possible replacement of the pound sterling by the euro (February).

Talks organised by the EU and USA were held at Rambouillet chateau (Paris) between Yugoslav and Kosovar Albanian (including KLA) delegations, under threat of NATO air strikes if a peace agreement, involving the continuance of theoretical Serbian sovereignty over Kosovo but the stationing of 30,000 NATO troops there to maintain peace, was not agreed (February–March). Kosovar Albanians finally agreed, but Yugoslavia refused (March).

Oskar Lafontaine (finance minister of Germany) resigned.

OSCE monitors were withdrawn from Kosovo. NATO began air strikes against Yugoslav army and Serbian infrastructure (March).

European Commission resigned in response to a critical report on fraud, nepotism and mismanagement by a commission of independent experts established by the European Parliament (March).

European Council meeting in Berlin agreed a package of budgetary, agricultural and regional policy reforms to improve the financial stability of the EU and prepare for its expansion into Eastern Europe.

NATO's Washington summit agreed as part of Agenda 2000 that the EU could use NATO equipment, personnel and infrastructure in operations that did not directly involve the USA (April).

Romano Prodi appointed new president of European Commission (May).

International War Crimes Tribunal indicted Milošević for organising murders in Kosovo (May).

EU announced economic/political 'Stability Pact' to stabilise the Balkan region.

The WEU member states agreed in principle to incorporate the WEU into the EU.

Treaty of Amsterdam took effect (May).

Yugoslavia agreed to NATO demands after 72 days of bombing, after almost one million Kosovar Albanians had fled Kosovo as refugees (June).

After 78 days, NATO bombing ceased after Yugoslav army fully agreed to NATO terms on withdrawal from Kosovo (10 June). Yugoslav forces withdrew, while NATO–Russian force (KFOR) of 51,000 troops under the auspices of the UN entered Kosovo, quickly followed by mass return of refugees, while many Kosovar Serb civilians fled to Serbia. Numerous mass graves of Kosovar Albanians discovered.

Elections to European Parliament showed a swing to the right in very low turn-out (June).

New government in Belgium, the first in 40 years without Christian Democrats (July).

IMF approved a US$4.5 billion loan to Russia.

President Yeltsin of Russia dismissed the government and nominated Vladimir Putin, head of the Federal Security Service, as prime minister designate.

Romano Prodi took office as president of the EU Commission (September).

EU published a major document, *Common Strategy on Russia*.

EU leaders strengthened cooperation on justice and home affairs at Tampere summit (October).

The Slovak government approved a plan for the country's accession to NATO.

In the Austrian general election, the far-right FPÖ won the second-largest number of seats.

The governing SP in Portugal was returned to power in the general election.

Russian government published its *Medium-Term Strategy for Development of Relations with the European Union.*

ETA, the Basque separatist group, announced the end of a 14-month truce (November).

A joint meeting of EU foreign and defence ministers, the first of its kind in the history of the EU, considered how to increase the military powers of the EU in the aftermath of the conflicts in Bosnia and Kosovo.

At a meeting of OSCE, 54 countries signed a European Security Charter.

EU leaders recognised Turkey as a candidate for EU membership at Helsinki summit and also agreed to start negotiations with six candidates for EU membership: Bulgaria, Latvia, Lithuania, Malta, Romania and Slovakia (December).

Scandal over undeclared donations to the CDU in Germany damaged the reputation of former chancellor Kohl.

In accordance with the 1998 Good Friday Agreement, a power-sharing cabinet was formed in Northern Ireland and power was devolved from the UK to the Northern Ireland Assembly. In addition, the first meetings took place of the North–South Ministerial Council and of the Council of the Isles.

Resignation of President Yeltsin of Russia.

Death of President Tudjman of Croatia.

2000   Negotiations for EU accession began with Bulgaria, Latvia, Lithuania, Malta, Romania and the Slovak Republic (February).

The far-right FPÖ in Austria became part of a new coalition government.

Conclusion of negotiations between the EU and 71 ACP countries to revise the fourth Lomé Convention on trade.

EU foreign ministers formally launched an IGC aimed at reforming EU institutions and decision making

Vladimir Putin elected Russian president (March).

Greece formally applied to join the EMU.

At a summit meeting in Lisbon, EU leaders launched a ten-year programme to make the EU the world's most competitive economic area by 2010 and predicted that the plan would result in an average annual economic growth rate of 3 percent.

Massimo D'Alema, Italian prime minister, resigned after his centre-left coalition government was heavily defeated in regional elections by the centre-right opposition led by Silvio Berlusconi (April).

In Greece, PASOK won a third successive term of office.

Eurocorps, comprising troops from Belgium, France, Germany, Luxembourg and Spain, took over command of the Kosovo peacekeeping operation from NATO.

José María Aznar was sworn in as prime minister of Spain for his second consecutive four-year term following a general election in which his party, the PP, won an absolute majority.

Referendum vote in Switzerland in favour of strengthening the country's commercial ties with the EU (May).

Russia's Foreign Policy Concept adopted (June).

On a visit to Germany, President Chirac of France advocated the creation of a two-tier Europe in which France and Germany would lead a 'pioneer group' of member states pushing ahead with integration.

Oresund Bridge linking Denmark and Sweden officially opened (July).

Denmark voted against joining Economic and Monetary Union in a referendum (September).

Lifting of diplomatic sanctions imposed on Austria by the other EU states because of the entry of the far-right FPÖ into a coalition government.

President Milošević of Yugoslavia overthrown (October).

Incumbent president, Aleksander Kwasniewski, re-elected in Poland.

Romania parliamentary and presidential elections (November/December).

George W. Bush elected president of the USA.

EU states (except Denmark) agreed to create a Rapid Reaction Force designed to give Europe the independent military capability to respond to crisis situations where NATO was not involved.

EU states agreed the Nice Treaty and proclaimed the Charter of Fundamental Rights of the European Union (December).

2001   Greece joined the euro zone (January).

Jorge Sampaio of the ruling SP re-elected president of Portugal.

EU justice and home affairs ministers agreed to accelerate harmonisation of the immigration and political asylum policies of the EU member states (February).

EU ban on exports of UK livestock, meat and dairy products imposed as a result of a foot and mouth epidemic in the UK.

A national referendum in Switzerland rejected a proposal to apply for EU membership (March).

Turkish government published its programme for meeting the requirements of EU membership.

Accession of Denmark, Finland and Sweden, together with non-EU members Iceland and Norway, to the Schengen zone (April).

Slobodan Milošević, former president of Yugoslavia, arrested.

A centre-right coalition led by former prime minister Silvio Berlusconi formed a government following its victory over the centre-left Olive Tree alliance in the Italian general election (May).

Following an EU–Russia summit in Moscow, Russia announced the creation of a committee to begin discussion of integration with, but not membership of, the EU.

Irish voters rejected the Nice Treaty in a referendum (June).

EU heads of government meeting in Gothenburg agreed a timetable for the enlargement of the EU.

Slobodan Milošević, former president of Yugoslavia, was handed over to the UN International Criminal Tribunal for the Former Yugoslavia (the war crimes tribunal) in The Hague.

UK Labour Party returned to power with a second huge majority.

In Russia, the Duma ratified the new 'Law on Political Parties'.

Terrorists hijacked four passenger aircraft in the USA. Two of the planes smashed into the twin towers of the World Trade Center in New York. A third plane demolished part of the Pentagon, and the fourth plane crashed in a field in Pennsylvania (September).

Polish parliamentary elections: a new left-wing government was formed under Prime Minister Lezek Miller.

Special European Council meeting in Brussels to set guidelines for EU response to 11 September terrorist attacks in the USA.

The Grand National Assembly in Turkey approved a number of amendments to the constitution designed to help Turkey to meet the EU's political criteria for opening accession negotiations (October).

European Council agreed the Laeken Declaration, which established the remit, membership and leadership of the European Convention (December).

2002   Euro notes and coins came into circulation in the twelve EU member states participating in Economic and Monetary Union (January).

Convention on the Future of Europe began work on a draft constitution for the EU (February).

Resignation of the Netherlands government under Prime Minister Wim Kok (April).

New centre-right coalition government in Portugal under Prime Minister José Manuel Durao following the victory of the PSD in March.

Opening of the trial of Slobodan Milošević, former president of Yugoslavia, at the International Criminal Tribunal for the Former Yugoslavia in The Hague.

Chirac re-elected president of France, defeating Jean-Marie Le Pen, the far-right (FN) candidate, in the second round of voting (May).

European Commission announced proposals for a major overhaul of the EU's CFP.

Extension of NATO mission in Macedonia.

Appointment of Lord Paddy Ashdown of the UK as high representative of the Bosnian Peace Implementation Council.

Elections to the French National Assembly resulted in victory for the centre-right UMP.

EU heads of government meeting in Seville agreed on a new plan to tackle illegal immigration (June).

50-year treaty establishing the ECSC expired and the functions of the ECSC were absorbed by the EC (July).

Introduction of major changes to Russia's criminal justice system.

Schröder government in Germany remained following general election (October).

Dissolution of the RPR in France and the end of a distinctively 'Gaullist' party.

EU Commission recommended EU membership for Cyprus, the Czech Republic, Estonia, Hungary, Latvia, Lithuania, Malta, Poland, the Slovak Republic and Slovenia.

France and Germany agreed to limit expenditure on the CAP after 2006 and pushed through this agreement in the face of opposition from some of the other EU states, including the UK, whose prime minister, Tony Blair, was critical of French refusal to reform the CAP.

In a second referendum, Ireland voted for ratification of the Nice Treaty.
The AKP (Justice and Development Party) gained an overwhelming victory in the Grand National Assembly elections in Turkey (November).
NATO summit meeting in Prague invited Bulgaria, Estonia, Latvia, Lithuania, Romania, Slovakia and Slovenia to join NATO in 2004.
In Turkey's general election, the Justice and Development Party (AKP) won an overall majority of seats in the Grand National Assembly.
An EU summit conference in Copenhagen approved the enlargement of the EU to include ten candidate countries: Cyprus, the Czech Republic, Estonia, Hungary, Latvia, Lithuania, Malta, Poland, Slovakia and Slovenia.
UN plan for peaceful reunification of Cyprus rejected by Rauf Denktash, leader of the self-declared TRNC.

2003 UK and Irish governments agreed a new plan to restore devolution to Northern Ireland (January).
Legislative elections in the Netherlands resulted in victory for the Christian Democratic Appeal under the leadership of Prime Minister Jan Peter Balkenende.
President Chirac of France and Chancellor Schröder of Germany drew up proposals for the election of a president of the European Council by the heads of government and the election of the president of the European Commission by the European Parliament.
The Federal Assembly of the Federal Republic of Yugoslavia (FRY) voted to replace the FRY with a loose union between its two constituent republics, Serbia and Montenegro (February).
Croatia applied for EU membership.
Former prime minister of the Czech Republic, Vaclav Klaus, elected president.
In the biggest backbench revolt since Tony Blair came to power in 1997, 122 Labour MPs supported an anti-war amendment to a government motion on the Iraq crisis.
In Finland's general election, the Centre Party (KESK) narrowly defeated the Social Democratic Party (SSDP).
US-led invasion of Iraq (March).
Assassination of Zoran Djindjic, prime minister of Serbia since 2001.
Grand National Assembly in Turkey voted against the deployment of US troops in Turkey for a possible war in Iraq.
At the Athens European Council, the Treaty of Accession was signed between the EU and ten prospective member states: Cyprus, Czech Republic, Estonia, Hungary, Latvia, Lithuania, Malta, Poland, Slovenia and Slovak Republic (April).
Hungary approved accession to the EU in a national referendum.
The heads of government of Belgium, France, Germany and Luxembourg met to discuss the enhancement of EU defence cooperation in the wake of the US invasion of Iraq, which each had opposed. They proposed the creation of an autonomous EU operational headquarters and agreed to invite other participants in the EU Rapid Reaction Force to join.
EU defence ministers reported that the EU's Rapid Reaction Force was ready for peacekeeping operations and that by the end of 2003 the EU should be able to deploy 60,000 troops abroad within 60 days.

Lithuania and Slovakia approved accession to the EU in national referenda (May).

European Council in Thessaloniki welcomed the European Convention's draft treaty establishing a constitution for Europe as a basis for intergovernmental conference negotiations for a new EU treaty (June).

Anneli Jaatteenmaki, the Finnish prime minister, resigned after being accused of lying about the use of classified government documents concerning the US-led invasion of Iraq.

Gordon Brown, UK chancellor of the Exchequer, announced that four of his five economic tests for taking the UK into the euro zone had not yet been met.

The European Commission offered the TRNC aid and an easing of trade restrictions to facilitate unification of Cyprus.

The Grand National Assembly in Turkey adopted a package of human rights reforms in order to comply with preconditions for negotiations with the EU on Turkey's accession to the EU.

The Czech Republic approved accession to the EU.

Death by suicide of Dr David Kelly, a biological weapons expert in the UK Ministry of Defence (July).

EU and USA reached agreement in principle on cutting agricultural subsidies and on improving market access to farm products from developing countries (August).

Assassination of Anna Lindh, Swedish foreign minister and pro-euro campaigner (September).

A majority of Swedes voted against joining the euro in a referendum.

Estonia and Latvia approved accession to the EU in national referenda.

Presidents of Belarus, Kazakhstan, Russia and Ukraine signed an accord forming a single economic space (EEP) on the territory of their countries.

Intergovernmental conference convened in Rome to discuss the draft EU constitution (October).

Amendments to bring Romania's constitution into line with EU law and to assist Romania's bid for EU membership were approved in a referendum.

The German Bundestag approved the government's 'Agenda 2010' economic and social reform programme.

EU finance ministers decided not to impose sanctions on France and Germany for breaching the budget deficit rules of the Stability and Growth Pact of the euro currency zone (November).

Eduard Shevardnadze, president of Georgia since 1992, forced to resign.

The Croatian Democratic Union (HDZ) won power in legislative elections.

Russian parliamentary elections: United Russia scored a landslide victory (December).

European Council in Brussels failed to agree the Constitutional Treaty.

The mandate of the EU-led military mission to Macedonia expired.

In elections to the State Duma in Russia, the result was a victory for the Unified Russia party.

New government formed in Croatia by the HDZ.

US government announced that it was lifting tariffs it had imposed on steel imported from the EU, Japan and other countries in March 2002.

2004   Resignation of Kostas Simitis, prime minister of Greece and leader of the ruling PASOK (January).

European Commission announced that it would take legal action in the ECJ challenging the decision of the EU finance ministers (25 November 2003) to suspend the rules of the Stability and Growth Pact.

French National Assembly approved a government bill empowering state schools to ban the wearing of Islamic headscarves.

Resignation of the centre-right coalition government in Latvia.

Russian presidential elections (March).

President Putin won a second four-year term in Russia's presidential elections.

Macedonia officially presented its application for EU membership.

Left won control of all but one of France's regional parliaments.

Islamic terrorists killed more than 190 people and injured more than 1,400 people in Madrid train bombings.

EU heads of government meeting in Brussels agreed to strengthen their cooperation in combating terrorism following the Madrid train bombings. They also decided to agree a text on the EU constitution by the time of the next summit (June 2004) and to request Wim Kok (Dutch prime minister) to produce a report on slippage in the 2000 'Lisbon strategy'.

PP lost power and the PSOE came to power as a result of general elections in Spain.

UN plan ('Annan Plan') to reunite Cyprus was supported by the UN, the EU and the governments of Greece and Turkey.

Albanian pogrom against remaining Serbian minority in Kosovo.

Greek Cypriot voters rejected UN plan ('Annan Plan') to reunite Cyprus in advance of EU accession (April).

Spanish government announced its decision to withdraw Spanish troops from Iraq.

Heinz Fischer became Austria's first Social Democratic president for two decades.

In a major policy reversal, Tony Blair, UK prime minister, announced that a national referendum would be held on the proposed EU Constitutional Treaty following agreement on a text.

EU justice and home affairs ministers reached agreement on the first stage of a Common European Asylum System (CEAS), establishing minimum standards for the treatment of political asylum seekers by member states.

European Commission recommended the opening of EU membership negotiations with Croatia.

European Parliament declared that Turkey had not yet met the political criteria required to enter EU membership negotiations.

Russian prosecutor-general's office announced that the major shareholders in the oil company Yukos would be charged with membership of an organised criminal gang.

Prime minister of Poland, Leszek Miller, resigned and was succeeded by Marek Belka (May).

Ten new member states joined the EU – Cyprus, the Czech Republic, Estonia, Hungary, Latvia, Lithuania, Malta, Poland, the Slovak Republic and Slovenia – the biggest enlargement to date.

Lionel Jospin, French Socialist leader, retired from frontline politics.

Tony Blair, UK prime minister, and Bertie Aherne, prime minister of the Republic of Ireland, announced a 'road map' to restore devolution to the suspended Northern Ireland Assembly.

Assassination of Mufti Akhmed Kadyrov, the pro-Russian leader of the separatist republic of Chechnya within the Russian Federation.

Meeting of presidents of Belarus, Kazakhstan, Russia and Ukraine to develop the Single Economic Space (EEP) on the territory of the four countries.

EU Council approved a new EU constitutional treaty (June).

Lowest turnout (45 percent) for European Parliament elections.

The centre-left in Italy scored major gains in regional and European Parliament elections.

In Lithuania's presidential elections, Valdas Adamkus, the independent centre-right candidate, defeated Kazimiera Prunskiene of the Farmers and New Democracy Union.

Resignation of Vladimir Spidla, prime minister and leader of the senior ruling coalition Czech Social Democratic Party (CSSD).

Christian Social People's Party (CSV/PCS), the senior party in the government coalition in Luxembourg, increased its share of the vote in a general election.

Olafur Ragnar Grimsson was re-elected to a third four-year term as president of Iceland.

Boris Tadic, leader of the Democratic Party (DS), was elected president of Serbia and Montenegro.

President Chirac of France announced that France would hold a referendum on the EU Constitutional Treaty (July).

Pedro Santana Lopes appointed prime minister of Portugal following the resignation of José Manual Durao Barroso.

Greece and Turkey signed an agreement on cooperation in the field of security.

The ECJ ruled that the EU Council of Finance Ministers had exceeded its powers when it had rejected the European Commission recommendation for sanctions against France and Germany for being in breach of the budget deficit rules of the Stability and Growth Pact.

EU foreign ministers decided to replace the NATO-led stabilisation force (S-For) in Bosnia by the end of 2004.

Resumption of trade (which had been suspended following the Turkish invasion of 1974) between the self-proclaimed Turkish Republic of Northern Cyprus (TRNC) and the internationally recognised Republic of Cyprus (August).

Resignation of Peter Medgyessy, prime minister of Hungary.

President Vaclav Klaus of the Czech Republic appointed a new centre-left coalition government.

Siege of school by Chechen separatists in Beslan in Russia's republic of North Ossetia (September).

Following EU pressure, the Grand National Assembly in Turkey dropped a proposal to criminalise adultery.

New government in Hungary under Ferenc Gyurcsany.

EU Council of Economic and Finance Ministers agreed in principle to reform the Stability and Growth Pact.

EU Council signed the new EU Constitutional Treaty in Rome (October).

European Commission announced qualified approval for the opening of EC accession negotiations with Turkey.

Resignation of Mehmet Ali Talat, prime minister of the self-proclaimed TRNC, and of his minority ruling coalition.

Parliamentary elections in Lithuania resulted in the Labour Party (DP) becoming the largest group in parliament.

José Manuel Barroso, European Commission president-designate, withdrew his list of proposed new commissioners when it appeared that the European Parliament would reject the list as a whole.

More than half of Italy's magistrates and judges signed a petition protesting against attacks on the independence of the judiciary by the Berlusconi government (November).

George W. Bush re-elected president of the USA.

Large demonstrations in the Ukraine in support of the opposition leader, Viktor Yushchenko, and in protest at the allegedly fraudulent conduct of the second round of the presidential elections.

Legislative elections in Romania resulted in victory for the Social Democratic Party (PSD) and its ally, the Humanist Party of Romania (PUR).

European Parliament approved a new list of commissioners presented by the European Commission president-designate, José Manuel Barroso.

EU leaders agreed to open EU membership talks with Turkey in October 2005 (December).

Collapse of a breakthrough in the peace process in Northern Ireland.

Silvio Berlusconi, prime minister of Italy, was acquitted of corruption charges by a court in Milan.

European Commission announced the suspension of disciplinary proceedings against France and Germany for breaching the Stability and Growth Pact by running budget deficits in excess of 3 percent of GDP.

New presidential election in the Ukraine resulted in victory for the opposition leader, Viktor Yushchenko.

EU formally took over responsibility from NATO for peacekeeping operations in Bosnia.

Traian Basescu, candidate of the Justice and Truth Alliance, elected president of Romania.

2005   In Germany, unemployment rose to 12.6 percent, or 5.2 million people, the worst unemployment figures in Germany since Hitler came to power in 1933 (January).

European Parliament approved the EU Constitutional Treaty.

EU Council of Economic and Finance Ministers again failed to agree on reform of the Stability and Growth Pact.

Presidential elections in Croatia resulted in victory for Stipe Mesic, the centre-left incumbent.

Spain voted in favour of the EU Constitutional Treaty in a referendum, the first referendum on the treaty in the EU (February).

European Commission launched its new Social Agenda.

In Portugal, the PSP benefited from massive disillusionment with the centre-right government and returned to power with its best ever electoral success (February).

EU foreign ministers postponed EU entry talks with Croatia on the grounds that it has not cooperated sufficiently with the hunt for Balkan war criminals such as General Ante Gotovina (March).

EU finance ministers agreed proposals for improving the implementation of the Stability and Growth Pact that amounted to a relaxation of the enforcement procedures of the pact.

European Council meeting endorsed a mid-term revision of the Lisbon strategy.

President Chirac of France announced that France would hold its referendum on the EU Constitutional Treaty on 29 May 2005.

Condoleezza Rice, US Secretary of State, criticised EU plans to lift its ban on the export of weapons to China.

President Chirac of France won the backing of EU leaders for a major revision of the proposed directive to open up the EU's services market on the grounds that the providers of services in Eastern Europe undercut the prices of services elsewhere in the EU through lower labour and environmental standards.

European Parliament approved plan for Bulgaria and Romania to join the EU in 2007, but EU enlargement commissioner warned that accession could be delayed until 2008 or later (April).

Greece and Italy ratified the new EU constitution.

Panel of Balkan experts and politicians under Giuliano Amato of Italy criticised EU policy in the Balkans and called for EU membership for Bosnia, Kosovo, Macedonia and Montenegro within a decade.

UDC ministers belonging to Berlusconi's Italian coalition government resigned following disastrous regional election results for the government. Berlusconi was invited to form a new government.

UK Labour Party returned to power with a reduced majority (May).

Austria, Germany and Slovakia ratified the new EU constitution.

Schröder, Germany's chancellor, announced that he was bringing forward the country's general election by a year following his party's defeat in the key industrial state of North Rhine-Westphalia.

French voters in a referendum rejected the new EU constitution.

EU and USA in dispute over subsidies for Boeing, the American plane-maker, and for the European Airbus (June).

Dutch voters in a referendum rejected the new EU constitution.

Bibliography

Abley, M. (2003) *Spoken Here: Travels Among Threatened Languages*, William Heinemann, London.

ACP Secretariat (http://www.acpsec.org).

Agh, A. (1998) *The Politics of Central Europe*, Sage, London.

Ambrosius, G. and Hubbard, W.H. (1989) *A Social and Economic History of Twentieth-Century Euope*, Harvard University Press, Cambridge, MA.

Andersen, S. and Burns, T. (1996) 'The European Union and the erosion of parliamentary democracy: a study of post-parliamentary governance', in S. Andersen and K. Eliassen (eds), *The EU: How Democratic Is It?* Sage, London.

Anderson, B. (1983) *Imagined Communities: Reflections on the Origin and Spread of Nationalism*, Verso, London.

Anderson, J. (1995) 'The exaggerated death of the nation-state', in J. Anderson, C. Brook and A. Cochrane (eds), *A Global World?* Oxford, Oxford University Press.

Anderson, J. (1997) 'Hard interests, soft power and Germany's changing role in Europe', in P. Katzenstein (ed.), *Tamed Power – Germany and Europe*, Cornell University Press, Ithaca, NY.

Andrén, N. (1967) 'Nordic integration', *Cooperation and Conflict*, 2(1): 1-250

Archer, C. (2005) *Norway Outside the European Union*, Routledge, London.

Archer, C. and Sogner, I. (1998) *Norway, European Integration and Atlantic Security*, Sage, London.

Arikan, H. (2003) *Turkey and the EU: An Awkward Candidate for EU Membership?* Ashgate, Aldershot.

Arter, D. (1999) *Scandinavian Politics Today*, Manchester University Press, Manchester.

Artis, M. and Nixson, F. (eds) (2001) *The Economics of the European Union: Policy and Analysis*, 3rd edn, Oxford University Press, Oxford.

Ash, T.G. (1993) *In Europe's Name: Germany and the Divided Continent*, Jonathan Cape, London.

Avery, G. and Cameron, F. (1998) *The Enlargement of the European Union*, Sheffield Academic Press, Sheffield.

Bache, I. (1998) *The Politics of European Union Regional Policy*, Sheffield Academic Press, Sheffield.

Bacon, E. (2004) 'Russia's law on political parties', in C. Ross (ed.), *Russian Politics Under Putin*, Manchester University Press, Manchester.

Bainbridge, T. (1998) *Penguin Companion to European Union*, Penguin, London.

Baldwin, M., Peterson, J. and Stokes, B. (2003) 'Trade and economic relations', in J. Peterson and M. Pollack (eds), *Europe, America, Bush: Transatlantic Relations in the Twenty-First Century*, Routledge, London.

Balibar, E. (1991) 'Es gibt keinen Staat in Europa: racism and politics in Europe today', *New Left Review,* 186: 15–21, Verso, London.

Baranovsky, V. (2001) 'Russia: a part of Europe or apart from Europe?, in A. Brown (ed.), *Contemporary Russian Politics: A Reader*, Oxford University Press, Oxford.

Batt, J. (2003) 'Democratisation in Central and Eastern Europe: a comparative perspective', in S. White, J. Batt and P.G. Lewis (eds), *Developments in Central and East European Politics – 3*, Palgrave Macmillan, Basingstoke.

Batt, J. and Wolczuk, K. (1998) 'Redefining the state: the constitutional process', in S. White, J. Batt and P.G. Lewis (eds), *Developments in Central and Eastern Europe – 2*, Palgrave Macmillan, Basingstoke.

BBC (2004a) 'Cyprus "spurns historical chance"' (available at http://www.news.bbc.co.uk/go/pr/fr/1/hi/world/europe/3660171.stm).

BBC (2004b) 'EU pledges aid for Turkish Cyprus' (available at http://www.news.bbc.co.uk/go/pr/fr/-/1/hi/world/europe/3656753.dtm).

BBC 'What the EU constitution says' (available at http://www.news.bbc.co.uk/1/hi/world/europe/2950276.stm).

BBC News Country Profiles (available at http://www.newsvote.bbc.co.uk).

Beck, U. (2003) 'Cosmopolitan Europe: a confederation of states, a federal state, or something altogether new?', in S. Stern and E. Seligman (eds), *Desperately Seeking Europe*, Archetype Publications, London.

Bell, D.S. (2000) *Parties and Democracy in France: Parties under Presidentialism*, Ashgate, Aldershot.

Bell, P.M.H. (1997) *France and Britain 1940–1994: The Long Separation,* Longman, London.

Berryman, J. (2000) 'Russian foreign policy: an overview', in M. Bowker and C. Ross (eds), *Russia after the Cold War*, Longman, Harlow.

Blazyca, G. (2003) 'Managing transition economies', in S. White, J. Batt and P.G. Lewis (eds) *Developments in Central and East European Politics – 3*, Palgrave Macmillan, Basingstoke.

Blinken, A. (2001) 'The false crisis over the Atlantic', *Foreign Affairs*, Council on Foreign Relations, New York, 80 (3): 35–48.

Borehardt, K.-D. (2000) *The ABC of Community Law*, Office for Offical Publications of the European Community, Luxembourg.

Borrás-Alomar, S., Chrisiansen, T. and Rodríguéz, A. (1994) 'Towards a "Europe of the Regions"? Visions and reality from a critical perspective', *Regional Politics and Policy*, 4: 1–27.

Bourne, A. (2003) 'Spanish autonomous communities and the convention on the future of the European Union', draft paper.

Bower, T. (1991) *Maxwell: The Outsider*, Mandarin, London.

Breslauer, G.W. (2001) 'Personalism versus proceduralism: Boris Yeltsin and the institutional fragility of the Russian system', in V.E. Bonnell and G.W. Breslauer (eds), *Russia in the New Century: Stability or Disorder?*, Westview Press, Boulder, CO.

Bretherton, C. and Vogler, J. (1999) *Europe as a Global Actor*, Routledge, London.

Brubaker, R. (1996) *Nationalism Reframed: Nationhood and the National Question in the New Europe*, Cambridge University Press, Cambridge.

Bruneau, T. (1997) *Political Parties and Democracy in Portugal: Organizations, Elections and Public Opinion*, Westview Press, Boulder, CO.

Brussels, 27 April 2004, see EU website.

Buechsenschuetz, U. (2004) 'Analysis: EU welcomes new members, but where is the enthusiasm?' *RFE/RL Newsline*, special issue, 'EU Expands Eastward', 3 May.

Buller, H. and Hoggart, K. (1994) *International Counterurbanisation*, Avebury, Aldershot.

Bulmer, S. and Paterson, W. (1992) *The Federal Republic of Germany and the European Community*, Oxford University Press, Oxford.

Burgess, M. (2003) 'Federalism and Federation', in M. Cini (ed.), *European Union Politcs*, Oxford University Press, Oxford.

Callaghan, J. (2000) *The Retreat of Social Democracy*, Manchester University Press, Manchester.

Cameron, D.R. (2004) 'The tough trials ahead for the EU's eastern expansion', *Current History*: 119–26.

Cameron, F. (ed.) (2004) *The Future of Europe: Integration and Enlargement*, Taylor & Francis, London.

Campbell, D. (1998) *National Deconstruction and Violence: Identity and Justice in Bosnia*, Minnesota University Press, Minneapolis, MN and London.

Caplan, R. and Feffer, J. (eds) (1996) *Europe's New Nationalism: States and Minorities in Conflict*, Oxford University Press, Oxford.

Carchedi, G. (2001) *For Another Euope: A Class Analysis of European Economic Integration*, Verso, London.

Çarkoğlu, A. (2003a) 'Conclusion', in A. Çarkoğlu and B. Rubin (eds), *Turkey and the European Union: Domestic Politics, Economic Integration and International Dynamics*, Frank Cass, London.

Çarkoğlu, A. (2003b) 'Who wants full membership? Characteristics of Turkish public support for EU membership' in A. Çarkoğlu and B. Rubin (eds), *Turkey and the European Union: Domestic Politics, Economic Integration and International Dynamics*, Frank Cass, London.

Çarkoğlu, A. and Rubin, B. (eds) (2003) *Turkey and the European Union: Domestic Politics, Economic Integration and International Dynamics*, Frank Cass, London.

Carlsnaes, W., Sjursen, H. and White, B. (eds) (2004) *Contemporary European Foreign Policy*, Sage, London.

Castles, S. (2000) *Ethnicity and Globalization*, Sage, London.

Castles, S. and Davidson, A. (2000) *Citizenship and Migration: Globalization and the Politics of Belonging*, Macmillan, Houndmills.

Castles, S. and Miller, M. (1998) *The Age of Migration*, Macmillan, London.

The Central Committee of AKEL (1978) July/August 1974: *Chronicle of the Contemporary Tragedy of Cyprus*, AKEL, Nicosia.

Christiansen, T., Jørgensen, K.E. and Wiener, A. (1999) 'The Social Construction of Europe', *Journal of European Public Policy*, 6 (4).

Chryssochoou, D. (2003) 'Democracy and the Democratic Deficit', in M. Cini (ed.), *European Union Politics*, Oxford University Press, Oxford.

CIA (2005) The World Factbook, February (available at **http://www.cia.gov/cia/publications/factbook/goes**).

Cini, M. (ed.) (2003) *European Union Politics*, Oxford University Press, Oxford.

Cohen, E. (1990) *Making a New Deal: Industrial Workers in Chicago, 1919–1939*, Cambridge University Press, Cambridge.

Cook, R. (2004) *The Point of Departure; Diaries from the Front Bench*, Pocket Books, London.

Council (2005) *Presidency Conclusions of the Brussels European Council (22/23 March 2005)*, Council of the European Union, Brussels, 7619/05.

Cox, M. (2003) 'Europe and the new American challenge after September 11: crisis – what crisis?' *Journal of Transatlantic Studies*, 1 (1: supplement): 37–55.

Cox, T. (1998) 'The politics of social change', in S. White, J. Batt and P.G. Lewis (eds), *Developments in Central and East European Politics – 2*, Palgrave Macmillan, Basingstoke.

Coxall, B. and Robins, L. (2003) *Contemporary British Politics*, 4th edn, Palgrave Macmillan, Basingstoke.

Crawford, K. (1996) *East Central European Politics Today*, Manchester University Press, Manchester.

Daalder, I. (2001) 'Are the United States and Europe heading for divorce?' *International Affairs*, 77, (3): 553–67.

Daalder, I. (2003) 'The end of Atlanticism', *Survival*, 45 (2): 147–66.

Danks, C. (2001) *Russian Politics and Society*, Longman, Harlow.

De Grauwe, P. (1997) *The Economics of Monetary Integration*, Oxford University Press, Oxford.

De Witte, P. (2003) 'Taking EU–NATO relations forward', *NATO Review 2003* (3) (available at http://www.nato.int/docu/review/2003/issue3/english/art2.html).

Dearden, S. (2005) 'Social policy', in F. McDonald and S. Dearden (eds), *European Economic Integration*, 4th edn, Prentice Hall, Harlow.

Debardeleben, J. (1997) *Russian Politics in Transition*, 2nd edn, Houghton Mifflin Company, New York.

Delanty, G. (1995) *Inventing Europe: Idea, Identity, Reality*, Macmillan, London.

Delors, J. (1988) *Report on Economic and Monetary Union in the European Community* (available on the EU website (http://www.europa.eu.int).

den Boer, M. and Wallace, W. (2000) 'Justice and home affairs: integration through incrementalism?, in H. Wallace and W. Wallace (eds), *Policy-making in the European Union*, 4th edn, Oxford University Press, Oxford.

Department of Economic and Social Affairs, Statistics Division (2004) *Statistical Yearbook 2000*, 47th edn, United Nations, New York.

DG Development (http://www.europa.eu.int/comm/development/index_en.htm).

Diez, T. and Wiener, A. (2004) *European Integration Theory*, Oxford University Press, Oxford.

Dinan, D. (1999) *Ever Closer Union*, Palgrave, Houndmills.

Dinan, D. (2004) *Europe Recast: A History of European Union*, Palgrave Macmillan, London.

Dockrill, S. (2003) 'After September 11: globalization of security beyond the Transatlantic Alliance', *Journal of Transatlantic Studies*, 1 (1: supplement): 1–19.

Drysdale, H. (2001) *Mother Tongues: Travels Through Tribal Europe*, Picador, London.

Duff, A. (1997) *The Treaty of Amsterdam*, Federal Trust, London.

Duff, A. (2003) 'A liberal reaction to the European Convention and the IGC, Federal Trust Online Paper 23/03.

Dunleavy, P. *et al.* (2003) *Developments in British Politics – 7*, Palgrave Macmillan, Basingstoke.

Dyson, K. and Featherstone, K. (1999) *The Road to Maastricht: Negotiating Economic and Monetary Union*, Oxford University Press, Oxford.

East, W.G. (1989) 'Historical geography', in G.W. Hoffman (ed.) *Europe in the 1990s: A Geographic Analysis*, 6th edn, John Wiley and Sons, New York.

ECB (2005) *Statistics Pocket Book* (available on ECB website).

ECB (http://www.ecb.int/ecb).

Eder, K. and Giesen, B. (eds) (2001) *European Citizenship between National Legacies and Postnational Projects*, Oxford University Press, Oxford.

Edmunds, T. (2003) 'NATO and its new members', *Survival*, 45 (3): 145–66.

Eickelman, D.F. and Piscatori, J. (1996) *Muslim Politics*, Princeton University Press, Princeton, NJ.

Einhorn, E.S. and Logue, J. (2003) *Modern Welfare States: Scandinavian Politics and Policy in the Global Age*, Praeger, Westport, CN.

El-Agraa, A.M. (ed.) (2004) *The European Union: Economics and Policies*, 7th edn, Prentice Hall/Pearson Education, Harlow.

Elder, N., Thomas, A.H. and Arter, D. (1988) *The Consensual Democracies?* Revised edn, Basil Blackwell, Oxford.

EMU (http://www.europa.eu.int/pol/emu).

Encarta Online 'Yugoslav Succession, Wars of' in *Microsoft Encarta Online Encyclopedia* (available at http://www.encarta.msn.com).

EPAwatch (http://www.epawatch.net).

Erdemli, O. (2003) 'Chronology: Turkey's relations with the EU', in A. Çarkoğlu and B. Rubin (eds), *Turkey and the European Union: Domestic Politics, Economic Integration and International Dynamics*, Frank Cass, London.

Esping-Anderson, G. (ed.) (1996) *Welfare States in Transition: National Adaptations in Global Economies*, Sage, London.

Ethier, D. (1990) *Democratic Transition and Consolidation in Southern Europe, Latin America and South-East Asia*, Macmillan, Basingstoke.

EU (http://www.europa.eu.int/development/).

EU (http://www.europa.eu.int/comm./employment_social/fundmental_rights/index_en.htm).

EU (http://www.europa.eu.int/comm/enlargement/arguments/index.htm).

EU (http://www.europa.eu.int/comm/external_relations/russia_docs/index.htm).

EU (http://www.europa.eu.int/comm/public.opinion/enlargement.en.htm).

Europa (2004): http://www.europa.eu.int/comm/fisheries/ First Application of the Reformed Common Fisheries Policy: Commission proposes long-term recovery plan for cod.

Europa (2004a) 'Enlargement: Candidate Country: Cyprus' (available at http://www.europa.eu.int/comm/enlargement/cyprus/print-index.htm).

Europa (2004b) http://europa.eu.int/comm/fisheries/ Introduction to the CFP – the Common Fisheries Policy (and factsheets).

European Commission (2000) *Regional Socio-Economic Studies on Employment and the Level of Dependency on Fishing*, Commision of the European Communities, Directorate General for Fisheries, Brussels.

European Commission (2003a) *Commission Communication on Immigration, Integration and Employment*, 3 June 2003, COM (2003) 336 final of 3.6.2003.

European Commission (2003b) *Going for Growth: The Economy of the EU*, European Commission, Brussels.

European Commission (2004a) *Communication from the Commission to the Council and the European Parliament: Area of Freedom, Security and Justice: Assessment of the Tampere Programme and Future Orientations*, COM(2004) 4002 final.

European Commission (2004b) *Enlargement and Agriculture*, European Commission, Brussels.

European Commission (2004c) *Equality and Non-discrimination Annual Report*, Directorate-General for Employment and Social Affairs, Office for Official Publications of the European Communities, Luxembourg.

European Commission (2004d) *The Common Agricultural Policy – A Policy Evolving with the Tmes*, European Commission, Brussels.

European Commission (2004e) *The Common Agricultural Policy Explained*, European Commission, Brussels.

European Commission (2004f) *Third Progress Report on Economic and Social Cohesion* (available at http://www.europa.eu.int/comm/regional_policy).

European Commission (2005a) Anti-discrimination unit website, Directorate-General for Employment and Social Affairs (available at http://www.europa.eu.int/comm./employment_social/fundmental_rights/index_en.htm).

European Commission (2005b) *Communication from the Commission on the Social Agenda*, COM (2005) 33.

European Commission (2005c) *Integrated Guidelines for Growth and Jobs (2005–2008)*, COM (2005) 141.

European Commission on the Press and Communication (2004) *Many Tongues, One Family: Languages in the European Union*, Office for Official Publications of the European Communities, Luxembourg.

European Communities (1982) *The Economy of the European Community*, Office for Official Publications of the European Communities, Luxembourg.

European Communities (1990) *Europe, A Fresh Start: The Schuman Declaration, 1950–1990*, Office for Official Publications of the European Communities, Luxembourg.

European Communities (2003) *How the European Union Works: A Citizen's Guide to the EU Institutions, 1950–1990*, Office for Official Publications of the European Communities, Luxembourg.

European Communities (2004a) *Working for the Regions*, Office for Official Publications of the European Communities, Luxembourg.

European Communities (2004b) *Freedom, Security and Justice for All: Justice and Home Affairs in the European Union*, Office for Official Publications of the European Communities, Luxembourg.

European Communities (2005) Equal rights in practice, *Newsletter of the Community Action Programme to Combat Discrimination*, spring 2005 (available at http://www.europa.eu.int/comm./employment_social/fundmental_rights/index_en.htm).

European Council (2000) *Presidency Conclusions*, Lisbon European Council, 23 and 24 March 2000.

European Parliament (2005) Committee on Citizens' Freedoms and Rights, Justice and Home Affairs (available at http://www.europarl.eu.int/comparl/libe/elsj/news/default_en.htm).

European Union in the US (2004) 'Facts and figures on the European Union and the United States' (available at http://www.eurunion.org/profile/facts.htm).

Eurostat (1997) *Europe in Figures*, 4th edn, Office for Official Publications of the European Communities, Luxembourg.

Eurostat (2004) *Portrait of the EU*, Office for Official Publications of the European Communities, Luxembourg.

Eurostat (2005) http://www.europa.eu.int/comm./eurostat/newcronos).

Everett, W. (1996) *European Identity in Cinema*, Intellect Books, Exeter.

Fontaine, P. (1998) *Europe in Ten Points*, Office for Official Publications of the European Communities, Luxembourg.

Foreign and Commonwealth Office (FCO), 'European leaders call for Europe and United States to stand united: joint letter by the leaders of eight European countries in the *Times* newspaper, Thursday 30 January 2003' (available at http://www.fco.gov.uk).

Freedom House (2003/4) *Nations in Transit: Democratisation in East-Central Europe and Eurasia* (see website for annual surveys: http://www.freedomhous.org/research/nattransit.htm).

Garrett, G. and Weingast, B. (1993) 'Ideas, interests and institutions: constructing the European Community's internal market', in J. Goldstein and R. Keohane (eds), *Ideas and Foreign Policy: Beliefs, Institutions and Political Change*, Cornell University Press, Ithaca, NY.

Gati, C. (1990) *The Bloc That Failed*, I.B. Tauris, London.

Geddes, A. (2003) *The Politics of Migration and Immigration in Europe*, Sage, London.

Genteleman, A. (2001) 'Back to the USSR', *The Guardian*, 29 May 2000, p. 2. Quoted in Danks, C., *Russian Politics and Society*, Longman, Harlow.

George, S. and Bache, I. (2001) *Politics of the European Union*, Oxford University Press, Oxford.

Gerstenlauer, H. (1985) 'German *Länder* in the European Community', in M. Keating and B. Jones (eds), *Regions in the European Community*, Clarendon Press, Oxford.

Giddens, A. (1998) *The Third Way: The Renewal of Social Democracy*, Polity Press, Cambridge.

Giesen, B. (2001) 'National identity and citizenship: the cases of Germany and France', in K. Eder and B. Giesen (eds), *European Citizenship between National Legacies and Postnational Projects*, Oxford University Press, Oxford.

Gildea, R. (2002) *France Since 1945*, 2nd edn, Oxford University Press, Oxford.

Gillespie, R. (1996) *Mediterranean Politics*, Vol. 3, Pinter, London.

Gillespie, R., Story, J. and Rodrigo, F. (1995) *Democratic Spain*, Routledge, London.

Gillingham, J. (2003) *European Integration, 1950–2002: Superstate or New Market Economy?*, Cambridge University Press, Cambridge.

Ginsborg, P. (2001) *Italy and its Discontents*, Allen Lane/Penguin Press, London.

Ginsborg, P. (2004) *Silvio Berlusconi: Television, Power and Patrimony*, Verso, London.

Glasser, S.B. (2004) 'Putin talk worries independent groups civil society activists on defensive', *Washington Post*, 1 June, 2004. Reproduced in Johnson's Russia List, 3 June.

Goldman, M.I. (2003a) 'Render unto Caesar: Putin and the oligarchs', *Current History*, p. 324.

Goldman, M.I. (2003b) *The Piratisation of Russia: Russia Reform Goes Awry*, Routledge, London.

Goodin, R. (ed.) (1996) *The Theory of Institutional Design*, Cambridge University Press, Cambridge.

Gordon, P. (2001) 'NATO after 11 September', *Survival*, 43 (4): 89–106.

Gower, J. (2004) 'Russian foreign policy towards the European Union', in C. Ross (ed.), *Russian Politics Under Putin*, Manchester University Press, Manchester.

Gowland, D. and Turner, A. (1999) *Reluctant Europeans: Britain and European Integration 1945–1998*, Longman, London.

Gowland, D. and Turner, A. (eds.) (2000) *Britain and European Integration 1945–1998: A Documentary History*, Routledge, London.

Grabbe, H. (2003) 'The implications of EU enlargement', in S. White, J. Batt and P. Lewis (eds), *Developments in Central and East European Politics – 3*, Palgrave Macmillan, Basingstoke.

Grabbe, H. (2004) 'The newcomers', in F. Cameron (ed.), *The Future of Europe: Integration and Enlargement*, Routledge, London.

Gray, M. and Stubb, A. (2001) 'Keynote article: the Treaty of Nice – negotiating a poisoned chalice?', *Journal of Common Market Studies*, 39, annual review.

Green Cowles, M., Caporaso, J. and Risse, T. (2001) *Transforming Europe: Europeanisation and Domestic Change*, Cornell University Press, Ithaca, NY.

Gstöhl, S. (2002) *Reluctant Europeans: Norway, Sweden and Switzerland in the Process of Integration*, Lynne Rienner, Boulder, CO and London.

Gunther, R. *et al.* (2004) *Democracy in Modern Spain*, Yale University Press, Yale, CN.

Gunther, R., Diamandouros, N. and Puhle, H.-J. (1995) *The Politics of Democratic Consolidation: Southern Europe in Comparative Perspective*, Johns Hopkins University Press, Baltimore, MD.

Guyomarch, A. *et al.* (2001), *Developments in French Politics – 2*, Palgrave Macmillan, Basingstoke.

Haas, E. (1961) 'The uniting of Europe and the uniting of Latin America', *Journal of Common Market Studies*, 5 (2): 315–43.

Haas, E. (1968a) 'Technocracy, pluralism and the new Europe', in J. Nye (ed.), *International Regionalism*, Little, Brown, Boston, MA.

Haas, E. (1968b) *The Uniting of Europe*, Stanford University Press, Stanford, CA.

Haas, E. (1970) 'The study of regional integration: reflections on the joy and anguish of pre-theorising', *International Organization*, 24 (4): 607–46.

Hakim, C. (1998) *Social Change and Innovation in the Labour Market*, Oxford University Press, Oxford.

Hale, H. (2004) 'The new Duma', *Russia Election Watch*, 3 (4) January.

Hale, W. (2003) 'Human Rights, the European Union and the Turkish accession process', in A. Çarkoğlu and B. Rubin (eds), *Turkey and the European Union: Domestic Politics, Economic Integration and International Dynamics*, Frank Cass, London.

Hall, P. and Taylor R. (1996) 'Political science and the three new institutionalisms', *Political Studies*, 44: 936–57.

Hamilton, M. and Hirszowicz, M. (1993) *Class and Inequality: Comparative Perspectives*, Harvester Wheatsheaf, Hemel Hempstead.

Hansen, J.D. and Nielsen, J.U.-M. (1997) *An Economic Analysis of the EU*, 2nd edn, McGraw-Hill, Maidenhead.

Hansen, L. and Wæver, O. (eds) (2002) *European Integration and National Identity: The Challenge of the Nordic States*, Routledge, London and New York.

Haseler, S. (2004) *Superstate: The New Europe and its Challenge to America*, I.B. Tauris, London and New York.

Healey, N. (2005) 'Economic and Monetary Union', in F. McDonald and S. Dearden (eds), *European Economic Integration*, 4th edn, Prentice Hall, Harlow.

Heclo, H. and Madsen, H. (1987) *Policy and Politics in Sweden*, Temple University Press, Philadelphia, PA.

Heffernan, M. (1998) *The Meaning of Europe: Geography and Geopolitics*, Edward Arnold, London.

Heidar, K. (ed.) (2004) *Nordic Politics*, Universitetsforlaget, Oslo.

Heywood, P. (1998) *Spain: A European Democracy*, Frank Cass, London.

Hill, C. (1993) 'The capability–expectations gap, or conceptualising Europe's international role', *Journal of Common Market Studies*, 31 (3): 305–28.

Hitiris, T. (2003) *European Union Economics*, 5th edn, Prentice Hall (Pearson Education), Harlow.

Hix, S. (1999) *The Political System of the European Union*, Palgrave, Basingstoke.

Hobsbawm, E. (1994) *Age of Extremes: The Short Twentieth Century, 1914–1991*, Michael Joseph, London.

HM Treasury (2003) *UK Membership of the Single Currency; An Assessment of the Five Economic Tests*, Home Office, London (available at http://www.hm-treasury.gov.uk).

Hoffman, S. (1966) 'Obstinate or obsolete? The fate of the nation-state and the case of Western Europe', in J. Nye (ed.), *International Regionalism: Readings*, Little, Brown, Boston, MA.

Hoffman, S. (1995) *The European Sisyphus*, Westview Press, Boulder, CO.

Holtom, P. (2005), 'The Kaliningrad test in Russian–EU relations', *Perspectives on European Politics and Society*, Brill Academic Publishers, 6 (1).

Hooghe, L. and Marks, G. (2001) *Multilevel Governance and European Integration*, Rowman & Littlefield, Maryland.

Hudson, R. (2004) 'Thinking through the geographies of the new Europe in the new millennium: dialectics of circuits, flows and spaces', *European Urban and Regional Studies*, 11: 99–102.

Huntington, S. (1991) *The Third Wave: Democratisation in the Late Twentieth Century*, University of Oklahoma Press, Norman, OK.

Hutchinson, J. and Smith, A.D. (1996) *Ethnicity*, Oxford University Press, Oxford.

IBRD (http://www.worldbank.org).

IMF (http://www.imf.org/external/ or http://www.imf.org).

IMF (2004) *International Monetary Fund Country Report No. 04/315, Russian Federation: Statistical Appendix*, IMF, Washington, DC.

Ingebritsen, C. (1998) *The Nordic States and European Unity*, Cornell University Press, Ithaca, NY.

Jeffery, C. (1997a) 'Farewell the third level? The German *Länder* and the European policy process', in C. Jeffery (ed.), *The Regional Dimension of the European Union. Towards a Third Level in Europe?*, Frank Cass, London.

Jeffery, C. (1997b) 'Regional information offices in Brussels and multi-level governance in the EU: a UK–German comparison', in C. Jeffery (ed.), *The Regional Dimension of the European Union. Towards a Third Level in Europe?* Frank Cass, London.

Jeffery, C. (1997c) 'Conclusions: sub-national authorities and "European Domestic Policy"', in C. Jeffery (ed.), *The Regional Dimension of the European Union. Towards a Third Level in Europe?* Frank Cass, London.

John, P. (1994) 'UK sub-national offices in Brussels: diversification or regionalization?', *Regional Studies*, 28: 739–46.

John, P. (1997) 'Europeanization in a centralizing state: multi-level governance in the UK', in C. Jeffery (ed.) *The Regional Dimension of the European Union. Towards a Third Level in Europe?*, Frank Cass, London.

Joint Statement (2004) 'Joint statement on EU enlargement and EU–Russia relations' (available at http://www.europa.eu.int/comm/external_relations/russia_docs/index.htm).

Jones, B. *et al.* (2004) *Politics UK*, 5th edn, Pearson Education, Harlow.

Jones, T. (2003) *The Dark Heart of Italy*, Faber and Faber, London.

Keating, M. (1995) 'Europeanism and regionalism', in B. Jones and M. Keating (eds), *The European Union and the Regions*, Clarendon Press, Oxford.

Keating, M. and Jones, B. (eds) (1985) *Regions in the European Community*, Clarendon Press, Oxford.

Kellas, J. (1998) *The Politics of Nationalism and Ethnicity*, 2nd edn, Macmillan, Basingstoke.

Keohane, R. (1989) *International Institutions and State Power – Essays in International Relations Theory*, Westview Press, London.

Kerremans, B. (2000) 'Determining a European policy in a multi-level setting: the case of specialized co-ordination in Belgium', *Regional and Federal Studies*, 10: 36–61.

Kerremans, B. and Beyers, J. (1997) 'Belgian sub-national entities in the European Union: second or third level players?', in C. Jeffery (ed.), *The Regional Dimension of the European Union. Towards a Third Level in Europe?*, Frank Cass, London.

Kesselman, M. *et al.* (2002), *European Politics in Transition*, 4th edn, Houghton Mifflin, Boston, MA.

King, R. (ed.) (2001) *The Mediterranean Passage: Migration and New Cultural Encounters in Southern Europe*, Liverpool University Press, Liverpool.

Kleinman, M. (2002) *A European Welfare State? European Union Social Policy in Context*, Palgrave, Basingstoke.

Knapp, A. and Wright, V. (2001) *The Government and Politics of France*, 4th edn, Palgrave Macmillan, Basingstoke.

Kofman, E. (2002) 'Contemporary European migrations, civic stratification and citizenship', *Political Geography*, 21: 1035–54.

Kohler Koch, B. (1996) 'Catching up with change: the transformation of governance in the European Union', *Journal of European Public Policy*, 3 (3): 359–80.

Kok, W. (2003a) *Enlarging the EU: Achievements and Challenges*, Report to the European Commission, 2 March.

Kok, W. (2003b) *Jobs, Jobs, Jobs; Creating More Employment in Europe* (available on the European Commission website at http://www.europa.eu.int/comm/).

Kolmakov, S. (2004) *Russia Election Watch*, 3 (5) February: 10.

Kopecky, P. (2003) 'Structures of representation: the new parliaments of Central and Eastern Europe', in S. White, J. Batt and P.G. Lewis (eds), *Developments in Central and East European Politics – 3*, Palgrave Macmillan, Basingstoke.

Kryshtanovskaya, O. and White, S. (2003) 'Putin's militocracy', *Post-Soviet Affairs*, 19 (4): 294.

Kubik, J. (2003) 'Cultural legacies of state socialism: history making and cultural-political entrepreneurship in post-communist Poland and Russia', in G. Eckiert and S.E. Hanson (eds), *Capitalism and Democracy in Central and Eastern Europe*, Cambridge University Press, Cambridge.

Ladrech, R. (2004) 'Europeanisation and the member states', in M. Green Cowles and D. Dinan (eds), *Developments in the European Union*, Palgrave, Basingstoke.

Lafontaine, O. (1998) The future of German Social Democracy, *New Left Review*, 72–87.

Lahav, G. (2004) *Immigration and Politics in the New Europe*, Cambridge University Press, Cambridge.

Landmann, T. (2000) *Issues and Methods in Comparative Politics: An Introduction*, Routledge, London.

Lane, D. (2004) 'The economic legacy: what Putin had to deal with and the way forward', in C. Ross (ed.), R*ussian Politics Under Putin*, Manchester University Press, Manchester.

Lane, D. and Ross, C. (1995) 'From soviet government to presidential rule', in D. Lane (ed.), *Russia in Transition: Politics, Privatisation and Inequality*, Longman, Harlow.

Lavdas, K. and Magone, J. (1997) *Politics and Governance in Southern Europe: The Political Systems of Italy, Greece, Spain and Portugal*, Westview Press, Boulder, CO.

Lewis, J. (2003) 'The Council of the European Union', in M. Cini (ed.), *European Union Politics*, Oxford University Press, Oxford.

Lewis, P.G. (2000) *Political Parties in Post-Communist Eastern Europe*, Routledge, London.

Lewis, P.G. (2003) 'Political parties', in S. White, J. Batt and P.G. Lewis (eds), *Developments in Central and East European Politics – 3*, Palgrave Macmillan, Basingstoke.

Library of Congress (http://www.lcweb2.loc.gov/cgi-bin/query).

Library of Congress Country Studies (http://www.lcweb2.loc.gov/frd/cs/cshome.html).

Light, M. (2001) 'Post-Soviet Russian foreign policy: the first decade', in A. Brown (ed.), *Contemporary Russian Politics: A Reader*, Oxford University Press, Oxford.

Linch, D. (2003) 'Russia faces Europe', Chaillot Papers, No. 60, May.

Lindberg, L. (1963) *The Political Dynamics of European Economic Integration*, Stanford University Press, Stanford, CA.

Lindberg, L. and Scheingold, S. (1970) *Europe's Would-Be Polity*, Prentice Hall, Upper Saddle River, NJ.

Lindley-French, J. (2003) 'The ties that bind', NATO *Review* 2003 (3) (available at http://www.nato.int/docu/review/2003/issue3/english/art2.html).

Linz, J. and Stepan, A. (1996) *Problems of Democratic Transition and Consolidation: Southern Europe, South America and Post-Communist Europe*, Johns Hopkins University Press, Baltimore, MD.

Lloyd, J. (2003) 'The closing of the European gates? The new populist parties of Europe', in S. Spencer (ed.), *The Politics of Migration*, Basil Blackwell, Oxford.

Lord, C. (2001) 'Assessing democracy in a contested polity', *Journal of Common Market Studies*, 39 (4): 641–61.

Lord, C. and Magnette, P. (2004) 'E pluribus unum? Creative disagreement about legitimacy in the EU', *Journal of Common Market Studies*, 42 (1): 183–202.

Lundestad, G. (1997) *'Empire' by Integration: The United States and European Integration, 1945–97*, Oxford University Press, Oxford.

Lundestad, G. (2003) *The United States and Western Europe Since 1945: From 'Empire' by Invitation to Transatlantic Drift*, Oxford University Press, Oxford.

Magone, J. (2004) *Contemporary Spanish Politics*, Routledge, London.

Maksymiuk, J. (2004) 'Analysis: Poland rides into EU on ebbing enthusiasm', *RFE/RL Newsline*, special issue, 'EU Expands Eastward', 3 May.

Malmborg, M. and Strath, B. (eds.) (2002) *The Meaning of Europe: Variety and Contentions within and among Nations*, Berg, Oxford.

March, J. and Olsen, J. (1989) *Rediscovering Institutions: The Organisational Bias of Politics*, Free Press, New York.

Marks, G. (1993) 'Structural policy and multilevel governance in the EC' , in A.W. Cafruny and G.G. Rosenthal (eds), *The State of the European Community*. Vol. 2, *The Maastricht Debates and Beyond*, Lynne Rienner, Boulder, CO.

Marks, G., Hooghe, L. and Blank, K. (1996) 'European integration from the 1980s: state-centric *v.* multilevel governance', *Journal of Common Market Studies*, 34 (3): 341–78.

Marquand, D. (1995), 'Reinventing federalism: Europe and the left', in D. Miliband (ed.), *Europe and the Left*, Polity Press, Cambridge.

Mason, D.S. (1996) *Revolution and Transition in East–Central Europe*, 2nd edn, Westview Press, Boulder, CO.

Maxwell, K., (1995) *The Making of Portuguese Democracy*, Cambridge University Press, Cambridge.

McCormick, J. (2001) *Environmental Policy in the European Union*, Palgrave, Basingstoke.

McDonald, F. and Dearden, S. (eds) (2005) *European Economic Integration,* 4th edn, Addison Wesley Longman, Harlow.

McFaul, M. (1997), 'Russia's rough ride', in L. Diamond, M.F. Platter, Y. Chu and H. Tien, (eds), *Consolidating the Third Wave Democracies*, Johns Hopkins University Press, Baltimore, MD.

McFaul, M. (2002) *Demokratizatsiya: The Journal of Post-Soviet Democratisation*, 10 (2): 111.

McFaul, M. (2003) 'The dangers of managed democracy', *Radio Free Europe/Radio Liberty, Russian Political Weekly*, 3 (49), 12 December.

McGiffen, S.P. (2001) *The EU: A Critical Guide*, Pluto Press, London.

McLeod, H. (1997) *Religion and the People of Western Europe, 1789–1989*, Oxford University Press, Oxford.

McNamara, K. (2002) 'Managing the euro: the European Central Bank', in J. Peterson and M. Shackleton (eds), *The Institutions of the European Union*, Oxford University Press, Oxford.

McNeil, D. (2004) *The New Europe: Imagined Spaces*, Edward Arnold, London.

Mecham, R.Q. (2004) 'From the ashes of virtue, a promise of light: the transformation of political Islam in Turkey', *Third World Quarterly*, 25 (2): 339–58.

Meehan, M. (2002) 'The Charter of Fundamental Rights', in J. Gower (ed.), *The European Union Handbook*, 2nd edn, Fitzroy Dearborn, London.

Mény, Y. and Knapp, A. (1998) *Government and Politics in Western Europe: Britain, France, Italy, Germany*, 3rd edn, Oxford University Press, Oxford.

Michaleva, G. (2003) 'At the starting line: September and the Duma vote', *Russia Election Watch*, 3 (1).

Michaleva, G. (2004) 'Election results 2003: another step towards autocracy', *Russia Election Watch*, 3 (4).

Middlemas, K. (1995) *Orchestrating Europe: The Informal Politics of the European Union 1973–95*, Fontana, London.

Miles, L. (ed.) (1996) *The European Union and the Nordic Countries*, Routledge, London.

Miles, L. (1997) *Sweden and European Integration*, Ashgate: Aldershot.

Miles, L. (2001) 'Sweden in the European Union: changing expectations?' *Journal of European Integration*, 23 (4): 303–33.

Miles, L. (2004) 'Sweden: "hitchhiking" and the euro referendum', *Cooperation and Conflict*, 39 (2): 155–65.

Miles, L. (2005) *Fusing with Europe? Sweden in the European Union*, Ashgate, Aldershot.

Miljan, T. (1977) *The Reluctant Europeans*, Hurst, London.

Millard, F. (2003a) 'Poland', in S. White, J. Batt and P.G. Lewis (eds), *Developments in Central and East European Politics 3*, Palgrave Macmillan, Basingstoke.

Millard, F. (2003b) 'The parliamentary elections in Poland, September 2001', *Electoral Studies*, 22: 367–74.

Milward, A.S. (1984) *The Reconstruction of Western Europe, 1945–1951*, Routledge, London.

Milward, A.S. (1992, 2000) *The European Rescue of the Nation State*, Routledge, London.

Moisi, D. (2001) 'The real crisis over the Atlantic', *Foreign Affairs*, 80 (4): 149–53.

Monnet, J. (1963) 'A ferment of change', *Journal of Common Market Studies*, 1: 203–11.

Moraes, C. (2003) 'The politics of European Union migration policy', in S. Spencer (ed.), *The Politics of Migration*, Basil Blackwell, Oxford.

Moravcsik, A. (1998) *The Choice for Europe: Social Purpose and State Power from Messina to Maastricht*, University College London Press, London.

Mudde, C. (2000) *The Ideology of the Extreme Right*, Manchester University Press, Manchester.

Nagle, J.D. and Mahr, A. (1999) *Democracy and Democratisation*, Sage, London.

NATO, (1949) 'The North Atlantic Treaty' (available at http://www.nato.int/docu/basictxt/treaty.htm).

Nevin, E. (1990) *The Economics of Europe*, Macmillan, Basingstoke.

Nichol, W. and Salmon, T. (2001) *Understanding the European Union*, Pearson Education, London.

Nikonov, V. (2003) 'A strange start', *Russia Election Watch*, 3 (1) October.

Nordal, J. and Kristinsson, V. (1996) *Iceland – The Republic*, Central Bank of Iceland, Reykjavik.

Nugent, N. (1999) *The Government and Politics of the European Union*, Macmillan, Houndsmills.

Nugent, N. (ed.) (2004) *European Union Enlargement*, Palgrave Macmillan, London.

OECD (http://www.oecd.org).

Oguzlu, H.T. (2004) 'Changing dynamics of Turkey's US and EU Relations', *Middle East Policy*, 11 (1): 98–105.

Olsen, J. (2003) 'Europeanisation', in M. Cini (ed.), *European Union Politics*, Oxford University Press, Oxford.

Olson, J.P. (2002) 'Four Faces of Europeanization', *An Arena seminar*, University of Oslo, Oslo.

O'Neill, M. (1996) *The Politics of European Integration: A Reader*, Routledge, London.

O'Reilly, K (2000) *The British on the Costa del Sol: Transnational Identities and Local Communities*, Routledge, London.

Osborn, A. (2004) *The Independent*, 14 May, in Johnson's Russia List, No. 8207, 14 May, p. 4.

OSCE (2003) Parliamentary Assembly International Election Observation Mission (IEOM). *Statement of Preliminary Findings and Conclusions Russian Federation State Duma Elections*, 7 December 2003.

OSCE (2004) Parliamentary Assembly International Election Observation Mission (IEOM) *Statement of Preliminary Findings and Conclusions Russian Federation Presidential Election*, 14 March 2004.

Padgett, S., Paterson, W. and Smith, G. (2003) *Developments in German Politics – 3*, Palgrave Macmillan, Basingstoke.

Papademetriou, D. (2003) 'Managing rapid and deep change in the newest age of migration', in S. Spencer (ed.), *The Politics of Migration*, Basil Blackwell, Oxford.

The Parliamentary Office and Edita plc (2002) *The Finnish Parliament*, Edita Prima Ltd, Helsinki.

Pehe, J. (2004) 'Consolidating free government in the new EU', *Journal of Democracy*, 15 (1), January: 36–47.

Peters, B.G. (2001) 'Agenda setting in the European Union', in J. Richardson (ed.), *European Union: Power and Policymaking*, Routledge, London.

Peterson, J. and Bomberg, E. (1999) *Decision-Making in the European Union*, Palgrave, Basingstoke.

Peterson, J. and Pollack, M. (2003) 'Introduction: Europe, America, Bush', in J. Peterson and M. Pollack (eds.), *Europe, America, Bush: Transatlantic Relations in the Twenty-First Century*, Routledge, London.

Petersson, O. (1994) *The Government and Politics of the Nordic Countries*, Publica, Stockholm.

Phinnemore, D. (2003) 'Towards European Union', in M. Cini (ed.), *European Union Politics*, Oxford University Press, Oxford.

Phinnemore, D. (2004) *Treaty Establishing a Constitution for Europe: An Overview*, Chatham House Briefing Note.

Pierson, C. (1998) *Beyond the Welfare State?* Polity Press, Cambridge.

Piore, M. (1979) *Bird of Passage: Migrant Labour and Industrial Societies*, Cambridge University Press, Cambridge.

Popescu, M. (2003) 'The parliamentary and presidential elections in Romania, November 2000', *Electoral Studies*, 22: 325–34.

Pridham, G. and Lewis, P. (1995) *Stabilising Fragile Democracies*, Routledge, London.

Prodi, R. (2004), 'Russia and the EU: enduring ties, widening horizons' speech by Romano Prodi, president of the European Commission, 23 April, Tretyakov Gallery, Moscow, Russia (Speech/04/198 on the EU website.)

Puchala, D.J. (1972) 'Of blind men, elephants and international integration', *Journal of Common Market Studies*, 42 (3): 267–84.

Putin, V.V. (2004) 'Address to the Federal Assembly of the Russian Federation', 26 May 2004 in Johnson's Russia List, No. 8225, 27 May.

Rees, W. (2003) 'Transatlantic relations and the war against terror', *Journal of Transatlantic Studies*, 1 (1: supplement): 76–90.

Remmington, T. (1999) *Politics in Russia*, Longman, Harlow.

Report of Wim Kok to the European Commission (2003) *Enlarging the European Union: Achievements and Challenges*, European University Institute, Florence.

Riekmann, S.P. (1997) 'The myth of European unity', in G. Hosking and G. Schöpflin (eds), *Myths and Nationhood*, Hurst in association with the School of Slavonic and East European Studies, University of London, London.

Richardson, J. (ed.) (2001) *European Union: Power and Policymaking*, Routledge, London.

Risse, T. (2004) 'Social constructivism and European integration', in T. Diez and A. Wiener (eds), *European Integration Theory*, Oxford University Press, Oxford.

Rosamond, B. (2000) *Theories of European Integration*, Palgrave, Basingstoke.

Rose, R. (2004), 'Advancing into Europe? The contrasting goals of post-communist countries', in A. Motyl and A. Schnetzer (eds), *Nations in Transit, Democratisation in East Central Europe and Eurasia*, Freedom House, Washington, DC.

Roskin, M.G. (1997) *The Rebirth of East Europe*, 3rd edn, Prentice Hall, Upper Saddle River, NJ.

Ross, C. (2002) *Federalism and Democratisation in Russia*, Manchester University Press, Manchester.

Roxburgh, A. (2002) *Preachers of Hate: The Rise of the Far Right*, Gibson Square Books, London.

Ruggie, J.G. (1993) 'Territoriality and beyond: problematizing modernity in international relations', *International Organization*, 47: 139–74.

Rupnik, J. (2004), 'Concluding reflections', *Journal of Democracy*, 15 (1), January: 22–85.

Rutland, P. (1994) 'The economy: the rocky road from plan to market', in S. White, A. Pravda and Z. Gitelman (eds), *Developments in Russian and Post-Soviet Politics*, Macmillan, London.

Rutland, P. (2003) 'The sorry state of Russian democracy', *Radio Free Europe/Radio Liberty*, *Newsline*, 3 (50), 18 December.

Sakwa, R. (1996) *Russian Politics and Society*, 2nd edn, Routledge, London.

Sakwa, R. (2002) *Russian Politics and Society*, 3rd edn, Routledge, London.

Sandholtz, W. and Zysman, J. (1989) '1992: recasting the European bargain', *World Politics*, 27: 4.

Sapelli, G. (1995) *Southern Europe Since 1945: Tradition and Modernity in Portugal, Spain, Italy, Greece and Turkey*, Longman, Harlow.

Sassoon, D. (1997a) *Contemporary Italy: Politics, Economy and Society*, Longman, London.

Sassoon, D. (1997b) *One Hundred Years of Socialism: The West European Left in the Twentieth Century*, Fontana Press, London.

Scharpf, F. (1999) *Governing in Europe, Effective and Democratic*, Oxford University Press, Oxford.

Schaub, A. (1996) 'Competition policy in the telecoms sector', *European Commission Competition Policy Newsletter*, 2 (1): 1–7.

Scheller, H.P. (2004) *The European Central Bank: History, Role and Functions*, European Central Bank, Frankfurt-am-Main.

Schlesinger, A.M. (1967) 'Origins of the Cold War', *Foreign Affairs*, xlvi (1 October).

Schmitter, P. (1970) 'A revised theory of European integration', *International Organisation* (Autumn): 836–68.

Schmitter, P. (2004) 'Neo-neofunctionalism', in A. Wiener and T. Diez (eds), *European Integration Theory*, Oxford University Press, Oxford.

Schonfield, A. (1973) *Europe: Journey to an Unknown Destination*, Penguin Books, London.

Schuster, L. (2004) 'The exclusion of asylum seekers in Europe', *COMPAS Working Paper No. 1*, University of Oxford Press, Oxford.

Scully, R. (2003) 'The European Parliament', in M. Cini (ed.), *European Union Politics*, Oxford University Press, Oxford.

Seleznev, L. (2003), 'Post-Soviet Russian foreign policy: between doctrine and pragmatism', in R. Fawn (ed.), *Realignments in Russian Foreign Policy*, Frank Cass, London.

Shackleton, M. (2002) 'The European Parliament', in J. Peterson and M. Shackleton (eds), *The Institutions of the European Union*, Oxford University Press, Oxford.

Shafir, M. (2004a) 'Analysis: Czechs still fear fireworks mark pyrrhic victory', *RFE/RL Newsline*, special issue, 'EU Expands Eastward', 3 May.

Shafir, M. (2004b), 'Analysis: Slovakia's EU run has left premier gasping', *RFE/RL Newsline*, special issue, 'EU Expands Eastward', 3 May.

Shaw, J. (2003) 'What's in a convention? Process and substance in the project of European constitution building', in J. Shaw *et al.*, *The Convention on the Future of Europe: Working Towards an EU Constitution*, Federal Trust, London.

Shaw, J. *et al.* (2003) *The Convention on the Future of Europe: Working Towards an EU Constitution*, Federal Trust, London.

Shohat, E. and Stam, R. (1994) *Unthinking Eurocentrism: Multiculturalism and the Media*, Routledge, London and New York.

Shore, C. (2000) *Building Europe: The Cultural Politics of European Integration*, Routledge, London and New York.

Simonian, H. (1985) *The Privileged Partnership: Franco–German Relations in the European Community 1969–1984*, Clarendon Press, Oxford.

Smith, G. (1999) *The Post-Soviet States: Mapping the Politics of Transition*, Edward Arnold, London.

Smith, G. (1988) *Soviet Politics: Continuity and Contradiction*, Macmillan, London.

Smith, K. (2003) 'EU external relations', in M. Cini (ed.), *European Union Politics*, Oxford University Press, Oxford.

Soborski, R. (2004) 'Anti-globalism and ecologism in comparative perspective', in J. Barry, B. Baxter and D. Dunphy (eds), *Europe, Globalization and Sustainable Development*, Routledge, London.

Socialist International (1998) *Socialist International Newsletter* 39, December (available at http://www.socialistinternational.org/9Newsletter/39/news39).

Soetendorp, B. (1999) *Foreign Policy in the European Union*, Longman, London.

Spinelli, A. (1972) 'The European adventure – tasks for the enlarged community', in M. O'Neill (1996), *The Politics of European Integration: A Reader*, Routledge, London.

Spybey, T. (ed.) (1997) *Britain in Europe: An Introduction to Sociology*, Routledge, London.

Steinberg, J. (2003) 'An elective partnership: salvaging transatlantic relations', *Survival*, 45 (2): 113–46.

Stepashin, S. (2004) 'Moskovsky Komsomolets', 20 May, 2004 in *RFE/RL Newsline*, 8 (96) Part 1, 24 May, 2004, p. 2.

Stern, S. and Seligman, E. (eds) (2003) *Desperately Seeking Europe*, Archetype Publications, London.

Stiglitz, J. (2002) *Globalisation and Its Discontents*, Penguin Books, London.

Stoker, G. (1998) 'Governance as theory: five propositions', *International Social Science Journal*, 155: 17–28.

Strathclyde University, Centre for the Study of Public Policy (2001) *New Europe Barometer*.

Tanyici, S. (2003) 'Transformation of political Islam in Turkey', *Party Politics*, 9 (4): 463–83.

Thomas, N. and Le Saux, F. (eds) (1998) *Unity and Difference in European Culture* University of Durham Press, Durham.

Thorhallsson, B. (2004) *Iceland and European Integration*, Routledge, London.

Tiersky, R. (ed.) (2004) *Europe Today: National Politics, European Integration and European Security*, 2nd edn, Rowman and Littlefield, Lanham, MD.

Tiilikainen, T. (1998) *Europe and Finland*, Ashgate, Aldershot.

Timmins, G. (2003) 'Strategic or pragmatic partnership? The European Union's policy towards Russia since the end of the Cold War', in R. Fawn (ed.), *Realignments in Russian Foreign Policy*, Frank Cass, London.

Timmins, G. (2004) 'Coping with the new neighbours: the evolution of European Union policy towards Russia', *Perspectives on European Politics and Society*, 5 (2): 357-74.

Tolz, V. (2001) *Russia*, Edward Arnold, London.

Tolz, V. (2002) 'Values and the construction of a national identity', in S. White, A. Pravda and Z. Gitelman (eds), *Developments in Russian Politics – 5*, Macmillan, Basingstoke,

Trade Negotiation Insights (http://www.ictsd.org)

Tranholm-Mikkelsen, J. (1991) 'Neofunctionalism: obstinate or obsolete?' *Millennium: Journal of International Studies*, 20 (1).

Traynor, I. (2004) 'US campaign behind the turmoil in Kiev', *The Guardian*, 26 November, p. 17.

Turner, A. (2001) *Just Capital: the Liberal Economy*, Macmillan, Basingstoke and Oxford.

UN (2004) 'Annan Plan: main articles' (available at http://www.cyprus-un-org/Main_Articles.html).

Unwin, T. (1998) 'Ideas of Europe', in T. Unwin (ed.), *A European Geography*, Longman, Harlow.

Vaizey, J. (1971) *Revolutions of Our Time: Capitalism*, Weidenfeld & Nicolson, London.

Veremis, T. (1997) *The Military in Greek Politics*, Hurst, New York.

Wallace, W. (2001) 'Europe, the necessary partner', *Foreign Affairs,* 80 (3): 16–34.

Wallace, W. (2003) 'Organised Europe; its regional and global responsiblities', in S. Stern and E. Seligman (eds), *Desperately Seeking Europe*, Archetype Publications, London.

Western European Union (WEU) Assembly (1964) *A Retropective Year in Europe*, WEU, Paris.

Western European Union (WEU) 'Western European Union Council of Ministers Petersberg Declaration' (available at http://www.weu.int/eng/comm.92-petersberg.htm).

Western EU Assembly 1963 (1964) *A Retrospective View of the Political Year in Europe*, Paris.

White, B. (2000) *Understanding European Foreign Policy*, Palgrave, Basingstoke.

White, S. (1993) 'Eastern Europe after communism', in S. White, J. Batt and P.G. Lewis (eds), *Development in East European Politics*, Macmillan, Basingstoke.

White, S. (2000a) 'Political parties', in M. Bowker and C. Ross (eds), *Russia After the Cold War*, Longman, Harlow.

White, S. (2000b) *Russia's New Politics: The Management of a Postcommunist Society*, Cambridge University Press, Cambridge.

White, S. and McAllister, I. (2004) 'Dimensions of disengagement in post-communist Russia', *Communist Studies and Transition Politics*, 20 (1), March.

White, S., Gardiner, J. and Schopflin, G. (1987) *Communist Political Systems: An Introduction*, St Martin's Press, London.

Willerton, J.P. (2001) 'The presidency: from Yeltsin to Putin', in S. White, A. Pravda and Z. Gitelman (eds), *Developments in Russian Politics – 5*, Macmillan, Basingstoke.

Williams, W. A. (1962) *The Tragedy of American Diplomacy*, Delta Books, New York.

Wilson, T. and Estellie, M. (eds) (1993) *Cultural Change and the New Europe*, Westview Press, Boulder, CO. and Oxford.

Woodworth, P. (2001) *Dirty War, Clean Hands: ETA, the GAL and Spanish Democracy*, Cork University Press, Cork.

World Bank (2004) Europe and Central Asia Region (http://www.worldbank.org).

Wright, A. (2005) *Who Governs Scotland?* Routledge, London.

WTO (http://www.wto.org).

Wyman, M. (1997) 'Elections and voting behaviour', in S. White, A. Pravda and Z. Gitelman (eds), *Developments in Russia Politics – 4*, Macmillan, Basingstoke.

Wyman, M. (1999) 'Elections and voting behaviour', in S. White, A. Pravda and Z. Gitelman (eds) *Developments in Russian Politics – 4*, Macmillan, Basingstoke.

Wyman, M. (2001) 'Elections and voters', in S. White, A. Pravda and Z. Gitelman (eds), *Developments in Russian Politics – 5*, Palgrave, Basingstoke.

Xanthaki, H. (2002) 'Cooperation on justice and home affairs', in J. Gower (ed.), *The European Union Handbook*, 2nd edn, Fitzroy Dearborn, London.

Xenakis, D. and Chryssochoou, D. (2001), *The Emerging Euro-Mediterranean System*, Manchester University Press, Manchester.

Yasman, V. (2004) 'Russia and the EU: a problematic future', *RFE/RL Russian Political Weekly*, 4 (17), 5 May.

Yergin, D. (1990) *Shattered Peace: The Origins of the Cold War and the National Security State*, Penguin, London.

Young, J.W. (1991) *Cold War Europe 1945–1989: A Political History*, Edward Arnold, London.

Zetter, R., Griffiths, D., Ferretti, S. and Pearl, M. (2004) *An Assessment of the Impact of Asylum Policies in Europe 1990–2000*, Home Office Research Study 259.

Zielonka, J. (2004) 'Challenges of EU enlargement', *Journal of Democracy*, 15, (1), January.

Index